A MEMOIR ⌣ .

HER ROYAL HIGHNESS

PRINCESS MARY ADELAIDE
DUCHESS OF TECK

BASED ON HER PRIVATE DIARIES AND LETTERS

By C. KINLOCH COOKE, B.A., LL.M.
BARRISTER-AT-LAW

IN TWO VOLUMES, WITH
PORTRAITS AND ILLUSTRATIONS

Vol. I.

LONDON
JOHN MURRAY, ALBEMARLE STREET
1900

Yours affectionately
Mary Adelaide

DEDICATED

BY PERMISSION

TO HER ROYAL HIGHNESS

THE DUCHESS OF YORK

PREFACE.

It was in response to a widely expressed wish, coming from all classes of English people, to possess some authentic record of Princess Mary's life and work, that the family of Her late Royal Highness entrusted me with the duty of preparing the Memoir which I am now permitted to place in the hands of the public.

The active interest shown in the undertaking by the Duchess of York and Prince Adolphus of Teck has in no small measure lightened my task. From the commencement they have been ever ready to help and advise, and I respectfully and gratefully acknowledge the valuable aid so graciously rendered. I further take this opportunity of stating that the proof-sheets were carefully perused by the Grand Duchess of Mecklenburg-Strelitz, the Duchess of York, and Prince Adolphus of Teck.

I beg also to tender my respectful thanks to the Prince of Wales, the Duke of Cambridge, and Prince Edward of Saxe-Weimar for assistance given me in the preparation of the Memoir. When the book was first contemplated, I had every reason to hope for the co-operation of the Duke of Teck, but the serious illness which succeeded his wife's death, I regret to say, made it impossible for him to take any part in the work he was so anxious to see accomplished.

As soon as circumstances allowed, the Duchess of York handed to me the Journal which her mother had kept, with more or less regularity, from the year 1853, together with such papers as Her Royal Highness considered would be of use for the purpose in view. These materials have formed the basis of the Memoir. Wherever it has been possible, I have let the Princess's words tell their own tale, but what to select and what to leave out is always a matter of extreme difficulty in contemporary biography, and the sense of responsibility in the present instance has been very real.

It was not altogether as a stranger that I approached my subject. A chance meeting with Her late Royal Highness in a country house, some twelve years ago, led to my being invited to White Lodge, and in the years that followed, it was my privilege to see something of Princess Mary's home life. During my editorship of the *English Illustrated Magazine*, the Princess wrote what she modestly called her "first humble effort in the writing line," which will be found incorporated in these volumes.

Princess Mary's father was the favourite son of George III., and the Duchess of Cambridge one of the most active and prominent ladies of her time in London society. For several years Princess Mary was the only English Princess about the Court, as the Queen had no sisters, and Her Majesty's daughters were children when their cousin attended her first drawing-room. The Queen often visited Cambridge House and Cambridge Cottage, and Princess Mary was a constant guest at Windsor Castle, while many happy hours were passed at Gloucester House, where the Duchess of Gloucester delighted to welcome her much-beloved niece. The Princess's letters contain touching allusions to the early days of the Queen's widowhood, and give expression to the grief felt by the nation at the death of the Prince Consort, with whom, as well as with the Queen, Princess Mary was a great favourite.

Her late Royal Highness was present at almost every State Ceremony that has taken place during the last fifty years, and generally noted down the people she met, and some account of the proceedings she witnessed. At her

mother's house; at her own apartment in Kensington Palace
(formerly occupied by the Duchess of Kent); and later on
at White Lodge, Princess Mary saw most of the crowned
heads of Europe, as well as the distinguished diplomatists,
artists, and *litterateurs* of the latter half of the nineteenth
century.

The Journal and letters afford an insight into Her
late Royal Highness's family life, her motherly care and
anxiety for her children, their bringing up and training.
From the same sources we learn something of the kindly
nature of the Duke of Teck and the devotion of the Princess to the husband of her choice. Princess Mary was
much attached to the Prince of Wales, and it pleased her
greatly when the Heir-apparent married her favourite
cousin Princess Alexandra of Denmark. As time went on,
the tie between Princess Mary and the Prince and Princess
of Wales became closer, and the friendship culminated in
the union of the Duke of York and Princess Victoria Mary
of Teck.

It would not be possible to deal with the life of Princess
Mary without alluding to the present Duke of Cambridge,
and soldiers and civilians who knew the Duke only as the
popular Commander-in-Chief of the British army will see
him portrayed in the following pages as a devoted son and
affectionate brother.

So extensive and continuous were the charitable and
philanthropic undertakings of the Duchess of Teck, that I
have found it expedient to deal with this phase of her life
in a separate chapter. To recite the various public appearances of Her late Royal Highness in the cause of charity
would merely repeat the records which from time to time
have found a place in the chronicles of the day. I have,
therefore, mainly relied upon information derived from
private sources for the account I have given of the self-deny-
ing work that afforded the Duchess such infinite pleasure and
occupied so great a portion of her later years.

Among the papers given to me by the Duchess of York
was a charming series of letters written by Princess Mary

to her former governess, which the grateful recipient sent, in her declining years, to Princess May as a birthday gift, neatly tied up with blue ribbon, and enclosed in a *bonbonnière* with the following letter:—

May 26, 1878.

MY DEAR PRINCESS,—Allow me to offer Your Highness every best wish for health and happiness on this your eleventh birthday, and to request Your Highness to graciously accept the box of bonbons. It is a treasure which for many years brought joy and happiness to myself, being the letters with which I was honoured by Her Royal Highness the Duchess, your illustrious parent, long ere she had reached the age of Your Highness, and for many years after. They are the reflex of the noble mind and generous tender heart which have so greatly endeared Her Royal Highness, not merely to those most honoured by her, but also to the whole British nation, which regards Her Royal Highness as more peculiarly its "own dear Princess." And that you, dear Princess, may be blest with the inheritance of the same glorious qualities of tender affection for your relatives, gracious condescension to inferiors, and universal benevolence is the heartfelt wish of Your Highness's obedient humble servant,

SOPHIA BARRY.

But for the kindly aid of the Honble. Mrs. Dalrymple, the very early days at Kew, whither the Duke and Duchess of Cambridge repaired soon after their return from Hanover in 1837, must have been passed over. Not only has this life-long friend of Her late Royal Highness recalled scenes of sixty years ago, and given us a delightful picture of Princess Mary as a child, she has also added to the interest of the Memoir by placing at my disposal a correspondence beginning when the Princess was but ten years old, and ending only with her death.

My thanks are likewise due to many other personal friends of Princess Mary's, who kindly gave me their letters, more particularly to the Duchess of Sutherland, the late Marchioness of Salisbury, Lady Geraldine Somerset, the Countess of Tankerville, the Dowager Countess of Aylesford, the Countess of Dunraven, Lady Elizabeth Biddulph, the Honble.

Mary Thesiger, Mrs. Bridges Taylor, Mrs. Alexander, and Mr. Peter Wells.

I am further indebted to the Countess Granville for letters addressed to the late Earl Granville; to the Earl of Hopetoun for the letters of the late Countess of Hopetoun; to Lord Rowton for the late Earl of Beaconsfield's letters; to Mrs. Atkinson Clark for her aunt the late Lady Holland's letters as well as her own; and to Miss Harrison for letters written to her father, the late Canon Harrison.

Among others who have been good enough to send me contributions, I would especially thank the Countess of Munster, the Honble. Alexander Nelson Hood, Miss Ella Taylor, who also lent her letters, Miss Pocock, the Bishop of Calcutta, and Sir Dominic and Lady Colnaghi.

I have received help in various ways from the Dowager Countess of Shrewsbury, the late Lady Caroline Cust, Lady Katherine Coke, Lady Eva Dugdale, Lady Hothfield, Lady Mount-Stephen, the Honble. Mrs. Percy Mitford, Madame Bricka, Earl Brownlow, the Bishop of Peterborough, the Honble. Sir Spencer Ponsonby Fane, the Honble. Arthur Walsh, Sir Edgar Sebright, Sir George Arthur, General Clifton, and Captain Mildmay.

The officials of different societies with which Princess Mary was associated supplied some of the information relating to her charitable and philanthropic work, while numerous incidents were told me by friends and fellow-workers of Her late Royal Highness. I wish to thank every one who has assisted me in this portion of the book, and in particular the Countess of Meath, the Bishop of Bristol, the Bishop of Stepney, Lord Rookwood, Lady Ellis, Mrs. Bevan, Mrs. Meredith, Mrs. Dalison, Mrs. Master, Mrs. Basil Ellis, Dr. Barnardo, and Mr. George Holland. Many of the facts connected with Princess Mary's efforts to resuscitate the British silk industry were given me by Sir Thomas Wardle, President of the Silk Association of Great Britain and Ireland.

Lord Esher kindly had the plans of White Lodge, Cambridge Cottage, and Kensington Palace specially prepared for the book. Mr. Harcourt of Nuneham Courtenay allowed me to inspect and copy the letters written by Adolphus Frederick, Duke of Cambridge to the late Countess Harcourt, and Sir Thomas Dick-Lauder contributed a drawing of the Villa Cedri.

In conclusion, I would add that my wife has been my *collaborateur* throughout, and her assistance has been most helpful in the compilation of the Memoir.

C. KINLOCH COOKE.

3, MOUNT STREET, W.,
   January, 1900.

CONTENTS OF VOL. I.

LIST OF ILLUSTRATIONS.

———

TABLE AND PLAN.

PROLOGUE.

THE CAMBRIDGE BRANCH OF THE ROYAL FAMILY.

THE title of Cambridge is one of the most distinguished in the peerage, and has always been associated with the family of the reigning sovereign. As a dukedom, it was first conferred upon each of the four children of James, Duke of York, afterwards James II.; but they all died in infancy, and the title ' remained in abeyance until Queen Anne bestowed it upon George Augustus, Prince Electoral of Hanover. When the Prince came to the throne as George II., the dukedom merged in the Crown, and was not revived until 1801, in which year Adolphus Frederick, youngest son of George III., and father of Princess Mary Adelaide, was created Duke of Cambridge.

In countless ways the Princess showed her devotion to her father, and from her own letters it is easy to trace the paternal influence upon that noble life which, to the great sorrow of the nation, passed away so unexpectedly on October the 27th, 1897. No record, therefore, can do justice to Her Royal Highness's memory which is not prefaced with something more than a passing reference to the founder of the Cambridge branch of the Royal Family and the grandfather of England's future Queen.

Adolphus Frederick was born at Kew on the 24th of February, 1774. He was a year younger than his brother Augustus, afterwards Duke of Sussex, and three years junior to Ernest, who became Duke of Cumberland, and ultimately King of Hanover. As boys, the three princes resided with their tutors, Dr. Hughes and Mr. Cookson, on Kew Green, in

cottages given them by their father, and when Adolphus
was thirteen the brothers were sent to Hanover, in order that
they might learn German and study at the University of
Göttingen. Every care was taken to maintain the dignity of
their position, and each prince was attended by "a governor,
a preceptor, and a gentleman," while the best professors,
including Heyne and Blumenbach, were engaged to give them
instruction. Adolphus proved an apt pupil, and, like his
brother Augustus, soon became proficient in the German
language, but Ernest did not find the task so easy, and never
really mastered the grammar.

Prince Adolphus chose the army for a profession, and to
perfect himself in military tactics visited the Court of
Prussia. At the age of nineteen he made practical acquaintance with the realities of war, serving as a volunteer in the
Flanders campaign of 1793, first under his brother the Duke
of York, and afterwards under Marshal Freytag. The Prince
was a great favourite with his father, and the King was
often heard to say that Adolphus had never given him a
moment's anxiety or concern. Nor were these amiable
qualities noticed only by an indulgent parent; they were
observed by all about the Court, and Lady Chatham,[1] writing
on the eve of the Prince's departure for the Continent, says—

The dear charming Prince Adolphus took leave of me this
night. I shall see him no more as he's to go in a few
days. I quite pity the King, and indeed all the family;
he has been so delightfully pleasant with them all that
they will be undone without him. You never saw such a
picture of a fond father as the King with him, or indeed
anything prettier than the son's constant affectionate attention to his Father, and with all this he's as lively as
any of them, and I dare say as well inclined to be wild in
a gentlemanlike way; a thorough gay young soldier; but
everything with him seems to give way to his sense of duty
in the Service and his love for the King.

During the progress of hostilities the Prince was wounded,
and narrowly escaped being taken prisoner. His state of

---

[1] Wife of the second Earl of Chatham.

health obliged him to return home, and it is characteristic
of him that he told the Prince of Wales "he had resolved
not to be taken. If he had not effected his escape, he would
have resisted, and got himself killed; he felt the disad-
vantage it would be to the war that he should be a hostage
in the enemy's hands."[1] Prince Adolphus did not remain
long in England, and within a few months, attached to
General Walmoden's corps and advanced to the rank of
major-general, he was again seeing active service.

A soldier's life with him was no sinecure; when there was
work to be done he did it, sharing the hardships of war
with his companions in arms on terms of equality. "The
weather has been very severe," he says, in a letter to Lady
Harcourt,[2] written in November, 1794, while encamped
"with a brigade under General Abercromby's orders," adding,
"I can assure you we have suffered a good deal. We are
at present making huts, and I hope in a few days they will
be ready. . . . My brigade is the only one of the Hanoverians
which is not in cantonments." Again, in the following
March, he writes to the same correspondent—

How glad I am for your's and Lord Harcourt's sake that
the General and his Lady are returning to England. Indeed
he has had a dreadful time of it. The fatigues and the bad
success have been very great, but so much the more honour
and comfort to him. . . . Thank God I have borne the Campaign very well. The cold was shocking, and the marches
we had to make horrid, but I luckily have escaped having any
limb frozen. What a comfort it is to me not to have quitted
the army this winter. I have shared everything with the
men, but I would not miss what I have seen and gone through
for the world. I wrote this to the King in my last letter, and
thanked him for having left me here.

It is not surprising that those with whom he served

---

[1] "Life and Letters of Sir Gilbert Elliot," vol. ii. p. 162.
[2] Wife of the second Earl Harcourt and Lady of the Bedchamber to
Queen Adelaide. Lord Harcourt was Master of the Horse, and both he
and Lady Harcourt were admitted to the close friendship of the King and
Queen, who were frequent visitors at Nuneham-Courtenay, the residence
of the Harcourt Family.

regarded Prince Adolphus as a diligent, brave and reliable officer, and in a very short time he was given another step in the Hanoverian service. But military matters did not alone engage his attention; he was also well versed in affairs of State. His affection for the King made him resist all overtures from the Prince of Wales, Fox, Sheridan, and other prominent Whigs of the day, and he never wavered in his allegiance to the Tory Party. A critical observer of political movements at home, he possessed an equally intimate knowledge of European complications. Commenting, in 1798, on the events in Ireland, he remarks, " I trust that all ideas of rebellion will soon be given over in that country. The firmness shown by the Government has undoubtedly contributed the most to the quelling of this unlucky rebellion; and had the other Governments on the Continent shown as much energy, I will answer for matters being quite otherwise than they are now." To another correspondent [1] he writes, some two years later: " I have lately heard from Berlin that Lord Carysfort has played with the Queen at Court, which I look upon in a favourable light; and the exclusion of the Russian ships from the embargo makes me hope that the disharmony which has taken place between the cabinets of London and Berlin has ceased, and that matters will be made up."

These letters were dated from Hanover, whither the Prince had returned to continue his studies, which had been interrupted by so much active service. Determined to take every advantage of his opportunities, as well as to make up for lost time, he rose at six o'clock, spending the greater part of the day at his books. He was fond of science, and devoted to music, particularly the violin, on which instrument he became a proficient player, and being a man of refined and cultivated tastes, delighted to have beautiful things about him, while scholars, artists, and musicians were numbered among his intimate friends.

Mrs. Trench, who was visiting Hanover about this time, emphasizes these characteristics, and thus records her

[1] Mrs. St. George, afterwards Mrs. Trench.

impressions of the Prince: "His exterior is highly pre-possessing. He is extremely handsome, tall, and finely formed. His complexion fair yet manly; his features regular yet expressive. His manners bear that stamp of real goodness which no art can imitate, no other charm replace; and though he presents himself with suitable dignity, his address immediately inspires ease and confidence. His conversation is fluent, various, and entertaining." On another occasion she notes: "Our company only consisted of our host and hostess, an officer who played the violin, some musicians, and Mr. Tatler, who educated the Princes Augustus and Adolphus, and who now lives with the latter as a friend. It was a delightful evening, and Prince Adolphus sang with very good taste, and has a charming voice. He is extremely animated, and there is a frankness and goodness in his manner that pleases even more than his graces and his talents." Describing the Prince's house, Mrs. Trench tells us that it was "very beautiful, both as to taste and magnificence. The rooms are chiefly hung and furnished with Lyons silks, and the ceilings, floors, doors, and windows are appointed in the most exquisite Italian style."[1]

This period of comparative ease and comfort was rudely interrupted in the spring of 1801, when the King of Prussia demanded and obtained military possession of Hanover. In the same year Prince Adolphus was created Duke of Cambridge, with the subsidiary titles of Earl of Tipperary and Baron of Culloden; and in 1803 he was transferred from the Hanoverian to the British service with the rank of full General. Meanwhile Prussia had handed back Hanover to this country, but on war breaking out between France and England a few months later, the electorate was menaced by the French army. For the relief of Hanover, the King's German Legion was raised, and the Duke of Cambridge placed at the head of the new force. Public opinion in Hanover had, however, undergone a change; the people showed little disposition to take advantage of the aid offered, and evinced a leaning towards the French. Accordingly the

[1] "Remains of Mrs. Richard Trench," pp. 37–39.

Duke asked and obtained permission to return to England, leaving the control of the forces to General Walmoden, who soon afterwards surrendered to Marshal Mortier. During his stay at home the Duke did not lead an idle life. He was given the command of the Home District, and received the colonelcy of the Coldstream Guards.

Subsequently Napoleon relinquished his claims to Hanover in favour of Prussia, but a quarrel with France once more deprived Prussia of possession, and in 1810 Hanover was annexed to Napoleon's creation of the kingdom of Westphalia. Three years later it was recaptured for the allies by Bernadotte's troops and restored to England, when the Duke of Cambridge, now promoted to the rank of Field Marshal, was again appointed to command in the electorate. In 1814 Hanover was raised to the dignity of a kingdom, with succession only in the male line, and two years afterwards the Duke was made Governor-General. The appointment, however, carried with it little or no political power, as Count Münster, who had guarded British interests at Hanover with signal ability for many years, was transferred to London, and all instructions to the Duke passed through him; he, in fact, drew up the Constitution which made provision for two representative Chambers, and came into force in 1819.

But if political power were wanting, the office of Governor-General of Hanover was an important one, requiring the exercise of much tact and diplomatic skill, and as an administrator the Duke of Cambridge showed marked ability, his conduct of affairs being characterised by wisdom and discretion. The people liked him, and he soon became a favourite in Hanoverian society. That he fully deserved his popularity is clear from the testimony of Sir James Riddell, who, writing to a friend in 1815, remarks—

At Hanover the Duke of Cambridge was extremely civil to me, and I dined with him three times during my stay there. It cannot be partiality alone to a son of one's own sovereign which gives him in my eyes superiority over every other Prince I have ever seen in Europe. His manners and address are most prepossessing. He inspires at first sight

confidence and respect, which at every successive interview
are increased. To judge of him by the common rules of good
breeding and elegance, he fails in none. His air is fine and
manly : he is perfectly well formed, and his countenance,
especially when lighted up by a smile, is most pleasing. I
have never heard a whisper of reproach on his moral
character. He pays that attention to the Sunday one would
expect of the son of George III.—assembling his family even
to the lowest menial, and giving them an example of the
most profound attention, while one of his aides-de-camp reads
an excellent form of prayer. He visits people in their own
way at their own houses. They seem to bear towards him
all the respect due to his high station, and all the veneration
due to his still more exalted virtues, with all the esteem and
affection which his very amiable manners cannot fail to
excite. The officers of his household appear to copy him in
most things, and are the most gentlemenlike men as well as
the pleasantest set of fellows you can imagine. Indeed,
these are expressions one would be tempted to make use of
in speaking of the Duke ! were he not—and every motion
reminds you of it—your Prince.

Although the Duke threw himself heart and soul into his
new duties, he never lost touch with his friends in England,
always manifesting a warm interest and sympathy in everything that concerned them. His thoughtfulness for others is
shown in the letter he wrote condoling with Archbishop
Vernon [1] on the death of his daughter, from which the following extract is taken :—

I cannot let the mail go off without a few lines to
express my very great concern at the melancholy event
which has occurred in your family. Knowing your's and
Lady Anne's affection for your children, I can easily conceive the deepness of your affliction at this severe blow
which has deprived you of a most excellent and amiable
daughter. The conviction you must have that she is happy
where she now is will, I am sure, be your greatest comfort,
and that you and Lady Anne may be preserved from any
further misfortunes is my sincere wish and fervent prayer.

When the news of the battle of Waterloo reached the
Duke of Cambridge he was spending the summer months

---

[1] Archbishop of York, and brother of the Countess Harcourt.

at the Villa Monbrillant,[1] and, writing to Lady Harcourt, thus expresses himself on the situation:—

I congratulate you on the glorious victory of the 18th gained by the Duke of Wellington over Bonaparte in person. I fear that the British loss has been very great, though I know no details of it, but to judge from the lists I have received of the loss of the Legion and the Hanoverians, I dread the arrival of the Gazette. There is one great comfort in the reflection that all those who have been killed died for the good cause, and I flatter myself that this great victory will bring about the downfall of the *Monster*, without which we can never expect to have peace in Europe.

The much-lamented death of Princess Charlotte in 1817 made it desirable that the King's sons should no longer delay the question of marriage. The Duke of Cambridge selected for his bride Princess Augusta, youngest daughter of the Landgrave Frederick of Hesse and of Princess Caroline of Nassau-Usingen. Princess Augusta had three brothers and two sisters. Her eldest brother, the Landgrave William of Hesse, was married to Princess Charlotte of Denmark, sister of Prince Christian, afterwards Christian VIII., and their second daughter Louise became the wife of Prince Christian of Schleswig-Holstein-Sonderburg-Glücksburg, who was subsequently chosen to succeed to the Throne of Denmark.[2] The younger brothers, Prince Frederick and Prince

---

[1] Monbrillant was built by one of the older Electors of Hanover for a lady to whom he was much attached. The story goes that while discussing with the Elector what name to give the Villa, the lady missed a diamond off some portion of her toilette, and exclaimed "Mon brillant!" Whereupon he said he would call the Villa "Monbrillant" to replace the jewel she had lost. Monbrillant was used by the Electors of Hanover as their summer residence and in turn occupied by the Duke of Cambridge.

[2] On the death of Christian VIII. in 1848, Frederick VII. became King of Denmark, and as he had no children the heir to the throne was Princess Charlotte, wife of the Landgrave William of Hesse. With a view of putting an end to the struggle over the Schleswig-Holstein Duchies, and providing a King and Queen for the throne of Denmark, at the suggestion of the Czar Nicholas, a marriage took place between Princess Louise of Hesse and Prince Christian of Holstein-Glücksburg; after protracted negotiations between the different Courts of Europe a Protocol was signed in London on May 8, 1852, by which it was agreed that in case of default of male issue in the direct line of Frederick VII., the crown of Denmark was to pass to Prince Christian,

TABLE SHOWING THE CONNECTION OF HER ROYAL HIGHNESS THE DUCHESS OF CAMBRIDGE WITH THE ENGLISH ROYAL FAMILY AND THE ROYAL FAMILY OF DENMARK.

GEORGE II. m. Wilhelmina Carolina of Brandenburg-Anspach.

FREDERICK m. Augusta of Saxe-Gotha. — MARY m. Frederick II., Landgrave of Hesse. — Other issue.

GEORGE III. m. Sophia Charlotte of Mecklenburg-Strelitz. — Landgrave FREDERICK m. Caroline of Nassau-Usingen. — Electric WILLIAM I. of Hesse.

GE IV. — WILLIAM IV. — Edward m. Victoria of Saxe-Coburg, Duke of Kent. — Other issue. — Adolphus Duke of Cambridge. — MARY m. Duke of Gloucester. — Landgrave m. Charlotte of WILLIAM Denmark. — Frederick. — George. — Louisa m. General von Decken. — Marie m. Grand Duke of Mecklenburg-Strelitz. — AUGUSTA m. ADOLPHUS Duke of Cambridge.

VICTORIA m. Albert, second son of Ernest Duke of Coburg and Gotha. — LOUISE m. Christian of Schleswig-Holstein-Sonderburg-Glücksburg, afterwards King of Denmark. — Other issue. — GEORGE Duke of Cambridge. — AUGUSTA m. Grand Duke of Mecklenburg-Strelitz. — MARY ADELAIDE m. FRANCIS Duke of Teck.

HARLOTTE m. opold of Saxe-urg, afterwards of the Belgians. — Other issue. — ALBERT EDWARD m. ALEXANDRA. Prince of Wales. — Other issue. — Victoria Mary. — Adolphus. — Francis. — Alexander.

GEORGE m. VICTORIA MARY of Teck.

EDWARD. — ALBERT. — VICTORIA.

George of Hesse, died unmarried. Princess Augusta's elder
sister, Louisa, married General von Decken, a distinguished
officer in the German Legion, and her remaining sister, Marie,
was united to the Grand Duke of Mecklenburg-Strelitz.

The ancestor of the present House of Hesse, one of the
oldest of the German dynasties, was Henry the Child, son
of Henry, Duke of Brabant, and Sophia, daughter of the
Thuringian Landgrave Louis. In 1263 the Duchess of
Brabant received by treaty the landgraviate of Hesse, and
two years later resigned it in favour of her son. Towards
the end of the thirteenth century the German Emperor,
Adolphus of Nassau, acknowledged Hesse as a part of the
Empire and its Regent as an Electoral Prince. The Hesse
family is essentially Protestant, and it was always a great joy
to Princess Augusta that she numbered among her immediate
ancestors Philip the Magnanimous, the champion and patron
of Luther.

"I am the happyest of men," the Duke of Cambridge
writes to Lady Harcourt from Cassel soon after his engagement, "and I really believe that on the surface of the globe
there does not exist so happy a Being as myself. Every hour
I feel that my esteem and attachment for my bride increases ;
and she is really everything both as to heart, mind and Person
that I could wish. . . . Truly, truly grateful do I feel to
Providence for having reserved this Blessing in store for me,
and Heaven grant that I may be deserving of it and not
forfeit my happiness by any misconduct." This attachment
deepened as years went by, and the union from the very
beginning was one of perfect harmony and great affection.

The marriage of the Duke and Duchess of Cambridge took
place at Cassel on the 7th of May, 1818, and was solemnised
in England three weeks later. The reception of the young
Duchess in this country was most cordial, but she must have
found it somewhat difficult to appreciate the attentions of the

and his wife Princess Louise, who upon the death of Frederick VII. became
King and Queen of Denmark. This collateral branch of the Cambridge
Family is specially interesting to English people, as the eldest daughter of
King Christian and Queen Louise is Alexandra Princess of Wales. Queen
Louise died in 1898.

British public, since Mr. Greville tells us that on the Sunday
after her arrival the Duke took his wife for a walk in the park,
" when she was so terrified by the pressure of the mob about
her that she nearly fainted." [1]   After a short stay in England
the royal couple returned to Hanover, where, on March 26,
1819, Prince George [2] was born, and three years later the birth
of Princess Augusta [3] took place.

Each year the system of governing Hanover from London
became more difficult, and matters were brought to a crisis
by the revolution in Paris during 1831.   The Duke lost no
time in representing the position of affairs to the King, who,
recognising the gravity of the situation, appointed him Viceroy
with full powers ; and Count Münster retired from the post
he had so long occupied.   Under the new *régime* the revolutionary spirit in Hanover disappeared, and it was admitted
on all sides that the Duke of Cambridge was in every way a
worthy representative of the British Crown.

[1] " The Greville Memoirs," vol. i. p. 2.
[2] The present Duke of Cambridge.
[3] Now the Grand Duchess of Mecklenburg-Strelitz.

CHAPTER I.

1833-1838.

Princess Mary's birth—Christening ceremony—William IV.—The Court at Hanover—A Masquerade—*Tableaux vivants*—Prince George—The Duke of Cambridge and his family return to England—Baron Knesebeck—The Queen's coronation—The village of Kew—The Gardens—Cambridge Cottage—The parish church—The Duke's kindheartedness—His popularity—The Duchess of Cambridge—Her characteristics and personality—Rumpenheim-on-the-Maine—Visit to Rome—Dear old England.

THE youngest daughter of the Duke and Duchess of Cambridge was born at Hanover on the 27th of November, 1833, and named Mary Adelaide Wilhelmina Elizabeth, after her god-parents, the Duchess of Gloucester,[1] Queen Adelaide, King William, and the Landgravine of Hesse-Homburg. In the following letters to Miss Swinburne[2] the Landgravine gives some interesting particulars concerning the birth and christening of her little godchild.

Hombourg, December 4, 1833.

Thank God my dearest Adolphus' mind is at ease about the Duchess of Cambridge; she has given him another little girl. . . . She was woefully alarmed about herself, which affected him, as he adores her to a degree that almost made him ill. . . .

Hanover, December 26, 1833.

. . . I found everything as it *should be* here; the Duchess well, thank God, with the finest baby you ever saw, and the

[1] Princess Mary, fourth daughter of George III.; she married her cousin Prince William, Duke of Gloucester and Edinburgh, in 1816.

[2] "Letters of Princess Elizabeth of England," edited by Philip Yorke, pp. 208, 209, etc. Princess Elizabeth was the third daughter of George III., and married the Landgrave of Hesse-Homburg.

image of George at that age . . . her prudence, courage, and good sense have gained her *great credit;* and she appears comfortably happy and full of my brother's amiable and devoted attachment and affection for her.   She is not out yet, and very wisely keeps quiet a fortnight longer, though perfectly well. Adolphus is a great deal better. . . . We had the trees for the children, beautiful sight, and they happy beyond measure; it was a pleasure to see them. The Duchess came into the room, then sat with us till near nine. . . .

Hanover, January 10, 1834.

. . . She [Mrs. Stephens] never appeared till Thursday, at the christening of my pretty little niece, who was christened by the names of Mary Adelaide Wilhelmina Elizabeth, but is to be called by the *two first.* I held the dear child for the dear Queen and myself. I never saw a finer sight. The Duchess of Cambridge sat in a beautiful dress, which Adolphus gave her from Paris, white crape and blonde over pink; she looked very well.   Everybody else in Court dresses, having on *man-teaux,* lappets, jewels, gold, silver, etc., etc. I performed my part, I was assured, very well; it made me rather nervous, I must confess; and the *heat* beyond all description; however, when the ceremony was over, and the Ladies, Gentlemen, Ministers, and the States had gone by the Duchess to make their compliments, and we were to quit the room, I managed to glide out into a cool corner to recover myself a little. The Duchess went walking about, talking to every one, and did it all famously. At ten we took leave, and I followed the Duchess into her private room, staid a little to talk over the event of the evening; and when I had seen her comfortably sitting by her fire, which I was flying from, I wished them *good night.*

I was proud of my nephew George, who is much improved in every way, and *Gussy*[1] is quite a dear; looked very well in white with blue ribbands, and behaved very well. I never saw my sister-in-law look to such advantage as the evening of the christening, you have no idea of the magnificence of the whole. I was as much amused as if I had been *Minette à la Cour.* . . . The child's dress amused me so—a *drap d'argent,* all tied *with pink* bows, and an enormous long train of the same, all trimmed with fine Brussels lace; two cushions of the same, so think what a weight to carry.

She behaved so well; had cried herself to sleep before, and looked so innocent and pretty. I was delighted with

---

[1] Princess Augusta of Cambridge.

her; [the] poor little soul started so when she was christened, and Mrs. Wood[1] assured the Duchess that the cold water had refreshed her in that *hot House*, for I really believe Greens would have shot up in the room. Never was I more happy when all was *over*.

Hanover, January 23, 1834.

. . . The baby is a *great dear*, thrives well, and appears to grow every time I see it; for she sleeps a great deal, so that she is not always *visible*; they are highly pleased with her, and she is a constant source of amusement to her mother. Not being used to such young children, she is too anxious about it.

At this period the Court of Hanover was considered one of the most agreeable on the Continent. The Viceroy's income, which on his marriage had been raised to £27,000 a year, allowed him to live in suitable style, and to keep up a sufficient amount of state, while many members of the Hanoverian aristocracy possessed fine houses, and there was no lack of balls and other entertainments, which were often attended by their Royal Highnesses. Sleighing was a favourite pastime in winter, and the Duke was fond of shooting and hunting the wild boar. Nor were social claims alone recognised, the welfare of the people was never for a moment forgotten, and Art in all its branches received every encouragement. Both the Viceroy and his royal consort were regular attendants at the opera, while nothing pleased the Duke better than a musical evening at the Palace, when he gathered together the best musicians, and would himself join in a quartette. "My sister-in-law's passion is the theatre," writes the Landgravine. "Yesterday I drove out for the first time in my drowska, dined at the Duchess of Cambridge's, my brother being gone-a-shooting; they went to the play, all the society with her." The annual exhibition of drawings and paintings, continued at Hanover to this day, owes its initiation to the Duke of Cambridge, and is still opened on his birthday. Intercourse with England was frequent, our

[1] The Grand Duchess of Mecklenburg-Strelitz is of opinion that "Mrs. Wood" should be Mrs. Page.

customs were introduced, and the Viceroy made a point of
noticing the young Englishmen who came out to Hanover to
study the German language and military tactics. Many of
the officers in the Hanoverian army had served in the King's
German Legion, and fought side by side with the British
troops in Spain and at Waterloo, while some had been
quartered in this country.[1]

The Viceroy's birthday was always marked by a special
fête; and the description given by the Landgravine of a
masquerade arranged in honour of one of these occasions
affords further insight into Court life at Hanover.

. . . Since I had the pleasure of hearing from you [Miss
Swinburne] I have been to *thès dançants*, assemblies, concerts,
masquerades, never more amused than with the last, though
the heat sometimes nearly overpowered me, but not at the
masquerade which was given on Adolphus' birthday by the
Duchess. Nothing ever succeeded better; I only wish you
could have been there. Adolphus' birthday being on a
Sunday, he would not as an Englishman have a ball at his
house. . . . Monday there was a dinner *chez moi* of near
thirty; it put me into a fever, but it went off well; they
quitted me at seven, when all the ladies flew home to dress;
this was a business on such a day, for, being the day on
which the Queen's birthday is celebrated in town, we had
double duties to perform; off I set *accomplished* at half-past
eight, and went in *without* seeing what I was desired not to
look at.

In a short time we got to the great room full of company;
480 there, about 190 excuses. After the common civilities
we found ourselves *all* placed within a chord, which proved
something was coming; we heard a fife and drum. First
arrived a company, or rather a guard of honour, dressed in
the time of George II., all gentlemen, admirable, followed
by a woman belonging to the camp, a gentleman who acted it
to perfection, also a fruit woman who was also a gentleman
of the Court about six feet and a half high; they were
followed by two men in black, which in former days were
called knights, to proclaim the Fair. . . . Instantly after

---

[1] Our uniform was worn up to 1837, when King Ernest adopted the
Prussian uniform; it was some time, however, before the army became
accustomed to the change, and many a Hanoverian soldier left the ranks
when he was no longer allowed to wear a red coat.

began the procession by Augusta of Cambridge dressed as a
fine lady at the beginning of the 17th century, with her
cousin, Louisa of Hesse, very pretty as a Danish peasant,
the little Augusta of Hesse as a Hessian broom-girl, then the
fine quadrille, magnificent Russians, Spaniards, Hungarians,
Turks, Polish, German, followed by two Chinese, a woman
and a mandarin, with their servant, a poppet show, a quack
doctor, Indians, ten, five pair, Greeks, harlequin and Columbine, the father and two Pierrots, then again peasants, Dutch
women, Swiss, Italians, etc.

They then begged the Duke to come to the Fair, which was
very pretty.   Booths in quantities, with ladies and gentlemen
all in character, musicians, Tyroleans, Chinese shop, fortune
tellers; . . . the shops were well stocked with things, and all
got some very pretty little remembrance—ribbons, gloves,
perfumes, fruit, etc., and one Chinese shop was attended by a
very rich lady, who gave us really some beautiful little things.
After walking round the Fair we had a little pantomime;
harlequin and Columbine danced very well. . . . My dear
little Augusta's *minuet de la cour*—perfection, with an air
and a grace which one seldom sees in so young a child.   She
acted her part capitally. . . . We then returned to the great
ball-room, where the fine quadrille was danced . . . the
stage dancing-master had given himself great trouble, and it
answered perfectly.   When all the shows were thought to be
over there appeared all the court cards, exquisitely done by
four ladies appearing as the kings, four gentlemen the queens,
the most laughable thing I ever saw . . . and the clock
struck four before we parted.   I was not the least tired, and
came away so amused that I shall never forget it, everybody
pleased and delighted, it was impossible to be otherwise, not
a rub the whole of the day.[1]

A favourite way of celebrating the birthday of the
Viceroy was by a series of *tableaux vivants*, when the
subjects chosen were generally connected in some way or
other with the Duke.   In 1834 the scenes consisted of
incidents in the lives of his ancestors, and included "The
marriage of Henry the Lion with Matilda of England at
Münden," "Saint Elizabeth of Hungary," and "Queen
Elizabeth of England receiving the tidings of the defeat of the
Spanish Armada."   Referring to the approaching festivity,

[1] "Letters of Princess Elizabeth of England," p. 179.

the Landgravine says, " She [The Duchess of Cambridge] has
asked five hundred people—in which she is perfectly right, for
it pleases all; as I can say with truth my brother is adored.
They dine with *me*, which saves their servants all the evening, and I am to have twenty-four at table." Writing after
the event, she remarks, " Countess Kneffstein was of all those
I saw the most perfect as St. Elizabeth, never can I describe
it—her piety, beauty, grace, dignity—I was quite wild,
it was something I had never seen before, and shall never
see again, for it was quite celestial." Another time the
attributes of the Duke were symbolised, and Miss Ella
Taylor [1] recollects, when quite a little girl, appearing in a
scene designed to illustrate the Duke's great charity. " I
was asked," she says, " to stand barefoot by my mother, who
was in a kneeling position. To this I strongly objected, but
yielded at last to the bribe of the Lord Chamberlain, who
promised me a fine wax doll if I would take off my shoes
and stockings." Even Princess Mary, young as she was,
had a part assigned to her in these representations, and years
afterwards she distinctly remembered sitting on the step
of the bed watching " Mama make up George for the
tableaux."

The royal parents liked to have their children with them
as much as possible, and a familiar sight in the Herren-
hausen Avenue was the Duke and Duchess taking their
daily promenade, followed by Prince George and Princess
Augusta. Studies were pursued with regularity and every
advantage afforded in the way of masters. Ample provision
was also made for the children's amusement, while little
dances were of frequent occurrence, and an old friend of the
family recalls a juvenile party at the Palace where Prince
George appeared in the uniform of the King's Rifles, at that
time dark green, covered with innumerable silver buttons.
Captain ——'s boy, now a general, was also there, very
naughty and sulky, and when the kind Duke went up to ask

---

[1] Daughter of General Taylor who held the appointment of Paymaster-
General to the German Legion. Both General and Mrs. Taylor enjoyed the
friendship of the Duke and Duchess of Cambridge.

him what was the matter, he struck his host a blow in the face
with his fist. The Duke good-naturedly laughed at the incident, which he never forgot, and in after years, when the boy
went to Sandhurst, always made a point of asking to see him.

Prince George was sent home at the age of eleven, in
order that he might receive an English education, and for
the next five years resided at Windsor under the care of the
King and Queen, returning occasionally to Hanover to visit
his parents. The Landgravine describes her nephew, at the
age of fourteen, as "very cheerful, extremely manly, civil,
obliging, in short quite a *dear*." A year later she writes[1]:—

Hanover, March 21, 1834.

. . . I am trying to stretch this house by taking out the
comforts, but leaving a row of small chairs round the *rooms*,
ornamenting my rooms with fine flowers and doing all I
possibly can to make it pretty, convenient and nice; it will
sound nothing to your English ears, for you are so used to
Crowds; but I am to have near three hundred people in the
Salle, where they are to dance. . . . This *Thé* is given to my
nephew George of Cambridge, who quits us soon for England
—it is his last ball here. . . . We don't talk of his departure,
for it is a great trial to his Mother; but he does so well in
England that those that love him must own the King and
Queen's education is perfect for him.

Hanover, April 2, 1834.

. . . The last week has been taken up in writing volumes
to England by George of Cambridge, who left Hanover this
morning. You may suppose what a trial it has been to the
Duchess; she is not quite well, so of course it goes the
harder; still between friends he is so well off under our
most perfect Queen's protection and care that he is a most
fortunate boy; and as they have now another *baby* which
is of all the pretty children you ever saw the prettiest, she
will serve with Gussy as their balm.

The weather is beautiful to-day, but I have such a headache that I must keep quiet, till I go to dinner at Adolphus',
which I would not miss for the world. . . . This week I
suppose we shall have nothing grand, as the Duchess of
Cambridge is not stout, and now out of spirits. On Monday

[1] "Letters of Princess Elisabeth of England," pp. 231, 233, 240.

the Cassino open their new Salle, and we are asked to it;
I believe it is to be a grand affair. . . . The Duchess had
a little dance on Monday for George, but she could not
appear, she was so unwell; so I was obliged to come forward
and do the honours to assist my Brother. . . .

Hanover, May 20, 1834.

I want him [Adolphus] to make a little Tour of a few
days just to recover himself; for the hot weather, much
business, and that business always going on, does him no
good; a few days' absence will be of use, and I am prevailing
upon him to go. . . .

The first two years of Princess Mary's life were passed at the
Viceregal Palace and the Villa Monbrillant. At the age of
three she was taken by her mother on a visit to England, and
the Duchess and her little daughter stayed awhile at Windsor
Castle. William IV. took a great fancy to his godchild, and
the gold chain and locket containing the King's hair, which
he gave her as a parting gift, were always kept among the
Princess's most treasured possessions. Both the King and
Queen were much attached to the Duchess of Cambridge, and
when she came to England Her Royal Highness invariably
spent a few weeks at the Castle. The Duchess, however,
was not a good sailor, and avoided, when possible, the dis-
comfort of crossing the Channel, so her visits to this country
were not very frequent, and she seldom remained for any
length of time.

Previous to Prince George's return to the Continent
in 1835, the King conferred upon him the Order of the
Garter, and his Aunt of Hesse-Homburg, who was then staying at Frogmore, thus describes the ceremony, "The chapter
was held at the Castle; a very numerous attendance of
Knights, and the finest dinner I ever saw in my life—the
plate, the fine, magnificent St. George's Hall, the splendour
of the whole thing was enough to make one feel proud, till
I thought of the littleness of all earthly concerns. . . . We
had a large assembly afterwards—all over by twelve, being
Saturday night." In the same year the Prince received a

H. R. H. Princess Mary of Cambridge
at the age of 2
In the collection of
H. R. H. The Duke of Teck.

commission in the Hanoverian army. He was a very good horseman, and his leading of the musical ride in the farewell festivities of 1837 won the admiration of the military staff.

At the death[1] of William IV., by virtue of the change in the laws of succession, the Duke of Cumberland became King of Hanover, and on the 1st of September, 1837, the Duke and Duchess of Cambridge left with their children for England. They were accompanied by Miss Kerr,[2] who had been lady-in-waiting to the Duchess for some years, Baroness Ahlefeld,[3] and Baron Knesebeck. The Baroness, after a short stay in this country, went back to Germany, but ever remained a dear friend of her royal mistress, whom she occasionally visited. Baron Knesebeck continued in the service of the Cambridge family until his death. In appearance he was tall and aristocratic, and his bushy snow-white hair and dark eyebrows made him a striking figure in any assembly. Although somewhat blunt and downright in manner, he was loved and esteemed by all who knew him, and much liked in London society. His devotion to his royal patrons knew no bounds, and Princess Mary grew up to regard him in the light of a favourite old uncle.

The first year in England was spent at Cambridge House,[4] Piccadilly, the lease of which the Duke had purchased when he gave up his residence in South Audley Street,[5] in 1830. Both Princess Augusta and Princess Mary were present with their parents at the Queen's coronation, and the Duchess, it was said at the time, looked regal in "a robe of estate of purple velvet, and a circlet of gold on her head;" her train was borne by Lady Caroline Campbell, and her coronet by Lord Villiers. Soon after the State festivities

---

[1] June 20, 1837.

[2] Second daughter of Lord Robert Kerr; she married, in 1841, Major-General Cornwall, A.D.C. to the first Duke of Cambridge.

[3] Baroness Ahlefeld lived to the great age of 103; she died in November, 1897.

[4] Cambridge House, after the death of the Duke of Cambridge, passed into Lord Palmerston's possession, and is now the Naval and Military Club.

[5] This house is now known as Alington House, and occupied by Lord Alington.

were concluded the Duke and Duchess of Cambridge removed to Kew, and took up their residence at Cambridge Cottage, which had been considerably enlarged for their reception.

Kew, in those days a pretty country village, had long been connected with the Royal family, but it is with the life and reign of George III. that the place is chiefly associated. In the Palace, leased by the representatives of the Capel family to his father,[1] George III. was brought up, and after he came to the throne part of every year was spent at Kew. Indeed, so attached was the King to the home of his youth that he purchased the freehold of the Capel estate, which included Kew House,[2] where he and Queen Charlotte resided, when the Palace was given over to the Prince of Wales and the Duke of York, while another house, long since disappeared, was reserved for the younger children. George III. also acquired many small properties on the south side of Kew Green, including the cottage which he gave to his son Prince Adolphus. This house, afterwards known as Cambridge Cottage, was in former years the residence of Lord Bute, the friend and adviser of Frederick, Prince of Wales, and later on of Mr. Planta, whose daughter[3] gave daily lessons at the Palace. The Duke of Cambridge took his wife to the Cottage for a short time after their marriage, but did not again occupy it until the summer of 1838.

If the glory of Kew had passed away with the abandonment of the Palace as a royal residence, many landmarks yet remained, and Princess Mary's young life was spent amidst the scenes which had awakened the interest and kindled the affections of her grandfather, George III. The Palace, though no longer tenanted, was still standing, the Gardens retained their original character, and the Village Green wore much the same aspect as in olden days.

---

[1] Frederick, Prince of Wales.

[2] Kew House was pulled down in 1802.

[3] Miss Planta died in 1834. "Miss Planta's part in the Court Calendar is that of English teacher; but it seems to me that of personal attendant upon the two eldest princesses. She is with them always, when they sup, work, take their lessons, or walk" ("Diary and Letters of Madame D'Arblay," vol. ii. p. 126).

Princess Mary and myself [writes a guest at Cambridge Cottage some twenty years later] were taken over the Palace by the housekeeper, Mrs. Murphy, an old lady of ninety, who had a cottage in the grounds. She, of course, remembered the old Royal family, and showed us the chair in which Queen Charlotte died—the only piece of furniture left in the Palace. The house is small and very plain, and the wainscotting in the drawing-room is what might be found in an old country house. The Princesses had rooms in the attics, with sloping roofs—so small that the Royal ladies were obliged to hang their hoops outside their doors, and Mrs. Murphy showed us the pegs placed there for this purpose. The gentlemen-in-waiting lived in a house close by; the kitchen was in another house, so that their Majesties must often have run the risk of getting cold dinners. In a secluded part of the grounds stands the Queen's Cottage, which the Princesses had built for their mother, and presented to her as a surprise on her birthday. It is a quaint little place, and the drawing-room is, as it were, papered with Hogarth's prints.

As far back as the sixteenth century rare plants were cultivated at Kew, and that the Capel family upheld the reputation of the estate is evident from the diary of Mr. Evelyn, who writes: " After dinner we went from Sheene to Kew, to visite Sir Henry Capell, whose orangery and myrtetum are most beautiful and perfectly well kept." The Royal owners jealously guarded the traditions of the Gardens, and it is in no small measure due to their zeal in the cause of horticulture that the present unrivalled school of botany, in the development of which Princess Mary took so keen an interest, owes its initiation.

The arrival of the Duke and Duchess of Cambridge was naturally regarded as a great event at Kew, which at that time had no steam communication with London, and was separated from the town of Richmond by two miles of country road. The principal houses stood on the Green, and many were occupied by ladies and gentlemen, at one time about the Court and now royal pensioners. In the immediate neighbourhood were a few farm-houses, while the usual cottages and quaint old shops familiar to Surrey village life completed the surroundings of Princess Mary's English home. The Duke was looked upon much in the same light as a country squire, a position he readily accepted, and willingly took an active part in all that concerned the welfare of the village and its inhabitants. In fact, so far as his rank allowed, he led the life of a private gentleman, and at his death the same simplicity was observed by the Duchess and Princess Mary.

Cambridge Cottage assumed its present proportions in 1840, when the east wing and portico were built. These additions contributed not a little to the size and picturesqueness of the house, and made the country residence of the Cambridge family, though unpretentious, a by no means insignificant building. The drawing-room and library were on the ground floor of the new wing. They communicated one with the other and overlooked an old-fashioned garden, full of lilac, may, and laburnum. In the choice of furniture, comfort rather than display was studied, but the Duchess possessed many pretty things and much valuable china, which she and Princess Mary always arranged with their own hands. The tapestry covering the chairs and ottoman in the drawing-room was a souvenir of Hanover days and a specimen of the untiring industry of the ladies about the Vice-regal Court. Another proof of their affection and regard was seen in the centre carpet, also worked by them, and sent to the Duke and Duchess of Cambridge after their arrival at Kew. The Duke's birthday was appropriately chosen for the presentation, and that date was embroidered on the border, together with the loyal and expressive words:—

> "Liebe, Treue, Dankbarkeit,
> Kennen weder Raum noch Zeit.
>
> "Sie belebten Herz und Hand,
> Bringen Gruss aus Deutchem Land.
>
> "Hohe! nehmt mit Huld entgegen
> Was sie Euch zu Fuszen legen."

The dining-room, hung with family portraits, opened into the library, which was a large and comfortable. room

Garden Room.   The Duchess of Cambridge's apartments.   Princess Mary's Sitting-room.

Dining-room.   Library.   Drawing-room.

CAMBRIDGE COTTAGE.

containing the piano and billiard table, and often used by
the family to sit in after dinner. Princess Mary's apartments were over the drawing-room; the schoolroom [1] faced
the garden, and her bedroom, small and simply furnished,
adjoined her dresser's room. Near at hand was the Duchess'
boudoir, where she received her intimate friends. In the old
part of the Cottage were the Duke's apartments and those of
Princess Augusta, who, after her marriage, still retained the
same rooms. Here, too, was the little library in which the
Duke often sat, and on the ground floor the "garden" or
breakfast-room.[2]

The parish church, so intimately associated with Princess
Mary's life, was situated on the Green within a hundred
yards of Cambridge Cottage. It was built in the reign of
Queen Anne, and the fabric had been enlarged from time to
time, while corresponding changes were made in the interior.
One of the more important alterations was carried out in
1805, when the members of the Vestry expressed their thanks
to the King "for beautifying the church and building a
gallery where their Majesties and the Royal family have
graciously condescended to attend divine service." This
gallery filled the west end of the church and was divided
into three parts. In the centre was the royal pew, used by the
Duke and Duchess of Cambridge and their children, the pews
adjoining being reserved for the equerries and ladies-in-
waiting. The interior of the church was very unpretending,
for there was no chancel and the communion table was of
the plainest description, while the raised benches on either
side of it were occupied by the school children,[3] the girls in

[1] Afterwards used by Princess Mary as her sitting-room.
[2] When the Duchess of Cambridge died, the Queen continued the tenancy
of the Cottage to the present Duke of Cambridge, who has made a point of
keeping the house and grounds just as they were during his mother's lifetime.
The old-fashioned furniture is still in the rooms, the same pictures hang on
the walls, and the garden is unchanged. Not long ago a member of the
late Duchess' household was in the library, and noticing that the piano
was not placed as in her time, mentioned the matter to the housekeeper,
Mrs. Mold, saying, "We can't have the piano so, Eliza; it must be turned
round, and put as it was when Princess Mary used to play to Prince Teck."
[3] The school originally endowed by Lady Capel in 1721 received special
assistance from George IV., and was called the "King's Free School."

red cloaks and poke bonnets. The Vicar[1] preached from a high pulpit, the clerk below making the responses. Towards the end of his life, being troubled with deafness and unable to hear the preacher from the gallery, the Duke sat in a large square pew near the pulpit. Close by were the schoolboys, and every Sunday he counted them. If any were missing, he would lean over his pew and say to the schoolmaster, " Simpson, there are two or three (as the case might be) boys not here to-day." " They are ill, Your Royal Highness," Simpson would reply in a necessarily loud whisper. " Send to the Cottage for soup for them," was the invariable answer.

The Duke was a strong Churchman, and in his simple way, very religious, but, as a friend of His Royal Highness used to say, " his religion sometimes took rather an unconventional form." He would frequently make audible remarks when the service was in progress. On one occasion, after the officiating clergyman had repeated the usual exhortation—" Let us pray," the Duke was heard to reply, " By all means." Another time he startled those near him by saying, " Shawms, shawms! what are they ? " During a very dry summer, the Vicar read the prayer for rain; at the close the Duke joined fervently in the " Amen," adding, in exactly the same tone of voice, " but we shan't get it till the wind changes." One Sunday, during the reading of the offertory sentences, when the words, " Behold, the half of my goods I give to the poor," were read, His Royal Highness astonished his fellow-worshippers by exclaiming, " No, no, I can't do that ; a half is too much for any man, but I have no objection to a tenth." Again, on hearing the text, " For we brought nothing into the world, neither may we carry anything out," he ejaculated, " True, true—too many calls upon us for that." The Duke at times expressed himself in a somewhat forcible manner. After hearing an eloquent preacher at the Temple Church, he observed to his friend Sir Frederick Thesiger,[2] as they were

[1] The Rev. R. B. Byam.
[2] Afterwards Lord Chancellor and raised to the peerage as Baron Chelmsford.

walking up the Strand together, "That was a d—d good sermon," a criticism which in no way implied irreverence, much less profanity, but one that might have astonished a less intimate friend than the late Lord Chancellor.

Lady Munster, whose mother[1] was State Housekeeper at Kensington Palace, recalls an incident in her early life showing the Duke's fondness for children. One day when she and her sister were leaving the Palace with their French governess, they met him entering the courtyard on his way to visit the Duke of Sussex. As the children passed he stopped them, saying, "Bless my heart! I know these children, don't I? Whose are they?" The governess replied, "*Ce sont les enfants*[2] *de* Lady Augusta Gordon, *Monsieur le Prince.*" "What," said the Duke, "both of them?" "*Oui, Monsieur le Prince, toutes les deux.*" "You mean both the ducks, nice little quack quacks," rejoined His Royal Highness, laughing heartily, and evidently much pleased with his pun.

Always charitably disposed himself, he was anxious that his children should develop the same virtue, and when the family were in Piccadilly it was his custom every day to give Princess Mary a sixpence for the sweeper who kept the crossing opposite Cambridge House. One morning the Princess forgot the sixpence, and on her return to breakfast mentioned the omission. The Duke immediately summoned the footman and ordered him to escort the Princess and her governess back to the park, so that the sweeper might not be disappointed. An amusing incident, illustrating the Duke's ready sense of humour, happened when a playmate of Princess Mary's was lunching at Cambridge Cottage. Some special cheesecakes had been handed round; there was one left in the dish which the servant was taking away. "Have another cheesecake, Miss ——," said the Duke. As he spoke he saw, in the looking-glass opposite, the footman

[1] Lady Augusta Fitzclarence, daughter of William IV. She married firstly the Honble. John Kennedy Erskine, and secondly Lord John Gordon.

[2] Wilhelmina Erskine, now Countess of Munster, and Millicent Erskine, who subsequently married Mr. Wemyss.

putting the delicate morsel into his mouth. "Bless my soul!" exclaimed His Royal Highness, "you're too late now, for it's down the fellow's throat."

The Duke was kind, courteous, and sympathetic, and a great favourite with the people. He liked and understood them, and they in turn appreciated his virtues and admired his personality. Without any pretence to eloquence he had a manly and unaffected style of speaking, and whenever he took the chair at a meeting it was sure to be a success. A zealous and indefatigable friend of charitable undertakings, he was Patron or President of almost every benevolent institution in London; and not only did he help with pecuniary support, but in many cases took a large share in the administrative work. He was always ready to recognise artistic merit, and manifested the same interest in the drama as in music and painting. When Macready retired from the management of the Theatre Royal, Covent Garden, the Duke of Cambridge presented the testimonial which had been subscribed for by "lovers of the National Drama."

The Duchess of Cambridge, a handsome, stately lady somewhat above the average height of women, was forty years of age when she came to live at Kew. Her features were striking, and the dark eyes and eyebrows made her appearance most attractive. When in repose her face wore rather a severe expression, but directly she spoke her countenance lighted up and a charming smile at once betrayed the gentle nature within. She had perfectly shaped hands, a point of beauty she retained to the last. Dignified in bearing and manner, as became a great lady brought up in the sentiments of the *ancien régime*, the Duchess was invariably kind and gracious to those about her. She personally attended to the management of the household, and in every way endeavoured to make her servants feel that she was their friend as well as their mistress. When Oppermann, the old German cook who had come over with the family from Hanover, died, the Duchess, on the day of his funeral, directed that every blind in Cambridge Cottage should be drawn down, and she herself remained indoors all day.

Punctuality was a strong point with Her Royal Highness, and she never allowed the carriage to be kept waiting longer than was necessary. Method and regularity were seen in every department, and it would have been difficult to find a household better ordered than that of Cambridge Cottage.

With her children the Duchess was most affectionate and considerate. She was the recipient of their childish confidences, and ever ready to sympathise with them in their joys and sorrows, yet the love and devotion she lavished upon them never caused her to forget her duties as a mother. " Train a child up in the way he should go" was a precept, the true inwardness of which, she fully appreciated, and that she succeeded beyond her highest expectations is shown by the splendid example which Princess Mary has left to successive generations.

The Duchess took great pleasure in her garden, and might often be seen picking the dead leaves off the roses or weeding the lawn with a long-handled spud. A true lover of nature, she delighted in birds, and was fond of watching their habits. During the winter months it was her custom to sally forth with a basket of breadcrumbs to feed the birds in Kew Park; the robins knew her quite well, and flew to meet her. She was naturally industrious and always had some needlework or knitting in hand. Charitable in the truest sense of the word, her immediate care was for the sick and poor of Kew, but she did not forget other claims, and every year handed over a sum of money to Mr. Walbaum,[1] to be administered among her German charities.

Her Royal Highness had much ability, and was a good conversationalist, while her keen sense of fun and humour made her a most delightful companion. She liked reading and being read to, and was an appreciative listener, a serious book being selected for the early part of the day, and lighter literature reserved for the evening. She was a thorough musician, possessing a beautiful soprano voice, and greatly enjoyed the opera. The Duchess was also warmly interested in politics; she was a frequent attendant at the

[1] The Rev. Charles Walbaum, Chaplain of the German Chapel Royal.

debates in the House of Lords, and never missed reading her daily paper. Such was the mother of Princess Mary, and it is not surprising that so amiable and accomplished a lady soon gained the affections of the people at Kew, became a favourite with the Royal Family, and a prominent personage in London society.

The Duke and Duchess of Cambridge paid many visits to Rumpenheim, near Frankfort, a favourite palace of the Hesse family, prettily situated on the Maine. In former years it was the home of Princess Mary of England, daughter of George II. and great-grandmother of Princess Mary of Cambridge. On her husband, the Landgrave of Hesse, embracing the Romish Faith, the Princess left Cassel and settled at Rumpenheim, then a small outlying *domäne*, in order to escape the Roman Catholic influence she feared for her children; it was during her occupation that the palace was enlarged, and made the handsome and convenient residence it is at the present day. In due course the property came to the Duchess of Cambridge's father, the Landgrave Frederick, and Miss Knight,[1] who dined at the Hessian Palace in 1824, records—

Rumpenheim has been built quite in the style of an old country house, with a print-room, and furniture such as was in vogue ninety years ago. The garden was laid out after the same model. Everything was remarkably neat, and the dinner very good. The Landgrave had not forgotten his English, and talked much of his visit to London and "Aunt Emily." I believe he was at that time called "the handsome Prince of Hesse," and he had certainly great remains of beauty.

The Landgrave Frederick was anxious to see the family connection kept up, and thought, not unwisely, that this end would best be attained by establishing a common place of meeting. Accordingly, he bequeathed Rumpenheim jointly to his six children,[2] accompanying the bequest with the wish

---

[1] "Autobiography of Miss Knight," vol. ii. p. 148.

[2] The Duchess of Cambridge outlived all her brothers and sisters, and became the sole owner of Rumpenheim. At her death, in 1889, the property

that his children and grandchildren should meet there every second year. This wish was respected, and biennial gatherings of his descendants took place regularly at the Palace. The different members of the family had their separate suites of apartments, and brought their own servants, but all dined together in the great hall. It was essentially a family party and in this way Princess Mary was enabled to make the acquaintance of the large circle of relations on her mother's side. As these reunions grew in number, lifelong friendships were formed, and often marriages were arranged. With Prince Frederick and Prince George of Hesse, who lived at the palace all the year round, their niece was a great favourite, and Princess Mary spent many happy months in the society of her uncles, aunts, and cousins at Rumpenheim.

When the Duchess and her daughters went to Hesse they often stopped on their way to explore some place of interest. Now and then a longer tour was undertaken, and in 1840–41 the family stayed several months in Italy, where Princess Mary's fair childish beauty won much admiration. Young as she was, the visit made a great impression upon her. It was the first and last time she ever went to Rome, and long afterwards she was fond of dwelling upon her Roman experiences. " I remember so well," she said on one occasion, "when I was a little girl in Rome with Mama and Augusta ; they used to go into the churches and galleries, but I was always left outside [1] under the charge of an attendant, whose one idea of amusing me was to run me up and down in front of the building the whole time." Save for these periodical excursions, Princess Mary passed her girlhood in what she delighted to call " dear old England."

---

passed to the blind son of her nephew, the Landgrave Frederick, but having inherited Philipsruhe, which is also on the Maine, he lent Rumpenheim to his brother, Prince Frederick Charles, who married Princess Margaret, youngest daughter of the Empress Frederick.

[1] The Duchess of Cambridge feared infection, and the chill atmosphere of the churches and galleries for the little Princess.

CHAPTER II.

EARLY DAYS AT CAMBRIDGE COTTAGE.

1838-1843.[1]

Princess Mary at four years old—Walks with papa—At the age of five—
Miss Draper's arrival—Ellinor Napier—First sorrow—The Honble.
Mrs. Dalrymple's recollections — The Queen's coronation — High
spirits—Fondness for dolls—Miss Howard arrives—Early visits to
Windsor — Fancy ball at Buckingham Palace — The Duchess of
Gloucester — Princess Augusta's marriage—New responsibilities—
Work in the parish—Birds'-nesting—Sir William Hooker—A village
acquaintance—The Rev. William Harrison.

WHEN the Cambridge family settled at Kew Princess Mary
was four years old. In the home circle, she had no companions of her own age, but this fact did not in any
way interfere with the happiness of her young days, for
every one was devoted to the little Princess, whose sunny
disposition and winning ways made her the pet of the entire
household. She was quite happy romping in the garden with
Vandal the nurse, who had been with her from babyhood,
or wandering about Kew Park making daisy chains with
Miss Kerr—but her greatest treat was a walk with "papa."
Often, in the spring and summer, the Duke would take
his little daughter into the adjoining meadows, where she
loved to gather primroses and other wild flowers; while during
the winter months, she might frequently be seen trundling
a hoop along the lanes, and running backwards and forwards
to her father, receiving at each turn some fresh expression of
paternal approval.

[1] Some of the personal recollections in this chapter refer to incidents
which occurred a few years later.

H.R.H. PRINCESS MARY OF CAMBRIDGE AT THE AGE OF 4.

From a painting by Reichmann.

Many years have passed since then, and the majority
of the villagers who witnessed those scenes have gone to
their long home; but a few still remain, and one old
inhabitant recollects seeing the Duke of Cambridge standing
on the Green, watching, with manifest delight, his little girl
jumping on and off a fallen tree, her merry sweet face
sparkling with delight at each success and her golden
ringlets waving in the wind.   Lady Munster remembers
Princess Mary walking in Kensington Gardens with her
stately mother. "The Duchess," says Lady Munster, "was
dressed in a long cloak of ermine, which struck my infantine
mind as too gorgeous for words.   She was accompanied
by a lady-in-waiting, and followed by a 'red footman,' as we
children used to call the royal servants; and I have not
forgotten my feelings of childish indignation that Princess
Mary was allowed to pick the flowers at her own sweet will,
unrebuked by the 'green man,'[1] a personage of whom we
stood in the greatest awe."

Even at the age of five the Princess had her own ideas of
what was becoming, and in after years, when recalling incidents of her childhood, told how the Queen Dowager gave
her a large bonnet covered with feathers, which the Queen
thought did not suit herself. She remembered being made
to drive from Kensington Palace to Marlborough House,
where Queen Adelaide then resided, to show herself in the
bonnet, and crying all the way because she did not think it
became her. The Princess never forgot the visits paid as
a child to the Duke of Wellington, with whom she was
a great favourite. She was often taken to see the Duke, who
entertained a profound admiration for her beautiful fair curls,
and would gently play with them as he talked to the little
Princess in the library at Apsley House.

When she was seven years old the question of education
had to be considered, and a competent and sympathetic
governess was found in Miss Draper, to whom her royal pupil
soon became warmly attached. But devoted as the Princess
was to her governess, the restraint proved somewhat

---

[1] Gatekeeper.

irksome at first, and no opportunity of escaping from the
schoolroom was ever missed; when remonstrated with she
would laughingly reply, "Oh, I know quite enough for this
world." If out walking with her father, all manner of
excuses were thought of to avoid returning at the appointed
hour, and a familiar plan of Princess Mary's was to run away
and hide, leaving the Duke to search for her as best he could.
Frequently she would fly into Mrs. Sears' shop on the Green,
and, concealing herself behind the skirts of the friendly shopkeeper, whisper excitedly, "Mind you say I'm not here.
Don't let papa know where I am." Whereupon the good
woman replied, "I can't tell a story, even for you, Princess.
But keep still, and I'll do my best." Presently the Duke
bustled into the shop, exclaiming, "Where's my Polly? I
know you've got her somewhere." With a solemn shake
of her head, and a pretence of looking round, Mrs. Sears
invariably asserted that she could not see the Princess.
"Well, well, she can't be far off," answered the Duke, good-
humouredly, starting to look elsewhere. As soon as this
little comedy had been enacted, the child, with a burst of
laughter, would emerge from the ample folds of the skirt that
had shielded her from view, and, running down the road,
spring on her father's back. The Duke fully entered into
the fun of the situation, and kissing the little truant, bade
her run in to her lessons, advice which Princess Mary
invariably followed, for with all her waywardness she was
seldom disobedient.

The Princess often visited the Royal Dairy,[1] and had her
special pets among the cows. When the grass in the wild
part of Kew Gardens was cut, the "Royal cows," as well as
those belonging to the various dairy-keepers in the district,
were turned in to graze, and one of her favourite games was to
drive the cows about for the amusement of seeing Kemble,
the old man in charge, chase them back into their allotted
pastures.

Sometimes the neighbours were invited to bring their

---

[1] The Royal Dairy stood in the yard of the house now occupied by the
Bank of Kew.

children to Cambridge Cottage, a privilege often accorded to
Lady Napier, whose daughters Ellinor[1] and Lucy were
about the same age as the Princess, and the three girls soon
became great friends. The untimely death[2] of Lucy was
Princess Mary's first sorrow, but in her own distress at the
loss of her playmate she did not forget to send Ellinor a
touching letter of sympathy, tenderly alluding to "that little
angel Lucy." Ellinor Napier was a great favourite with
the Duchess of Cambridge, and just the companion she
desired for her daughter. The two children saw much of
each other, and the intimacy ripened into a lifelong
friendship.

" My earliest recollection of Princess Mary," writes Mrs.
Dalrymple, " was when, accompanied by Miss Kerr, she
paid her first visit to our house at Kew. I can distinctly
recall the occasion and the appearance of the little Princess,
then barely six years old. She was seated in a wickerwork
chair, her long fair hair falling in ringlets over her shoulders.
The refined features were beautifully moulded, the blue eyes
full of expression, and rendered more striking by long black
eyelashes and dark pencilled eyebrows, while the lovely
mouth, dimpled cheeks, and well-formed chin, completed a
model of beauty in childhood. The complexion with its
delicate tints called to mind the inside of some rare shell,
and according to the varied emotions of the most tender,
sensitive heart, so would her colour be ever changing, reflect-
ing all her feelings and the index of her joys and sorrows.
Although a large child for her years, she was very upright in
figure, and even at this early age, the setting of the well-
shaped, classical head on the neck, gave a grace, a dignity,
and free movement which was noticeable all through her
life. Her feet were finely formed, and she inherited her
mother's beautiful hands and long tapered fingers. She was
attired in a short white frock and blue sash, with embroidered
spencer of muslin and large white hat, short white socks,
and walking shoes with strap and button. We were both
observant children, and I recollect that while I took note of

[1] Now the Honble. Mrs. Dalrymple.   [2] Lucy Napier died in 1842.

all the details of her looks and dress, nothing meanwhile escaped the Princess regarding myself.

"We were children together in our games and sympathies. Saturday, the weekly half-holiday, was the day on which the verdict was passed respecting our conduct during the week, and was either a day of encouragement or one of dire distress and tears.   At half-past twelve a little note of three inches square, fastened by a large thick red seal and crown, such as a child delights to make, was handed in by a servant in royal livery, whose appearance on first acquaintance filled me with amazement.   Those precious notes were carefully cut open round the seal and eagerly read.   The welcome lines generally ran thus: 'Dear Ellinor,' or 'Dearest dear Ellinor, Mama says will you come at 3 o'clock and go a walk with me, remain to tea at six, and tell 'your servant to come for you at 8 o'clock.   Yours affectionately, Mary Adelaide,' or, 'Your affectionate friend, Mary.   P.S.—You must come, dear.'   The writing was round text, firm and clear, without a blot or mis-spelt word.   As time passed on, these notes became longer and the writing smaller, with an occasional postscript added, 'I have been in disgrace,' or, 'I have something to tell you.'   By which I understood there had been what the Princess called a 'battle.'

"Princess Mary's thirst for information on all subjects was insatiable.   Before our day of meeting a number of questions was prepared and counted over and over again on her fingers.   As soon as we were alone the questions began, and when the fingers were exhausted, the thumb was brought into action.   This was the signal that the last question, generally the most difficult to answer, was reached. Often she expressed dissatisfaction that I did not sufficiently enter into detail, and, being a child myself, I had frequently to admit ignorance of the matter on which my opinion was asked.   Moreover, the Duchess had told me that 'Mary was too curious on some points,' and that I was not to indulge this curiosity, but pass on to some play or other.

"The schoolroom at Cambridge Cottage, furnished with all the taste of a young lady's sitting-room, was a charming

room upstairs, and the three windows, crescent-shaped, overlooked a sunny garden, in spring-time and summer, gay with
flowers. The walls were hung with pictures of the Duke
and Duchess and other members of the family, and arranged
on cabinets were china ornaments and presents which had
been given from time to time to Princess Mary. Near the
window stood the bird-cage, and next it, on a tray, a
collection of very tiny scarlet flower-pots containing trees,
each tree, a representation in miniature of its kind, standing
from six to seven inches high. One, an oak with gnarled
trunk and branches, was regarded as a great curiosity. I
understood the culture to be Japanese. In other parts of
the room were toys of every description, dolls' houses,
games, and needlework. Opposite the sofa stood the table
for study and a most uncomfortable chair with a high back
and narrow seat. In summer the Princess wore cotton or
muslin frocks, and as security against ink-spots, deep
holland cuffs from the wrist to the elbow, with apron or
pinafore to match.

"When a change of book or subject was required, she
would seize that moment of comparative freedom to execute
a pirouette on one toe, a performance which, with the figure
swinging round and one limb extended, invariably ended
in misfortune, and a sharp 'crack' on the back in consequence. I was often present during arrears of work or
holiday tasks, and well recollect how these innocent imita-
tions of the ballet usually knocked down a chair or dragged
off a table-cover. But it must not be thought that such
outbursts of gaiety indicated a dislike to school-work. On
the contrary, the Princess had begun to take great interest
in her lessons, particularly in history and geography. Whilst
reading about acts of tyranny or injustice the tears would
stream from her eyes. She wept in a manner totally
unlike any other child, the tears flowed, rapidly chasing one
another down her face, and it was only when she considered
herself unjustly punished that her expression changed to
one of defiance. She delighted in discussing different
characters in history, and one day, brandishing a long ruler

in her hand, turned round suddenly and said to me, 'Can it be possible that when I go to Heaven I shall meet that murderer Henry VIII.? Never! I can't believe it—such a bad character. But there, you see, Christ died for all.'

"Children though we were, we had our serious conversations. I remember once saying to the Princess that not only had she the love of her parents and her brother and sister, but that numerous advantages were at her feet, the result of her station in life. 'Yes,' she replied, 'I am Princess Mary Adelaide of Great Britain and Ireland, and,' striking herself on the chest, 'I feel it *here*.' One summer afternoon we were swinging lazily to and fro in the garden, when a heated argument arose about the early Christian martyrs and people dying for their faith. The Princess became very excited, and asked me whether, if my father were alive, I would lay down my head on the block for him and be beheaded? 'No,' I replied, 'I do not believe I could; perhaps I might, but I do not think so.' 'Oh, what a cowardly thing to say!' quickly rejoined the Princess. 'I would die for any one I loved, for any cause that was dear to me. I would die for my dear father twice over if needful.' What I said then I do not exactly remember, but I know that my remarks only aggravated matters; the Princess lost all patience with me, and a battle royal ensued. At last I jumped out of the swing, and, curtsying very low, said, 'I regret that in spite of Your Royal Highness's exalted position, I must leave you.' This had the desired effect, and we were soon sobbing on one another's necks. But the Princess was not satisfied with the atonement made, and after she returned home wrote me a loving little letter.

"Our walks in Kew Gardens were full of liveliness and activity. I was a very fleet runner, and we often had races together. Other amusements were making buttercup and daisy chains, climbing into the old mulberry and crab-apple trees, hiding among the rhododendrons, and collecting wild flowers and grasses. Frequent visits were paid to the beautiful white lily—the first Victoria lily—which floated on the portion of water assigned to it at Kew. Sometimes we went to the hot-houses and orangery with Mr. Smith, the Curator; all the time the Princess would be asking the most intelligent questions, and Mr. Smith used to turn to whoever was in charge of us and remark on the fact.

"Princess Mary often spent an evening at our house. On one of these occasions, when she was seven years old, I remember her talking about Scotland to my brother, Lord Napier. She became much interested in his description of our home, and, turning to me, said, 'I want to come and stay with you at Thirlestane, but I know that royal visits are very expensive, so you must send in the bill to me.'

"Christmas, the New Year, and birthdays were times of special enjoyment. Great preparations were made, and mysterious pieces of needle-work engaged upon. Christmas at Cambridge Cottage in 1841 is vividly impressed upon my memory. It was the last occasion on which my dear sister Lucy was able to be present, and her lovely face and sweet gentle manner particularly attracted the Princess. The schoolroom was gay with holly berries and flowers, while the entrance hall, with long wreaths of evergreens entwined round the pillars, looked like fairyland. Against a sloping border of laurel leaves and holly berries, relieved by Christmas roses and other flowers, were tables, placed at equal distances, and on them numberless presents, from loving hearts far and near, were tastefully arranged. It was at Christmas, I think, that the Duke gave Princess Mary his annual gift of pearls. I and my sister also received presents, and the poor of the parish were not forgotten. It was a real pleasure to see the dear Princess's beaming face and that bright smile which all through her life gave a radiance to her countenance, and was sunshine to those who had the privilege of associating with her.

"The Duchess of Gloucester was deeply attached to her god-child, and often gave little entertainments at her house in Piccadilly [1] in honour of the Princess's birthday. At other times the Duchess would have exhibitions of ventriloquism for her niece's amusement, or 'little wonders' of about six

[1] Gloucester House.

years old who played the violin and piano. When I was
invited, the Princess took the greatest interest in my dress
as well as her own.   Sometimes she complained that she
thought her dress was not sufficiently attended to, and that
in her position it pleased the people to see her looking
smart.   I suggested that as she and I rushed about the
bushes so much her plain frocks were more convenient and of
little consequence if torn.   One evening I went to Cambridge
House and found the Princess very prettily dressed in white
and blue.   After looking at me, she said, 'Do not hold that
lace-edged handkerchief in your hand, dear; Mama does not
like to see children dangle their handkerchiefs.   Just put it
in your pocket.   I and all sensible people use—well, wait
a bit, I'll fetch it;' and she returned holding out a large
hem-stitched linen handkerchief.

"Except when standing, the occupants of the Royal pew
in Kew Church could not see the congregation.   This
troubled the dear Princess much; she thought it very dull,
and I sympathised with her, as the sermons were often long
and wearisome.   My family occupied a large square pew on
one side of the church near the schoolboys, who were kept
in order by the master with a long stick.   The Princess
wished to see me in church, as she was anxious to know how
I behaved, and the restlessness for which she was continually
reproved was a frequent jump up and down, that she gave
for no other reason than to have a look at me.

"Occasionally I went to Cambridge Cottage on a Sunday
afternoon, and I shall never forget the kind consideration of
the Duchess.   She knew and appreciated my mother's views
on sabbatarianism, and always took care to avoid any game
or amusement in which she thought my mother might not
like me to join.   During these visits we usually read books,
or tore lint for the sick and wounded.   One Sunday afternoon, when the Duke was unable to go to church, he read all
the service aloud to himself in the library, and I recollect
being much impressed with the earnest manner in which he
prayed for his children, mentioning each by name.   The
Duke was kindness itself, and used to make great fun with

us. He asked all sorts of questions, and one day an answer
I gave pleased him greatly, although I felt shy at the time.
Patting me kindly on the head, he said, 'Well done, you
must be a philosopher!' and from that moment he always
called me 'Phil.'

"The Princess was expected to learn off by heart the
Psalms and collect for the day. On one occasion when I
was staying for a few days at Cambridge Cottage, she
appeared at my bedside early one morning, and with a very
grave expression, said, 'Hear this collect, and see if I know
it perfectly; I am very anxious about it.' Now, it so happened that the Princess used to ask me many questions about
the church in Scotland, especially regarding the country
churches in the hills, and if the collie dogs still followed
the shepherds into the sacred edifice. That morning her
manner puzzled me; however, I took the Prayer-book, and
she began to repeat solemnly the third collect for Good
Friday. The first part was said very naturally, then she
fixed her beautiful eyes upon me, saying with great emphasis
and fervour, 'Have mercy upon all Jews, Turks, Infidels,
Presbyterians, and all such hereticks, and take from them
their ignorance.'

"Princess Mary had the greatest admiration for her sister,
Princess Augusta. 'I wonder if I shall ever be as clever.
Augusta never gave Mama any trouble,' she used to say;
'I am always getting into scrapes.' Again, 'Augusta is so
handsome. What do you think of her?' Then she would
ask me, 'What do you think of George? He is very handsome and clever, is he not? In fact, we are a promising
family. But then look at the Father! look at the Mother!'
accompanying her words with one of her overwhelming
'dunches,' followed by an apology in the shape of a hug
which took all power of speech from me for the moment—
and how we laughed!

"An excellent mimic, she delighted to take people off; but
her powers in this respect were always used in a good-natured
way, and she was especially careful not to make fun of any
person born with an infirmity. She paid the utmost respect

to old age.   One day we were walking in Kew Park, watching a mason repairing a shelter, or, as Princess Mary called it, 'that hideous temple!'   While we were looking on, the man injured his hand with the tool he was using.   The Princess immediately ran to his assistance, saying, 'He is an old man, I must help him,' and with her own handkerchief she bound up his wounds.   'Now I hope the hand will soon be all right, my man,' she said, and ran back to where I was standing.   Meanwhile the mason had recognised her, and was quite overcome with gratitude.   The Princess liked to talk to me about Kew Gardens and their associations; we seldom passed the old Palace without her expressing the hope that it would never be 'torn down.' It was, she said, a building after her own heart, of great historic interest.

"She had a warm regard and great respect for Mr. Ward, a clergyman who gave her lessons in Latin and Scripture History.   He was rather striking in appearance—dark, with large deep-set eyes, regular features, and the mouth, from its peculiar shape and slightly projecting teeth, gave to his voice a deep and solemn sound.   Clerical in dress, he usually wore a double row of hem-stitched frills to his shirt-front. He had a peculiarly quiet manner, and an earnest way of speaking to the Princess regarding her impulsiveness, a fault which troubled her very much and which she was especially anxious to control.   Mr. Ward also had good influence over the Princess in inducing steady application to work, and helped her to realise the seriousness of life and the many responsibilities which awaited her as she became older and would affect others by her example.   The Princess had a splendid memory: it mattered little what the subject was, she grasped it quickly and retained easily what she had been taught.   Her tutor said that she learnt in a week what it took his best pupil three weeks to overtake.

"Most unfortunately Mr. Ward was not always punctual, and often failed to arrive at the hour fixed by the Duchess. Naturally this fault caused a good deal of inconvenience, and in the end he received his *congé*.   One day an urgent appeal reached me to go and see Princess Mary. I found her in great distress. We went together into the garden, where she poured out her sorrow and regret to me at the prospect of losing her good kind teacher, 'to whom she could say anything without being frightened.' She allowed it was not right of him to be unpunctual. 'But then, Ellinor,' she added, 'we all do something stupid, and his other pupils may be tiresome and lazy, and help to make him late. I feel I shall make an ass of myself when the time comes.' 'Oh no,' I said, 'you can never be an ass, but you may be a British lioness,' a remark which made her laugh, and she promised to submit when the new tutor arrived. The best resolutions were formed, but when the day of Mr. Ward's departure came, the Princess was nowhere to be found. After considerable search had been made, stifled sobs were heard coming from her bedroom, the door of which was locked and for a time nothing could persuade her to unfasten it. At last she opened the door, her face bathed in tears and she herself utterly exhausted, but penitent, very penitent 'because, Ellinor, it would have vexed my dear old friend to see me like this; and then I have made an—no, after all, I was just as you said I should be—a young lioness!'"

At the Queen's wedding, although only a child of seven, Princess Mary appeared quite to understand and appreciate what was going on around her, and her appearance in the procession at the Chapel Royal, St. James's, won golden opinions from her royal relatives. In describing the pageant a chronicler of the day records that "H.R.H. the Duchess of Cambridge led her young daughter, the Princess Mary, by the hand, and the mother of so beautiful a child was certain not to be seen without interest," thus endorsing the view of every one present.

About this date Vandal's place was taken by Louisa Frazer, "an exceedingly superior person, gentle, patient, and well-educated" as she is described by one who knew her when she came to Cambridge Cottage. The Princess felt deeply the separation from her old nurse, and at first refused to be comforted, sitting up till past midnight sobbing her heart out, and repeatedly saying that she knew her nurse would come back. Before long, however, the sympathetic influence of Frazer reconciled her to the change, and she warmly. reciprocated the devotion of her new attendant, who, first as dresser, and afterwards as housekeeper, spent the remainder of her days in the service of Princess Mary. Frazer's connection with her beloved mistress's life was something deeper than that of an old and valued servant; she became a friend and trusted confidante.

Full of fun and frolic, Princess Mary was the life and soul of Cambridge Cottage. Lessons over, a favourite amusement was to play about the corridors with her little friends or the faithful Frazer, and the house echoed with peals of laughter as the Princess ran from room to room, either pursued or pursuing. "Catch her, papa! Catch her, papa!" she would cry, as one or other of her companions ran past the Duke's apartments. Upstairs and downstairs she flew with eyes flashing, cheeks burning, and her bright hair falling about her shoulders. In at one window and out at the other, over the lawn and over the flower-beds, until she would sink down exhausted and out of breath. At Christmas-time Princess Mary was always in very high spirits. One Christmas Eve, having heard that Owen the steward, an old family servant, used to kiss the maids under the mistletoe which hung in the hall, she made up her mind to see the fun, and, watching for what she thought was a favourable opportunity, crept downstairs and hid behind the evergreens that decorated the pillars. Owen caught sight of her frock, and feeling sure that she was up to some mischief, made a movement as if to seize her. This greatly delighted the Princess, who ran out from her hiding-place laughing gaily, convinced that the steward had taken her for one of the maids, and that her little plan had been a complete success.

Mary, who was schoolroom maid at Cambridge Cottage, has a vivid recollection of the Princess's merry disposition. She is a very old woman now, but her face lights up with pleasure as she recalls memories of the days spent in the royal household at Kew. Her reminiscences take her back to the

H.R.H. Princess. Mary of Cambridge
at the age of 6.

In the collection of H.R.H. The Duchess of York.

time when the Princess delighted to ride on Prince George's rocking-horse, which, though long since discarded by its owner, had been carefully stored away. When "Miss Clark and Lady Arabella"[1] came there were fine romps in the old nursery; Mary had to get out the rocking-horse, and all three children mounted it at the same time, to the great glee of the little Princess. One day she had been naughty during her morning lesson, and the Duchess directed that she was to have bread and water for luncheon, a punishment Princess Mary particularly disliked. "But she was not going to let any one see it," said the old servant, "and when I went up to the schoolroom with the bread and water, Princess was sitting on the piano with her legs dangling in the air, and singing to herself as though she were quite happy."

Princess Mary had a large and varied collection of dolls. She delighted to wash and dress them, and take them out for walks, while for her "baby dolls" she entertained quite a motherly affection. "I remember," writes Lady Munster, "the visits we used to pay to Cambridge House, and I can see, as though it were yesterday, Princess Mary's fair head looking out from one of the top windows as we drove up, while she kissed one hand violently, and held up her doll with the other. King Louis Philippe had, I think, given it to her, and it was magnificently dressed, with a beautiful tiara, bracelets, necklace, and brooches, all of real diamonds, rubies, and other stones. When we (my sister and myself) were taken up to the Princess's nursery, she was generally playing with this doll, and I used to think how hard it was that I, always considered so like her, should not have a doll with diamonds and rubies too!" Nor did this love for dolls disappear with childhood; even at the age of fifteen or sixteen the Princess would sometimes take a doll into Kew Gardens. Now and then a weeding out took place, and the children of the household were made

[1] Lady Arabella West, youngest daughter of the fifth Earl of Delawarr, who assumed the surname of Sackville before West in 1843. Lady Arabella married Sir Alexander Bannermann, Bart.

happy with the gift of a "Princess Mary doll," reluctantly cast aside by reason of some physical defect, or to make room for a fresh arrival. Yet, in spite of these occasional removals, the collection grew, and when the Princess married, many of the dolls, which years before she had tended so carefully, were still in her possession.

As her daughter grew older the Duchess thought a change in the schoolroom desirable, and wished to secure the services of a more advanced English governess. Upon the recommendation of Mr. Evan Nepean, domestic chaplain to the Duchess of Gloucester, Miss Howard was selected for the post. She resided at Fulham, and drove over to Cambridge Cottage every morning. The Princess was now nine years of age, and work became more settled, but in the words of a lifelong friend of the family, "Miss Howard had no ordinary pupil to deal with; Princess Mary required far more than mere teaching. It was necessary to give a loving sympathy to the child who had a hard struggle with her own nature, so excitable, impulsive, and emotional was she, yet so earnest and anxious to do right." The new governess succeeded in gaining the confidence of her pupil, and Princess Mary began to take a more serious interest in her lessons. Still, things did not always go smoothly, and Miss Howard had occasional "battles" with her pupil. Once, when the family were at Cambridge House, she thought it her duty to refuse the Princess permission to take a walk with her father in the Green Park. The Duke felt the privation quite as much as his little daughter, and was inclined to be vexed with Miss Howard for being what he considered too strict. But a week afterwards he came to her and said, "You were right, Howard, not to let Mary go with me to feed the ducks, and I was wrong."

The Princess naturally attracted a great deal of attention when out walking in Kew, and Miss Howard, fearing that so much notice might not be good for her, mentioned the matter to the Duchess, who replied, "Oh, that will never do Mary any harm. She will soon get used to being noticed by the public. But," added Her Royal Highness, "be sure you see that she always responds." There was no need, however, to prompt the Princess on that point. From very early days she had never failed to return the salutations of all who greeted her, for it was not in her nature to slight or ignore the humblest individual. When thanking or taking leave of any one, her manner had a warmth and heartiness which endeared the Princess to the village people, and in her little kingdom of Kew she ruled the hearts of rich and poor alike.

Ever considering the sensibilities of others, she was scrupulously careful not to wound them by word or deed. Once, during her schoolroom days, she went into a shop at Richmond to buy something. When paying for the purchase she gave a sovereign to the young woman who had served her, and on receiving the change instantly put it into her purse. Her governess noticed the action, and said, in perhaps too audible a tone, " Princess, you must count your change ; you should always do so to see if it is correct." Princess Mary replied, " No, I should not like to do that ; I am sure it is correct." Then, turning to the shopkeeper, she smiled reassuringly, and said, " Good morning," fearful lest the remark about the change should have hurt the young woman's feelings.

Whenever the Queen invited Princess Mary to Windsor Miss Howard was in attendance, and on these occasions it was her duty, each evening, to take her pupil down to see the Queen, and to fetch her again before Her Majesty went in to dinner. She also accompanied Princess Mary to Germany, and the following extracts from a diary kept by Miss Howard show the consideration she invariably received from her royal patrons :—

Rumpenheim, August 20, 1843.—Arrived to-day ; thus ended a week's journey which I shall always remember with the greatest pleasure and much gratitude for the kind treatment I experienced from their Royal Highnesses the Duke and Duchess of Cambridge, at whose table I was always a guest.

Dresden, December 28.—We left Dresden on our return

home : the Duchess was most anxious that I should see everything, and frequently invited me to drive in her chariot.

Miss Howard had been ordered a particular kind of wine, and the Duke was always mindful that it should be handed to her at meals. When the family was at Rumpenheim, the Duchess expressed her regret that Miss Howard's wine was not to be procured in the neighbourhood. " Oh yes, it is," said His Royal Highness ; " I have brought it from England." In 1845 the Queen gave a fancy dress ball at Buckingham Palace,[1] and Princess Mary was allowed to go and look on at the festivities. The Duke was anxious that Miss Howard and her sister[2] should also see the sight, and very kindly made the necessary arrangements. When the day of the ball arrived, he said, " I suppose, Howard, your sister knows that she is to go in full dress." " No, sir," replied the governess, " she thinks that she is to stand in the corridor to see the guests as they pass into the Palace." " Then you must drive at once to Fulham," said His Royal Highness, "and tell her to put on full dress, as she is going with us. You have plenty of plumes, Howard, so you can soon dress her up." Miss Howard's sister, now an old lady of eighty-seven, remembers seeing the Queen dance two minuets, and describes Princess Mary as looking beautiful with her fair hair down her back, and wearing a green velvet frock cut low at the neck, and a string of pearls round her throat. The dress was given to her for the occasion by the Duchess of Gloucester.

No member of George III.'s family was more widely known

---

[1] The dresses and uniforms worn by the Queen's guests were designed to illustrate a period (1740-50) in the reign of George II. Her Majesty and Prince Albert, preceded by the grand officers of state, opened the ball with a polonaise, followed by the Duc and Duchesse de Nemours and other distinguished guests. A minuet was then danced in the Throne Room, the Queen and Prince George of Cambridge being partners, the Duchesse de Nemours dancing with Prince Albert. Quadrilles, minuets, and strathpeys succeeded, and the ball closed with Sir Roger de Coverley led by the Queen and Prince Albert.

[2] Mrs. Hatchard.

and respected for kindly acts and good works than the Duchess of Gloucester. Before her marriage she spent much time in ministering to the wants of the poor, and all her life was a liberal supporter of charitable institutions. After her husband's death[1] the Duchess retired for a time to Bagshot Park, and later on removed to the White Lodge in Richmond Park, which the Queen placed at the disposal of her aunt as a country residence. Writing of her sister from St. James's Palace in February, 1835, the Landgravine of Hesse Homburg says[2]—

. . . I have the comfort of seeing my dearest Mary much better than I expected, and acting with great good sense, much delicacy, and a great deal of good excellent feeling, but it is always a difficult thing for a widow to set out right I well know from fatal experience, all she does is fraught with good sense and judgment—that I must say. Of course, she must make various changes, which she is doing well, and with a delicacy to all those she is obliged to part with, which shows the sweetness of her character and the goodness of her heart. . . .

The Duchess of Gloucester is described by one who knew her well, as of medium height, and remarkably good-looking, with small and regular features, blue eyes, and a particularly sweet smile ; her bright and pleasing manner showed a genuine desire to make all whom she invited to her house welcome and at ease. Princess Mary was considered to be like her aunt, in many ways, more especially in her smile and gracious manner. Both the Princess and her mother were constant visitors at Gloucester House and White Lodge, while nothing was ever done at Cambridge Cottage without first consulting " Aunt Mary."

The marriage of Princess Augusta of Cambridge[3] to the

[1] Nov. 30, 1834.

[2] " Letters of Princess Elizabeth of England," p. 271.

[3] The wedding was solemnized at the Chapel Royal, Buckingham Palace, with all the splendour of a State function. The ceremony took place at nine o'clock in the evening, in the presence of the Queen and Prince Albert, the King of Hanover, the King and Queen of the Belgians, the Duke of Cambridge, who gave his daughter away, the Duchess of Cambridge, Princess Mary and Prince George of Cambridge, the Duchess of Kent, the Duchess of Gloucester, and other royal and distinguished personages.

Hereditary Grand Duke of Mecklenburg-Strelitz, which took place on the 28th of June, 1843, opened a new era in Princess Mary's life. She was no longer the "younger sister," and the responsibilities of her new position awakened qualities that, but for this change in the home circle, might have lain dormant for some years longer. She felt the separation keenly; but, child as she was, her one thought was for her mother, and her great aim henceforward was " to fill Augusta's place." With the altered condition of things, Princess Mary naturally enjoyed more of the Duchess's society, and the tie between mother and daughter became closer. As the Princess grew older her waywardness disappeared, and she began to think more of serious things. With all her young strength she fought against her natural failings, and her unselfish disposition showed itself in constant thought for others, while an anxiety to please was noticeable in every action.

When she was fourteen the daily governess system at Cambridge Cottage came to an end, and from that time her education was entrusted chiefly to masters, an alteration which marked the advent of the *grande-gouvernante*. Baroness Hammerstein, who came as lady-in-waiting to the Duchess, had charge of the Princess for a few months, but relinquished her post when Baroness Böse arrived to superintend the Princess's studies. This lady's temperament, however, was hardly suited to the task she essayed, and at the end of a year the engagement terminated. The Duchess decided to dispense with further assistance in the schoolroom, and to assume the direction of her daughter's education.

Left to the care of her mother, Princess Mary had more opportunities of taking part in the work of the parish, and thus early in life came to know much of the trials and sorrows of the poor. She inherited the strong and generous feelings of her parents, and was never happier than when engaged in helping those in distress. On one occasion Baron Knesebeck had made some inquiries about a poor woman in the village, with a view to placing the facts before the Duchess. Struck with the urgency of the case, he hastened to explain the circumstances to his Royal mistress.

During the recital Princess Mary was standing by, dressed for walking, and her tender heart was much moved by the tale of the woman's poverty. Impulsively taking off her jacket, she held it out to the Duchess, saying, "Mama, send this to the poor woman,"—and it was sent.

The village children she regarded as her special care, and was ever doing or saying something to brighten their lives. She might often be seen wending her way through Kew, bent on some errand of mercy, and no cripple was passed by without a smile of recognition or a word of sympathy. In her visits about the parish, Princess Mary found a boy who was deformed and unable to walk. She constantly went to see him, and was most anxious that he should get out into the air. At last she thought of having a little hand-cart made, which she sent him as a present from herself. This was before the days of perambulators, and it was necessary to have the cart built on purpose. The Princess personally superintended the work, and her delight was great when she met her *protégé* being wheeled about the village.

The sights and sounds of country life were very dear to her. She loved flowers, and delighted in the songs of birds. Many a time she waited in the Mortlake Lane on the chance of hearing the nightingales, and the daughter of a neighbouring farmer was particularly requested to send word to the Cottage whenever she heard them sing. Sometimes a message came after dinner, yet the Princess went all the same, and once stayed at the farm as late as ten o'clock. It always roused her indignation to see any one molesting birds. One afternoon when walking by the river she came upon a village schoolboy birds'-nesting. The boy, who knew the Princess could not bear to have the nests taken, ran off and climbed into an elm tree. Walking up to the tree, and espying the boy among the branches, where he thought himself hidden, she called out, "Now then, Tom, I know who you are. What have you been doing?" "Nothing, Your Royal Highness," the boy replied from his lofty perch. "Oh yes you have! Don't tell a lie. You've been birds'-nesting.

Come down, and don't be a coward as well as cruel." And
the boy had to come down, show what he had taken, and be
reproved.

The Gardens at Kew were a source of endless pleasure to
Princess Mary, and she made great friends with the Director,
Sir William Hooker,[1] who taught her the first principles of
gardening. He was inclined to be chary of cutting his flowers,
but the Princess generally managed to get her own way, and
he often gave her leave to fill her basket. On one occasion
some rare calceolarias, of which Sir William was specially
proud, had attracted her attention. She obtained permission
to gather some, and ran off by herself to the hot-house.
Presently she reappeared with her arms full of the beautiful
blossoms, and with much pride showed her spoils to Sir
William, whose consternation was great as he realised that
instead of the few calceolarias he had intended her to take,
she had picked nearly all his precious flowers !

If a face specially attracted Princess Mary, inquiries were
sure to be made, and an invitation to Cambridge Cottage
sometimes followed. In this way she came to know Fanny
——, whose parents occupied a farm near the royal residence. At the age of seventeen Fanny left school and came
to reside at Kew. The Princess soon noticed the new arrival
in church and about the village, and being taken with her
appearance, deputed Mr. Scard, the churchwarden, to bid her
call at the Cottage. Fanny thus describes her reception—

The Princess, who was sixteen years old, came quickly
towards me, smiling, with her hand extended. She was
tall and dignified, and her dark eyebrows and eyelashes
contrasted with her hair, which was quite golden. Her
eyes were blue, her cheeks dimpled with smiles, and her
complexion the soft colour of a monthly rose. She had a
small mouth, good teeth, and a well-shaped nose. Indeed,

[1] William Jackson Hooker was born at Norwich in 1785. At the age of
twenty-five he was appointed Regius Professor of Botany in the University
of Glasgow, and was knighted in 1836. Five years later he was made
Director of the Royal Gardens, Kew, which at that date only covered fifteen
acres. He died in 1865, and was succeeded by his son, who had acted as his
father's assistant for some years.

Winterhalter's picture, taken two years before, is a perfect likeness. The painter caught her expression as she came down the staircase to meet him, and told the Duchess he had seen the Princess as he meant to paint her.

Continuing her recollections, Fanny says—

Not long afterwards the Princess, attended by Baron Knesebeck, came to see me at the farm. I had not been told of the honour in store for me, and when the Baron entered the room where I was sitting, and said that Princess Mary had come to pay me a visit, it was some time before I grasped his meaning. Nor did I understand what he intended to convey when he added that she was waiting outside, until, chancing to look through the window, I saw a face peeping over the fence, and to my dismay recognised the Princess, who, tired of waiting, had climbed up the steep bank in order to see why the Baron did not return. Then my mistake dawned upon me, and I hurried out to pay my respects. After this I went often to Cambridge Cottage, and the Princess was a frequent visitor to the farm. She was invariably kind and considerate to me, and any little gift of mine was always graciously accepted. Knowing she liked gingerbread-nuts, I used to make them and take them to her, and every year I worked a pair of mats for her toilet-table. Nothing was ever put aside, and my basket of wax flowers was assigned quite a place of honour in her room. On New Year's Day, forty-nine years ago, the Princess gave me a glass case, which I greatly prize, containing four precious little volumes of Sir Walter Scott's poems, with Her Royal Highness's name inscribed in each.

The Princess liked me to be with her when she was dressing for dessert, and on these occasions I was sometimes the recipient of small confidences. I remember a very becoming bonnet which she used to wear, fancy straw, with little drops of black beads all round and a bunch of pink roses outside. One day when the family were leaving Kew for London, she was looking at the bonnet and said, "I think I shall have it cleaned for next summer, as George admires it so much." Her Royal Highness was most precise, and her things were kept in perfect order. She was very particular about her shoes being put one inside the other, and if ever I forgot to perform this little office to her satisfaction she would not fail to remind me of the omission. One day she remarked, "I have not a small foot, but I do not think it is a bad shape, do you?" The reply needed no consideration, for the Princess had a very beautiful foot. I was much struck with the tidiness of her desk, which on one occasion it was my privilege to pack; nothing was out of place—pens, paper, envelopes, and letters were all neatly arranged.

Her Royal Highness was not always punctual. I recollect once bringing some wall-flowers for her; the carriage was at the door and the Duchess seated in it, but the Princess was not down. Presently she made her appearance, and, evidently vexed with herself for being late, passed me by without speaking. The drive was a short one, and when the carriage returned Princess Mary, all smiles, took the flowers, saying, "For me?" "No," replied Frazer; "they are mine, Princess. You did not speak to Fanny when she brought them." The reproof was at once accepted, and taking the wall-flowers to her room, the Princess said she was very sorry she had not spoken to me, and was most kind and gracious. My father had some violets planted especially for her; she came herself to gather them, and always said that no other violets were so sweet. The Princess was very fond of Frazer, who fully entered into her young mistress's love of fun. Sometimes the Princess playfully seized her dresser round the waist and whirled her round and round till both were breathless. Then setting her down, she would look at Frazer, who was very small and slight, and say, "I should like to whirl you round again, only I am afraid that I should *break* you."

I shall never forget one very warm afternoon in the middle of summer when the royal ladies called at the farm to make inquiries about a poor person in the village. Quite unceremoniously they walked in, and found me lying on the sofa fast asleep. As I awoke I heard the Princess say, "See, Mama, how tired she must have been." It may easily be imagined that the position was a most embarrassing one for me, but the kind Duchess only smiled, and the Princess did all she could to put me at my ease.

Knowing how I wished to see the Queen, Princess Mary obtained an order for me to stand in the hall at Buckingham Palace, where I saw Her Majesty and the Prince Consort pass to their carriages on their way to the Drawing-room at St. James's Palace. After the ceremony I went to Cambridge House, and the Princess, looking so sweet in a pink muslin gown, took me to the Duchess of Cambridge's rooms. Her Royal Highness was very tired after the Drawing-room, but smiled at me most graciously, and taking off a beautiful necklet of pear-shaped emeralds and a diamond rose and spray—a wedding-present, I think, from George IV.—gave me the jewels to look at. Before I left, the Princess went upstairs to fetch an etching of Winterhalter's portrait that she had promised me, and coming down, tore her muslin dress, but she was not in the least put out, and never even stopped to look at the rent; her one thought was to give me pleasure. She placed the picture in my hands and kissed me. The etching still hangs in the room into which the Princess used so often to come.

Princess Mary's religious instruction was mainly entrusted to Mr. Harrison,[1] who succeeded his father as Domestic Chaplain to the Duke of Cambridge. Mr. Harrison did not reside at Kew, but often stayed at the Cottage, where he always met with a hearty welcome. Both Princess Mary and her mother were much attached to him, and corresponded frequently with him upon spiritual matters. "I cannot sufficiently express how much I feel indebted to you," the Duchess writes to Mr. Harrison on one occasion, "for having so soon and so kindly complied with my request respecting the form of daily prayer to assist and direct my thoughts. The one you have written for me exactly answers all I wish; but should any other thoughts or advice occur to you I shall feel most grateful if you would send them to me." Princess Mary also wrote in the same simple, earnest way to this good man, and always consulted him when any difficulty arose in her daily life. From his advice and teaching she derived much benefit, and was truly grateful for the sympathetic care with which he watched over her spiritual welfare.

[1] The Rev. William Harrison was select preacher at the Foundling Hospital, and the first incumbent of St. Michael's Church, Chester Square. He was appointed Honorary Chaplain to the Queen, and in 1877 made Honorary Canon of St. Albans. He died in 1882.

CHAPTER III.

CHILDHOOD : LETTERS.

1843–1847.

Princess Mary's ninth birthday—Death of the Duke of Sussex—Princess
Augusta's marriage—Rumpenheim (1843)—Hanover revisited—At
Dresden—Festivities at Strelitz—The Keeleys—Princess Helena's
christening—Visit to the Queen Dowager—The Duke of Wellington's
statue—Princess Mary's thirteenth birthday—Ball at Gloucester House
—New Year's Eve at Windsor—Miss Howard's departure—Baroness
Hammerstein arrives—Jenny Lind—Letter in French—Grisi and
Mario—Life at Rumpenheim (1847)—Princess Mary's fourteenth
birthday.

FROM the incidents related in the preceding chapter, some
impression may be gathered of Princess Mary as she appeared
to those about her in early years. The outlines of the picture
are filled in by the Princess herself, who tells the story of her
youth in a series[1] of letters to her friend Ellinor Napier,
and her former governess, Miss Draper. The handwriting
is free and distinct, there are no ruled lines, and the sheets
are often crossed.

Her daily life, her aims and ambitions, her joys and sorrows,
are all set forth in this correspondence, which discloses a
nature, generous, tender, and true, not without faults, but
showing a spirit of humility and an earnest desire to improve,
rarely seen in one so young. Each page bears the impress
of the warm heart and noble qualities which endeared
Princess Mary to all as a child, and gained for her in later
years the love and respect of the English nation.

The letters begin soon after the Princess had celebrated

[1] To the series are added two letters addressed to the Rev. William Harrison.

her ninth birthday, and the first is written to Miss Draper—
" Draperchen," as she was affectionately called by her royal
pupil.

Cambridge Cottage, January 2, 1843.

MY DEAREST DRAPERCHEN,—I have not forgotten you yet,
and hope I never shall. I must first announce to you the
intended marriage of my sister with my cousin Frederick.
I shall be very melancholy when she goes, and am afraid
Mama will feel it very much, she will be so lonely; but
I must try and be good to comfort her. Mama thinks I
am improved in my conduct, which I am sure you will be
delighted to hear. I am very sorry Mrs. "Teatotum "[1] was
so ill on the journey, but am sure that she had *no sooner
reached St. Peter's*[2] than she began to recover, and I hope by
this time she is quite well. Your beautiful birds Mama has
had mounted and put in a handsome case, and they look
lovely; they are at present in the little room, but they are
going to London with us. I had a beautiful table at Christmas, and a great many nice presents. I had also a very
fine Birthday, and dined with Papa and Mama; afterwards
I played at Lotto Dauphin, and had a delightful evening. I
am sorry your present is not arrived that I might thank you
now for it, but I am equally obliged for your kindness in
thinking of me and for your dear letter which arrived, as
you wished, on my Birthday. Mama and Augusta send you
their love, and I hope you will accept the same from your
very affectionate and *troublesome*

MARY.

Cambridge House, May 14, 1843.

. . . I thank you for your charming letter and lovely present
which has lately arrived. We have just sustained a great
loss in the death of the Duke of Sussex.[3] He suffered a great
deal shortly before his death; it is a dreadful loss for the
poor Duchess of Inverness[4] and the whole family. We have

---

[1] Mrs. Tatham.   [2] St. Peter's, Rome.

[3] Sixth son of George III.; he died at Kensington Palace, April 21, 1843,
and by his death the inhabitants of Kensington lost a kind friend.

[4] Eldest daughter of the second Earl of Arran; she married Sir George
Buggin, and at his death in 1825 assumed her maternal surname of Underwood.
She afterwards married privately the Duke of Sussex, and in 1840 was
created Duchess of Inverness.

just left Kew, and I am so sorry, for the flowers are now so beautiful, it is such a pity, I enjoyed it so much. . . . In your last letter you asked me to tell you all that was settled about Augusta's marriage, but her writing to you has prevented me. . . . I have been once to the opera this season and hope soon again to have that pleasure. My conduct, I think, is improved, but there are a great many faults still to cure, but I do hope and think that I am not so passionate, and that when we next meet you will find most of my faults corrected. I have seen Aby Clark and Arabella West; they do not seem much altered since last year. Mama was much affected on reading your kind sentiments with regard to my sister. . . . My brother is also, I am sorry to say, about to leave us; perhaps you have read in the papers he is going to Corfu. I like the idea of Fritz [1] becoming my brother-in-law. I know him better than any other cousin, for when we were in dear Italy he was always with us. My dear Papa is, I am delighted to say, quite well and in good spirits again. Miss Howard sends you her compliments, and begs me to tell you that I wrote this note without any help. . . .

Cambridge House, August 8, 1843.

EVER DEAREST DRAPERCHEN,—. . . I was concerned to hear of the death of your sister, who I have so frequently heard you speak of, and who so kindly sent you the birds for me. I was going to write to you before your letter arrived to tell you, as I promised, all about dear Augusta's marriage. I must first say the separation from my dearest sister was a very sad one, and poor Mama has not yet recovered it, but we are now very soon expecting to meet them at Rumpenheim, which will be a great happiness; we leave England next week for Germany. I am afraid, dearest, there is no chance of our coming to Italy. How much I should like to meet you there! Mama thinks you are so much interested in Augusta that you will like to know her bridal dress, and Miss Howard has promised to help me describe it. She wore Brussels-lace over white satin, trimmed with orange flower and myrtle; the train was white, shot with silver, also trimmed with Brussels-lace and flowers; she had a wreath of the same flowers on the front of her hair, and behind that, three superb tiaras given her by Mama, Fritz, and the Queen Dowager, one of them fastened her veil of Brussels lace at the back of

---

[1] The Hereditary Grand Duke of Mecklenburg-Strelitz.

her head; her necklace was of diamonds, also given by the Queen Dowager. So, you see, she was splendidly dressed, and I assure you she looked most lovely, and was the admiration of everybody. You who know her will not be surprised to hear that she had innumerable presents.

On Monday I had two teeth out, and I am pleased to tell you Mr. Parkinson gave me a very good character, and Papa gave me a new bonnet. We have been very busy packing to-day, therefore the lessons have been rather neglected. I have been learning some pretty pieces of music lately and some duets to play with my cousins, and Miss Howard says I may tell you I have been getting on very nicely, but she cannot prevail on me to look at my notes. I have received a letter from dear Augusta since her arrival at Strelitz, she is very well and happy. I have seen Mr. Hutchinson,[1] who delivered your kind message, for which I thank you a thousand times. . . . I have had my friends, you so well remember, Aby and Arabella, every Saturday afternoon, and I have been much with the Beauforts. And now, dear Draperchen, good-bye, and ever believe me your very affectionate, although *once very troublesome pupil*,

MARY.

Cambridge Cottage, March 6, 1844.

Very many times do I thank you, dearest *Draperchen*, for your elegant and beautiful paper-knife and kind remembrance of me when so far distant. I mean to place it in the lower part of my cabinet which Mama gave me for my pretty birds. It always remains in my room in Cambridge House, where I hope you will some day come and see it. I was very sorry to hear of the death of your poor sister. What a dreadful affliction it must have been for you, dearest, to lose two sisters in so short a period; but let us hope and trust that they are now rejoicing in Heaven.

I will now tell you something of my travels. I was much pleased with the journey to Rumpenheim, where I spent two happy months. . . . We then went to Hanover with many of our relations, *too numerous* to name, for indeed we were so large a party that we started in eight carriages and four. It was really a pretty sight, as all the villagers attended us to the ferry-boat. Perhaps you do not know that Rumpenheim is on the Maine, and as there is no bridge,

---

[1] The Rev. J. Hutchinson, sometime Chaplain to the British Embassy at Rome, where the Duchess of Cambridge made his acquaintance, and afterwards resident Chaplain to the Duke of Cambridge.

we of course crossed over in boats. At Hanover we stayed
four days, and I did indeed enjoy myself. The first evening
the King gave a grand concert, and invited me ; also he
invited me to a very grand ball ; I danced two Quadrilles,[1]
and Mama allowed me to remain till eleven o'clock. I like
the Crown Princess [2] very much ; her Mama, Papa, and sisters
were staying there. The youngest, Alexandrina, is thirteen,
and a nice companion for me. I dined twice with her at the
Crown Princess's, and we went to the play in the evening.
I was much pleased with my cousin.[3] Poor fellow! his
blindness is a great affliction ; but he is very cheerful, and
appears very happy.

From Hanover we went by rail-road to Dresden. It was
the first time I had tried it, and I liked it very much. We
arrived safely at Dresden, after two days' journey. The King
and Queen of Saxony live there ; they were very kind to
Mama and me. The brother of the King, Prince John, heir
to the Crown (as the King has no children), was also very
attentive to us. He is married, and has eight children. I
was very great friends with them, and often went to spend
the evening with them. At Dresden I spent my tenth
birthday. The King and Queen heard of it, and gave a party
the day before in honour of it. I had a holiday, and enjoyed
it much ; dined at the Austrian Minister's, and drank tea at
Prince John's. I received many very pretty presents. The
King and Queen also invited us to their grand Christmas,
which is kept with lighted trees and presents. To Mama they
gave two beautiful Dresden figures, and a china ink-stand and
candlestick, with views of the different places we had seen ;
to me they gave a handsome china soup-basin, saucer, and
ladle, also a complete band of monkeys in china, besides a
doll, an antique necklace and earrings. After we had
looked at our presents we plundered the tree, and then
played till bedtime.

[1] " *Hanover, October* 30, 1843.—I dined with Princess Mary, and afterwards dressed for the Grand Ball. . . . When I went to take the Princess
home before supper, the Hereditary Grand Duke, who was talking to the
Duchess, said, ' Is that Miss Howard ? ' On Her Royal Highness answering
in the affirmative, the Grand Duke rose from his seat and expatiated on the
charms of my little Princess, who looked lovely, and danced through two
quadrilles without knowing a step or figure, but with such perfect ease and
elegance as surprised me " (Extract from Miss Howard's diary).

[2] Princess Marie of Saxe Altenburg married the Crown Prince of Hanover,
afterwards George V. She is still living, and is the mother of the Duke of
Cumberland, Princess Frederica, and Princess Mary of Hanover.

[3] Prince George of Cumberland, Crown Prince of Hanover.

From Dresden we came back to Frankfort, and stayed there ten days; and then we returned to *Old* England, travelling the greater part of the way by rail-road. We had a most beautiful passage across from Calais, only an hour and three quarters, in a new iron boat named the *Princess Alice;* even dear Mama did not suffer. Miss Howard was with us all the time, and was much delighted with everything. . . . Poor dear Papa, I am sorry to say, has a slight attack of the gout, and is obliged to keep his room. I go and sit with him sometimes. George is still at Corfu; he frequently writes, and is quite well; so is Augusta, who wrote me a funny letter last week. She has been riding in a sledge, and gives an amusing account of it. Dear Mama is quite well. And now, having written you a very long letter, . . . I remain your affectionate *ancient pupil,*

MARY.

Cambridge Cottage, July 23, 1845.

MY DEAREST ELLINOR,— . . . Our departure is arranged for the 30th, so I fear there is but little chance of our meeting until next year. . . . I am very much pleased at your sister Anne[1] having become Maid of Honour to the Queen. I hope she will like her new appointment. Pray tell me in your next letter when her first waiting begins. I went last Thursday to the Opera, to see the *Pas-de-Quatre* danced by the four first Dancers, Taglioni, Carlotta Grisi, Cherito, and Grahn. It was quite *enchanting.* They all received quantities of flowers. Last Saturday was Augusta's Birthday. I had a holiday, and went to dine and drink tea at Lady Wilton's, where I enjoyed myself very much. We were a party of 16. Monday there was a breakfast at Mr. Vincent's,[2] at Campden Hill, where I also was. You will think me very gay lately. Next Friday is dear Mama's Birthday, and I intend to give her some china, but I have nothing as yet. Lady Augusta Cadogan,[3] who takes likenesses, is now doing mine for Mama as a surprise. It is considered like, but is not finished. She is coming again to-day. We have three dear little puppies, which Mama has received from Mrs. Weaver at Kew. They are quite *lovely,* and are called Norma, Roma, and Ritta. I can fancy

[1] The Honble. Anne Napier; she married Captain the Honble. George Hope, R.N., fifth son of the late Earl of Hopetoun.

[2] A friend of the Duchess of Gloucester's.

[3] Lady-in-Waiting to the Duchess of Cambridge.

you laughing at the grand names. My address will be Rupenheim, Frankfort-on-the-Maine, and any letters sent to Cambridge House or Cottage are sure to be forwarded. . . .

Strelitz, December 11, 1845.

MY DEAREST DRAPERCHEN,—Many thanks for your pretty letter and lovely present, which much pleased me, particularly as it shewed that I was not forgotten. My Birthday was a very happy one; everybody was very kind, and my presents were both handsome and numerous. From Mama I received some gowns, some things in bronze, and a bracelet; Augusta gave me a very fine gobelet; the Grand Duke and Duchess gave a bracelet, and I received many other presents besides. In the evening there was a Ball, where all the children, myself included, were costumed, and we danced a Polka of four pairs in Greek costume; it was much applauded. We have had much pleasure lately in the visits of Countess Rossi (Mademoiselle Sontag formerly) and Madame Schröder Devrient. Countess Rossi sings beautifully, and the Grand Duke gave several concerts, at which she sang. Madame Schröder Devrient is more an actress than a singer; she has appeared in *Norma, Romeo*, and in *Lucrezia Borgia*, and to-night she will perform *tableaux* at the theatre, and will also sing some parts out of different Operas.

. . . I have a great deal to do for approaching Christmas: I am making a pair of slippers for Mama, and some mats for Aunt Marie; but although Miss Howard is allowing some time to do the things in, I fear they will not be finished in time. Strelitz is very pretty, but the weather we are now having is anything but agreeable, it rains and snows alternately, which is very good for the progress of my work. I have a German Master here, who teaches me German History and Grammar. He is a very nice man, *only he smells most charmingly of tobacco!* We stay here till the beginning of January, much to Augusta's satisfaction; but I fear Papa is not of the same opinion. How is Rome looking? Pray give *my best love to it, and tell it* how we all wish to be once more in its gates. The Palace here is large and comfortable; Augusta's rooms are *charming*, consisting of a bedroom, dressing-room, two sitting-rooms, and a large drawing-room. Mama lives next to her, and Fritz lives underneath. I have the same rooms as my late cousin Louisa had. They consist of a room for Miss Howard, two sitting-rooms, and my bedroom, where Frazer also sleeps. Augusta has begun again to ride, to see if she likes it; if so,

Fritz will give her a horse. Yesterday I went to see her ride. She looks very well on horse-back, and her habit much pleased me. I would have given everything to have been on the horse instead of her; but I hope that pleasure will soon come, when we return to *dear old England.* I must wish you a merry Christmas and a happy New Year. . . . And now good-bye. Ever your very affectionate *late pupil,*

MARY ADELAIDE.

Strelitz, December, 1845.

MY DEAR ELLINOR,— . . . Strelitz now presents a wintry scene, and the lake will soon be entirely frozen. This is the grand time, for everybody *takes a walk upon the ice,* and they are already beginning to drive about in sledges. . . . To-day there is a great fair; it will be very amusing, and all the shops are arranged for Christmas. . . . Have you been to many parties lately? There have been several dances at which I have been, I have also made the acquaintance of a number of very nice children here who come sometimes and drink tea with me; some of them speak English. . . . *I hope Kew is quite well,* and happy to hear that we are coming back in January. Give my compliments to everybody, and my best love to your dear Mama and sisters. Ever yours sweetly affectionately,

MARY ADELAIDE.

Cambridge Cottage, March 8, 1846.

MY DEAREST DRAPERCHEN,— . . . After having remained three months at Strelitz, we are now comfortably established at Kew; having left Gussy quite well, and hoping to see us soon again in *dear Old England.* We were very gay indeed at Strelitz, and I have been to six balls since we have been away. . . . At Berlin I went to a grand Concert given by the King, and I dined with the children of the different Princes several times.

Our Christmas at Strelitz was charming. We came into a large concert-room, a platform had been made, so that the upper part of the room was much raised, in the middle stood the tables of Mama, of my Aunt, and of the Grand Duke; on the sides were our tables. The tables were covered with presents, and a tree stood on each, with a festoon of green leaves round the table, and from this festoon was suspended a pretty kind of lamp, with flowers instead of lights in it. In the background was a large landscape, and the room was prettily lighted. My table was *covered* with presents and my tree *quite loaded* with Bonbons. After our tea the amusing part of the evening began. It is the custom in the north of Germany to have *Juhl-klaps*, or jokes which are thrown in by the servants. I received amongst other things a couple of prints of Polka-Dancers, dressed in red and in blue, as in remembrance of the 27th of November. In some of the jokes there were ridiculous verses. With a quantity of chocolate which I received was a little piece of paper with these words, "For the private picking of Queen Gormandiza." The best joke of all was this, I was dressed up as Lady Augusta de Noiman, with a long black gown, a Turkish shawl trailing on the ground, a pink bonnet, *black curls*, and *a long nose;* in my hand there was a paper, with "Souvenir from Augusta de Noiman" on it, which I was to bring to Gussy, and in it was a quantity of black hair. William Norman, son of one of the *Dames d'honneur*, was dressed as Baron Noiman, and brought Mama a letter of funny nonsense. The whole evening was excessively amusing.

We at last left Strelitz, and after some days, and a day at Dresden, arrived at Calais. In consequence of high winds, we were detained there five days, with nothing to do but to go shopping. . . . After a tolerable passage of three and a half hours in the ship *Charon*, as the *Princess Alice* was then being repaired, we arrived at Dover extremely sick and uncomfortable. But we may thank God that we did not leave Calais the day we expected, for the same night there was a fire in our house at Kew, and two rooms have been so much damaged that they cannot be as yet used. It appears that there was something wrong in the fireplace of Papa's bedroom, and, as there had been a great deal of fire made there previous to our arrival, to make it comfortable, it caught fire and extended to the upstairs rooms, which are those belonging to Mama's dressers and to the maids. However, they have got two new rooms, and nothing worse happened. These new rooms have been built since we were away, together with another small back room. That same afternoon there was an *accident on the very railway* by which we should have come.

We have not long ago celebrated dear Papa's birthday, upon which day I put on my Polka costume to show him. I gave him a pair of mats of my own work, and a large pretty glass to drink out of. In the evening we dined in town with Aunt Mary, and heard there Parry, the great comic singer, and also the Ethiopian serenaders: these consist of five men who are Americans by birth, but wear black masks and sing amusing songs, one of them plays the Tambourine, another the Accordian, two others play the Guitar, and the last plays with *four bones*, which he *rattles together*, and which give a peculiar sound. Next week is dear George's Birthday; I believe I shall give him a couple of mats and a flowerpot, but I am not quite sure. I have been twice to the Pantomime, and have been much amused with Keeley. The French Play and the Italian Opera are both open now. The Opera has been newly done up, and Mama says she never saw anything half so frightful; it is a bright yellow satin, curtains, boxes, and everything alike, and is painful to the eyes. Costa is no more the director, but Balfe. Mama has now with her Baroness Ahlefeld; I do not know whether you know her or not. Mama's *dame d'honneur* is Lady Augusta Cadogan. Next week is the second drawing-room, to which Mama will go, not having been to the first. Give my compliments to anybody I know at Rome, *particularly to the dear old Pope.* Pray do not allow the *dear vespers to convert you.* How is Prosperi?[1] Tell the Piazza del Popolo, the Church of St. Peters, the Vatican, and the Pincio that I have not forgotten them. Mama sends you everything that is kind and agreeable, Miss Howard, who is quite well, sends you her compliments, Frazer sends you her duty, and *I send you my love —Darling.* . . .

Cambridge House, June, 1846.

MY DEAREST ELLINOR,—I congratulate you on the appointment of your brother,[2] and hope that he likes the place, although Naples is rather far off. Mama thinks it will agree with Lady Napier, because the climate is very warm. . . . I like Benedict very much; he is very strict, but civil and satisfied with my three first lessons, which pleases me very much, as I think I gain confidence as I proceed. What do you say to the Queen's having another little girl? I saw her on her Birthday, when she was looking very well, and the day after, the child[3] was born. Papa has seen the baby, and says that it is a fine little child. The time here passes very much in the same way every day: in the morning I have lessons, and in the afternoon I frequently drive out with

---

[1] Monsignor Prosperi, whose acquaintance the Duchess of Cambridge made at Rome. He visited England in 1853, and was a welcome guest at Cambridge Cottage.

[2] Lord Napier and Ettrick: he was appointed Secretary of Legation at Naples, May 27, 1846.

[3] Princess Helena.

Mama; I have had young friends several nights lately, and every Saturday evening Lady Wilton's two little girls [1] come and drink tea with me, when we work and read some amusing book together. . . .

Cambridge House, July 5, 1846.

Many thanks for the pretty picture, which will take its place in my small album, and will be much valued as your work. We should have been at Kew last Sunday but for the heat; I was particularly sorry, as I hoped there might have been a chance of your remaining in Kew till Monday. Mr. Ward told me that he understood that you had lost some valuable articles in the train, but I hope you will find them again. Last Monday I went to a party at Lady Wilton's, to celebrate her eldest girl's birthday ; Miss Howard went with me. We dined there, and afterwards went to the Colosseum ; in the evening we danced. Tuesday I shopped, and bought for Augusta's Birthday, to send her, a sash, which is very pretty. . . . To-morrow there will be a grand dinner here ; I suppose it will be the last; I do not know whether I shall appear. Mama is very well and has been very busy buying presents for Gussy, she will receive two beautiful china vases, four gowns, and, I believe, different smaller things. . . .

Cambridge House, July 13, 1846.

MY DEAREST DRAPERCHEN,—We are going to-day to Dover to receive dear Augusta, only think what happiness ! . . . I must now tell you how I spend my time. In the hot weather, from 8 o'clock till 9, I walk; from 10 till 2 I am occupied in lessons with Miss Howard; in the afternoon I have one or two hours lessons, as it happens; twice a week Mr. Ward, whom I think you must remember, gives a Latin lesson ; once a week a dancing lesson with Mrs. Worsly ; and once a week a music lesson with Monsieur Benedict, Augusta's music master. Is not this lesson a great indulgence ? . . . We are much interested in a book called "Gertrude ; " it is in two volumes, and very prettily written. I am sorry to hear that the dear old Pope is dead, but I congratulate you that you will be present at Pope Pius's coronation. Think of me when you are in St. Peter's ; pray write me a long description of it. In Kew some alterations have been made in our *Cottage;* the fire which I wrote to you about, I suppose, has, I think, *done good*—that is to say, that in consequence of two

---

[1] Lady Elizabeth and Lady Katherine Grey-Egerton.

small rooms just above Papa's room being burnt, they have been altered into one room, the windows of which are long and open on two little balconies; these form Augusta's sitting-room.[1] The rooms have been now papered up that way, and also the wall of the passage. But now I must wish you good-bye, . . .

I have just time to add this: Dear Gussy had a good passage and was quite well; she looks lovelier than ever, though she is rather tanned.

Cambridge House, July 19, 1846.

My dearest Ellinor,— . . . Next Saturday is dear Mama's Birthday. The Queen gives the christening that evening, and has invited me; so if I behave well I shall go. To-day is Augusta's Birthday; she has received very fine presents indeed. I gave her a pen-wiper with Tom Thumb and his carriage on the outside, and also one of those *very* broad sashes. She has been to Kew with Mama, and thinks her room quite charming. . . . Last week little happened to me; yesterday the Wiltons came as usual. I am sorry to say it was their last night, as they leave town to-morrow. We have, however, happily finished our book. I have been very busy working at the slippers, which must be finished by Mama's Birthday; they are advancing rapidly. . . . I was happy to hear by your dear letter that Eliza is better. When will Anne take her waiting? I hope I shall see her if I go to the christening. Mr. Ward told me that he heard you had got back your portmanteau and cloak; I congratulate you on it. Poor Ahlefeld has lately lost a notebook, containing money to the amount of 15 pounds. It has been advertised, but she has as yet heard nothing; I fear it is a lost case. Pray write to me soon, and tell me everything about everybody. . . .

Cambridge House, July 31, 1846.

. . . I went to the christening, which went off very well; the baby cried a little, but not much. All the children were there, and looked very nice; they were all in the chapel with the exception of little Alfred. The two eldest came down after dinner. At the Banquet the Archbishop of Canterbury took me in, and I sat between him and the Duke of Wellington. Pray tell your Mama that I spoke with him

---

[1] This room is known as the Grand Duchess's sitting-room to the present day, and the same paper still remains on the walls.

a great deal about your sister Nina, also about her, and you, dearest, were not forgotten. There was an evening party after dinner, and we left the Palace at twelve o'clock. My slippers were finished in time for dear Mama's birthday, and I have now a new work, which is very pretty. It is a bag, worked with straw; it is not very difficult, and I intend to give it to " Mizzard." [1] . . . "Wardikins" [2] gives me no lessons this week, as he is gone down to Powell, to enjoy himself there; but next Monday he returns to find new pupils in his house. . . .

Cambridge Cottage, August 23, 1846.

. . . This last week I have been very gay. On Tuesday I went to the Opera; Wednesday I lunched with Aunt Mary, who had been so kind as to invite some young friends to meet me. We drove to Hampton Court, where we saw some of the *Lions*, and then returned to Richmond, where we amused ourselves till after 9 o'clock. Yesterday I had a half-holiday (I mean to say a whole one), as Miss Howard went to the marriage of her first pupil, Miss Mary Hay. The weather has been remarkably fine, and admits of sitting out in the garden. To-day dear *Wardikins* preached a very fine sermon. . . . The mulberry trees are getting ripe; I have been there once with Miss Howard, but we did not get much fruit; however, we are all going to try to-day. Our garden is prettier than ever, and is very full of sweet flowers. I have seen in your pew the last two Sundays three girls dressed alike, and a lady with them; tell me if those are the Kinlochs? and if the one girl with curls is your favourite Isabella? There is a little one, [3] who sits in your place, and I often think, "Get out of the way, you *little Imp*, and make room for dearest Ellinor Napier!" Give my best love to your mother and to Eliza and Georgiana. I hope your sister Maria and her darling chicks are quite well? Is your little cousin Henrietta still with you? Have you heard from Lord Napier and Nina? [4] . . .

Cambridge Cottage, September 6, 1846.

. . . Last night we went to the Colosseum and saw it lighted up; it is very pretty, and looks very natural. We

---

[1] Princess Mary used to say people did not pronounce their words properly, and that she often heard Miss Howard called "Mizzard," so she adopted the contraction as a nickname for her governess.

[2] A favourite name of Princess Mary's for Mr. Ward.

[3] Now Lady Fairfax, wife of Admiral Sir Henry Fairfax.

[4] Lady Napier.

afterwards supped with George. . . . This week has been rather a gay one for me, for I have had two holidays, which Miss Howard spent at Brighton. She has been so kind as to bring me a pretty little straw basket from there. Augusta and I have got a new work; it is a cushion for Mama, and each will do a side; the work is very pretty, one side straws and shades of red, the other, straws and shades of green. I hope again to see you before you start for Scotland, for I do not think there is much chance of your remaining in dear England! Mama is going to-morrow to the Queen Dowager at Cassiobury, and will remain till Saturday; I shall stay here, for there is no room to lodge me there. The Duchess of Gloucester has invited me to come to Richmond on Tuesday and on Thursday, which will be very pleasant, and she will probably pay me a visit on Wednesday. The Queen Dowager and the Princess of Prussia (who I suppose you know has just come with the Queen Dowager to England) were here on Wednesday last; they lunched, and saw the Gardens, with which the Princess was so much pleased that she may perhaps come again to see them more comfortably, as we were much hurried last time.

. . . Mr. Hutchinson (whom I think you must remember) is staying here for some days; he is, I am sorry to say, going, in less than a fortnight, to Rome. He had hoped to get a curate, which would have enabled him to remain here for some months longer, and he had, in fact, already engaged one, but this man's mother will not permit him to go, and so poor Mr. Hutchinson will go himself. He has been very ill at Rome, and has been to Vichy, in France, to recruit his strength; he still, however, looks pale and thin, and not as merry or as strong as formerly. To-day Mrs. de Burgh [1] has brought her little boy, who is three years old, to pay us a visit; he is Augusta's godchild, and is called Augustus after her. He is a remarkably fine child, with a fine head of hair; he behaved very well, and seemed to be much amused. He has been very ill last week, together with the youngest child, Minna, and they have much alarmed poor Mrs. de Burgh, who is looking very pale and delicate. Mama and Augusta desire their love to you, and pray remember me to Anna Maria Rede, who I hope is quite well, together with the rest of your cousins. Mama thinks of having my picture taken by Buckner. . . . And now, after this *werry lang letter* (admire my Scotch), which it must tire you to read, I remain, your very affectionate though *tiresome* Friend,

MARY ADELAIDE.

---

[1] Wife of Mr. Hubert de Burgh of West Drayton.

Cambridge Cottage, September 14, 1846.

MY DEAR DRAPERCHEN,— . . . My lessons go on very steadily. Mr. Ward comes to me three times a week, and I have lately re-begun Italian, which had been given up when I had Latin lessons. In music I am learning a duet called the " Grande Valse," . . . and hope that I am improving. I am sorry to say that Ellinor Napier is going in a fortnight to Scotland. I have hardly seen her this summer, for they have been travelling about, and now will leave us, I fear, for this year, and not return till next spring. I miss her very much, for she is a charming companion. However, we keep up a very regular correspondence, which consoles us a little. The weather is quite beautiful, and I think that my favourite Kew is this year more lovely than ever. . . .

Aunt Mary is very well, but in Aunt Sophia [1] there is no amendment, but she bears all pain with the greatest possible fortitude. All the Cambridge family is quite well, and enjoying the fine air and weather of the country. . . .

Cambridge Cottage, September 20, 1846.

MY DEAREST ELLINOR,— . . . To-morrow week my uncle Frederick (one of Mama's brothers) is coming here from Germany, and he will probably stay here this winter; this will be a great pleasure for us all. The weather is delightful; we hope it will remain so, as to-morrow the Princess of Prussia is coming here to luncheon, after which she will see the Gardens, and remain for dinner. Yesterday our George gave her a luncheon; Augusta declares that he got *paler and paler* out of nervousness. I was not there, but they said it went off very well. . . . Mama has been reading a sermon to me this morning, as we are only going to church this afternoon. . . .

Cambridge Cottage, October 11, 1846.

. . . I am going to-day with Mama to Cassiobury, where we remain till Monday next. This is a great pleasure, and I am going *without* Miss Howard . . . I went to town the other day to see the statue of the Duke of Wellington placed upon the Arch, but we only saw the procession, as the statue was drawn up the following day. All the horses had branches of laurel on their heads, and the statue was escorted by three or four bands of music, cavalry, and foot soldiers. We saw the whole from Aspley House, where there was a large

---

[1] Fifth daughter of George III.

party. Dear Mama went last Wednesday to Windsor Castle on a visit to the Queen, to present my uncle; she remained there until yesterday. Augusta stopped to take care of me and Fritz. To amuse ourselves while the others were away, and *to lessen the grief of the separation*, we sang, and played billiards both nights! I have just learnt an accompaniment of a pretty song of Augusta's by Donizetti, and she and dear Mama wish me to learn some more things to be able to accompany them. I was very much delighted at your visit to Kew, and I only wish that it could be often repeated, for I always think that next year you will be presented, and then you will be *almost too* grand to come to poor little me in my schoolroom. . . .

Cambridge Cottage, October 18, 1846.

I hope that my last letter has safely reached you, and that amongst the numerous visits you have been making you have not quite forgotten me. Yesterday was Frederick's Birthday; we saw him late in the afternoon, as Augusta and he have been at Windsor and only returned that day. The Queen and Queen Dowager united in giving him Gussy's picture done by Winterhalter, besides which the Queen gave him studs, and Albert an inkstand. His other presents were too numerous to mention. I gave him a paper weight of marble which Knesebeck sold to me. Lady Augusta Noiman is just come to England for a short time, and dined with us yesterday; she is grown very thin indeed, but I hope that her native land will do her good. . . . Aunt Mary, who has been making a *ronde* of visits in the north of England, will return to Richmond Park next Tuesday; we shall all be charmed to see her. . . . Adieu, dearest. . . .

Cambridge Cottage, December 6, 1846.

. . . Dear Augusta has left us, and I am sure you can fancy *how dull dear Kew* feels without her. . . . My Birthday was spent very happily; I send you a list of my presents. . . . At the charming ball given by Aunt Mary on the *auspicious event*, I amused myself very much; there were a good many people, and it went off very well, but Gussy, I fear, could not much enjoy it, as she had to take leave of all her friends. . . . We are expecting dear George to-morrow, from Ireland; he will probably come to London to-night. I suppose you have heard that he is to be removed from Limerick to Dublin, of which he is very glad. . . .

[*Enclosure.*]

From Papa and Mama, a blue Turkish shawl, silk dress, and two broad sashes. From Fritz and Augusta, a Wat-not (I don't know how to spell it) for books. From the Queen, a necklace. From the Duchess of Gloucester and Princess Sophia, a set of writing things in gold and ebony, a silk gown and bonnet. From the Queen Dowager, a necklace. From the Duchess of Kent, a writing-desk. From the Duchess of Inverness, a bracelet. From Uncle Frederick, a ring. From Knesebeck, a large flacon with lavender water. From Miss Howard, a small flacon in a pretty stand. From Mr. Mildmay, a china vase. From "Wardikins," a Bible. From Mr. Byam, a religious book. From Frazer, a cake. From Mrs. Hargreaves[1] a china jug; and from Alsfeldt, a pair of slippers.

Cambridge Cottage, January 10, 1847.

. . . You seem to be very gay indeed, and to be quite making up for the quiet of poor dear Kew. . . . Mama and my Uncle are gone on visits to Lord Brownlow at Belton, and to the Duke of Rutland at Belvoir Castle. Papa, however, is staying here; without this last comfort I don't know how I *could* have borne a separation of more than a week from dear Mama, with only Miss Howard to console me. We shall probably go to-morrow to London, to lunch at Aunt Mary's, and then pay a visit to Aunt Sophia. . . .

I am studying Italian very busily, and think it a beautiful language, and long to speak it correctly. In French Miss Howard and I have been reading " Belisaire," by Madame de Genlis; we found it very interesting, and we are now going to begin " Picciola," which I hear is very pretty, but more in the style of a novel without *too much love*. . . . I send you the portrait of Scotland; I hope you will *be pleased* with it. I certainly think that Diana Vernon, Scotland's maid, is highly flattered.[2] Hoping that you will forgive me, I remain your humble servant, or *affectionate* Friend and *Loveress*,

MARY ADELAIDE.

Cambridge Cottage, January 24, 1847.

MY DEAREST DRAPERCHEN,—A thousand thanks for your charming present, which has been generally admired. . . . Our Christmas was a very pretty one, although not half as

---

[1] Housekeeper at Cambridge Cottage.
[2] A little coloured print was enclosed.

gay as if Augusta had been here. I received a number of pretty presents, as I also did on my birthday. The Duchess of Gloucester gave a charming ball, which went off very well, and much amused me, there being a number of children besides grown-up people.

We paid a visit to the Queen at Windsor on New Year's Eve, and left there on the 2nd. The Queen gave me a bracelet with her hair, and was very kind to me. The little Royal children are sweet darlings; the Princess Royal is my pet, because she is remarkably clever. The Prince of Wales is a very pretty boy, but he does not talk as much as his sister. Little Alfred, the fourth child, is a beautiful fatty, with lovely hair. Alice is rather older than him, she is very modest and quiet, but very good-natured. Helena, the baby, is a very fine child, and very healthy, which however they all are.

. . . We are reading part of the Family Library, namely, one volume of " Universal History," by Lord Woodhouselee, a book which is both instructive and interesting. I learn still Latin, and also Italian, with Miss Howard, in which I trust I am progressing. In work, of which I am very fond, I am finishing the half of a large cushion for dear Mama, and am also doing another cushion for Miss Howard; they are both in the straw-work, with wool . . .

We shall go to London next month, I fear; at this I am horrified. . . . To exchange the green lawns and gardens of *dear old Kew* for that *horrid* London with all its smoke and dirt is too shocking to think of. . . . What do you say to the Spanish marriages?[1] For a long time I heard

---

[1] The Princess alludes to the marriage of Queen Isabella of Spain to her cousin Don Francisco de Asis, Duke of Cadiz, and that of the Infanta Louisa Fernanda to the Duc de Montpensier. Both marriages took place at Madrid on October 10, 1846. By this means it was hoped to secure the reversion of the Spanish throne for the House of Orleans, but the subsequent birth of children to Queen Isabella deprived the Montpensier union of all importance. These marriages were in direct opposition to the promise given by Louis Philippe to Queen Victoria at Eu in 1845. "The King," says Her Majesty's Journal of that date, "told Lord Aberdeen as well as me, he never would hear of Montpensier's marriage with the Infanta of Spain (which they are in a great fright about in England), until it was no longer a political question, *which would be, when the Queen is married, and has children*. This is very satisfactory." That Her Majesty regarded the Spanish marriage as a breach of faith on the part of Louis Philippe is seen from her reply to the letter in which Queen Marie Amélie announces the Montpensier betrothal. After referring to her own refusal to arrange a marriage between the Queen of Spain and Prince Leopold of Saxe-Coburg, "solely with the object of not departing from a course which would be more

so much about them that I was sick and tired of hearing nothing but that. I envy you in your dear Italy, enjoying the beauties of the Pamphili Gardens. The weather has been very cold, but these last days much milder, and to-day it rained. Our conservatory has been in great beauty, for all the camelias were out, and it looked most enchanting. . . . Ever your very affectionate late pupil, *very troublesome*,

MARY ADELAIDE.

Cambridge House, February 24, 1847.

MY DEAR ELLINOR,— . . . Miss Howard has left me, and you can imagine I was very sorry to lose her. Baroness Hammerstein has come as *Dame d'Honneur* to Mama; but she is present at all my lessons, and is constantly with me, and has the entire charge of me, but has nothing to do with the teaching. I have four masters—Mr. Ward for Latin Divinity and English History; Mr. Walbaum for German, geography, and Universal History; M. Ori for French; and Benedict for music. You can fancy how much I have to do.

To-day is dear Papa's Birthday, and he received from Mama, jointly with Aunts Mary and Sophia, my picture done by Winterhalter,[1] the Queen's painter, during our stay at Windsor. It is considered an excellent likeness, and gave Papa great pleasure. I made for him two markers, and I intend to give him (when it is finished) a white cover for the top of a chair in crochet stitch. We are going to-night to Aunt Mary's to dinner. Last week we went to the Haymarket and Princess' theatres, and were at both places much amused. We have also lately seen the model prison of Pentonville, which is a very interesting sight, and not at all disagreeable. . . . Will you grant me a favour? namely, will you send me, some time or other, work and drawings of your own, or of your sister's, to be exposed for sale at the fancy Bazaar, to be given for the German Hospital, in which we are all much interested? It will be held in the middle of May, so you have time enough; but I can assure you that any addition would be thankfully received. . . .

agreeable to the King, although we could not regard the course as the best," Her Majesty goes on to say, "you will therefore easily understand that the sudden announcement of this double marriage could not fail to cause us surprise and very keen regret " ("Life of the Prince Consort," by Theodore Martin, vol. i. pp. 305, 368).

[1] See Frontispiece.

Cambridge Cottage, March, 1847.

. . . Will you come and drink tea with the Baroness and me to-night at seven o'clock? Pray bring your music, and do not tell your servant to fetch you before half-past nine. . . . If you would not like to leave dear Anne so short a time before her marriage, tell me so, and, of course, I shall not wish you to come, for I quite understand your feelings. If you like to come, be assured you will be received with open arms by your devoted and affectionate Friend,

MARY ADELAIDE.

Cambridge Cottage, May 26, 1847.

MY DEAR DRAPERCHEN,— . . . We have been to-day to the Irish Bazaar,[1] under Lady Londonderry; some of the stalls were very handsome. The best was Aunt Mary's and Madame Rothschild's. . . . Ellinor Napier came with us last Sunday to town and remained with me till yesterday. I fear it is one of the last times I shall see her, as she leaves next month for Scotland, and will probably go in the winter to Naples. . . . The Grand Duke Constantine came here to-day, to pay Papa and Mama a visit; he seems a very nice young man, rather good-looking, with much fun about him; he is going to marry Princess Alexandra, fourth daughter of the Duke of Altenburg and sister of the Crown Princess of Hanover. I knew her when we were at Hanover last, but I hear that since then she has entirely changed in manners and appearance, and has grown a very handsome and amiable young lady. You can imagine how sorry I am to leave *dear sweet charming Kew.* . . . I hope you will soon come and see me; we lunch at two o'clock, and that hour is the best if you wish to see me, but more particularly Mama. I have a good many lessons, but the afternoons are free, all but Mondays and Thursdays, when Mr. Ward comes from three to half-past four. . . .

Cambridge House, June 3, 1847.

MY DEAR ELLINOR,— . . . Yesterday the little Wiltons paid me an evening visit. We played charades, but alas! you were wanting to make them quite perfect. The Baroness

[1] The Bazaar was in aid of the Distressed Irish. It was held in the Cavalry Barracks, Regent's Park, and all the great ladies in London were present. The Duchess of Gloucester's stall was presided over by the Ladies-in-Waiting upon Her Royal Highness. On the first day £1000 was taken by the stall-holders.

sends her love.   Poor Papa is becoming so shockingly deaf at times, that we can hardly make ourselves understood by him. . . . I hear that Lady Jocelyn [1] is going to take your house, but it is to be altered.   The children will go in October, she in March.   What a *remplacement* for dear "Long Nosie"! . . .

Cambridge House, June 5, 1847.

MY DEAR DRAPERCHEN,— . . . I thank you for your kind letter and grammatical corrections; I am delighted you take the trouble to correct me, and am very thankful to you, dear. . . . We have been twice to Kew this week, on Monday and Thursday, you cannot think how beautiful it was.   We went about 3 o'clock, and drank tea there in the open air, and cut asparagus.   *Only think of that !*   Ellinor Napier leaves Kew and England next Monday, I am sorry to say; I fear I shall not see her again for more than a year. . . .

Cambridge House, June 10, 1847.

MY DEAREST ELLINOR,—You may imagine how pleased I was to hear of the marriage of dear Eliza; I immediately inquired if Mr. Hay [2] was a "Bon Parti," and when Mama said "yes" I almost jumped with joy, particularly as before we left Kew you said the Napiers never would make good marriages.   However, you are mistaken, and so much the better, for though *Scotch people never like to be mistaken,* yet I am sure you are too good-natured, and too full of sisterly affection to mind it in this instance.   I am sure you will be sorry to lose her, but if it be for her happiness, of course one must not repine. . . . The next letter we receive will be the announcement of your marriage; pray prepare me for that beforehand, *lest I should faint on hearing it.*

You will, I trust, be glad to hear that I am going with the others to Germany; you cannot think how pleased I am, and I assure you I shall show myself worthy of this great pleasure.   We go to Rumpenheim, where the whole family is assembled. . . . I was last night at the Lumley Opera House, where I heard Jenny Lind in the "Fille du Regiment." She sung very well, but Mama says her voice is much weaker than when she first came; the fact is, she is *too weak* for the large house, unless she *screams,* and of course *this*

---

[1] Lady Francis Cowper, extra Lady of the Bed Chamber to the Queen, married, in 1841, Robert Viscount Jocelyn, eldest son of the third Earl of Roden.

[2] Now Admiral Sir John Dalrymple-Hay, Bart.

fatigues her.   Carlotta Grisi danced very well—I think you
would have liked to have seen her again.   I forgot to say *our
departure* is fixed for the middle of the week after next. . . .
I remain your affectionate *big* friend,

MARY ADELAIDE.

Cambridge House, June 12, 1847.

. . . A thousand thanks for your darling letter with such a
charming description of Kirouchtree.   You will really become an *English Madame de Sevigné!*   I should have
answered your last letter, in which you wished me goodbye,
but I knew not how to forward it to you, and therefore did
not write.   You cannot think how I dread seeing Kew, when
I know I cannot send for you to take a charming *toddle* with
me alone in the delightful gardens.   Alas! those pleasures
are over for ever, I fear; but we must think of the many
pleasant hours we have passed together.   Papa has been
unwell for some days this week, but thank God he is now
much better. . . .

There is to be a review next Wednesday, of which George
is to have command—the Duke of Wellington gave it to
him, and it gives George much pleasure.   I am very glad of
it, and I must confess I am doubly pleased, as there are so
many foreigners here just now.   I hope Mama will go and
take me with her.   Mama is quite fatigued, for she has been
out almost every night this week; however, to-day she is
gone to Kew for a little quiet.   Arabella West and the two
little Wiltons have been to see me. . . .

Yesterday we went to the exhibition of pictures of foreign
masters now dead, and which belong to people here.   There
were some fine pictures done by Rembrandt, Holbein,
Collins, Cuyp, and Guercino.   We also went the other day to
see the exhibition of American plants down by Belgrave
Square.   The Azaleas and Rhododendrons were quite splendid,
and of all different colours; all shades of lilac, pink, white,
rose-coloured—in fact, quite beautiful.   Monday we are most
likely going to a concert of Monsieur Benedict, but it is not
quite certain.   My lessons go on the same. . . . I have a
French Mistress besides Monsieur Ori, a Madame Esquerel, a
very nice person apparently.   My chief occupation with her
is to read and talk.   I hope you are employing your delicate
fingers for the German bazaar, and that fishing will not
make you forget to work for it.   As for me, I am getting on
very rapidly with my work, and it will soon be finished.

Aunt Mary is quite well, and is going to give a Ball next Thursday to the Weimars [1] and the other foreigners. . . .

Cambridge House, June 27, 1847.

MY DEAR DRAPERCHEN,— . . . I am studying very busily just now, and trust I am getting on nicely with my lessons. . . . I went to Covent Garden to see Grisi and Mario in the "Dui Foscari," and was perfectly enchanted. It was quite magnificent. Yesterday Mr. Mitchell gave a fête to the children of Royalty and nobility, which consisted of a piece, or rather part, of a comedy called the "Gamin de Paris." Then a concert of three children, two playing the harp, and one the violin; they did it remarkably well. Then came a dance by Mademoiselle Baderna. Then a child walked upon a globe; this was a most wonderful sight. The child stood upon it while it went backwards and forwards, and danced upon it. Then there came several Bedouin Arabs, who made the most wonderful leaps I ever saw; one man holding six others on his head, forming a kind of Pyramid; then one jumped over six men, head over heels, and alighted safely on his feet. Then there came the Ethiopian serenaders, and the whole ended with a "Pas de Fleurs." The Queen was there with her three dear little children, who all amused themselves very much. To-day we have been to church and heard a fine sermon preached by Mr. Harrison. Then we paid a visit to the Queen of the Belgians, and to Aunt Sophia. . . . I have written out for you the little prayer you were so kind as to make for me, and which, although it has unfortunately not yet benefited me, will certainly, I trust, be not long without its good fruits. . . . Believe me ever yours affectionately,

MARY ADELAIDE.

[*The Prayer.*]

Almighty Father, I pray Thee to look down on Thy erring child, and teach me to subdue my proud rebellious nature. Grant that I may be humble and submissive to my dear parents, and to all that are given authority over me; and whenever I may offend Thee by pride, self-will, or disobedience, I beseech Thee to make me sincerely penitent and sorry for my transgressions, and send me Thy grace, that I may endeavour to amend my conduct for the time to come, and walk in Thy blessed ways, through Jesus Christ our Lord. Amen.

[1] Prince and Princess Edward of Saxe Weimar.

Cambridge House, July 11, 1847.

DEAREST DRAPERINECHEN,—As Frazer is going to Brighton to see her friends, I could not resist charging her with a short note conveying to you the (I trust) *welcome news* that I am going with the rest to Germany. Our departure is fixed for the middle of next week, so I hope to see you once again ere we are off. . . . We shall go to Rumpenheim, and I believe remain there about two months, and then return here. . . . Dear Aunt Sophia has been very unwell these last days, having been seized with violent spasms; she was a little better yesterday. . . . Believe me your affectionate,

MARY ADELAIDE.

Rumpenheim, Août 3, 1847.

MA CHÈRE DRAPERCHEN,—Enfin Je trouve un moment pour vous écrire que nous sommes arrivés à Rumpenheim, et qu'à Bonn nous avons rencontré Augusta et Fritz. Augusta se porte bien et elle a l'air d'une rose fraiche. Fritz est beaucoup mieux, il part Jeudi prochain pour Kreuznach. Je suis charmeé d'être à present réunie avec mes trois cousines dont l'ainée a justement mon age. . . . Monsieur Ullrich, notre ecclesiastique, me donne des leçons deux heures par jour, et demain j'attend une Maîtresse de musique qui viendra deux fois la semaine. Papa est parti Dimanche dernier pour Hanovre, et hier notre Tante Louise est arrivée. Le jardin ici est très joli; il est rempli de fleurs, et nous y avons une escarpolette et un carousel. Il y a aussi une petite voiture dans laquelle nous conduisons de temps en temps la petite Alexandrine.[1] La Duchesse de Kent a diné ici Samedi dernier; elle est maintenant à Soden tout près de Rumpenheim. Les promenades autour du château sont jolies; nous allons souvent dans les champs cueillir des bouquets de fleurs champêtres. La Baronne m'a prié de vous faire ses amitiés. Pray give my compliments to Mrs. *Teatotum*, et Aimez toujours vôtre Affectionée

MARIE ADELAIDE.

Rumpenheim, August 8, 1847.

MY DARLING ELLINOR,— . . . We left London on Friday, 23rd of July, and went *per* rail to Dover; after a walk in the town we went on board with favourable wind and fine weather. Mama went into the cabin, but I remained on

---

[1] Princess Alexandra, now Princess of Wales.

deck. The first three hours I was perfectly well, but then the wind changed suddenly, and a fresh breeze springing up, Mama and I were seized at the same moment and continued ill till we got to Ostend. The following morning we were off again at seven o'clock; in about an hour we reached Bruges, where we stopped and saw three churches, a room full of pictures in the Hospital, and a curious chimney-piece with statues of oaken wood. In about two hours we again started, and arrived the same evening at Aix-la-Chapelle. Next morning we were *en route* at half-past six, and arrived at Cologne about ten, where we were met by a man sent by Fritz and Augusta to say they awaited us at Bonn; of course we hurried on *per* rail to Bonn, and you can fancy how delighted we were to be united, after a separation of nine months. After a *Déjeuner à la Fourchette* we proceeded to Coblence, where we were received by—who do you think? Colonel Girardot [1] and family. . . I saw Anna the next morning, and was *led by her to the carriage !* . . . The same evening we arrived at Rumpenheim, and found all the family quite well. Our party consists of twenty ladies and two gentlemen. My little cousins are charming, much grown, and much improved, but more of this another time. . . .

Rumpenheim, August 19, 1847.

. . . You cannot think how much I have thought of you these last days, and I quite jumped when it struck twelve o'clock yesterday morning, for that was the moment I fancied Eliza became Mrs. "Johnny" Hay. . . . The heat, my dear, is overpowering. . . . I have a large room at the top of the house all to myself, but am shut in, on one side by Mama's bedroom, on the other by her sitting-room. . . . I am reading "Waverley" and "La Henriade." "Waverley" I am delighted with, and have just brought Edward to that interesting period when he is taken prisoner and examined by Major Melville of Cairnvrechan. How often do I think of you while reading, and wish you could help me to pronounce the Scotch! . . . We are an immense deal in the garden, which is much improved since we were last here. . . . We have a swing and a Carousel! Adelaide,[2] the eldest of my younger cousins, is a month younger than I am; she is a very pretty and amiable girl. Her sisters Bathildis [3] and Hilda are two nice

---

[1] Colonel Girardot lived on Kew Green.

[2] Princess Adelaide of Anhalt-Dessau, who afterwards married the Duke of Nassau, and is now Grand Duchess of Luxemburg.

[3] Princess Bathildis married Prince William of Schaumburg-Lippe.

little girls, particularly the former, who is so good and gentle, although she suffers considerably with her spine. Heaven grant she may be preserved to us. There are also the three dear little children of Cousin Louise,[1] who are quite charming.

Rumpenheim, August 31, 1847.

. . . A thousand thanks for your darling letter, which enchanted me. You cannot think how I feel for you, dear, as you know I have gone through this before; to lose your two favourite sisters at a time when, as you are entering the world, you have more need of their advice and companionship, is a great trial. . . . I am enjoying myself very much here, for although we do not go out much, yet there are such a number of us that we are very happy together.

My day is spent in the following manner. I get up at half-past six o'clock, and when dressed take a walk in the garden. At nine the Baroness and I breakfast together. After that I prepare my lessons, and at ten the Clergyman here gives me a lesson till twelve. Then I write my journal and prepare for *Wardikins*, and a little before one o'clock I lunch; from one to two o'clock I practise, and twice a week a music mistress from Offenbach comes to me. After this we walk for an hour, and then I learn something more and dress for dinner, which is at four o'clock. From six to seven we read English and French, and after that I may do anything I like. Tea is at eight, and at nine Adelaide and I go to bed. My cousins have a very clever, agreeable governess, of whom they are very fond. We walk generally in the fields round the *Château* and there we find very pretty wild flowers. In the large garden we have got a small concealed little nook appropriated to our own use, and of this we have formed a garden, and next to it we have made what *we* call a house, that is to say, we have trained the bushes over so as to cover it, and then, having swept the leaves away, we call it a dining-room, bedroom, and kitchen, or rather we divide it into such; this little property occupies us in our free hours, and amuses us very much. . . .

Rumpenheim, September 16, 1847.

MY DEAR DRAPERCHEN,—I am afraid you will think I have almost forgotten how to hold my pen, but so much has happened since I last wrote that I hardly know where to

---

[1] Wife of Prince Christian of Holstein-Glücksburg, afterwards Queen of Denmark.

begin. A short time ago we were very busy in preparing a surprise for the Birthday of my cousin Louise. On the evening of that day, which was a partial holiday, we proposed to form a cabinet of wax figures, and it succeeded very well. We were placed on high tables, and certainly there never in all the world was such a varied assembly of figures seen. Augusta danced the minuet with cousin Fritz. I represented a young Savoyarde girl, and my two little cousins Hilda and Bathildis made dancing monkeys. The most charming of all the automatums was little Freddy,[1] dressed as General Tom Thumb, and placed on a table in the middle. We enjoyed ourselves very much. Last week we went to Frankfort to the *Messe*, or fair, and spent the day in *flying about* and shopping.

On Sunday, it being a beautiful day, we walked to a wood at some little distance and cooked ourselves a rural luncheon, and had all kinds of fun ; indeed, we are such a party that we amuse ourselves constantly in this kind of rural way, for I think the less the number the less the fun. Yesterday we drove to Bergen, a small village upon the top of one of the hills which lie opposite to Rumpenheim ; there, under the shade of a charming arbor of vine leaves, we had our luncheon, and at the same time enjoyed the beautiful view, for the eye glanced downwards on hills of vines, thence to the Maine, and over a small wood, on to Rumpenheim, and other places in the distance. I longed at that moment to have taken a sketch of the lovely scene. . . . Papa left us a week ago, and I suppose he is now at Richmond with Aunt Mary. We expect George here to-day. . . . You ask me when we shall return. I believe certainly not before the end of October, as Kew will not be ready for our reception till then. . . .

Cambridge Cottage, December 10, 1847.

My DEAREST ELLINOR,—I hasten to answer your very kind letter, and to thank you for your congratulations upon my (14th) Birthday ; I am growing so old that I am almost frightened to think how little I know for my age. Indeed, a Birthday becomes a very serious thing now ; but I trust I shall improve year by year, and, with God's help, become a blessing and comfort to every one. You may imagine how sorry I was at the thought of losing the dear Baroness,[2] as in her I lose an amiable companion

---

[1] Prince Frederick, now heir apparent to the Throne of Denmark.

[2] Baroness Hammerstein, who a few weeks later married Mr. Featherstone Stonestreet.

and a kind friend; but yet it may be for the best, and perhaps I shall improve more under Baroness Böse, . . . who is very clever indeed, very amiable, and *remplie de talents:* she draws and plays beautifully, and is in every way a most accomplished person; besides, she is no stranger to us, for we saw her at Rumpenheim lately, she having been a year with my little cousins. She will probably come here in the beginning of January. The Baroness leaves us the 20th of this month, and for the period intervening between her departure and the arrival of the other I shall be under Mama's care, and sit entirely in her room.

Mama left us to-day to go on a visit to Lord Salisbury, and will only return on Monday; so to console myself, I have invited *Wardikins* and the *Dot*[1] to take tea with me to-night, and on Sunday we drive to town to pay some visits. I had a letter the other day from the Princess Royal, in answer to one I wrote her on her birthday; she writes very well indeed for a child of her age. I had the most beautiful presents on my birthday from my dear parents, family, and friends, and their kindness has prostrated me with gratitude. Indeed, the great, great kindness of Mama to me no words can express, and if formerly I loved her, I now adore her, and I long to make up for dear Augusta, for it is very lonely for poor Mama, and she bears this privation with the greatest fortitude. . . . My Aunt, the Landgravine of Hesse, and my cousin Augusta, together with Uncle George, are now in Italy, and by this time most probably at Rome. I believe they intend to visit Naples. Poor Aunt Sophia has been suffering from a severe attack of influenza, and they are alarmed for her, as, in addition to her other sufferings, this will weaken her so. Aunt Mary is well. George is at Dublin, and I fear we shall not see him this Christmas, owing to the unsettled state of affairs in Ireland. . . .

I am stitching away as hard as I can at the music-stool, to finish it for Papa at Christmas. I have not been drawing yet, though I hope to do so with the Baroness Böse. The things you sent for the German Bazaar are very pretty, and most acceptable. Pray write to me again about your dear family, and tell me everything about the Baby[2]—how he is dressed, and whether he has your "tiny" nose or Nina's. I hope the air of Naples will recruit your strength; and I am happy to learn you are going to be so busy, as occupation is good for a

---

[1] Daughter of Colonel Girardot; she was very small of stature, and Princess Mary christened her "the Dot."

[2] The present Lord Napier and Ettrick.

youthful mind. Lady Augusta Cadogan had a letter from a friend a short time ago, who tells her the house of Lord Napier is the one which gives the most entertainments of any ; so I hope you will dance away, and be the *Belle* of the season. Pray do not run away with an Italian in your haste to get married. . . . Papa is, thank God, very well. We are just now in mourning for the Elector of Hesse, Mama's cousin. Kiss the dear little unknown baby, and believe me ever your affectionate *amie*,

MARY ADELAIDE.

CHAPTER IV.

GIRLHOOD: LETTERS.

1848–1849.

Arrival of Baroness Böse—Death of Princess Sophia—M. Brasseur—Visit to Cowes and Osborne—Princess Louise's christening—Unrest at Strelitz — Visit to Brighton — Theatricals at Windsor — Baroness Böse's departure—Continental complications—Attempt on the Queen's life—Lord Palmerston—Letter in French—Visit to Plas Newydd—Welsh customs and scenery—Penrhyn Castle—Manchester and Liverpool—At Windsor—Mr. Hutchinson succeeds Mr. Ward—Letter to Mr. Harrison.

Cambridge Cottage, January 1, 1848.

MY DEAREST DRAPERCHEN,— . . . Pray accept my best thanks for your letters. I wish you most sincerely a happy New Year. . . . The Baroness left us on the 20th, and arrived that same day at the Isle of Wight, where she remains till her marriage. Till Baroness Böse arrives, Mama performs the part of *Grande-Gouvernante*, and no one can do it better than she does; my only sorrow is that I am not *half so good a pupil* as I ought to be. Our Christmas went off very well. The room was beautifully decorated; there were four fine trees, and these were connected by wreaths of laurel evergreens and holly. My table was a very handsome one; and, indeed, after such a Birthday, was more than I could have possibly expected. We were at the Lyceum last Wednesday; the Pantomime was not *particularly* amusing, but the richness and beauty of the scenes and dresses made up for it. Next Tuesday we are going to Windsor till Thursday; and towards the end of the week to Drury Lane Theatre.

Now I must announce to you, in due form, a marriage which I think will give you pleasure. *The spinster Miss Sophia Howard is going to bestow her lovely hand* on Doctor Laumann, a Doctor of Civil Law, who has a large establishment of boys at Fulham. He is very comfortably off, and in future will probably become rich; he is a widower with six children, who are, however, all at school. She is a very happy bride. . . .

Cambridge Cottage, January 24, 1848.

. . . The long-expected Baroness is at length comfortably established at Kew. I like her already very much, and feel that I shall be very happy with her. I wish you could see her, but fear there is no chance of that as yet. I am sure you must have been quite shocked at the death of poor Sir Henry Mildmay; the account of which you undoubtedly read in the papers. It is most awful and appalling for his family and poor Mr. Mildmay [1] was very much cut up at this dreadful intelligence. He immediately went to Ireland to fetch his brother, and the burial took place yesterday at the family place. I have not seen Mr. Mildmay since the sad event. Mama and Papa leave us to-morrow for Burghley, whence they proceed to the Duke of Rutland's; however, they return on Saturday, and we must do the best we can to make this week pass as pleasantly as possible without them. . . . The Queen has sent to Uncle Frederick the Order of the Bath; this is a very kind attention on her part. . . .

Cambridge House, May 31, 1848.

. . . I have this instant received your letter, and I hasten to assure you that it is not from any want of affection on my part that you have not heard from me so long; but indeed I ought to be ashamed of my negligence towards one whom I always have and shall love, and to whom I am so much indebted. Though my faults are numerous, I trust ingratitude is not one of them, and how could I ever forget the kindness and affection I have always experienced from you. The sad event which plunged us in mourning occurred on Saturday; but, thank God, my poor dear Aunt Sophia [2] did not suffer

---

[1] Second son of Sir Henry St. John Mildmay, Bart., who died January 17, 1848. Mr. Mildmay was an officer in the Austrian service (Radetzky's Hussars), and during the war between France and Austria in 1839, was employed as British Commissioner at the headquarters of the Austrian army; he was subsequently appointed equerry to the Duke of Cambridge.

[2] In consequence of ill-health Princess Sophia lived much in retirement at her residence near Kensington Church, where she died on May the 27th, 1848, at the age of 70. In moving an address of condolence with the Royal Family in the House of Lords, Lord Landsdowne bore testimony to Her Royal Highness's "long life of virtue, charity, and excellence, in every position, public and private, in which she was placed."

much in her last moments, and died without a sigh, with Mama's hand in her own. She had been insensible for two hours before death released her from a life of suffering, and, I doubt not, she is now reaping that reward in Heaven to which the patience and sweet temper with which she bore her sufferings, and her generosity and kindness to every one, entitled her. Dear Aunt Mary bears this trial with great composure, and Papa and Mama, although deeply grieved, are tolerably well.

We were very much cheered yesterday by the arrival of my dear brother, who is remarkably well; I think we feel more pleased at seeing him this time than we have ever felt before, because he has been exposed to more dangers. You no doubt are aware that my dear sister hopes to make me a little Aunt very soon, which event makes Mama very anxious, as she cannot be with her during her confinement, and dear Augusta cannot come here; but we must trust to a higher Power that all will go off well. What a dreadful state of things! Almost every country in Europe is torn by dissension. Anarchy and confusion pervade every land. You can fancy how anxiously *we* all await the issue of the Danish war; but I am happy to say the Danish cause appears to be flourishing. My cousin Fritz,[1] who is heir presumptive to the throne of Denmark, on the death of his mother the Landgravine, is now here, as is also George of Mecklenburg. They are both flying from party to party and amusing themselves very much. As for us, this sudden mourning has shut us up almost entirely; we have been to Kew twice this week, and intend going there again on Friday and on Sunday next. The funeral takes place next Tuesday; it is to be at Kensal Green, where my Uncle Sussex lies buried. I saw my poor Aunt on Monday, and, of course, was much affected, as it was the first time I had ever seen death, and the sudden change appears so awful. . . . Her face was not much altered, but her countenance looked so peaceful and composed, no longer, thank God, convulsed with suffering.

Ellinor Napier remained a week in London, and thence proceeded to Scotland, to join her sister Eliza, who married last year. There are now only *two Honorable Napiers* to be disposed of—Ellinor herself, and her elder sister, Georgina, who is nearer thirty than twenty, or, I believe, past the age at which ladies generally like remaining stationary. Mr.

---

[1] Eldest son of the Landgrave William of Hesse. In accordance with the terms of the Protocol signed in London, May 8, 1852 (see footnote, pp. 8, 9), he renounced his right to the Danish Throne.

Mangold is very busy teaching me to play on the piano; he is strict, but a very good master. Monsieur Brasseur,[1] my French master, I like very much. He is remarkably gentlemanlike, and quite a first-rate master; so, you see, my lessons go on famously, and it will be my own fault if I am not well instructed and accomplished, and good also, I may say, for every one take pains with me. . . . I remain your very affectionate *ci-devant* Pupil,

MARY ADELAIDE.

Cambridge House, June 17, 1848.

MY DEAREST ELLINOR,—You cannot think with what pleasure I received your letter, and how agreeable was the news it contained. You may indeed be thankful that all has gone off so well, and that you have a dear little nephew. I hope Augusta will ere long make me the same present that Eliza has offered to you.

My brother is now here; he came some little time ago from Dublin, but was obliged to return there last week, as something was apprehended, but the country being quiet he returned here on Thursday, and I expect him this afternoon to take a *tête-à-tête* walk with me. Our mourning keeps us quite out of the world, but next week I think Mama will go to the Opera. I have very little to tell you. We have been at Kew several times lately, and the gardens are looking more beautiful than ever; we get the loveliest bouquets you can conceive from thence. We have seen the Queen once since we have been in London; she looks so young when surrounded by her six dear little children. The baby Louise is the finest child I ever saw, very large beautiful eyes, a sweet little mouth, and a very pretty good-humoured expression.

I saw Mrs. Laumann (Miss Howard that was) not long ago; she is very happy indeed, and appears to like her new position amazingly; she has indeed a most comfortable life with no *wicked* little children to educate. . . . Dear Mama is kinder to me than ever, and day by day I think more and more how undeserving I am of such a Mother, who lives only for others, and watches over me with such constant and loving care. Oh, Ellinor, what a blessing it is for you and me to have such kind mothers to lead and advise us! Aunt Mary bears the loss of my dear Aunt Sophia with great

---

[1] Monsieur Brasseur was also French master to the Prince of Wales, and in later years often stayed at Marlborough House. Towards the end of his life he lived entirely in Paris, and the Prince always went to see him when His Royal Highness visited the French capital.

composure and calmness, though she is deeply grieved. For my poor Aunt Sophia it is a great release, for she has exchanged the sufferings of this world for the eternal happiness of the next, and she is no doubt now in the presence of her God and Saviour. With best love to your Mama and Eliza, and a kiss to the little heathen unknown thing,[1] believe me your very affectionate and attached friend,

MARY ADELAIDE.

Cambridge House, July 31, 1848.

DEAREST DRAPERCHEN,—I thank you a thousand times for your affectionate congratulations on the happy event which has made me an Aunt. You will be glad to hear that Mama has had very good accounts from Strelitz to-day; dear Augusta is going on very well, and her little darling also. They say he is a most beautiful child, very much like the first, and his hands are the same as Augusta's. He screams a great deal, which makes my sister very happy, as they say it is very good for little babies to make a noise; the little gentleman came rather unexpectedly on Saturday (22nd) morning at seven o'clock, the Doctor and nurses from Hanover had not arrived, so my sister was surrounded by Mecklenburghers.

The people of Strelitz were so happy when they heard that they had a little *Erbprinz* that they fired the cannons, and the bands of the " Burgergarde " began to play before the Palace; they dined in the open air, and in the evening they illuminated the whole town. My sister's picture was hung out at every window, surrounded with lights. . . . Mama and Papa are, as you may imagine, very happy, and so indeed are all the inmates of Cambridge House—indeed, I may say the whole family, for Aunt Mary was at Osborne when my letter reached her to announce the arrival of another little grand-nephew, and the Queen was, she says, as delighted as she herself at this agreeable news. We all now look forward with great pleasure to seeing Augusta soon in dear old England again. . . .

During this whole season I have only appeared once in public, and that was at the christening;[2] but to make up for this Mama took me constantly to the Opera—indeed, she has hardly ever been there without taking me. Every Sunday I dine with the others in the evening, and always drive out

---

[1] Eldest son of Admiral Sir John and Lady Dalrymple-Hay.
[2] The christening of Princess Louise.

with Mama; so, you see, I am quite a great Lady now, and I hope to become more and more so by my conduct. I am getting on pretty well with my studies. I have had a French master and a music master twice a week all the time we were in London. I hope we shall not remain all the autumn at Kew, but wander away and go for a short time to the Isle of Wight; for though we love Kew very much, yet it is rather dull to remain there for so long a time without Augusta, whom we cannot expect before October, as it would not be prudent for Baby or Mama to travel before three months. . . .

On Mama's Birthday we went a large party to the dear Covent Garden Opera. Mama has not been looking well for some time, but the news from Strelitz has done her good. The death of my poor Aunt very much upset her, for she saw her so much, and was so fond of her. Aunt Mary has given us all gold lockets with the name of Sophy engraven on them, and her hair inside. The gentlemen have rings very much like our lockets, with hair inside. . . . Pray give my compliments to Mrs. *Teatotler*. . . .

Cambridge Cottage, September 7, 1848.

DEAREST ELLINOR,— . . . Augusta is going on as well as possible, and dear little Adolphus laughs and crows all day long. He has ten names and twelve Godfathers and Godmothers! . . . We returned from Cowes last Monday. Our cottage there was a very pretty one, commanding a view of the sea, but very small. Downstairs there was a dining-room and two sitting-rooms, and upstairs were all the bedrooms, *et voilà tout*. However, we spent nearly three weeks very pleasantly there. The weather was against us, for it rained latterly almost every day. We made excursions to Shanklin Chine, Carisbrooke Castle, Ventnor, and Black-gang Chine, besides which we used every day to take long walks in the fields and lanes, and along the beach at Cowes. We were several times at Osborne, with the interior of which I am quite enchanted. On the birthday of the Duchess of Kent we went there, and were present at a dinner the Queen gave to the sailors and royal labourers, after which these men played at different games for the amusement of the royal party. On Albert's birthday the Queen gave a morning dancing *fête*. . . .

Nothing can exceed the Queen's kindness to me; she gave me a water-proof cloak, and is going to give me some flounces of Newport lace. The children are much grown, and very much improved. The Princess Royal looked very well indeed at the *déjeuner*. . . . Dear Kew looks gay and pretty, and since we have been here the weather is most favourable. I am busy now making up for three weeks' holidays, and getting on nicely with studies and accomplishments. I like the Baroness very well, but she has her peculiarities, and we do not always agree, *cependant ce n'est que pour quelques années*, and she is very clever, and really has my welfare at heart, and is anxious to assist me *en toúte chose;* I must put up with little disagreeables and make the best of it. . . . Mama is going to Chatsworth, the Duke of Devonshire's country seat, next week, and thence most probably to Heaton, Lord Wilton's place in Lancashire; so I shall be left alone for about a week. Although I shall miss dear Mama most dreadfully, it is more easy to bear now, as Aunt Mary is at Richmond, and she is so extremely kind that that somewhat makes up for the loss.

I cannot help feeling that Aunt Mary has grown much older in the last few months; the death of my dear Aunt Sophia gave her a dreadful shock, but I hope and trust that she will still be spared to us, for you cannot think how fond we are of her. We young people—that is to say, George, Augusta, and I—love her as a second mother; she is quite an angelic Being, her sweetness of temper is *beyond,* and I trust that one day I may follow her bright example, and resemble her in mind and heart as well as in name. Indeed, dear Ellinor, though I say it who should not say it, I think that I really have improved, and do improve, and that I am *far, far* less passionate than I used to be. I think, also, that I am growing more religious, and feel more anxious to do my duty; so I trust, with God's assistance, that I may soon become an altered Being.

With Mr. Ward I am now reading Jewish History, and in the intervals between his lessons I read parts of "Nichol's Help" for him, upon which he afterwards gives me questions to answer. With Mr. Walbaum I do German, history, geography, arithmetic, and literature—in short, all the important branches of education. Sellé[1] gives me a music lesson twice a week, and French and other things I do with the Baroness's assistance. *Ainsi vous voyez ma chère, que mon temps est bien rempli.* Mama talks of reading some interesting English book in the winter with me. Dear Mama looked fatigued and ill when we left town, but Cowes did her a world of good, and she is looking very well now, and yesterday

[1] Organist at Kew Church.

rode for two hours and a half without being tired afterwards.
I hope you read those two articles in the *Morning Post* about
my brother and sister; they really were very complimentary,
and gave us all great pleasure. Thank God dear George is
very popular in Ireland, and I feel quite proud of him, and
long to say to every one, *he is my brother !* . . . Ever your
affectionate friend,

MARY ADELAIDE.

P.S.—Love to Lady Napier, to Anne, and to your other
sisters; 1000 kisses to yourself.

Cambridge Cottage, September 10, 1848.

DEAREST DRAPERCHEN,— . . . We have most excellent
accounts from Strelitz; Augusta and her darling little
Adolphus, George, Frederick, Augustus, Victor, Ernest,
Adalbert, William, Gustavus, Wellington, who is now
seven weeks old, are very well indeed. The Baby has
quite an English face with the exception of the nose. He
is growing so very fast that he has nearly outgrown his
little frocks. . . .

Cambridge Cottage, October 5, 1848.

MY DEAR ELLINOR,— . . . The people demanded of the
Grand Duke alteration in the law of election and the dis-
missal of the ministers. He has remained firm in refusing to
dismiss the ministers, and only promised them to deliberate
with the Grand Duke of Schwerin upon what measures could
be adopted to conduce to their welfare. As they appeared to
be dissatisfied with the reply, and continued sending deputa-
tions, and affairs became more and more alarming, it was
thought better that in case the people, who were by this time
in a state of great excitement, should endeavour to storm the
Château, my sister, the baby, and my Aunt should leave the
town. They left, and went to Hohenzieritz, a small *Château*
situated at about two hours' distance from Strelitz. The
Grand Duke followed them, but my cousin George remained
in the town. Fritz was at a bathing-place, and was to
return to Strelitz on the same evening that all this took
place.

The people contented themselves with breaking the
windows of the houses of the ministers. As towards evening all again became quiet, the whole of the family returned.
They have since been threatened with invasions of great
bodies of Republicans, but fortunately as yet, these have not

arrived, besides which they are now much more comfortable, as their "Battalion" of troops has since returned from
Schleswig-Holstein. I can assure you that had these troops
been at Strelitz when the riot occurred, my sister and the rest
would never have left the castle. We heard from Augusta
the other day, who says that universal suffrage now prevails,
in consequence of which labourers are chosen at the elections
for the purpose of forming a Constitution. What a pity it
is too for Lord Palmerston to meddle with it, or to make
as great a mess of it as he has done of all the other places
he has kindly interfered with, to the great detriment of the
Monarchical government and to the advantage of the radical
party ! Write soon, and tell me all the news of yourself. . .

Cambridge Cottage, October 30, 1848.

DEAREST DRAPERINECHEN,—You must have thought me
shockingly and naughtily remiss in answering your kind
letter. . . . You can imagine that the dreadful events which
have taken and do daily take place on the continent make
every one very unhappy, and though I am generally gay
and merry, yet I often feel very serious in thinking of
the present, and endeavouring to anticipate the future,
and am as much interested in all that is going on as
any one. I trust that Germany may soon be restored to
peace and prosperity, but to judge from the accounts which
are daily received this appears very improbable. In
Strelitz matters are going on tolerably quietly at present, but
if once things begin to wear a sanguinary aspect at Berlin,
the radical party will break out again at Strelitz; so this
is only a calm previous to the eruption of a volcano.
. . . Augusta does not speak of coming here at present, but of
course if any revolution were to break out she would take
refuge in her own country ; for, say what she will, she's
English, and proud of being so, and she writes that should
she fall, her fall would be most comfortable, as she would
tumble upon Kew and a host of affectionate relations and
friends. She would certainly not stoop *to conquer* but to
gain. . . . My little nephew is, we hear, a very fine child,
and thrives delightfully. . . .

Dear Kew looks very smart in its autumnal dress of red,
orange, and green. We are living very quietly and comfortably, which is a great advantage to me, as I can attend nicely
to my studies, and make good progress in the literary and
accomplishment world. By way of enlivening me, we take
long drives in the pony-phaeton, which have additional

charms for me, as I then get a *tête-à-tête* with Mama. I am now agreeably occupied preparing presents for Christmas, and am very busy doing a cushion for my brother; if possible, I shall work another for my sister, a penwiper for Knesebeck, a basket for Mama, and perhaps some mittens for Mr. Mildmay. All the *Journaux des jeunes personnes* are in requisition to furnish patterns for the industrious. In the evening I read to Mama for an hour (from six to seven o'clock) a very nice English book, the "History of Lorenzo de Medicis," by Mr. Roscoe, which is apparently a most instructive and interesting historical work. Yesterday we were rather alarmed on receiving the news that Aunt Mary, who has just been to Windsor, had returned to London with a kind of erysipelas in her cheek caused by the bite of a gnat. As my Aunt is very much subject to this, and has several times been in great danger with it, we were much frightened; but I am thankful to say that we have received good accounts this morning. Mama is gone to town to pay her a visit.

Yesterday Mama received a letter from the Queen inviting us to Windsor next Thursday to stay till Saturday. On Wednesday we are going to Chelsea to hear Mr. Harrison preach for the benefit of the Society for the Propagation of the Gospel, it being the anniversary of its establishment. Thence we shall go to town to pay Aunt Mary a last visit before she proceeds to Brighton, where she intends to stay for some little time. I have great hopes that Mama will go down there, and spend a few days with her, in which case I might perhaps be allowed to accompany her, and should see you. How delightful that would be! . . . Are you not quite enchanted with the news that the Hungarian Regiments in the Austrian Service have declared themselves in favour of the Emperor? It is almost too good to be credible. Our pretty neighbour, Lady Jocelyn, dined here yesterday, and I was quite struck with her beauty; she is certainly one of the most fascinating persons I have ever seen in all my days. We have also new neighbours at Kingston, for the Prince and Princess of Parma have taken a house there for a few months. The Princess is quite charming, clever, pretty, and agreeable, and she has a great affection for Mama, and makes me call her "Louise." They are constant visitors at Kew, and she once brought her two children—little Marguerite, two years of age, and a Baby called Robert.[1] They are now in Scotland, but I suppose they will come back very soon. Mama is very busy making

---

[1] The present Duke of Parma.

improvements and alterations in her garden, and the adjoining one. But now I must bid you adieu, and ask your forgiveness for troubling you with such a long letter. . . .

Cambridge Cottage, January 9, 1849.

DEAREST DEAR ELLINOR,—Will you forgive me for not having thanked you sooner for your kind congratulations? . . . I should have done so had not the dissipation of a Brighton life and some visits we received here prevented me. . . . God grant that I may grow in grace as well as in stature. But few years remain to me in which to improve in heart and mind, and it must and will be my earnest endeavour so to employ the time granted to me as to render me fit to encounter the temptations of the world and to resist them, thus behaving in a Christianlike manner and doing my duty in that station of life in which I may hereafter be placed, be it high or low, rich or poor. Forgive me for beginning my letter in so serious a manner, but having confided to you my good resolutions, I shall now proceed to tell you what has passed since my last letter.

We went to Brighton about the end of November, to pay a visit to Aunt Mary and to spend my birthday with her, and we enjoyed our stay there very much indeed. Brighton is a very pretty town and much frequented this year, as people are unwilling to visit the continent in the unsettled state in which it at the present moment is. The shops are extremely pretty, and the Promenades and streets looked very gay with the crowds of smartly dressed people walking about. Nothing could exceed the kindness of Papa and Mama and my Aunt, and numberless were the handsome and useful presents I received from them and my other kind friends on my birthday, when I enjoyed myself very much. Young Princess Metternich,[1] a very charming girl whose acquaintance I had made in London, came in the morning of the 27th and spent the day with me. In the evening we had a little party, and, after having played a round game, we danced till twelve o'clock. We walked out twice every day, and in the afternoon Melanie Metternich generally accompanied me; so that I saw a great deal of her, and I like her exceedingly. She is pretty, clever, agreeable, and remarkably gay and merry, and besides all this, is so kindhearted that one cannot long be with her without becoming good friends. Aunt Mary received people every evening. Twice

[1] Princess Melanie Metternich, who afterwards married Count Zichy.

we went to the Metternichs' (after dinner), where I saw the
Prince, who was extremely kind to me, and it was very
interesting to me to see a man who for so many years has
governed the Austrian Empire, preserved in a great measure
the Balance of Europe, and for whose cleverness and talents
as a statesman all European countries have had the greatest
respect.[1]

Princess Lieven[2] and Monsieur Guizot[3] were also at
Brighton, and of the former we saw a great deal, and I was
obliged to talk French to her, which frightened me out of
my wits; but she was very indulgent, and took a great deal
of notice of me. Aunt Mary gave another little dance in
honour of your humble servant, and I returned to Kew quite
sorry to leave Brighton and Melanie Metternich, and very
grateful to everybody for their kindness. As an agreeable
consolation Mama promised to invite Melanie and her eldest
brother, Prince Richard,[4] to Kew for a few days. Accordingly,
in the middle of December they arrived, and we were all as
happy as possible. We went to Exeter Hall to hear
Mendelssohn's "Elijah," in which Jenny Lind sang the
principal part. The music is very fine, and the choruses
quite splendid. The next day we danced and sang all the
morning in the Library, and afterwards I sat and worked

[1] Prince Metternich was first Minister of Austria from 1809–1848: he died
in 1859.

[2] Princess Lieven was a clever and brilliant woman, and in her day a
power in social and political life. It was said of her that she combined "*la
raison de la Rochefoucauld avec les manières de Madame de Sevigné.*" As the
wife of the Russian Ambassador accredited to St. James's during the period
which preceded the downfall of Napoleon, she was seen a good deal at Court
functions in this country, and to the end of her life maintained her connection
with London society. Princess Marie Liechtenstein, who met Princess
Lieven very often at Holland House, describes her as "in appearance
dignified, in manners simple, with the intellect of a man, and the pliability
of a woman." Her last years were passed in Paris, where her *salon* was a
favourite resort with the great men of the day. She died in 1857 at the
age of seventy-three.

[3] M. Guizot, the well-known French historian and statesman, was born
in 1787, and died in 1874. After the fall of the monarchy he came to London,
where he spent the remaining years of his life. He was a close and devoted
friend of Princess Lieven's, and when the Princess was on her death-bed,
and no longer able to speak to Guizot, who, with his son, was watching by
her bedside, she traced in pencil the words, "*Merci de vingt ans d'amitié et de
bonheur.*"

[4] Was Austrian Ambassador at Paris in the time of Napoleon III.; he
assisted the Empress Eugénie to make her escape from the French capital
after the unhappy events of 1870.

with Melanie. In the evening George arrived, looking remarkably well and in very good spirits. We played at a round game and then danced about till very late. As the following day was a Sunday these riotous proceedings were put an end to; but we were very gay nevertheless, and very sorry to part on Monday. The Metternichs are to pay us another visit soon, and, to keep up our friendship, Melanie and I write to each other. I live in hopes that the Prince and Princess will take a House in our neighbourhood next spring, which will be quite delightful to me.

The Christmas holidays have been very happily spent by the inmates of Cambridge Cottage, and I have received a number of *cadeaux!* Our Trees were arranged in the Conservatory, which was hung with festoons of evergreens, from which transparent lamps were suspended. The whole was well lighted up, and looked remarkably pretty, and the three trees were quite covered with bon-bons and fruit. Several people came down to spend Christmas with us, and had my dear sister been with us we should have been *perfectly* happy; but we must not grumble, as we continue to receive good accounts of herself and the darling Baby, and probably may expect to see them this spring. On New Year's Day we had no grand doings, and as it was a holiday I went to town with Mama and paid some visits. Poor Aunt Mary is suffering from a fit of Influenza, which has weakened her extremely, and although the Doctors say she is much better, yet Mama is very anxious about her, as she cannot get her strength back again, and is in very low spirits.

Last Wednesday we went to Windsor Castle to remain till Friday. The visit went off very well indeed. The Queen and the children are looking very well, and the latter much grown. The poor little Prince of Wales has disfigured his face by falling on an iron-barred gate, and the bridge of his nose and both his eyes are quite black and bruised, but fortunately no bones were broken. The first evening we danced till twelve o'clock. Next day, the weather being very cold, we went to see the gentlemen skate and play at Hockey; I found time to write some letters and pay a visit to the Duchess of Kent. Dinner was very early, and at eight o'clock the Play began. *Used Up* and *Box and Cox* were chosen for that night, and I was much pleased at seeing two very amusing pieces. They were very well acted, and we all laughed a great deal. The Theatre was well arranged, and the decorations and lamps quite wonderfully managed. It was put up in the Rubens-room, which is separated from the

Garter-room by one small room where the Private Band
stood. In the Garter-room was the Buffet, and in the
centre hung one of the beautiful chandeliers from the
pavilion at Brighton. The four elder children appeared at
the Play, and the two boys wore their "kilts." The two
little girls had on white lace gowns, over white satin, with
pink bows and sashes. Princess Royal wears her hair in a
very becoming manner, all twisted up into a large curl, which
is tucked into a dark blue or black silk net, which keeps it
all very tidy and neat.

We are going to the Priory (Queen Dowager) next Monday
for a few days, and after that I shall stay here and attend
diligently to my lessons; so you must not expect to hear
from me for some time, as I have a great deal to do. In
the working department I am embroidering two things—a
pair of slippers and a cushion; the pattern of the latter is
rows of pink and red roses on a white ground; the pattern
of the other is red leaves shaded on black. . . . Pray write
to me soon, a long letter, full of news about yourself, and
do not scold me for not writing! or think I like you less!
because *that* would be very foolish and nonsensical of you.
Adieu. I wish you and yours a happy New Year. Believe
me to be ever your very affectionate friend,

MARY ADELAIDE.

Cambridge Cottage, April 9, 1849.

DEAREST DEAR DRAPERINECHEN,— . . . Very much has
happened since we met at Brighton. . . . The Baroness Böse
has left me for good. . . . I will not say anything about her,
excepting that she has returned to Germany, and is looking
out for a situation. I pity her extremely, for she has not
made herself friends. . . . I trust, with the assistance of dear
Mama and my kind friends, I shall get rid of all the faults
that have made me till now so very unamiable. You have
no idea how kind Mama is, and how she gives up her time
to me, and superintends my music-lesson, besides reading
with me in the evening. We have now two very interesting
books, one is Macaulay's "History of England," the other is
French, on the Littérature Française, giving a brief biography
of all the great French writers in verse and prose. My
lessons go on as usual—indeed, the only difference since
the Baroness left us, is that I am a great deal more with
my Mother, and I declare I have grown a great deal older
in these last two months. The mornings I spend alone in

my little sitting-room, and am fully occupied in preparing for my masters.

I am sorry to say poor Papa is still confined to his room—to his chair, I should say—for he cannot walk yet, and the gout, I fear, is coming on again in his knee; he is getting very tired of being in his room so long, for it is now more than three weeks since he was first attacked. In the beginning it came in his wrist, fore-finger, both knees, and one foot. Now it is in one foot and one knee, but we trust the dose which he took again last night will do him good, and that in a few days he will be able to stand. Mama had intended to go to Belvoir and Melton, and I was to go for a week to the Queen Dowager's, but of course all visits were given up when we found that Papa was unable to move. We have therefore been leading a very retired and quiet life, and for the last week have been going every day to church.

On Good Friday, as Mama took the Sacrament, I got permission to stay and see it administered. I was much edified by seeing it given, and I confess had a great longing to take it myself. However, I trust I shall have that privilege next Easter. We have been reading serious books all this week, and I now take a great interest in religious matters, and attend much more to them than I used formerly to do. . . . My piece of good news I have kept to the last, to surprise and delight you. It is that Augusta expects to be here for the Birthday of Aunt Mary, which is the end of this month. . . . This is happiness indeed, and we are delighted at it also on my brother-in-law's account, for he has been seriously unwell of late, and Augusta is quite anxious about him; but how can he get well when he is so constantly worried and harassed by all the sad events that occur in poor Germany? Frederick has such very monarchical principles that he is not at all suited to these unhappy times and the republican spirit that appears to be innate in all classes at present. Heaven preserve England from following the example of her sister countries! The Baby is thriving, and very intelligent and amusing. I am longing to see the little darling and his dear parents. What a happy party we shall be when we are all again united! For my brother intends to come over when Augusta arrives, he not having seen her for more than a year and a half.

How charming is the news from Austria! *Vivat* Radetzky! who has behaved *en grand seigneur*, so nobly and so generously. Our friends the Parmas are going to leave us, at which we are very sorry, though it is much better they should go and return to their Duchy. The Duke has abdicated in favour of our friend who is now *Charles 3rd;* they are going to Olmutz, to the Emperor of Austria, where they intend to await the proper time to return to Parma. Are you not glad that Charles Albert (the coward) has been compelled to fly? They say that they think he will come here; I can hardly believe it, as he will be very ill received. . . . I am quite furious with him and his want of honour.

Now I have in conclusion to ask you, in Mama's and my name, a great favour. We shall probably not go to London till the middle of May, and then of course Mama will go out of an evening, and I shall mostly stay at home. My lessons and occupations will take me all the morning and a part of the afternoon, and then I shall probably go out with Mama and Augusta, or Fritz will take me for a walk, so all day I shall be very happy; but of an evening I shall be rather dull, so I wanted to know if you would get Mrs. Tatham to be so kind as to take a house in or very near London for the month of June, and, if possible, of July, and you would then be able to be so kind as to take pity upon poor lonely me, and spend the evening with me, when I should be most *charmingly & pleasantly & usefully employed* in reading and working with dear Draperinechen. If you could arrange this for a month or six weeks, Mama and I would owe you a debt of gratitude. She, because she would then feel that her precious daughter was well employing her time, and very happy; and I, because you were sacrificing your time to a worthless body who, but for you, would feel very dull about 8 o'clock of an evening. . . . Now, dear creature, pray consider this *mighty question,* and do as you think right and proper. You know it would be quite like *old times,* when I was a naughty little girl *aged seven,* and your very unworthy pupil. . . . Kew is looking charming, and sends its love to you. All the trees are getting green, and violets abound. *Addio! cara mia Draperina. Les môts me manquent.* Goodbye. I remain your most affectionate

MARY ADELAIDE.

Cambridge Cottage, April 11, 1849.

DEAREST SWEETEST DRAPERINECHEN,—How very kind of you to come to London for me! I assure you that Mama and I fully appreciate your affectionate kindness, and are truly grateful for it. . . . Papa is getting much better, but is still unable to stand, as the left foot and knee are not quite well yet. I perfectly agree with all you say about

Radetzky and the Italian affairs, and I think it very probable that, as you say, the Ministers have followed the example of the Spartans in fomenting the revolutionary spirit of the age, in order to show what misery and ruin it leads to in the end; but I confess I think you take a too high and honourable view of Charles Albert's character. After his treachery and double dealing I should hardly think him capable of acting so well, and sacrificing himself for the good of Italy; I should rather have said that he had been guided and led on by his ambition, and had hoped to have thereby become King or Emperor of Italy. Be that as it may, your idea of this *entr'acte question* is much the most Christian and the most noble. Pray express to Mrs. Tatham how grateful I am to her for so kindly acceding to my wishes, and with my kind and thankful compliments to her, and a love and kiss to yourself, believe me to be, ever your very affectionate and grateful

MARY ADELAIDE.

Cambridge Cottage, May 21, 1849.

MY DEAREST DEAR ELLINOR,—Many thanks for your amiable and interesting letter, which I hasten to answer, as I know how anxious you must be to hear something about the Cambridge family, and particularly about the baby Adolphus, with a minute description of whom I shall begin this long epistle. He is a beautiful child, with large dark blue eyes, dark eyebrows and eyelashes, a little tiny nose, a sweet little mouth with six teeth, and a fresh rosy complexion. He is very good tempered and good humoured, cries very seldom, and begins to know us all now. There is the prettiest expression about his dear little face that I ever saw, and the fat little creature is a great pet, and he and I are the greatest possible friends. He is very much like the English family, and like his own dear Mama, who is grown very thin, and looks much older than when we last saw her. However, she already begins to look better, and to get her colour back again. You can fancy how delighted we all are to be again united, and I confess I never felt till this moment what a blessing it is to have a darling sister to whom one can confide all one's little joys and griefs, with the full conviction that they will interest her, and that she is always ready to give one kind advice, and when necessary an affectionate scolding.

Fritz, and indeed we all are, very unhappy at the

melancholy accounts we receive of the fearful state of the
Continent, every part of which seems torn with anarchy and
confusion.   In Dresden, happily, the troops have been victorious, but in Baden the state of things is dreadful; the
poor weak Grand Duke is concealed somewhere near Frankfort, his troops having declared against him, and that horrible
Struve, who, if you remember, was imprisoned some months
ago for inciting the people to revolt against their sovereign,
is now one of the members of the Provisional Government.
At Frankfort an outbreak is expected; my Uncle Frederick,
who has lately been at Rumpenheim, has therefore left that
place and was going to Cassel, for, to be in the *voisinage* of
Frankfort at such a moment is anything but agreeable.   The
letters he wrote to Mama from thence were very interesting,
and of course contained the newest accounts.   We are to
leave dear Kew on the 28th, on which day we shall install
ourselves in smoky London; however, strange to say, I do
not so very much object to going to Town this year, for I
shall be very glad to have my masters again, and to see a
very little of the world.

The Metternichs have taken a house at Richmond for
several months, at which I am quite delighted, for Melanie
is a great friend of mine.   I am sure you would like her. . . .
She often has very serious kind talks with me.   I am very
pleased to have such a friend, and Mama is also very fond of
her.   The others, that is to say Mama and Augusta, have been
to London several times lately, but I had only accompanied
them twice; the first time I went to a dance at Buckingham
Palace, where I heard the inimitable Strauss, and the second
time I drove to town to see the ladies dressed for the Birthday drawing-room.   Mama was in blue, with ornaments of
pearls and diamonds; Augusta in white and pink, with
sapphires, both looking remarkably well.

Yesterday morning we again went to London to church,
and after having lunched with Aunt Mary, we drove with
her to see the Queen, who was looking well, though a little
nervous, of course, after her fright on Saturday.   She was
returning home from her drive, and was very near the Palace
on Constitution Hill, when she was shot at by an Irishman,
a plasterer by trade, but fortunately the pistol, which appears
to have been loaded only with gunpowder, did not wound
any one.   The man, who made no attempt to escape, was
taken upon the spot, and the populace would have torn him
to pieces had not the police carried him off.   He was
examined yesterday, but I do not know what was the result

of the examination. Some say he did it to make himself notorious, others from poverty, as he wished to be hanged or drowned. They cannot convict him, as no bullet can be found, but I think he will be severely punished. . . . What horrifies every one is that it should have happened on the day the Birthday is celebrated. The Queen wrote a very pretty letter on the unhappy affair to Aunt Mary, in which she does not mention the man by any other way than as *foolish*. She says she was not frightened, but that it was very annoying and disagreeable, and took away all comfort in going out. Alfred, Alice, Helena and Miss Macdonald [1] were in the carriage with her.

I fear this unfortunate event will have a very bad effect in Germany, where they will think that England is in a state of revolution, which I trust will never be the case, though if we are spared it we may thank the devoted attachment of the people to their Royal Family for it, for Lord Palmerston and his *emissaries* are doing as much harm as they can. . . . I hope that we may soon get rid of him, and that his successor will do all in his power to make up for all the horrors we have done abroad. . . . These democratic principles will one day bring us all to the scaffold. . . . I sincerely congratulate you upon the birth of a second nephew and on your happiness in having such a charming sister-in-law as Nina seems from your accounts to be. In these melancholy times it is a great blessing to belong to a nice united family, and this you and I enjoy in the highest degree. With compliments and affectionate messages to your Mama and sisters, and a love and a kiss to yourself, I remain, your most affectionate and attached friend,

MARY ADELAIDE.

Cambridge Cottage, le 9 d'Août, 1849.

MA CHÈRE AMIE,—Mille remerciments pour votre aimable petite lettre. Je serai charmée de vous voir Jeudi prochain à *luncheon-time;* mais comme Maman et Auguste ne seront pas à Kew ce jour, car elles me quittent Mardi pour Portsmouth d'où elles ne reviendront que Jeudi soir, elles m'ont chargé de vous prier de venir nous voir Vendredi si cela vous est possible à toute heure qui vous conviendra. Il faut que je vous dise encore une fois ma chère Miss Draper, combien

---

[1] The Honble. Flora Macdonald was appointed Maid-of-Honour to the Queen in 1847, which post she resigned in 1874, on her appointment as Woman of the Bedchamber. In 1897 she was made Extra Woman of the Bedchamber.

je vous suis reconnaissante pour les bontés que vous avez eu
pour moi pendant notre séjour à Londres. Je tâche de me
rappeler de vos bons conseils et d'en profiter en les suivant;
et je suis persuadée qu'en me laissant guider par Maman et
en y mettant de la bonne volonté je réussirai à me défaire
de beaucoup de mes défauts. Je suis bien fachée d'apprendre
que Mrs. Tatham a été souffrante, mais j'espère qu'elle
reprendra ses forces à Paris et que le climat Français lui
conviendra mieux que celui de sa propre patrie. Je suis très
heureuse ici, continuant mes études à peu près d'après votre
liste et faisant dans mes heures de récréation de longues promenades à pied et en voiture. Les jardins sont en grande
beauté maintenant et il y à touts les jours une foule de
monde qui vient de Londres pour les voir, ce qui n'est pas
agréable pour les habitants de Cambridge Cottage. Le Baby
vous fait ses amitiés et vous remercie pour votre baiser. Il
grandit de jour en jour mais ses dents le font souffrir un peu
dans ce moment, cependant il est bien gentil et veut absolu-
ment vous faire la conversation. Quel dommage que vous
n'avez pas vu Mr. Barry à Brighton; il aura été désolé de se
voir appeler par le devoir à Bordeaux, au lieu de se rendre à
Atlingworth Street pour vous voir. Espérant de vous voir
Jeudi prochain en tous cas, je vous fais mes adieux en vous
priant de garder un agréable souvenir du temps que nous
avons passé ensemble à Londres, votre bien affectionée,

> MARY ADELAIDE.

> Plas Newydd, Isle of Anglesey, September 7, 1849.

DEAREST ELLINOR,—How surprised you will be when
you read the funny Welsh name of this place, and when
you hear that I am located here for a month at least, and
in a fine large country house, situated on a rising eminence overlooking the Menai Straits and surrounded by
mountains and hills, making quite a pendant to your Highland home! But to explain this wonderful mystery I must
tell you that Lord Anglesey has lent us this house for some
time, and it is in the Isle of Anglesey, and that we are here
for the sake of the whole family, who wish for a complete
change of air. We arrived here yesterday, rather fatigued,
having left Kew a little before eight, and travelled 250 miles
by rail to Bangor, where we got into the carriages, drove over
the famous Suspension Bridge, and arrived here about 6
o'clock. The country we passed through from Chester was
beautiful, and we did nothing but go from one window to the
other to see the different views. At Conway station we

jumped out of the carriage to see the beautiful Gothic archway under which we had passed. This station is in the
middle of the fine ruins of an old Castle covered with ivy; I
had only a glimpse of it, but that was sufficient to show that
it is well worth the trouble of coming to see it, and I am sure
one of the many excursions we propose making will be to
this place.

The house we are now in is very large and comfortable,
built rather in the castle style, with a long terrace in the front;
a very nice garden surrounds the house, and there is a fine
wild park. My room is very comfortable and spacious, with
four windows, from each of which a lovely view is before me:
hills covered with fields, corn-fields, and cottages, to the left
wooded scenery; and when I turn my head round, the Menai
Straits, with a view of the hilly part of the Isle of Anglesey
and the tubular bridge which is being repaired, in the distance. My room is arranged at once as sleeping and dressing-
room, and as sitting-room with a sofa and writing-table,
and a piano, which having been played on for forty years at
least, has become useless from old age. It is but fair to let
it rest (the keys being toneless and tuneless), and so I use it
only to put the quantities of pretty music I brought with me
upon.

We were all sorry to leave Kew, which is now in great
beauty, and our neighbours the Metternichs. Melanie was
very unhappy at the thought of not seeing me for so long a
time, but we are in hopes of meeting again in Wales, as I
think that Mama will ask her to pay us a visit, which will
give us both the greatest possible pleasure. Poor Mama has
been very low these last few days, as on leaving Kew she
took leave of her old Dresser, dear old Alsfeldt, who is going
away after having served Mama most faithfully for upwards
of thirty years. She says her health is declining, and as she
begins to feel quite unable to do much, she declared she could
not stay, and is going to Germany. This is a dreadful
blow to dear Mama, who loved her very much, and makes us
all very unhappy. I took leave of her yesterday with many
tears, and she starts for Hamburg to-morrow. It has been
raining all this morning, but I hope it will clear up, as I am
most anxious to get out. I shall not send this letter away
till I have seen some places and given you a description of
the Welsh scenery and the wonders of Snowden, etc., etc.
I must now leave off, as I am going to read French with
Mama; for though I have holidays, I shall occupy myself
some hours every day.

September 8.

Though it rained all day we took a walk in the afternoon round the grounds; the trees about this place are beautiful, and we talk of having a picnic some fine day under them. The kitchen-garden is very large, and the walls are covered with peach trees—the fruit will be ripe in another week. The way to it leads through a lovely little wood, quite wild and countrified. To-day the weather is very fine, and I believe we are to make some excursion either by water or land. As a reward for your telling me about your three little nephews, I shall write to you about my own little Adolphus, who is improving every day, becoming more intelligent, more amusing, and more companionable. He is growing very fast, and is so heavy that one can hardly carry him. He has not begun to walk yet, but I think he will soon, as he is very fond of putting his feet to the ground and standing up. He calls me "Amma," that is to say, according to my construction, Aunt Mary. When you ask him to do what he dislikes he says, "No, no, no," and puts you away with his dear little hands. He is in general very obedient and extremely amiable and generous, but he begins to have a will of his own.

September 9.

We are just returned from a most charming expedition on the water to the Menai Bridge. We got out of the boat, and walked up a slippery wet beach and a stony hill to get to it, then crossed the bridge, and went some little way beyond. On our return we again passed under the tubular railroad bridge, which is being repaired, as the machine which was raising it up broke, so that as yet no railroad has passed through it. It is the most wonderful thing of its kind, and we are to go and see the interior some day, with the Engineer to explain it to us. All I know of the tubes is, that they are made of metal plates joined together; if they were of solid metal they could not bear their own weight, and would break in the middle. We had a charming boat, with four men to row us. On returning, the tide was against us, and so strong that we were hardly able to get on at all, and had to row in all directions to avoid the current, which is particularly strong near the rocks. I am very much amused at being in *Britain* and not understanding the language of the people. Most of the poor people speak nothing but Welsh, and do not understand English at all; so that our cook has got an interpreter when he wants to buy fish or things of that sort. The women here wear the peasant's dress and charming white caps with frills, and black *wide awakes* or *beaver* hats, like the men, stuck on the top of their heads. They ride two and two on the horses, one person sitting on a saddle, the other on a pillion behind. I saw some riding in this way, but they were too far for me to distinguish them quite clearly. Some of the women wear large dark cloaks with hoods very much like the Malines peasants. Goodbye for to-day.

September 14.

I am looking out of my window at Snowden and thinking how I wish you could be here to take a trip with me to see this beautiful mountain. Plas Newydd is quite charming and the walks too delightful. We walked, before our aquatic tour, along a path above the beach, and had a most splendid view of the whole way, stumbling every now and then on a little waterfall which gushed out of the rocks and tumbled over the stones down into the water, so cool and sparkling, much nicer than champagne. On Saturday we had lovely weather and in the afternoon we drove to Sir Richard Bulkeley's place, called Baron Hill, which is close to Beaumaris and about eight miles from here. It is a very fine place, the house quite new, and furnished in French style, and almost too grand to please me. The gardens are also laid out in the French style, which I do not admire, but the Vinery is beautiful and the grapes quite magnificent. Lady Bulkeley has been so kind as to send us some, together with some splendid peaches. On Sunday we had Divine Service performed in the little Chapel which is in the house; in the afternoon we took a long walk on the beach and in the grounds.

Monday we went to Carnarvon to see the famous old Castle where Edward II. was born. I was delighted with it, and particularly pleased to see the tiny apartment in which it is *supposed* he first saw the light; we went to the top of the Eagle's Tower, whence there is a fine view of the mountains and surrounding country. Yesterday we made a charming excursion to Penrhyn Castle, which belongs to Colonel Douglas Pennant, Lord Morton's brother. We started at twelve o'clock, crossed the Menai Bridge, and were received with shouts of joy at the little town of Bangor, through which we passed, and all the shops hoisted their colours as we drove by. Penrhyn Castle is a splendid place, built during these last years, but in the ancient style, and uniting modern comforts with ancient architecture; it is built of Anglesey marble (unpolished), and the rooms downstairs are wainscotted with wood and gilding, they are large, but very comfortable, and the library can form one large room or two smaller rooms. At the end of it there is a little nook like a Boudoir, in a round shape, where any one desirous of writing letters without being disturbed or interrupted can retreat to. Besides these there is a large drawing-room, a smaller one which is seldom used—as Lady Louisa thinks it very gloomy—an immense dining-room, and a beautiful hall with a billiard table. The bedrooms and rooms for the family are in the Keep, which I have not yet seen.

Colonel Douglas inherited this beautiful place from his 1st wife, a Miss Pennant, the mother of his five children. His second wife is a charming person, Lady Louisa Fitzroy, and she has two little girls. Some of the neighbours had been invited to the luncheon to meet us, and we sat down a large party. Afterwards we all drove to the slate quarries which belong to Colonel Pennant, where we were received in style by 2,200 workmen employed here, and the peasantry with cheers and a royal salute, which had a splendid effect, the royal standard being put up in different places, and the band of the miners playing the National Anthem. I was very much interested in seeing the different ways the slate is prepared for use, and having walked round a part of the quarry and seen the men at work, we went to a place of safety from whence we could see the blasting. Between 500 and 600 pieces of the rock were blasted, and the whole thing ended with the Royal salute and the cheers of the people. Colonel Pennant then took us to a pretty cottage of his, close to the quarry, a peaceful little retreat where the family sometimes take their luncheon; it overhangs a lovely waterfall, which we went to see. We did not return home till seven o'clock. To-day we remained quietly at home, and took an exploring ramble in the afternoon from a quarter to three till nearly six o'clock.

September 16.

Yesterday we drove to see the Fall of the Swallow, a beautiful waterfall close to Capel Cury, and about twenty-one miles from here. The scenery we passed through on our way was partly picturesque and romantic, and partly wild, terrific, and gloomy. We started at twelve o'clock and did not return till nine, but this did not signify as the waterfall was well worth seeing. I shall now conclude this long epistle, which I hope will not tire you. . . . Ever your affectionate friend,

MARY ADELAIDE.

Windsor Castle, November 7, 1849.

DEAREST DRAPERINECHEN,—I take advantage of a holiday at Windsor to thank you for your kind note. I should have answered the letter you wrote me from Boulogne if I had not been very much occupied just then; for while at dear Plas Newydd we were continually *par voie et par chemin*, and had but few leisure hours. Our stay in Wales has done us all a great deal of good. . . . The Welsh scenery is certainly very beautiful, and reminds one much of Switzerland, at one moment being picturesque and romantic, the next wild and grand. The excursions on foot, in the carriage, and in the boat were also very agreeable, and I assure you we enjoyed our *séjour* at Plas Newydd of all things.

On our way home we went to Heaton, and I spent a charming week with my friends Elizabeth and Katherine. We went to see Manchester and its principal factories, and I was much interested to see how cotton is manufactured; how silk is woven, how gowns are embroidered, and how steam-engines are made. We went also to Liverpool, and saw the *Lions* of that town, the Docks, Mansion House, concert room, Blue-Coat school, the Town Hall, and one of the great warehouses, where tea, silk (in its raw state), and wines and spirits were kept, also brown sugar. I returned to Kew much pleased with all I had seen and heard, but not the less inclined to pursue my studies with renewed ardour.

The week after we arrived at Cambridge Cottage the Metternichs left Richmond, to our infinite sorrow and disappointment; they are gone to Brussels, where they have taken a house for a year. Melanie, and indeed the whole family, were very unhappy at leaving us and dear England, and we are now consoling ourselves by keeping up a most regular correspondence, and I am happy to say I have very good accounts from Brussels. Elizabeth and Katherine also write to me very often, so you can imagine I have a pretty good deal to do to answer their kind letters. Poor Papa is not quite well; he was prevented from coming with us by a slight attack of gout in the knee, which I believe was caused by his having over-walked himself last week at Newmarket, when on a visit to the Duke of Rutland. Aunt Mary is just gone to the Bedford Hotel, Brighton, where she intends to stay about a month. The poor Queen Dowager is sinking, and the doctors do not expect her to live a fortnight longer. Her sufferings, which they say are now diminishing, have been dreadful, and it will be a very happy release. I am glad we saw her on our return to Kew, and I think she took leave of us for ever, for her manner was so warm and kind and she seemed pleased to have seen us all again.

Baby has frightened us tremendously lately; he was very ill for several days, and we thought it must be cholera, but I believe it was only his teeth, as he was just then cutting the eye-teeth. He looks pulled down but much better, thank God. . . . I hope and trust he will not have the chicken-pox, for the Queen has just had it, and Princess Alice has caught it from her; and I am afraid I shall be the next victim, as I have the honour to be at the Castle, in which case I fear Baby will have it too. . . .

Towards the end of November we expect Mr. Hutchinson, who is to be Papa's resident Chaplain, and to superintend my religious education. You can imagine how painful it was to me to separate from poor dear Mr. Ward; but I trust it is for the best, and that I shall improve under Hutchinson's care, and become in heart and mind a true Christian. . . . Ever your affectionate

MARY ADELAIDE.

Letter to the Rev. William Harrison.

Cambridge Cottage, November 29, 1849.

MY DEAR SIR,—Pray accept my very warmest thanks for your kind letter, and good wishes for my 16th birthday, which I received yesterday evening on our return from Brighton, where we have been spending a few days with the Duchess of Gloucester. My Birthday is now hailed with different feelings than it used to be; I feel I am no longer a child, and that my confirmation is approaching; and then the question occurs to my mind, "Am I prepared for it ?" This is a very serious consideration, and the happiness or misery of my future life depends on the answer I am able to give; but if I fervently pray to God to bless my very humble endeavours to become a Christian, and live as a child of God, I trust I shall be able one day to answer truly and sincerely in the affirmative. It must be my endeavour in my new year to make up to dear Mama the blank caused by the return of my sister and brother-in-law, and our dear little treasure, to Germany. I am now of the age to begin to be a companion to dear Mama, and I trust she will find that the pains she has taken with me, and all the love she has bestowed upon me, have not been wasted. If I perform this pleasant duty to the best of my abilities, I may hope for the favour of God; and I am sure I shall then reward the hopes of all my true friends, amongst whom I reckon you, dear Mr. Harrison. I trust Mrs. Harrison is quite recovered, and request you to give her my kind remembrance and best thanks for her good wishes for the 27th, which I was much pleased to find you had not forgotten as being my birthday.

I was very sorry not to have had the pleasure of seeing you at Plas Newydd, where, on receiving your kind letter, I had hoped to have seen you; but I trust your excursion to Scotland delighted you as much as our stay in Wales did us, and that you derived benefit from the mountain air. I suppose that we shall pass the winter very quietly at Kew, as Mama will not like my studies to be again interrupted. I fear there is no chance of seeing you soon again, as I imagine you are now too occupied at Birch to think of going to town; but should anything induce you to come to London, I need hardly say how pleased Mama and I should be if you could come down to Kew. With Mama's kind compliments to yourself and Mrs. Harrison, and in the hope of seeing you ere long, I remain, dear Mr. Harrison, your very grateful and attached

MARY ADELAIDE.

CHAPTER V.

GIRLHOOD : LETTERS—*Continued*.

1850-1852.

Death of the Queen Dowager—The Queen and the Royal children—Death of the Duke of Cambridge—In retirement at Plas Newydd—Princess Mary's seventeenth birthday—Preparing for Confirmation—The ceremony at Kew Church—First Communion—Visit to Melton—Opening of the Great Exhibition—Rumpenheim (1851)—August at Ischl—A fortnight in Vienna—Christmas at Strelitz—Apartments at St. James's Palace—Music lessons with Mr. Müller—First Drawing-room —London season—First Court Ball—Alterations at Kew—General election—Lord Derby's cause—Summer at Ryde—A true Protestant —Death and lying-in-state of the Duke of Wellington.

Cambridge Cottage, January, 1850.

DEAREST DRAPERCHEN,—A thousand thanks for your kind letter, which I have just received. I trust you will forgive me for not having written sooner to thank you for the charming tiny Indian deity, which gave me great pleasure as a pledge of your affection for me; but I must candidly confess to you that the death of the poor dear Queen Dowager [1] quite put it out of my head, though I ought to have remembered it, as it always stands upon my table. In return for your kind good wishes for the New Year, pray accept mine, both for 1850 and for many succeeding years; and I trust that each one will find you in health and happiness, surrounded by those dear to you. We have passed a quiet but very agreeable Christmas; our Trees and Tables were . arranged in the conservatory, which was hung with evergreen wreaths, and being well lighted up, looked extremely pretty. I was quite the *enfant gâtée* and received a number of beautiful presents from Papa and Mama and other friends.

We are just returned from Windsor where we have been

---

[1] Queen Adelaide died on December 2, 1849.

staying a day and a half. The Queen was exceedingly kind
and gracious, and the children are great darlings. It is quite
a pretty sight to see them all together; the handsomest are
certainly Alfred and Helena, but they all have nice counte-
nances, and I think the Princess Royal is very quick and
clever. I am now again resuming my usual occupations.
My lessons with Mr. Hutchinson get on very well. In the
mornings we read the Lessons and the Prayer-book, and the
afternoon hours from five to seven o'clock are devoted to
the study of Hume, which, notwithstanding its eight volumes,
interests me very much indeed. I am already at the reign
of Edward III., and have been reading to-day the war between
England and France, up to the battle of Crécy. Mama is
generally present at these lessons, and indeed at the morning
lessons also. My studies with dear Walbaum get on most
prosperously: French History, Mythology, Geometry,
Geography, and so forth. The piano is also not forgotten,
and Mr. Müller is pronounced by Mother and Daughter to
be an excellent master and a charming man. He assures me
he shall make a first-rate player of me, and that my progress
and improvement is great, more even than he could expect
after only eight lessons. He is indefatigable during my
lesson, which lasts two hours and a half, and the only
digression he permits himself is to ask in *touching accents*,
that would bring jealousy to the heart of poor Mr. Barry,[1]
after Miss Draper, *his kind friend*. . . . You know that Papa
and Mama gave my sister a little marble statue of her first
Baby; well, Dolphin calls it his "little Bother," and kisses
it, and wants it to come and play with him. Is not this
touching for fourteen months old ? Now I must say good-bye,
and subscribe myself your very affectionate and loving

MARY ADELAIDE.

Cambridge Cottage, March 7, 1850.

MY DEAREST ELLINOR,—Ten thousand thanks for the
"Songs of the Holy Land," and for your kind letters. . . .
We are living very quietly and sedately at Kew, and I am
studying all day long. . . . From Strelitz we have good
accounts; Baby grows very fast, runs about and tries to talk;
he is Augusta's plaything and the delight of her life, and
poor *we* miss him terribly. He minds neither heat nor cold,
wind nor weather, and we cannot be sufficiently grateful for
this, and for his general good health : they say he looks like

---

[1] Miss Draper was engaged to be married to Mr. Barry.

a little rosebud, so fresh and rosy, with his large clever blue eyes and fair, such a pet. I am so sorry that you have not seen him. Ahlefeld is now with us, but she has made us rather anxious of late, as she has been very unwell indeed, but she is now slowly recovering. My Uncle Frederick has also passed this winter with us, but I fear he will leave us in about a fortnight, when Mama intends to pay a few country visits, and I shall stay quietly with Ahlefeld at Cambridge Cottage. With kind love to your Mama, and many congratulations to you on Captain Hay's good conduct in China and his promotion. Your affectionate friend,

MARY ADELAIDE.

Cambridge Cottage, April 18, 1850.

DEAREST DEAR DRAPERINECHEN,—Your last kind and affectionate letter having informed me that your marriage is to take place on the 22nd, I hasten to address you once more as " dear Draperchen," and send you my most heartfelt and affectionate good wishes and congratulations on this great and I trust happy event. That you may enjoy every blessing this world can afford, and that each succeeding year may find you in health, happiness, and prosperity, and surrounded by those dear to you, is the most earnest and sincere wish and prayer of one who truly loves you, and whose whole heart rejoices in the happiness of her own Draperchen. I shall think of you all next Monday, and shall drink " Mrs. Barry's " health with Mama, and may it bring you good luck, my dear. . . . To all these other friendly wishes, I must add the selfish one that ere long I may see your dear face again. May God bless and preserve you, my dearest Draperchen, and may you ever remember with love, your naughty, but truly affectionate,

MARY ADELAIDE.

Cambridge House, May 26, 1850.

DEAREST ELLINOR,—Mama has permitted me to invite you to drink tea with me to-morrow evening at seven o'clock, should you be disengaged. How can I imagine that such a *charming individual* as yourself should not have a thousand engagements ! But I flatter myself that as the fashionable world keeps very late hours, and seldom receives before reasonable people have gone to bed, you may perhaps, for old acquaintance's sake, be prevailed upon to give me your agreeable company till *ten* o'clock. It will be a great pleasure and treat to me. . . .

Letter to the Rev. William Harrison.

Plas Newydd, Isle of Anglesey, August 14, 1850.

MY DEAR SIR,—I hope you will forgive me for not having before answered your very kind letter, for which I now return you my warmest thanks, but my own deep grief, and that of all around me, rendered me quite unequal to write to you sooner. I have indeed lost[1] the best of Fathers, and day by day I begin to feel more and more what I have lost in him, whom I so deeply, so devotedly loved, and whom I now so sadly mourn. . . . How comforting for us is the knowledge that he is only taken from us for a while, and the hope that ere long we shall be reunited with him, never more to part. As we sat by his death-bed and watched his fine countenance, lighted up with a placid, happy expression, unlike the one of suffering which had rested upon it for the last days, all fear of death seemed to have passed away, and we felt that he was now thoroughly happy, and that it would be selfishness to wish him back again amongst us. But yet it was hard and almost too difficult for us to say with sincerity of heart, "Thy will be done, O Lord," and humbly and confidingly to resign ourselves to the divine dispensation. Dear Mama has borne this trial with such wonderful fortitude, and such entire submission to the will of God, that it has endeared her, if possible, more to us all. She indeed sets us a perfect example of patient resignation, and it must now be our, more especially my, most earnest endeavour to be her comfort and support. God's assistance and dear Papa's example will, I trust, aid me in the performance of this duty to my *only* parent.

Mama desires me to return you her best thanks for the kind sympathy expressed in your letter to her, which she at present is unable to answer; and with my kindest remembrance to Mrs. Harrison, I remain, my dear Sir, yours very sincerely and gratefully,

MARY ADELAIDE.

Plas Newydd, Isle of Anglesey, August 26, 1850.

DEAREST DEAR DRAPERCHEN,—Your affectionate letter reached me at a moment when all my thoughts and feelings

---

[1] The Duke of Cambridge died at Cambridge House, July 8, 1850.

were absorbed in the deepest grief, and I was to go through the last sad scene and attend the remains of my beloved Father to the silent and desolate grave.   You will, therefore, I trust, forgive my apparent neglect in not having before returned you my most affectionate thanks for your kind expressions of sympathy, and will now accept them together with my most sincere hope that you will pardon me for my delay in writing to so fond, so true a friend.

We have indeed sustained a severe loss, and one that can never be repaired, in the death of the best of Friends and Fathers, and our happy and gay little family circle has been suddenly and fearfully converted into one of mourning; but it is the hand of God which has inflicted the wound, and He alone can heal it and give us the strength of faith and mind to say in truth, "Thy Will be done."   It is a consolation for us to know that our grief is shared by the nation, and that *his* goodness and truly Christian virtues are appreciated, which are now reaping their reward in a better and a happier world, where sin and sorrow are unknown, and all is peace and heavenly bliss in the presence of God and our Saviour. It would be the height of human selfishness to wish our dear Papa back again amongst us, and yet how difficult it appears *not* to do so.   But we must find comfort in the hope of being one day reunited with him, never more to be separated, and this is the only consolation I can offer to your sad heart, which so lately has suffered a bereavement as severe as ours.

No one can feel with and for a mourner so deeply as one who herself mourns, and be assured, my dear friend, that I warmly sympathise with you and long to see you, that we may have the melancholy satisfaction of *exchanging* our tears.   Dear Mama is truly resigned and wonderfully composed, though but slowly recovering from this severe shock.   She desires her kindest remembrance to you, and earnestly hopes that you may long continue to enjoy every blessing and all happiness in your new position.   I think you will remember our having been here last year.   Lord Anglesey has kindly offered us his house again, where we are, I believe, to remain till the end of September, when I suppose we shall return to Kew, which will be very painful for us all. . . .

Cambridge Cottage, December 9, 1850.

. . . A thousand thanks to you for the pretty Swiss cabinet and the kind letter which accompanied it, and brought me the many dear good wishes you so affectionately

THE ROOM AT CAMBRIDGE HOUSE IN WHICH H.R.H. ADOLPHUS FREDERICK, DUKE OF CAMBRIDGE, DIED.

From a drawing at Gloucester House.

express for my happiness and welfare. That the next year may be happier for us than the last has been, is my most earnest hope and prayer, and that on the 31st of December, 1851, we may not again have to look back on sad events and mourn the loss of near and dear friends. My Birthday was spent as happily as the sad recollections of the past would permit, for though overwhelmed with kindness by all around me, I could not forget that the blessing and congratulations of my own dear Papa were now wanting, which had formerly so much conduced to my pleasure and gaiety on that day. As a Birthday gift from Mama, and in memory of the mournful scenes we have passed through together this year, I received the hand of Papa in marble; so very like and so well done. That and his dear picture are all that now remain to remind us of Him, who was the life and soul of our little circle. . . .

My confirmation, which is to take place on the 19th of this month, occupies my time and thoughts. My whole mind, and I think I may say heart, are directed to this most serious and solemn step, which concerns not only my earthly but my heavenly happiness. It is now my most earnest prayer that God may grant me His Fatherly aid, so that I may be enabled to keep the solemn promises I make, and as a true Christian, become a blessing to my widowed Mother, and one day reunited with Papa in a better and happier world. . . . Believe me, dearest Draperinechen, your very affectionate and attached

MARY ADELAIDE.

Cambridge Cottage, January 6, 1851.

DEAREST DEAR ELLINOR,—Several months have passed since last you heard from me, my dear friend, and now I take up my pen to beg your pardon most humbly for all my misdeeds, and to wish you a very happy New Year, and that you and yours may enjoy in this and many many succeeding ones every blessing and all happiness. But to explain the cause of my long silence. You must know that after our sad loss we all went into Wales, too thankful to escape from London, which dear Papa's illness and death had made quite hateful to us, and that Mama might somewhat regain her strength and spirits. We spent about two months and a half at Plas Newydd, which has become dearer to us than ever by the many recollections it brought to our minds of him so fondly loved, so deeply mourned, and returned to Kew much benefited by our stay in Wales.

I am thankful to say Mama got through the first few days here pretty well, and bore this last trial with the same Christian fortitude and resignation to the Divine Will with which she closed my own dear Father's eyes and followed his revered remains to the grave. Ah! Ellinor, that was a sad procession down the aisle in our dear little Kew Church, to the vault where the coffin was temporarily deposited until the little Chapel can be finished, which we shall erect close to the Church to his memory. I cannot tell you what I felt! And yet I was comforted when I thought he was now happy with his Maker and his God, there where I hope we shall one day be reunited. When I think about it all, I feel so grateful to God that I was permitted to be with him during his illness, at least to be near him; and the last day I never left him, for he liked to have me with him, when Mama was for a moment called away, to fan him and to bathe his temples with *eau-de-Cologne;* and then he would press my hand and whisper, "Charming," "Dear." I felt happy then, and still hoped; but the same evening all was over, and the spirit had returned to God who gave it. His will be done.

On the following morning, between five and six o'clock, *seven hours* after dear Papa had breathed his last, poor Augusta, who had travelled night and day to reach England in time, arrived. She could say nothing but "Too late!" and sunk down by the side of the body. Thank God, we have an agreeable, I might say hallowed recollection of my dear Father, as when I kissed his forehead for the last time a sweet and heavenly smile played on his lips, and but for their marble hue I could not have believed that they were closed for ever. Deeply as we felt our bereavement then, we seem to miss him more now that weeks and months have rapidly passed away, and we feel sadly the want of that love and kindness he so fondly bestowed on us all. But we would not recall him; he is happier by far, and we only pray to be one day reunited with him in a better and more glorious world. I have written these details, as I know they would interest you, but I confess they have cost me many tears.

Since our return from Plas Newydd, all my time and thoughts have been devoted to preparation for my confirmation and the examination by the Bishop of London, which preceded it. The ceremony took place in our little Kew

Church, in the presence of the Queen and the whole family; George acting for the first time as *Father* on this occasion. You can imagine what my feelings were when I stood before the Altar and received the Archbishop's blessing, and how firmly I resolved to keep the vows and promises I made there before our heavenly Father. Dear Papa's blessing was sadly wanting; but he was no doubt present in spirit, and knew what I felt and determined in those words "*I do.*" I seem to have grown ever so much older since, and feel so grateful to be now fully a Christian and admitted to the Lord's Supper. As I was confirmed on the 19th of December, I took the Communion for the first time on Christmas Day, and I returned home afterwards with a feeling of happiness and inward peace such as I had never known before.

My sister and her darling boy are still with us, and as George and Fritz have now both joined us—the one from Ireland, the other from Germany—we are rather a large family circle; but he who was once its very life, soul, and pride is gone, and his place cannot be supplied by any one. We kept our Christmas on New Year's Day, when we all enjoyed ourselves very much, and interchanged quantities of presents. I had received magnificent ones at my Confirmation, but was not forgotten, I assure you, on New Year's Day. We have been of late very anxious about dear Aunt Mary, who has been confined to bed with a very severe attack of influenza, but, thank God, she is slowly recovering, and may almost be termed convalescent. . . . What a dreadful year this has been! How many friends one has lost, and such near and dear ones! May this New Year prove a happier one to us all, and may we, in the course of its spring, meet again. . . . Ever believe me to be, dearest Ellinor, your affectionate and true friend,

MARY ADELAIDE.

*   *   *   *   *

Melton, March 18, 1851.

DEAREST ELLINOR,—*Bon jour!* How do you do? I hasten to reply to your very kind letter. . . . You will wonder by my date where in the world I am! Well, I am at Melton on a week's visit to the Wiltons, and as you know the girls are great friends of mine, you will, I am sure, rejoice at my having this treat after the very secluded life we have led at Kew. We are a very small party here: only the family,

Etta Somerset,[1] and ourselves; and this evening a *beau*, Lord
Forester, is to arrive, to keep Lord Wilton company, for we
are quite a convent of ladies. Unfortunately, to-day it rains,
so that I have as yet seen nothing of Melton or the country
around it. . . .

March 19.

. . . Luckily the weather promises more favourably to-day,
so I hope to have a long walk and scramble in the fields.
The house and garden here are charming, and the former so
comfortable. I suppose you saw by the papers that Augusta
left us at the end of January, to our infinite regret.
Politics, of course, and affairs of state recalled my Brother-
in-law, but you will laugh when I say that hardly anything
has been achieved or settled since they left, and that their
very sudden departure was quite unnecessary. . . . What an
anxious winter you have had, poor dear, with so many sick
people to nurse! and now I hope that your visit to old
England will do you good, where I promise you a most
hearty and affectionate welcome. . . .

Cambridge Cottage, May 2, 1851.

. . . How can I sufficiently thank you for the lovely locket,
which will be treasured by me as the gift of a very old
friend, and always worn for the sake of the dear kind giver?
I have not had an instant to myself these last few days, or
you would long since have received a letter of thanks from
me; but I know you will forgive me, and that you understood
my look of thanks at the Exhibition.[2] I was so delighted at
seeing you, and at finding you had so good a place. Were
you not pleased and proud of the loyalty of our countrymen,
and at everything going off so remarkably well? . . . With
love to Lady Napier, and many kisses to you for the darling
locket. Ever yours most affectionately,

MARY ADELAIDE.

Cambridge Cottage, June 23, 1851.

DEAREST DEAR DRAPERCHEN,—Pray accept my most affectionate thanks for your kind letter, which I purposely delayed

---

[1] Lady Henrietta Somerset, third daughter of the seventh Duke of
Beaufort; she married Mr. John Morant of Brockenhurst in 1855.

[2] The Great Exhibition of the Industry of All Nations, held in Hyde
Park in 1851, opened May 1, and closed October 15. The building was
known as the Crystal Palace, and was afterwards moved to Sydenham. The
idea of the Exhibition originated with the Prince Consort, who personally
superintended all the arrangements connected with the undertaking.

answering, as I thought you might like to hear something of the State Opening of the Crystal Palace—the wonder of the world, and the one only subject of conversation in society at the present moment.

The Duchess of Kent was kind enough to take me to the grand Ceremony under her chaperonage, which was very agreeable! and I confess it was so splendid a sight that I would not have missed seeing it for all the world, and I am very grateful to dear Mama for letting her precious chicken go. The truly loyal and enthusiastic reception given by John Bull to the Queen was very gratifying, and *we English* Royal family had a right to be proud of our country, and happy that foreigners should witness its loyalty. I would not have exchanged my title of Princess of England at that moment for that of Empress of the whole world.

The interior of the building was magnificent, and a good proof of what England could do. High above all the nations of the world in her contributions, she is far superior to them in many things, backward in none, sculpture excepted, which has never been our *forte.* You see how patriotic I am, though at the point of going abroad for some months. I regret to say we are about to leave England to join Mama's family at Rumpenheim; thence, in the course of the summer, we shall proceed to Ischl for the fashionable bathing season, and afterwards make a tour in Germany, on our road to Strelitz. I suppose we shall return home in the course of the winter, as we cannot leave Aunt Mary too long alone. . . .

Rumpenheim.

I had advanced thus far with this letter when active preparations for the journey so entirely engrossed my time that my unfinished letter was, I am almost ashamed to confess, laid aside to be dispatched at leisure. I therefore now take up my pen to tell you that we arrived here in a high state of preservation, and found my Uncles well, and ourselves heartily welcomed by them. Mama is all the better for the change of air and scene; I have not seen her looking so like her own dear self for some time. As for me, the country life we lead here suits me of all things, and my Uncles spoil me so terribly that I fear my precious head will soon be quite turned. The neighbourhood of Frankfort and Biebrich, the Duke of Nassau's Place, is remarkably agreeable, especially Biebrich, as it has once again become a family seat by the marriage of the Duke with my cousin Adelaide, the one nearest my own age, and consequently my playfellow and pet companion. We are just returned from paying a visit of a few days to her, and then spending a couple of days with the Metternichs at the Johannisberg; and I assure you this has been a week of great enjoyment to me, thanks to our kind friends.

To-day I have settled down, like a good little girl, to my morning's occupations, and have been reading for two hours with the village clergyman, who comes to me five days in the week; so that *mental* improvement is not suffered to be neglected. . . . From what you say, I cannot help imagining that you, dearest, no longer belong to England's Mother Church. Pray tell me the true state of the case in your next. . . . My heart is truly Protestant. . . . It is because I love you that I wish you to be one with me in Faith ! . . .

Strelitz, December 16, 1851.

. . . In what agitated times we live ! Poor Paris is once again the scene of disturbance and trouble, and no very peaceable dwelling-place for you, poor dear. I do most sincerely trust that if things begin to wear a more serious and warlike appearance, you will pay a visit to your family in England, for Heaven knows how it may all end. But now to speak of the past year.

Our journey has been quite delightful; the family meeting at Rumpenheim very pleasant (not having seen them for four years), especially the two months we spent there with my two Uncles. In the first days of August we reached Ischl, having stopped on our road thither at Nuremberg and Munich, to take a general view of what ancient and modern art offers of interesting and remarkable in these two cities; and at Salzburg to explore the finest parts of the adjacent country, the scenery of which is splendid. At Ischl we stayed five weeks, spending the days in climbing the hills and enjoying from their summits the most lovely views, and our evenings in society. The *société de Vienne* make Ischl their summer residence, and consequently one leads a season-like life, balls, *thès causants* and *petits soupers*, following each other in quick succession. Ischl is also the resort of Majesty and Royalty, and it was here that I had the pleasure of dancing twice with the young Emperor.[1]

Our departure was hastened by our wish to see the Manœuvres of the Garrison of Vienna, under the command

¹ The present Emperor of Austria.

of the Emperor, and, taking the road by Linz and down the Danube, we reached Vienna in time to see 20,000 troops manœuvre and defile before the Emperor, on the memorable field of Aspern, where the Archduke Charles defeated Napoleon. You can imagine that my military heart beat high, and that the 11th of September is a day that will ever be noted by me, as it was on that day I saw so many Austrian Regiments that had distinguished themselves in the Italian and Hungarian campaigns. During our fortnight's stay at Vienna we saw everything interesting there. The Picture Gallery at the Belvedere is very fine indeed, as also the collection of Spanish pictures at the Esterhazy Palace. Besides this, the Palaces, shops, and Theatres afford an endless source of interest and amusement to the visitor, while the kind reception of the Imperial family greatly heightened the charm of our *séjour* there. . . . We remained one day at Prague, to see its Hratschin or Imperial Palace, and the other *lions* of this far-famed city, which bears the stamp of fallen grandeur; and thence to Dresden, where I had spent two happy months eight years ago, and where I now enjoyed the delight of *vegetating* for ever and ever in its beautiful Picture Gallery—the finest in Germany—and of spending nearly every evening at the play.

After a month's stay at Dresden, where we had a miniature family meeting—George, Uncle Fritz, *en route* for Italy, and my cousin Louise (my favourite one), with her husband and four children, having spent some time with us—we travelled on to Strelitz, our temporary home, which we shall not leave till the end of January, when, by way of Hanover, we journey home to dear old Kew. After leading a wandering life for three months, I assure you I am not sorry to be once again in tranquility, and able to follow the camel's example, and feast my mind upon all I have seen and heard and done. Till now we have been leading a tolerably quiet life; but the season will soon begin here in good earnest, and I hear of nothing but balls, and parties, and amateur theatres in prospect. And now that I have wearied you out with this long letter, I must say fare thee well, and remember that *nothing* will ever alter the feelings that I have towards you, and that I only hope and pray that the step[1] you have taken may conduce to your own happiness and peace of mind here and hereafter. God bless you. . . .

---

[1] Mrs. Barry had recently been received into the Church of Rome.

MY VERY DEAR ELLINOR,—I have never yet acknowledged your birthday letter, but I assure you that my time has been so terribly broken in upon of late, that I am only just beginning to get rid of the heap of letters that still remained on my table unanswered. My Birthday brought with it heaps of charming presents and congratulatory letters, and just as I was in the midst of answering them, my Aunt begged me to sit to her for my picture; after this came the preparations for Christmas, and last, but not least, "the Carnival," beginning with a Court ball, January 1st. The season here is short, but brilliant; however, the balls were to me the least fatiguing part of the affair, as we got up amateur acting, and I had to act the part of maid in a charming piece called *Der Gemahl an der Wand*, and an infinite degree of talent did I reveal, so that I am no more in doubt as to my being able to earn my bread should everything at some future day turn topsy turvy! Besides this, to please the dear old Grand Duke, who is all kindness to me, I joined in a great musical piece to be performed on four pianos, a *potpourri* of several Operas, and we played it at a grand concert, to the general satisfaction of the delighted listeners. This, of course, required much practice and several repetitions before the eventful evening arrived, and you can fancy how nervous and anxious I felt.

Our three months' *séjour* here has been one of great enjoyment to me, and makes a glorious finishing stroke to our delightful journey, which will ever be remembered by me with gratitude and pleasure. We start about the 10th of next month for Hanover, where we are to remain about a week previous to our returning home to dear old England, which I quite long to see again. Perchance we shall meet ere long in London, so till then adieu, and God Almighty bless you, my own dear friend, and with an earnest heartfelt prayer that you may regain health and strength in the New Year. . . .

MY DEAREST DRAPERCHEN,—You can imagine how pleased we all are to find ourselves once more at home, after being absent for upwards of *nine months;* I have been so busy unpacking and arranging my things . . . and, indeed, this is no small matter, for I have been away long enough to forget how I used to arrange them. Dear Kew is quite unchanged,

as pretty and peaceful as ever, and so you will, I trust, find
it when you come and pay us a visit here this spring; for
we shall only have a *pied à terre* in Town for this season, as
Mama wishes not to be hurried in her plans for the alterations
to be made in our apartments at St. James's.[1] At present they
look dismal and gloomy enough, but when newly furnished
and painted, and perhaps a conservatory added, I think they
will be very handsome and comfortable.

We are living at present in a state of retirement at Kew, and
recruiting our strength, in order to be prepared to brave the
fatigues of the season; our pretty constant visits to Gloucester
House forming just now our chief recreation. But both
Mama and Daughter enjoy this quiet life of all things; and,
what with letter-writing, work, *books*, and music, we find
plenty of occupation, and only think our mornings *too short*
for all we have to do. Dear Aunt Mary is looking remarkably well, and considerably *rajeunie* since we left. George
has been appointed Inspector-General of Cavalry, which post
established him for good and all in Town, much to our
delight. He is now at Dublin, but will shortly arrive here
to commence his new career. . . . I must tell you that your
protégé, Mr. Müller, who has really awakened in me a perfect
passion for the piano, has already given me a lesson since my
return. He was enchanted to see us again, a feeling I very
much shared in, but I schooled myself to good behaviour,
and did *not* fall into his arms! . . .

Cambridge Cottage, March 23, 1852.

MY VERY DEAR ELLINOR,—Finding you are coming to town
for a day, I write to know whether there is any possibility
of our meeting, and if so, when and where? Now, in my
own head I settled that it would do charmingly if you were
to come to Gloucester House on Tuesday evening, as there
will most likely be a party there; a little hint to Aunt
Mary on the subject, and your invitation would be sent to
Prince's Gate immediately, and if you could come at half-past
nine o'clock we should be able to have a nice chat ere people
began to arrive. But would this suit you, is the question?
Think it over well, as I fear it is the only chance we have of
meeting, for it is rather a busy week with us, what with the

[1] After the death of the Duke of Cambridge, the family gave up Cambridge House, and the Duchess and Princess Mary removed to the apartments
in St. James's Palace now occupied by the Duke and Duchess of York, and
called York House.

Drawing-room and all; and as we shall be in town Monday morning, it would not be very convenient to come up either of the following days early.

You can fancy how rejoiced I was to find myself once more in dear old England, and see all the well-known faces again . . . and yet, curiously enough, now that I am once more settled down at Kew, and engaged in my usual occupations, it seems to me as if I had never been away, and all our wanderings on the face of the earth were a dream. Since our return from the Continent we have been leading a tolerably retired life; occasional dinners in town, and frequent morning visits *thither and from* thence making a pleasant break. However, next Thursday I am fairly to be launched into the wide deep of the world at the Drawing-room. My dress consists of a train of white moiré antique, trimmed with bugles, and down each side in front, with branches of white roses; the petticoat, white tulle with roses; and on my head two feathers and lappets, fastened by turquoise brooches; the corsage to match. *Celà sera joli n'est-ce pas?* And now I must really conclude, petitioning you for an answer. . . .

Cambridge Cottage, April 21, 1852.

MY DEAREST DRAPERCHEN,—I received your kind note at Windsor, but delighted as I was at the thought of seeing you again, I was deeply grieved at the event which hastened your coming, and beg to assure you of my most heartfelt sympathy. How thankful you must be that you arrived in time to receive your dear Mother's blessing, and even to attend on her in her last hours, for sad experience has taught me how soothing and comforting this is to one when *all* is over. I need hardly assure you that Mama and I are both longing to see you, and if you were to come down to-morrow between two and three o'clock you would be certain to find us. . . . Luncheon as it used to be is done away with, but still starvation does *not* ensue at Cambridge Cottage; it is only a diminution of provisions! I say this in case you might come intending to make your *dinner* here, as you used sometimes in bygone years to do. You may have seen by the newspapers that I made my *début* at the last Drawing-room, and am therefore virtually *out!* . . .

Cambridge Cottage, May 2, 1852.

MY DEAREST ELLINOR,—Many thanks for your kind letter upon your arrival at Thirlistane. I thought it most kind of

you to write when you were so busy. I must begin by giving
you a sad bit of Parish news : poor Fanny White died last
Wednesday ; Mrs. Arnold White[1] is quite resigned, but it
is a fearful blow to her, more especially as she knows that
Annie's days are also numbered, for I fear she will hardly
last through the summer, that is to say if it be a hot one.
Mama and I went to see them the other day, and it was
quite touching to see how resigned they are, particularly
poor Annie. . . .

St. James's Palace, May 5, 1852.

. . . We came up to Town yesterday for the first time, to
stay at St. James's, and do not return to Kew till Friday next.
The apartments are really beginning to assume an air of
comfort, and with the help of the " Woods and Forests " and
Mama's good taste, I think we shall manage to make them
look handsome and *feel* comfortable. And now for some
news concerning the *wicked* world. I have not been out
much at present; a visit of two days to Windsor, which I
enjoyed excessively ; a Concert and banquet of fifty-four
people with music in the evening at Miss Coutts's ;[2] a little
hop (my first in London) at dear Aunt Mary's ; a dinner and
evening party at Lord and Lady Derby's, and two journeys
to the Opera; *voilà les grands évènements,* I might almost say
the " bill of fare " of the last five weeks.

To-night is the first great Court ball, when I shall wear
my petticoat from last Drawing-room with a wreath of roses
for the back of my hair to match ; to-morrow we go to the
Haymarket with Aunt Kent, and afterwards to a party at
Lady Jersey's, given in honour of Clementina's[3] birthday.
On the 10th there is a concert at the Palace; on the 13th a
Drawing-room for the Birthday, when I shall be *blue,* and an
evening party at Lord Derby's ; and on the 14th the Duke of
Wellington gives a Ball in honour of *licke me!* Much to my
delight he announced his intention of doing so to me on his
birthday, the 1st of May, when I met him at Miss Coutts's
and congratulated him. Before I conclude I must wish you
joy for your approaching birthday, and good health and
happiness for many many years to come; and I also
congratulate you on your brother's appointment to St.
Petersburg.[4] . . .

[1] Formerly Dresser to Queen Adelaide.
[2] Now the Baroness Burdett-Coutts.
[3] Lady Clementina Villiers.
[4] Lord Napier was transferred from Naples to St. Petersburg, April 7, 1852.

. . . We are leading a somewhat unsettled life, eternally
en chemin between Kew and London, popping up to Town
whenever any agreeable festivities are taking place, and back
again for a few days' rest in the country to gain *fresh roses*
(how *poetical* I am growing!) for the next occasion. On the
whole I enjoyed my season very much, though, of course,
there are bitters to be endured besides the sweets, and some
tiresome parties will occur. I need not enumerate the places
I have been at, the newspapers will enlighten you on this
point; suffice it to say that I find myself mostly surrounded
by a knot of pretty and agreeable girls *toutes à mes pieds*,
whom I like excessively, and whom I call by their *Christian
names*. I value, when there chances to be room, and my
danseurs are all excessively civil, and some of them very
agreeable. Next week we go to Ascot, that is to say, to
Windsor, for the Thursday, the Cup day at Ascot, and I am
in great glee at the thoughts, as it will be the first race I
have ever been at. Only think of George's gallantry in
giving me a new gown and bonnet for the occasion! The
former is a lilac *chiné;* the bonnet *green* crape, trimmed
with blonde and pink roses ; so pray admire his taste! . . .

. . . We are in a great state of mind at a terrible event
which is to take place at Kew. The new part of the house
which we inhabit, comprising library and drawing-room and
the rooms above, has given way, and, though propped up with
iron girdings, it is not considered safe, and consequently that
whole side of the house is to be pulled down and built up
again! Is not that pleasant? Meantime we are obliged to
take up our abode in the other side, cramming the rooms as
full as ever we can. They begin operations in July, and for
the first six weeks the dust and dirt will be such that we
must not think of staying there; but the question is, where
are we to go? Perhaps to the Isle of Wight for a time, but
my next letter will be able to tell you more ; the house will,
however, not be quite finished before November. . . .

. . . We have been stationary here since the 30th of last
month, and there is nothing can exceed the beauty of the
weather, it has been most enjoyable. We have led a terribly

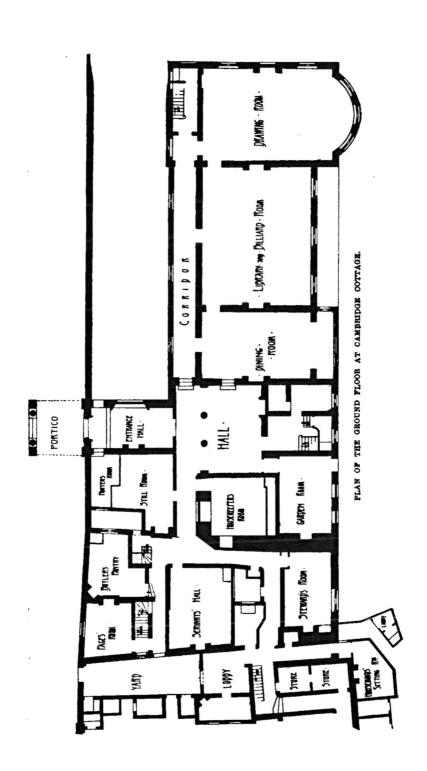

PLAN OF THE GROUND FLOOR AT CAMBRIDGE COTTAGE.

idle life, quite on the pattern of the Italian *Dolce far niente*, spending our days and evenings out-of-doors, dining early and driving out late; but the heat was too great for anything else. I have no news for you, for no one seems to think of anything but the elections. Some are sanguine about them, while others are very low, and I spend my life in perusing the lists of members returned, and hoping that the ministerialists may have the advantage. You cannot think what an active politician I am becoming, and what a staunch friend I prove to Lord Derby's [1] cause. . . .

10, Brigstocke Terrace, Ryde, July 28, 1852.

DEAREST DRAPERINECHEN,—I have not heard from you for so long that I begin to imagine either that you mean to cut me or that you are not well. I therefore make a *great effort* considering my usual idleness, and begin, or rather renew, the correspondence. You will see by the date of this that we are at Ryde, where we have taken a house, owing, you know, to their being obliged to pull down part of the Cottage at Kew, which had given way. We are very much pleased with our new abode, as the house is both airy and comfortable and commands a charming view of the sea. . . . The Isle of Wight is too lovely, and would well deserve the appellation of the *Emerald Island*. . . . Yesterday we went, on our way home from Shanklin, to a breakfast at St. Clair, a lovely place belonging to a Colonel Vernon-Harcourt, which is situated on the seashore at a short distance from Ryde; the gardens are beautifully laid out, and the house itself is charming.

And now to return to the past, for I suppose you are anxious to know how I liked my first season? Well, I enjoyed it very much indeed, particularly as I got more

---

[1] Lord Stanley was a vigorous opponent of the Free Trade policy accepted by Sir Robert Peel in 1846, and was regarded for many years as the leader of the Protectionists. He succeeded to the Earldom in June, 1851, and in the following February, on the resignation of Lord John Russell, who had suffered defeat on the Militia Bill, was invited to form his first Administration. Lord Derby accepted the invitation, but being in the minority the position was by no means an enviable one, and hoping to secure a working majority, he took an early opportunity of appealing to the country. It is to this appeal that Princess Mary makes reference in her letter to Mrs. Dalrymple. Unfortunately for Lord Derby the result of the elections made little or no material change in the balance of parties, and a few weeks after the new Parliament had met, the Ministry suffered defeat on Mr. Disraeli's Budget, whereupon Lord Derby resigned, and was succeeded by a Coalition Ministry, with Lord Aberdeen as Prime Minister.

acquainted with the people. I am, however, not at all *blasée*, for as I only numbered fourteen balls (besides a few dinners and parties) I did not overtire myself; and then Mama always contrived to get a few days' country air between the trips to Town. The season was so short this year, in consequence of the Elections, that we were able to spend the month of July in the country, much to our delight, particularly as the weather was so hot and lovely and the gardens in such great beauty. . . .

Augusta is now at Dresden undergoing a *Cure de Homœopathie!* under the care of the famous Doctor Wolff, which I hope will be attended with good results. We missed her and her dear boy terribly on their several birthdays, and longed for wings to join them, or rather for a fairy wand to conjure them over to *dear old England.* How you will laugh at me for being such a John Bull! On dear Mama's birthday we dined at Osborne *en honneur du jour*, which was spent most quietly *en famille*, George coming over from London and my cousins from Shanklin to spend it with Mama. The Queen paid Mama the charming attention of sending her a copy of George's picture by Winterhalter, which she had done a short time ago for herself. It is his very image, and as I sit looking at it I can almost fancy that it is the *original.* What do you say to the Elections? I hear the Government is in high spirits about them; turning out Sir George Grey has been such a triumph to our party; and then Liverpool! that was quite glorious. I must now say goodbye and ask pardon for writing such a *very* long letter. . . .

10, Brigstocke Terrace, Ryde, August 5, 1852.

MY DEAR ELLINOR,—Your kind letter found me enjoying the sea and country air at this nice place. You cannot think how much we like Ryde; our house is airy and comfortable, and, as it lies rather high, commands a charming view of the sea, and a sloping field under our windows greatly improves the prospect; the rooms are nice-sized though not large. We do not want for society, for the Lysters, Cadogans, Heneages, Damers, and others of our acquaintance have also sought refuge here from the turmoils and heat of London. Besides which Aunt Mary has been paying us a ten days' visit, and my Cousin George,[1] of Mecklenburg, with his Russian wife, who is a very pleasing and agreeable person, are staying at Shanklin, which is not far off, for the benefit of sea-bathing.

[1] Brother of the Hereditary Grand Duke of Mecklenburg-Strelitz; he married in 1851 the Grand Duchess Catherine of Russia.

Ryde itself has never been gayer than this season; and crowds of well-dressed people throng the pier at all hours of the day, but most particularly of an evening, so that Mama, out of kindness to me, dines rather early, which enables us to promenade on the pier while the band is playing, sometimes even till after dark. We have been undergoing lately a very pleasant round of luncheon-breakfasts, to see all the pretty Villas and Places in the neighbourhood. The three principal rivals are Colonel Vernon-Harcourt, Lord Downes, and Sir Augustus Clifford, and I really hardly know to whose place to give the preference; St. Clair, Binstead, and West Field are each lovely in their way, and nothing can equal the civility of their owners. The Wiltons were to arrive at Cowes yesterday, so that I am looking forward with much pleasure to seeing them again very soon. No lack of fashionable society there! . . .

Cambridge Cottage, September 9, 1852.

MY DEAR DRAPERCHEN,—We are once more *at home*, but what a home! One half of the house is a scene of desolation, and as all the partitions are pulled down it looks like a shell scooped out, whilst the old part which we are now inhabiting serves as *lumber-room* for all the furniture; so that we dine in the little garden-room and sit in what used formerly to be Papa's little library. Great was our regret at leaving Ryde and all our acquaintances there, but *un doux devoir nous rappella à notre poste*, namely the knowledge that dear Aunt Mary would miss us as she is now staying at Richmond. We found, as we expected, that she was quite longing for us, more particularly as she has greatly improved the place during our absence, and much wished to show it to us in all its glory and before the flowers are gone. . . . We had not a single *wet day* during our stay at Ryde, and greatly enjoyed the long excursions we made to Freshwater and Alum Bay, and to Shanklin, Ventnor, and to Black Gang Chine. The more we saw of the lovely island, the more we wondered at the English travelling for ever in search of picturesque scenery when our own country affords so much for admiration, though certainly on a smaller scale. Pray admire my John Bull feelings! In this, as in other instances, I do not think it likely that I shall ever become a disciple of yours. I leave to you the *Italian school;* whilst I retain my own dear country *and her Church*, to which I pray God I may ever cling with a *true Protestant heart.*

On Monday last, the day we left Ryde, we cruised round

Spithead, and the ships there, out of compliment, saluted and manned their yards and rigging. At Portsmouth, or rather in the harbour, we were received by the Admiral, who took us in his barge to the *Victory*, the ship on which Nelson fell, and the *Neptune*, 120 guns. You can imagine how delighted I was at inspecting two line of battle ships; it was indeed a treat, and a day ever to be remembered by me. You will be glad to hear that my Brother, who is at present at Berlin, found Augusta looking very well on his visit to Strelitz. It was his first visit, so you can imagine how pleased they all were; he will remain at Berlin till the Manœuvres there are over, and then return home for more Inspections. . . . I have no more news for you excepting that Mama likes Lady Suffield,[1] who has been staying with us at Ryde, very much. She is a very nice companion, and seems quite attracted to us all. . . . You will find us at Kew for the next four weeks. And now adieu. . . .

MARY ADELAIDE.

Cambridge Cottage, September 27, 1852.

MY DEAR ELLINOR,— . . . It is now three weeks since we left the Isle of Wight, to establish ourselves in this half-demolished house. . . . We shall not be able to get into St. James's or our own apartments here till November, and that is a long time to look forward to; but *time flies so fast*, and we have plenty to do and think of, about furnishing, till then.

The sad loss we have all sustained by the death of the dear and revered old Duke,[2] was a *great blow* to us, to whom he has always been so particularly kind. I have had a letter from poor Lady Douro,[3] to whom I immediately wrote, telling me that up to the last there was no pain or struggle, so that those around him could scarcely tell the exact moment when he ceased to breathe. England has sustained an irreparable loss, and I am happy to say this seems universally felt. *We* are, of course, all in mourning, and shall continue so for some little time longer, as we are going to pay the Wiltons a visit next week at Heaton, and they quite adored him, so

---

[1] Lady-in-Waiting to the Duchess of Cambridge.

[2] The Duke of Wellington died at Walmer Castle, September 14, 1852.

[3] Daughter of the eighth Marquis of Tweedale and wife of the Marquis of Douro, eldest son of the first Duke of Wellington. Lady Douro was Bedchamber Woman to the Queen (1843–58), and afterwards became Mistress of the Robes.

it will be more in accordance with our mutual feelings. George has been appointed Colonel of the Fusilier Guards, which we are very glad of. But I think Lord Hardinge's [1] appointment does not give universal satisfaction, as *many* wished that Lord Fitzroy Somerset [2] should get the post, the business of which he has in point of fact carried on for many years. . . .

Cambridge Cottage, November 25, 1852.

. . . We have been leading a very quiet life at Kew, particularly since our return from Heaton and Worsley, where we paid most delightful visits to the Wiltons and Ellesmeres. . . . Now that the lying-in-state and funeral of the dear old Duke are over, I am sure you will like to hear from me my impression of the splendid yet mournful pageant. We went with the Queen to the lying-in-state at Chelsea, and I cannot tell you how affecting a scene it was. The sombre appearance of the dimly lighted Hall, lined with Grenadiers, their arms reversed, contrasted with the illumination of the furthest end, where the bier stood, behind which rose a laurel wreath, encircling *his* immortal name, and a curtain of what seemed cloth of gold, which *reflected* the light, had a magnificent effect; indeed, I do not think I ever saw anything better done, with a view both to appearance and feeling. I have since heard people say that it was too like a *Chapelle ardente*, but I confess *I* did not see any signs of *papacy* anywhere. The evening preceding the 18th we came up to town to sleep at Gloucester House; from the balcony of which we saw the military part of the procession pass soon after eight o'clock the following morning. Infantry, artillery, and cavalry, all looked so magnificent! and George, commanding them, *so* well! that there was a sort of melancholy pleasure in seeing them march slowly by, while the

[1] Viscount Hardinge succeeded the Duke of Wellington as Commander-in-Chief of the British Army.

[2] Lord Fitzroy Somerset was the youngest son of the fifth Duke of Beaufort. On Lord Hardinge being appointed Commander-in-Chief, he became Master-General of the Ordnance, being at the same time raised to the Peerage with the title of Lord Raglan, as a mark of respect to the Duke of Wellington, whose military secretary he had been for many years. He served throughout the Peninsular War on the Duke's staff, and lost an arm at Waterloo. As Commander-in-Chief of the Army in the Crimea, he rendered his country the greatest service, and writing to King Leopold after Balaclava Her Majesty says: " Lord Raglan's behaviour was worthy of the Old Duke's —such coolness in the midst of the hottest fire."

bands played funeral marches by some of the *old* composers. They were chosen by Albert, and were very appropriate.

When we had seen the one soldier out of every Regiment in the service pass, we hurried into our carriage, and drove by the back streets to St. Paul's, where we saw the rest of the procession from the gallery round the Dome. As soon as the car had arrived we took up our places in the Church in front of the Peeresses, where we could see and hear everything. The Church itself, with its wreath of gas, and *black walls*, against which the uniforms looked very fine, was occupied by *16,000* persons. The ceremony was finer and more impressive than anything I ever saw before. The words of the chaunts, particularly of the Dirge, and the music were beautifully chosen, and most affecting. While the coffin was being lowered the Dead March in Saul was played, which quite *upset* me ; and immediately afterwards came the Lord's Prayer, responded to by the *whole* congregation. The behaviour of all classes was most exemplary, and it was indeed *the nation's heartfelt tribute* of respect to the memory of her *greatest Hero*.

The meeting of Parliament has brought numbers of people to London, exclusive of those who came up only for the funeral; so that we went to Town on Tuesday last to see some friends and dine at Lady Jersey's, where a few people came in the evening. On my Birthday we are to dine at my Brother's, and to go to the Play afterwards. How terribly old I am growing. Nineteen!—it is quite a serious consideration. I hope, indeed I know, you will think of me on the 27th, when this letter will in all probability reach you, dearest, and pray that I may continue as happy as I now am with dear Mama ; our only drawback being our anxiety about Augusta, who is still far from strong. Poor Fritz has completely lost the sight of *one* eye, but the Doctors do not think the sight of the other will be affected by it ; but still it is very sad! They are to come over in the spring, please God. Dear Aunt Mary is recovering, and will leave Brighton for London some day this week, the weather proving fine. . . . Adieu, dearest. Ever your *own*,

MARY ADELAIDE.

Cambridge Cottage, November 29, 1852.

DEAREST DRAPERCHEN,—How very very kind of you to send me such a darling fan, and a *Paris* one into the bargain ! I hope you will accept my most affectionate and warmest thanks for it, and for all your good wishes, which I hope will be fulfilled. You will not wonder, perhaps, at my telling you that my Birthday-table stamps me as a complete spoilt child! Indeed, the list of my presents, which are both lovely and useful, appears quite endless, for they poured in from all sides. Furniture, trinkets, work, and *objets de vertu*, and a sufficient quantity of each to furnish two Birthday-tables, at least. I spent a *very very* happy day, the pleasure of which was greatly enhanced by the Queen's granting a petition I had made to get a poor little pensioner of mine into the Consumptive Hospital. I must now say good-bye, or I shall never save the post. With many kisses for the lovely *cadeau.* . . .

Cambridge Cottage, December 31, 1852.

. . . Pray accept my best wishes for the year 1853, and my most affectionate thanks for the beautiful Portuguese matting, which is *du meilleur gout*, and will ornament my new sitting-room at St. James's, where I intend to place it under my writing-table. I long to give you a *hug* and a *kiss* for it. I hope you will tell Mr. Barry how much I admire it, and his taste in ordering it. We spent Christmas Eve very happily, but very quietly, as we had no tree, on the plea of being too old for such juvenile pastimes. So Mama and I consoled ourselves by dressing a large tree up for the servants and school-children, which succeeded remarkably well, and gave general satisfaction. In the course of the evening we interchanged our presents, making the most of them by packing them up and sending them in directed, but without the name of the donor being attached. On Christmas Day we dined at my brother's, and afterwards adjourned to Aunt Mary's, who had asked a few people, and had very kindly provided a tree covered with loveliest bonbons for the occasion. I received beautiful presents from Mama and all my family, principally *des objets de toilette*. To-night we dine at Gloucester House. . . . And now, dearest, you must let me say *Adieu*, for it is nearly dressing-time. With much love and many thanks, I remain, ever your affectionate

MARY ADELAIDE.

CHAPTER VI.

AT HOME AND IN SOCIETY.

1853.

Princess Mary at nineteen—Girl friends—Country house visits—Doctor Quin—The Duchess of Inverness—In Kew Gardens—Taste in dress —Home occupations—Journal opens (Jan. 1, 1853)—Twelfth Night at Windsor—Visit to Middleton—Day at Blenheim—Charles Mathews —Belvoir Castle—At Badminton—Birth of Prince Leopold—Letter to Mr. Harrison— Kew Gardens opened to the public on Sunday —Conferring honorary degrees at Oxford—Visit of the King and Queen of Hanover—Bazaar at Wellington Barracks—Madame Rachel—First dinner-party at St. James's—Trip to Hatfield—The camp at Chobham —Picture-galleries—Thanksgiving Day at Female Orphan Asylum— Visit to Arundel Castle—Goodwood Races—Off to Scotland—Drum-lanrig Castle—Hamilton Palace—Princess Mary's impressions of Scotland—Letter to the Honble. Ellinor Napier on her marriage—The play at Windsor—Princess Mary's twentieth birthday—Sits to Mr. Wells for the collection of miniatures at Windsor—Christmas at Kew.

THE Duchess of Cambridge went a good deal into general society, and, following in the steps of the Duchess of Gloucester, was a frequent visitor at the country homes of the old aristocracy. In this way Princess Mary had the opportunity of choosing her own friends, and was able to meet, without the restraint of Court etiquette, the distinguished men and women of the day, advantages which her social qualities and natural ability allowed her fully to appreciate. With her attractive appearance, wonderful charm of manner, rare gift of sympathy and eagerness to share with others the pleasures that fell to her lot, she soon won all hearts, and in a very short time established herself a universal favourite.

Describing Princess Mary at the age of nineteen, Lady Caroline Cust [1] said—

Princess Mary was strikingly handsome, and her beautiful hair and dark blue eyes were much admired; she was dignified and graceful in her movements, and a remarkably light dancer. Always bright and animated, her ready wit and keen sense of humour kept us continually amused. The Princess had a splendid memory, and if she heard a good anecdote, would repeat it word for word. Her power of grasping subjects was exceptional, and she derived pleasure as well as profit from conversing with people of merit and distinction. She was passionately fond of music, possessing a beautiful mezzo-soprano voice, and sang with great feeling, while the opera and theatre afforded her intense enjoyment. Princess Mary inherited her father's taste for art; she was an excellent judge of pictures, but a kind critic, and always tried to find some redeeming feature even in an inferior work. "It is not a good picture," she would say, adding quickly, "but that is well drawn," or, "That is a pretty bit of colour," calling attention to some point that had hitherto escaped notice. If she saw an historical subject, she recognized it at once, and was generally able to give the exact date of the event. She was fond of going out, and usually went with her mother, but was sometimes chaperoned by the Hereditary Grand Duchess. Society in those days was less cosmopolitan than it is now, and Princess Mary only attended balls and parties given at the great houses. She saw much of her royal relatives, and had many friends of her own age, her chief companions being Lady Katherine and Lady Elizabeth Grey Egerton, Lady Henrietta and Lady Geraldine Somerset, Lady Elizabeth and Lady Agneta Yorke, Lady Arabella Sackville West and Lady Rokeby's daughters. The Duchess of Cambridge entertained a good deal, and often gave dinners and receptions when in residence at St. James's.

After the London season, the Duchess and her daughter returned to Kew, where time passed very pleasantly. They were on friendly terms with their neighbours, and intercourse with the different members of the French royal family, then

---

[1] Second daughter of the first Earl Brownlow. Lady Caroline Cust was appointed Lady-in-Waiting to the Grand Duchess of Mecklenburg-Strelitz in 1853, an appointment she held until her death in 1898.

living at Twickenham, was frequent. During the hot weather, many happy hours were spent in the shady garden, reading, writing, or working, and receiving friends—for the Duchess was most hospitable, and any one she had met and noticed, either in London or abroad, was cordially welcomed at Cambridge Cottage. Country visits were generally paid in the autumn. The Princess was an easy and charming guest to entertain; she was never bored, but always fresh and ready to join in fun of any kind, and from the time she came down in the morning till she went to bed at night every hour of the day was occupied. Often, after breakfast, and in the interval between tea and dinner, she sang and played to her friends, or delighted them with an effective recitation of some favourite poem. Rural pursuits were thoroughly to her taste; no one liked a cross-country walk better than Princess Mary; and though she did not ride, she enjoyed driving to the meets, and entered with enthusiasm into the day's sport.

Many agreeable dinners were given at Kew during the winter months. The Duchess of Cambridge lived in the world of affairs, and was personally acquainted with the leading foreign diplomatists. Members of the Austrian Embassy were special favourites, and the Ambassador Count Colloredo, and his successor Count Apponyi, were constantly invited to Cambridge Cottage. Besides the diplomatic corps, the Duchess entertained the prominent military men at the Horse Guards whose duties kept them in town at this time of the year. Sometimes she would have a little dinner-party of five or six people, and occasionally the home circle was augmented by one or two intimate friends, who drove down from town and stayed the night. A much-favoured visitor was the homœopathic physician, Dr. Quin,[1] who was a

---

[1] Dr. Quin was born in London, 1799. He was appointed physician in attendance on the exiled Emperor Napoleon, who died, however, before the doctor could take up his duties. He became a convert to the Hahnemann system, and in 1844 formed the British Homœopathic Society, of which he was the first President. Six years later, mainly owing to his exertions, the London Homœopathic Hospital was founded. For a time Dr. Quin was resident physician to the household of Prince Leopold of Saxe-Coburg, and

great wit, a perfect linguist, and a good talker. The Duchess appointed him one of her physicians in ordinary, and was a firm believer in the medical doctrine he preached. He suffered from asthma, and when dining at Kew generally remained to sleep, as his royal hostess was anxious that he should avoid the night air. On these occasions Princess Mary attended to his comforts, and saw that his room was well warmed. Now and then it was absolutely necessary for him to return to town after dinner; and when that was the case, his greatcoat was brought into the drawing-room, while the Duchess, with her own hands, wrapped the comforter, which she herself had knitted, round his throat. Towards the close of his life, Dr. Quin's asthma increased, and at last he was unable to leave his rooms. All through the period of his enforced confinement, Princess Mary and her mother were very kind and attentive to their old friend, and by many gracious acts showed their appreciation of his estimable qualities. His apartments were near Victoria station, and the Duchess of Cambridge's first experience of a lift was when she went to see Dr. Quin.

After settling down for the winter at Kew, the Duchess seldom drove to town in the evening, except to attend a theatre, or to dine with the Duke of Cambridge or the Duchess of Gloucester, and occasionally with the Duchess of Inverness, who still lived at Kensington Palace,[1] and was quite a personage in London society. She was small of stature, old-fashioned in dress, and quaint, rather than distinguished, in appearance, but her kindness of heart and general *bonhomie* secured for her a large circle of friends and acquaintances. The furniture of her apartments, and all her surroundings, were reminiscent of days gone by. She was most hospitable—in fact, no visitor ever left her presence without hearing the words, "Come and dine." Her entertainments were void of ostentation, but she was always careful

resided at Marlborough House. He was *personâ grata* in London society, and in later years became a friend of the Prince and Princess of Wales. He died in 1878.

[1] In the apartments now occupied by the Princess Louise and the Marquis of Lorne.

to observe the respect due to rank, and whenever the Duchess of Cambridge and Princess Mary dined with her, a gentleman was deputed to receive them at the entrance; and as they passed down the long corridor which led to the reception-room, the footmen, drawn up on either side, and wearing semi-royal liveries and nankin tights, bowed low. The small dining-room, fitted up as a tent, lacked ventilation —some of the Duchess's guests called it stuffy—but the dining-room used on great occasions was large and very convenient.

The Duchess of Cambridge and Princess Mary enjoyed their drives round about Kew; the neighbourhood still retained its rural aspect, and in spring-time the orchards were white with blossom. Many an afternoon was spent in Coombe Wood, gathering primroses and listening to the nightingales, while Kew Gardens were visited almost every day.[1] The Princess took great interest in the planting out of the flower-beds, and had long discussions with Sir William Hooker and Mr. Smith on the subject. She and the Director, however, were not always of the same mind; he only thought of science, Princess Mary of beauty.

One day the Duchess and her daughter were taking their usual walk in the Gardens, both clad in voluminous circular waterproof cloaks. When some distance from the Cottage a heavy shower came on, and they turned their steps homewards, meeting on the way two poorly clad children. Without a moment's hesitation each child was given shelter under the folds of a "royal mantle," and brought back to Cambridge Cottage. Shoes and stockings were quickly taken off and dried, the little ones regaled with hot tea, and as soon as it was found that they lived at Brentford, a fly was fetched, and they were sent home. Next morning the father, a poor shoemaker, called to express his gratitude, when it transpired that the children had only lately recovered from scarlet fever. This was no solitary instance of kindness on the part of the royal ladies. Similar actions were of almost

---

[1] A private entrance led from the garden of Cambridge Cottage into Kew Gardens.

daily occurrence. They passed unrecorded, it is true, but the poor people of Kew and its neighbourhood treasured them up, and an old resident writes: "Few have any idea of the great charity shown by the Princess and her mother to those in humble circumstances."

For one occupying so exalted a position, Princess Mary's daily life was simple, and there is no doubt she preferred it to any other that accident or circumstances might have rendered necessary. According to custom Miss —— called at Cambridge Cottage, to take the Princess's directions on a parish matter, and was astonished to find her in the garden running round and round the flower-beds as hard as she could go. "Why are you running so fast, Princess?" Miss —— ventured to inquire. "To get rid of the etiquette," was the reply; "we have just had a visit from the Emperor of ——." Though this story is characteristic of Princess Mary as a girl, it would be a mistake to suppose that state and ceremony were distasteful to her; she quite appreciated a Court function, and was very proud of being a "Princess of England." Kind and affable to all alike, her gracious manner soon set people at their ease, but she never lost sight of her position, and always maintained a dignity which made familiarity impossible.

The Princess had great taste in dress, and disliked anything that was *outré* or conspicuous; she possessed the gift of knowing what was effective as well as becoming, and invariably wore a colour that suited her. Without being extravagant, every little detail was studied, not from the standpoint of vanity, but with the eye of an artist and the desire to appear at her best. She was very careful about the way her things were made, and noticed directly if the work was not well done. Miss Burt, who was dressmaker at the Cottage from the time the Cambridge family settled at Kew, recalls with pride and pleasure that for many years she "dressed" Princess Mary. She recollects taking a new gown home and the Princess saying, "Burty, I am so glad to have one of your well-made dresses. I feel so comfortable and safe in yours; now, these other dressmakers often put such slight work in, that I am afraid to move about lest the stitches should give way and my dress drop off!" But it was not always that Miss Burt was in favour with her royal mistress; once when ordering a dress to be trimmed with rows of graduated velvet up to the waist, her dressmaker unwisely replied, "But, Your Royal Highness, I don't think I could get so many widths in that colour." "Then," said the Princess, with raised head and an air of command, "get it made, Burt."

Princess Mary was just as particular about the dress of her acquaintances in the village, and anything at all brilliant in colour and extravagant in style was met with disapproval, or, to use the words of one of the villagers, "with raised eyebrows, compressed lips, and bent-down motion - of the head," so that the girl never ventured to wear the offending garment again. On the other hand, neat and quiet attire was sure to receive approbation.

I remember the day [writes one, who as a child was much noticed by the Princess] when my sister and I were in Kew Gardens wearing our first black silk frocks. They were made very plainly, and we wore black straw bonnets trimmed with pink rosebuds. During our walk we met Princess Mary with other members of the Royal Family. She gave us one of her gracious smiles, accompanied by two or three nods of approval and a prolonged sideway glance. Not long afterwards a message was brought by one of the ladies at Cambridge Cottage to say that Her Royal Highness wished us to know that she considered we were the nicest dressed girls in the gardens. Another time I was walking with a friend, who had on a new dress—her first long one— and was enjoying trailing it along the ground. We did not know that the Princess was near; she, however, had come quietly across the grass behind us, and picking up my friend's skirt, shook it, then placing it in her hand, said, "Emily, Emily, don't trail your dress, my dear; you will spoil it and make it so dirty."

Princess Mary's entry into society was not allowed to interfere with the continuation of her studies; singing and music masters came regularly, she practised with the same diligence as when in the schoolroom, and kept up her knowledge of English, French, and German literature. Reading aloud, a recognized custom at Cambridge Cottage, was an accomplishment in which the Princess excelled; she read with much power and expression, and it was often said that she made even a dull book seem interesting. Perhaps works of history and biography attracted her most, but she also appreciated a good novel, becoming absorbed in the plot, and entering with enthusiasm into the vicissitudes of the different characters.

She was always cheerful and contented, taking life as it came, and never thirsted for change or amusement. To "dear little Kew," with its wealth of flowers, local interests and responsibilities, she was devoted, with the routine of St. James's Palace she was equally pleased; indeed, whatever her surroundings, the Princess found in them something to occupy and amuse her. She threw herself heart and soul into everything she did; nothing was thought too trivial, and whether it were work or play, ministering to the sick, tending to the wants of the poor, or fulfilling her religious duties, she invariably brought all her powers of resource into action.

Little difficulty would be found in gathering further testimony of so charming a personality; but enough has been said to show how Princess Mary strove to carry out both at home and in society, the precepts learned from her parents, and to what advantage she used the many gifts with which nature had endowed her. The events of her life, and the way in which she passed her time, are recorded in the Journal which about this date she began to keep with more or less regularity, and which opens, in the year 1853, with a visit to the Queen at Windsor.

Journal.—Cambridge Cottage, January 1, 1853.—George came down to breakfast—an event! Lord William Paulet [1]

[1] Lord William Paulet, brother of the thirteenth Marquis of Winchester, was appointed equerry to the Duke of Cambridge in 1851, and served as Assistant Adjutant-General to the Cavalry Division in the Crimea. Later on

and Captain Clifton[1] rode over to wish us joy of the New Year, and walked with us till four o'clock. We dined at Aunt Mary's—a party of twelve; a few people came in the evening, and we played a round game. . . . *January* 5.— . . . At six o'clock we left Kew for Windsor Castle, which was reached just in time for dressing. At dinner Van de Weyer[2] and Lord Hawarden were my neighbours.

Windsor Castle, January 6.—A rainy day! We breakfasted punctually at a quarter to nine, and then I wrote letters. . . . After luncheon, at two, we drove down to Frogmore, and on our return I read "Corinne" to Mama. At six o'clock the children's Christmas-tree was lighted, and we joined their little party. Some people arrived for dinner, and I sat next to Albert. Very agreeable! In the evening the Twelfth Cake appeared, and we ended up with snapdragon, which was great fun. *January* 7.—We were in the breakfast-room by a quarter to nine, and, as it rained, we went with the Queen and Albert to look at the Chapel, the new armoury, and the theatre; returned to our rooms by 11.30, when the Colloredos[3] came to see us. In the afternoon Victoria and Alice played to me and Ada Hohenlohe.[4] Arthur paid us a visit as a Scotch Fusilier—too lovely! Dinner at a quarter to seven: I sat next to Count Colloredo and Leiningen.[5] Six of the children appeared at the play— *Henry IV.*, by Shakespeare—but it was not at all dull. Old Bartley acted "Falstaff" to perfection. *January* 8.—After breakfast we said good-bye to the Queen. Aunt Kent came and took us for a drive. We returned on foot to the Castle, and then left by rail for Richmond.

Cambridge Cottage, January 10.— . . . We started at half-past one for a visit to Middleton,[6] and waited at the

he commanded the South Western District, and was made Adjutant-General of the Forces in 1865. He became a Field-Marshal in 1886, and died in 1893, in his ninetieth year.

[1] Aide-de-Camp to the Duke of Cambridge, and later on appointed Equerry to His Royal Highness.

[2] M. Silvain Van de Weyer was Belgian Minister at the Court of St. James for many years. He married the heiress Miss Bates, and lived at New Lodge, Windsor. A well-informed, distinguished, and very agreeable man, he enjoyed the intimate friendship of King Leopold, and was much regarded by Her Majesty.

[3] Count and Countess Colloredo.

[4] Princess Adelaide, daughter of the Queen's step-sister, Princess of Hohenlohe-Langenburg. She married, in 1856, Frederick, Duke of Schleswig-Holstein-Sonderburg-Augustenburg.

[5] Prince of Leiningen, step-brother to the Queen.

[6] Middleton Park, the Oxfordshire seat of the Earls of Jersey.

H.R.H. The Duchess of Cambridge.
In the collection of H.H. The Duke of Teck.

Ealing station in pouring rain for the train; reached Heyford at 4.30, where Lord Jersey met us, and were at Middleton by five o'clock. We dined at eight, Lord Jersey and Lord Maidstone sitting next to me. Afterwards we played at the " race game " in the grand saloon.

Middleton, January 11.—Breakfasted upstairs with Mama, and spent the morning talking and working in the drawing-room ; Clemmy[1] played to us. After luncheon, as it was a wet day, we made a tour of the house and wrote letters. Lord Chesterfield and Evelyn[2] arrived. My neighbours at dinner were Lord Jersey and Lord Bathurst—very pleasant. In the evening we played at " Post," a game which is now *bien en vogue. January* 12.— . . . At one o'clock we started for Blenheim ; Clemmy, Lord Bathurst, Mr. Hardinge,[3] and myself in the barouche. The Duchess of Marlborough (number three),[4] Lady Allan Churchill, and Lord Alfred received us, and took us over the house to see the splendid pictures in the drawing-rooms, also the library, chapel, and collection of rare old china in the rooms only meant for summer use. We had luncheon, and afterwards some of us took a run, just to look at the garden and cascades. . . . In the evening we played at "Proverbs." *January* 14.—After a downstairs' breakfast, we walked out to see the village, the almshouses (one old woman was 93), schools, and stables. When we had finished, I went with Lord Bathurst and Lady Chesterfield to the farm, returning by a nursery and a wood, where it was knee deep in mud. Came home dead tired, and read quietly till tea-time ; then I sang and played to Lady Chesterfield. *January* 15.— . . . We inspected the china closet and offices, and dawdled about in the drawing-rooms till one o'clock, when we had some luncheon previous to starting. I was *very, very* sorry that the visit was over. I enjoyed myself gloriously, and Clementina does the honours to perfection. We reached Kew soon after five, and sat down three[5] to dinner, as usual.

Cambridge Cottage, January 21.—I walked with the Baron and Hooker to choose the fir trees for transplanting, and

---

[1] Lady Clementina Villiers.

[2] Lady Evelyn Stanhope, only daughter of the sixth Earl of Chesterfield. She married the Earl of Carnarvon in 1861.

[3] The Honble. Arthur Hardinge, second son of Viscount Hardinge. He was created K.C.B. for military services, was equerry to Prince Consort, and after a brilliant career in India appointed Governor of Gibraltar.

[4] The third wife of the sixth Duke of Marlborough.

[5] The Duchess of Cambridge, Princess Mary, and Baron Knesebeck.

gardened all the afternoon. Mama read "Castle Avon," a
very interesting novel, to me for two hours before, and again
after dinner. *January 22.*— . . . We drove to Richmond
Park to see the gentlemen shoot, sharing their luncheon, and
nearly perishing with cold. . . . Went up to the play at six
o'clock—the Lyceum ; Charles Matthews acted admirably,
and the scenery in the pantomime is wonderfully well done.
January 24.—Up before seven, and off at 9.30 to the King's
Cross station, reaching Belvoir Castle soon after three. . . .
The Wilton girls flew to see me just before dressing time.
At dinner the Duke[1] and Lord Granby were my neighbours.
    Belvoir Castle, January 25.—After breakfasting punctually
at ten, I took a walk with the Wiltons. . . . In the afternoon we all went down to the saw-mill, and peeped at the
rehearsal in the green room. The evening was spent in
dancing country dances till half-past twelve. *January 26.*—
We sat in the gallery working, playing, and singing till
luncheon-time. . . . Walked in the kitchen garden, and,
falling in with George,[2] we had a jolly run round the Duke's
Walk—in all 4½ miles. On my return, I went with George
to his room, drank tea with him, and spent a very happy
hour. In the evening Jim[3] arrived, and we played at
"Post" till 12. *January 27.*—. . . . Mama, Lady Wilton,
Peppy,[4] and I took a walk on the road leading to the reser-
voir, I sticking in the mud, thanks to my clogs! . . . After
dinner we had *tableaux* and dancing till late.
    January 28.—Started at 11.30 for Harlaxton, Mr. Gregory's
place, about five and a half miles off, where we were met by
Lady Brownlow and Lady Caroline Cust. The place itself is
very fine, though in an unfinished state, and I should say
only covetable in part. We had a sort of second breakfast
in the dining-room, and hastened back to Belvoir, in time
for a late luncheon there. I practised in the gallery, and
then attended to the toilet of · the two Denbigh girls.[5]
We dined at seven, on account of the play beginning shortly
after nine o'clock, and for which the three Jerseys arrived.

[1] The Duke of Rutland.
[2] The Duke of Cambridge.
[3] The Honble. James Bosville Macdonald, son of the third Lord
Macdonald, Colonel 21st Hussars and Equerry and Private Secretary to the
Duke of Cambridge; he married in 1859 Elizabeth Nina, daughter of Lord
Wallscourt, and died in 1882.
[4] Lady Elizabeth Grey-Egerton.
[5] Lady Mary and Lady Jane Fielding, daughters of the seventh Earl of
Denbigh, who was Master of the Horse to Queen Adelaide.

The first piece, *The Captain of the Watch*, was the best
acted ; the second was *The Prize*, but the Fieldings were not
very successful in it. Mr. Stafford[1] is an actor *jusqu'aux
bouts des doigts*—in short, nothing could be more perfect.
Mr. Cochrane, Mr. Marley,[2] and Miss Wortley[3] were the best
of his troop. The whole finished with a supper.
January 29.—We drove in the barouche to the meet. An
unpursued fox crossed the fields and road in sight, and we
saw the gentlemen leap a hedge after another one. This
was all our sport! Luncheon over, I went with Lady
Adeliza and Lady Elizabeth[4] to visit the Mausoleum, which
is very fine, and was designed by Wyatt. Then rested
in my own room till dinner-time. In the evening we worked;
Lady John Manners sang and Clemmy played. *January* 30,
Sunday.—Divine service in the Chapel. What a glorious
Murillo hangs over the altar, to be sure! Walked to the
Kennels with Lord Forester to see his " precious pets." On
our return, Lord John[5] took me to the kitchen, steward's room,
and housekeeper's room. Then I played with Lady John's
baby, and had a long talk with dear Mama. In the evening
every one wrote their names on my " sheets,"[6] and the band
sang and played hymns. *January* 31.—All the gentlemen
went out hunting, and we walked—Lady Adeliza and I arm-
in-arm—round the Duke's Walk ; then I sang to her in the
green room. We took our departure immediately after
luncheon, much to my regret, for our visit to Belvoir was really
quite delightful. . . .
Cambridge Cottage, February 10.—I had my first music
lesson with Mr. Müller. . . . In the afternoon Count Kielmansegge[7] called and presented his nephew, who has come
over to join our navy as a volunteer; a very nice gentlemanlike young man. The weather was wretched, so instead of
going out I finished a letter and read to Mama. We dined
at five, and went to the Adelphi to see *Uncle Tom's Cabin*

[1] Mr. Stafford O'Brien, who assumed the name of Augustus Stafford. He
was a well-known man about town and a writer of plays.

[2] Brother of Lady John Manners.

[3] The Honble. Victoria Stuart-Wortley, Maid of Honour to the Queen.
She married, in 1863, the late Sir William Earle Welby-Gregory, Bart.

[4] Lady Adeliza Norman and Lady Elizabeth Drummond, daughters of the
Duke of Rutland.

[5] Lord John Manners, now Duke of Rutland.

[6] Sheets of note paper on which all the guests wrote their names, a
custom Princess Mary continued all her life.

[7] Hanoverian Minister at the Court of St. James's.

and the pantomime, in which Flaxmore acts well. George, Mr. Norman, the two Damers, Elphinstone, and Cecil Forester were in our box. *February* 20.— . . . Drove to Town and called at the Palace, but the Queen was just going out; then paid Aunt Mary a long visit, and Mama settled with Morant about St. James's. On our return from Badminton [1] we hope to find St. James's considerably advanced, though I fear it will not be habitable before May, or thereabouts. . . . Count Trauttmansdorff [2] came down with accounts of the Emperor; thank God the attempt on his life was frustrated! [3] . . . *February* 24.—Dear Papa's birthday. George came to breakfast, and we went to the vault. . . . *February* 25.—Up early and packed. At a quarter-past twelve we started for the Ealing station, where we joined the train, reaching Badminton at half-past five; rested, and dined at eight o'clock. We were a party of twenty-five, and in the evening we played at *des petits jeux*.

Badminton, February 26.—I went out hunting with the Duke [4] in his phaeton, and we were out nearly four hours, and had great fun. On my return I had a bit of luncheon, and then the girls fetched me and we sang and played in the drawing-room. At dinner the Duke and Lord Granby were my neighbours, and in the evening we danced till midnight. *February* 27.—Church at twelve; then to the stables. After lunch saw Lord Cardigan's and Mr. Calthorpe's [5] horses, finishing up with a walk and being caught in a snowstorm. In the evening we amused ourselves with "Words." *February* 28.—A frost, consequently no hunting. Played at billiards and worked all the morning. In the afternoon Etta took Suffie [6] and me for a long drive, and we walked over to the Roman Camp to see the view in the Vale. We dined in the hall, and danced till one o'clock. *March* 1.—We young girls sat in Etta's room and chatted, and after lunch drove over to Dodington to see "Dody" [7] and her four children. On our return we dressed up our heads to imitate old pictures, coming down to dinner in powder. The Duke and Lord Chesterfield sat next to me, and afterwards we danced.

---

[1] The principal seat of the Dukes of Beaufort.

[2] Chargé d'Affaires at the Austrian Embassy during the absence of Count Colloredo.

[3] On the 18th of February an attempt had been made to stab the Emperor of Austria at Vienna.

[4] The Duke of Beaufort.   [5] Afterwards Lord Calthorpe.

[6] Lady Suffield.

[7] Lady Georgina Codrington, daughter of the seventh Duke of Beaufort.

March 2.—After seeing the gentlemen mount we left Badminton, having spent a most charming visit, and returned to Kew, arriving about five.

Cambridge Cottage, March 11.— . . . At one o'clock started for Town. Lord Douro and Lord Fitzroy[1] met us at Apsley House and took us over it, and into the *dear* Duke's[2] own rooms. Paid Aunt Mary a visit, where we saw the future Princess Henry's sapphires, then drove out shopping for George's birthday, were very successful, and finally went to St. James's. *March* 22.—Attended morning prayers. Poor Mama had a headache, so after I had walked and practised, I drove up to town with Frazer to see Aunt Mary and the Duchess of Inverness. Home again by half-past six and found Mama up and reading. I finished the newspaper to her. . . . The fire at Windsor Castle is, thank God, not very extensive, the dining-room and a few servants' rooms alone having suffered. In the evening we finished " Ladybird," which is very well written and so interesting.

March 31.—Lord Chelsea[3] came down and went for a walk with us; in the earlier part of the morning I had made up my book with Knese,[4] which was right to a halfpenny! Mrs. Taylor[5] and her three children arrived, and we spent the afternoon hiding the Easter eggs, in which amusement Davison[6] joined, finishing up with a glorious tea! We dined with George, where we had a charming party of twelve, including the Mandevilles, John Stanleys,[7] and Elphinstones. *April* 4.— . . . Paid the Queen a visit and saw the three youngest children; then on to Aunt Mary's, where we found Lady Howe and Lady Ailesbury,[8] who had come there by appointment to see us. After dinner Mama began reading the French *brochure* on the dear Duke of Wellington. M. Maurel is the *only* Frenchman who really does Wellington justice, and thoroughly appreciates his character. *April* 5.— Wrote a letter before breakfast, and afterwards walked round

---

[1] Lord Fitzroy Somerset.   [2] The late Duke of Wellington.

[3] Father of the present Earl Cadogan.   [4] Baron Knesebeck.

[5] Wife of Mr. Bridges Taylor, Her Majesty's Consul for Denmark. He was a nephew of General Sir Herbert Taylor, who was private secretary to George III., George IV., and William IV.

[6] Sir William Davison, formerly Equerry to the late Duke of Cambridge.

[7] Mr. and Mrs. John Stanley. He became a baronet on the death of his brother and assumed the surname of Errington. She was the only daughter of Baron de Talleyrand.

[8] Maria, second wife of the first Marquis of Ailesbury, well known for many years in society as "Lady A." She died in 1893.

the Park with Knese. Drove with Mama to Mr. Byam Martin's [1] to see his magnificent camellias. We were soon joined by the Queen of the French,[2] Princess Clementine,[3] and the Nemours,[4] and (*par parenthèse*) a very pushing Mrs. —— . . .

April 7.—. . . Finished the "Light of the Forge" and wrote a long letter to Mr. Harrison. At half-past two we learnt that the Queen had a boy [5] born at one o'clock, and, thank· God, all goes well. We went for a walk, and were joined by Lady Marian Alford,[6] who came to announce her sister's marriage with Frederick Leveson-Gower. I rushed about the Gardens to get some flowers for her. Practised for half an hour, dressed and dined at six; drove up to the Opera at Covent Garden, and saw the *Barbiere di Sevilla*—Ronconi perfection !

Letter to the Rev. William Harrison.

April 7, 1853.

DEAR MR. HARRISON,—Having carefully perused your little work, I cannot but express to you how thankful and pleased I am that you should have been so kind as to bring me a copy of it. The "Light of the Forge" is indeed both interesting and instructive, and many a lesson have I found therein; for, though more especially addressed to the *Sick*, I think that the *Whole* cannot but benefit by it. One part, in which you speak of the daily occupations, and the method or plan by which they should be regulated, came *very home* to me, and this is one of the reasons which induced me to trouble you with this letter. I think that were I to lay down some kind of rule how to spend the several hours of the day, I should save a great deal of time otherwise wasted, and consequently get through a great deal more, and read more, by myself, than I am at present able. Perhaps you would kindly give me your advice on the subject, or even draw up a little plan, reserving time for practising the piano, and two hours reading History, etc.,

[1] A gentleman who had a villa on Ham Common, and a conservatory filled with *one* splendid camellia tree.

[2] Queen Marie Amélie, widow of King Louis Philippe.

[3] Daughter of King Louis Philippe.

[4] The Duc and Duchesse de Nemours: he was the eldest son of King Louis Philippe, and married Princess Victoria of Saxe-Coburg and Gotha.

[5] Prince Leopold.

[6] Mother of the present Lord Brownlow, and Princess Mary's intimate friend. Lady Marian Alford was very talented; she possessed many artistic tastes, and had a charm of manner which attracted every one.

with Mama, which would prove of great assistance to me.
I need hardly add that I should be very grateful to you if
you would recommend a daily course of Scripture Reading
to occupy the hour before breakfast.

I read the Bible and a prayer for every day in the year the
first thing each morning, besides my own private devotions;
but now that I grow older, I feel that if I were to devote a
little more time in the morning to sacred thoughts and
subjects, it would raise the tone of the mind, and improve it
in every way. You, dear Mr. Harrison, are one of my oldest
and truest friends, and I therefore now appeal to your judgment to guide me in this matter, and I know you will forgive
me for troubling you. You cannot imagine how glad Mama
and I were to see you again, and how often we have since
spoken of your kind visit; it was a great treat to us both, so
you see the "World" does not make us forget old friends; on
the contrary, I think it makes one cling more firmly to them.
I am looking forward to the pleasure of another visit from
you when we are in Town, and when I hope to have a long
conversation with you, for I assure you I at times feel very
anxious about myself and my neglect of my duty to my God
and to those around me. Prayer is at such times a very great
comfort to me. . . . I doubt not that you remember me in
your prayers, and that they will be answered. . . . Pray
believe me, dear Mr. Harrison, your very sincere and grateful
friend,

MARY ADELAIDE.

Journal.—Cambridge Cottage, April 11.—Wrote to Aunt
Louisa [1] before breakfast, and walked with Frazer; practised,
and started for town at two o'clock. Went first to the
Palace to see Albert and my tiny godchild, and then on to
St. James's. . . . *April* 13.—After luncheon we paid a visit
to Orleans House, where we met Miss Coutts; then took a walk
on Ham Common. . . . Dined at Aunt Kent's to meet George,
the party of nine being made up by her suite; Ada and
Speth [2] were my neighbours. Thence we adjourned to the
French play; Lafont and Mdlle. Page—not very amusing.
On arriving at Gloucester House we found Aunt Mary
sitting up to receive us.

Gloucester House, April 14.—I came down rather late to
breakfast, and busied myself all the morning with my work

[1] Princess Louisa of Hesse.
[2] Baroness von Speth, for many years Lady-in-Waiting to the Duchess of
Kent; she died at a great age in Her Royal Highness's service.

and receiving visits. The Ellesmere girls[1] and Suffie came before luncheon; Lady Raglan and daughter, dear little Arthur,[2] George, Lady Barrington and Mary,[3] the Jerseys, and Countess Colloredo paid their respects in the afternoon. . . . Went to Lady Mandeville's dance, and enjoyed myself very much, valsing twice and staying till half-past one.

Cambridge Cottage, April 17.— . . . In the afternoon we started for town, and saw the Queen on her sofa; then went into the garden to see the seven children at play; and at five o'clock on to Aunt Mary's. . . . Home for dinner and worked all the evening. *April* 21.—After my music lesson, which lasted from eleven till one, I took a walk in the Gardens, Hookey[4] *raining* camellias upon me, and on my return read Perthe's "Leben" to Mama. We dined with George; the Wiltons, and a host of eldest sons and young peers formed the party; my neighbours were Lord Bath and Lord Wilton. Afterwards there was an evening party at the Colleredos'. *April* 25.—Dear Aunt Mary's birthday! May she be spared to us a few more years! Before breakfast, I put away all my letters, and from half-past eleven till one practised and read to Mama. Mr. Johnston[5] came and began "The Monastic Life of Charles V.," by Mr. Stirling of Keir. . . .

April 26.—. . . We started for Coombe, and enjoyed ourselves immensely, digging out tufts of yellow primroses and wild violets, and listening to the nightingales—the first I have heard this year. . . . Dined at six, and went to the Opera. The *Puritani* was given, it being Mario's *début;* Ronconi sang beautifully, and Mdlle. Bosio very well. Suffie, Lord Fitzroy, and the Normans were our party. *April* 28.— Arranged and put away some of my things before breakfast, after which I completed all domestic arrangements about moving the furniture. Saw Miss Burt. . . . Visited the National Gallery[6] with Suffie and the Cadogans. The Exhibition is a very fine one this year, John Leslie particularly

---

[1] Lady Alice Egerton, afterwards Countess of Strafford, and Lady Blanche Egerton, who married the seventh Earl of Sandwich.

[2] Prince Arthur.

[3] The Honble. Mary Barrington, now Mrs. Sartoris.

[4] Sir William Hooker.

[5] The Rev. — Johnston, at one time Chaplain to the British Embassy at Vienna: he used to go regularly to Cambridge Cottage to read aloud to the Duchess and Princess Mary.

[6] The Royal Academy Exhibitions were then held in the building on the north side of Trafalgar Square.

distinguishing himself by two beautiful pictures of the German school. We called at St. James's, where they are getting on well. . . . Dined with Aunt Mary and went to a charming ball at Norfolk House.[1] I danced eleven times, and was home by three. Slept at Gloucester House.

Gloucester House, May 5, Ascension Day.—Attended morning service at Grosvenor Church (Mr. Nepean's). . . . At three we walked down to St. James's, where we stayed upwards of two hours; dined at Aunt Kent's, and then on to hear *Lucrezia* at Covent Garden. Grisi, Mario, and Ronconi —divine! *May 6.*— . . . The Vincents and Kielmansegge dined with us. Aunt Kent came in the evening, and at eleven we went to a rout at Lady Jersey's in honour of Clem's birthday. Home at Kew by two o'clock.

Cambridge Cottage, May 7.—Dear Mama's wedding-day! It poured, but we went to Papa's grave. . . . Mr. Johnston read to us from a quarter-past one till three. In the afternoon I practised, and ran about the house to see that Mr. Harrison's rooms were nice and tidy. He arrived at six, and we spent some little time with him before dinner. . . . *May 8, Sunday.*—Mr. Harrison gave us a splendid sermon in the morning, for the benefit of our schools, and in the afternoon preached on the Song of Solomon. . . . *May 10.*—Mr. Harrison came to read and pray with me before breakfast, and then took leave. I was so *very* sorry. Wrote my journal and had my music lesson. . . . Geraldine Somerset came in the afternoon, and we sent her home with a large nosegay. Dined with Aunt Kent—Colonel Seymour[2] being the only *beau!*—and went to the French play; *Les demoiselles de St. Cyr* was given. Lafont, Regnier, and Mdlle. Brohan admirable.

May 13.—Drove up to town, going first to St. James's, where my rooms are the very pink of perfection; thence to Lady Suffield's; and, lastly, walking across the Park with George, to Aunt Mary's, where we saw Lady Jersey and Lord Winchester. Then shopped for the Queen's birthday; after some little time we found what we wanted, and reached

---

[1] The Town house of the Dukes of Norfolk.

[2] Afterwards General Sir Francis Seymour. As a lieutenant in the 19th Regiment he was appointed by King Leopold to travel with his nephew Prince Albert, and in 1839 accompanied the Prince on a tour through Italy. He served with the Scots Fusilier Guards in the Crimea; was appointed Groom-in-Waiting to the Prince Consort from 1860, and on the death of the Prince held the same position in Her Majesty's Household. Later on he became Master of the Ceremonies, and was created a baronet in 1869.

home by eight o'clock. Knese read to us after dinner, and I finished a hand-screen for the Bazaar. *May* 15, *Sunday.*—Church. . . . Mama and I walked in the Gardens, which were open for the first time on Sunday to the public. The Taylors dined with us, and in the evening we made the tables and a hat move! Suffie is all electricity! We nearly died of laughing. *May* 18.—George reviewed our Militia on the Green. I finished packing, moving, and arranging things. . . . The Danish Minister and his wife [1] paid us a visit, and we showed them the Gardens. At five we left dear little Kew for St. James's.

St. James's Palace, May 19.—I spent the morning helping Mama, and unpacking all my china from dear old Cambridge House. . . . Miss Mitford [2] drove us to Aunt Mary's, whence we proceeded to the Enclosure, Regent's Park, for a walk, returning home to dress for the dinner at the Duchess of Inverness's. We were a party of twenty-one; I sat between Lord Otho Fitzgerald and Lord Anson. It was *very* agreeable; and in the evening we danced. *May* 21.—Madame Nestor came to try on a wreath.[3] . . . We drove to the station to receive my sister. It was a happy meeting. We took her to the Hotel, and there I waited to go with Fritz and darling Doppus [4] to my Aunt's. The whole party dined with us.

May 24.—The Queen's birthday. We went to the Horse Guards' Parade, which was very fine. Home to breakfast at half-past eleven. . . . At 4.30 we drove *à quatre Princesses* round and round Hyde Park and down Rotten Row. Augusta dined with us, and I read "Larpent" to Mama till ten o'clock, then dressed for the ball at Lord Breadalbane's—a very grand one. Gussy and I stayed till nearly three o'clock! *May* 27.— . . . At half-past five we drove to the House of Lords and heard Lord Derby speak on the legacy duty in reply to a wooden, bitter speech of Lord Aberdeen's.[5] In the evening we went to the Colloredos' ball, where we stayed till 3.30 a.m.! *May* 28.—Lord Normanby paid Mama a visit, after which we proceeded in *festal attire* to pay our respects to the Queen, Aunt Kent, and Aunt Mary. We dined at

[1] M. and Madame de Bille.

[2] Sister to the Earl of Redesdale and a friend of the Duchess of Gloucester's.

[3] Princess Mary was very fond of wreaths for her hair, and generally wore one in the evening.

[4] Prince Adolphus of Mecklenburg-Strelitz.

[5] A coalition Government had recently come into office (December 28, 1852), with Lord Aberdeen as Prime Minister.

seven and went to the Opera (Queen's box). *Ernani*—
but Bosio, who had been taken ill, was unfortunately replaced
by a dreadful woman! Ronconi and Tamberlik were as good
as ever, but the *female* spoilt the *ensemble* terribly.

May 29.—Mama was taken ill in the middle of the night,
and had to send for Quin. With this information they
awoke me in the morning, and on rushing to Mama as soon
as dressed I found her very low about herself and in bed.
She, however, wished us to go to Church, so I fetched
Augusta, and we went to Grosvenor Chapel to hear the
Bishop of Oxford preach for the Cambridge Asylum. His
allusions to dear Papa were both touching and true. The
collection amounted to upwards of £126. On our return I
wrote to the Queen, and stayed with Mama till five o'clock,
when we went to see Aunt Mary and the poor dear Duchess
of Beaufort, who is terribly cut up at the death of her father.[1]
In the evening we had a charming dinner at George's, and
I sat next to Lord Derby. *May* 30.—Dear Mama had a
bad night, but was better in the morning. . . . Lunched at
Gloucester House, and drove to Lady Howard's[2] *town breakfast*, where Mario sang to perfection. Everything was charmingly done, and the entertainment lasted till after seven
o'clock. Sir William Fraser[3] and Katty[4] were my neighbours
at the breakfast.

May 31.— . . . Walked with Lilli,[5] Knese, and Lühe[6] out
shopping to Garrard's, through the Burlington Arcade to
Barry's, and thence home. . . . In the evening we dined
with the Queen, a family party and suite. I sat next to
Albert. *June* 1.—Mama had a good night, and I found her
up and dressing. After breakfast I wrote notes, and then
took my work and sat with her, she being *en robe de chambre*,
ensconced in an armchair in her bedroom. Shortly after

[1] Mr. Charles Culling Smith. He married Lady Anne Wellesley, only
sister of the Duke of Wellington, and after the death of his wife in 1844
lived with his daughter at Beaufort House.

[2] Wife of Sir Ralph Howard, Bart. She entertained a good deal both at
her house in Belgrave Square and at Craven Cottage, Fulham. Her
garden parties, or breakfasts as that form of entertainment was then called,
were very popular with London Society.

[3] Lady Howard's eldest son by her first marriage with Sir James Fraser,
Bart. Sir William's brothers were General Sir Charles Fraser, V.C., and
General Keith Fraser, who commanded the 1st Life Guards.

[4] Lady Katherine Grey-Egerton.

[5] Sister to the Hereditary Grand Duke of Mecklenburg-Strelitz.

[6] Equerry to the Hereditary Grand Duchess of Mecklenburg-Strelitz.

poor Augusta arrived with a bad headache, so I was a sort
of general nurse. . . . A dinner of twenty-nine at the
Wiltons'. His lordship and Lord Otho Fitzgerald were my
neighbours. . . . I did thoroughly enjoy myself. *June* 2.—
I went to the drawing-room arrayed in blue. It was a very
full one, and lasted from 2 till 4.30. We drove to my Aunt's
en grande toilette to show ourselves. Home by six to undress
and prepare for the dinner at Aunt Kent's previous to the
Opera—*Ugonotti;* Mario and Grisi superb! *June* 5.— . . .
Mama went out for her first drive, and after luncheon had quite
a rout. The Queen and Albert, Aunt Mary and Aunt Kent,
Lord Raglan, the Duke of Genoa, and Lady Jersey came to
see her in the course of the afternoon. . . . I dined with my
sister at the Granvilles', a party of fourteen, and sat next to
Lord Granville. In the evening, who should walk in but
Panizzi[1] and Monckton Milnes![2]

June 7.—Up at six, breakfasted, and was in the carriage
by eight. Started from the station at half-past, picked up
three Wiltons at Slough, and were at Oxford soon after ten
o'clock. Dr. Bull received us at the station, and took us at
once to the theatre, where the undergraduates gave us a
cheer. The ceremony itself was very imposing, and the
reception of Lord Derby, my brother, and Disraeli most
enthusiastic. After Lord Derby's Latin speech, and the
nineteen new doctors had had the dignity conferred upon
them, there were several Latin speeches and two beautiful
English odes, in which the names of Wellington and Derby
(Stanley) were blended. When all was over, we were taken
to the house of the Warden of All Souls' College, and rested
there till the luncheon, which the fellows gave us in the
Hall, was ready. The Sub-Warden, Mr. Stopford, did the
honours, and I sat between him and George. They then
took us to the Library and Chapel. Magdalen College was
our next point, with its cloisters and beautiful Chapel;
whence we proceeded to inspect Christ Church Hall and
Chapel, which is also the Cathedral. We then walked to
Merton College, rested ourselves in the garden, visited the
Chapel, and drove to Parker's shop, where an interchange of
presents, consisting of books bound in fine old Oxford style,

---

[1] Sir Antonio Panizzi, who succeeded Sir Henry Ellis as principal Librarian
of the British Museum in 1856. He was an intimate friend of Lord
Palmerston, Mr. Gladstone, and Macaulay, but perhaps his most celebrated
friendship was with Prosper Mérimée, the emissary of Napoleon III. Sir
Antonio retired from the post he had filled with so much ability in 1865.

[2] Afterwards Lord Houghton.

took place. As it was very warm indeed, we sat in the garden of St. John's College till 5.30, when we returned to Grey's[1] rooms in Christ Church, where he gave us a substantial tea, Mr. Birch[2] joining our party. At eight o'clock we left Oxford, and were at St. James's by half-past ten.

St. James's Palace, June 10.—Drove to Kew, where Mama took her first walk. We spent a delightful afternoon in the garden, drinking tea and haymaking. Home by six. . . . Mrs. Barry came, and we had a chat together. . . . I joined Augusta at Aunt Mary's evening party, whence we adjourned to Stafford House, where upwards of eight hundred people were assembled. *June 12, Sunday.*—Augusta and I attended morning service at St. Paul's[3]—Mr. Liddell's church. At 1.30 we started off, a large party, in three carriages, with the Duke of Genoa and suite for Chiswick, where we went over the House[4] and part of the grounds. I was in the second carriage with Lilli, Fritz, and Azeglio.[5] We drove on to Kew, and showed the Duke the finest glass-houses, and then took him on to the terrace to see the view of Syon.[6] On our return we had tea, which all the Italians *did great justice to,* and afterwards they explored the wonders of the Cottage! At half-past six they returned to London, and we stayed half an hour longer, discussing the events of the day. Home by eight o'clock. Fritz peeped in during the evening.

June 13.—After taking my music lesson at Gloucester House I remained there all the afternoon, working for the Bazaar, and saw Lady Bessborough, Lady Cowley, Lady Truro, and Elizabeth Yorke. On my return home I worked away till dinner-time. In the evening we went to Lady Antrobus's concert; Mario and Miss Pyne did not sing—thanks to the influenza. The Duke of Genoa was there. *June 14.*— . . . We lunched in the Passage[7] and sat there

---

[1] Viscount Grey de Wilton. He married Lady Elizabeth Craven, and succeeded his father as Earl of Wilton in 1882.

[2] The Rev. Henry Birch, Rector of Prestwich; he was Lord Grey de Wilton's tutor at Eton, and from 1848–51 had charge of the Prince of Wales's studies.

[3] St. Paul's Church, Knightsbridge.

[4] Chiswick House, then the residence of the Duke of Devonshire. It was here that Fox died in 1806, and Canning in 1827.

[5] Marquis d'Azeglio, Sardinian Minister at the Court of St. James's.

[6] Syon House, Isleworth, belonging to the Duke of Northumberland.

[7] Up to 1868 Her Majesty's Drawing Rooms were always held at St. James's Palace, and from the passage windows in the Duchess of Cambridge's apartments a good view could be obtained of the ladies and gentlemen who

with our work to see the drawing-room. The Duke of Genoa came to take leave. . . . Dressed for an early dinner with Augusta, and thence to the Opera with Aunt Kent. *June* 15.— Suffie and I drove out shopping for the Bazaar. We made our purchases at the Pantheon and Soho, spending £10—George's kind gift. At 4.30 we paid the Queen and the Duchess of Coburg[1] a visit, and went on to the Regent's Park Gardens, as it was *un jour de promenade* there. The gardens were very full, and the show of American plants quite beautiful. Dined *tête-à-tête* with Mama and dressed for the Court Ball, which was a magnificent one, as the toilettes were first rate. I danced a great deal. Home by two o'clock.

June 16.—A very late breakfast, after which I went over to Aunt Mary's to take my music lesson; returned home in the afternoon and found the Hamiltons[2] with Mama. At half-past three we started off in a carriage and four to meet the King and Queen of Hanover on the Woolwich road. One of our horses lost a shoe, so we had to get out on the other side of Greenwich and take a walk in a market garden with an avenue of magnificent walnut-trees and a charmingly civil owner. We then returned to Greenwich and sat in the Square of the Hospital till six o'clock, when we went to see the old pensioners at tea. While in the hall the carriages of the Hanoverian party passed us, but by dint of shouting and running we stopped them, and Greenwich was witness to our tender meeting. We all drove back together, and on reaching the dear King's House[3] we found Aunt Mary waiting to receive him. The Queen and Aunt Kent joined us shortly. We returned home to dinner, but spent the evening *en famille* with the King and Queen. *June* 17.—. . . At half-past three we paid a visit to the Hanoverians, where we were joined by the Queen, Aunt Gloucester and Aunt Kent. We then drove in the Park, stopping in Rotten Row to hear the music; home to dress for the grand dinner *en famille* (*c'est à dire avec la suite*) at Court.

June 20.—. . . We went to Aunt Mary's about the things belonging to our stall at the Bazaar.[4] Lunched with the

had the privilege of the *entrée*, as they entered the Palace from Ambassador's Court.

[1] Wife of the reigning Duke of Saxe-Coburg and Gotha, elder brother of the Prince Consort, and formerly Princess Alexandrina of Baden.

[2] The Duke and Duchess of Hamilton. The Duchess was the youngest daughter of Charles, reigning Grand Duke of Baden, and a distant cousin of the Emperor Napoleon III.

[3] The house in Grosvenor Place occupied by the Hanoverian Legation.

[4] The Bazaar was in aid of the Royal Cambridge Asylum, and held at the

Hanoverians, home again at three, and had a peep at Ellinor
Napier. Then Lady Wilton arrived with her contributions
to the Bazaar. From four till six we drove with the Queen
of Hanover round the Park. . . . Dressed for the Concert at
Court, where the Cologne singers performed some very fine
choruses. Mario refused to sing! *June* 21.—Off by the
quarter-past eight train to Staines; thence in the Queen of
Hanover's carriage to the camp at Chobham. The weather
kept fine during the military business of the day, and it
only rained on our drive back. The troops looked *gloriously
beautiful*, and the manœuvres, which we witnessed from a
hill, rejoiced my soldier-like heart. We lunched with the
Queen in her tent, and returned to Staines in our own
carriage. . . . Dined at seven, to be in time for the Opera
Rigoletto. The Hanoverians went with us. *June* 22.—
Very busy all dressing time writing notes; went down to a
late and hasty breakfast, and started at 11.30 for the Bazaar,
to be in time to receive Majesty and Royalty at twelve.
We remained there buying and helping till three, when we
adjourned to a luncheon at Grosvenor House. Afterwards we
walked about to see the pictures; the four Rubens' and " Mrs.
Siddons," by Sir Joshua Reynolds, particularly delighted me.
At about five we returned to the Bazaar, and remained till it
closed. . . . After dinner we drank tea with dear Aunt Mary
and Lady Brownlow, and then went on to the Clanricarde ball.

June 23.—. . . At a quarter-past twelve I began to dress
for the Drawing-room, which was anything but a full one—
plenty of royalties there, however. As soon as it was over
we changed our dresses, had a cup of tea, and hurried to the
Bazaar, where we found business very brisk, and assisted as
shopwomen. It was most successful, and realised upwards
of £1500 free of all expenses. Returning home we dined
in great haste to get to the Opera—*Lucrezia Borgia*—in
time. The King invited us all to his box, and we stayed to
see Plunket in the *divertissement. June* 24.—Helped Mama
to arrange the china in the " Red " and " Green " drawing-
rooms. . . . Went with the Queen of Hanover and her children
to the Zoological Gardens. Dined with the Hanoverians, and
accompanied them to the Montrose ball,[1] where Augusta and

Cavalry Barracks, Hyde Park. The Duchess of Gloucester had a stall, over
which the Hereditary Grand Duchess of Mecklenburg-Strelitz and Princess
Mary of Cambridge presided for their aunt. Among the things on sale at
the Duchess of Gloucester's stall was an ottoman worked by Her Royal
Highness and a piece of embroidery worked by the Queen.

[1] The Duchess of Montrose gave the Ball in honour of the Duchess of
Cambridge and Princess Mary.

I stayed till past three! *June* 25.—. . . Went at five o'clock to a *déjeûner dinatoire* at Gloucester House in honour of the Hanoverian children,[1] who did not, however, arrive till six. There were the Marionettes and tea for the juveniles, and a magnificent dinner with some very fine catches and glees for us grown-up people. The little *fête* went off charmingly, but unfortunately, thanks to the King and Queen's coming so late, we got to the French play just as the second act of *Adrienne Lecouvreur* was over. Rachel acted wonderfully well, as far as I could judge, having lost the thread of the piece, but did not charm me.

June 26.—I despatched two notes for Mama between breakfast and the Chapel Royal. . . . Although a rainy afternoon, we drove down with the Queen to Kew, and took her over the Cottage and to dear Papa's tomb, on which she placed a wreath of flowers. Home again by six, to put the finishing stroke to the arrangement of the drawing-room, and dressed for the *first* little dinner-party given *at home*, and in honour of the King and Queen of Hanover. We were fourteen in all, my neighbours being the Queen and Mallortie.[2] The Hamiltons came in the evening. The " Red " drawing-room looked perfectly lovely when lighted up. *June* 27.—In the morning Mama took me down to Kew, where we had a *tête-à-tête*, for a wonder, and did not return till eight o'clock. Dressed after dinner for a very *oppressive* party at the Jerseys' for the King, and a very nice ball at the Exeters'.

June 25.—. . . The Hanoverians lunched at Stafford House, where we joined them afterwards, to see the pictures ; these, especially the Murillos, delighted me. Before five I began to dress for the christening,[3] which was in state, in honour of the King. Prince Hohenlohe took me into the Chapel and in to dinner. The children—English, Hanoverian, and Mecklenburg—appeared before the banquet, Dolphus[4] looking lovely in his *kilt*. In the evening there was a party, and we listened at a respectful distance to the strains of instrumental music till midnight. *June* 29.—At 11.15 we left London in company with the Hanoverians *per* train for

[1] Prince Ernest, now Duke of Cumberland, Princess Frederica, who married Baron von Pawel Rammingen, and Princess Mary of Hanover.

[2] Comptroller of the Household to the King of Hanover.

[3] The christening of Prince Leopold, the sponsors being the King of Hanover, Prince Hohenlohe, the Princess of Prussia and Princess Mary of Cambridge.

[4] Prince Adolphus of Mecklenburg-Strelitz.

Windsor. The day was most propitious, and we went
rambling over the *dear old castle*, and admiring all the
treasures it contains. At two we sat down to a grand
luncheon in the breakfast-room, and then walked down to
St. George's Chapel; thence we drove to Frogmore,[1] where
Aunt Kent was waiting to receive us. After spending half
an hour there, we drove on through the kitchen gardens
and Park to the Royal Lodge and Virginia Water; paid
Whiting[2] a visit, and then returned to the station. Home
again by seven o'clock, and dined with the King—that is
to say, Mama dined with him, while I dined upstairs with
the Queen, who suffers much from her foot, and is quite
lame. Their Majesties and ourselves drank tea at dear
Aunt's. . . .

June 30.—I had a quietish morning till eleven o'clock,
when Elizabeth Yorke came to see me, and Lady Napier and
Ellinor also paid me a visit. Shortly after three we started
for Richmond, where the Buccleuchs gave a breakfast
to meet the King. Unfortunately there were several very
heavy showers of rain, which prevented our walking at all.
The *déjeûner dinatoire* was served in a large tent, and we sat
down upwards of seventy people. My neighbours were the
Duke of Hamilton and Lord Sydney;[3] during dinner some
glees were sung, and the band played. We left about half-
past seven, and were in town again just in time to dress
for the concert at Aunt Mary's, which was very successful,
though not *de première qualité*. I was thoroughly tired out.

July 2.—. . . Etta Hamilton[4] came and found me showing
off my pink room to Count Decken. We waited at home till
half-past four, in expectation of a visit from the Princess of
Prussia, who did not arrive till much later; then we drove
to Grosvenor House, where there was a kind of breakfast,
which was very good fun, as there were *loads* of people. . . .
On our way home we took a drive down Rotten Row.
Dined *à trois* and dressed for a small evening party at the
Palace, where we were treated to a concert. . . .

---

[1] The Duchess of Kent lived at Frogmore House.

[2] Formerly page to Queen Adelaide, and afterwards in the service of
Queen Victoria.

[3] Earl Sydney was Groom-in-Waiting to King George IV., Lord-in-Waiting
to King William IV., and Lord-in-Waiting to the Queen. He was Lord
Chamberlain 1859–66 and 1868–74.

[4] Lady Harriet Hamilton, eldest daughter of the first Duke of Abercorn.
She married the second Earl of Lichfield.

July 3, Sunday.—Attended church at St. James's to hear Jackson the new Bishop of Lincoln preach. . . . The King and Queen arrived to pay us a farewell visit. The Queen afterwards took a drive with us to Hampstead to see the pretty cottages, and we were home again in time to dress for a nice little dinner at George's. In the evening we went over to Aunt Kent's, where *the* Queen, the Coburgs, and the Prince of Prussia came to meet the Hanoverians, and there we took leave of the latter. *July 5.*— . . . After lunch I drove to Kew with Mama and Augusta, and spent the rest of the day there. We gathered roses and had a *heavy tea* in the garden. . . . Went to Lady Cardigan's ball—a very grand concern, with a sitting-down supper for us ; home by two o'clock. *July 6.*—In the morning I was pleasantly disturbed in my meditations by a visit from the Princess of Prussia. . . . At three o'clock we left London for Mrs. Lawrence's villa,[1] where there was a very sumptuous breakfast, though but few people we knew ; the weather was lovely, and we did not leave till past seven as the gardens were very enjoyable ; both Arabella and Libbet Yorke [2] were there.

July 7.—At noon we drove to the National Gallery, where Mr. Grant and Sir Charles Eastlake [3] met us, and we spent upwards of two hours in looking at the pictures. Mama and I then called on poor Madame de Bille [4] previous to her leaving England. Ada Hohenlohe came to take leave of me, and on going to Mama's room I found Aunt Kent and the Prince of Prussia there. At five we drove to Kensal Green to see dear Aunt Sophia's and Uncle Sussex's tombs. . . . Dressed in a tremendous hurry for, as we supposed, a dinner quite *en famille* at Aunt Mary's ; but lo ! and behold, just as we were going to start she arrived in great state under the impression she was going to dine with us. Both cooks being out we saw ourselves reduced to utter starvation ; however, thanks to the cleverness of our kitchen-maid, we had a very tidy little dinner by about nine o'clock, and drank tea at

[1] Mrs. Lawrence was the wife of the distinguished physician of that name. He was appointed Sergeant-Surgeon to the Queen in 1857, having long been Her Majesty's Surgeon-Extraordinary, and was created a baronet for his professional services just before his death in 1869. The villa at Ealing was famous for its rare orchids and other flowers.

[2] Lady Elizabeth Yorke.

[3] Sir Charles Eastlake was then President of the Royal Academy. He was succeeded in the office by Mr., afterwards Sir Francis, Grant in 1866.

[4] M. de Bille died suddenly of heart disease on June 19, 1853, at the Danish Legation. Singularly enough, his predecessor, Count Reventlow, succumbed to the same complaint.

Aunt Mary's. *July* 8.—Third anniversary of dear Papa's death. We spent the day at Kew, and visited the vault to put flowers on the coffin. It was a very touching sight to see Dolphus kneeling at the foot of the coffin. In the course of the afternoon Ellinor Napier arrived, and shortly after this we sat down, a party of seven, to a frugal dinner. We then took a walk and gathered heaps of flowers, returning at about ten o'clock to London.

July 9.—Prepared for our trip to Hatfield,[1] . . . and on arriving at the station found a large number of *élites* waiting for the train. We reached Hatfield about one o'clock, and had a short walk before luncheon, losing our way in the Labyrinth. . . . Saw all over the house, and walked to the stables, which are the oldest part of all, and then drove to the "Vineyard"—very pretty indeed; after this we returned to the house, drank tea, and started for home by the 6.15 train. Dressed in great haste for the Opera to hear *Le Prophète*. *July* 11.— . . . Went to Norfolk House for the Raffle.[2] . . . Dined at the Hamiltons', my neighbours being the Duke and Prince Poniatowski; there was an evening party and a splendid concert—Mario, Grisi, and Ronconi did their best to please.

July 12.—Off at eight o'clock to Chobham for the day. The weather was perfectly lovely, and the drive from the Windsor station through the Park enchanting. We saw the manœuvres from the hill occupied by the Rifle Brigade, and when the troops were out of sight we looked into a few of the soldiers' and officers' tents and walked to the "Crescent," where some of the married men live. We went to the lower ground to see them march past, and then to Lord Seaton's for lunch. On our way back we drove through the Camp, stopping at George's tent and at the stables of the 13th Light Dragoons. . . .

July 13.—We devoted the day to the arts, and set off at twelve o'clock with Stephens[3] to see the Exhibition of Amateur Artists, in which Mr. Lumley[4] and Mrs. Carew Mildmay particularly distinguished themselves, and that

---

[1] The seat of the Marquis of Salisbury.

[2] A means of getting together funds for charitable purposes, much in vogue at this time.

[3] Colonel Stephens, equerry to the Duke of Cambridge.

[4] Mr. Augustus Savile Lumley; he succeeded to Rufford Abbey on the death of his elder brother, and died in 1885. He was popular in London Society, and much sought after for country-house parties, being a clever actor and an excellent leader of cotillons.

of the New Society of Painters in Water-colours. Shortly
after we reached home, Mr. Norman Macdonald[1] fetched
us to see the funeral car of the dear old Duke of Wellington
at Marlborough House; we then visited the Vernon Collection of pictures and a collection of old china, Indian and
Turkish things exhibited in the rooms above, part of which
came from the great Exhibition. At four o'clock Aunt Kent
arrived. . . . We drove to a morning party at Lady Hastings',
where she sang and Piatti played on the violoncello. . . .
Dined at Lady Foley's, and on to a ball at the Grahams',[2]
which was very nice.

July 15.— . . . Started at three o'clock in pouring rain
for Craven Cottage—Lady Howard's place—where there was
to be a breakfast; we were almost the first to arrive. As
Mario *se fit attendre* we had a *déjeûner dînatoire* first, and
then a charming concert, in which Mario was sole performer,
returning in time to go with Aunt Kent to the German
play; Devriant acted admirably in *Donna Diana. July* 17.—
We attended church at the Female Orphan Asylum this
morning, as it was "Thanksgiving Day" for the five
apprentices, who were rewarded after church with a purse
of five guineas for having served their time to the satisfaction of their employers, and only returned home after
we had seen the children at their dinner. . . . We drove
to Kensington Gardens, and walked there to see the *beau
monde.* On our way home we paid Marie Hamilton[3]
a visit, and then dressed for a dinner of fifteen at
Beaufort House. I sat between Lord Forester and Mr.
Calthorpe.

July 19.—Augusta's birthday! Immediately after breakfast we paid her a visit in honour of the day, and were
joined there by Aunt Mary on the same errand. On my
return I found Monsignor Prosperi with Mama. Clementina,
Mr. Hutchinson, and Miss Mitford paid their respects, and
in the afternoon we went to see the Zulu Kaffirs. Home
again early, on account of *our* grand dinner (12) at half-past
six o'clock. Shortly after eight we adjourned to the Opera,
where, to our disappointment, *Le Prophète* was given, and
we finished the evening with a *petit concert* at Madame

---

[1] Comptroller of Accounts to the Lord Chamberlain's Department. He
died in 1855, and was succeeded by the Honble. Spencer Ponsonby, now Sir
Spencer Ponsonby-Fane, G.C.B.

[2] Sir James and Lady Graham. Sir James Graham at this time held the
post of First Lord of the Admiralty.

[3] The Duchess of Hamilton.

Walewska's,[1] at which Prince Poniatowski sang. *July* 20.—
. . . I shopped with Mama and Knese in the morning,
poking about the furniture shops in Bond Street. . . . Dined
at Lord Derby's, and on to the Colloredos' ball, where we
stayed till half-past three !

July 21.—Could think of nothing all the morning but dear
Peppy's happy face last night after Dudley de Ros had
proposed to her. This is indeed a charming marriage, though
the gossips perhaps may not approve. . . . Took my last
music lesson at Gloucester House. . . . Drove to Hampstead Heath, where Doppus had a donkey ride. . . . At
eleven we went to Lady Jersey's "tea-table"[2] party, and left
at 12.15. *July* 22.—Doppus's birthday ! Augusta and I took
him to Madame Tussaud's exhibition, including the Chamber
of Horrors ! . . . At two o'clock we started for Kew; Doppus
followed with the Hamilton children, and I devoted the
whole afternoon to playing with them. . . . Aunt Mary,
Lady Caroline Murray,[3] and Monsignor Prosperi dined with
us in honour of the day. The evening found us at Beaufort
House, where Bosio, Ronconi, and Gardoni gave us a charming concert. Prince Poniatowski also sang.

July 23.—I spent the great part of the morning arranging
my things, packing up, and settling bills. In the afternoon
we went to see and hear Albert Smith's ascent of Mont
Blanc. . . . We dined with Aunt Kent, who took us to the
German play to see Devriant as "Wilhelm Tell," *mais ce
n'est pas son meilleur rôle.* *July* 25.—Dear Mama's birthday !
Augusta, Fritz, and Doppus came to breakfast, after which
we offered her *nos petits cadeaux.* Aunt Kent, Aunt Mary,
Miss Coutts, Marie Hamilton, George Mecklenburg, and the
Duchess of Inverness all came to wish Mama joy of the
day. . . . Dined at George's.

July 26.—Packing morning ! so that I had heaps to do,
besides which I wrote my journal, which I had neglected doing for several days. At four o'clock we left for
Arundel Castle,[4] where we arrived just before seven. Our
luggage did not come till very late, so that we sat down
to dinner long after eight o'clock. In the evening we
danced.

July 27, *Arundel Castle.*—Breakfast at ten ; then we
drove in the park and grounds. I went in a phaeton with

[1] Wife of the French Ambassador.
[2] A small evening party of intimate friends.
[3] Lady-in-Waiting to the Duchess of Gloucester.
[4] The country seat of the Dukes of Norfolk.

Constance Grosvenor,[1] Suffie, and Azeglio. Home again to luncheon soon after two o'clock, and remained in our rooms till 4.30, when we explored the laundry, Fitzalan Chapel, Church, and Tower in the flower-garden; then walked down to the dairy, where we had tea. We dined at eight, my neighbours being Trauttmansdorff and Elphinstone, and afterwards we danced. *July* 28.—Frazer awoke me with the sad and shocking news of the sudden death of Mr. Calthorpe's poor servant, who died in the night in an apoplectic fit. This threw a gloom over everything. We started at 11.30 for the races at Goodwood, I in a barouche with Constance, Adeliza, and Fritz. The weather was rather showery, but the view of the surrounding country from the stand quite beautiful. The day was a very unlucky one on the course, for the *blacklegs* won, and the Cup was carried off by a *French horse*, to my horror! We had luncheon in the stand, and remained till five o'clock to see Lord Derby's horse "Sortie" run, and I am happy to say it beat Charles Greville's horse and won the Stakes (£600). We then drove to the house,[2] where the Duchess of Richmond had tea for us, and after we had seen the rooms we returned home. In the evening we played at a round game of cards, and laughed immoderately.

July 29.—After breakfast we retired to our respective rooms, and at twelve took a long walk, returning home by the dairy and looking in at the Keep and its inmates the owls. Luncheon over, we went the round of the Castle, to see all the rooms, and paid an especial visit to Azeglio's "dressing-box!" At four o'clock we started in carriages for the "Decoy" (wild ducks), where we had tea; but owing to the rain were obliged to return home early. . . . In the evening we had great fun in guessing eyes, or, rather, finding out people by their eyes. *July* 30.—This morning, as it was *le jour du départ*, we remained some time in the drawing-room writing autographs; then Lord Foley took us for a long walk through the fields and down into a charming valley, but it poured with rain, and we well-nigh stuck in the mud! On our return we had a morsel of luncheon, and then, to our great regret, bade adieu to Arundel and its kind owners. The train deposited us at Brighton, where George[3] and Catherine had given us a *rendez-vous*. The Bedford

[1] Youngest daughter of the second Duke of Sutherland. She married in 1852 the present Duke of Westminster, and died in 1880.
[2] Goodwood House.
[3] See footnote, p. 128.

Hotel was witness to the *entente cordiale* between England and Russia, and we there partook of a second luncheon or, rather, dinner. At six we started for town, the others returning to Ryde, and reached Kew by about 9.30. Dined for the *third* time in the course of the day, and hurried to bed.

Cambridge Cottage, August 1.—I spent the greater part of the morning settling myself comfortably down and putting the finishing touch to the arrangement of my room. After luncheon I drove with Mama and Augusta to White Lodge ; we visited my Aunt's kitchen garden, and devoured quantities of gooseberries ! . . . *August* 5.—We had a perfect rout, as Aunt Mary and her party came over from Richmond, and Lady Caroline Cust, Lady Hardwicke, and Libbet drove down from town to see us. After they had left, we had a walk, and then did our hair before dinner at eight, dressing afterwards, and starting at ten for Mr. Henry Greville's.[1] The concert was beautiful. Mario, Grisi, and Bosio, all in high force, and the music well chosen. . . . *August* 6.— . . . Shortly after twelve the Crown Prince and Princess of Würtemberg arrived. The latter is *un peu passée*, but still very good-looking, and her manners most taking. They went on to the White Lodge to lunch, where we joined them. . . . A quiet evening, with a good deal of laughter and fun over some new songs. *August* 8.— . . . Mama left for the dinner at the Palace in honour of Olga,[2] and to console myself for the loss of the rest of the party, I put Doppus to bed and afterwards took a walk with Freieisen[3] in the twilight. . . . Had tea, practised a little, and went to bed early.

August 10.—We were off by nine o'clock to Chobham ; Count Perponcher[4] going with us in the carriage, and Knese on the dicky. . . . George had taken command for the day, and put us into a capital place on the top of a hill, behind the enemy, so that the troops manœuvred all round us and we saw everything. We lunched at Lord Seaton's, and then drove through the camp, passing by the Guards' tents, and paying Lord George Paget and Colonel Forester a visit in their tents. . . . *August* 12.— . . . Wrote to the Grand Duke,[5] as it was his birthday ; practised, and at four o'clock

---

[1] A brother of Mr. Charles Greville, who was Clerk of the Council under George IV., William IV., and Victoria, and of Mr. Algernon Greville, Private Secretary to the Duke of Wellington.

[2] The Crown Princess of Würtemberg, *née* Grand Duchess Olga of Russia, afterwards Queen of Würtemberg.

[3] Dresser to the Duchess of Cambridge.

[4] Prussian Minister at the Court of St. James's.

[5] Grand Duke of Mecklenburg-Strelitz.

set off with the Baron for a six miles' walk, going up to
the Star and Garter to see Marie Hamilton, and coming
home by the Park. . . . After dinner we drove to town for
Bruno's concert in honour of the two Russian sisters. Olga
disappointed me ; . . . she was dressed à l'Espagnole. Marie [1]
only appeared at a distance in the green-house, but we paid
her a visit while at tea. We did not get home till two
o'clock, owing to Olga's keeping us waiting at the beginning
of the evening.

Letter to the Honble. Ellinor Napier.

Cambridge Cottage, August 20, 1853.

. . . I lose no time in writing to you to say that our
departure is definitely fixed for Monday, when we proceed
to Drumlanrig on a visit. Thence we go to Hamilton for
a week, and on to Eglinton Castle for a few days, and we
are to be at Edinburgh on the 6th of September. We
shall remain there a short time, to see all that is worth
seeing, and then post away on the 10th to Taymouth,
finishing up with a visit to Scone. That is at present the
plan of our journey, or rather tour, and I lay it before you
with the intent that you should meet us somewhere if
possible—for instance at Edinburgh, where you might perform the part of cicerone with great effect. I, however,
still indulge a secret hope that you may be asked to the
Buccleuchs'. Augusta and her dear little boy are at present
with us, and intend accompanying us to Scotland. . . .

Journal.—Cambridge Cottage, August 22.—Up at 5.30 !
Breakfasted at half-past seven, and were off before eight for
the Euston Square Station, where George put us into our
carriage. We had ten hours and a half of rail before reaching
Thorn-Hill Station, where the Duke [2] received us, and we
arrived at the Castle in about half an hour, whither he had
preceded us. The Duchess insisted on our dining with them
en robe de voyage, as our luggage could not arrive till rather
late. We were eleven at dinner, and spent a quiet evening,
being rather tired.

Drumlanrig Castle, August 23.—After breakfast we walked
up and down on the terrace, and at 12.30 started for a
walk, beginning with the gardens, then climbing up the

[1] The Grand Duchess Marie of Russia had married Prince Romanowski,
Duke of Leuchtenberg.

[2] The Duke of Buccleuch.

opposite hill, to get a very pretty view, and also in search of wild raspberries. In the afternoon we took a charming drive along the Duchess's walk overlooking the Nith, and made the complete circuit of the hills surrounding the Castle, for the sake of different views. Our party was joined in the evening by the two Custs and a Captain Higginson,[1] and we played at curling. *August* 24.—At breakfast we found two new-comers in Mr. and Lady Louisa Oswald. . . . Prepared for the expedition up Cairn Kenna, and started shortly before one o'clock in carriages. We drove to the foot of the Cairn; the rest of the ladies then mounted their ponies, but I walked, and at the steepest part was *dragged* up by the gentlemen by means of a leathern strap. The view from the top was very grand, though Arran was lost in a mist. We all walked down again, and had a picnic luncheon at the foot of the hill, which was capital fun. On our drive home we inspected a farm. We were twenty at dinner, including the Weimars and Sir James Fergusson. In the evening we played at curling.

August 25.—A wet day! Consequently, we ladies sat in the *grand commun* with our work. . . . Practised at curling under Mr. Fletcher's direction; after lunch the curling was resumed till half-past four, when, clad in linsey-wolsey and waterproofs, we walked down the kitchen garden, and made an invasion on the gooseberry bushes; then to the gardener's house, where we fell upon the scones and oat cake. On our way back we visited Jenny Melrose and another cottager.

August 26.— . . . Had two games at curling with the gentlemen, then looked at the Duchess's rooms, and at three o'clock sat down to a luncheon-dinner. As the weather had somewhat cleared up, we went out on the terrace for a little while; and a little later, to our great regret, left the Castle. The Duke took us a charming drive along the Nith to the station, and at half-past five we were off, the Weimars going with us the whole way, but the Oswalds got out at their own place. At ten o'clock we reached Hamilton, and were conducted to our Gobelin rooms, had a *petit souper*, and hurried to bed.

Hamilton Palace,[2] *August* 27.—At twelve o'clock we sat down to a *déjeûner dînatoire.* . . . The Duke brought out a perfect curiosity shop of fine things to show us. Marie and a Marquis Rostin sang. In the afternoon we drove to

---

[1] Now General Sir George Higginson.
[2] The seat of the Dukes of Hamilton.

Bothwell Castle, a beautiful ruin overhanging the river, which we explored in a pouring shower. We then went over the house itself, which belongs to a Lord Douglas, and seems very nice and comfortable. . . . We were eighteen at dinner, my neighbours being Lord Eglinton and Mr. Norman. Afterwards we played at " Post." *August* 28.—Attended morning service at the Episcopalian Church; the singing was particularly good. . . . At four o'clock we braved the storm and drove to Chatelherault, but the rain came on so heavily that we could only see the " Pavilion " itself and the Duke's kennels. . . . In the evening we turned tables and hats. *August* 29.—After breakfast there was a great deal of music and singing, in which the French Marquis bore a principal part. . . . We drove to Wishaw, Lord Belhaven's place; his Lady did the honours, and, after giving us some tea, she took us to the garden, which is charmingly situated. We reached home again at dressing-time. Most of the authorities at Glasgow had been asked to dinner, so that we were thirty-seven in number. I sat next to Lord Northampton and Sir Archibald Alison, the historian. We had a capital ball of about 140 people, which we kept up till past three o'clock.

August 30.—A late breakfast at twelve, after which some Tyrolese minstrels sang to us very prettily in the gallery, or throne room. At two o'clock we started in shut carriages, as it poured, for Calderwood, Sir William Maxwell's place, where we found a party invited to meet us. We were promenaded from room to room and back again; then regaled with Miss ——'s moderately good singing; and, lastly, treated to the " German chorus," in which we ourselves were constituted chief performers! Finally, we departed. . . . The drawing-rooms at Calderwood were very pretty indeed, and the place itself must be quite beautiful on a fine day. On our return I went up to the children, and sat with them at their supper. At dinner I was placed between Lord Henry Lennox and Henry Murray.[1] In the evening we played at curling. *August* 31.—A fine day for a wonder! We went to see the Mausoleum and the garden, close to which stands the "carousel" imported from France, in which we rode till it made us feel quite uncomfortable. After luncheon we made an expedition into the bowels of the earth, to inspect the coal-pits; the road winding along the banks of the Avon was exquisitely picturesque. Thence we proceeded to the meadows near Chatelherault, to see the white buffaloes, and passing the remains of the Caledonian Forest,

---

[1] Brother of the sixth Earl of Dunmore.

went to the ruin of Cadzow Castle. . . . We sat down a party of thirty to dinner. In the evening the Maxwell family gave us some music, and "The Piccadilly Mob" was recited by Sir William.

The remainder of this Scotch tour is unrecorded, and the Journal is not again resumed until the return of the Princess and her mother to Kew some weeks later; but Mrs. Dalrymple, who duly performed the part of cicerone at Edinburgh, recalls:

I met the Duchess of Cambridge and her daughter at the Douglas Hotel, and we went all through the old town together, visiting the different public buildings. Princess Mary was especially interested in the Advocates' Library and Donaldson's Hospital for the deaf and dumb, where she was much amused by the matron telling her that the children, as soon as they knew how to speak a few useful sentences, ought to prove valuable servants, because they would never be able to gossip. With this view the Princess agreed, but remarked that they might be able to gossip with the pen! Another day Roslin and its chapel and Hawthornden were visited. We also drove out to Dalmeny, and had lunch there.

Letter to a Friend.

Cambridge Cottage, October 15, 1853.

We are leading a very quiet life just now, diving into the pages of Macaulay's History and Lamartine's "Girondins," by way of study, and feasting on the recollections of our Scotch tour by way of recreation. The journey was, indeed, very enjoyable, and I delighted in Scotland with its picturesque *underground* scenery—for we did not penetrate far into the Highlands, so that we failed to see any of the wild parts—its Castles and Palaces, and above all its Capital. Edinburgh is, indeed, one of the finest cities from an architectural and picturesque point of view I have ever seen. Arthur's Seat, immediately above, and the Calton Hill, and the Castle, rising, as it were, out of the City, present magnificent features to the eye. The old part of Edinburgh, which looks as if it had stood there from time immemorial, and reminds me very much of Nuremberg and other old German towns, is curiously interesting. We spent several days at Edinburgh, which formed a break in the midst of our visits, for with this exception we went from one nobleman's seat to another, and as there was a party at every place to meet us, we got rather tired of for ever doing the agreeable. However, I thoroughly enjoyed myself, and am sure we are all most grateful for the great kindness and attention we met with everywhere.

Since I last wrote to you, my old friend, Elizabeth Egerton, has entered the holy state of matrimony; her marriage with Captain de Ros, Lord Ros's only son, took place at Heaton, on the 12th of this month. Ellinor Napier, my other great friend, is also about to follow her example, and is to be married on the 10th of November to Mr. Dalrymple, second son of Lord Stair. So, you see, I shall very soon be an "old maid." . . .

Journal.—Cambridge Cottage, October 24.—Up at seven o'clock and went to dear Gussy's room, where we had a last and very sorrowful breakfast together. At half-past ten we bade her farewell, and Mama and I wandered about the Park for three hours, each with a book, picking violets and feeding the goat. . . . The King of the Belgians, with his two sons and daughter-in-law,[1] a blooming rosebud, arrived; after they had left we had tea, and Knese read the second volume of Larpent's "History of the Duke of Wellington." . . . In the evening we played bowls, and I read poetry aloud. *November 5.*—On coming out of my room I was greeted with, " Remember, remember, etc.," and had a good view of the Guy Fawkes drawn up opposite the passage windows. When the boys had shouted the stanzas, I practised with Colonel Stephens, piano and violin, then lunched and walked with Mama to gather violets; after which we sat in the dark looking at and enjoying the bonfire—a glorious one !

Letter to the Honble. Ellinor Napier.

Cambridge Cottage, November 6, 1853.

MY DEAREST ELLINOR,—Many thanks for your dear kind letter. And so this is the last time I am to address you as Ellinor *Napier.* . . . You cannot think *how* heartily I sympathise with and feel for you "in weal and woe," and therefore at this moment my thoughts are oftener present with you than

---

[1] The Duchess of Brabant, now Queen of the Belgians, a daughter of the late Archduke Joseph of Austria. She married (August 22, 1853) Prince Leopold of Belgium, who succeeded his father as King in 1855.

H.R.H. Prince George of Cambridge
at the age of 8.

H.R.H. Princess Augusta of Cambridge
at the age of 6.

From miniatures at Gloucester House.

ever. I shall think of, and pray for you, darling, on the eventful day. . . . And I must beg of you to reserve me a wee bit of your bridal wreath, if it be divided among the brides-maids; indeed, I claim it as a *right* in virtue of my being your *oldest, nearest,* and *dearest* friend! . . . I have but little more to say—and that refers principally to your dear mother, for whom I feel more than I can express. Pray tell her so, with my kindest love; and now God bless you, my darling Ellinor, my *childhood's* friend, and may every earthly blessing and all happiness be showered upon you, and remember that whenever, upon your arrival in London, you feel inclined to wend your way down to Kew, you will be received with open arms by your fond and affectionate friend,

MARY ADELAIDE.

Journal.—Windsor Castle, November 16.—We reached here at seven. I sat next Lord Waterpark and Colonel Grey[1] at dinner, and played patience with Aunt Kent in the evening. *November* 17.—Breakfast at 8.45, and sat talking with the Queen in the breakfast-room till ten o'clock, when we went out with her, and on our way back paid a visit to Frogmore. . . . The rest of the morning was spent in writing letters and talking to Aunt Kent. Luncheon over, the Queen, Albert, and I took a stroll, and were home by 4.30, when the three eldest girls came and played to us, and we had a romp; at a quarter to six I began to dress, as we dined at 6.45. My neighbours were Lord John Russell[2] and Sir Charles Wood.[3] After dinner we had the play—two farces, *Speculation* and *Little Toddlekins,* in which Charles Matthews was principal performer. I enjoyed it very much indeed. *November* 18.— . . . We retired to our rooms till 11.30, when we had a

---

[1] Colonel the Honble. Charles Grey, Private Secretary to the Prince Consort, and afterwards Equerry and Private Secretary to the Queen.

[2] Third son of the sixth Duke of Bedford. He was 47 years a member of the House of Commons, and twice Prime Minister. On Sir Robert Peel's resignation in 1846 the task of forming an Administration was entrusted to Lord John Russell, who carried on the affairs of the country till 1852. During Lord Aberdeen's Government (1852-5) Lord John led the Lower House, first as Foreign Secretary, then without portfolio, and lastly as President of the Council. He was raised to the peerage as Earl Russell in 1861, and on the death of Lord Palmerston (1865), was again summoned to form a Cabinet, but in the year following he was defeated on the Reform Bill, and retired from public life. He died in 1878 at Pembroke Lodge, Richmond Park.

[3] President of the Board of Control. After filling many important offices in the Government he was created a peer, with the title of Viscount Halifax.

short walk with the Queen, and at twelve drove to see the hounds hunt a *hare*. . . . The Aumales[1] came to luncheon. . . . In the course of the evening the little Duchess of Brabant paid me a visit, and we sang and played together. Alas! in the midst of our fun I learned the sad intelligence that the Duke of Beaufort and Sarah Esterhazy[2] were *no more*. . . . At dinner I sat next to Lord Abercorn; afterwards we all played at "vingt-et-un." *November* 19.—We saw the Duchess of Brabant's picture by Ross,[3] and went with the Queen to her room to say good-bye. Then we started by train for Richmond, and reached Kew soon after twelve. I immediately wrote my letters of condolence, and in the afternoon sat working in Mama's room while she read to me.

Cambridge Cottage, November 21.— . . . I joined Mama and Hooker in Gardens, where we walked about for up-wards of two hours, selecting shrubs and plants for our own garden. . . . We drove to Lady Alice Peel's[4] to luncheon, the party consisting of the Colloredos, Mr. Reeve,[5] and a *Turk*. The luncheon was on a grand scale, but we were nearly frozen to death with cold. . . . *November* 27, *Sunday.*— My 20th birthday! I received my presents before breakfast, to which George and Stephens came down. After church Mrs. Barry arrived. . . . At six, Mama and I drove to town to see Aunt Mary, and we went on to George's to dinner. We were a small party of twelve, and I sat between George and Lord Mandeville. *December* 7.—Breakfasted in my own room, and at eleven o'clock was pleasantly surprised by the arrival of the painter, Mr. Wells, who came to take a rough sketch of me; this lasted for over an hour, then I went out into the garden and trotted about till luncheon-time. In the evening we played bowls, and Knese began to read us the novel called "Mary of Burgundy."

---

[1] The Duc and Duchesse d'Aumale. He was the fourth son of Louis Philippe, and she the daughter of the Prince de Salerno, a Neapolitan Prince, who married the Archduchess of Austria, sister to Marie Louise, the wife of Napoleon I. At this time the Duc and Duchesse d'Aumale were living at Orleans House, Twickenham.

[2] Eldest daughter of the fifth Earl of Jersey, and wife of Prince Nicholas Esterhazy, son of the eminent Austrian diplomatist.

[3] Sir William Ross, who painted many of the royal miniatures in the collection at Windsor Castle.

[4] Lady Alice Peel lived at Marble Hill, Twickenham. She was the daughter of the first Marquis of Ailsa, and wife of General Peel, a brother of the great Sir Robert Peel, and at one time Secretary of State for War.

[5] Editor of the *Edinburgh Review*, and compiler of the "Greville Memoirs."

Letter to the Honble. Mrs. Dalrymple.

Cambridge Cottage, December 11, 1853.

. . . I have entered into my new year overwhelmed with kindness from all sides. In honour of the day we dined at my kind brother's, to meet a few friends. My greatest treat, however, on that day was to see dear Aunt Mary quite herself again in looks and strength. Hers has been a most wonderful rally, and I am sure we ought to feel most particularly grateful to God for sparing her to us, at a time when so many of our friends are in the deepest affliction; for instance, the poor Beauforts and Jerseys. But I must not write you a melancholy letter, darling; on the contrary, it should only speak of your happiness, which I trust will daily become more real as you settle down into everyday life. And now I am going to ask you a favour! I am sitting for my picture for the collection of Miniatures at Windsor; and as this is no very pleasing task, I thought you might perhaps kindly take pity on me and "run away" to Kew some morning, when Mr. Dalrymple is on guard. It would be a real treat to me to see your dear face again, and would consequently call up the requisite smiles upon my own visage. If you say "yes!" I will send you a line to inform you of the days and hours the Painter has chosen. And now, ere I conclude, let me thank you for the much-treasured favour, and the wedding-cake, which proved most excellent! With much love and a kiss, dearie, then adieu! . . .

Journal.—Cambridge Cottage, December 12.— . . . In the afternoon we went out walking, and trotted from one glasshouse to the other in search of flowers to fill our vases with. I practised and read a little to Mama, and at half-past six went to dress for our *fête*—a grand dinner of twenty people to the Aumales! It went off very well indeed. *December* 17. —I sat to the painter from 11.30 till three, Mama and Knese keeping me company. Then lunched, after which the Queen's dressmaker tried on my gown, and I read with Mama till six o'clock, when I dressed for the dinner at the Duchess of Inverness's, where we sat down a party of twenty-three, my neighbours being the Duc d'Aumale and Lord Chelsea. There was a small party in the evening. *December* 20.—I remained in my own room all the morning writing to Mrs. Taylor and working. Mama lunched with me, and I then received Countess Colloredo in my own *sanctum*. At 4.30 the Duchess of Aumale and her Mother paid us a visit, after which I took my work to Mama's room, and she read the newspaper to me. George dined with us.

Letter to Mrs. Bridges Taylor.[1]

Cambridge Cottage, December 20, 1853.

MY DEAREST MRS. TAYLOR,— . . . I am delighted to find that you do not dislike your distant home, and that your house is so comfortable.   At the same time I really think it does you the greatest possible credit to *settle down* so happily and contentedly at Elsinore. . . . I hope the winter which has set in so very severely will not do you and little Emily[2] any harm. . . . The particulars you enter into respecting your new habitation interested us all very much indeed; I read your letter to Mama and Knesebeck at breakfast, the morning I received it, and we had a long talk about you afterwards. And now before giving some account of ourselves, let me wish you in the old standard, *John Bullish* way: "A merry Xmas and a happy New Year," with many many happy returns of them—and health and prosperity to you all ,in this and each succeeding year! . . . The visit of the dear King and Queen of Hanover in the course of the season was a great treat to us, and we kept the gaieties up gloriously till the last days of July. . . . For about a month after our return (from Scotland) to Kew we made up a happy family circle, George also honouring us with his presence; but alas! it broke up on the 24th of October, when Augusta left us to return to her northern home.   Since then our party has been again reduced to *three* individuals, who lead a very quiet and comfortable life with now and then a slight *dash* of *society* to enliven them.   Last month we were summoned to Windsor by *royal command*, when I had the opportunity of making the acquaintance of the young Duchess of Brabant, to whom I have taken a great fancy.   She is nice-looking, and very gay and cheerful when you get more acquainted with her. . . . Our thoughts are just now devoted to the preparations for Xmas; on Monday next, as the Day itself falls on a Sunday, we give a tree to the children of the servants, and a day or two later to the school-children.   Lord Palmerston's resignation[3] forms just now the chief topic of conversation

[1] See footnote, p. 147.
[2] Now Lady Alston.
[3] Lord Palmerston had accepted the post of Home Secretary in Lord Aberdeen's Administration, but finding himself in conflict with Lord John Russell's views on reform and foreign policy, tendered his resignation to the Prime Minister.   The difference in the Cabinet, however, was quickly settled, and Lord Palmerston continued at the Home Office till the Government went out in 1855, when he became Prime Minister.

everywhere; and no one seems to know who will replace
him! The last report says: that as Sir George Grey has
refused, Sir James Graham will give up the Admiralty to Lord
Panmure (late Fox Maule), and undertake the Home Office.
But all agree in thinking the Ministers rather *shaky*, and the
Conservatives are in good spirits. . . . Mama talks of spending a part of this winter in Town; we have consequently
been very busy hanging up pictures at St. James's. Knese
sends you his *love!* and hopes to hear from you soon. . . .
Mama joins with me in kindest remembrance to Mr. Taylor,
and much love to yourself and the children, and Believe me
ever, dearest Mrs. Taylor, your very affectionate

MARY ADELAIDE.

Journal.—December 24.—At four o'clock we began to
make our preparations for the exchange of presents; and as
soon as it was dark the *Bell*[1] summoned me to Mama's room,
where I found a little Christmas-tree on my present table.
I then read to Mama, and at seven we started for George's,
where a tree awaited us—a palm tree without lights, but
covered with bonbons, and quantities of presents. We were
not home till past twelve.

---

[1] A bell was always rung to summon the party into the Christmas-room.

CHAPTER VII.

A YEAR OF ANXIETY.

1854.

Visit to Hatfield—Home-life at Windsor—Prince Consort reviews the troops—War with Russia proclaimed—Letter on the Duke of Cambridge's appointment to a command—His departure for the Crimea —The Duke at Vienna—State opening of the Crystal Palace—Ascot races—A day at Frogmore—Grisi's farewell performance—Londoners at Kew—Letters from the Front—The cholera—Visit to Ashridge— News of Alma—Princess Mary's twenty-first birthday—Duke of Cambridge at Inkermann—The *Retribution* in a gale.

THE year 1854 was a memorable one for this country, and Princess Mary's patriotic spirit was thoroughly aroused when it became known that war with Russia could no longer be averted. She was most enthusiastic over the preparations for the approaching campaign, and hailed with pride and satisfaction the Duke of Cambridge's appointment to a command. But with all her military ardour, she would fain have seen peace maintained, for she realised acutely the terrible responsibility and individual suffering which war involved. The separation from her brother was a sore trial to her, and the months that followed his departure for the East were months of constant anxiety. The arrival of letters from the Duke was eagerly awaited by his mother and sister; copies were made and sent round to different members of the family, while Princess Mary, when writing to her friends, never failed to give them the latest accounts of "George." As the year wore on, the anxiety at Cambridge Cottage increased, and the Duchess and Princess

Mary remained at Kew during the winter months, to be in
closer touch with the various channels of information.

Journal.—Cambridge Cottage, January 1, 1854, *Sunday.—*A
happy New Year to us all! Church; we stayed for the Holy
Sacrament. . . . *January* 4.—Mr. Müller arrived unexpectedly,
and I played the piano with him from eleven till one o'clock,
when Mr. Wells was announced; he had been delayed three
hours by the snow, coming from London by rail. . . . Then
I took a walk with Knese, and we pelted one another with
snowballs! Read our new novel, "One in a Thousand,"
by James, which seems very interesting, in the evening.
January 7.—After breakfast we saw Mr. Hills,[1] to inquire
after the little Duchesse d'Aumale and the "Infant Prince," [2]
and I arranged my account-book with Knese. At one
o'clock we started for town, and stayed some time at St.
James's hanging pictures. . . . Dined with George, and
spent the evening at Aunt Mary's, where we found a nice
little party and splendid Twelfth Cake! *January* 13.—I
sat to Mr. Wells from eleven to one o'clock, when the
picture was pronounced "finished." . . . *January* 16.— . . .
We reached the King's Cross station by five, to go to Hatfield,
where we arrived shortly before six; were most kindly
received, and had tea in the drawing-room (King James's).
At dinner we sat down, a party of twenty-four, I next to
Lord Derby, and in the evening we danced till twelve.

Hatfield, January 17.—After breakfast at a quarter to
ten I went to King James's room, to hear the Montagu
girls [3] sing. Later on we drove out—five of us in the
Irish car—and saw the gentlemen start on their shooting
expedition. On my return I visited the "Ladies' Barracks."
Lunched at 1.30, then had a walk, and spent the rest of the
afternoon in getting up a chorus, "Viva la compagnie," for
the evening, and drinking tea in the library. We were
thirty-eight at dinner, and, after our chorus, which went off
grandly, we played *à des petits jeux. January* 18.— . . .
"We girls" amused ourselves singing and playing at billiards
till luncheon-time. Lady Salisbury [4] then showed me her

---

[1] Mr. Hills was medical attendant at Cambridge Cottage, and lived at
Richmond.

[2] The Duc de Guise.

[3] The Honble. Mary, the Honble. Harriet, and the Honble. Magdalen
Montagu, daughters of Lord Rokeby.

[4] Second wife of the second Marquis of Salisbury.

rooms, and carried me up to the nursery, where I had a good romp with the children. When tea was over, we all went upstairs, to rest and prepare for the earlyish dinner—seven o'clock. At half-past nine the county people began to arrive, and shortly afterwards the ball commenced. It was kept up with great spirit till past two. I enjoyed myself immensely, and danced eleven times. About six hundred people came. *January* 19.—A late breakfast! . . . We stayed in the drawing-room, conversing, singing, giving and collecting autographs till half-past one, when we took leave of our kind host and hostess, and returned by special train to town. On our way to Kew we called to see Aunt Mary, and met George and Lord John Russell there. . . .

St. James's Palace, January 26.—Arrived at St. James's, and at once began our arduous task of unpacking, settling, and arranging. I put my own room to rights, but was principally employed in Mama's rooms; it was not till four o'clock that we gave ourselves a respite to go and see dear Aunt Mary, take a flying peep at Ellinor Dalrymple, and pay Marie Hamilton a visit. We spent the evening at the Lyceum; the scenery in the extravaganza is wonderfully beautiful and quite fairy-like. *January* 31.—. . . On coming back from Aunt Kent's I tumbled into the dressmaker's, and soon after into Mr. Hutchinson's clutches! At one o'clock we went over to the St. James's Palace garden with Marie Hamilton and her children, Mrs. John Stanley, and Lady Georgina Bathurst,[1] and saw the Queen pass on her way to Parliament.[2] After walking up and down the garden we returned with Lady Georgina and drove to the Palace to see Her Majesty in her crown and train (not robes). At five o'clock we were at the House of Lords to hear the Debate. Lords Carnarvon, Derby, Clanricarde, Clarendon, Malmesbury, and Grey spoke; and we remained till eleven to hear Lord Derby. *February* 1.— . . . We proceeded to the new Paddington Station, and were at Windsor by seven. The Queen, Albert, and some of the children came to see us before dressing time. . . .

Windsor Castle, February 2.—Breakfasted at a quarter to nine, and went out walking with Victoria[3] and Alice directly

---

[1] Lady-in-Waiting to the Duchess of Gloucester.

[2] Her Majesty went in the customary procession to the House of Lords, but the circumstances of the occasion gave unusual interest to the ceremonial, and the park and streets were thronged with enthusiastic spectators.

[3] The Princess Royal.

afterwards ; we trotted down to Frogmore to see Aunt Kent, and then visited the kitchen garden, where the girls picked me a beautiful nosegay. . . . In the afternoon I walked with the Queen, Albert, and the two younger girls, as far as the new model farm. The little ones then took me to their room to hear Helena play. We dined at a quarter to seven, and the play (*The Tempest*) began soon after dinner ; all the characters were very well performed, and I was much interested and in part amused by it. *February 3.*— . . . My young cousins took me to Adelaide Cottage,[1] and to the kennels and poultry yard, where we fed the chickens. On my return I found Peppy waiting to see me ; she sat with me till one o'clock, when we went to the library, and Mr. Glover[2] showed us some prints of the three last Tudor sovereigns, and a collection of original drawings by Holbein, besides several miniatures. On our way to luncheon we saw the three Esquimaux that have lately come over—the first ever imported to this country. . . . At six the children played their pretty little operetta, *Les deux petits Savoyards,* in which they all acted wonderfully well. We dined at eight, and in the evening danced till midnight. *February 4.*—Left the castle directly after breakfast and were in town before eleven. . . .

St. James's Palace, February 5.— . . . After dinner I read aloud part of the *Times* epitome of the Turkish Blue Books, in eight columns! *February 11.*— . . . I helped Mama to stow away temporarily all her rare, fine old china in one of the cabinets, then took my music lesson, and after this there was a perfect *levée* of people. By four we were quite tired out, and after a snug little tea I began to read Macaulay to Mama. . . . We dined at George's, Lord Chesterfield and Lord Clanricarde, Marie Hamilton, the John Stanleys, and Lord Chelsea making up the party. *February 12, Sunday.*—We went to the Chapel Royal, and afterwards I walked with Mama and Knese in Hyde Park, to see the vulgar *monde ;* then paid Aunt Mary a long visit. On our way home we walked up Piccadilly. Tea, and I read till six in my own room ; when I went to Mama and found her deep in converse with poor Madame de Brunnow,[3] who was much affected on taking leave.

---

[1] The pleasure house on Virginia Water.

[2] The Queen's Librarian.

[3] Wife of Baron Brunnow, the Russian Ambassador. He first came to England in 1839 on a special mission relating to the Turco-Egyptian question, and at the end of the same year was accredited to the Court of St. James's as the representative of his Sovereign. This position he held uninterruptedly till July 7, 1854, when he was recalled to St. Petersburg, on account of the

Letter to Mrs. Bridges Taylor.

St. James's Palace, February 13, 1854.

. . . *War* and the Eastern Question are now the ruling topics of the day, and though I *pray* for *peace* you can imagine how warmly I am enlisted in my own country's cause. We are still in the greatest possible uncertainty respecting George, who has of course applied for a command; but his fate is still pending. On Saturday next the three Battalions of Guards, etc., are to embark for Malta (in all, they say, *10,000* men), preparatory to being sent on to Constantinople. Lord Raglan will have the command, but is not to go quite yet. I hear the Baltic Fleet, consisting of *20* sail of the Line, is the finest one that ever left our shores. . . .

Journal.—February 15.— . . . Shortly before two o'clock Albert came, and after luncheon we prepared for a visit from the Queen, who sat with us nearly three-quarters of an hour. At five Lady Caroline Cust arrived. . . . We dined at the Duchess of Inverness's, a party of thirty, and I sat next M. de Isturitz[1] and Lord Mandeville. In the evening there was an impromptu "hop." *February* 16.—We went out shopping, and after selecting a chandelier for the dining-room, visited the old part of the National Gallery, which I had never seen. The Secretary took us round, and we stayed some little time admiring the productions of the old Masters. On my return I wrote for the Madeira mail, but was interrupted by a farewell visit from Ellinor Dalrymple, and before I had quite finished my epistle, Princess Royal and Alice came with Miss Hildyard.[2] I then joined Mama at Aunt Mary's, where I heard the good news that George is to command the 1st Division[3] in the event of a war. Hurrah! We were home in time to receive Wales and Alfred, who arrived almost immediately afterwards with Mr. Gibbs,[4] and remained with us nearly an hour. . . .

hostilities pending between England and Russia. At the beginning of 1858 Baron Brunnow returned to his post in London, where he remained as Russian Ambassador until his retirement from diplomacy in 1875.

[1] The Spanish Ambassador.

[2] English governess to the Princesses.

[3] Writing to Baron Stockmar, Prince Consort says, "Twelve thousand men will be assembled in Malta within a few days. Lord Raglan received the command; the two Divisions will be led by George of Cambridge and General Browne."

[4] Mr. Frederick Gibbs succeeded Mr. Birch as tutor to the Prince of Wales in 1851, and continued to act in that capacity until his retirement in 1858; he died in 1898.

February 20.—Breakfasted punctually at ten, and then drove to the Wellington Barracks to see the Grenadiers and Fusiliers once more before they embarked for Malta. Albert reviewed them, and we followed down the lines. I hope we shall soon have them back again with fresh laurels to add to former ones! On my return, I studied my French lesson, and then had a very kind visit from Miss Coutts. After lunch M. Brasseur arrived, but I was called away from his lesson to take leave of Edward Weimar.[1] Brasseur was kind enough to stay till nearly six o'clock, and then I practised. I spent the evening with Aunt Mary playing "Casino." *February 26, Sunday.* — After Divine Service at the Chapel Royal, Mama and I walked through the Green Park to Gloucester House, and thence drove to the Palace, where we were joined by the Queen and her children in the garden. Albert took us to see the new ball and supper rooms, and galloped us over the new offices, which are now on a very grand scale.

March 4.—Called at Gloucester House ; Hawkins's [2] report was a little more satisfactory. . . . We dined at the Palmerstons', a party of twenty-three, and I sat between M. de Walewski and Lord Palmerston. In the evening there was a party, and the Hungarian band played. *March* 6.— . . . George took us to his apartments to see his canteen (the Queen's present) and his bed, table, and chairs. As Mama had a headache, and was obliged to lie down, I went to the Buckingham Gardens, where I played with the children and walked with the Queen. . . . *March* 6.—A shocking fog! We drove to Gloucester House and found Aunt Mary a little better; then enquired after Lord Londonderry, who had just *expired*. . . . Later on Countess Colloredo came to tell us that dear Princess Metternich was no more. . . . *March* 8.—George breakfasted with us, and I occupied myself writing letters of condolence till half-past two, when we left for Drury Lane, where we were to patronize the benefit for the soldiers' wives: we were *cheered* on entering, but the tragedy of *Virginius* was very badly acted. As soon as the performance was over we returned to Gloucester House, and found Aunt Mary on the sofa, *plaiting*, thank God! . . . Home by half-past six, when Mama finished Perthe's "Leben" to me, whilst I worked and wept over *Carolinen's letzte Lebenszeit!*

March 12, Sunday.—We attended church at St. Michael's,[3]

---

[1] Prince Edward of Saxe-Weimar was leaving for the Crimea.
[2] Medical attendant to the Duchess of Gloucester.
[3] St. Michael's Church, Chester Square.

as dear Mr. Harrison preached for the Scripture Readers, and on our return had a nice long visit of upwards of an hour from Count Gröben.[1] . . . Accompanied by Knese and Lord William Paulet, we walked in Hyde Park to see the world! it was very full and most amusing. After tea I read a sermon to Mama, and we dined with George, my neighbours being Lord Raglan and Jim. *March* 16.—After breakfast we arranged the drawing-room. . . . Augusta Gordon and her two daughters had tea with us; when they left we put the finishing stroke to our arrangements for the evening, and I read "Marguerite" to Mama. Our *first* little *dinner-party* in the new dining-room went off delightfully; fourteen *personales*. Lord Derby and Mr. Norman were my neighbours. A few people came in the evening. *March* 18.—After breakfast we went with Captain Stephens to the British Institution, where the modern artists are at present exhibiting, and coming back were caught in the rain. . . . At three we drove to Gloucester House, and on to Mr. Swinton's[2] studio, where many of our friends were to be seen. On our return the Queen paid us a visit.

March 25.—We saw George's picture by Mr. Crawley. . . . Paid Aunt Mary our accustomed visit, and took a short walk in the Regent's Park Gardens, where we had the amusement of watching a tender *tête-à-tête*. We dined at the Palace in honour of George's birthday, and there was a hop in the evening, which was very nice. *March* 26, *Sunday.*— Dear George's Birthday! He breakfasted with us, and we went to the Chapel Royal. . . . We had a little dinner-party of twelve for him; Lord Raglan and his son, Lord Burghersh, Kielmansegge, the three equerries, Quin, and our three selves.[3] *March* 27.— . . . At half-past four we drove to the House of Lords, to hear *the Message from the Queen proclaiming war*, which was delivered in *solemn silence!* . . . I heard that poor Parma[4] had been stabbed. *March* 31. —We drove down the Fulham Road, stopping at the nursery which used to be Mr. Knight's, but which is now Mr. Veitch's, and took a walk in some market-garden fields

---

[1] General Count Gröben, who had come over as special envoy from the King of Prussia, to urge the Queen to reconsider the proposals of Russia which had been rejected by the conference of Ambassadors at Vienna.

[2] Mr. James R. Swinton, who made a great reputation as a painter of portraits; he married the Honble. Blanche de Ros, daughter of the twentieth peer.

[3] The Duke of Cambridge always dined with his mother on his birthday, when His Royal Highness's equerries were invariably invited.

[4] The Duke of Parma was assassinated March 27, 1854.

beyond. At half-past four we had a kind of luncheon-dinner, and then went to the House of Lords to hear the debate on the Queen's Message, which I thought too personal and jocose! We were home again by nine and had a *stiff tea* downstairs.

Letter to a Friend.

St. James's Palace, March 31, 1854.

. . . Most gladly do I accept your congratulations on my dear brother's appointment, though now that the time for his departure is drawing near my heart somewhat fails me, and the military ardour which the departure and, previous to it, the splendid farewell review of the Guards, called up, is now exchanged for the feelings of a sister, about to part with her only brother for an indefinite period, perhaps for ever. I can quite enter into your feelings with regard to the war, and have hitherto anxiously hoped it might yet be averted. . . God grant our troops a speedy and glorious return, and may He watch over and guard our men. George is delighted at having a command. . . . My British heart quite glories in the noble spirit shown by our country on this occasion, and my only regret is that so many brave hearts must, I fear, cease to beat ere peace can again be restored. You will, I suppose, know that George will pass through Paris on his way to the East; he is, I believe, to accompany Lord Raglan, and will therefore start about the middle of next month, but nothing decided is known on the subject. . . . I hear talk of enlisting and forming more regiments, so as to be able to send out a very efficient force, which I am glad of. Poor Augusta is in no enviable position just now, as all the Mecklenburg family are complete *Russians.* My Cousin George, too, who married the Grand Duchess Catherine, is now in the Russian service, and will in all probability be opposed to George on the Balkans! . . .

Journal.—April 1.—Visited Mr. Wells's *atelier*, to see his pictures for the Exhibition; thence to Hyde Park, where we walked down Rotten Row, chaperoned by Knese. When I arrived home, I found Mrs. Layton, who had come to thank me for getting her boy (thanks to George) into the Bluecoat School. We dined early, and went to the Opera (opening night). *Guillaume Tell* was given, with Ronconi, Tamberlik, and a new singer, Mdme. Marai—*pas mal. April 2, Sunday.* —The weather was quite lovely, so we drove to Kew, and sat in the garden while I read the morning service to Mama.

After tea, I went to church; then we walked in the Botanic,[1] and Sir William Hooker gave us *lots* of flowers. We were not home again till nearly eight o'clock. *April* 7.— . . . We dined at the Palace, a farewell dinner to George! He and Sir John Burgoyne were my neighbours. All the children appeared.

April 9.— . . . George took us to his apartments[2] to see them once more before he leaves. Lady Suffield then came to me for a minute; also Jim Macdonald, to say good-bye, and Countess Colloredo. We drove to the Palace at half-past four, where I spent a couple of hours very pleasantly with the children. On our return home Lord Raglan came to take leave, and we dined with Lord Adolphus Fitzclarence in George's honour. Count Kielmansegge, Lord Stanley of Alderley, and Lord George Paget were the guests.

April 10.—A very sad day! At ten o'clock we went to the Palace to be *daguerreotyped* (photographed), previous to which the Queen took me for a walk. I did not return till past twelve. George joined us at Gloucester House, where we left him, and hurried back to see his servant (Dickens[3]), before they started. George ran in at seven o'clock for a few minutes on his way to Lord Adolphus's, where he dined; and Mama and I spent a *dreadful* hour watching for him to return to us for the *last adieu*, which he did at eight o'clock, and jumped into his brougham with Jim at ten minutes past. God Almighty bless and guard him! Knese went with him as far as Calais. *April* 11.—Breakfasted with Mama, after which I wrote some notes, packed and arranged my things, saw Clemmy (*en larmes pour cause*), and Lord William Paulet. We then went over to dear George's apartments, where I stole a dagger off his writing-table. . . . We reached Kew about half-past five.

Cambridge Cottage, April 14, *Good Friday.*—Breakfasted in my own room and read preparatory to taking the Holy Sacrament; we were in church from eleven o'clock till two. After luncheon I went out walking with Frazer in the Gardens, which were very full—7,270 people! *April* 19.— . . . I made up my account-book with Knese. . . . The little Shepherds[4] came to hide the eggs, and we took them into the King of Hanover's garden. At seven o'clock Mama and I walked in the Botanic, but were frightened by

---

[1] The Botanic Garden was then separated from the pleasure grounds, or arboretum, by a wire fence.

[2] The Duke of Cambridge had apartments in St. James's Palace.

[3] Now steward at Gloucester House.

[4] Children of a page in the service of the Duchess of Cambridge.

an impudent man and a very wild party! Aldridge [1] *escorted*
us home! Mama finished "Florence the Beautiful" to me
in the evening; the latter part of it is very interesting.
April 21.— . . . Count Kielmansegge came to tell us that
George had gone to Vienna. . . . At one o'clock we started
for Frogmore, and after luncheon, as the weather was
showery, sat in one of the summer-houses: the air was
loaded with perfume from the lilacs, and the garden was in
great beauty. On our return I read to Mama and finished
"Still-leben and Welt-leben" and "Marguerite." The Baron
interrupted us, to tell us that he had seen Major Purves in
town, and had arranged everything with him; so Mama has
an *equerry*!
    April 26.—The day of Humiliation and Prayer! [2] Morning
service with Form of prayer. . . . To church again in the
afternoon. *April* 27.—We started for St. James's at 11.30
and dressed there for the Drawing-room, which was a very
shabby one! Suffie and Hélène [3] came to see us in our
trains. We were home again by three. On our return to
Kew I read our new novel, "The Heir of Redclyffe," to
Mama. *April* 28.—I got up late, with a terrible cold, and
went for a walk with Frazer. At one o'clock we drove to
town for the opening view of the Royal Academy, with Suffie
and Colonel Stephens. The collection of pictures is greatly
inferior to the one last year. . . . Dined with Aunt Kent
and went to the French play—*L'Abbé de l'Epée* and *La Partie
de Piquet*—very good indeed. *Mama* applauded some verses
recited by Lafont.
    May 1.— . . . An early dressing, and at six o'clock we
drove to Gloucester House, to dine with Aunt Mary, and
then went to the children's ball at the Palace, which was
a very pretty sight, and lasted till nearly twelve o'clock.
May 4.—I had my music lesson with Müller, and read the
Times to Mama. Lunched, and walked up to William's
Lodge [4] in the rain; and thence drove to Twickenham, to
see the Aumales. When we got home we played at battledore and shuttlecock, and *hung pictures*. I read in the
Morning Chronicle about the Vienna *fêtes* and George's visit
there. In the evening there was a dance at the Granvilles',

---

[1] Foreman of the outdoor department at Kew Gardens, in which capacity
he had charge of the trees and shrubs in the Botanic Garden.

[2] This day was set apart to be observed as a day of prayer and supplication
for the success of our forces by sea and land.

[3] Daughter of Count Kielmansegge.

[4] In Richmond Park.

and we did not get home till after two. *May 5.—* . . . A
heavy shower kept us indoors till four, when we drove to
Richmond Park, to look at the hawthorns in full blossom!
It was quite lovely. We waited in anxious expectation
Colonel Phipps's[1] reply concerning the *Box*, which only
arrived just as we had finished tea. Dined with Aunt Mary,
and went to the Opera with the Wiltons, Mandevilles, and
Lord Colville: *Fidelio.* Cruvelli *cold*. Tamberlik beautiful!
May 11.—Mrs. Simpkins came to try on my ball dress;
wrote to Augusta. . . . After luncheon we started for Claremont, paid the Nemours a visit, and found the Aumales with
them. Thence we drove to Hampton Court, walked in the
garden and along the avenue; but the chestnut trees had
been destroyed by the frost. Mama gave a dinner to her
Court!—Suffie, Lady Caroline Cust, and Major Purves.
May 12.— . . . Left at five o'clock for St. James's, and
waited patiently for *two hours* for our ball dresses. We
were, however, dressed in time, and reached the French
Ambassador's before the Queen had arrived. . . . We stayed
till two o'clock, and I was *amused*.

Letter to Mrs. Bridges Taylor.

Cambridge Cottage, May 12, 1854.

. . . Knesebeck has given me your kind message of thanks,
which indeed I hardly deserve, as Mama prompted me to
write to the Queen on ——'s account. I now therefore
hasten, after thanking you most affectionately for your last
dear letter, to copy out for you the Queen's answer on the
subject: "I fear, my dear Mary, I cannot hold out much
hope for Mrs. ——, as the list of applicants (some of very
long standing) is *so* large; but I shall *not* forget her." This
is not very satisfactory, but yet I do not despair, for I think
she may yet be successful some time hence. I know Lady
——, who has lately got an *apartment* at Hampton Court,
applied for it through Aunt Mary *several* years ago, and had
almost given up all hopes of it when it was suddenly and
quite unexpectedly offered her. *Esperons donc*, and do not
let —— be too much cast down about it. . . . There is little
in the way of parties going on, and I imagine that the season
will be a very dull one. All eyes are at present directed to
Madame Walewska's *Bal Costumé*, which is to take place this
evening, and at which Her Majesty is to be present. We

---

[1] Second son of the third Lord Normanby; afterwards Sir Charles Phipps.
He was Keeper of the Queen's Privy Purse, and treasurer of the Household
to Prince Albert.

are going up for it, and you shall have a line to-morrow to say how it went off.

St. James's Palace, May 13.

True to my promise I hasten to tell you that the ball went off very well indeed. All the Royal Family were of course in *usual* dress, but I saw a great many fine costumes. There were four quadrilles. Lady Wilton's Spanish Quadrille—lovely! Lady Barrington's *Poudré* Quadrille; Lady Stanley of Alderley's Quadrille—Roses and Violets, in the dress of shepherdesses—pretty! Lady Waldegrave's Quadrille, *du temps de* Marguerite de Navarre—very rich, but out of character with the ball in general. The costume *poudré* predominated. I saw young Du Plat,[1] who has just taken his first waiting as Equerry to Albert. His father,[2] who has arrived from Warsaw, was also there.

Letter to a Friend.

Cambridge Cottage, May 16, 1854.

. . . We have been here ever since dear George's departure, and I think the country air and change of scene have done us all a deal of good, for the last few days of our stay in town were a sad trial. Each day one or more of our friends came to bid us good-bye, previous to starting for the East; and then came the terrible parting with dearest George. We *all* broke down at the last; and when the crowd gave him a parting cheer, it seemed to impress the fact more vividly on our hearts and minds that his destination was *War!* But the remembrance that God would watch over and protect him at all times, and, above all, in the hour of greatest need, comforted and lightened the trial. God grant unto *him*, and to our forces by sea and by land, a speedy and a glorious return.

His visits to Paris and Vienna have been most successful, and his reception at both places very gratifying. Louis Napoleon behaved with admirable tact and good judgment during George's stay in Paris, and the latter has a *very high opinion* of him. Lord Clarendon[3] has written two most kind

[1] Captain Du Plat, R.A., now General Sir Charles Du Plat, extra Equerry to the Queen.

[2] General Du Plat, Consul-General at Warsaw.

[3] Lord Clarendon had succeeded Lord John Russell as Minister of Foreign Affairs in 1853. He continued in the same office under Lord Palmerston [1855–8], and in Earl Russell's Administration [1865–6] was again Foreign Secretary, which post he occupied for the fourth time when Mr. Disraeli was Prime Minister in 1868.

letters to Mama, speaking in the most flattering terms of George, and informing her of the complete success of his missions. Who would ever have thought that George would distinguish himself in the *diplomatic* line? I had the last account from George, as he wrote to me from Trieste on the 2nd of this month, just before embarkation. He hoped to reach Constantinople on the 6th or 9th instant. His letter is written in good spirits, and is full of praise of the Emperor of Austria, who has quite won his heart. I hear George's visit has greatly contributed to the revival of the good old alliance between Austria and England. . . ..

Journal.—St. James's Palace, May 17.—Tried on my gown, after which we dined and dressed for the Queen's ball. I danced *nine* times, and we were home by two o'clock. *May* 19.—I was at my work before breakfast, and remained in my room the whole morning to finish the blotting-book for the Queen's birthday. . . . At 9 o'clock we went to the Palace, to hear the Cologne singers—quite beautiful; a small party. *May* 20.—Soon after breakfast the toilette for the drawing-room began. Mrs. Laumann, her sister, and Suffie came to see me *en grande tenue.* Being the Birthday Drawing-Room, it lasted till a quarter to four. From the Palace I went to show myself to Aunt Mary, then home, undressed, had tea, and hurried back to Gloucester House, where I had appointed Lord Bathurst to meet me and receive the screen which I had been working for him. . . .

Cambridge Cottage, May 24.—I had my usual music lesson from eleven till one, then went for a run with Mama. Marian Alford came in the afternoon, but she was obliged to leave early; so to console ourselves we *feasted* on *cream cheese !* Later we drove to town for a grand dinner of twenty-three at the Van de Weyers'; our host and the Duke of Newcastle [1] were my neighbours. In the evening we went to a charming ball at Lady Craven's, and did not get home till a quarter to three!

St. James's Palace, June 1.—We sat in Aunt Kent's garden, where Mama read letters and the newspaper to me whilst I worked. . . . At four o'clock we drove to Gloucester House, and made a *visitation* there, the Duchess of Kent and the Queen joining us. Dined at Lord Combermere's, and in the evening a Miss Thellusson recited à la Rachel, and we listened to some indifferent music. Then on to a very hot and crowded ball at Lady Hume Campbell's. *June* 3.—

---

[1] Secretary of State for War.

. . . Dined at seven to be in time for the opera—Grisi's *supposed last representation of Norma.* Her acting was quite *splendid;* the voice weak but good in parts. *June* 7.— . . . We went with Purves and Stephens to the Old Gallery of Watercolours, and in the evening to Lord Breadalbane's state ball, where I danced till nearly half-past two. The Queen was there.

June 10.—At 1.30 we accompanied Aunt Kent to Sydenham, where we waited three-quarters of an hour before the Queen arrived. As soon as we were under the canopy " God save the Queen " was sung by Novello and a splendid chorus under Costa's direction ; then came the Address and presentation of books, followed by a promenade round the building ; the prayer and Hallelujah, and " God save the Queen " once more sung brought the whole thing to a close. . . . Schlütter dined with us, and we adjourned to the Haymarket to see *The Knights of the Round Table* and *Buckstone's Journey round the World. June* 14.—Mr. Assheton Smith came to see us, and at four we drove to the Paddington station, and were at Windsor by half-past six. There was a grand banquet in St. George's Hall.

Windsor Castle, June 15.—We breakfasted at a quarter to nine, and at half-past twelve started for Ascot Heath in eleven carriages. I was in the third with Alice, Countess Walewska, and the Duchess of Sutherland. The weather was tolerably fine and the stands well filled. We were home again by half-past five, and in the evening there was a second grand banquet, at which the King of Portugal and the Duke of Beaufort were my neighbours. A ball in the Waterloo Gallery brought the day to a close. *June* 16.— Breakfast at the usual hour; after which we drove with the Queen to see the Blues reviewed in the Park near the Long Walk, and then proceeded to their Barracks; on our return the 46th (all Irishmen) was drawn up in the Quadrangle of the Castle and manœuvred before us. We took leave of the Queen and drove down to Frogmore, where we lunched. Reached town before five, and had a visit from dear Olivia Cowley;[1] dined with Aunt Mary, and in the evening, though Mama was far from well, we went on to the ball at Lansdowne House.

St. James's Palace, June 19.— . . . I received Lord Eglinton, Marie Hamilton, and the Ellesmere girls. The afternoon was spent at Gloucester House, where we met the Queen and Albert; and afterwards we took Lady Wilton

---

[1] Wife of Lord, afterwards Earl Cowley, British Ambassador at Paris.

to the Regent's Park Gardens to see the American plants
(a kind of show day). We dined at Lady Marian Alford's,
and I sat between the Duke of Wellington and Lord
Carlisle. In the evening there was a party at which ladies
preponderated, and Mario, Bosio, and Belletti sang, *mais la
musique trainait un peu.* *June 22.*— . . . We went out
shopping to Wardour Street in search of a sideboard, and to
Duke Street for china. . . . In the evening we were again at
the Opera—*Lucrezia Borgia* was given by Grisi for the last
time, they say, and one act of the *Barbiere* with Lablache
and Bosio.

June 23.—After writing to George we started for Kew,
where Knese joined us. . . . We worked assiduously at
the Rosary, and gathered plenty of flowers, returning to town
at half-past eight. *June 25, Sunday.*— . . . At five we went
to Aunt Mary's, and found her *tête-à-tête* with the Duchess of
Buccleuch, and thence to the Kensington Gardens, where
we promenaded with *le beau monde.* We dined with Aunt
Kent to meet Her Majesty, a party of twenty, which included
the King of Portugal, who sat next to me. *June 28.*—
Eleventh anniversary of Gussy's wedding-day! After a late
breakfast I practised, as Mama went with Aunt Kent to
Claremont. . . . I was at the Palace by a quarter to six, to
accompany Her Majesty on her drive—*very pleasant* indeed.
We dined at Lord Derby's, and went on to Lady Ashburton's [1]
ball.

June 30.— . . . In the afternoon the Somerset girls [2] and
Arabella West came to see me. . . . We dined with the
Westminsters, a party of twenty, and at eleven o'clock
went on to the Duchess of Inverness's ball, which was completely spoilt thanks to the Duchess of Sutherland's *dance!*
and was quite a *bear garden.* *July 1.*—I spent the morning
arranging the rooms for the party, and stripped my own room
of pretty well everything in honour of the other rooms. At
half-past three we started for Ealing, but Mrs. Lawrence's
breakfast was anything but amusing, as we found but few
acquaintances there. We were home again about seven,
and went to the Opera to hear *Don Pasquale.* Lablache
perfect, Grisi very good, Ronconi and Mario ditto! *July 3.*—

[1] Lady Ashburton was widely known for her hospitality, and great social
qualities. She gathered around her, both at Bath House and at her country
residence, the Grange, Alresford, the chief literary men and women of the
day, and was an intimate friend of Thomas Carlyle. Her younger sister was
the first wife of Count Walewski.

[2] Lady Henrietta and Lady Geraldine Somerset.

. . . Our dinner of 24 *personnes* in honour of Aunt Kent went off beautifully, my neighbours being Lord Westminster and Count Colloredo. The two drawing-rooms looked lovely, and at eleven we dispersed and went to Lady Breadalbane's ball, at which I danced till dawn!

July 4.—I woke with a headache, and poor Mama was ill nearly all day and nursed herself for the evening; so that I breakfasted in my own room, and then arranged the rest of the rooms for the evening party. Aunt Mary and Lady Caroline Murray came to see them about four, and everything being complete I had a nap till it was time to dress, when I found Mama much better. Our second dinner of twenty-four went off as well as the former one. I sat next to Lords Clarendon and Breadalbane. The evening party of 350 people was not too crowded, and the suite of rooms, I believe, was greatly admired. *July* 6.— . . . Dined with the Jerseys, and in the evening went to the Ellesmeres' and danced in the hall at Bridge-water House. *July* 9, *Sunday.*—Attended Divine service at the Chapel Royal, after which ˙Mama had a visit from a Florentine sculptor. At three o'clock I had *mon petit diner*, Mama eating to keep me company! . . . About seven we had a very jolly young ladies' tea-party of nine, which lasted till nearly eleven o'clock.

July 10.— . . . At a quarter to four Mama and I *dined*, and at half-past were at Gloucester House for the juvenile *fête* given to the Queen's children. It went off most successfully, and the children danced till past seven, when we hurried home to dress for the French play, and saw Madame Cabel in *Les Diamants de la Couronne. July* 13.—Spent the day at Kew, where, as usual, we worked away at the rose trees till four o'clock, when we had dinner, and afterwards went into the great garden for some flowers. Home in time to go to the Olympic Theatre, where we saw the Wigans in *The Jealous Wife.* Hélène Kielmansegge, Lord Forester, Chotek,[1] and Mr. Norman came to our box. *July* 17.—A very busy morning! I wrote my French exercise, tried on my gown for a second time, and was ready for M. Brasseur at half-past twelve. . . . After trying on my gown for the *third* time, I joined Mama, and we went with Charlotte Lyster[2] and Libbet Yorke to the Botanic Gardens. We dined at

---

[1] Count Chotek, Councillor at the Austrian Embassy.
[2] Lady Charlotte Lyster, daughter of the sixth Earl of Shaftesbury. She married Mr. Henry Lyster, of Rowton Castle, Shropshire.

Miss Coutts's to meet the young Rajah[1]—a party of forty-six. Lords Bruce and Mandeville were my neighbours, but most of the guests were unknown to us, and in the evening, after having heard *La Tort*, and a little Portuguese boy sing, we went on to Lady Rokeby's ball.

July 18.— . . . We started for the Euston Square Station, where we joined a large party of about fifty, and steamed off to Moor Park, Lord Robert Grosvenor's[2] place. From the Watford station, Victoria Grosvenor drove me in her pony phaeton to the house; whence we walked up, in a broiling sun! to the top of a hill, and had a *cold collation* under a tent. Returning to the house I took a peep at the rooms, the *hall* and large dining-room both being particularly well worth looking at; Oggy[3] then drove me, in her straw phaeton with four donkeys abreast, to the kitchen garden and lodge, where we had coffee and tea, and danced and played *aux petits jeux*, the elders joining. We reached town shortly after ten o'clock.

Cambridge Cottage, July 23, *Sunday.*—A heavenly morning! After morning service I put away some of my things, and joined Mama in the garden under the chestnut tree; the heat was intense, but we sat in the garden all the afternoon, and went out again after dinner. *July* 25.—In honour of the day I awoke dear Mama at eight with a *clove!*[4] When she had received her birthday presents we sat down to breakfast, and then established ourselves in the drawing-room, as that was the coolest place. In the course of the afternoon visitors *poured* in. . . . We sat out in the garden, and Katty and I enjoyed a nice long *tête-à-tête*. We were a party of eleven at dinner, the Lysters, Redesdales, Lord Forester, and Quin making up the number—a charming evening. Thus ended a very happy day. *July* 26.—In the afternoon we started for the Richmond station, and reached Frogmore soon after 4 o'clock. The *déjeûner dinatoire* in honour of Mama's birthday took place at five, the Van de Weyers, Bruces, Cowpers, and Colonel Hood[5] being the guests; we then adjourned to the garden, where we had

---

[1] The Maharajah Dhuleep Singh.

[2] Lord Robert Grosvenor was the third son of the first Marquis of Westminster. He was sometime Groom of the Stole to the Prince Consort, and married a sister of the first Earl Cowley. In 1857 he was created a peer, with the title of Baron Ebury.

[3] The Honble. Victoria Grosvenor.

[4] Clove carnations were very favourite flowers with the Duchess of Cambridge.

[5] Now Lord Bridport.

coffee and *danced*, the band of the Blues being in attendance. Their gallant colonel did not get his card of invitation till too late! At eight o'clock the party broke up, and Aunt Kent accompanied us to the station.

July 27.— . . . We drove up to town for the Opera. *Lucrezia Borgia* was given; Grisi was in very good voice, but poor Mario was taken suddenly hoarse, and quite unable to sing the last act, in consequence of which the audience got up a *row*, and would not suffer the orchestra to play the overture to *Othello*. At last the people were pacified, and the next piece, *La Proba d'une Opera seria*, came off quietly. Lablache was perfection in it, and Grisi sang (to *calm* the public mind) an air out of *Anna Bolena. August* 1.— . . . We arrived just before two o'clock at the Foleys',[1] and the *photographing* process began at once. Suff[2] and Lady Mandeville were the only other guests, and after a snug little luncheon we were photographed *en groupe;* and, lastly, Louise[3] and I together, looking out of a window. At four o'clock we went over to the Wiltons', to congratulate the whole family, *rayonnant de bonheur*. Dudley, Grey, and Alice[4] took me to see the tiny baby,[5] which lay in Katty's arms. We then returned to Kew in a pouring shower, but as the weather cleared up I went into the garden, and weeded away in my new brown Spanish hat.

Letter to a Friend.

Cambridge Cottage, August 3, 1854.

. . . I am very much rejoiced to find myself down here again, and away from the noise and bustle of London. The season has not been a gay one, although balls have been very numerous; indeed, how could it be otherwise, if we consider how many of those nearest and dearest to us are absent, and that in a cause of danger? We are leading a regular country life down here, and spend the greater part of the day in the garden, reading, working, or *weeding*, which is a very favourite occupation of mine. . . . I cannot, however, say that Kew is a particularly *quiet* place in summer, as thousands of people flock down to the Gardens, and I am

---

[1] Lord and Lady Foley.
[2] Lady Suffield.
[3] Lady Mandeville, daughter of Comte d'Alten of Hanover; she became Duchess of Manchester August 18, 1855, and is now Duchess of Devonshire.
[4] Lady Alice Grey Egerton.
[5] The only child of the Honble. Dudley and Lady Elizabeth de Ros.

just now regaled with the shouts of a hundred school children, who are having a treat in the Gardens and on the Green. This seems quite the rage now, for nearly every day some school from London, or its environs, is transported hither in vans, or steamboats. The Duchess of Buccleuch is at her Villa at Richmond, but too unwell to see any one. . . .

Journal.—Cambridge Cottage, August 7.—A lovely day. After breakfast we took Du Plat for a walk, and wandered all over the Houses and Gardens. On our way home we were met by Mr. Hutchinson, and went with him to see the Victoria Regina[1] in blossom; then established ourselves in the garden, as it was too fine to go indoors. We dined at six, and drove up to town for Grisi's *farewell performance.* The first act of *Norma* and three acts of *Huguenots* were given. Grisi and Mario were *beyond,* and the house rose to give her a last cheer. We threw her *our* bouquets, and she must have received a hundred! She left the stage much affected—almost in tears. Home by half-past one. *August* 11.—At breakfast we learned the sad news of the King of Saxony's death. . . . We sat in the garden, and I began to weed at a great rate. At five we drove to the White Lodge, and as Aunt Mary had not returned from the Crystal Palace, Miss Sneyd joined us, and we transmitted our weeding mania to the Liddell children! After dinner Knese began reading Mrs. Beecher Stowe's "Travels" to us. (There was a cricket-match on the Green, at which Kew lost.)

August 16.—Before breakfast I had a run, and at eleven Walbaum arrived and read Stein's "Memoirs" to us while we worked. . . . We dined at Lord Adolphus Fitzclarence's, Lord Canterbury and Mr. Norman making up the party, and afterwards went to the Haymarket to see the Spanish dancers, who are very good indeed; between the dances we had *As like as Two Peas,* which would be all the better for a little curtailing. *August* 18.— . . . We had dinner at half-past six, and went to *Cremorne,* where Lord Adolphus and Mr. Norman met us. We were quite *incog.,* and enjoyed the monkey performance, horsemanship, fireworks, and looking on at the dancing very much. We left at a *respectable* hour, and were home by half-past twelve. *August* 22.—Lady Georgina Bathurst arrived to escort me up to town, and, accompanied by Knese, we were at St. George's by half-past twelve for the christening. Lady

---

[1] See p. 36.

Wilton received me at the Vestry door, and I held the baby [1] with *composure* and *courage!* I then drove to the Wiltons' in the *family coach* with the young de Roses, and as it was early the Montagus, Katty, and Grey sang till luncheon time. We sat down a party of twenty, and afterwards chatted till four, when I returned to Kew with Lady Georgina, where we found Aunt Mary sitting with Mama.

August 24.— . . . I read the newspaper and *Edinburgh Review* to Mama in the garden, and we had a good laugh. About five we went out driving, and got out at Lord Dysart's Avenue; after being civilly refused admittance to his garden, we were invited into Mrs. Fitzgerald's pretty garden and boudoir. *August* 26.— . . . We drove to Wimbledon to see Mrs. Marryat.[2] The old lady received us very graciously, and after sitting with her for some little time, a friend took us into the garden, which is very tastefully laid out, though to see it in its *glory* one ought to come when the roses are in bloom. We reached home about half-past seven, having met the Maharajah! on our way back. *September* 1.—Walked and breakfasted, after which I read "Eine Abendnachts Betrachtung" to Mama, and we had a long talk on serious subjects. I then made some alterations in my bookshelves. After luncheon Lady Ailesbury arrived, and we had an agreeable visit from Lady Truro. When she left we drove in the *pony phaeton,* and on our way home called at Chiswick, but unluckily the Duke [3] was at dinner.

September 4.—A very dissipated day! Immediately after breakfast . . . M. de Gersdorf [4] arrived and gave us all the particulars of the poor dear King of Saxony's death and funeral, and talked most agreeably till one o'clock, when he left, and Mrs. Cockerell was announced: next came Knese to bid us adieu before leaving for Amport, and, last of all, we for the hundredth time altered the what-nots. . . . We took the dressers over to the Cambridge Asylum. I peeped in at some of the old women's rooms, and walked home by the fields at Coombe. In the evening I began reading "The Earl's Daughter" to Mama, but nearly fell asleep over it. *September* 7.—Immediately after breakfast we started for Harrow, where Lord Rokeby met us and took us on to

[1] See footnote, p. 193. The child was named Mary after Princess Mary, who was her godmother.

[2] Mrs. Marryat's flowers had a great reputation.

[3] The Duke of Devonshire.

[4] M. de Gersdorf had come over to announce the death of the King of Saxony to the Queen.

Hazelwood, a twelve-mile drive, with his own horses. On arriving there we found the Richard Grosvenors[1] with their son and daughter; Grey and Lady Clarendon soon after joined us. After sitting a little out-of-doors, overlooking the garden, which is lovely, we had an early dinner, then went over the house and into the garden, where we assembled round a tea and coffee-table. . . . We returned to Kew by half-past nine.

Letter to Mrs. Barry.

Cambridge Cottage, September 1, 1854.

. . . Pray accept my best thanks for your kind letter and the hope or rather wish you cherish of seeing me one day Empress of ——, but I honestly confess I am *too* fond of my English home ever willingly to resign it for any other. . . . That home is now in great beauty, and we have been enjoying this lovely weather of all things, and have been leading an *out-of-doors* life. Dear Aunt Mary is our neighbour at Richmond Park, and scarcely a day passes without our meeting. She is wonderfully well, thank God, and enjoys her country drives immensely; she has even been twice to the Crystal Palace, and went all over it in her garden-chair. . . . Our plans are to stay a few days next week with Lady Marian Alford, and to pay some visits in Lancashire in October. Meantime, we are making the most of our time, and I am having a French master and am going through a *cours de Littérature* with him. Once a week Mr. Walbaum, whom you may remember as my German master, comes down to read to us an historical work; and on Thursday a German violin-player, whom I am to accompany on the piano, will make his first appearance here. So, you see, I am relapsed into a *school-girl*. But I have forgotten to inform you that when winter sets in and drives us indoors, the clergyman here is to read the second volume of Macaulay to us; so that I hope and trust that I shall get through a good deal of needlework this winter, which is much wanted at St. James's! . . .

Journal.—*September* 14.—I copied French Littérature both before and after breakfast, but was interrupted by a summons to go and look at the *curling table* sent us by the Duke of Buccleuch. Mr. Deichman, the violin-player, gave me my

---

[1] Lord Richard Grosvenor, now Lord Stalbridge, and his first wife, a daughter of Lord de Vesci.

first lesson. The Dowager Lady Cowley arrived just before luncheon, and spent the afternoon with us; we took her into the gardens, and it was quite a treat to hear her talk of bygone days! *Elle sait se bien causer.* Major Purves played curling with us in the evening.

Letter to a Friend.

Cambridge Cottage, September 16, 1854.

Our last letters from George were dated Therapia, August 30th, and report him as nearly well. . . . When the troops encamped for change of air near Varna, he moved into the town, and thence went to Therapia, where at Lord Stratford's[1] house, with every comfort, he soon got better, and was to return to Varna and embark with his division for the Crimea on the 2nd of September. God speed them! But it is an anxious time for those who have friends and relations in the East. The cholera and sickness are, I am thankful to say, subsiding, but I fear the allies have greatly suffered; and though the French have lost by far the greater number of men, several of our officers have either succumbed or are invalided. Sebastopol once ours and they will be amply avenged and repaid for all that they have gone through.

George informs us that Lord de Ros and General Cator of the Artillery, both invalided, are to return home directly, and that Sir John Burgoyne, who succeeds Cator, has arrived. The cholera, which seems to be everywhere, has been raging terribly in the less healthy parts of London, so much so that some streets have been marked with the *black flag;* but I hear this morning that the accounts are better, so that it is to be hoped it is on the decrease. Poor Lord Jocelyn fell a victim to it; you can imagine how much his death shocked *us,* who had seen him in church in perfect health the Sunday before! On the very morning of the day he died Lady Jocelyn accepted for herself and *him* an invitation to come over and dine with us on the day but one following. These sudden deaths and visitations are certainly very awful, but they lead one to think very seriously, and to put one's trust in God alone. . . . Lady Jocelyn was with her husband till the last. Lady Palmerston writes me word that she says

---

[1] Youngest son of Mr. Stratford Canning, and first cousin of George Canning the statesman. In 1852 he was raised to the peerage with the title of Viscount Stratford de Redcliffe. He was one of England's most distinguished diplomatists, and achieved an historic reputation when Ambassador at Constantinople (1841–1858).

the happiness of her life is gone; but that the desire of
preserving herself for her children, who are a great comfort
to her, saves her from utter despair. Poor thing! . . .

Letter to the Honble. Mrs. Dalrymple.

Cambridge Cottage, September 17, 1854.

. . . I must transcribe a few lines out of George's last
letter to gratify your sisterly feelings! "I find Lord Napier [1]
a most delightful person. He is quite *dans les meilleurs
pensées*, quite Austrian, and not at all violent in his political
views. In short, he suits me to perfection." If you will let
me know where Lady Napier (Dowager) now is, I will send
her a similar copy, as I think it may please her, so pray do
not forestall me. . . .

Journal.—Cambridge Cottage, September 18.— . . . We
drove over to the White Lodge to see the cricket-match, and
dear Aunt took me into her postchaise, whence I saw it all
comfortably. About five we went into the house for tea,
which was arranged in the gallery; [2] the Aumales and
many of the neighbours were present under the tents.
The Duchess of Gloucester's people beat the Sheen*ites.*
. . . I read the *Illustrated London News* aloud in the evening. *September 19.*—After breakfast I packed up a few
things, and at three o'clock we started for the Willesden
station, where the train picked us up, and we reached
Ashridge [3] about five. Lady Marian and the family received
us most kindly, and we had time to walk about the garden
a little, where the Hardwickes and Lady Clarendon joined
us. After tea we went up to our very nice rooms. We
were a party of twenty-four, and I sat between Lord Winchester and Lord Northampton at dinner. In the evening
we played at "Bebec" till twelve.
Ashridge, September 21.—At breakfast Lord Clarendon
received the telegraphic despatch containing the good news
that the armies had landed at Eupatoria [4] (afterwards found to
be "the Old Fort") on the 14th instant, and were marching

---

[1] Lord Napier had recently been appointed Secretary of Embassy at
Constantinople.

[2] Afterwards known as the Green Corridor.

[3] Ashridge Park, the Hertfordshire seat of Earl Brownlow.

[4] The British and French troops landed at Eupatoria on September 14,
1854, and did not evacuate the Crimea until July 12, 1856, during which
period the battles of Alma, Tchernaya, Balaclava, and Inkermann were fought,
and the fortress of Sebastopol was reduced by siege.

to Sebastopol! Hurrah! Cheered by this, we started for Woburn,[1] and a charming sixteen miles' drive we had, changing horses at Dunstable. The Duke and Duchess of Bedford received us most kindly; but the guests staying in the house were all strangers to us. After lunching in the breakfast-room, the walls of which are hung with Canalettos, we were taken through the drawing-room, and shown the apartments the Queen occupied, and the Duchess's *private* rooms. The Van Dycks are beautiful, and the corridors are hung with family and historical portraits. Next we visited the garden, sculpture gallery, Chinese dairy, stables, tennis court, and riding house, all on a grand scale; and then sat down to the Duchess's tea-table, which was covered with the loveliest china imaginable. Finally, we departed, charmed with the interior of the house, but agreeing with Paschol in looking upon the exterior as resembling *un quartier-général de Cavallerie.* . . . After dinner we danced. *September 23.*— . . . By degrees people began taking leave, and our party rapidly diminished. Lady Marian piloted the remainder of us over the house, and into the offices and cellar, with its gutta-percha spider. We took our departure after luncheon, dear Lady Marian accompanying us to Berkhampstead, whence we steamed back to Willesden, with Lord Winchester as our *compagnon de voyage.*

Cambridge Cottage, September 27.—We started in the phaeton for the pond in Richmond Park, where Colonel Liddell[2] awaited us, but had little fishing sport before our luncheon under the trees. In the afternoon, however, Mrs. L. Franks and "Carolina"[3] joined us in the punt, and we caught quantities of roach. Aunt Mary took a peep at us in her brougham, and when it got chilly we hurried up to the Lodge for tea. After a tender leave-taking we drove home. *September* 30.—I worked the whole morning to try and finish a sachet, but did not succeed in doing so. . . . Drove up to St. James's, where we found several letters from dear George. When Mama had finished her household affairs, we walked down with Knese and Major Purves to the Turkish Bazaar at Hyde Park Corner; it is very interesting, and remarkably well done. Thence we returned to Kew, and I read to Mama "The Earl's Daughter" till dressing-time. In the middle of dinner we received a letter from the Duke of Newcastle, with the good news that our troops had gained a great victory on the Alma—September 20th—Hurrah!

---

[1] Woburn Abbey.   [2] Equerry to the Duchess of Gloucester.
[3] Lady Caroline Murray.

And carried the entrenched camp of the Russians *by the bayonet* after two hours and a half of fighting. In the evening I read the 2nd edition of the *Times* to the others.

October 1.—At church we had a very fine prayer of Thanksgiving for the Harvest. . . . We heard from the Duke of Newcastle that George was *so far safe!* and then went out walking in the great garden, whither we were followed by the Turkish Ambassador, Alimster, and his Lady, to bring us news of the *taking of Sebastopol!* and by the Portuguese Minister and Lady, to wish us joy of the victory. In the evening we heard from Lord Clarendon. . . . Finished my sachet! *October* 3.—No authentic news arrived. The anxiety and suspense are dreadful to bear. . . . . *October* 5.—We found by the newspapers that the telegraphic news of the surrender of Sebastopol was false, as proved by Lord Stratford's despatch, dated the 28th. Went to bed very low-spirited. *October* 6. —In the afternoon, as it rained heavily, I helped Mama to choose some worsteds for her work, and then played at curling with her. . . . No news.

October 8, *Sunday*.—Whilst we were dressing, Ramstahl[1] brought down a charming letter from George (dated Sept. 21). . . . We drove to town, and shortly after reaching St. James's Lord Burghersh[2] arrived; he gave us a full description of the battle of Alma, which must have been *glorious*. His *auditoire* was further increased by Charles Bentinck[3] and Colonel Stephens. The Duke of Newcastle kindly peeped in to bring Mama the *Gazette*. Poor Horace Cust was killed—the only one of our friends at present upon the sad list. We were home again by half-past three, had some luncheon, and hurried to church. . . . Dined *à trois* at 7 o'clock. An exciting day! *October* 9.—Major Purves, the Aumales and Countess Colloredo arrived, and on their departure Mr. Norman Macdonald, who stayed till 4.30, when the Walewskis walked in. *"Tous pour féliciter."*[4] . . . *October* 10.—I wrote the whole morning, partly for mama and partly on my own account, to answer kind notes of

[1] The Duke of Cambridge's valet, and afterwards steward. He was forty-three years in the Duke's service.

[2] Lord Burghersh had arrived in London with despatches from Lord Raglan, containing particulars of the battle.

[3] General Sir Charles Bentinck, who had been invalided home from the Crimea.

[4] They came to congratulate the Duchess of Cambridge upon the brilliant manner in which the Duke had led his Division, consisting of the Guards and the Highland Brigade, at the battle of Alma.

congratulation. A letter arrived from George, dated Bala-klava, September 28th, which had to be copied twice over. In the afternoon we drove to Chiswick, where the dear Duke of Devonshire was waiting for us in the garden, and took us into his charming sitting-room. After dinner I read the German newspapers to Mama, and then finished "The Earl's Daughter," shedding many tears over the sad end.

October 17.— . . . Wrote letters all the afternoon till five, when I finished Mrs. Beecher Stowe's "Sunny Memories" of her travels in England and elsewhere, to Mama. The book is full of Americanisms, and, with the exception of the last few pages, is uninteresting, and "self" predominates too much. After dinner we began reading Dickens's new book, "Hard Times." *October* 19.— . . . Soon after six we started for the Richmond station, where we picked up Lord Burghersh, and were at Windsor Castle in time to dress for dinner. The Clarendons, Victor Hohenlohe, Colonel Sir C. Hamilton, and the Bernstorffs [1] were the guests. The Queen talked a long time, and we did not *sit* down before eleven o'clock.

Windsor Castle, October 20.—After an early breakfast we re-mained in our rooms till nearly eleven o'clock, when we went out driving with the Queen; going through a lovely part of the Park and passing Cranbourne Tower, we returned to the Castle by the fruit garden, and getting out by the Terrace, took a turn with Her Majesty. In the afternoon Mama and I drove down to Frogmore to see Aunt Kent, who is still far from well, and quite shut up; the Queen and Albert there picked me up and took me over the model farm, with its *cow-stables* and *pig-sties*. When we reached home, the Bernstorffs and little Leopold paid us a visit, and I suc-ceeded in finishing the mittens for dear George. Whilst I was dressing, Victoria and Alice came to me. At dinner I sat between Lord Clarendon and Lord Waterpark. We were twenty-one in number. In the evening Sainton played beautifully. *October* 21.—Returned by train to Kew. . . .

Cambridge Cottage, October 28.—Directly after breakfast I went out walking, or rather *running*, with Knese. I then wrote to George. . . . In the evening Knese read Napier's description of the siege of Badajos to us, *trop à propos*. . . . The *telegraph* said the bombardment of Sebastopol was opened on the 17th, and a fort *silenced* from the sea. . . . We finished dear interesting "Hard Times."

[1] Count and Countess Bernstorff. He was Prussian Ambassador at the Court of St. James's.

Letter to Mrs. Bridges Taylor.

Cambridge Cottage, November 15, 1854.

. . . Would that Sebastopol *had then* fallen, when the *false* report reached us through that *horrid* telegraph, which is enough to drive one *wild!* However, your rejoicings were fully justified by our *glorious victory* at *Alma*, which will be chronicled in the annals of our history as one of the noblest feats of arms ever achieved by British troops. That dear George was so honourably mentioned in the Gazette, or rather Despatch, and gained Lord Raglan's approval was, as you may imagine, *very gratifying indeed* to us; and truly thankful were we that God in His mercy spared him on that day when so many of our brave countrymen fell to rise no more. . . . The present state of suspense is terrible, and one can only pray to be enabled to bear it with patience and submission. Need I say how truly *I* can sympathise in all *your* fears? Knese has had a charming letter from your brother [1] written in excellent spirits, and describing *everything* most interestingly.

Our last accounts from dear George were dated October 28th, and entered into all particulars concerning the *dearly won* victory of the 25th [2] and the glorious one of the 26th. He says, "Our Light Cavalry were by some mistaken order pushed too forward, and made a most brilliant and glorious charge, actually took 10 Russian guns in the very centre of the Russian Army, which they however could not bring away, and returned with very great loss, being, in fact, nearly destroyed." This loss was, I think, hardly compensated for by that sustained by the Russians next day, which is computed to be about 1,000 men. Canrobert's telegraphic Despatch informs us that a great battle has been fought and *won* by us on the *5th of November,* [3] but we tremble for the results and anxiously await the arrival of a Despatch from Lord Raglan. Thus much from the seat of war!—as for ourselves, we are staying quietly at Kew, having given up all the visits for this autumn, and doing our best to distract our thoughts by occupying ourselves and *reading* a great deal. . . .

How sad is the sudden death of poor Lady Strathmore (the pretty Miss Barrington that was) at Florence. The poor

---

[1] Lieut.-Colonel James Halkett, Coldstream Guards, fourth son of the first Baron Halkett; he was dangerously wounded at Inkermann.

[2] Battle of Balaclava.

[3] Battle of Inkermann.

Duchess of Sutherland feels the death of her son, Lord Frederick Leveson Gower, who died of cholera in the East, most deeply I hear, and tendered her resignation, but the Queen would not hear of it. The Duchess had also requested that her year's *salary* might be devoted to the Patriotic Fund, which I think *very nice* of her. The poor Wynns grieve most deeply for their son and brother,[1] who was killed at Alma. . . .

Letter to a Friend.

Cambridge Cottage, November 8, 1854.

We shall be charmed to see you here on Friday afternoon at about three o'clock. But I cannot promise that you will find Mama in very good looks. Poor thing! she is pale and harassed. This dreadful state of suspense begins to tell upon our nerves as well as spirits ; and all one can do is to pray that those near and dear to us may be mercifully spared, and that the hitherto glorious campaign may be speedily brought to a victorious end, crowned by the taking of Sebastopol ! . . .

Journal.—Cambridge Cottage, November 27.—My 21st birthday ! May the coming year bring peace and happiness. Dear Mama came to wish me joy privately, and before breakfast I received my lovely presents ; after which we stayed in the library, birthday fashion, and I read my letters (twelve in number). . . . At seven we started for town to dine with dear Aunt Mary; the Mandevilles, Lord Adolphus, and Mr. Norman were the guests. A few friends came in the evening, which made it very nice.

Letter to a Friend.

Cambridge Cottage, December 9, 1854.

Many thanks for your kind letter and good wishes on the return of my Birthday, which has indeed been much saddened this year by the absence of my beloved brother, and that, too, at a post of danger. However, dear Mama and all my kind friends endeavoured by *additional* kindness to make up for the absence of both brother and sister, and I have, therefore, really no right to complain.

[1] Major Arthur Watkin-Wynn, son of Sir Henry Watkin-Wynn, for many years our Minister at Copenhagen. He was killed when in command of his Regiment, the 23rd Royal Welsh Fusiliers.

We have received several very interesting letters from dearest George since the battle of Inkermann, and I will endeavour to give you some account of their contents. The first of these, dated the 8th, contains a most interesting account of our glorious, but alas! dearly purchased victory at Inkermann, and bears witness to the gallantry and heroism of our brave troops, and the deeds of valour performed by them. Well may we feel proud of our noble countrymen! George was himself so hotly engaged in the battle, that they all say it is a wonder he escaped; for five hours and upwards he was in a perfect hailstorm of shot and shell. As it is, he had his horse shot under him, and a ball grazed his arm, tearing up his sleeve, but fortunately not wounding him, as it was turned by a pair of gold buttons he wears with *our hair* in them (is not that *touching?*) and consequently only inflicted a slight contusion. He was so worn out after all the fatigue he had undergone, that Lord Raglan sent him on board for a few days' rest, in the hope that he would be enabled to recruit his strength; but in this he was grievously mistaken. . . .

Dear George's second letter, dated the 13th, informs us that he was on board the *Retribution*, trying to get rid of a kind of aguish fever which was hanging upon him; but that it was blowing a gale, and he, not being at all a good sailor, was therefore far from comfortable. Little did we think what would follow! His third letter, dated the 18th, contains a terrible and heartrending account of the awful storm of the 14th. For twenty-four hours they expected every moment that the *Retribution* would share the fate of the *eight* transports, which were driven on the rocks before their very eyes, and went down with all on board. The gale began at six in the morning of the 14th, and increased momentarily in violence; by 12 o'clock the ship had lost *two* of her anchors and her rudder, and it was only by throwing the large guns and shot overboard and keeping her up to her one remaining anchor, which, though *damaged*, held on by steam, that, under God's blessing, she was miraculously saved. At two a thunderbolt struck the ship, and then there was a tremendous hailstorm, after which the storm began to abate, but the sea ran so fearfully high that they spent the night pitching and tossing at *only 200* yards' distance from the rocks, and it was not till noon on the 15th that a steamer was able to come off and take them into harbour. . . . George speaks in the highest terms of Captain Drummond, to whose coolness, courage, and determination he considers himself, under God's blessing, mainly indebted for preservation.

December 11.

. . . I have kept my letter back until to-day, hoping that another mail would have arrived, as it was due yesterday, but in vain. . . . I will not conclude this without proffering a small request. I am endeavouring in a humble way to collect subscriptions amongst my friends, with which to supply the soldiers' widows in the Cambridge Asylum and the girls in the Female Orphan Asylum with the materials for knitting socks and stockings for our brave soldiers. These will then be sent to the Committee of the " Crimean Army Fund." It thus becomes a twofold charity, and any subscriptions down to one shilling will be most thankfully received. Perhaps you will kindly interest yourself in my little plan, and mention it to any friends who would be willing to contribute. We have this instant received letters from George, dated Constantinople, where he arrived on the 27th. He is, thank God, much better, and only wants a little rest and relaxation for a few days before returning to his post. . . .

Journal.—Cambridge Cottage, December 14.— . . . We went to see Aunt Mary, and found Lady Canning [1] with her ; shortly after Miss Mitford arrived, and Bentinck,[2] Lady Jersey, and Clemmy paid their respects. We also had a visit from a Lieutenant O'Reilly, who brought us a sketch of the *Retribution* during the storm, done by his son, the senior Lieutenant of that ship. It made one shudder to see what dangers George had been exposed to. . . . Whilst waiting for the carriage, I read in the *Globe* the sad news of the death of dear Lord Frederick Fitzclarence,[3] and on our way home we stopped to call upon the Duchess of Inverness, who confirmed it. *December* 20.—We drove to town on a shopping expedition, and after buying Christmas presents called at Gloucester House. . . . Lord Rokeby came to wish us good-bye before starting for the Crimea.

December 25, *Christmas Day.*—After our return from church, we went to look at the Christmas dinner in the hall. . . . Dined with dear Aunt Mary, the Kielmansegges, Miss

[1] Wife of Earl Canning, and daughter of Lord Stuart de Rothesay. She and her sister, the Marchioness of Waterford, were two of the most beautiful women of their day.

[2] Count Bentinck, Netherlands Minister at the Court of St. James's.

[3] Second son of William IV., Lieut.-General, Colonel of the 36th Foot. He married, in 1821, Lady Augusta Boyle, daughter of the fourth Earl of Glasgow.

Adams,[1] and Lord Chelsea forming the party.   A few
friends came in the evening, and we had a round game.
December 27.— . . . Draperchen arrived, and I took a walk
with her.   Soon after five we gave the school-children their
tree and presents. . . . We had a dinner-party of ten—
4 Davisons, Prince Radali (Wilding), Chotek, and Stephens
—and music in the evening.   *December* 31.— . . . I paid
some bills, and received my money . . . read to Mama till
nearly dinner-time, and after a dinner *en famille* Knese read
Lord Carlisle's Diary to us; and thus ended the old Year.

[1] Companion to the Duchess of Gloucester.

CHAPTER VIII.

COUNTRY HOUSE VISITS.

1855.

New Year's Day at Windsor—Return of the Duke of Cambridge from the
Crimea—Belvoir Castle—State visit of the Emperor and Empress of
the French—Distribution of Crimean medals—Death of Lord Raglan
—Shrubland Park—Ashridge—Moor Park—Rowton Castle—Heaton
—Knowsley—Battledore and shuttlecock with the Queen—Wimpole
—Day at Cambridge—State visit of the King of Sardinia—Hatfield—
Princess Victoria Gouramma of Koorg—Return to Kew.

THE Duke of Cambridge remained five weeks at Constantinople, in vain trying to shake off the attack of fever which
had necessitated his leaving the Crimea. At last he was
advised by his medical attendant to apply for leave of
absence, and, most reluctantly, on the 1st of January, 1855,
started on his homeward journey. Hostilities were continued
for some months longer, and the fall of Sebastopol did not
take place till the following September.[1] In these circumstances, as may be imagined, the season was most unsettled,
and the Duchess of Cambridge and Princess Mary spent a good
deal of time at their rural abode. Towards the end of August
they started on a tour of country house visits, and did not
settle down again at Kew till late in December. During the
year Princess Mary assisted at the State visit paid by the

---

[1] After the battle of Alma the allied troops laid siege to the southern
portion of the town of Sebastopol, and on October 7 the first bombardment
took place. Earthworks were thrown up under the fire of the besiegers, and
the place was gallantly defended for eleven months. At last the memorable
siege terminated by the retirement of the Russians to the north side on
September 8, 1855, and the fortifications were then blown up by the attack-
ing forces.

Emperor and Empress of the French to the Queen at
Windsor, and also at the festivities arranged in honour of
the King of Sardinia,[1] who, according to Court gossip of
the time, desired an alliance with the Cambridge branch
of the Royal Family.

Journal. — Windsor Castle, January 1.— . . . We
reached Windsor from the Paddington Station by seven
o'clock, and the Queen and Albert came to see us immediately on our arrival. . . . In the evening there was a
grand concert in St. George's Hall.   Beethoven's "Praise of
Music" and Mendelssohn's "Walpurgis Nacht" were performed by a very large orchestra, the singers being Mrs.
Clara Novello, Mr. and Mrs. Weiss, and Mr. Sims Reeves.
It was very fine, and lasted till twelve o'clock. *January* 2.
—After breakfast the children .recited, and at eleven we
drove with the Queen to the Meet.   In the afternoon we saw
the Christmas presents, and I walked down to Frogmore
with Vicky[2] and Alice.   On our return I played to them,
and heard Alice play; then I went to my room, where we
were honoured by a visit from Leopold.   About five my
cousins fetched us to see them dance, and, after paying Lady
Canning a visit, the Queen sent for me. . . . In the evening
we *worked for the soldiers. January* 3.—The Queen walked
with us and took us over the model farm and kennels; then
we drove down to Frogmore, lunched with Aunt Kent, and
returned to St. James's in the afternoon by train, just in
time to receive Princesse Clementine, her spouse,[3] the
Duchesse d'Aumale, and the Princesse Salerno. . . .

Letter to a Friend.

Cambridge Cottage, January 16, 1855.

The papers will have informed you that George is on his
way home on *sick leave*. . . . He was three weeks at an Hotel
at Pera when, at Lord Stratford's *urgent* request, he removed
to the British Embassy in order to receive a visit from the
Sultan. . . . Lord Raglan wrote him a very kind letter, and
after submitting his case to a Medical Board he set sail for
Malta, where he is still detained by fever and extreme weakness; so that we do not expect him to arrive till the end of
the month. . . . We intend taking up our abode in town next

[1] Victor Emmanuel II., afterwards King of Italy.
[2] The Princess Royal.   [3] Prince Augustus of Saxe-Coburg and Gotha.

week, in order to be nearer my brother whenever he comes.
Yesterday we had a charming visit from Lord Cardigan,[1] who
is looking much pulled down from his protracted illness, but
seems in very good spirits. He talks like a brave soldier as
he is, and is very modest about himself. Bentinck is rapidly
recovering, and will, I believe, be able to return ere long
to the seat of war in command of the 4th Division. I am
sure you will have grieved to hear of the death of *our dear
friend* General Du Plat; he is a terrible loss to his country
just now; I hear Colonel Crawford of the Grenadiers is to
succeed him. . . . Lord Raglan's last despatch sounded
methinks more hopeful.

Journal.—St. James's Palace, January 30.—I wrote my
first cheque under Knese's superintendence. . . . We heard
that the Ministers were out,[2] and received a letter from George
from Paris. . . . I went over to Mama's room to see Lady
Wilton, and shortly afterwards the good news reached us that
George had arrived in his apartments and would be with us
in a few minutes. At a quarter to seven the dear brave
fellow (*our hero*) made his appearance. It was a *happy*
moment, and God be thanked for it. . . . We took him on to
Aunt Mary's, where we spent the evening *en famille. January*
31.— . . . The staff paid their respects, namely Jim, Colonel
Tyrrwhit,[3] Captain Clifton, and Dr. Gibson. . . . George dined
with us, and the Kielmansegges had a jollification in the
shape of a punch bowl in honour of his return.

Letter to a Friend.

St. James's Palace, February 7, 1855.

. . . George is daily regaining strength, thanks to "dear old
England," as you say, but he certainly looks pulled down and
worn, and cannot yet shake off the effects of fever, of which,
thank God, he has had no return since Malta. He has grown
much thinner, and *we* think much handsomer, as his features
are quite pointed, and, moreover, set off to great advantage
by a splendid beard, to which I have quite lost my heart.
Mama is still suffering from the effects of the influenza. . . .

Journal.—St. James's Palace, February 7.—After reading
German with Mr. Walbaum for two hours, I saw Major

---

[1] Lord Cardigan led the famous charge of the Light Brigade at the battle
of Balaclava.
[2] Lord Aberdeen's Ministry.
[3] Equerry to the Duke of Cambridge.

Purves about the contributions to the Crimea and Scutari.
. . . Rigged Frazer out for the play, and went on reading
till half-past ten, when George came in, and we looked at
Colnaghi's prints of the war. *February* 13.— . . . I took
my music lesson, astonishing Mama and Mr. Deichmann
by playing some of my *old, difficult* pieces. . . . In the
afternoon we paid dear Aunt Mary a visit, where we met
the Queen on the stairs, and on our return to St. James's we
received the young Maharajah and Sir John Logan. While
we were talking George returned from Windsor, and remained
chatting with us for some time. . . . In the evening I sang
—oh wonders ! !

February 22.—Breakfast over, we hurried on foot to the
Palace to see 29 of the sick and wounded of the Coldstreams.
It was a sad and touching scene ! Later on we drove along the
Thames from Westminster to Vauxhall Bridge to look at the
floating ice. . . . In the evening we finished Lord Carlisle's
Diary; interesting but very light reading. *March* 2.— . . .
At half-past four o'clock we drove to the House of Lords,
where we heard Lord Clarendon announce the death of the
Emperor Nicholas,[1] which took place between twelve and one
the preceding night, owing to paralysis of the lungs. On
our return home I read a French pamphlet entitled " Sur la
conduite de la Guerre · d'Orient," and supposed to be written
by Prince Napoleon. Dinner over we adjourned to the
Princess's Theatre, where the Mandevilles, Counts Trauttmansdorff and Chotek joined us, and we saw three acts of *Louis XI.*
and the pantomime, which was very good. *March* 28.—We
left St. James's at ten o'clock for the King's Cross station,
and reached Belvoir Castle about three ; the Duke [2] and
Lord Charles Manners received us. . . . We sat down thirty-
four to dinner, and in the evening I played at whist with
some of the ladies.

Belvoir Castle, March 29.—After breakfast we had some
singing in the ball-room. Lady Wilton, Suffie, Katty, and I
then set off for Croxton Park, where we arrived just in time
for the second race. We lunched in the tent, and did not
return to Belvoir till after the last race. . . . In the evening
a cockney conjuror exhibited very well till nearly one
o'clock. *March* 30.— . . . Katty and I scribbled verses at
Grey's dictation, and directly after luncheon we drove to the
course. . . . Great excitement prevailed in our stand during
the last race but one, which was won by Lord Wilton on his
own horse " Orson." We danced in the evening till long

---

[1] The Emperor of Russia.   [2] The Duke of Rutland.

past one o'clock, two large parties from neighbouring country houses joining us. *March* 31.— . . . A charming drive to the meet, but we did not see much sport, and at three o'clock returned to lunch. Afterwards we adjourned to the gallery, and Lady Sandwich sang delightfully, Lady —— the *reverse*. We were a smaller party at dinner than last night. . . . I played at whist. It was an eventful game, as a large lamp was upset close to me, which covered me with oil, though, thank God, I escaped being hurt. *April* 1.— . . . I drank tea with Lady Sandwich in her room when we concocted an April fool letter for Lord Granby. . . . Dinner was most exciting, as our joke came off, and was *quite* successful! In the evening we sat round the table and talked. *April* 2.—We took leave of the family *à regret*, and reached Grantham in *too* good time. On our arrival in town we drove at once to Gloucester House; had tea, and then left for *licke* Kew, where Knese received us.

Cambridge Cottage, April 9.—We drove to town for some shopping. First we went to Mrs. D——, " at Paris," then to Mme. M——, " gone to Paris," lastly to Mme. P——, and reached Gloucester House about four, where we had to see milliners in plenty. . . . *April* 14.—Dressed early and started for Aunt Mary's at 6.15, as I had to try on my blue ball gown. . . . We dined at eight, Lord Hardwicke, Libbet, Lord Winchester, and Colonel Foster making up the party. Mary Yorke and Lady Cadogan came in the evening. *April* 17.—Mama read to me a review in the *Quarterly* of the life and last moments of the Emperor Nicholas, and at half-past four we started for Richmond, reaching Windsor *per* train at six. From George's windows we saw the Queen and her French guests return from the review, and then I hastened to dress. In the Garter Room I first set eyes upon the present Emperor and Empress of the French. The grand banquet in their honour was given in St. George's Hall. It was a magnificent affair; seventy-six guests were present, and my neighbours were M. de Walewski and Lord Breadalbane. A dance in the Waterloo Gallery till one o'clock finished the evening.

Windsor Castle, April 18.—We breakfasted at nine o'clock, the Emperor Napoleon being of the party. I then drove down to Virginia Water with Vicky and Alice, and paid Mrs. Whiting a visit. On our return I saw the Queen, and after choosing my wreath for the evening, went over to see the Empress Eugénie. I was back soon after one to be *coifféed*, then lunched with the Imperial guests in haste, dressed in

manteau de cour, and was present at the Chapter of the
Garter,[1] which was over by half-past four. We took a short
drive with the Queen, and after tea I dressed for a second
banquet of eighty persons in St. George's Hall. *April*
19.—Soon after ten o'clock we left the Castle, and in less
than two hours reached St. James's Palace garden, where,
mounted on the porter's lodge, we saw the Queen and her
guests pass *en route* for Buckingham Palace. Later on, from
the same post of vantage, we watched the procession on its
way to the City.

St. James's Palace, April 20.— . . . Walked over to
George's apartments to dine with him, returning home to dress
for the Concert at the Palace, which lasted till half-past
twelve. Said good-bye to the French guests, changed our
costumes, and drove back to Kew, which we reached at two
o'clock. The visit of the Emperor and Empress has gone off
very well indeed, thanks to his tact and agreeable cleverness,
and her pleasing and unassuming manners. *April* 23.— . . .
Drove to the Palace to see the suite of rooms occupied by the
Emperor and Empress, and thence to Gloucester House,
where we met the Duchess of Inverness, Wales, and Alfred. . . .
May 3.—We drove to the Royal Academy, to have a private
view of the Exhibition of paintings, which offers no *chefs
d'œuvre*, but many gems. We found the Queen there. . . .
In the afternoon returned to Kew.

Cambridge Cottage, May 6, *Sunday.*—George came down to
breakfast and to attend church, as the Bishop of Lincoln
preached the charity sermon for our school. The collection
was a *very good* one, amounting to £69! We received the
Bishop and Mr. Byam Martin at luncheon. . . . I read an
" Address," by Mr. Ryle,[2] to Mama till dressing-time. *May*
14.—It was a morning divided between gardening, writing,
and trotting through the spare rooms. . . . At half-past four
we made our dinner, and afterwards started for Town, where
we were joined by Louise Mandeville and the suite, who
accompanied us to the House of Lords, where we heard Lords
Ellenborough, Lansdowne, Hardwicke, Granville, and Derby
speak on Lord Ellenborough's motion.[3] We did not get to
St. James's till half-past eleven, when we had tea and went

[1] At four o'clock the Queen invested the Emperor with the Order of the
Garter in the Throne Room.

[2] Now Bishop of Liverpool.

[3] The motion condemned the conduct of the war. Lord Ellenborough
was supported by Lords Hardwicke and Derby, and Lord Granville and Lord
Lansdowne were among the peers who opposed. The Government secured
a majority of 110 in a House numbering 250.

to bed. *May* 15.— ... Suffie took me to see dear Katty after her terrible fall from her horse, and afterwards Mama, George, and I went to the London Bridge station, where we had the happiness of receiving dear Gussy and her boy. . . .

St. James's Palace, May 18.—We had a hurried breakfast before going to the Horse Guards, whence from a balcony, unfortunately too far off to admit of a very satisfactory view, we witnessed the distribution of the Crimean medals by the Queen, to the officers and men of the army and navy, about 700 in number, George being the first to receive the medal. The parade was over by half-past twelve, and after making a fruitless expedition to the Riding House,[1] we returned to St. James's, but were sent for to the Palace, to see the men, who had received the medals, amusing themselves in the garden, whence we followed them to the Riding House, where they dined. After bidding the Queen good-bye, we went to luncheon at Gloucester House. On our return we rested till seven, when we had tea and I was *coiffée* for the concert at Court. The music was more lively than the last time, and Lablache and Gardoni were a great addition, but the company was not brilliant. *May* 19.—The Birthday drawing-room! Lady Hooker and Mrs. Laumann came to see us in full dress. The city people greatly predominated over the aristocracy, and rank, fashion, and beauty were wanting.

June 6.— ... I walked in the Palace gardens, the heat was intense, and saw the Maharajah's horses and saddles being exhibited to Her Majesty; returned home about six o'clock, dressed and dined at the Derbys', a party of twenty-two, but owing to my cold I did not feel well enough to *enjoy* either dinner or ball, and only walked two quadrilles. *June* 12.— ... We started *à quatre* with Engel[2] for Kew, *viâ* Fulham and Richmond Park, where we got out and walked to look at the hawthorns, and were met by Sir Edward Bowater,[3] who took us to see his pretty cottage and garden. . . . *June* 17, *Sunday.*—We attended Divine service at the Chapel Royal, and heard a beautiful sermon preached by Mr. Anderson. After luncheon we received *l'Ambassadeur,* M. de Persigny,[4] and then Gussy, Dolphus,

---

[1] Riding School at Buckingham Palace.

[2] Fräulein von Engel, Lady-in-Waiting to the Hereditary Grand Duchess of Mecklenburg-Strelitz.

[3] Sir Edward Bowater lived at the Thatched House in Richmond Park. He was appointed Governor to Prince Leopold in November 1861, and died at Cannes a month later.

[4] M. de Persigny had succeeded Count Walewski as French Ambassador.

and I paid the Princess Royal and Alice a visit. . . . Dined
with George to meet Crimean heroes; Sir John Burgoyne [1]
and Admiral Dundas [2] were my neighbours.   *June* 18.—
Mama, Knese, the Major,[3] and I went out walking, and
peeped into some old china shops in Pimlico. . . .
     June 20.—George came to breakfast, after which we
hurried over to his apartments to see his photograph coloured;
. . . At four we started for Mr. Vincent's villa, and found a
great many *people* assembled there, but few acquaintances.
Concert at Court in the evening.   *June* 21.—We spent the
day at Kew, and sat in the garden all the afternoon, dined
early, and then went into the Botanic to see the rhododendrons and cut some flowers; there we met Lord Elcho and
Lord Ossulston.   We left again at eight, and after a comfortable tea at St. James's, dressed for the ball at Eglinton's,
which was too hot and crowded to be enjoyable, 850 people
being asked to it.   *June* 22.—At breakfast we learnt that
our attack on the Redan had failed.   I took my music lesson,
and Mrs. Barry arrived.   Then Arabella West and Mrs. de
Burgh came in for a moment. . . . Drove in the afternoon
to Kensington Gardens, and walked in the fashionable part.
June 24, *Sunday.*—On our return from the Chapel Royal,
Mama held a consultation with the suite about her party.
Princess Doria and her daughter came later. . . . I called
to see the Princess Royal, and she kept me with her for the
rest of the afternoon.   The Palace gardens were very enjoyable, and I walked with the Queen till past seven.
     June 26.—Mama, Gussy, Knese, and I went to St. George's
to see Etta Somerset's wedding—all smiles and no tears!   On
our way home Knese and I got out and trudged down St.
James's Street, where the happy pair, Mr. and Lady Henrietta
Morant,[4] passed us. . . . After a bit of luncheon we saw Lord
Winchester, and attended a very good concert at Lady
Middleton's, where we partook of an early dinner at six
o'clock.   We were home by eight, had tea, and dressed for
a charming ball at the Duke of Beaufort's.   *June* 27.—I
spent the whole morning arranging the rooms for our party,
and most of the afternoon putting up the flowers. . . . Then
drove to Hampstead and back, . . . and was ready before

---

[1] To Sir John Burgoyne is ascribed the credit of devising the celebrated
flank march to Balaclava.
[2] Admiral Dundas succeeded Admiral Sir Charles Napier in the command
of the Baltic Fleet.
[3] Major Purves.
[4] See footnote, p. 118.

eight to receive the Queen. Our grand dinner of twenty-four went off admirably; the Duke of Buccleuch and Lord Breadalbane sat next me. The evening party which followed was an undoubted success, and greatly enlivened by Lavassor.[1]

June 30.—A wretched day! George and Augusta came to tell us that *dear* Lord Raglan had died on the 28th. What a loss to the country and his friends! Of course we gave up Miss Coutts's breakfast and the Opera, and, after seeing Suffie, started for Kew, stopping on our way at poor Lady Raglan's to inquire after the family. Sat in the garden till six, when we dined out-of-doors. . . .

July 5.—Gussy and I paid a short visit to Aunt Kent, and then we started at a quarter-past ten for Holly Lodge, where Miss Coutts gave the Aumales and us a luncheon. I sat next George and had Azeglio on my other side. . . .

July 6.— . . . Dined at the Palace to meet King Leopold, and went on with Gussy to a ball at Lady Lyndhurst's.

July 7.—Accompanied George and Augusta to see the exhibition for the Patriotic Fund at Burlington House. . . . After receiving the new French Ambassadress, Comtesse Persigny, we started for Lady Shelley's place at Fulham, where there was a children's breakfast. Dined quietly, and went to the Opera to see *Don Pasquale* and a short ballet called *Vivandière. July* 17.— . . . After luncheon we went to the Panopticon, where we heard the organ play, were edified by lectures upon music and electricity, and saw the luminous fountain and the diver. . . . In the evening we had the Queen's box at the Opera, and saw *Favorita.*

July 18.—Breakfasted early, and visited the Royal Academy, where we stayed from half-past twelve till half-past two. On our return we had tea, and took a drive round the Park. . . . Dined with the Palmerstons: and in the evening they had a charming *petit bal* for me, which I much enjoyed.

July 25.—Dearest Mama's birthday! I was with her at a quarter-past eight to wish her joy. Major Purves joined us at breakfast, and directly after Davison walked in: we then laid our offerings at her feet, and a very pretty birthday table it was. At three Mama, Gussy, Doppus, and I started for the Crystal Palace, where we were met by George, Fritz, Knese, Purves, Jim, Lady Marian Alford, Libbet Yorke, Quin, and Norman Macdonald. After seeing the fountains play, and being mobbed whilst wandering through the courts,

[1] A Society entertainer.

we sat down in the centre to hear the band, and had a peep at dear Lady Wilton, who kindly chaperoned Katty down. At 6.30 we dined, a party of fourteen, in the Pompeian Court. It was a very merry party, and we toasted Mama in grand style. The only *contretemps* that occurred was the upsetting of a dish of cream over poor Mama. We took another ramble through the Palace, which had a fairy-like appearance by moonlight, before starting on our homeward journey; stopped *en route* to drink tea at the White Lodge.

Cambridge Cottage, August 6.— . . . Had a visit from the Aumales and Lady Caroline Murray, and dressed for an early dinner, at which we were honoured by Edward Weimar's presence; it was such a treat to see him again after all he has done and undergone. At seven we started for the French play to see Rachel in *Lady Tartuffe*, a most interesting and well-acted piece. *August 22.*— . . . At half-past one we left for the Shoreditch station, changing carriages at St. James's. Suffie and Major Purves met us there, and soon after we steamed off for Shrubland Park,[1] Lord Winchester and Mr. Graham Vivian accompanying us. We reached our destination about seven, where the Middletons received us most kindly, and refreshed us with tea. We sat down twenty to dinner, I between Lord Sydney and Sir William Fraser. In the evening Mr. Spence played and sang to us, and we had a round game, at which I was the winner.

Shrubland Park, August 23.—We breakfasted at ten; then sat in the morning-room looking at Mr. Vivian's photographs, and chatting till Sir William Middleton took us over his beautiful garden and the grounds more immediately surrounding the house. On our return we were photographed on the flight of steps, and after luncheon were done again in groups by Mr. Vivian. At 4.30 we started for a drive all round the place, Lily Montagu and I *tête-à-tête* in a post-chaise, which we liked of all things. Tea refreshed us when we got home, and we watched the sunset till dressing-time. In the evening the Montagu girls sang charmingly, and Mrs. —— atrociously and with *grande prétention*. *August 24.*—Began the morning with a good game of ball, and then rested in the drawing-room and were sung to, sketched, and photographed. In the afternoon the grounds were thrown open to the public for the good of the East Suffolk Hospital, and at half-past three we all

[1] The seat of Sir William Middleton.

promenaded *en procession* to an iron gate to deposit our donations, after which we sat down *en évidence* in a hut and listened to the band of the Grenadiers.

Later in the day Lord Sydney, my cavalier, took me to the group of Spanish chestnuts where we rested, and were joined by the rest of the party. At seven we returned to the house, and almost directly sat down to dinner, Lord Sydney and Lord Winchester on either side of me. We then dressed in haste, whilst the guests assembled and opened the ball with a Polonaise; we danced till past one o'clock. *August* 25.—Breakfasted at 10.30, and played at ball on the terrace till summoned to prepare for departure. After taking a last look at Shrubland Park and the surrounding country from the tip-top of the tower, we left the Middletons' hospitable roof and travelled up to town in company with nearly the whole of our party. Bidding them all a tender farewell at the Shoreditch station, we hastened to the Euston Square terminus, where Doppus, Engel, and the Baron met us; thence we proceeded by train to Tring, which we reached so late that George and Jim overtook us by the later train and drove with us in the omnibus to Ashridge. Dear Lady Marian gave us a warm welcome. We dined at half-past eight *en toilette de voyage*, a party of nineteen, and in the evening chatted *very agreeably*.

Ashridge, August 26, Sunday.—Service was performed in the chapel, after which Lady Marian and I had a poetic chat together, which we continued in the afternoon. I went for a two hours' walk with George and four of the gentlemen, and then rested till dressing time. In the evening we gave "Words" and conversed. *August* 27.—We sat in the drawing-room and library all the morning, and I played to the others. Drove in the afternoon through the woods and round by the common. Engel, Lord William Graham, and Jim were my companions on this occasion; at Peacock Lodge we got out and walked up to the house. We were twenty-four at dinner. In the evening we played at whist, and Mama *faisait des patiences*. *August* 28.—I spent the morning looking over Lady Harry Vane's album, and copying scraps out of it. Directly after luncheon we went out driving; I was in a barouche with Lady Alwyne Compton, Mr. Dickins,[1] and Lord Cranley. On our return to tea we found some of the

---

[1] Mr. Charles Scrase-Dickins of Coolhurst; he married Lady Elizabeth Compton, daughter of the first Marquis of Northampton and Aunt to Lady Marian Alford.

neighbours and their children assembled on the lawn, and had a capital game at ball. . . . Lord Salisbury and Jim were my neighbours at dinner.

August 29.—In the morning we inspected Lord Lonsdale's pack of hounds; then I played and sang to some of the party, and wrote to Aunt Mary. After luncheon Lady Alwyne, Count Palffy, Jim, and I drove in Lady Marian's sociable: we made a tour of the nearest country places—Mr. Halsey's, Lord Cranley's, and Sir Thomas Sebright's—returning home to tea in the garden and a game at croquet and ball. Sat in the library in the evening; Lady Alwyne played to us, and Suffie and Jim danced a jig! *August* 30.—The party began to disperse after breakfast, and Lady Marian carried me off to her room for a quiet cose, then we sat out in the garden till luncheon-time. At about half-past two we left.dear Ashridge for Berkhampstead—Lady Marian driving me in her pony phaeton—where we paid Mr. Hutchinson [1] a visit, and were regaled with tea on the lawn in front of his house. The five o'clock train carried us back to Willesden, and we reached Kew by seven.

Cambridge Cottage, September 10.—I was up before half-past five, and with Augusta by six, and at a little before seven Gussy, Dolphus, and Engel left us after a sorrowful leave-taking, Knese accompanying them. Mama and I went into their now-deserted rooms, then I finished my toilet and read. Spent the morning in the great garden, where we walked and weeded till it was time to drive over to the White Lodge to luncheon. We went out fishing in the Park with the Liddells, but had very poor sport. Home by half-past seven, and partook of a heavy tea in the little room; we sat upstairs afterwards, and Hardy [2] brought us the evening papers containing the intelligence (official) that Sebastopol was in possession of the Allies, the Russians having evacuated it on the 9th, and destroyed their ships. Hurrah!!! The morning papers had brought us the news of the capture of the Malakoff by the French.

September 25.— . . . Directly after luncheon we started in the landau with the dressers for Moor Park, which we reached about five after a charming drive through the Harrow country. The Robert Grosvenors received us most kindly; we had tea, and I went up with Mary Montagu to her room. Lord Robert

---

[1] Lord Brownlow had presented the living of Berkhampstead to the Rev. J. Hutchinson.

[2] Page to the Duchess of Cambridge.

H.R.H. Princess Mary of Cambridge as a girl.

From a miniature at Gloucester House.

and Bo Grosvenor[1] were my neighbours at dinner. The three Rokebys and Honoria Cadogan made up the party. . . .

Moor Park, September 26.—In the morning we younger ones played at billiards and battledore and shuttlecock in the beautiful hall. And then I drove in the donkey carriage up to the kitchen garden, whence we walked to the large lime tree and home. Punctually at two the elders set out for Hazelwood, whilst I went to see my old nurse Vandal, now Mrs. Macpherson, wife of the butler, and afterwards lunched with the children. Oggy drove the Montagus and me in the pony phaeton over to Hazelwood,[2] *viâ* Cassiobury, and on our arrival we had tea; the garden was looking lovely, and after sitting out and wandering over every part of the place, we returned home about six. In the evening I played and sang.

September 27.—After Lady Rokeby had read us her husband's letters about the attack on the Redan and the fall of Sebastopol, I wandered out into the garden, and recited to Lady Robert and the girls. The elders went for their drive about two, and we followed them in the pony phaeton, passing through Chenies, the most picturesque and prettily built village I have ever seen. It belongs to the Bedford family, and their vault lies under a chapel built on to the church. We proceeded to the old Manor House for tea, and lastly to Lord Wriothesley Russell's pretty rectory. On our drive home we were taken through a charming specimen of a Hertfordshire lane. In the evening we had music, in which I took part, and about twelve we went upstairs, but not to bed, for after holding a council, I was summoned by Lady Robert, and deputed to petition Mama to stay over another day, which I succeeded in doing about one o'clock, after we ladies had aroused the poor Baron from his slumbers !

September 28.—We were driven all over the Park by Oggy with the donkeys at full speed, and shown the site of Cardinal Wolsey's castle, the moat, and the fine old lime tree, which was set on fire a short time ago by some of the London Sunday mob. I then walked with Lady Robert to the cricket-ground, and at half-past three we drove in the pony phaeton through the grounds of Mrs. Marsh, who wrote "Emilia Wyndham," to see a beautiful view and into Oxey Wood; but as it began to rain, we turned homewards, stopping, however, at Norwood, to see the church built by Lord Robert. Had tea in the drawing-room, where we remained chatting till past six. On going up to

[1] The present Lord Ebury.
[2] Belonging to Lord Rokeby.

our rooms, we were startled by a flash of lightning, which
proved the precursor of a thunderstorm, in the midst of which
Lady Robert set out on foot to attend the choir practice at
Norwood; but, to our no small relief, the pouring rain forced
her to return. In the evening Oggy danced a ballet, and we
had a round game, which turned out a tremendously noisy
one. *September* 29.—Lady Rokeby and Mary left, and we
amused ourselves in the hall, as it rained. . . . After luncheon
we bade adieu to our kind hosts, an hour and a half's drive
bringing us back to Kew. Dined at the White Lodge, where
we sat down seven to dinner, and in the evening I played at
patiences with Aunt Mary.

Cambridge Cottage, September 30, *Sunday.*—At church we
had the prayer of Thanksgiving for the fall of Sebastopol,
which was too *lukewarm* to please me. . . . *October* 3.—A
rainy day! . . . I saw Mr. Johnston, then went to my own
room, and, with the single interruption of half an hour for
luncheon, wrote till five o'clock. After tea Mama and I
had a game of ball till seven, when I settled my bills
with Frazer, and read "The Heir of Redclyffe" to Mama,
amidst floods of tears, till dressing-time! *October* 11.—I
got up at half-past six, as the luggage had to go early,
and at 9.30 we left for Willesden, where the train picked
us up. It poured all the way, and we had a damp and
chilly journey, though it was "all serene" inside our
carriage. At the Wellington station we were cheered by a
number of people collected on the platform to see us pass,
and saluted by a cannon. We arrived at Shrewsbury
about four, and were received in great state by Colonel
Forester, Colonel Hill of the Militia, and several of the
inhabitants; a guard of honour was drawn up outside the
station, and Mama and I drove off in a post-chaise and
four to the sound of "God save the Queen," and amidst
great cheering. The old town was decked out for the
occasion, and the people had all turned out to have a peep
of us. Three-quarters of an hour's drive brought us to
Rowton Castle, and dear Charlotte's *open* arms! We had
tea in the drawing-room, and warmed ourselves by its fire
till dressing-time. Dined at eight, the Newports and Colonel
Hill forming the addition. In the evening I played at whist,
and our second rubber was not over till half-past twelve!
Colonel Forester was my partner and we played against the
Newports.

Rowton Castle, October 12.— . . . I sang and played to
Lady Newport, and at twelve, as the weather had cleared,

we started for Powis Castle;[1] a longish, but very pleasant
drive through picturesque Welsh scenery, brought us to
Welshpool, when our "reception" began. The town was
decorated and dressed up with laurels and evergreens, and
to crown all, sported a grand triumphal arch, while the old
church sent forth its merry peal. In the Park the Militia
were drawn up, and a little further on the school children,
who cheered most lustily. The Powises received us at the
entrance of their fine old Castle and conducted us through
long oaken and rather ghostly looking corridors to the drawing-room, which is a very handsome room, and shares with
Lady Powis's sitting-room the advantage of a glorious view.
The Howard de Waldens and a few neighbours, with the
family, made up the party in the house. We had a grand
luncheon in the tapestried dining-room, and then were shown
some of the bedrooms and taken to the terrace and garden.
After this we had a beautiful drive through the Park and
up a very high hill, whence I got a peep of Snowdon.
On returning to Powis Castle we had coffee, and then set
off on our homeward journey amidst the schoolchildren's
parting cheers and martial honours, reaching Rowton about
seven. . . . *October* 13.—Breakfast over, I settled down in
the *hall* to write a letter, and we went into the garden for
a little while, where Mama and I had each to plant a tree.
Luncheon: then started for Shrewsbury, stopping on our
way to see Miss Borton's picturesque cottage and the old oak
in her grounds under which Owen Glendower sat to witness
the battle of Shrewsbury. After passing through the old
town we saw the late Lord Hill's column, and on our way
home got out at several shops. We returned to Rowton for
tea, and sang till it was time to dress for dinner.

October 14, *Sunday.*—We drove to church, a distance of
four miles. The road was very pretty, and the old Welsh
church picturesque in the extreme, but alas! *damp* and *chilly*.
The service was remarkably well performed. Lunched at
two and went out walking, first to the dairy, next through a
little wood to the keeper's lodge, lastly we retraced our steps,
and, passing through the garden, went on to the kitchen
garden. Later I made a tour of inspection through the
offices, rested a little in the hall, and betook myself to Mary's
room. We sat down nine to dinner, and afterwards amused
ourselves with guessing words. *October* 15.—Breakfasted at
ten, repacked my bag, and played and sang to the rest till it
was time to leave. We bid the Lysters adieu with *real*

---

[1] The seat of the Earls of Powis.

regret and started for Shrewsbury, which was reached about one o'clock. Lord Powis met us there, and conducted us, after about a quarter of an hour's waiting, to our carriage, in which we were shortly after whisked off *en route* for Manchester. At Stoke the London train joined, bringing Lady Rokeby, Lily, Lord Winchester, Jim, and Bo. We reached Manchester by 4.20, and Heaton shortly after five, where a warm welcome awaited us after our cold journey. We had tea in the schoolroom, and then dispersed to our several rooms, dressed, and dined at eight, a party of fifteen. In the evening we worked and talked.

Heaton, The pretty Convolvulus Bedroom,[1] *October* 16.— Breakfasted at ten, then we young ladies trotted up to Katty's charming sitting-room, and later on went to the stables, escorted by some of the gentlemen, to christen Katty's mare, and for a long walk in the grounds. Blanche Egerton, her brother, and Lord Fordwich rode over to luncheon, and we played billiards. Had tea in Katty's sitting-room, and then sang choruses without end. The Dean of Manchester and Mr. Birch dined;[2] conversation, work, and music in the evening. *October* 17.—We played at ball in the library, and then set about preparing the *tableaux*. The afternoon was spent in the schoolroom cutting out flowers and stars, and making wreaths. We had tea in Katty's room, in the midst of which Louise Manchester and Lady Newport arrived, and afterwards I went with Louise to her room.

October 18.—Busied ourselves with the *tableaux*. . . . Some of the party went over to Worsley[3] to luncheon, in spite of the rain, but I prudently stayed at home, and after luncheon Lady Rokeby dressed me up and cut out draperies upon me preparatory to the *tableaux*. The others returned in time for tea in Katty's sitting-room, and we had a rehearsal *des poses*. In the evening I played one rubber and then joined the younger party and had a game of "Consequences." Lord Otho Fitzgerald made his appearance after dinner, and Lord Canterbury also arrived very late. *October* 19.—We adjourned for a while to the library to watch the progress of the stage scenery, and then I took my knitting to the saloon and looked at Lord Otho's book of photographs. Luncheon

[1] Princess Mary became much attached to the rooms she occupied on her different visits, and sometimes would imprint a kiss of adieu upon the wallpaper as she passed out of a room where she had spent a very happy time.

[2] Whenever the Duchess of Cambridge and Princess Mary came to Heaton the Rev. H. M. Birch was always invited to dine.

[3] Worsley Hall, belonging to the Earls of Ellesmere.

over, the others started for Manchester, and I went to my
room and wrote for some time, after which I joined Lady
Rokeby, the stage manager, and her *aides-de-camp*.   On
the return of the rest of the party we had a strictly private
rehearsal, and then four of us partook of a heavy tea in
Katty's room, previous to lying down for an hour's rest.   At
nine I began to dress, and shortly after half-past the *tableaux*
began.   They were seven in number—*A Dutch Scene; Faith,
Hope, and Charity ; The Novice's Dream; Night ; The Pleiades;
The Bouquet* and *The Water Nymph.*   I acted in five; they were
very successful, and lasted till twelve, when we all appeared
in the saloon and had tea.   *October* 20.— . . . After luncheon
we started on an expedition to Schwabe's Chintz works,
Katty driving us in the Irish car; but on arriving there we
found the works closed, as it was a half-holiday, and had to
content ourselves with an inspection of the warehouse.   We
returned to the Park by a circuitous route, and after getting
over an iron fence we, of the car, walked home.   Dined at
7.30, and in the evening sang any number of choruses, to
cover Lord Winchester's embarrassment whilst proposing to
Mary Montagu, and the latter's confusion whilst accepting
him !   A grand cheer and a game at ball, in which the
cushions took part, closed this auspicious and eventful
evening.

October 21, *Sunday.*—Breakfasted a little before ten, and
as the rain came down in torrents several of us remained at
home and read prayers in the drawing-room, the Duke of
Manchester officiating as clergyman. . . . In the evening the
choir sang psalms and hymns.   *October* 22.—Lady Rokeby,
Mary, Lord Winchester, the Newports, Colonel Parker, and
Mr. Grosvenor left, after signing their names for us.   Lord Otho
then photographed the remainder of the party.   In the afternoon we left dear Heaton, carrying the *beaux restes* of the
party with us to the number of twelve, and the three o'clock
train from Manchester conveyed us (ten in one carriage) to
Heighton, where Lord Derby received us, and half an hour's
drive landed us at Knowsley.   From the drawing-room
windows we watched the party arrive, and then had tea, and
retired to our rooms till dressing-time. . . . After dinner
we young people played at *vingt-et-un.*

Knowsley, October 23.— . . . Our host took us to the library
to see a very fine collection of water-coloured copies of family
portraits. . . . We *all* indulged in a grand game of ball in
the dancing-room, Lord Derby at our head, and when quite
tired out sang choruses till tea-time ! . . . then to my room

to finish a letter, where I found Katty, Mandy,[1] and Lily reposing! After dinner we danced away till past one! *October* 24.—At twelve o'clock, fifteen of us started for Liverpool; Mama, Lady Derby, Lady Wilton, and I in the coach, and the rest in the omnibus. The Mayor and Mrs. Tobin received us at St. George's Hall and conducted us over it. It contains a concert room, a criminal and civil Court, into the latter of which we peeped whilst a case was being deliberated on, and a fine Hall, where we stayed awhile to hear the splendid organ. Next we drove to the Town Hall with its large Ball-room and suite of reception rooms, where the Mayor gave us luncheon, and then followed the Mayor in his carriage to get a sight of the Wharf and chief streets and public buildings of Liverpool, returning to Knowsley in time for tea.

October 25.— . . . The Bectives arrived in place of the Wiltons and Salisburys, and after dinner we had *tableaux* arranged by Mr. Lumley; *Bolton Abbey, The Prisoner Condemned, The Dying Bride, Naomi and her Daughters-in-law*, and *Titian's Daughter* were the subjects chosen. I took part in the last two. *October* 26.—The gentlemen started on a shooting expedition, and Mama, Lord and Lady Howe, and I sallied out for a walk; first we visited the kitchen garden and fruit-room, and next invaded the clergyman's cottage; he kindly acted as cicerone, and took us to the lake and boat-house, with its carved luncheon-room, and lastly to the newly constructed bridge. On our return poor Mama went to her room, as she was suffering from headache, and I joined the others, who were being photographed by Mr. Vivian. After luncheon I sat with her, conversing, knitting, and writing, till five, by which time she felt so much better that she went with me to tea. When the shooters came in we adjourned to the billiard and dancing rooms, where we played and sang till dressing-time. We were twenty-six at dinner (Jim having left), and danced all the evening. *October* 27.— . . . Bade adieu to our kind hosts and the remains of our gay party, and started for Heighton, where about twelve a slowish but very steady train picked us up, and landed us at Willesden after a comfortable and prosperous journey. . . . Reached Kew at eight, and retired to rest early.

Cambridge Cottage, October 29.— . . . We spent an hour with dear Aunt Mary, and then proceeded to the Paddington station, *en route* for Windsor. George and Colonel Tyrrwhit travelled

---

[1] The Duchess of Manchester.

down with us, and we reached the Castle about half-past six. The Queen, little Arthur, and shortly after Albert, came to see us. . . .

Windsor Castle, October 30.—We breakfasted before nine, and I played with the children in the corridor, as it was a wet day, then joined Mama in her sitting-room; after reading the Bible with her and knitting, Aunt Kent paid us a visit. We lunched at two, and Albert took us through the state rooms lately occupied by Napoleon and Eugénie, and to the library, where we were joined by the Queen, Vicky, and Alice. In the print-room Albert showed us some of the oldest collections of the ancestors of the Saxon House. We retraced our steps by the new underground passage, across the court-yard, and returned to our rooms, where I read and wrote till dressing-time. The Persignys, Clarendons, and Lord Panmure having arrived, we sat down twenty-five to dinner. *October* 31.—A wet day ! . . . I joined the elder girls in the corridor, and knitted with them for an hour, then read with Mama and wrote letters till the Queen sent for me to play battledore and shuttlecock with her. After luncheon we saw the Ambassadress [1] and her baby, and I played with the little ones, and read and sang to Vicky and Alice till five, when I went to my room, and afterwards joined Alice in the schoolroom to play duets with her. On returning I found the Queen and Albert with Mama. *November* 1.— . . . We bade Her Majesty adieu, and left Windsor at ten o'clock by the Paddington line, George remaining there to shoot. We were at Gloucester House shortly before eleven. . . .

Cambridge Cottage, November 5.— . . . I walked on the Richmond road with the Baron till about four ; practised, and was just settling myself down to write when I was sent for to look at the bonfire. In honour of Inkermann, the village people fired a salute with small cannons, and the fireworks, though humble, were in great profusion; I watched the bright scene till dressing-time. *November* 19.—We left for the King's Cross station, whence we started off about half-past twelve, in company with Major Purves, Lord Somerton, and Count Palffy. Lord Hardwicke, Libbet, and Lord Royston received us at the Royston station, amidst the waving of flags and cheering, and at half-past three we reached Wimpole,[2] where we found a large family party to meet us. . . . Lady Hardwicke took us first to our rooms, then to her boudoir, and lastly to the south drawing-room, where some

[1] Comtesse Persigny.
[2] Wimpole Hall, the seat of the Earl of Hardwicke.

of the party were assembled. About five, we young ladies betook ourselves to Libbet's and Mary's sitting-room, where we chatted till it was time to dress. After dinner the Yorke nieces joined our party, and we had some music and played whist at two tables.

Wimpole, November 20.— ... Established ourselves in the large drawing-room, and wiled away the morning with work, chat, and music. In the afternoon we drove over to Bourne, an Elizabethan house belonging to Lord De La Warr, and now rented by Mr. Pemberton, whose wife received us most kindly. The Vincents and Lady Caroline Duncombe were staying in the house. After tea Mrs. Pemberton took us upstairs to see a fine old carved chimney-piece, and the room in which Arabella West was born. In the small library we were shown part of a carved bedstead once slept in by Queen Elizabeth, and now converted into a chimney-piece. . . . The evening's amusement consisted of private theatricals, in which the family of Yorke were *sole* performers, and highly distinguished themselves. Mr. Eliot Yorke,[1] Mary, Libbet, and Lady Hardwicke were *first-rate.* The Prologue was written and spoken by Mr. Eliot Yorke. The evening concluded with a supper, as a good many of the neighbours had been asked to witness the performance.

November 21.—Started before twelve, in two carriages and an omnibus, for Cambridge, where we got out at Trinity Lodge, the Vice-Chancellor's (Whewell's [2]) abode. After taking a survey of the old apartments, and awaiting the arrival of the rest of the party, we drove to King's College Chapel, one of the finest buildings I have ever seen. The stained-glass windows, representing parallel passages in the Old and New Testaments, are beautiful ; and on the screen which separates the chancel from the rest of the Chapel, the cypher and arms of poor Anne Boleyn were pointed out to me, this being the only instance of their ever having been carved as a pendant to the arms of Henry VIII. The organ is a magnificent one, and a psalm was chanted for us to hear the effect ; after a hasty survey of the dining-hall at King's College, we were taken to see Trinity College Chapel, with its monuments and fine organ, and the old dining-hall, containing a very good picture of the late Duke of Gloucester as a child. We then returned to the Lodge

---

[1] Brother of the fourth Earl of Hardwicke.

[2] Dr. William Whewell, one of the greatest scholars of the nineteenth century. On the resignation of Dr. Wordsworth, in 1841, he was appointed Master of Trinity College, Cambridge.

for luncheon, at which Whewell and Lord Royston were next
to me, and afterwards inspected old manuscripts, amongst
others Prince Henry's copybook, Milton's works, and Sir
Isaac Newton's letters. We walked to Trinity College library,
and thence to Lord Royston's very nice rooms; then drove
to the Fitzwilliam Museum, but it was too dark to see
anything of the collection of pictures, and the only thing
I thought worthy of notice was the model of an ivory palace,
or tomb, erected by the Chinese Emperor to the memory of
his favourite and most lovely wife, and in which her ashes
repose. Returned to Wimpole about five.

November 22.— . . . We settled ourselves in the south
drawing-room, where we cut out and made paper flowers for
the ball-room, under Mr. Eliot Yorke's superintendence.
Later on the Grantham Yorkes joined us, and we sang glees
and catches till luncheon-time. In the afternoon we again
returned to our morning's quarters, and had lots of fun; the
nieces and cousins joined us from the Rectory, and we sang
till tea-time, then went upstairs to rest, and I read to the
girls in my room, and wrote to Vicky. In the evening we
had a charming ball, which we kept up till three o'clock.
November 23.—Breakfasted at eleven, after which I was
taught tricks at cards, and sat to Count Palffy for my
picture. I went to look at the Chapel, the work of Sir J.
Thornhill, the decorator of St. Paul's, and in the afternoon
drove with Mama, Lady Bloomfield, and Libbet to see a very
pretty little Chapel, belonging to old Mr. Cust, the Canon
of Windsor; the beautiful *wood carvings* are from Belgium
and Italy, the altar is Flemish, and the pulpit Italian; Mr.
Yorke and Mary accompanied us on horseback. It was
dark when we returned to Wimpole, and we drove at once to
the Rectory, where tea was prepared for us, and after roam-
ing all over the house, we walked home across the churchyard. We had some music in the evening, held a chapter of
the Order of the *Whistle*, of which Count Palffy and *Cardigan*
were duly elected *Knights*, and played at French Blindman's
Buff till twelve. *November* 24.—I got up early (having sat
up talking to Mary and Libbet till three), and went to
prayers in the Chapel at half-past nine. Soon after ten we
took leave of the whole party. Lord Hardwicke accompanied
us on horseback to the station, whence we steamed off with
Lord Somerton, Count Palffy, and Mr. Robert Liddell in our
carriage. . . .

Cambridge Cottage, November 27.—My 22nd Birthday!
May it usher in a bright and happy year for me, throughout

which I may be *blessed*, and do my duty to the best of my
ability, and may God vouchsafe unto me many and many
happy returns of this day.   Dear Mama took me into the
Drawing-room before breakfast, where I found my presents
spread out, *und nie wurde ein Geburtstags Kind mehr ver-
zogen !*   Whilst we were at breakfast George arrived and we
had a succession of visitors in the course of the morning. . . .
Count Palffy and the Duc d'Ossuna[1] came with splendid
bouquets about four *pour féliciter*, and on their departure I
wrote to the Empress Eugénie till dressing-time.   We
started at seven for town, and had a little chat with Aunt
Mary before dinner.   *November 29.—* . . . Attended St.
James's Church to witness the wedding of Lord Winchester and Mary Montagu.   We were in a pew by the altar,
and saw everything to perfection.   It was a very pretty
and *cheerful* wedding, whence *tears* were quite banished.
On our way through the vestry we exchanged greetings
with the whole party, and congratulated the " *happy
pair.*" . . .

December 1.—We heard from George that the King of
Sardinia would pay us a visit on the morrow, and this
entailed plenty of note writing on our part for *attendants*,
and a little arranging of my presents in the drawing-room.
. . . *December 2, Sunday.* — A very disturbed day !   I
breakfasted in my own room, and did not go to church on
account of my cold.   Major Purves came early, and about
half-past twelve we betook ourselves, with our work and
our books, to the drawing-room, to await the arrival of His
Sardinian Majesty.   Mrs. de Burgh made her appearance
about one, George very soon after, and at half-past the
King and his suite arrived in three carriages.   The interview lasted about half an hour, the suite remaining in the
library until called in by the King to be presented. . . .   I
sat talking in Mama's room till Mrs. de Burgh left, and
then read the evening service to Mama.   *December 3.—* . . .
Reached Windsor by six, and found Lady Caroline Murray
awaiting us there.   The Queen came to see us for a few
minutes, we being next door to Her Majesty as we were lodged
in the late King's rooms.   The Banquet was in St. George's
Hall, and the guests ninety in number; we met the King
of Sardinia in the Garter-room.   I sat between Count

---

[1] The Duc d'Ossuna was a Spanish Grandee.   He was an intimate friend of
the Duchess of Inverness's, and when he came to London, called to see her
every day, though he did not speak English, and the Duchess knew very
little French.

Cavour, the Sardinian Prime Minister, and the Duc de Pasqua, *Grand Chambellan* to His Majesty. . . .

Windsor Castle, December 4.—The King breakfasted with us *en famille* at a quarter to nine, and on returning to our rooms Lady Caroline Murray kept me company while Mama walked with the Queen. (The King spent the day in London.) In the afternoon I went up with the two youngest boys [1] to see their nurseries, and played with them in the corridor till five. After writing for some little time in my room, Vicky walked in, and insisted on paying me a visit in my own *sanctum;* then we paced the corridor together. Dressed in haste for the Banquet in St. George's Hall, at which I sat between the King and Count Cavour. *December* 5.—The King was not present at breakfast, as he had gone to town by the seven o'clock train. . . . On returning from walking with the Queen I finished a letter, and drove with Mama to Frogmore, to spend an hour with Aunt Kent. The King came back for luncheon, and directly it was over the investiture of the Garter took place, at part of which ceremony Mama and I were bidden spectators. We then remained with the children in the corridor, and saw the stag-hounds and harriers from Vicky's schoolroom. The rest of the afternoon was spent with Vicky and Alice in their room. The evening passed as usual, and at its close we said good-bye to the King of Sardinia. His visit has been quite an affair of state and grandeur. In this pageantry His Majesty must have found himself rather out of place, as he is naturally very shy, which he conceals under a brusque manner. He is also far from prepossessing in appearance, but remarkably soldier-like, frank, and, I believe, clever.

December 6.—I got up early, after being awakened at half-past four by the King breakfasting next door to me, previous to his departure at five; breakfasted with the Queen and the children, and bidding them good-bye, Mama and I started for town. . . . Sat with Aunt Mary for a little time, then drove to the King's Cross Station. Steamed off in company with Lord Sydney for Hatfield, and were received by Lord Salisbury at the station. We found only the ladies at home, and, luncheon over, we established ourselves in the library till four, when I went with Mandy to her rooms. On my return to the library for tea, I found quite a party assembled. . . . Lord De La Warr and the Duke of Manchester sat next me at dinner, and we danced till twelve.

[1] Princes Arthur and Leopold.

Hatfield, December 7.— . . . I spent the afternoon with Mandy in her room, and had tea in the library, where photographs were inspected till dressing-time. Dinner at seven, followed by a grand county ball, at which three hundred neighbours were present, and we kept the dancing up till three. My spirits rather flagged at last. *December 8.*—A great many of the party had left by early trains. At twelve we bade our kind hostess good-bye, and were accompanied by Lord Salisbury to the station; the Manchesters, Mr. Egerton, and Lord Chelsea went up to town in the same carriage with us.

During the autumn the late King of Hanover's house, adjoining Cambridge Cottage, was prepared for the reception of the Indian Princess Victoria Gouramma of Koorg. Colonel Drummond had been deputed to bring the Rajah of Koorg and his daughter to this country, and Her Majesty undertook the guardianship of the child, who was to be brought up in the Christian faith. The Indian Princess was baptized in the Chapel at Buckingham Palace—the Queen herself standing sponsor—and was entrusted to the care of Mrs. Drummond, who went to reside with her charge at what is now known as Church House.[1] On their return to Kew the Duchess of Cambridge lost no time in making the acquaintance of her new neighbours, and Mrs. Drummond,[2] recalling these days, writes—

The trust assigned to me proved an onerous one, and I had to put up with much annoyance in consequence of the Rajah's refusal to go back to India. Princess Mary and her kind mother entered into all my anxieties, and never lost an opportunity of lessening or removing them. The Mutiny necessitated my husband's return to India, and the Duchess and the Princess redoubled their kindness to me when I was left alone. Many may remember the happy

[1] Church House was bought by George III. at the same time that His Majesty purchased Cambridge Cottage, and given by him to his son Prince Ernest, afterwards Duke of Cumberland and King of Hanover. In 1831, the Herbarium buildings, on the north side of Kew Green, another property belonging to George III., were assigned to the Duke of Cumberland for life, and this residence has ever since been known as Hanover House.

[2] Now Mrs. Alexander.

home of the Royal mother and daughter, but few perhaps
can call to mind such numberless loving little traits of
unselfish thought for others, as myself. I became accustomed to the kindly voice calling out, "May I come up?"—
to the warm welcome always extended to me at the Cottage,
to invitations to the young Indian Princess and my own
little girls to play games or to look for Easter eggs, and,
above all, to the ready sympathy that never failed.

Journal.—Cambridge Cottage, December 24.—We had a visit
from our little neighbour the Princess Victoria Gouramma of
Koorg and her chaperone, Mrs. Drummond, and when they
left, we arranged the Christmas-tree and drawing-room, and
ticketed the presents for the steward's room. George, Major
Purves, and Count Chotek arrived at half-past seven, and we
had the *splendid* Christmas-tree before dinner; the table
with our presents looked very tempting, and the *pleasure* was
general. Afterwards we knitted, chatted, and relighted the
tree. The guests left at half-past eleven, and Mama and I
sat talking till twelve. *December* 25, *Christmas Day.*—After
church we took a walk, and then went into the Christmas
room, to feast on the tree and gifts. . . . Read a sermon to
Mama, and dressed at six for the dinner at Gloucester House ;
the guests included Lord Burghersh, Colonel Steele, Lord Chelsea, the Gordon Hallyburtons,[1] Colonel Tyrrwhit, and Miss
Adams. In the evening there was a party, at which grown-
up people were mixed with juveniles, and a Christmas-tree
covered with bonbons, which we all drew for, but from
which the lights were, thanks to Colonel Liddell, banished.
December 31.— . . . I sat to Sir William Ross, *en robe
décolletée,* for two hours; then drove to London, lunched with
George, called upon Aunt Mary and the Duchess of Inverness, and was home by seven. I spent the evening alone
with Mama; we poured lead, and indulged in some New
Year's Eve tricks. I was up when it struck twelve, and
prayed that 1856 might prove a bright year and one of *peace,*
and be succeeded by many happy years for us.

[1] Lady Augusta and Lord John Gordon had assumed the surname of
Hallyburton.

CHAPTER IX.

HAPPY DAYS.

1856.

Sir William Ross completes the miniature—March past of the Artillery—
Princess Royal's Confirmation—Visit to Egerton Lodge—Proclamation of Peace—Herr Hallé's first lesson—Laying the foundation-stone
of Wellington College—Ascot Races—Prince Oscar of Sweden
arrives—A day at Farnborough—Entry of the Guards into London
—The Duke of Cambridge appointed Commander-in-Chief—Review
of the troops by the Queen—Dinner to the Coldstreams—Princess
Mary's impressions of the season—A month at Baden—Rumpenheim—Return to Kew—Visit to Windsor—Sir William Dunbar
—Princess Mary's twenty-third birthday—Festivities at Cambridge
Cottage.

PRINCESS MARY had now entered upon her twenty-third
year, and as yet showed no disposition to turn her thoughts
in the direction of matrimony. It was far from her intention to marry in accordance with any political arrangement,
and the missions to this country for the purpose of bringing about a betrothal with some foreign Prince seldom
advanced beyond the initial stage. That the visit of Prince
Oscar of Sweden,[1] in the summer of 1856, was undertaken
with a similar object in view soon became an open secret,
but while the Princess enjoyed his society, she never contemplated an alliance with the heir-presumptive to the
Swedish throne.

Her life was very happy, and her interests were many.
The thought of exchanging her English home for one in a

---

[1] Third son of Oscar I. On the death of his elder brother in 1872 he
succeeded to the throne of Sweden, and is now the reigning sovereign. He
married, in 1857, Princess Sophia, daughter of Duke William of Nassau.

foreign land had ever been distasteful to the Princess, and, above all, she refused to bestow her hand where she could not give her heart. Seeing that she went so much into general society, it is hardly surprising that suitors, other than those of royal birth, aspired to wed her; but had Princess Mary wished to select a husband from the ranks of the English nobility, the wish must have been abandoned, for such a union would not, in those days, have received the sanction of the Sovereign.

Meanwhile, her public appearances became more numerous,. and her visits to Windsor more frequent. Both the Queen. and Prince Albert were much attached to their young: cousin, who was also a great favourite with the royal chil-- dren. The reviews of the troops by the Queen following the Proclamation of Peace had a special attraction for· Princess Mary, and her pleasure was naturally enhanced by the appointment of the Duke of Cambridge to the post of· Commander-in-Chief, an appointment which was received with acclamation by the army, and cordially endorsed by public opinion. The position of affairs on the Continent during the last two years had interfered with the visits of the Duchess of Cambridge to her relations in Germany, but now that matters had assumed their wonted aspect, she decided to pass the autumn abroad, and mother and daughter spent a very gay month at Baden, before joining the family circle at Rumpenheim, where they remained until their return to Kew, towards the end of the year.

Journal.—Cambridge Cottage, January 1.— . . . The Christmas-tree was lighted for the school-children, to whom we gave the accustomed presents. *January 2.*—After a late breakfast I read with Mama and walked till 1 o'clock, when Mr. Walbaum read with us till 2.45, and again for an hour after luncheon. We then had a visit from the Lavradios,[1] and I read till it was time to dress for our dinner-party of twelve *personnes*—the Oxholms, Hochschilds, Count Collo- redo, Karolyi[2] (*père et fils*), Chotek, and Trauttmansdorff. Conversed all the evening. *January 10.*— . . . I finished my‾

---

[1] Count Lavradio, the Portuguese Minister, and his wife.
[2] Afterwards Austrian Ambassador at the Court of St. James's.

accounts with Knese, and counted out *half-crowns* for the
Soldiers' Widows till my brain was in a perfect *whirl !*   In
the afternoon we drove over to the Cambridge Asylum, and
after dispensing our bounty in money and mittens to 20
widows, returned home. . . . I read a beautiful sermon,
entitled "Religion in Common Life," by Caird, a Scotch
divine, which he had preached before the Queen. *January*
15.— . . . Reached Windsor Castle by six; hardly were we
settled in our snug rooms when I began to read "Night and
Morning" to Mama, till interrupted by a visit from the Queen
and Albert.   I had to dress in a hurry, amidst the caresses
of five cousins ! . . .

Windsor Castle, January 16.— . . . I went with the
Queen to see the girls sketch, and walked with her *tête-à-tête*
till about 12. . . . In the afternoon I played with the
younger children, the Maharajah joining us.   We dined
a party of twenty-nine, and in the evening we danced.
January 17.—I passed the morning writing letters, whilst
Mama walked with the Queen.   Luncheon over, I took Leo and
Arthur up to the nursery, and on coming down again to the
sitting-room, Her Majesty came in, followed by Sir William
Ross with my miniature; after duly inspecting it she departed, and Mama read to me whilst I knitted.   At 4.30 we
paid Helena and Louise a visit, and were honoured with one
from Leo, I assisted at his supper in the day-nursery, hurried
down to see the Queen, who was waiting to pay *us* a visit,
and dressed in haste for the seven-o'clock dinner.   In the
evening we had theatricals in St. George's Hall : *The Jealous
Wife*, in which Kean acted remarkably well—his worse
half detestably !—but it was a very ill-chosen piece for such
a stage.

St. James's Palace, January 26.— . . . Mama dropped me
at Louise Mandy's, by whose couch I sat and chatted for
nearly an hour, and was introduced to the *tiny fat baby*.[1] . . .
We dined with George; the guests consisting of General La
Marmora and Lord Hardinge, who were my neighbours,
Azeglio, the Sardinian aide-de-camp, Sir Edmund Lyons,
Admiral Dundas, of the Baltic fleet, General Jones, General
Airey, Colonel Brownrigg, and Hélène Kielmansegge as
dame d'honneur.   In the evening Captain Drummond of the
Retribution came in. *February* 15.— . . . At twelve we
drove to Hyde Park, and walked up and down Rotten Row,
where we were joined by Major Purves and Count Kielman-
segge, and met George and loads of people we knew !   Home

[1] The present Countess of Gosford.

to luncheon, and had a visit from Lord Adolphus Fitzclarence.
. . . . We spent the evening at the Haymarket, and saw
The Busybody and *The Little Treasure;* Buckstone and Miss
Blanche Fane acted *very* well. *February* 20.—We had a
visit from Mr. Hutchinson, and watched the Levée for a
little while. Davison made his bow, and whilst we were at
luncheon the *Equerries* showed themselves in the *new
uniform !* Colonel Kinloch came to present his son to
Mama. . . . We had a dinner-party of sixteen, the Aumales
and Lady, the John Stanleys, Shelburnes, Lord Chelsea, Count
Colloredo, Baron Bentinck, Sir Edmund Lyons, Sir Benjamin
Hall,[1] and " Poodle " Byng.[2] In the evening the Hardwickes
and a few other people came in.

February 26.— . . . At two o'clock we drove to the Park,
escorted by Knese, and walked up to Cumberland Gate,
whence we proceeded to Montagu House, and, after picking
up Lady Rokeby, to the New Road, to choose a centre for
the fountain at Kew. We were unsuccessful in our search
at different stone masons, and then took Lady Rokeby
to the Regent's Park gardens. We dined with the Persignys
at the French Embassy, à 25 at eight o'clock. In the evening they had a very nice ball, and I danced till two a.m.
February 29.— . . . Mama dined at George's, to meet the
Queen, and I was to go there in the evening, but just as I
was sitting down to dinner with Knese, I was told Lord
Granville's carriage was waiting to take me over in his
Lordship's stead, as he was prevented by gout from making
the *fourteenth* at the table. I accordingly hurried over and
found them at soup, and a place left for me between Lord
Panmure and Sir Edmund Lyons. M. de Persigny, Van de
Weyer, Sir James Scarlett,[3] and *the suite* including Lady
Churchill, made up the party. The Princess Royal and
Lady Caroline Barrington[4] came in the evening. *March* 4.—
. . . At one we drove down to Kew to inspect the alterations 24
workmen were carrying out in our garden. . . . Dined with
Mama, and went with Rose Fane[5] to the Haymarket, where
the Purveses and Colonel James Halkett met us. Covent
Garden Theatre burnt down.

[1] First Commissioner of the Board of Works, afterwards raised to the
peerage as Baron Llanover.
[2] The Honble. Frederick Byng.
[3] General Sir James Scarlett, a distinguished officer in the Crimea. He
was the second son of Lord Abinger.
[4] Lady Caroline Barrington was entrusted with the superintendence of
the Princesses' studies.
[5] Now Lady Rose Weigall.

March 6.— . . . Drove to the British Museum to see the Nineveh, or rather Nimroud Marbles, with Sir Henry Rawlinson as our guide.   Home for luncheon, after which I called at Gloucester House, where I found the Queen and Vicky. . . . Tiny Hamilton[1] and Hélène Kielmansegge accompanied us to the Olympic, and we saw *Still Waters run deep* acted by Wigan to perfection, and *The Discreet Princess*, which came very tamely after that most interesting piece.   *March* 8.— . . . At the Regent's Park Botanic Gardens, where we had given George a *rendezvous*, we met Baron Goldsmid, the old millionaire; he was introduced to us by Sir Walter Stirling,[2] and took us to see his fine villa, where a large family party was assembled.   Home at six, and I sat with poor dear sick Knese. . . . *March* 10.— . . . Dressed early, to be in readiness to receive our dinner guests.   The Queen dined with us, and Mama had invited the Granvilles, Sydneys, Duke of Newcastle, Lord Lansdowne, Lord Eglinton, Lord Westmorland, and Count Kielmansegge to meet her. . . . Afterwards the Queen played at whist, and I looked over albums with Vicky, whose *first dinner* out of the palace it was.   We broke up shortly after eleven. *March* 12.— . . . Little Leopold arrived before I had *begun* breakfast, and before I had *finished* Mr. Harrison was announced; he sat with me till twelve. . . . We had a dinner-party of twenty people.   The Persignys, Prince de la Mossowa, Count Jaucourt, Breadalbanes, Cravens, Lady Jersey, and Clemmy, Hélène Kielmansegge, Count Vitzthum,[3] Lord Dufferin, Jim, General Ashburnham, Colonel Steele, and Mr. Norman Macdonald.   We had a small party in the evening to take off all stiffness, and it was over before twelve.

March 13.— . . . Soon after luncheon we drove to Woolwich to see the artillery corps, which had just landed, and had brought back the greater part of the *siege train* from the Crimea.   Lord Hardinge, Lord Panmure, and Colonel Maude[4] received us at the Artillery Barracks, where the Queen, Albert, and Victoria shortly after joined us.   As soon as the men had disembarked, they marched past us, looking worn and travel-stained, it is true, but *noble* and *soldier-like* to a

[1] Lady Louisa Hamilton, now Duchess of Buccleuch, Mistress of the Robes to the Queen.

[2] Of Faskine.

[3] The representative of the King of Saxony at the Court of St. James's.

[4] Afterwards Sir George Maude, Crown Equerry and Secretary to the Master of the Horse.

degree; and taking them generally they were a fine body of men, although sent home as being the *least efficient* part of the service. We next walked down the lines counting the medals for distinguished conduct in the field, the east wind blowing a perfect hurricane, and then placed ourselves on a platform to see the March Past. The royal salute was given, and the Queen took her departure; we followed her example, first inspecting the Russian guns taken at Alma and Sebastopol. *Sunday, March* 16.—After church we walked till three, and on our return home found a letter from the French Ambassador announcing the Empress Eugénie's safe confinement and the birth of a *boy*.[1] A very civil *billet* was penned in reply. . . .

Windsor Castle, March 20.— . . . At a quarter to twelve we assembled for dearest Victoria's Confirmation, which took place in the private Chapel, the Archbishop of Canterbury officiating. The ceremony was very short (the service for the day being omitted), and not solemn enough for my feelings, although the anthems were fine and well chosen. It was followed by a great deal of standing in the green drawing-room, where the Queen held a kind of *tournée* in honour of the Ministers, who had come down for the confirmation; after which dear Victoria, who looked particularly nice, and was very much impressed with the solemnity of the rite, received our presents on the occasion, and about half-past one we sat down to luncheon *en famille* as usual. We said good-bye to Her Majesty at a quarter to three, when Alice accompanied me to my room, and stayed with me for some time. I paid Vicky a flying visit, and got ready for our departure. We were back again at Kew soon after five. . . .

Cambridge Cottage, March 26.— . . . Dearest George's birthday! He rode down to breakfast, which was set out in the dining-room, as his presents were also arranged there—and much approved of they were. Sir William Davison came shortly before one, at which hour Kew Green fired *a royal salute*, and then George left us. . . . Colloredo came to take leave of us, as he is appointed to Rome. . . . *March* 29.— Up at seven, and directly I was dressed, packed my bag and breakfasted. Left at 10.5, after bidding Knese adieu, for Willesden, where the train and Major Purves picked us up, and we landed at Melton at 3.30. Lady Wilton met us at the station, and Katty and Peppy received us at dear Egerton Lodge. We were fifteen at dinner, and in the evening I

---

[1] The Prince Imperial.

played at whist. The party in the house at present consists
of the Manchesters, Hélène Kielmansegge, Jim, Mr. Craven,
and Lord Forester, besides the family, including Sim.[1]

Egerton Lodge, March 30, Sunday.—We breakfasted punctually at ten, and went to church, where a charity sermon
awaited us; then basked in the sun until luncheon was
announced. Early in the afternoon the youth of the party,
under Lord Wilton's and Jim's wing, and accompanied by
the Lloyds,[2] set out for a walk across country. We jumped a
brook and numberless fences; at the last fence I stupidly
twisted my foot, and thereby lamed myself, so we rested
at a farm-house, where the hospitable inmates (Farmer
Clayton and his wife) regaled us with apples and milk,
after which a two miles' walk across some pretty fields
took us home. I bathed and rubbed my foot before joining
the rest in the schoolroom, where I lay on the sofa until
dressing-time. In the evening we conversed, and Katty,
Mr. Leslie,[3] and Sim played trios on the piano, concertina,
and violin.

March 31.—Peace was proclaimed!! Katty, Hélène, and
the gentlemen, with the exception of Jim, went out hunting.
. . . I sang to Alice in the *sunny* drawing-room, and *received*
Count Chotek; and on Katty's return from hunting, I established myself in her room, to keep her company whilst she
was resting, Louise and Hélène dropping in upon us occasionally. We dined in the gallery at two small round
tables, and in the evening the *élite* of Melton came, and we
had a charming dance, which was kept up with great spirit
till 2.30. Ten couples altogether. *April* 1.—I was down at
breakfast about half-past ten, and the first of the young ladies
to appear! Lord Forester, Mr. Craven, and Sim left, and
shortly after M. de Jaucourt arrived. . . . Lord Granby
came over to see Mama, and we drove to Ashby Pasture—
Mama and Lady Wilton leading the way in the pony
phaeton, and nine of us following in the break—to gather
violets, which we found growing in *abundance* in the fields
and under the hedges along the road, returning home just
in time for tea in the schoolroom. . . . In the evening
we had a ladies' whist, until Lord Wilton made a fourth.
April 2.— . . . Sat in the drawing-room with my work all

---

[1] The Honble. Seymour Grey Egerton, youngest son of the second Earl
of Wilton. He succeeded his brother in the Earldom, and was father of the
present peer.

[2] Mr. and Lady Francis Lloyd.

[3] Now Sir John Leslie, Bart.

the morning, ànd in the afternoon 12 of us set out for a
"cross country" ramble, which proved great fun; we
returned home in a shower and the *steady ones* accompanied
Lord Wilton to the stables. . . .

April 3.— . . . I played duets (the "Stabat Mater,"
"Lombardi," and Mendelssohn's "Lieder") with Katty in
the drawing-room, whilst the rest worked or talked.
Soon after twelve Mama, Lady Wilton, M. de Jaucourt, and
I started in the coach (as it was raining) for Belvoir Castle,
where Lord Granby, Lady Adeliza Norman, Lady Elizabeth
Drummond, Mr. Norman, and Mr. Mules received us. We
took a peep *en passant* at the dear Gallery which was *en
papillotes*, as it is too large for their small party, and then
went on to the Chinese sitting-room at the end of the ball-
room, which Suffie and I shared on our two visits to the
Castle, but which is now the *grand commun*. There we
found Mr. and Mrs. Lumley, Cecil Drummond, Victoria
Wortley, Miss Gooding, and Sir F. Trench. We lunched in
the adjoining room, and then Lady Elizabeth and Lord
Granby took us to see the dear Duke, who is still shut up in
his own apartments, owing to his throat complaint. . . . We
were at Egerton Lodge again about five, and found the party
there just returned from a wild and *very wet* walk *à la*
Lady Mandy! tea in the schoolroom, and then I sang a
little, and went to Louise's room till dressing-time. We
were surprised just before dinner by the *walking-party*,
headed by Louise and Grey, appearing in masks and long
cloaks. Dined at 7.30, and after the ladies' game at whist,
we young people adjourned to the Gallery to dance and play
at games, and went through the Lancers, singing the music.
To bed at 1 a.m. *April* 5.—I was down early, collected
my autographs, and saw the gentlemen start for the meet.
Soon after eleven we took leave of our dear hostess, and proceeded to the station, where the train picked us up, after a
short delay. We travelled up to town—six of us—*vià*
Peterborough, in a remarkably uncomfortable carriage, and a
very seedy party we were! for poor Grey was quite asthmatic
with a heavy cold, Jim had a terrible headache, and Hélène
looked very much the worse for wear! whilst we were all
rather tired. . . . After stopping on our way at Gloucester
House, we reached Kew about eight, where dear Knese
tout-à-fait rajeuni received us.

Cambridge Cottage, April 14.— . . . Directly after luncheon
I flew to the arms of Aunt Kent, who had arrived with her
grandson, Ernest Leiningen. They left soon after four, and

I took an hour's walk with Knese, and then occupied myself (writing away) until dressing-time. We dined at six and went to the Haymarket, where we saw the greater part of *The Evil Genius*, a ballet performed by the Spanish Dancers, and *Court Favour*, in which piece Miss Blanche Fane acted remarkably well. The Newports and Colonel Tyrrwhit were in our box, and George joined us later. Home by half-past twelve, and waited upon myself, as poor Frazer was in bed.

April 19.—A damp cold day. I read to Mama while she worked in my *snug* room for an hour. We then played at billiards (I with a cue for a wonder) till dressing-time, and started at seven for Gloucester House, where we dined. . . . In the evening fourteen ladies came in with a very small sprinkling of men. Geraldine Somerset was there, and took joy on her recent appointment to be Mama's lady.[1]

April 24.— . . . We drove to the Palace by appointment to see the Queen and present Geraldine Somerset, and went on to the Duchess of Beaufort's, where we made a *visitation*.

April 25.—Dear Aunt Mary's birthday (the 80th). Quite a summer's day, so that we wandered about our garden; we lunched at Gloucester House, and being joined by George, presented our gift. At three we went to the Exhibition of the Painters in Water Colours, where we enjoyed a private view of a *very good* exhibition. Home (at St. James's I mean) by five o'clock. . . . We dined with Aunt Mary, and Lady Cowley, Lord Adolphus, Jim, and Liddell made up the party; at nine we went on to the Palace for a children's ball, given in honour of Alice's birthday, and I danced two quadrilles. We returned to St. James's to change carriages, and reached Kew by 1.30 a.m.

St. James's Palace, April 29.— . . . Perched on our balconies, we witnessed the Proclamation of Peace before the archway at St. James's! I then had several things to settle respecting my toilette, and began to dress for the drawing-room, which was *very full*. There were few pretty *débutantes*, but a number of our friends and acquaintances (*17 at least*) presented on their marriage.

Cambridge Cottage, May 4, *Sunday*.—At Church we had the Thanksgiving for Peace. . . . Mama read a Sermon to me whilst I worked, and we talked very seriously till luncheon-time. . . . We went out walking, and Knese and I returned

---

[1] Lady Geraldine Somerset had been appointed Lady-in-Waiting to the Duchess of Cambridge, and continued to hold that position until the Duchess's death in 1889.

home about five, leaving Mama in the King of Hanover's garden, indulging the fond hope of hearing the nightingales. I had not been home ten minutes before Count Karolyi and Count Chotek came, and we all four set out to join Mama. Count Karolyi left at six, but his *confrère* stayed to dine with us, and we sat talking with our *impromptu* guest till past seven, when we sent him to the Baron, who rigged him out for dinner. *May 8.*—Soon after luncheon we left for Gloucester House, where we met Brunnow, the *peace envoy! ganz der alte* and very little changed in person since we had last seen him two years ago. . . . We dined with George at seven, and then hastened back to St. James's to dress for the Court Ball. At 9.30 we drove to the Palace, and shortly after made our triumphal entry into the new State Ball and Concert Room, Albert's creation and *child*, as he calls it, which is very handsome, and on a grand scale. It was the Princess Royal's *début*, and a very fine ball; I danced ten times!

May 15.—. . . I strolled amongst *les beaux restes* of the lilacs, and then saw Mr. Johnston about the Bazaars. Mama read Palmer's trial for the Rugeley poisoning case to us. . . . Dressed at six o'clock and started for the Opera (Lyceum!), where we saw *Lucrezia Borgia*, in which Grisi and Mario were, alas! very weak, and a bad ballet. *May 16.*— . . . After writing out the cards for our Bazaar contributions, I stitched away, and whilst we were looking over some work George came to tell us that poor dear Adolphus Fitzclarence had had a paralytic stroke, and his life was despaired of. He was down at Sir George Wombwell's place. This was *sad news* indeed! . . . We then finished our selection of the work to be given away, and dressed for a dinner at Lady Jersey's, which was followed by a small evening party there, and a charming ball at Lady Craven's, at which I danced till 2.30. *May 19.*—I got up early and worked for two hours at my stool for the bazaar; breakfasted rather late in consequence. Mama then read with me, and I worked in her room till one o'clock. . . . Received in a letter from George the sad account of poor dear Lord Adolphus Fitzclarence's death, and wrote letters of *heartfelt* condolence, which occupied us for some little time. Mama set out for a walk in defiance of the weather, and I was preparing to accompany her when a hailstorm frustrated my attempt. . . . On her return, Mama got through all the speeches on the vote of Thanks to the Army and Navy whilst I worked.

St. James's Palace, May 21.— . . . Began to arrange my books and things, and put my sitting-room to rights. We drove in the afternoon to all manner of glass shops, in hope of finding hanging baskets in Bohemian crystal for the Queen, but in vain. Dined with Aunt Mary, and played at whist till nearly eleven, when we went to Lady Spencer's ball. *May* 22.—I divided my morning between Madame M——, who came to consult with me about my Court dress, and ticketing and arranging our work and contributions for the St. Anne's Bazaar. . . . We visited a wholesale shop in the city, in St. Paul's Churchyard, more like an *immense Bazaar* than any other place, where Mama made several purchases. Dressed for an early dinner and hurried to the Opera to hear *Rigoletto.* Geraldine, Louise Manchester, Jaucourt, Count Pourtalés, and Mr. A. Lumley were in our box. It was a great treat. . . . *May* 23.— . . . At two o'clock Mama left for Kew with Lady Rokeby, *her head gardener !* Libbet came to see me and I drove to Louise Manchester's, and picking her up as a chaperone, proceeded to the Regent's Park Gardens. . . . Louise made me come home with her to have tea and see the children. After dinner at Gloucester House we went on to Lady Antrobus's concert, which was *first rate,* and thence to Lady Stanley of Alderley's ball—pretty, but crowded.

May 27.—Before I had finished dressing, Helena and Louise arrived with Fraulein Ilhardt.[1] And after their departure I helped to make the yellow drawing-room *liveable;* we had a succession of callers all the afternoon—Lady Melbourne, Prince Frederick William of Prussia, the Prince Regent of Baden, and dear Lady Marian Alford. Drove to Gloucester House, and found Aunt *downstairs.* Helena, Louise, and Arthur came in whilst we were with her. Dined with George, and then dressed for a State ball at the Turkish Embassy, given in honour of Her Majesty. Upwards of 500 people being present, the crowd and heat were awful, but the temporary supper-room was beautifully arranged. *May* 28.—I practised until the arrival of Herr Hallé,[2] my new music master, who gave me his first lesson of an hour. We then went to the flower show in the Regent's Park, accompanied by *la suite;* the azaleas, roses, and geraniums were dazzlingly beautiful. . . . Dined at Lord Clarendon's.

May 29.—The Queen's Birthday kept, and the National holiday for Peace! Hargrave and Mary assisted at my toilet, poor sick Frazer only doing my hair. Breakfasted,

---

[1] Governess to Princess Helena and Princess Louise.
[2] Afterwards Sir Charles Hallé.

and at about twelve I began to dress, surrounded by 3 hand-maidens! The Drawing-room lasted nearly two hours, and we did not get home till half-past four; undressed, had tea, and then drove through Oxford Street, Regent Street, and Pall Mall to see the preparations for the evening's illuminations. Dressed for dinner, at which George made the fourth, and then went to the Palace for the fireworks, the crowd falling back to let us pass. We stood from 9.30 till 11.30 on the leads of the garden entrance, a *half-constructed* tent —quite a temple of the winds—forming our only shelter from the cold night air, watching the fireworks, which consisted almost entirely of splendid bouquets of comet rockets and showers of gold rain, ending with a grand discharge of rockets surmounting the words "God Save the Queen" in letters of fire. They were on the whole very fine, but there was too great a sameness for the length of time. When the display was over we had tea in the large ante-room down-stairs; and shortly before twelve we left and drove up to the Horse Guards, the front of which was brilliantly illuminated; then home, when we went up to Hardy's room just to get a peep at Pall Mall.

June 1.—. . . After luncheon we had a number of visitors. Lord Cadogan, the Prince of Wales and Alfred; then, just as I was settling down to write out texts on cards for the Consumption Hospital Bazaar, the Princess Royal and Alice walked in with Miss Hildyard, and on their departure I went to Mama's room, where I found Albert. . . . I worked for the Bazaar all the evening.

June 2.—Directly after breakfast we started for the Queen's private station at Vauxhall, and entered the second State carriage, where we awaited Her Majesty's arrival; *got under way* about twelve. Mama and I enjoyed the journey down to a temporarily erected station beyond Farnborough very much. We then followed in the *cortège* in our own carriage, and after proceeding about half a mile, alighted and joined the Queen in a tent, whence we passed in a kind of procession into the quadrangle marked out for the site of the Wellington College. Lord Derby then read a very fine address, which the Queen answered equally well, and after this laid the stone of the College. Luncheon in a second tent followed, at which Wales and Albert were my neighbours, and afterwards we adjourned to a platform in front of the quadrangle, whence we saw 13,000 men (partly militia) march past and fire volleys, under George's command, the only *contretemps* being the death of a poor sergeant of the Rifle Brigade, who broke a blood-vessel internally, and dropped down dead just after passing the Queen. . . . Home soon after six o'clock. We dined at the Palace, and I sat between Albert and the Turkish Ambassador.

June 5.— . . . We went to the Princess's to see the *Winter's Tale*, but were neither edified nor amused; the piece being dull, heavy, and coarse! the dresses and *mise en scène* fine.

June 6.— . . . At twelve Mama took me down to Marochetti's studio to sit for my bust, which is to be Lady Marian Alford's property. She met us there, and Mama left me under her care and returned home. I spent a very pleasant morning, and Lady Marian took me back to St. James's. In the afternoon Mama and I visited the Exhibition of the Old Masters at the British Institution; the Duchess of Beaufort and her girls joining us there. On our way home George met us, and inveigled us into going to the Bazaar held in the tents at the Wellington Barracks for the benefit of the children of the Guards, for whom a school is to be erected. The Brownriggs *en faisaient les honneurs*. On our return I had to choose a mantilla, then dined, and dressed at nine for the fancy ball at the Hanover Square rooms for the benefit of the Academy, which Her Majesty likewise honoured with her presence. We were first conducted up into a grand box, and afterwards to a *haut pas* immediately under it. It was a *very pretty sight!* Lady Jersey's *Starry* Quadrille was particularly successful, Lady Wilton's and Lady Rokeby's ditto of the Elements *partially* so, and Lady Harewood's *poudré* Quadrille very pretty. The Alliance Quadrille was somewhat a *failure*. We went up into the box again after the Queen had left, and were joined by some of our friends, amongst others Louise Manchester, who, in the costume of Cybele, Goddess of Towers, was to my mind the *Queen* of the evening.

Cambridge Cottage, June 9.—About half-past eleven Lady Marian Alford arrived to take me to Marochetti's, and I sat and stood for my bust from about 12.30 till nearly 4.30, Lily [1] and Lord Northampton keeping me company part of the time, and dear Lady Marian the whole, whilst Lord and Lady John Russell's visit to the studio occasioned a short pause in the sitting. I then had a delightful *tête-à-tête* with Lady Marian at her *fairy-like abode*,[2] where we partook of a very late luncheon, and at six she drove me back to Kew in her pony-phaeton over the Hammersmith Suspension Bridge. On our arrival we took a walk in the great garden, and meeting *Hookey* in an amiable mood! we returned home with

---

[1] The Honble. Lily Montagu.   [2] Alford House, Prince's Gate.

two baskets full of flowers! . . . *June* 11.—Prepared for our visit to Windsor. . . . About three Lady Marian carried me off to her house, and gave me some luncheon, after which she galloped me back to St. James's, where I had just ten minutes to change my dress in before leaving for Windsor by the 4.30 train from Waterloo Bridge. Reached the Castle before six, and walked down to Frogmore, but Aunt Kent was out, and we met Speth and dear little Leo. Alice came to me whilst I dressed. We dined—seventy-five *personnes*—in St. George's Hall at eight, and I was next to Albert. There was a small party in the evening, and we danced in the Waterloo Gallery.

Windsor Castle, June 12.—I got up at 7.20; we breakfasted soon after nine, and I went with George, Albert, the Regent of Baden, and Prince Frederick William of Prussia to see St. George's Chapel, returning by the Terrace. At twelve we started *en cortège* for the Ascot Races, I in the second carriage with Vicky, Wales, and Albert. The Queen was greatly cheered on her arrival by the assembled crowds, for the course was more numerously attended than usual. I enjoyed the races of all things, and had great fun in the stand. Luncheon was partaken of about 2 o'clock, and we took our departure in drizzling rain at a quarter to five. On our return Mama and I had tea together, George joining us, and soon after the Queen and little Leo paid us a visit. We again dined in St. George's Hall. A ball followed in the evening, to which many more were invited than on the previous night, and it was kept up till past one o'clock. *June* 12.—After breakfast we took leave of the Queen, and returned by train to Waterloo Bridge, Lord Eglinton going up with us in the same carriage. . . .

St. James's Palace, June 16.—We drove down to Kew, and on our arrival I went with Freieisen into the Gardens to gather the large wild daisies and grass for my bouquet at the Court ball. I then rested a while in the little room,[1] where Mama was working at her frame. . . . We settled to stay at Kew, as Ristori's acting was very doubtful, and sat in the garden (*I* Schiller in hand) till six. After tea Mama read "Barnaby Rudge" to me whilst I worked. *June* 20.— . . . We had a dinner-party, of eighteen. The Hardwickes and Libbet, Middletons, Somertons, Lady Marian Alford, Lords Malmesbury, Eglinton, West, and Valletort, Count Chotek, and Mr. Graham Vivian, besides four at home; and a very talkative and pleasant party it was. In the evening we adjourned to Lansdowne House for a concert. *June* 21.—

---

[1] The garden-room.

Mr. Walbaum read to us, and afterwards I looked at pink and white tulle for a ball gown. . . . Dined at seven, preparatory to going to the old Opera (Haymarket) to see Mdlle. Piccolomini in *La Traviata.* Her acting is very good, and Calsolari has much improved in singing. Marie Taglioni danced one *pas* in the *divertissement* afterwards. The Sandwiches and Count Jaucourt were in our box.

June 22.— . . . Shortly before five George came in, and had not left us long before Prince Oscar of Sweden arrived, and paid us half an hour's visit. We then took a drive round Hyde Park, which looked bright and gay with promenaders. . . . *June* 23.—At 4 o'clock we drove to the exhibition of Barker's pictures of the Allied generals before Sebastopol. George and several others are very like ! . . . Went to the Lyceum with Geraldine, Miss Mitford, and the Major, to hear and *see* Ristori, the famous Italian actress, in *Pia del Tolomei :* she reminds one of a first-rate German actress, and is grand and beautiful. Lady Marian Alford joined us later. *June* 24.—I was up at eight for Frazer's sake. . . . After luncheon Sir William and Lady Gomm,[1] fresh from India, came to see us, and on their departure we drove to Hyde Park to hear the band ; as we were sitting in our carriage Prince Oscar rode up and spoke to us. We dined at the Wiltons', and a charming *hop,* or rather ball, followed, which Prince Oscar honoured with his presence, dancing away remarkably well, and with much spirit.

June 25.— . . . Hastened over to welcome Lord Rokeby home again from the Crimea. George came in, and Mama and I went to see the poor dear Princess Royal, who is laid up with a burnt arm. . . . Dined at the Palace at 8 o'clock, a party of forty, I between George and Albert ; a short concert followed, at which Wagner, Noq, and M. Le Forêt sang, and on to a hot and crowded ball at Lady Ashburton's. *June* 26.— . . . To Grosvenor House for a ball the Westminsters gave in honour of Her Majesty : we danced in the dining-room and supped in the gallery ; the heat was intense. *June* 28.— . . . Started after tea with Mama for our sylvan retreat.

Cambridge Cottage, June 29.— . . . Joined Mama in the garden, read a sermon to her, and we sat and talked under the Persian lilac. Soon after five Count Chotek arrived, and was almost immediately followed by George and Prince Oscar; they walked with us to see the glass-house and Gardens and

---

[1] Lady Gomm was the eldest daughter of Lord Robert Kerr, and married, in 1830, Field-Marshal Sir William Gomm, Colonel of the Coldstream Guards,

we returned to tea, when Prince Oscar and George took
their departure. *July* 4.— . . . We called upon Princess
Charlotte of Belgium,[1] and missed seeing the King as he was
out; returned home to dress for the dinner at Sir William
Middleton's, and shortly before ten went on to Gloucester
House, to be in time to receive the Queen, in whose honour
dear Aunt Mary gave a very pretty ball, at which Prince
Oscar and the Belgians were also present.

St. James's Palace, July 7.—Hélène Kielmansegge arrived,
and at half-past twelve we started for the Waterloo Bridge
Station, whence we steamed away for Farnborough, accompanied by George, Edward Weimar, and Prince William of
Hesse Philippsthal. At Farnborough, Mama's landau conveyed us to the Camp, George preceding us on horseback.
He took us first to the North Camp, where, after passing the
huts of the Jägers and other German troops, we got out and
walked through the tents occupied by the horses of the 4th
and 5th Dragoons (heavy), just returned from the Crimea;
thence to the South Camp, where we lunched in the mess-room
of the Grenadier Guards. It rained heavily whilst we were
at luncheon, and consequently the review was put off till the
next day. To make up for this disappointment we drove all
through the South Camp, getting out every now and then to
see some of the men of each regiment of Guards and of the
79th Highlanders, who had served through the *whole* of the
war. We then drove up to Lord Hardinge's tent, but found
every one terribly upset there, as the poor old man had had
a paralytic stroke whilst in the Queen's Pavilion; bidding
George adieu, we started on our return to the station, the *Coldstreams* turning out to give us a *cheer* on our way back! . . .

July 9.—At 11 o'clock we drove with Geraldine to the
Palace to see the Guards pass, with Lord Rokeby at their head;
this we did from the balcony of the centre drawing-room, fronting the Mall. It was a glorious and *soul-stirring* sight, and one
I shall never forget. The men cheered as they passed under
the balcony, and we waved our handkerchiefs to them. We
then waited for some time downstairs before the order came
to start (in procession) for Hyde Park; I drove in the third
carriage with Victoria, Alice, and Charlotte of Belgium, the
crowd cheering us all the way. Upon reaching the ground,
we followed Her Majesty down the line, after which the
whole brigade of Guards, under George's command, marched
past, gave the Royal salute, and finally three, or rather *any*

[1] Sister of the present King of Belgium. She afterwards married the
Archduke Maximilian, and became Empress of Mexico.

number, of *cheers* for the Queen. We returned home to luncheon, in the middle of which we rushed to the window to see the *dear* Coldstreams go by on their way to the Tower. *July* 10.— . . . The afternoon was entirely taken up with receiving visits; first the young Prince and Princess Kinsky, she *jolie comme un ange ;* next Lady Marian Alford ; after that Rose Fane, Lady Falkland, Colonel Gordon Drummond, and the Prince and Princess of Prussia, with their daughter. *July* 11.— . . . Prince Oscar of Sweden came to take leave, and at 4.30 we started for Craven Cottage. It was as usual a very pretty breakfast, Lady Howard having invited hardly any but acquaintances. The band of the 1st Life Guards played on the lawn. . . . Were home again soon after eight, when Mama and I dined *en robes de chambre* in her boudoir. Tea at nine, and dressed for a *grand* and charmingly first-rate ball at dear Apsley House. Prince Oscar was there, and bade us a second time good-bye.

Cambridge Cottage, July 14.—Mama surprised me before I was up with the pleasant intelligence that George had been appointed *Commander-in-Chief* by the Queen. Breakfast over, Gouramma and I went into the Gardens to gather roses. At six we returned to town, George coming in for a minute to be congratulated, and dined at the Palace to meet the Prussians. A dance followed, which was kept up till 1.30, and a very nice party was invited for it. *July* 16.— . . . At twelve we started with Knese and Geraldine for the Waterloo Bridge Station, whence we steamed, though but slowly, down to Farnborough, where we had to wait until our carriage could be got off the truck and ready. We then skirted the camp, and drove at once to Lord Panmure's tent ; George met us there, and we had some luncheon, after which, it being a quarter to four, we proceeded, escorted by Major Clifton, to the ground, and there awaited Her Majesty, in whose rear we drove down the line of several regiments just returned from the Crimea. We saw them march past, walked down the line for the Queen to notice those who had distinguished conduct medals, took up a position on a hill to see a manœuvre of cavalry, artillery, guards, and rifles, with Colonel Brownrigg as our cicerone, and finally witnessed a *general* march past of the *14,000* men. We returned to Farnborough, and were whirled back to town in the *Parliamentary* train.

St. James's Palace, July 18.— . . . Charlotte Lyster and Tiny Hamilton arrived to accompany us to the Tower ; we started a little before one, and were received by Colonel Gordon Drummond and a number of the officers of the

Coldstreams (both past and present), and by the Combermeres. The men of the second battalion were drawn up in front of the officers' mess-room, and we saw them march off to the dinner which was provided for them at Mama's expense. As soon as the *1,000* were seated we followed to an immense store-room given up to them for the occasion, and which the men had decorated with evergreens, and with colours and trophies, over which hung my dear Father's picture. We walked round the tables, the band playing, and feasted our eyes upon the bronzed happy faces of our *heroes!* Colonel Gordon Drummond made a very pretty speech, and the men gave three hearty cheers for dear Mama. It was altogether one of the most delightful and thrilling sights I ever beheld, and one not to be forgotten! We had luncheon in the officers' mess-room with a large party, the wives and belongings of the officers mustering pretty strongly, and I sat between Colonel Gordon Drummond and Colonel Upton; afterwards we went to see the old Chapel, and what used to be the mess-room of the officers, which is now held in veneration as having been the cell for prisoners of distinction.

July 24.— . . . Returned home in time to dress for a breakfast at the Duchess of Somerset's, Wimbledon. We got there about half-past five, and found a great number of people assembled on the lawn and steps, but rather a *disette* of men one knew. After a little promenading and talking, we *grandees*, to the number of eight, sat down to a private dinner, at which the only two men of our party were my neighbours. Then we sat out and talked, and at dusk we young people took off our bonnets and danced away indoors. We left about a quarter-past ten. *July 25.*—I was with Mama at 10.30 to wish her joy of this *dear day,* and gave her my birthday presents before breakfast, at which George assisted. At two o'clock the Duc d'Ossuna called, and in the afternoon Aunt Kent, attended by Lady Augusta Bruce, came to see us; on her departure the Duchess of Inverness arrived, to whom I showed the presents. . . . I drove with Mama to the Regent's Park Botanical Gardens, where we sat reading her birthday letters for some little time. . . . Dined with Aunt Mary, who, unfortunately, was not well enough to appear; in the evening she received us and a small party of Mama's friends upstairs, and Lily Montagu confided her shortly-to-be-announced marriage with Gerald Wellesley, the Dean of Windsor, to me this memorable evening.

Cambridge Cottage, July 29.—Lady Marian Alford chaperoned me to Marochetti's for the final sitting. Mama joined us there later, and pronounced the bust to be "an *excellent likeness!*" *August* 1.—Drove over to Orleans House with Mama at half-past eleven to meet Queen Marie Amélie at a French breakfast *à la fourchette.* The Duchesse d'Aumale was on her *chaise longue,* so that the Duc had to do the honours; we sat down to breakfast a party of twelve, comprising, in addition to the Princesse de Joinville, Condé, M. le Trot, and the French suites; we afterwards established ourselves in the centre room between the conservatories, where the little Duchesse had placed herself, and conversed. Home by half-past two, and sat with Mama and Mrs. de Burgh till tea-time, enjoying the *dolce far niente,* as I found it too hot to move. *August* 4.— . . . I wrote to Ellinor Dalrymple. . . . We dined at eight, and afterwards drove over to the White Lodge, where we were much alarmed at hearing that dear Aunt had had an attack of faintness and oppression on returning from her drive.

Letter to the Honble. Mrs. Dalrymple.

Cambridge Cottage, August 4, 1856.

. . . It is a very long time since you have heard from me, and I really must take up my pen to recall myself, and the happy days of our childhood that we spent together, to your recollection. I should have written before to thank you for your kind letter, but that I could not find a spare hour to devote to you in the whirl and bustle of the season— and what a fatiguing, unsatisfactory season it has been! Concerts and agreeable dinner-parties are quite out of date, and with them all real social enjoyment vanishes; instead of which we have had any number of hot, dull, crowded balls, at which one's gown is torn to shreds. . . . I can assure you there are very few days out of the two months we were in town that I should care to have over again, and these were chiefly spent in soldiering! The entrance of the Guards into London, the dinner Mama gave to the Battalion of the Coldstreams, lately returned from the Crimea, laying the foundation-stone of Wellington College, and our two visits to Aldershot form the principal exceptions.

Of course the foolish report of my *supposed* intended marriage did not tend to make the season very agreeable to poor me! And I rejoice to find myself once more at Kew, in the perfect enjoyment of peace and quiet, "the world

H.R.H. The Duchess of Gloucester
from a water colour drawing made in 1849 by Edwin D. Smith.

forgetting, by the world forgot"! Not that I take at all a melancholy view of things in general, quite the reverse; but I want a little rest after the wear and tear of London, and have, I am truly thankful to say, too many resources *in myself* ever to feel a want or craving for outward excitement. . . . You can imagine how delighted we were at dear George's appointment, and the manner in which it has been received by the army and country at large, proves how great and universal is his popularity. I only trust he may fully realise the hopes centred in him, which I venture to flatter myself he will. He is charmed with his post, and deeply touched at finding himself *so popular!* . . .

Journal.—Cambridge Cottage, August 11.— . . . Mr. Hills brought a better account of Aunt Mary, and Mama settled with Knese to start (D.V.) on Saturday for Germany. . . . *August 15.—* . . . Went with Mama to the White Lodge to bid dear Aunt good-bye, and she gave me a ring as a keepsake; she seemed stronger and looked *charming*, played at patiences with us, and bore up well at the parting. God in His mercy grant us a happy meeting in a couple of months, and spare her to us yet awhile. Amen.

August 16.—George came down to breakfast, and then wandered up and down the garden with us. . . . At three we bade the servants and our dear cottage good-bye and started for the London Bridge Station, whence we steamed off to Dover at 4.30. The wind rose every hour, so that by the time we reached Dover (7.15) it *seemed* to *me* to be blowing a gale. Captain Smithett and the military and naval authorities received us at the terminus, and conducted us to the entrance (at which the 93rd Highlanders were drawn up), and down the Admiralty pier, where we had to embark on account of the tide not serving inside the harbour. This promenade afforded us an extensive view of the stormy and foaming brine. I lay down at once in one of the paddle-box cabins, and, though giddy and uncomfortable, kept well throughout the rough and stormy passage, which quite upset poor Mama and most of the others. On arriving at Calais (9.45) we walked to the Hotel, in spite of the thunderstorm. Mama went to bed soon after, and about 11 o'clock we had dinner, five[1] of us, as Smithett and his son joined us, and then retired to rest for rather more than five hours.

[1] Lady Geraldine Somerset and Baron Knesebeck were in attendance upon the Duchess of Cambridge and Princess Mary.

Calais, August 17.—I was up at a quarter to six; breakfasted at 7.15, and left the hotel soon after for the station,
where Smithett awaited us to say good-bye. At Lille, which
was reached at 10.45, we had to wait an hour and a half,
and employed the time in walking up and down the nearest
streets, and resting in a smart green waiting-room, *garnie de
bouquets de fête fanés,* and inhabited by a tame and remarkably sociable sparrow! We arrived at Liège about eight
(having stopped at *forty* different stations in the course of
the day!) and went at once to the nearest inn, l'Hôtel de
l'Univers. After a tea-supper, we tidied ourselves somewhat, and rested on sofas till twelve, when we were hurried
over to the station, where we had half an hour to wait.
Fortunately it was a lovely moonlight night, and we quite
enjoyed sitting out-of-doors. About 1 a.m. we started in
the night train for Cologne, but could get little sleep on
our road, as the guards were perpetually disturbing us to
look at the passport, tickets, and so forth; we waited
some time at Verviers, and reached the station, or rather
terminus, at Cologne about 5.30, but, thanks to the dilatory
proceedings of the Prussian railway authorities and the bad
driving of the postillion, who in turning a sharp corner
jammed us against a wall (fortunately without injuring the
carriage), and then came down with his horse, we did not
get to the hotel till 6.15. Here a hasty toilet was performed preparatory to an indifferent breakfast, and we
walked down to the steamer which weighed anchor at
7.45. Mama sat in the carriage [1] at first, but as the smoking
around us was very unpleasant we shifted our quarters
and seated ourselves under the awning, until driven away
by the preparations for the *table d'hôte.* At about one
o'clock we had an excellent luncheon, *de petits poulets et
compôte,* in our carriage, after which we again sat out, and
were joined by a French gentleman and his wife, very nice
people seemingly, in whose company we spent the rest of the
day admiring the scenery of the Rhine, which really is *very
beautiful* in some parts, though perhaps on the whole there
is not enough change to please one. Towards the evening it
set in for rain, and the last part of the journey from Bingen
to Mayence, which we reached by a quarter to eleven, was
performed in the dark. We drove at once to the Hotel du
Rhin, where we found everything *very comfortable,* and directly
after supper hurried to bed.

Mayence, August 19.— . . . Breakfasted at 10.30-and-

---
[1] The carriage was taken-on-board the steamer. . .

went out on the balcony, where we found oleander and pomegranate plants in full blossom (they abound in these parts, and are to be seen before all the inns and railway stations). At 11.20 we left by train for Ludwigshafen, and came in for a fearful thunder shower on our way; we got there about one, and after waiting in the storm for horses to be put to the carriages, drove through Mannheim *en route* for the station, where we had to spend a considerable time in the royal waiting - room. At last we continued our journey, reaching Baden about 7.30, just as the weather was clearing up a little. We were received at the station by Mr. Heneage[1] and Mr. Hamilton,[2] and at the Hôtel d'Angleterre, whither we at once drove, by Mrs. Heneage and Mary;[3] they had procured a charming apartment for us, with a balcony commanding a view of the hills and of the promenade. On their departure Lord Westmorland walked in, and at half-past eight we dined *fort bien*. The Austrian band from Rastatt was playing on the promenade, and we listened as well as we could from the balcony.

Baden, August 20.—We breakfasted about ten, arranged the sitting-rooms, unpacked, had a visit from Mr. Hamilton, wrote to Aunt Mary, and then saw the Cavendishes,[4] Princesse Radziwill, and the Heneages, who all escorted us to the *réunion* on the promenade at a quarter to four, where we made the acquaintance of one or two people, rested under the trees till past five, and went home to dinner. Sat on the balcony for some little time, changed our dress, and returned to the promenade about 7.30. It came on to rain, and we waited under the booths for the arrival of our *coterie;* but as no one appeared we went to Marx, the bookseller's shop, to order a book. Soon after we met the Heneages, and fell in with Mrs. Cavendish and Lord Westmorland, who insisted upon taking us through the Kursaal. I watched the gambling in two different rooms, returning home about nine.

August 22.— . . . I walked with Knese and Geraldine towards Lichtenthal. Home shortly before 1 o'clock to receive the Fürstenbergs, our acquaintances from Ischl; we then had a visit from Countess Apponyi, and went on the promenade, where the Russian Chargé d'Affaires, M. de Stulipine, and some French gentlemen were presented to us,

---

[1] Mr. Charles Heneage of the Life Guards, and gentleman Usher to the Queen. He married a daughter of the second Lord Graves.

[2] British Chargé d'Affaires at Carlsruhe.

[3] Eldest daughter of Mr. and the Honble. Mrs. Heneage.

[4] Mr. and Mrs. George Cavendish.

and we found the Oubrils, whom we knew at Frankfort.
. . . On our return I read the English papers to Mama, and
then dressed for a very pretty ball given in the *Salle des
Fleurs* by the Cavendishes in our honour. At first I felt *very
shy*, as of course there were endless presentations, but when
those were happily got over, I soon danced my shyness
away. A sitting-down supper followed, at which M. de
Serre and M. de Stulipine were my neighbours, with the
latter of whom I afterwards danced the cotillon. We were
home by two, and I thought it great fun.

August 24, Sunday.— . . . We walked up to the Roman
Catholic Church, in which the English Protestant service
is performed at eleven. The clergyman, Mr. Lateward, gave
us a very good sermon, and the singing was excellent. . . . In
the afternoon we went on the promenade to hear the Baden
military band, and sat with the Cavendishes, Rumbolds,[1]
Lutteroths, Comtesse Lottum, Mrs. St. John, and the Apponyis till five, when we hastened home to dine. We then
took a charming drive up to and round by the Fremersberg and the Jagdhaus, returning soon after eight, and proceeding at once to the *réunion* on the promenade, where we
sat with the rest of the *société*, or walked up and down till
ten o'clock, the band playing indoors to attract people to the
gaming tables.

August 25.— . . . At a quarter to three we started for a
picnic. We got out at Ebersteinburg and walked up to the
ruins of the Burg, from a window of which we had a splendid
view. After scaling the highest tower and resting a little,
we trotted down again to the carriages, and drove on to the
Alte Schloss, where we sat down (27) to a very eatable
picnic-dinner in the open air. Before it was over I hurried
up to the tip-top of the ruined castle to see the sun set, and
we had a glorious view of Baden itself, its environs, and the
plain. Strasburg was, however, invisible, owing to the haze.
We were home again about nine o'clock, having thoroughly
enjoyed ourselves. *August 26.*— . . . In the afternoon I
took my music over to Mrs. Cavendish's, where I spent two
hours very pleasantly *faisant de la musique* with her, Mrs.
Rumbold, and the two brothers. . . . Returned home to
dress, and then proceeded to an upper room at Weber's,
where we found Princess Lieven,[2] her *demoiselle de compagnie*,
and the Cavendishes, to hear the Austrian band, which

---

[1] Mr., afterwards Sir Horace Rumbold, now British Ambassador at Vienna,
and Mr. and Mrs. William Rumbold.

[2] See footnote on p. 94.

played most beautifully for about two hours. We then adjourned to the *Salle des Fleurs*, where the gentlemen of the Club had arranged to give a dance *en notre honneur*, the Austrians forming the orchestra. We stayed till after twelve, and I danced a great deal, but it was not so *animé* as the Cavendishes'.

August 27.— . . . We paid the Fürstenbergs a visit in their new and pretty little house, and saw their children; then called at Princess Radziwill's, but she was not well enough to see us, and afterwards went on the promenade, seating ourselves under the trees with a large circle of acquaintances to listen to the music; Le Prince de Bauffremont came *pour nous faire ses adieux.* After dinner, which was at 4.15, we drove through Lichtenthal and the picturesque village beyond to Geroldsau, where we left the carriage to have a good view of the cascade, which is beautiful in its fall. Home soon after seven to dress for the representation of the pretty opera, the *Sylphe*. . . .

August 28.—Walked to the *Trink Halle*, and afterwards went into the Kursaal to watch the gaming tables. Just as we were coming out Mr. Hamilton joined us, and as it was beginning to rain we returned to the Saal, and sat there till one. I then took advantage of Mrs. Cavendish's absence to practise at her house, and had a romp with the children, returning home to prepare for a walk up to Yburg. The Heneage girls, their father, Geraldine, Major Purves, and I made up the walking party; Mama, Knese, Mrs. Heneage, and Mrs. Purves going up in the carriage. The walk would have been a charming one had not the sultriness of the weather rendered the continued though gradual ascent very fatiguing; the last bit before we reached the ruins of the Yburg was particularly steep. We were rewarded, however, by the *beautiful view* from the top of the tower, commanding Baden, the Fremersburg, the *beginning* of the Black Forest, and Strasburg in the distance, with the ranges of the Vosges and Jura. I returned home in the carriage in the proud consciousness of having walked nearly six miles !

August 29.— . . . Joined Mama on the Promenade, where we found most of the *société réunié*, and made the acquaintance of Princess Léonie de Béthune. . . . Home at 4.30 to dinner, after which we drove up to the Neuen Schloss, and were shown over the best rooms, which are dull, rather dark, small, low, and very heavily furnished. One or two of the private rooms, however, command a very fine view of the town and its surroundings. We drove down the hill by a different road, getting out at the station to receive the Queen of Holland;[1] most affectionate was the meeting, and we drove with her to the Hotel. . . . The Queen then came and sat with us for about an hour and a half.

August 30.— . . . Just as I was beginning to write, the Queen of Holland came in, next a French woman with sleeves and collars, whom we sent away in a hurry to receive the Margravine William of Baden and her three daughters, so *höflich und unterthänig!* Shortly after we had a visit from the Grande Duchesse Stephanie[2] *causant à merveille*. . . . At three we accompanied the Queen of Holland on a drive round the Fremersberg, during which she quite charmed us with her agreeable conversation, and on our return we called on the Grande Duchesse Stephanie at her *charming* abode, which is fitted up with the greatest possible taste. . . . Had a visit from the Regent of Baden[3] before making a hurried toilette and accompanying the Queen to the Grande Duchesse Stephanie's, where we found a small tea-party *réuni*.

August 31, *Sunday*.— . . . Walked to Church, the Queen following us thither in the carriage, and driving us back. I found her places for her, and was delighted to hear her responding in capital English, and with all her heart seemingly. Mama and I then paid a *visite d'adieu* to the Grande Duchesse Stephanie, after which we drove to the station to receive dearest Augusta, and found all the English already assembled there to greet her. Soon after 3.30 the train arrived, and almost before it had stopped she was in our arms! Engel and M. de Lühe accompanied her. We drove her at once to the Hotel, and sat with her till past five, when we hastened to dress for the dinner with the Queen of Holland. *September* 1.— . . . The Queen came to fetch us for a joint expedition to Rothenfels, and the drive thither was very enjoyable. We took the longest, and by far the most picturesque, road across the hills, reaching Rothenfels about half-past two, where the Markgraf William, his wife, and daughters received us most kindly at their prettily situated, but simply furnished, country house. . . . An hour and a half's drive along the plain, between fruit trees and fields,

---

[1] Queen Sophie, first wife of William III., King of Holland. She was a Princess of Würtemberg.

[2] Wife of the late Grand Duke Charles of Baden and daughter of Comte Claude de Beauharnais. Their daughter, Princess Mary, married the Duke of Hamilton (see footnote, p. 156).

[3] The present Grand Duke Louis of Baden. He succeeded his father as Regent during the lifetime of his elder brother, who was mentally afflicted.

brought us home again, when we dressed in a hurry, had a *déjeûner à la fourchette*, and started again (this time, however, without Her Majesty) for the Fremersberg, the Luitzen's place, where a *fête champêtre* awaited us, which, unfortunately, was quite spoilt by a violent thunderstorm. The amusement of the evening began with a conjuror, after which the garden was illuminated with coloured lamps, and we began to dance in a tent, but just as the Bengal fires were being lighted around it, and we were in the middle of a quadrille, the rain came down and drove us indoors, to wait downstairs in the small, hot, and crowded rooms until they could clear the drawing-room upstairs. I danced twice, and then came down to supper at a small round table for six. We were perfectly *ravenous!* Home by torchlight at a quarter to eleven.

September 2.—Soon after ten I followed the others to the Queen of Holland's apartments, to bid her good-bye; M. de Tuyll was also there, which made it less *à l'aise.* We saw the dear Queen depart *à grand regret,* and then sat down to breakfast. . . . Geraldine and I went over to Mrs. Caven-dish's, where Mrs. Rumbold joined us; I played and she sang *delightfully;* Mama and Gussy came to hear her, and the former was induced to join in the singing. In the afternoon we set out for a charming drive beyond Lichtenthal, leaving the road to Geroldsau on our left, and taking the so-called Holz-Weg, which led us on and on through a lovely valley with picturesque villages, till at length we got out where it ended in a steep footpath, and climbed up a little way. . . .

September 3.— . . . At three we started for the Favorita [1] (where the Villebois' [2] had prepared a *fête* for us), and got there soon after four. The *château* was built by the Markgräfinn Sybil, and we went over the quaint little rooms with em-broidered hangings, fitted up in the Louis XIV. style, and the kitchen, with its beautiful Venetian glass and old china. We sat down to dinner in the hall, 50 covers being laid, Lord Augustus Loftus and M. de Stulipine being on either side of me, which made it very pleasant. . . . We after-wards adjourned to a room at the end of a long open gallery, tastefully illuminated with coloured lamps. The Austrian band had failed at the last moment, so that the Villebois' had to send in all directions for *music,* but luckily, at 8.30, the

---

[1] Formerly a little *Jagd-Schloss* belonging to the Duke of Baden. Now a kind of pleasure garden.

[2] Mr. and Mrs. Henry Villebois, of Marham.

Carlsruhe military band marched in, playing "God save the Queen;" later in the evening Bénaget sent his band, and in consequence dancing was kept up with great spirit till about eleven.

Rumpenheim, September 17.—Breakfasted at ten, and wandered about the garden till one o'clock, when Madame de Bethman and her sister Fraulein Bose (de Nassau) came to see us *des Liebhaber Theaters wegen*. . . . I assisted at Dolphus's dinner, then unpacked, looked in upon Knese, who was ill, and arranged my things. We dined at five, and shortly before eight the Malets,[1] with their *attachés*, were announced. . . .

September 20.— . . . I joined Mama and Augusta in the garden, and we walked through the village to Pastor Ulrich's, who regaled us with *Zwetschen Kuchen* and nuts, and on our way home Geraldine and I had a frolic in the mud with Dolphus. . . . Worked away at a *tableau* till dinner-time, and directly afterwards went up to dress: at seven we started for Frankfort to see the two pieces—got up at Baden by the Rumbolds, Cavendish & Co., in our honour—acted at Madame de Bethman's. Before the play began, several presentations *du corps diplomatique* were made. . . . The performance opened with a melodrama entitled *Rudolphe, où frère et sœur*, in which Mrs. Rumbold was perfect, Mrs. Cavendish *pas mal*, though painfully shy, M. Fleuriot good, and M. de la Rochefoucauld rather stiff. In the second piece (a comedy entitled *Embrassons nous Folleville*) Mrs. Rumbold and Horace highly distinguished themselves, and Willy Rumbold acted very well. We afterwards had the pleasure of congratulating our friends on their complete success, and after bidding them and our kind hostess adieu, reached home about twelve o'clock.

September 22.—I was up at seven to finish a letter to Lady Marian. . . . We started for Frankfort *en route* for Biebrich. Close to the Mayence line station the leader postillion's horse fell, and we had to *jump* out of the carriage; we escaped with the fright, for neither man nor horse was hurt. We reached Biebrich shortly before one by train, and the Duchess of Nassau's carriage conveyed us to the *Château*, where we were received by Adelaide[2] and her Lady, Fraulein Lohn. After tidying ourselves in our late rooms, Adelaide

---

[1] Sir Alexander and Lady Malet. Sir Alexander was Envoy Extraordinary and Minister Plenipotentiary to the Germanic Confederation at Frankfort, and also Minister Plenipotentiary at Hesse-Cassel, Hesse-Darmstadt, and Nassau. He married the daughter of Mr. John Spalding.

[2] Duchess of Nassau. Now Grand Duchess of Luxemburg.

took us to her own apartments, which are new and charmingly fitted up, where we lunched. Little Willy[1] came in whilst we were at luncheon, but was nervous at seeing so many new faces and burst into tears, talking away as prettily as possible all the time. As it rained, we spent the intervening time in Adelaide's sitting-room, and at four went down to dinner in the *rondelle*, ten of us, including our respective suites. Afterwards we inspected the Duke's rooms, and shortly before six left for the station, where we took a most affectionate leave of our kind little hostess, and returned home with no further accident than the horses getting over the traces just before Oberrath. We were home by half-past eight, and had tea, pancakes, and *Zwetchen Compote* in the Gallery. . . . *September* 23.— . . . Geraldine, Dolphus, and I started on foot for Offenbach; and after paying a visit to the *pfeffernuss Laden*, had the amusement of waiting at the door of the *Leder Fabrik* for some time, till by giving our name we at length induced the subordinates to send for a foreman; after making several purchases we returned home in my uncle's carriage. . . . During the evening I accompanied Mama and Gussy while they sang.

September 24.— . . . At four o'clock Mama and I set out for Frankfort with Augusta. . . . We had nearly half an hour to wait at the station, as the passengers did not choose to come in time, and were *waited for*, and this prolonged leave-taking quite overcame poor dear Gussy. At length, with a heavy heart, we saw her and darling Dolphus whirled away, and, escorted by Mr. Edwardes,[2] we returned to the carriage and drove back to Rumpenheim, sad and sorry at heart to think of the dear faces we should miss on our return. . . . *September* 26.—I awoke with a headache and a terrible fit of the *blues*, which I am ashamed to say I indulged in till 11.30, when I went down to a solitary breakfast. We lunched at Frankfort with the Malets, in company with the legation, then went to the Stadelsche Institut, attended by Sir Alexander Malet and Mr. Edwardes, to see Lessing's famous picture, "John Huss before the Council of Constance." The collection of pictures is altogether very fair; one a fine head of a monk by Moroni, and several good specimens of the Dutch school. . . . We took leave of our *beaux*, and were home by 5.30. *September* 29.— . . . I wrote to the Princess Royal till two, when Knese joined us in the garden, and we

---

[1] Eldest son of the Duchess of Nassau, and now Hereditary Prince of Luxemburg.

[2] Secretary of Legation at Frankfort.

afterwards walked to the Tannenwald. Left at 4 o'clock for
Frankfort to dine with the Malets at five. We were sixteen
at dinner, and in the evening there was a party comprising
the corps diplomatique and a few Frankfort acquaintances ;
a good many people were presented to me. The Austrian
Jäger band played.

October 1.— . . . Started at eleven o'clock with Mama,
Uncle, and Geraldine for Frankfort, where we took post
and proceeded to Homburg. We alighted at the Euro-
paischer Hof, and after ordering *ein Gabel-Frühstück,*
walked over to the Kursaal, with its reading and playing
rooms (three roulette tables, at one of which gold was circu-
lating freely), and then through the newly laid out pleasure-
grounds and *die älteren Anlagen* to the four springs—*Eliza-
bethen, Stahl, Kaisers,* and *Ludwigs.* We returned to the
inn soon after two to our supposed *luncheon,* which turned
out to be a regular dinner; *pas mal* but awfully dear ! . . .
Soon after three o'clock we went to the promenade before the
Kursaal to hear the music, and then walked through the old
part of the town to the Château, and paid the Landgravine
Gustave [1] a visit, who was in bed, poor thing, with the rheumatism and a cold. She seemed delighted to see Mama, and
make my acquaintance; her daughter, Princess Elizabeth, is
much to be pitied, for her lot in life is dreary beyond description. Towards the close of our visit, in walked Prince
Frederick of Dessau, who is staying with his sister, and he
accompanied us as far as the garden gates; he has altered
but little during the nine years since we have seen him. Returning to the promenade to await, the carriage, we found it
deserted *car c'était l'heure du diner.* . . . The weather had
been lovely and the day so pleasant that our souvenir of
Homburg is a very agreeable one, and we settled, that what
with its rows of new and prettily built houses, its fine
pleasure-grounds and numberless walks, the place in itself
is prettier than Baden. . . .

October 2.—A wet morning ! . . . I wrote and visited
Frazer before going down to the Gallery to see General
Schmerling, *der mir aus der Seele sprach,* and thus quite won
my heart. We dined at five, and afterwards I played at
patiences in the Gallery, but as Uncle became very violent
on the Neapolitan question, I retreated to the next room to
write a letter for Mama. *October* 3.—Set out for Frankfort
viâ the ferry, *en souvenir* of the *old Rumpenheim* of bygone

[1] Daughter of the Hereditary Prince of Anhalt-Dessau, and widow of
the late Landgrave Gustave of Hesse-Homburg.

days.[1] Mama, Geraldine, Freieisen, and I drove in Uncle's
barouche and four to Madame Hehnel's (Countess Kesselstadt
a beauty!), thence we went on foot to the china shop and
the great glass shop, and finally paid Fraulein Stein a visit
up three pair of stairs. . . . *October 5, Sunday.*— . . . Went
to church, where we saw the sacrament administered to
fifty-three communicants; the service lasted in consequence
till nearly twelve. In the afternoon we drove to Wilhelmsbad,
where, after seeing the Carousel, the splendid old oak and
the *Spiel Saal*, we were joined by Count Rossi[2] and his
daughter on our way to the Hermitage. We paid a visit to
the Hermit, and then sat in front of the lodging-house to
hear the music (the Bavarian military band in plain clothes).
It was a lovely afternoon, and the place was therefore much
frequented; a good many people were coming in as we left,
about half-past four. . . . *October 7.*— . . . Set myself to
write my journal, but was interrupted twice in the course of
the morning, first by a visit from M. Ulrich, and afterwards
by what turned out a very pleasant visit from four Hessian
officers from Hanau. Just as I had joined Mama and Uncle
in the garden, the Danish minister, Bülow, and his wife,
arrived, and sat with us on the terrace; we afterwards
feasted upon raspberries in the new kitchen garden, and
then, accompanied by Geraldine, I made a round of visits. . . .
Count Rossi and his daughter came at four, and she sang
charmingly with her high, melodious, touching voice. In
the evening I played a little at Uncle's desire, and Marie
Rossi sang again.

October 8.— . . . My Uncle had a visit from *l'homme
d'affaires* du Prince ——, who came to ascertain whether *I*
were likely to marry, and if not, whether his Prince,
aged 25, with *une principauté bien arrondie par des heri-
tages et un battalion*, might come forward as a suitor for
my hand. Whereupon my Uncle made a diplomatic reply
and bowed him off! I had just time to run up and put on
my things when it struck two, and, bidding good-bye to the
servants, we crossed in the ferry, accompanied by Uncle and
Dreyer. After another tender farewell, we drove off in
Uncle's barouche and four, and on turning the corner we
had a sight of Prince ——'s ambassador, and a carriage full
of ladies, who bowed most respectfully. . . . At the Frankfort station we were met by the whole of the English

[1] See p. 57.
[2] Count Rossi had married the celebrated singer, Mdlle. Sontag, and lived
at Kesselstadt, near Hanau (see p. 60).

Legation and Hoffman, to say good-bye; we reached Mayence, or rather Cassel, by four o'clock, and the Hotel du Rhin half an hour later. The afternoon was so fine that we took a drive through the City, which is a very strong fortress. The public buildings have almost all been turned into barracks for the Austrians and Prussians. Thence we proceeded up to the Lustgarten, where the Austrian band plays, to have the finest view of the town, and then drove round part of the fortifications, returning by another gate. We sat down to an excellent dinner, and afterwards the moon shone so brightly that it tempted us to take a walk on the bridge and gaze upon the Rhine, with the moon's rays and the city lights reflected in its waters; it was a calm evening, and everything hushed around.

October 9.—By nine o'clock I was seated with Mama and Geraldine in the landau, whence we never stirred all day, on board the *Prinzen von Preussen*. We enjoyed the lovely scenery on both banks of the Rhine, from Bingen to Boppart of all things, besides several pretty peeps, and feasted our eyes upon the towns, villages, and churches that are built upon its banks; but as we went on the scenery lost its picturesque character, and became so flat and monotonous that we grew weary, and we were very thankful to reach Cologne and the Hotel Dietz by seven, where dear old Alsfeldt awaited us. We were off again about eleven. At Verviers, in the middle of the night, we had to change carriages, and were bundled into a delightful Belgian Government carriage, in which we slept most comfortably and undisturbed till we got to Malines, at a quarter to seven, where we had coffee and *des pistolets* (hot rolls) brought us! At Lille, Mama, Geraldine, and I wiled away the time *d'attente* by paying a visit to the nearest church, which is a fine pile of buildings. We met Colonel Maude returning from Russia at the station, and when Mama had retreated into the carriage, I paced up and down with him till it was time to start. Smithett received us at the Calais terminus at seven, with the assurance of a lovely passage, and we spent the intervening time until the tide would serve in purchasing *rose soap* at the corner of the market-place, and watching the passengers on the *Queen of the French* from the pier. The English Consul, Mr. Bonham, and Smithett accompanied us. At five we went on board the *Empress*, and performed the crossing in one hour and thirty-five minutes from pier to pier. It was an excellent passage, and I felt sorry not to have been on deck. Everybody kept

well, and with a firm foot and a thrill of indescribable pleasure
I again stood on *English* ground! Sir Henry Barnard and
Captain McIrvine received us, and conducted us to the Ship
Hotel; Captain Smithett dined with us. How delicious the
English fare seemed to us all, after having lived two months
abroad!

October 11.— . . . The 42nd and 93rd Highlanders marched
past our hotel; it was a splendid sight, and an attention
paid by General Barnard to Mama. The band played for
half an hour under the windows. Captain Smithett, Sir
Henry Barnard, General Cameron, and Captain McIrvine
paid their respects, and escorted us to the station, where the
Highlanders were drawn up to receive us. We started by
the twelve o'clock *so-called fast* train, but did not reach
London Bridge before 4.15, *just an hour* behind our time.
The train consisted of 46 carriages, besides several trucks,
and 3 engines!! George's carriage conveyed us through the
crowded thoroughfares to his apartments, where we sat down
at once to a late luncheon without waiting for him, he
having gone up to Gloucester House in the hope of meeting
us there, but he soon joined us. At 5.30 we bade him good-
bye, deposited Geraldine at Stable-Yard with real regret,
and then drove to Gloucester House, where we found dearest
Aunt Mary looking better and more *rajeunie* than we could
possibly have hoped; this was joy indeed! She kept us till
nearly seven, when we proceeded in our carriage and four to
the dear little Cottage, to which bright faces welcomed us *et
ou tout respirat le comfort*. After all there is no place like
home. I ran up to Alsfeldt's room to see that she was comfortable, and then visited Hargrave, whom I found in bed,
recovering from an illness. We dined at eight, and as it
smoked in the Library, Mama and I sat upstairs in the
evening; but the lamp had gone out, and the room therefore
was not odoriferous! To bed early.

Cambridge Cottage, October 12, *Sunday.*— . . . We heard a
new preacher from Mortlake, who aspires to succeed Mr.
Johnston, but is not gifted with a good delivery. On coming
home Sir William Hooker followed us in, and then we
went up to see the Baron's new bedroom above the kitchen;
a nice sunny room. Took Alsfeldt into my *sanctum* and
showed her my things. Mama and I had a walk after
luncheon, and fed the ducks with which Sir Benjamin Hall
has peopled our pond. . . . Arranged my books, and saw
the glass unpacked. George came to dinner, and we sat
in the Library. *October* 14.— . . . Breakfast over I ran down

to the hall to see Knese's new brougham, and read with Mama
till luncheon-time. We drove over to Orleans House to
wish the Aumales and Princess Salerno good-bye before their
departure for Spain and Sicily, and soon after our return
started for St. James's to dine with George. It was a remarkably pleasant dinner, as Sir George Brown made himself
most agreeable, and gave us much interesting information on
the subject of the late war. *October* 21.—My morning occupations were interrupted by the arrival of the Hereditary
Prince of Tuscany, who, together with his *Chargé d'affaires*
at Paris, talked so agreeably that we sat for two hours in
the Library. Went to dress at four, and drove to Gloucester
House, where we found red cloth and full liveries in expectation of a visit from Tuscany. Lady Caroline Murray and
Colonel Tyrrwhit received us, and Lady Truro was with dear
Aunt. There must have been some mistake, as the Prince
never came, but our visit was a very unsatisfactory and disturbed one in consequence.

Letter to a Friend.

Cambridge Cottage, October 28, 1856.

. . . We thoroughly enjoyed our stay at Baden; the
weather was delightful, and enabled us to lead such an
out-of-doors life as quite brought back the gloom chased
away by the late hours and fatigues of a London season,
and did us all a world of good. The scenery of the surrounding country, lovely and picturesque beyond description
—in a word, a *perpetual landscape*—we were never tired of
exploring, and as we were fortunate in finding a pleasant
English set, besides a few agreeable foreign acquaintances,
we had plenty of gaiety in the way of picnic and *fêtes* given
in our honour at Baden itself and in its environs. There
were plenty of Russians, headed by the ex-premier Count
Nesselrode and Princess Lieven; but the latter, finding Baden
no field for politics, did not prolong her stay; also, amongst
other "lions," old Rossini, the great composer, with whom I
spoke, and who has given me his autograph. People from
all parts of Europe were constantly passing and repassing,
and this made the place a very *magic lantern!* The Queen
of Holland spent three very pleasant days with us, and
during her *séjour* we were joined by dear Augusta, who
accompanied us to Rumpenheim, where we met darling
Adolphus, now a fine noble-looking boy, and from his sweetness of disposition a greater pet than ever. He spent a

week with us before escorting his mother back to her *northern* home, from which she was unwilling to be absent any longer, as my poor brother-in-law is in a very sad state, being as nearly blind as possible. It is a fearful trial for both, and I own I have but little prospect of his ever even partially recovering the sight of the remaining eye, although the oculist who has lately been to Strelitz left them just the shadow of a hope. . . . After their departure we remained at Rumpenheim for another fortnight. . . . Our homeward journey was performed with courier speed, for we reached Dover in less than 22 hours after leaving Mayence. We shall now settle down to our accustomed occupations with redoubled zeal to make up for our long holiday and the full conviction that however charming and agreeable "there's no place like home." . . .

Journal.—Windsor Castle, October 31.—A wet morning. . . . Stayed in the breakfast-room and the one adjoining talking and criticising a newly arrived posthumous bust of Albert's mother;[1] then I went to Alice's room, sat with her and Miss Hilyard, and afterwards with Vicky, when she showed me her scraps of drawing and composition. . . . Began to copy one of Vicky's poems, and at one o'clock drove with Mama and Geraldine to the Deanery, to see dear Lily Wellesley. The house is charming, her own sitting-room, with its view of Eton, the very pink of perfection, and she seems, as it were, cut out for the place, with its Gothic cloisters and chapel; unfortunately, the Dean was out. We returned to the Castle to lunch. The little boys carried me up to the nursery, and then, as it had cleared, we went out driving in open carriages, I in the second, with Vicky, Lady Jocelyn, and Lady Sydney. Home by five. Lady Sydney came to our room for a little while, but our conversation was interrupted by the entrance of dear little Arthur with his *drum*, upon which he performed in the most approved fashion! Leopold was our next visitor, and after having a good game of romps with him, I assisted at his supper in the nursery. Just as Mama had sent for me to hear Alice play, the Queen summoned me to *her own* room, where I had a very satisfactory and pleasant *tête-à-tête* with Her Majesty. At 7.30 Arthur conducted me back to my room, and Alice came to me whilst I dressed. We dined, a party of twenty, at eight o'clock. *November* 1.—We breakfasted a little after nine,

[1] Duchess of Saxe-Coburg and Gotha, only child of the Duke of Saxe-Gotha Altenburg by his second wife, Princess Caroline of Hesse.

Her Majesty being *en retard,* and after bidding her adieu reached Kew about twelve.

Cambridge Cottage, November 8.—In consequence of the Brabants having on the previous evening announced their visit, we were dressed in full *pontificalibus* before 10.30, and established ourselves in the library. They arrived shortly after, attended by M. and Madame de Lannoy, and remained till half-past eleven. She is much improved in looks, and they were both as nice as possible. On their departure we breakfasted for the second time, and who should tumble into our meal but Major Purves, just returned from Scotland. . . . We dined at 7.30, and I read "Barnaby Rudge" aloud till bedtime. The interest of the story is now at its height, and one could go on reading it for hours! *November* 14.— . . . We received the sad intelligence of poor Prince Leiningen's death, and after taking my *first* music lesson with Mr. Sellé (Beethoven *à quatre mains*), I wrote notes of condolence till long past dressing-time. . . . In the evening I read "La Mission de la Femme" to Mama; the latter part of it is most beautifully written, and applies to every daughter of Eve. *November* 22.— . . . Emily Somerset arrived, and after changing our dress we went down to the Library to receive the Chreptovitches,[1] thus setting our private seal to the new alliance with Russia! *November* 23.— . . . Went to Church: a Sir William Dunbar officiated on trial. The sermon was beautiful, but the voice not quite loud enough for our pew. After luncheon I sat reading for a little while in my own room, but at 3.30 put down "The Wide, Wide World," and hastened with Mama to afternoon service. On our return we found Count Chotek (just returned from Russia) and Count Jaucourt awaiting us; then General Halkett,[2] *our dear friend* from Hanover, came and sat with us till dressing-time. The General and George dined with us, and the former made himself so agreeable that we sat up till nearly twelve.

November 27.—My 23rd birthday! ushered in with sunshine! May this prove a bright omen for the coming year, and may my *growth* in *grace* increase year by year. I was awakened by Frazer's voice congratulating me, and got up in good time, but my numerous early visitors hindered me

[1] Count Chreptovitch had arrived in London on September 1 as Russian Envoy Extraordinary and Minister Plenipotentiary.

[2] General Sir Hugh Halkett. He commanded the Hanoverian Legion at Waterloo, and was employed as ambassador on various occasions. In 1848 he commanded the 10th Corps of the army of the Confederation in the war against Denmark.

whilst dressing. Dear Mama came to me at ten, and shortly after I was summoned down to the drawing-room, where George, Knese, and Walbaum were awaiting me. After receiving my presents, which proved to be the very things I had long been wishing for, we sat down to breakfast. George left, and we adjourned to the drawing-room, where our circle was increased by the arrival of several visitors. By four our friends had taken their departure, and I sat with dear Mama talking cosily, and reading to her and Alsfeldt my birthday letters. I then began a letter to the Queen, dressed, and proceeded to George's to dinner. The Duchess of Beaufort, Lord Granville, Cecil Forester, Count Chotek and Count Jaucourt, Colonel Forster, Knese, and Clifton made up the party, and at about ten we all adjourned to Gloucester House, where we found the Kielmansegges, Somerset girls, Liddells, Lady Georgina Bathurst, and the Duchess of Inverness. As we were too numerous for a round game, we conversed, and did not get home till after twelve. Thus ended a day rendered very happy by the kind affection of my *family* and friends.

November 28.— . . . Drove with Mama to Richmond Park and the Kingston Gate to meet George, who was out shooting with the two Liddells, and as soon as he came up with us he told us of poor Elver's dreadful accident, he having been thrown, with his head on an iron bar, from his horse in the stables. Adolphus Liddell had provided a *warm pie* luncheon, which he insisted on our partaking of by the roadside, but this sad event cast a gloom over everything, and it being besides raw and damp we got into the brougham again, and after following the sportsmen as far as Dan's[1] cottage we returned home. . . . A cosy tea, then I went to my room and alternately wrote and indulged in day-dreams till dressing-time. *December* 11.— . . . We went out driving and walked up and down Putney Heath. I then called upon Mrs. Drummond, and on my return hastened to Mama, who was sitting with Alsfeldt, to carry her the good news that Sir William Dunbar had for the present accepted the curacy. . . . To my room and read Elizabeth Barrett Browning's last new poem (a most extraordinary though highly interesting work), "Aurora Leigh," till 7.15, never taking my eyes off the book. At nine o'clock Gouramma made her appearance, and I played duets with her.

[1] Dan was one of the Duke of Cambridge's keepers. He lived in a cottage in Richmond Park, and died in 1890, after being sixty years in the royal service.

December 16.— . . . Drove to town on a very unsatisfactory shopping expedition. We saw Count Kielmansegge at Gloucester House, who announced his daughter's marriage to us, and dear Hélène herself all smiles and blushes! . . . Looked over the things I had bought abroad for presents, and walked to the school, escorted by Gouramma and Mrs. Drummond, to assist at the girls' singing lesson, previous to which Miss Newman put some scriptural questions to them, which Lady Hooker ably illustrated. *December* 24.— . . . After taking a peep at the tree I finished my letter to Gussy, and then joined Mama in the drawing-room to help decorate the tree and arrange the presents and *bonbonnières*. This occupied us till past six, when we set out our gifts for Alsfeldt, Freieisen, and Frazer in Mama's room. We dined at half-past seven, Major and Mrs. Purves, Count Chotek, and Dr. Quin, making up the Christmas party, and a very merry dinner it was, thanks to Quin! When the gentlemen came out from dinner, the drawing-room door was thrown open and we beheld the tree in all its glory! It was a *blaze* of *light* and looked lovely! my presents delighted me, and we spent the evening admiring our different gifts and gazing at the tree.

December 25, *Christmas Day.*—The morning was both raw and foggy, so much so that my room became quite dark twice during my dressing. George arrived per rail from town, and *fly* from Richmond, and accompanied us to Church; though the fog had cleared off it was too wretchedly cold for walking, so we took George into the drawing-room to see our tree. He lunched with us, and we took a peep at the dinner in the servants' hall, and filled two *bonbonnières* for Aunt Mary. At 3.30 we attended afternoon service, and at six I dressed for the Christmas dinner at George's, previous to which he gave Mama a cabinet, and received, in his turn, our presents. We sat down a party of eleven to dinner, the guests being Edward Weimar, Prince William Philippsthal, Cecil Forester, Jim, Knese, Lord William Paulet, Colonel Tyrrwhit, and Mr. Norman Macdonald. At 9.30 we adjourned to Gloucester House, where a small party of "elders and youngsters" was assembled to do honour to a pretty though dimly lighted Christmas Tree. . . .

Letter to Mrs. Barry.

Cambridge Cottage, December 26, 1856.

. . . Our preparations for Christmas so entirely engrossed my time and thoughts of late that I have never been able to finish my letter to you, but your kind appeal to my sympathy having this morning reached me, I hasten to assure you that I do with all my heart feel for you in this severe trial. I only trust and pray that the blessing of this holy season may rest on you, to comfort and support you, and one whose happiness is, I know, dearer to you than your own, in this time of trouble and adversity, and that the year we are about to enter on may bring with it the realisation of the hopes you indulge in . . . and a brighter prospect for the future. At a season of such universal rejoicing, it cannot but make me very sad to know that one I love so dearly has lately experienced so much sorrow ; but I earnestly hope that many happy days are yet in store for you, and that every blessing may attend you in the course of '57, and many succeeding years. As soon as ever you return I trust you will come and see us, and pour out your heart to me. . . . Wherever we may be a hearty welcome awaits you. Little did I think when arranging our tree, and with childish glee admiring it lit up on the 24th, or when spending the evening of Christmas Day so merrily at Gloucester House, that a heart fondly devoted to me was burdened with grief and anxiety. Mama unites with me in sympathy for past and present trials, and every good wish for the future. . . .

Journal.—Cambridge Cottage, December 31.—George and Count Chotek came down to dinner. In the evening we sang and played, and the bell-ringers gave us two tunes. Cut a flame pudding for the ring, poured hot lead, and finally ushered in the New Year (1857) with a game of romps, pledging one another in a loving cup of mulled claret.

We separated at half-past twelve, when I knelt down in prayer, giving thanks for past blessings, and imploring future mercies.

CHAPTER X.

CLOUD AND SUNSHINE.

1857.

Visit to Windsor Castle—Egerton Lodge—Illness and death of the Duchess of Gloucester—Christening of Princess Beatrice—Handel Festival at the Crystal Palace—First distribution of the Victoria Cross—Stay at Strasburg — Sight-seeing in Paris — Nôtre Dame — The Palais de Justice—Palais du Luxembourg—St. Cloud—The Madeleine—*Père la Chaise*—Versailles—The Tuileries—St. Germain—Fontainebleau—Hôtel de Ville—Chantilly—The Indian Mutiny—The Manchester Exhibition—Visits to Heaton and Knowsley—Revels at Ashridge—Death of the Duchesse de Nemours—Introduction to the woolsack.

Journal.—Windsor Castle, January 14.— . . . Mama and I reached here at six o'clock, and very soon Albert, the Queen, Arthur, and Leo paid us a visit; Alice came to me whilst I was dressing. The Comte de Flandres, the Shaftesburys, Barringtons, and two Stockmars[1] are staying at the Castle. In the evening we played at patiences and conversed. *January* 15.— . . . I went out walking with the Queen, and as it poured with rain in the afternoon I played with the children and walked up and down the corridor with

---

[1] Baron Stockmar and his son. Baron Stockmar entered the service of Prince Leopold as private physician in 1816, and after the death of Princess Charlotte, which took place in the same year, until 1831, acted as the Prince's private secretary and Comptroller of the Royal Household. When Prince Leopold accepted the Belgian crown, Baron Stockmar left England and returned to Coburg. He conducted the negotiations which preceded the alliance between Queen Victoria and Prince Albert, and after the marriage returned for a time to the English Court, where he remained as the confidential friend and adviser of the Prince Consort until the passing of the Regency Act in 1840. From that date until his death he resided with his family at Coburg, paying occasional visits to the Queen and Prince Consort, with whom he kept up a regular correspondence. When the Princess Royal married, Baron Stockmar's son was appointed Secretary to Her Royal Highness.

Vicky. . . . About half-past eight we adjourned to the theatre and saw the *School for Scandal*, a piece in five acts, amusing and interesting, *mais avec des longueurs!* and, besides, the parts were not well distributed. *January* 16.—Breakfast over, the Queen, Mama, Vicky, Albert, and I had a long walk in the grounds, and round by the river. On our return I fetched Geraldine, and trotted down to Frogmore to sit to Amalie Hohenlohe, Aunt Kent taking us back to the Castle in her carriage. In the afternoon I had a nice long walk with Vicky, assisted at Arthur's *drumming lesson*, and drove down to the Deanery to tea, where I met Mama and Geraldine, who had been to Chapel, and the de Roses with my *darling godchild.* . . . We dined at eight, the new guests being Prince Edward Leiningen, Lavradio, Lord Lansdowne, Lord Shelburne, Lord Burghersh, and Lord Waterpark. *January* 17.— . . . We took leave of Her Majesty, and by 11.30 were on our way back to Kew.

Cambridge Cottage, January 20.—I had to settle with Frazer, respecting *mes paquets* for Melton, beginning with music, and just looking over a few songs, and then choosing the gowns, flowers, and trinkets. . . . We had a charming visit from Lord Napier, and in the evening a country neighbour dinner. *January* 21.— . . . At ten o'clock we started for Willesden, where the Baron handed us over to the Major and bade us good-bye. We were picked up by a terribly slow train, which landed us at Melton about three. Lady Wilton, Katty, and Alice met us at the station, and on reaching Egerton Lodge I went upstairs to write to Adela Norman on the death of the *dear* old Duke of Rutland,[1] which sad news the morning's paper brought us.

Egerton Lodge, January 22.—No hunting. . . . In the afternoon ten of us set out for a cross-country walk (our *but de promenade* being a brook which Lord Wilton jumped, but the rest of the field *declined*), during which we very nearly stuck in a ploughed field, and were caught in pelting rain. Home by 5.30, after going over about six miles of country, and as soon as I had changed my drenched things I had tea in the schoolroom and rested. . . . After dinner I recited, and we played at all sorts of games in the breakfast-room, ending with waltzing and dancing round the mulberry-bush. *January* 24.—Most of the gentlemen having gone out hunting, Katty gave me a lesson at billiards. . . . We walked up to Mr. Grant's[2] cottage, and he showed us the two pictures he is working at—one of Sir James Scarlett,

---

[1] The fifth Duke of Rutland.　　　　[2] See footnote, p. 160.

the other of Mrs. Peel, *née* Lethbridge. . . . In the evening, after playing two rubbers of whist, I joined the young people in the next room, and we played at the game of "Neighbours" and "La mer est agitée" till twelve o'clock. *January 25, Sunday.*—We walked to church. Home to luncheon, when Sir George Wombwell and his wondrous parrot made their appearance, to our no small amusement. Count Pourtalés and Lord Cavendish also came in for a while. . . .

January 27.—Ten of us, headed by the Earl,[1] and escorted by Mr. Craven[2] and Count Pourtalés, started for a walk along the Buxton Road and across snowy fields. Alas! I put my foot in a hole and somewhat sprained it, but soon forgot the pain in the fun and enjoyment of the passing hour. We returned home for tea, and afterwards I sang to Katty and Jim in the drawing-room. . . . We danced very merrily amongst ourselves in the dining-room till about one o'clock. My foot was terribly swollen, and I could not sleep for the throbbing. *January 28.*—Watched Mama and Lady Wilton play a farewell game at billiards, and then bidding them all a tender adieu, we left Melton at noon for Kew. . . . I lay on the sofa, as my foot was very painful, then gave myself a real treat and read the "The Bride of Abydos." . . .

St. James's Palace, February 4.— . . . About four o'clock we landed at St. James's, where we at once feasted our eyes on the new conservatory—*a perfect gem!* Major Purves and Knese appeared to welcome us, and after a little peeping about we settled down to tea in Mama's boudoir, when she read me Lord Derby's speech. *February 11.*—I was dressed just in time to read prayers over to Mama before breakfast. . . . Arranged my books and work, then walked with Mama and the Equerries to see George's chariot at Hooper's, and, lastly, up and down Pall Mall. . . . Dressed soon after seven for a little dinner at home, which included Lady Cowley, Lord Eglinton, Lord Chelsea, Count Karolyi, General Ashburnham, and Colonel Forester. The evening passed off very pleasantly. *February 17.*— . . . Leo came, and stayed till nearly twelve, when Knese returned from St. George's, where Hélène Kielmansegge was married. Mama and I went to the wedding breakfast. Hélène received us, looking lovely in her Brussels lace and veil, but disappeared just as we sat down to a splendid *déjeûner* of eighty *couverts.* Count Kielmansegge, who sat next me, made a very pretty, touching speech on proposing the health of the bride and bridegroom, and *à propos* of the bridesmaids

[1] The Earl of Wilton.   [2] Nephew of the second Earl of Craven.

we had two funny speeches from Lord Giffard and Sir James Fergusson. Afterwards we went upstairs to bid *Lady Arthur Hay* good-bye. Home to change our dress, and then walked with Knese down to Grosvenor Place to see "the happy pair" drive by. *February 18.*— . . . After paying our respects to the Queen, we drove on to Hyde Park, and got out at Rotten Row. . . . Arranged the rooms for the evening's *entertainment.* . . . Mama *generously* bestowed on me her *emerald* necklace! Dear darling Mama! For which I have now given up the fine *row of pearls.* . . . Lady Sandwich, the Newports, George, Lord Canterbury, Jim, and Colonel Higginson dined with us, and a few friends came later.

February 24.—Dear Papa's birthday. I was hurried out of bed to see Lord Ellesmere's funeral pass. . . . At half-past twelve we started for Kew. After a visit to the vault "in memoriam" we called to see Gouramma and the Drummonds, and took a walk in the gardens, the sun shining warmly and brightly. We were at St. James's again by four, had an early dinner, and then went to the House of Lords to hear the debate on the affair in China;[1] Lords Derby, Clarendon, and Lyndhurst spoke, but it was too legal and argumentative to be interesting. We stayed till ten o'clock—five hours! *March 7.*— . . . Directly after breakfast I went for a drive in Fulham fields and Hyde Park with Lady Sandwich in her basket sociable. In the afternoon we drove to the Houses of Parliament, where Mama had given Sir Benjamin Hall a *rendez-vous*, to see the Queen's statue by Gibson. He took us over both Houses, including libraries, halls, and the cloisters. . . . Lord Chelsea called and held forth on politics from six till half-past seven! *March 12.*— . . . Proceeded to Gloucester House and found the Prince of Wales with Aunt Mary. Home by half-past four, had coffee, and hastened to the boudoir to see dear Quin, a *semi-convalescent* man! . . . Just as I was going down to dinner Taylor met me in the passage to make his farewell bow as footman, which quite upset me. I read the "Buckingham Memoirs" to Mama in the evening.

[1] Disturbances had taken place in Canton in consequence of the policy pursued by the British Representative at Hong Kong. The matter gave rise to much diversity of opinion in this country, and on February 24 Lord Derby moved a resolution of censure on the Government, which was, however, negatived by a majority of 36. The same issue was fought in the House of Commons, and the Government defeated. Lord Palmerston then appealed to the country, when he was again returned to office with an increased majority.

March 13.— . . . Constance Grosvenor came in at five o'clock, and Mary Yorke[1] treated me to a sight of her bright and beautiful face. Clemmy Villiers arrived soon after, and dragged me into a *very warm* political discussion, in which Geraldine, who was there at its commencement, supported me. We dined at Lord Eglinton's, a party of twenty-two; Lord Salisbury and our host were my neighbours. Home by eleven, as there were several evening parties going on. *March* 17.— . . . We had just time to have some coffee before going to the House of Lords to hear Lord Derby make his electioneering statement, to which Lord Granville replied; it was a most interesting debate. Home, and dressed in haste for dinner, at which Geraldine made the fourth, and then adjourned to Drury Lane to see *A Curious Case* (Charles Matthews acted very well) and *Betsey Baker*, in which the Keeleys were inimitable.

March 21.— . . . I fetched Lady Salisbury, and drove with her to the Regent's Park, around the greater part of which we *scampered* in the *keenest* of north-easterly winds. . . . Mama and I went to Lord Cadogan's to see his collection of rare old china, glass, and other *objets de vertu*—such treasures!—and had tea in his Lordship's room, where Lady Adelaide Cadogan also joined us. *March* 24th.— . . . In the afternoon Lady Sandwich chaperoned me to the Concert of the Royal Academy (presided over by Lord Westmorland), in a small locality near Hanover Square, which Albert also patronised. The selection of music was entirely serious, and some of the voices were very good, but all seemed nervous, as we were very near to them. *March* 27.— . . . We paid our respects at the Palace, where also we saw Alice and the four younger children. Her Majesty kept us with her quite an hour. . . . The carriage picked us up and we drove to the Houses of Parliament, and, with Mr. Fincham for a guide, inspected the great bell (Big Ben), destined for the Clock Tower. . . .

April 2.— . . . At half-past six Mama, Geraldine, and I left for the Blue Coat School, George and Lord Burghersh preceding us. On arriving there we went up at once into the great hall (which reminded me so much of St. George's Hall at Windsor), where the *800* boys were assembled, and after taking our places a psalm was sung, prayers were read, and then the boys sat down to their milk and bread and butter supper, during which we walked round the different tables. As soon as these were cleared, the boys marched

---

[1] Lady Mary Yorke married Mr. Craven in 1857.

past in procession; an anthem and "God save the Queen" were sung, and lastly, as we passed down the Hall, they cheered as stunningly and loyally as possible. It was altogether one of the most interesting sights I ever beheld, and I came away perfectly *enchanted !* *April* 14.— . . . Wrote to Lord Shaftesbury on Doctor Laumann's account, and drove, in the afternoon, to Richmond Park, stopping at Aunt Mary's kitchen garden to see the gardener's poor wife who is going blind. . . . On reaching home, George's groom informed me that the Queen had a little girl[1] I wrote to Victoria, and presently a letter came from Albert.

Cambridge Cottage, April 16.—Mr. Hills brought us a very bad account of Aunt Mary, and at half-past three we started for Gloucester House, where we were joined by Aunt Kent and Victoria. . . . Dear Aunt did not feel equal to seeing us, and the doctors considered she was not *out of danger.* Albert came in, and on his departure we sent Major Purves to telegraph for George and Gussy. I then sat with Mama in the small front drawing-room, talking and reading till nearly eight o'clock. It was *dismally wretched* work, more especially as we were not permitted to see her. We dined, and afterwards sat with Lady Cowley (whom Aunt had asked to make up her rubber) awaiting the doctors' last *Ausspruch.* They did not think her worse, so we left, but with heavy hearts, and found Knese and the establishment watching for us. *April* 17.—Another anxious day! Dr. Ferguson's afternoon report was so unsatisfactory that we left at eight for town, and, to our great comfort, Aunt Mary saw us for a few seconds, her first words being " Were you not astonished ? " She did not appear much changed in face, but feeble and oppressed. Later, George came in and we returned to Kew.

April 18.— . . . I dropped Mama at Gloucester House, and went on to Clarence House to take my lesson with Mr. Hallé. Soon after three Mama called for me to go to the Palace, where Albert received us, and took us to see the dear little fat Baby. She has one of a suite of apartments down-stairs, hung with Dutch, French, and Spanish pictures, which Albert showed us. From thence back to Gloucester House. Aunt Mary was dozing, and I watched her for some time; but on rousing up she just spoke to me, and as I was going out of the room kissed her hand. . . . Aunt Kent and the Hohenlohes came about five, and Hawkins told us that he felt much alarmed, as torpor was stealing over

[1] Princess Beatrice.

the brain. At this moment Albert and the Princess Royal arrived. . . . Aunt was so *very ill* (apparently dying) that Mama, in alarm, was about to send for George, who at that instant came in; but the crisis or momentary danger passed off, and she was able to speak. . . . We sat for some time with Nepean and Edward Weimar. *April* 20.— . . . A *tolerable* account, and a telegraph from Berlin, announcing Gussy's arrival at Calais for that evening. We drove to town, and I established myself in the great drawing-room at Gloucester House, but was soon after fetched by Mama to see Aunt Mary, who spoke to us both. . . . The Prince of Wales called, and sat with us for some time. . . .

April 21.—I waited downstairs till dearest Augusta and Dolphus came, and went with them to the morning-room, whilst George somewhat prepared Aunt Mary for their arrival. Presently Augusta went in behind Mama to look at her. . . . I found she had recognised and spoken to Gussy. Thank God! The Hohenlohes and Albert then paid us a visit, and I was fetched to take a peep at dear Aunt, who gave me a sweet smile when I kissed her hand, but did not speak. Whilst we were in the room behind the screen, George brought in the Prince of Wales. . . . The doctor came in later, and reported Aunt much the same, only the pulse fluctuating. We left at 10.30. *April* 22.— . . . Aunt Mary recognised each of us, but did not speak, for her breathing was very much oppressed. I returned to the drawing-room to write to Millicent Wemyss, but was interrupted by the entrance of Victoria and Alice; the latter I took round to have a glimpse of dear Aunt, and presently Vicky came in. . . . I sat in a corner of the bedroom till called away to tidy myself for dinner at eight o'clock, and after taking another look at the beloved invalid, we went home.

April 23.— . . . Mr. Hills came to tell us that Aunt Mary had had a quiet night, and some refreshing sleep. . . . We started before two for Gloucester House, where we saw Colonel Liddell and Lady Georgiana, and changed carriages to go to the Palace. The Queen was on her sofa in her sitting-room, looking wonderfully well, all over *pale lilac* for Leiningen. Albert took us in, and Her Majesty sent for the younger children and the Baby. At 4.30 we returned to Gloucester House, and heard that Aunt Kent was in the sick-room. . . . On her departure I went by the back way to the bedroom, where I found Mama and the Prince of Wales.

Aunt Mary knew us, and I stayed there for some time. . . .
Gussy came back rather later, when dear Aunt recognised
her and *looked upwards!*   Soon after six I left the room.
April 25.—*Her* 81st birthday! but, alas! we *dared* not keep
it, except *sacredly*, as it were. . . . A better account of the
invalid, who had passed a third quiet night. . . . We reached
Gloucester House about four o'clock.   Gussy and Dolphus
went into the bedroom, but I stayed outside.   Soon after
the Duchess of Inverness came, and I went to Aunt's room
to look at her dear face asleep, but left to make way for
Albert, and the three eldest children, to whom she spoke. . . .
Later on I returned; dear Aunt beckoned *me* up, and I went
to the bottom of the bed; presently George came in, so that
we all three stood by Her. . . .

April 27.—Hills brought a fair account of the night, but
found her weaker. . . . Mama went into the bedroom, and
Aunt Mary spoke to her for some minutes, asking her
different questions; Gussy followed, and was recognised;
Mary Edwards told dear Aunt that I was coming; upon
which I went forward, but she did not know me, and
said "To-night?" (meaning, was I coming that night?)   I
then left the room, but a minute afterwards was sent
for back, as she had again asked if I were coming that
night.   Upon being told that I was in the house, and asked
if she would see me, she assented by a nod.   When I
had kissed her hand, she asked me if Mama were come—
were in the house?   And on my saying, "Would you like
to see her?" replied distinctly, "Where is she?   By all
means let her come."   Mama then approached the bed, but
Aunt did not speak.   On our coming away she put up her
hand as if to kiss it to me.   Hawkins next went in, and
she said to him, " The Queen is coming to-day," which much
startled him.   Her eyes were wide open, and she looked
round the room very much as dear Papa used to do in
his last illness. . . . About ten o'clock Ferguson came to
see her, and sent for Liddell; the mind was evidently
wandering from excessive weakness, as she had repeated to
Ferguson about the Queen's coming to see her, and asked
Liddell "If he had got the house?"   We went in the last
thing to look at her dozing, and returned to Kew with
heavy hearts. *April 28.*— . . . A letter from George with
bad news. . . . We drove off at once, and on our arrival
went to the bedroom, where we sat watching dearest Aunt
for some time. . . . I took an unfinished letter into the
morning-room, and wrote on undisturbed till the arrival of

dear Wales, who had a few minutes' *tête-à-tête* with me before
going in . . . .

April 29.— . . . By a quarter to eleven we left for town,
having received from George a worse account; . . . her state
had undergone a marked change in the night, and she had
been gradually getting weaker and weaker. Liddell and
Lady Georgiana met us with sorrow-stricken faces, and on
going into the bedroom, we found George, Hawkins, Hills,
Lady Caroline, and Mrs. Liddell. A great change had taken
place, and we felt, alas! that *her* hours were numbered. It
was *a sad, sad scene.* Tears were on every face, but, thank
God! she did not seem to suffer. On their raising the much-
loved patient to feed her, she half unclosed her eyes, but the
sight seemed *gone.* We then left the room for a while, and
Lady Caroline read some meditations on the approach of
death to me. Afterwards I returned to the bedroom, and
sitting down on the couch at the foot of the bed, watched
Her as she lay perfectly quiet, and seemingly unconscious
from exhaustion, except when aroused to be fed. She could
swallow but little. On Aunt Kent's being announced I
followed Mama and Miss Adams into Mrs. Gold's [1] room,
where I completely gave way; in the midst of my tears I was
sent for to see Aunt Kent, who was much overcome.

Presently I was called away to speak to the Prince of
Wales and Albert, who were waiting in the morning-room.
I went into the bedroom with Mama. . . . Wales approached
the bed and kissed her hand, but Albert remained by the
door. . . . Directly after dinner we followed the doctors into
the bedroom; a great change for the worse had taken place,
and on consulting Hawkins he at once decided upon our
staying all night. . . . We afterwards went in again for a
few minutes, just to look once more at her sweet face, and
then sat in the drawing-room till past eleven, when Mama,
Gussy, and I retired to the small front drawing-room, where
three sofas had been prepared for us, and taking off my
jacket I wrapped myself in a shawl and lay down to rest
and think, but not to sleep. Nepean and all the suite
(save Lady Georgiana, who left at twelve) remained in the
house. . . .

All was quiet till three o'clock, when George came to fetch
Mama, as the last stage before death had set in. Gussy and
I were desired not yet to follow, but got ourselves ready.
At 3.30 Mama sent for us into the bedroom, where a most
trying and *heart-rending* scene awaited us; pressure on the

---

[1] Dresser to the Duchess of Gloucester.

brain having set in, she was breathing heavily, the pulse was beating feebler and feebler, and death had set its stamp upon her much-loved features. I could not cry, but stood watching her for a few minutes, and then withdrew to call Lady Caroline and Mrs. Liddell, Colonel Liddell having met me at the door. Mr. Nepean followed us in, and at a sign from Mr. Hills, who believed she was then passing away, read the prayers for the dying whilst we knelt in tears around the bed. During the prayer the breathing was quieter and less oppressed, and directly afterwards she unclosed her eyes, and then stretched herself as if to her last sleep ; but it seemed as though the body would not suffer the soul to flee away and be at rest, for the heavy breathing returned, and again she hovered between life and eternity. There was no consciousness, and the doctor assured us no suffering, but the struggle with death was most distressing for us to behold as we sat or stood by the bed, and lasted till 5.15, when, with another stretch and a momentary convulsive contraction of the face, all was over, and with the dawn of day the gentle spirit returned to God who gave it. A stifled sob broke from all present, and most of us bent in silent prayer.

There were present in the room, besides our four selves, Lady Caroline, Miss Adams, the Liddells, Nepean, Hawkins and Hills, Mrs. Gold, McEwan, the Nurse, and "little Mary" the wardrobe maid. Her own housemaid had just before left the room. . . . As soon as the first burst of grief had somewhat subsided, we knelt in the great drawing-room while Mr. Nepean read the prayers for the *mourners.* We then wandered sadly from room to room while they unbarred the shutters and drew the blinds, weeping for Her who had gone to her long but happy rest, in whom *we* had all lost a *second mother;* but God's will be done. . . . At 6.30, after bidding George and the others adieu, we left for Kew in *Her* undress carriage with a pair of horses; it was a lovely morning, but the drive was a *sad* one.

May 1.— . . . At noon we started for Gloucester House. . . . We were taken to the back drawing-room, the shutters of all the front rooms being barred, and oh! how dismal did the house appear now that she who had been its life and charm had fled. . . . We went into *the bedroom.* Mrs. Gold met us there and insisted on our taking one more look at that dear inanimate form. The face was more like herself than on the previous morning, but alas! how we missed the sweet smile of welcome she *always* gave us. The features, too, were more marked, and not so

prettily chiselled as we remembered hers to have been; in
a word, all told us it was but the wreck of Her we had loved,
and it comforted us to think that her *spirit* was with God
and the loved ones that had gone before, so that it would
be selfishness to wish her back again, for our loss was her
gain. . . . We drove in the chariot to the Palace. I just
saw the Queen, who was very kind, and Albert, and then
went over to see Victoria and Alice. We afterwards called
at Clarence House. . . .

With the death of the Duchess of Gloucester, the last of
George III.'s children passed away, and rich and poor alike
shared in the sorrow which had befallen the Royal Family,
while the loss of so near and dear a relative was s very sad
blow to Princess Mary, who had long regarded Gloucester
House as her second home, and her Aunt as a second mother.
It was characteristic of the unostentatious manner in which
the Duchess of Gloucester had lived that she should have
desired a simple funeral, and in accordance with the wishes
expressed by Her Royal Highness, she was buried at Windsor
with as little ceremony as was consistent with the respect
due to her exalted station.

Letter to a Friend.

Cambridge Cottage, May 16, 1857.

. . . Your last kind letter reached me but a few days
before all was over, and I knew not just then what to say
in reply. . . . The general decay was so very gradual that
there was a possibility of her precious life being prolonged,
though for only a short period. But it was not to be, and
I feel that it was mercifully ordained, for a life of lingering
pain and intense weakness would have been fearfully trying
to her, and has she not exchanged all this for the "peace
which passeth all understanding," and the blessed inheritance of the children of God? I think I shall never forget
that fortnight of anxious watching. . . . It was a peaceful
end . . . and we strove to picture to ourselves Her happiness
in the presence of her God, where we may hope she is,
through the Saviour's atonement, reaping the reward of her
work of love on earth.

To us who, as you well know, loved her with, I may say,

filial affection, her loss can never be repaired, as she was the centre around which we moved, and there is a void in our hearts and daily life which we shall realise by-and-by more fully than even now. Dear Mama has borne this sad trial better than I had dared hope, although her nerves were at first terribly shaken; but since the 8th, the day on which we paid the last tribute of respect and love to *Her* memory, and were present at the thrillingly solemn and affecting service in St. George's Chapel, Windsor, she has recovered in some degree her wonted composure and cheerfulness, which the presence of Augusta and dear Adolphus greatly tends to promote. This very lovely summer weather, also, has done her a world of good, as it enables her to spend most of the day in the garden, which is just now in its greatest beauty; a bouquet of lilacs, laburnums, and horse-chestnuts. . . . We drove over to the White Lodge to take a last look at everything as *she* had left it. Alas! how sad it made us. We went over the house and garden, and my heart ached to see it all so desolate. . . .

    •   •   •   •   •

Journal.—Cambridge Cottage, May 30.— . . . We started, six of us, in the open landau for the Crystal Palace, which was reached, *viâ* Clapham, about one o'clock. We at once directed our steps to the centre, where the *flower and fruit show* had drawn the crowd together, made the circuit of the raised stands, visited *en passant* the tropical part of the Palace and some of the courts, and finally repaired to the picture-gallery—a poor concern, the foreign collections appearing to more advantage than the English. After going down to see the *antediluvian* animals, we proceeded to the Queen's balcony to overlook the grand fountains which began to play soon after 4.30. The *coup d'œil* was beautiful, what with the waters and the 12,000 people collected to see them play. Unluckily a shower came on, which drove every one indoors. We waited for some time in the pavilion for the crowds to disperse, but on coming out found, to our no small alarm, that a very loyal mob had collected to see us pass; we had not gone far before we met Edward Weimar and the Prince of Meiningen,[1] who joined us in our tour through the exhibition courts to see the carriages, china, and glass, and round the upstair gallery, which is occupied by rows of shops, and from whence we had a capital view of the people feeding! On going down

---

[1] Prince George of Saxe-Meiningen.

again some of us paid a hurried visit to the Pompeian court, and soon after 6.30 we bade the Princes adieu and set out on our homeward journey *viâ* Norbury Road and Tooting. . . .

May 31.— . . . On joining Mama and Gussy in the garden I found Lord Londonderry sitting out with them under the lilac bush; he much amused us with his Irish fun and jokes. Lady Caroline Cust arrived about four, when his Lordship departed. . . . We dined at eight with Quin for our additional guest, and spent a very jolly evening, as the little doctor was in high force. *June* 9th.— . . . Mama and I drove in pouring rain to Richmond Station, reaching Windsor Castle at six, and were greeted by Albert almost immediately on our arrival; after tea, Helena, the Queen, and Arthur came to see us. We dined at 8.15; the Prince of Meiningen, Edward Weimar, the Duchess of Sutherland, and the other Court dignitaries were the only guests.

Windsor Castle, June 10.— . . . I got up at 7.30, after a wonderful night, and was dressed in capital time. At half-past ten I went out walking with Victoria, Alice, Albert, George, Prince Meiningen, and Edward, in spite of the showery state of the weather; after going down one of the avenues and along the Thames by a new road, we took shelter in a lodge, and then walked through the kitchen gardens to the Shaw Farm, where we saw a tremendous horse, " Great Britain," and rested in a pretty room built for Her Majesty. Home, and I then held a council respecting my dress for the christening. In the afternoon Alice came to me for a few minutes and Aunt Kent followed, attended by dear Lady Augusta Bruce, whom I entertained. At five I went out driving with the Queen, Mama, and Victoria; after passing through a perfect *haie* of rhododendrons in full blossom, we skirted Virginia Water, and only returned about seven, when I paid George, who had been at Ascot, a flying visit. We sat down seventy-two to dinner in the St. George's Hall, numberless visitors having arrived at the Castle, and there being besides many dinner guests. In the evening the Prince Frederick William of Prussia arrived, and the Queen left us to receive him. He made his appearance about eleven, when we established ourselves round the table, and the band struck up in the Waterloo Gallery.

June 11.— . . . At 12.15 we started *en cortége* for Ascot, I being in the second carriage with Alice, Albert, and Meiningen. The races were remarkably well attended, and I do not think I ever saw the course look gayer or more crowded. Lord Zetland's horse won the Queen's Cup. . . . There was

another banquet in St. George's Hall, and in the evening we
talked a good deal as the gentlemen came up to the round
table. The music thundered away in the Waterloo Gallery
till 11.30, when we hurried to bed. *June 12.*— . . . Bade
Meiningen and Edward Weimar good-bye, and put on our
things to accompany the Queen and children on the terrace to
see a wonderfully clever monkey, and then walked a little way
with Her Majesty, Victoria, Albert, and Frederick William of
Prussia, before taking leave of them. . . . Drove to the station
en route for Kew, where we arrived at half-past twelve.

St. James's Palace, June 16.— . . . At 11.30 I dressed in
pure white for the christening at the Palace at twelve. We
assembled in the *royal* waiting-room on the ground floor,
where the Archduke Ferdinand Max was introduced to us,
and then moved in procession into the Chapel, George con-
ducting me. When the Archbishop held the little baby at
the font, Beatrice Mary [1] gave a scream, but was quite good
all the rest of the time. The ceremony over, we went up to
the throne-room, and afterwards lunched in the great ball-
room, which looked very fine by daylight. We then adjourned
to the concert-room, where Her Majesty made a kind of
tournée, and were home by half-past three, when Gouramma
and Mrs. Drummond came to see us in full dress. . . .

June 18.— . . . At three I drove to the Palace to sit to
Winterhalter for a water-coloured drawing.[2] Victoria was
there when I arrived, and Albert, followed some time afterwards by the Queen, looked in upon our proceedings. . . .
We dined at the Rokebys'. . . . I sat by Louise Manchester
all the evening and we had quite a *tête-à-tête,* as none of
the others came up to our sofa. It was very pleasant.

June 19.— . . . At twelve we started with Geraldine
and the Major for the Crystal Palace, where we alighted
at the Queen's private entrance, and were conducted by Sir
Joseph Paxton[3] to Her Majesty's box in the corner of the
gallery opposite the Orchestra. Immediately on our arrival

---

[1] "Little Beatrice is an extremely attractive, pretty, intelligent child,
indeed the most amusing baby we have had."—The Prince Consort to Baron
Stockmar, April 2, 1858.

[2] See illustration facing next page.

[3] Joseph Paxton rose from humble origin to be superintendent of the
Duke of Devonshire's gardens at Chatsworth. He built a grand conservatory
for the Duke, which formed the model for the Great Exhibition Building of
1851, and for his services in connection with that undertaking was knighted.
Later on he was asked to prepare the designs for the Crystal Palace at
Sydenham, and was ultimately appointed Director of the gardens and grounds.
He died in 1865, after representing Coventry in Parliament for eleven years.

the performance of Handel's Oratorio "Israel in Egypt" commenced, with which I was much delighted. Some of the Choruses were *thrillingly* beautiful, others sublime. The solos were for the most part lost upon us, as we were not near enough to hear them. Between the first and second parts I trotted down to the photograph gallery *avec la suite*, and Paxton to partake of *his* luncheon, and, on my return, found Mama with the Duchess of Wellington. The Oratorio and "God save the Queen" were over soon after four. . . . Dead tired, and broiling with the heat, we at length got to our carriage, and were home by six, when I laid down and slept till dressing-time. . . .

June 20.—. . . I had to try on the diadem of stars for the drawing-room before starting with Geraldine on foot for the Palace about one o'clock to take my third sitting. Mama I left consulting with Baron Bentinck about the Queen of Holland's visit. Winterhalter was very cross at having to shift his quarters for the day, and packed me off again at 2.15, Albert and Victoria having looked in upon us shortly before their luncheon-time. . . . *June 22.*— . . . Occupied myself till one, when Mama and I drove to the Palace for a fourth sitting, and found Aunt Kent with Winterhalter. Just as we were *bien en train*, Her Majesty sent for me to her room *und empfang mich ganz schwesterlich.* . . . At eleven we went to Mr. Henry Greville's *soirée musicale.* Mario and Grisi did their very best *pour nos beaux yeux*, and Cimbatta and the Misses Pyne seconded them.

June 23.— . . . Mama assisted at my toilette for the drawing-room, and at a quarter to two I left with Geraldine for the Palace, where I awaited Her Majesty in the Closet and saw eight of the children. Victoria and I occupied the second carriage, and at once went up with the Queen. The drawing-room was neither well nor very *fashionably* attended, and lasted an hour and twenty minutes. I returned with Victoria to the Palace, and thence drove home. . . . Went to Her Majesty's Theatre with Geraldine and the Major to hear Alboni in the *Sonnambula.* She sings well *mais elle était embarrassée de sa personne* which certainly does not suit the part. The rest of the singers were very second rate. . . .

June 24.— . . . Drove with Knese to Sir William and Lady Gomm's to see their charming house and fine collection of Dutch pictures. She also showed us her bed and dressing rooms, beautiful Indian shawls, and china-closet, after which we were refreshed (for the heat was intense) with ice, fruit, and sherry. . . . Went to the first Court Ball, and were

H.R.H. Princess Mary of Cambridge in 1857
from a portrait at Cambridge Cottage.

home by two, having wished the Archduke and Prince of Meiningen good-bye.

June 26.— . . . At 9.15 we drove to the Palace, whence we proceeded in the Queen's *cortège* (Mama, Aunt Kent, Victoria, and Alice, in the first carriage ; I in the second, with Helena, Louise, and Lady Ely ; Her Majesty, Consort, sons, and George leading the way on horseback) to the enclosed ground in Hyde Park, to see the distribution of the Victoria Cross for *valour.*[1] We drivers alighted, and witnessed it all from the centre platform, in front of which the *sixty heroes* were drawn up! The Queen decorated officers and men with her own hand, and then followed the review, or rather march past, in slow and quick time, of the troops. In spite of the intense heat, no accident or *contretemps* occurred. We returned to the Palace amidst great cheering, and reached home about twelve. . . .

The season was naturally a quiet one for the Duchess of Cambridge and Princess Mary, and soon after taking part in the stirring scene which attended the first distribution of the Victoria Cross, they left England for Rumpenheim, to spend the remainder of the summer with their Hessian relations. Early in September, accompanied by the Heredi- tary Grand Duke and Grand Duchess of Mecklenburg- Strelitz, they proceeded to Paris, where some weeks were passed in seeing the sights of the French capital.

*   *   *   *   *

Journal.—Rumpenheim, September 3.— . . . We bade the family adieu *les larmes aux yeux,* drove off from the Casino, and crossed the ferry in the carriage, the rain not ceasing till we reached Frankfort. At 10.30 our train started ; the country, after we had passed Darmstadt, became very pic- turesque, as the road wound along under a range of hills. At Heidelburg we got out, to have a glimpse of the ruins of the old Castle from the high-road. After passing Carlsruhe, we found ourselves quite *en pays de connaissance*, and at Oos the Cavendishes were awaiting us. We saw them for a few minutes, and all our Baden recollections revived at sight of them, and of our old haunts—the Alt-Schloss, Fremersberg, Yburg, Windeck la Hub, etc. Later in the afternoon we reached Kehl, being nearly an hour behind our time, and

[1] The decoration was instituted on January 29, 1856, and this was the first distribution.

drove across the Rhine to Strasburg, where we alighted at the Ville de Paris about 5.30. We had dinner at once; and as it was too dark to go out, and too early for bed-time, we took a box and went to the French play. However, it was a most *tiresome lark*, as the three pieces were indifferently acted, and *très peu de chose*; the theatre itself is a good-sized building, but was very empty, and the heat intense.

Strasburg, September 4.— . . . We sallied out on foot to see the "lions" of Strasburg, and walked round the Minster or Cathedral, the architecture of which struck us as being finer and more perfect than that of the Cölner Dom, although it has a somewhat unfinished appearance, from there being but one tower, the corresponding one never having been put up, on account of a belief that the foundations were not strong enough to bear it. Crossing the market-place, we entered what used to be the house of Erwin of Steinbach, the architect and decorator of the Cathedral. Here we saw the mutilated and defaced remains of Gothic groups and statues, the results of the French revolution, some executed by Sabina, Erwin's daughter; the works of the old clock; and a spiral stone staircase, designed by Erwin, the most elegant and perfect thing of the kind I ever beheld. After peeping into the courtyard of what was once an episcopal palace, and now belongs to the Emperor, we went into the church itself, supported by huge pillars of red sand-stone, which have a fine effect; but in other respects the interior is very plain. I was much interested in the far-famed astronomical and mechanical clock, designed by Schwilgue to replace the old one, in 1842. . . . From the Minster we walked to the Protestant church of St. Thomas, to see the monument erected by Louis XV., and carried out by Picalles to the memory of Maurice Maréchal de Saxe; also the embalmed bodies of a Count of Nassau and his little daughter—a very unpleasing spectacle! We returned home by a *place* in the centre of which stands the statue of General Kleber (who was murdered in Egypt), and rested for a little while before restarting in the carriage for the Cathedral, to hear the great clock strike twelve, when the 12 apostles appear and pass by the Saviour, who blesses them, and the cock crows. This takes place once in the twenty-four hours.

We left for Paris at 12.20, and after passing Saverne, where there is a large *château*, the country, which had been undulating and picturesque, suddenly closed round us, and the line of rail passed through a valley shut in by a range of wooded hills with the first tints of autumn on them. This scenery certainly justifies the appellation "*La Belle France.*" After a while it lost its picturesque character, but continued *riant* and pleasing. Nancy is very prettily situated. At Epernay, which was reached shortly before eight, we walked up and down the platform whilst the passengers were feeding—half an hour being allowed for the *table d'hôte*—a most provoking arrangement. We did not get to Paris before 11.25, and were received by the German *commissionnaire* of the British Embassy, followed by Mr. Henry Howard; we drove along the Boulevards with their lighted *cafés*, which greatly enliven the otherwise dimly illuminated streets, to the Hôtel—in the Rue des Champs Elysées, where, to our surprise and dismay, we were shown into a succession of small rooms (which, however, have since turned out tidy and comfortable). The disagreeable impression was somewhat dispelled by the tea, which proved to be excellent, and hot chicken; *our midnight meal!* To bed about one a.m.

Paris, September 5.— . . . At 11.30 we started in the carriage, and, passing the Church of the Madeleine, drove along the Boulevards, of which the "Italiens" is the most fashionable, by the *portes* St. Denis and St. Martin, and the fountain called "*le château d'eau,*" opposite the spot where the "Temple" once stood, to the Colonne de Juillet, 1830, on the Place de la Bastille, under which the bodies of those who fell in that revolution were buried, and which was erected by Louis Philippe, on the site of the Bastille. Thence we proceeded down the new Rue de Rivoli, *un chef d'œuvre* of the present Emperor Napoleon, turning off by the Hôtel de Ville, a splendid building, *par le* Pont Neuf, on which Henry IV. was assassinated, and across the Seine to Nôtre Dame, the exterior of which is very fine. The interior of the Cathedral has, however, been greatly marred by the ceiling and arches having been painted in stucco for the christening of the Prince Imperial. The lamp over the spot where the Duc de Bordeaux and the Prince Imperial were baptized was a gift from Charles X. We saw the building in detail as we joined a party of spectators led by a verger. The Sacristie contains the splendidly embroidered clerical robes worn on State occasions, and the vessels used at the Altar; also the ball that killed Affre, Archbishop of Paris, on the barricades in 1848, together with his picture, and that of the late Archbishop, murdered in the beginning of this year by a priest whom he had suspended. . . . The Emperor and Empress [1] were married in this church.

We went down to the Palais de Justice, and leaving the carriage, turned into a small court to our left, whence, by a narrow turret stone staircase (the main entrance being under repair), we ascended to the "*Sainte Chapelle*," founded by St. Louis, to deposit in it the relics he had brought from Palestine. It is built in the Byzantine style, and the dome richly gilt; the walls are painted in fresco and arabesque, in the style of the Alhambra, and there are two niches in them, once the Oratories of St. Louis and his mother, Blanche of Castille; Louis XI. had a secret oratory, the *grille* of which is still there. The stained-glass windows are beautiful. The whole has quite lately been restored; indeed they are still working at it. *De plein pied* with the Chapel after crossing an open corridor is the "*salle des pas perdus*," a large hall so called from the individuals under trial awaiting here their sentence. *La Morgue*, where dead bodies are exposed to be recognised, and *la conciergerie*, the prison of Marie Antoinette and Louis XVI., are near this hall; beneath are prisons.

Re-entering the carriage, we drove to the Palais du Luxembourg, where Marie de Medicis resided as a widow. Ascending a fine staircase, we passed through two rooms that reminded me of Munich, and then into a long richly gilt and decorated throne-room, which has not yet been inaugurated, and at the end of which is the Emperor's robing-room (formerly Napoleon's study). A narrow oak passage leads to la Salle du Sénat, formerly Chambre des Paires, remarkable for carved oak panels, and immediately opposite is the library, with a fine central view of the garden. Downstairs we were shown the *salle des gardes*, with pictures by Philippe de Champagne exhibited in it, and the bedroom of Marie de Medicis; the last-named room has a beautifully painted ceiling by Rubens and Philippe de Champagne, and the walls, richly gilt, are painted in compartments by the latter artist and Nicolas Poussin. The trap-door under a now closed-up issue, by which Marie de Medicis was wont to cause the visitors who were obnoxious to her to pass out, when they were never heard of again, is no longer shown. Her chapel has been destroyed, and in its place is a very pretty one built by Louis Philippe, in which the children of Senators are married.

The picture-gallery being under repair, we seated ourselves

[1] Napoleon III. and the Empress Eugénie.

in the garden for a while, and then drove home, crossing
the Seine *par le* Pont des Saints Pères, and the court of the
Tuileries and Louvre, and along the Rue de Rivoli, and the
Place de la Concorde, on which Louis XVI. and Marie
Antoinette were guillotined. It was a little before four o'clock
when we reached the hotel, and we had a visit from Lord
Cowley, her Excellency being laid up with *une migraine.*
We dined at 5.30, and an hour later went for a drive to the
Champs Elysées and the Arc de l'Étoile, begun by Napoleon
and finished by Louis Philippe, in *commemoration des victoires
de l'Empire*—a fine but overpoweringly colossal archway.
Thence along the Empress's drive, reminding one of Rotten
Row, to the Bois de Boulogne, which owes its attraction to the
present Emperor. We drove round the artificial lake, by
sundry *châlets* or *cafés*, and the Pré Catalan (a kind of respectable Vauxhall), and, returning by the same route, passed up the
Boulevards, now alive with people walking up and down and
sitting under the awning of the lighted *cafés.*

September 6, Sunday.— . . . After breakfast we went to
the English service at the Chapelle Marbœuf, a chapel purchased by Bishop Spencer, and heard an excellent sermon
preached by a young man, Mr. Pigou;[1] the prayer for India
was most affecting. . . . Lunched and set out for St. Cloud,
where the annual fair was taking place ; on our way thither
we passed a fine cascade in the Bois de Boulogne, which
was filled with people, and took the *route de* Longchamps
by the race-stand, a somewhat gaudy edifice. The town
and *château* of St. Cloud are very prettily situated on a
wooded hill overhanging the Seine. The porter declined
to allow our carriage to enter the gates, so we were obliged
to walk up to the *château ;* of the interior we had but a rapid
and unexplained *aperçu,* as it was a public day, and our new
laquais de place, un imbécile ! The walls of the apartments
we looked into appeared to be decorated in the style of the
Luxembourg, and hung with paintings, chiefly by Rubens and
Canaletti. From the courtyard we had a fine view of Paris.
Descending the hill, we entered the Park gates where the
fair was being held, a gay and busy scene, to attract *le bas
peuple,* but as a shower came on, we took shelter under the
trees until *les grandes eaux,* strangely miscalled, began to
" throw up mud," as the old Irishman remarked in our hearing. We then left, and returned home by the merry suburb
of Boulogne, the Bois and the Champs Elysées. Dined at
six, and afterwards drove along the partially well lit Rue de

[1] Now Dean of Bristol.

Rivoli, passing by the Tour de St. Jacque, the oldest monument in Paris and sole remains of the church of that name, and round the Boulevards home. . . .

September 7.— . . . A little after eleven we drove to the Madeleine, commenced in 1764 for a church, transformed by Napoleon into a Temple of Glory, and finished as a church by Louis Philippe. Mass was being celebrated, so that we had only a peep at the interior. . . . The dome over the chief altar is painted in sacred and profane subjects—old Napoleon is represented amongst the Apostles "*parce qu'il était un grand génie*," remarked our wise *laquais de place.* The exterior, built on the model of the Parthenon, with columns all round, is striking and fine. Thence, by the Rue de la Paix and the Place Vendôme, in the centre of which stands a bronze column wreathed with bas-reliefs of Napoleon's victories and surmounted by his statue (the bronze of which was provided by cannon taken from the enemy), to the *hôtel monstre du Louvre.* In the immense dining-room (*à* 400 *couverts*), we met ——, sillier than ever, who forced himself upon our notice. We then drove by the *faubourg* St. Antoine *le foyer des révolutions au delà de la place de la Bastille* along the Rue de la Roquette to the Cemetery of Père la Chaise, which covers a hill from the summit of which one has a panoramic view of Paris. . . . Our *laquais* did nothing but lose his way, so that we spent two hours in wandering about under a broiling sun in search of the tomb of Abélard and Héloise, which is close to the entrance.

We next proceeded *viâ* the shabby streets of the Faubourg St. Germain to the Panthéon or church of St. Geneviève, desecrated in the time of the revolution, and dedicated to Philosophy. It is built in the shape of a Greek cross, with a fine dome, and rows of Corinthian columns all round the interior, giving it the appearance of a grand hall. The relics of St. Geneviève de Brabant are preserved in a large coffin above the chief altar, in front of which a priest holds watch night and day. . . . Opposite is the École de Droit or "Polytéchnique," the cradle of revolution! On our way home we passed through the fashionable streets of the Faubourg St. Germain, by Government buildings and the church of St. Clotilde, built in the modern Gothic style, beautiful though scarcely finished ; the first stone was laid by Queen Marie Amélie. The façade of the Corps Législatif is very fine. . . . At 8.30 Lady Cowley and Mr. Monson,[1] one of the *attachés*, fetched us to go to the Opéra Français. The

---

[1] Now Sir Edmund Monson, British Ambassador at Paris.

house is fine but dark. . . . As we three unprotected females were driving home our carriage was stopped by a drunken coachman, and a row ensued, in the middle of which Mr. Howard came to our rescue. *September* 8.—Lady Cowley came in a britzska to take me out shopping. . . . I was greatly disappointed with the shops themselves, the windows and premises of which are not to be compared with those of London.

September 9.— . . . We met Mr. Howard at *le chemin de fer du Nord*, and he accompanied us to Versailles. Driving at once to the *château* we devoted ourselves to *l'aile du Nord*, which comprises the Chapel, lovely in its gilding and painted ceiling; *les chambres des Enfans de France* in bygone days —now containing a series of French historical pictures; *l'Aumonerie*, where lived the Clergy, now called "*Les Croisades*," as the walls are covered with pictures of the French crusades. Louis Philippe, to his shame be it spoken, did away with all historical *souvenirs* in the *château* and turned it into a museum or pictorial history of France. Upstairs *de grandes salles*, built at the end of Louis XIV.'s reign, and filled with war pictures by Horace Vernet, chiefly taken in Africa and commemorating *les faits d'armes* of Louis Philippe's sons; there are one or two pictures of battles in the Crimea, *par exemple* the Alma *without* the English troops! How characteristic of a Frenchman! In the corridors adjoining are the statues of the Duc d'Orleans by Pradier, and of Jeanne d'Arc by Princesse Marie d'Orleans. The second storey, which was once occupied by *la suite*, is now a portrait gallery, and the paintings are by the older French masters, chiefly *du temps de* Louis XIV. and XV.

September 10.— . . . About three o'clock we went out to the Chapelle Expiatoire, erected by Louis XVIII., to the memory of Louis XVI. and Marie Antoinette, over the spot in the Rue des Mathurins where their bodies lay twenty-one years, until removed by Louis XVIII. to St. Denis; in the *Jardin d'entrée* are buried the bodies of the brave *Suisses* butchered by the people as they defended the King. On the monument of the King is the letter he left, containing his last will and wishes, and on that of the Queen her very touching last letter to Madame Elizabeth (January 21, 1793). . . . We proceeded to the Chapelle Ferdinand, Avenue de Neuilly, which marked the place where the Duc d'Orleans was killed[1] (July 13, 1842); he was carried from where he

---

[1] The Duc d'Orleans was driving, when his horses ran away, and in jumping from the carriage he was mortally injured.

fell into a grocer's shop close by, and died at the end of four hours without having spoken. His widow bought the shop and ground, and erected this Chapel; the monument is very handsome, the recumbent figure of the Duc in uniform, with his military cloak draped about him, is by Triqueti, the angel kneeling at his head by the Princesse Marie d'Orleans, his sister. In the pavilion opposite is the canoe which the Prince de Joinville brought the Duc d'Orleans from Canada. One clock marks the hour of the accident, 11.50 a.m.; another the hour of his death, 4.10 p.m.

We drove on to the Tuileries. The apartments of Louis XVI. and Marie Antoinette are in the Pavilion de Flore, now inhabited by the Empress. In the *Galerie de la Paix* is a picture of Napoleon III., by Müller, and a portrait of the great Napoleon by Horace Vernet hangs in the *Salon Blanc;* the *Salon Louis XIV.* contains a picture of the King and his brother, as children with Anne d'Autriche, and one of Louis XIII. . . . The view up the Champs Elysées from the centre window of the *Salle des Maréchaux* (the ballroom) is charming. . . . Lastly we visited the *appartements de l'Impératrice*, where there are some very fine Gobelins. . . . We spent the evening at the Théâtre Porte St. Martin, where *Les Chevaliers du Brouillard* (Jack Sheppard) was very well given indeed. *September* 15.— . . . Arrived at St. Germain about 2.30, and walked to the far-famed terrace to see the glorious view over the Seine. We hired what they called a *char-à-banc*, but what was really an English brake; it was made to hold about six, and we went ten in it! Our efforts to squeeze in Herr von Wenckstern were very absurd, and he was obliged to stand on the step. We drove for two hours or more in the beautiful forest—principally oak trees. . . . *September* 16.—George arrived soon after nine o'clock, having come to pay the Emperor a visit at the Camp at Châlons. . . . We all dined together at a *café* in the Rue Mont Orgueil—a most out-of-the-way place, in a *quartier* rather the equivalent of Covent Garden—with a very dirty, most uninviting entrance, but when once upstairs we found a comfortable room, and had a very good dinner, and a very jolly one. Thence to the Théâtre Français, where we saw *Tartuffe*. George and his staff go off to Châlons to-morrow morning at half-past six.

September 18.— . . . We went a large party to Fontainebleau, arriving at 1.30. . . . The courtyard by which we entered is the one that witnessed the sad, mournful scene of Napoleon's adieu to his Guards. One of the most lovely things in the *château* is in the Emperor's apartments, a bath-room, which was transported there from the *Garde Meuble*, opposite the Tuileries, where it was used by Marie Antoinette when she had been privately and *incognito* to balls; the walls and ceilings are all looking-glasses, with little cherubs, etc., beautifully painted. We saw, also in the Emperor's apartments, the small round table on which Napoleon signed his abdication, and the window in which it stood at the moment—bitter moment!

In the *cabinet de l'Impératrice*, formerly that of Marie Antoinette, the window fastenings were wrought in iron and gilt by Louis XVI. himself; they are wreaths of ivy leaves. In the *Petits Appartements* Louis XIV. gave hospitality for some time to Christine de Suède, and near one of the windows she had her secretary, Monaldeschi, murdered. Louis Philippe also allowed Marie Christine d'Espagne to inhabit them for some time. Marie Louise likewise occupied them for a little while. . . . We walked across the garden to the *Chapelle de la Sainte Trinité*, and getting into our carriages under the *perron*, drove by the canal, the beautiful gardens, charming green avenues, the Park, to the *Treilles du Roi*, on which grow the celebrated grapes called "*Chasselas de Fontainebleau*," past the *château* again, and out by the *Cour des Adieux*. Thence we drove into the Forest; such fine trees! . . . I think Fontainebleau quite the most beautiful place we have yet seen.

September 19.— . . . We spent some time at the Hôtel de Ville. The *Salle du Trône*, begun by Henri II. and finished by Henri IV., is the only portion of the present building that is old; the rest was built in Louis Philippe's time. The painting of the ceilings is very fine; the *Grande Galerie* and the ballroom are particularly handsome, and the staircase reminded me of that in the *Cour des Adieux* at Fontainebleau. Then we visited the Conciergerie, the most interesting, the most sad and touching *souvenir* in Paris! The prison inhabited by Marie Antoinette during the last fearful days of her tearful life! A very low room, a few feet square,—scarce space to move between the wretched pallet which served for her bed and the wall—a bare brick pavement, and halfway across was a low *paravant*—all that divided her from her brutal guards, who could see her every movement! Here, exposed to misery, cruelty, and insult, she spent seventy-six long, weary, bitter days! One cannot stand in the room without feeling choked by tears! The place where her wretched pallet was is now occupied by an altar, on which is the crucifix she used. There are two pictures of the unhappy Queen being taken from the Temple; one depicts her parting from her daughter and Madame Elizabeth—Simon and his wife looking on—and in the other she is taking the sacrament, the last morning of her life (October 16, 1793), administered to her by a priest, Magnan, at the peril of his life. A third picture, said to be very like, is in the little adjacent space, now opening into the cell, but then divided by a dead wall. Next to this is a room, since converted into a chapel, where the Girondins had their last supper the night before their execution, and in which Danton and Camille Desmoulins were imprisoned. We also saw the room where the present Emperor was confined during thirty-seven days before he was transferred to Ham. Prisoners are only kept there while their trial proceeds—until judgment is pronounced. Many *détenus* were in the courtyard, and we passed between a crowd of them in a narrow pitch-dark passage.

September 20.—The Persignys called, and when they had gone we drove to see the Walewskis' house, which is beautiful. Her sitting-room, looking into the garden, is perfection; one might be in the country, miles away from any town! Then to the Corps Législatif, formerly Chambre des Députés, on the *emplacement* of the old Palais Bourbon, which belonged to the Condés. Afterwards we went to the Palais Royal, but could not see it, being *en papillottes!* and lastly, to the church of St. Germain l'Auxerrois, the bell of which gave forth the dread signal on the night of the Saint Barthélemi.[1] All but the façade was burnt down in 1830, so the rest is modern; it is a pretty church. . . . Finding the singing at St. Roch over, we walked in the gardens of the Tuileries, and sat in the Champs Elysées, which was very crowded.

September 21.— . . . Started by rail for Chantilly. At the station of St. Leu Lord Cowley met us with a carriage and a covered brake to take us all, he himself riding. We drove, leaving Chantilly on our right, to the Parc d'Apremont, where Lord Cowley has the shooting. In the centre of the Parc, whence radiate all the avenues, is a famous old stone table called "La Table," once the *rendezvous de chasse* of the Prince de Condé. Over this table a tent was spread, and a grand luncheon provided. We found there Lady Cowley and her two daughters—Feodore[2] and Sophie:[3]—the

[1] The Massacre of St. Bartholomew's Day, August 24, 1572.
[2] Now Lady Féodorowna Bertie.
[3] Now the Dowager Lady Hardwicke.

Duc and Duchesse de Valmy, Lord Howden, and others. After luncheon we went (in a real *char-à-banc,* holding fifteen, and drawn by four horses abreast) a lovely drive to Chantilly. The old Castle was pulled down and destroyed in the great Revolution, and nothing left but the Capitainerie, where the Cowleys live. We walked on the terrace, which is the roof of the remains of the old Castle, now offices, and had a fine view of the racecourse and forest. A wide and deep moat surrounds the house. We dawdled in the *Château* and garden for some time, and about four o'clock went for a drive, having overcome the considerable difficulty of getting into the *char-à-banc!* We drove first through the great stables, built by the Prince de Condé—all of stone, and containing 150 stalls; then through the forest, to what is said to have been a chapel, where Queen Blanche came daily to pray for St. Louis when he was at the Crusades; it is pretty, but bears little appearance of its former state. We were back about six, after a charming expedition, for Lord Cowley was most amusing, and dined in the gallery—a beautiful room, where used to hang the Gobelins tapestries, pictures of the battles of the great Condé, which the Duc d'Aumale has now had brought over to Orleans House at Twickenham. At 8.30 we left, and as we drove away our eyes feasted upon the prettiest illumination possible—a line of lights round the moat, the front of the house and the boundary wall, with two Bengal lights, pale lilac, turning first to yellow, then to rich crimson. The reflection in the water enhanced the beauty of the scene, making the house look like some fairy palace.

September 24.—Breakfasted at seven a.m. Left the Hotel for the station, whence we started at eight o'clock. We were at Calais by four, and had to hurry off to save the tide at Dover. We crossed, in the *Prince Frederick William,* a new and powerful fast boat, in an hour and thirty-five minutes. It was such a lovely evening, so warm, and the sea more beautifully blue than one can conceive, and smooth as glass. We slept at Dover as usual at the Ship.

Letter to a Friend.

Cambridge Cottage, September 26, 1857.

. . . I thoroughly enjoyed our stay at Paris, although far too *John Bullish* to think that gay pleasure-hunting city at all to be compared with dear *grand* old London, the emporium of the world! The busy, sight-seeing, theatre-going life we led presented a funny contrast to the *dolce far niente* at Rumpenheim. The public buildings, the Louvre[1] in particular, promenades, and neighbouring *châteaux* delighted us, while the out-of-doors life of the inhabitants which makes the Boulevards charmingly attractive, amused us greatly. In the streets and shops we were much disappointed, both of which are on a very inferior scale (the latter I mean as regards premises, the contents being ruinously tempting) to those of London. . . .

In the progress of the Indian Mutiny[2] Princess Mary displayed an anxious interest, and writing on the 27th of September, from Cambridge Cottage, she says: "I felt very pleased to be in dear little Kew church again. . . . Sir William Dunbar preached on the *sad* events in India, and in the afternoon I read some letters from India with details of the *horrors* perpetrated." Her heart went out to those in danger and distress in a far-off land, and by womanly sympathy and practical humanity she brought a ray of light into many a darkened household. The stories of massacre, which thrilled the country with horror and indignation, made a deep impression upon the Princess, while the deeds of valour, constantly recorded, won her warmest admiration. A few days later the Duchess and her daughter left Kew for Heaton and Knowsley, where the Manchester Exhibition proved the chief attraction.

Journal.—Heaton, October 3.— . . . At two o'clock we[3] started for the Exhibition at Manchester; Mama in the coach and I following in the omnibus. The building is a fine one, and the disposal of the interior very effective. . . . We began our tour by inspecting the Hertford collection;

[1] The account of the visit to the Louvre is missing from the Journal.

[2] The Indian Mutiny began with the rising of the Sepoys at Meerut, May 10, 1857.

[3] The House party during the week included the Duke of Cambridge, the Duke and Duchess of Hamilton, the Duchess of Beaufort, Lady Geraldine Somerset (in waiting on the Duchess of Cambridge), Lady Edith Somerset (now Lady Londesborough), the Duke and Duchess of Manchester, Lord Canterbury, Lord Valletort, Lord and Lady Newport, Colonel "Jim" Macdonald (in attendance on the Duke of Cambridge), Colonel Cecil Forester, Mr. Corry, Mr. Augustus Lumley, and Count Chotek.

next the old Italian, Spanish (particularly fine, on account
of the numberless glorious Murillos), Flemish, French, and
German schools; and finished with just a peep of the
modern English school. We were delighted with everything, and marked our favourite pictures in the Catalogue
presented to us by Mr. Fairbairn, who, as chief of the
committee, took us round. . . . The Duke and Duchess
of Hamilton, and Jim having arrived and Sim being off
the sick-list, our party at dinner numbered twenty-one.
October 5.—We paid our second visit to the Exhibition,
and on alighting at the door I tumbled out of the
omnibus and fell into the *mud*, without, however, hurting
myself. The crowd inside was tremendous, but police and
detectives cleared a space for Mama and our party. We
began with the modern English school, three saloons and
two vestibules, including Sir Joshua Reynolds, and had
luncheon in the Queen's room, afterwards going round the
old masters, inspecting some of the cases with curiosities, and
ending with a peep at the Scheffers in the gallery. We were
home about five, and after tea in Katty's room I read some
of Moore's Irish melodies to a *select circle*. George, Lord
Canterbury, and Mr. Corry arrived. In the evening we
played at " Do you like your neighbours ? " and " Post " till
nearly twelve. I then paid Louise Manchester a visit, and,
after undressing, had a long cose with Geraldine till three
o'clock, when I got into bed quite chilled.
    October 6.— . . . We set out again for Manchester, accom-
panying George to the barrack-yard of the 4th Dragoon
Guards (commanded by Colonel Hodge) to review the Regiment. The men went through the sword exercise and other
evolutions to George's satisfaction, and looked particularly
smart and well. Proceeding to the Exhibition, where the
crowd was excessively loyal, and pressed forward to touch
His Royal Highness and my humble self, we again visited
the Hertford collection, I acting as cicerone, then the water-
colours, and, passing through an Oriental saloon, went to the
modern English school. After lunch I pioneered George
round the old masters till all were fairly tired out. . . .
    October 7.—The Day of Humiliation! Breakfasted punc-
tually at ten, and then drove to Prestwich to church. The
service for the day was *cold* and unnaturally merciful,
leaving a blank in every heart. Mr. Birch gave us a
fine sermon. £50 was collected. . . . In the evening we
amused ourselves at intellectual games — historical characters — whilst Louise and the men played at whist.

October 8.— . . . We drove over to Manchester early in the afternoon. It was a half-crown day, so the crowd was select, though not less numerous. . . . Whilst studying the Dutch school we met Lord Granville, who joined our party. We next visited *à fond* the water-colours and portrait-gallery, and then took our seats in front of the orchestra to hear the second part of the concert led by Mr. Hallé. At its conclusion we went up into the gallery to see the original drawings by ancient masters—Raphael, Canaletto, Claude, Rubens, and Sir Peter Lely—and at 5.30 we started on our return. . . . The Earl having forbidden dancing, to *spite* him we lit a fire in the library and had a quadrille! But the smoke and cold drove us into the further drawing-room, where we consoled ourselves by playing at "Blindman's buff," in which game Lady Newport had a nasty, and poor Katty a very severe, fall, as she hit her head against a table and went off to bed quite stunned. *October* 9.—Lady Wilton took me to her carpenter's shop, where I planed away till the carriages were at the door and the party grew impatient, so taking a tender leave of Katty and Heaton, I hurried into the omnibus. . . . We left by train for Knowsley at 3.30, where the Derbys and Emma [1] received us, and in the midst of tea the Hardwickes, Libbet, and Agneta arrived. I afterwards went to my suite of rooms (those in which the robbery was committed), and Emma sat with me till dressing-time. . . . We dined *à* 20, Lord Newport, Mr. Corry, Lord Cowper, and Lord Chelsea, making up the party.

Knowsley, October 10.— . . . We passed the morning working and singing *entre nous jeunes dames,* and at 2.15 prepared for our expedition to the boat-house, where we were to lunch, and whither Emma drove me in the pony-phaeton. Lord Canterbury and Mr. Lumley joined our luncheon, after which they, the Yorkes and Emma, rowed us young folks on the lake. We then had a walk in the Park, and heard the red deer belling, much to my dismay! Home by five o'clock, and had tea in Emma's room, to which the gentlemen were admitted; our snug little party was, however, broken up by Mama's departure to her room. . . . In the evening we danced till shortly before twelve. *Sunday, October* 11.— . . . Lord Derby, in consequence of the rain, read prayers most impressively in the Chapel. . . . The weather cleared in the afternoon, and we drove to the pretty village church, St. Mary's, for the service: on our return I walked with Lord

[1] Lady Emma Stanley, only daughter of Lord and Lady Derby; she married the Honble. Sir Wellington Talbot.

Derby to the stables, the finest thing at Knowsley. . . .
Soon after ten the chaplain read prayers to us in the chapel,
and we finished the evening with a nonsensical story from
Mr. Corry's pen. Separated about eleven, and I wrote my
journal after undressing.

October 12.— . . . We started, a party of sixteen, for the
Manchester Exhibition, where Lord Wilton, Mr. Fairbairn,
and Mr. Deane received us, but found to our discomfiture it
was a shilling day, and that 25,000 people were in the building.
To improve matters we were conducted *viâ* the second class
refreshment room, which was filled to suffocation, and very
nearly made us all ill, to the organ loft, where we had to sit
patiently, and be stared at whilst our party was collecting.
At length we made a desperate push for the gallery, and
inspected again the original drawings by Michael Angelo,
Raphael, and others. Then Lord Wilton insisted upon our
having luncheon. . . . Afterwards I set off with him to explore
the neglected walls on one side of the modern saloons, bade my
pet Sir Joshuas and Gainsboroughs good-bye, looked again at
the Murillos and old school, including Masaccio, the Hertford
room portrait gallery, and china; then *rendez-vous-d* with
the rest at 4.30 in the Queen's room. Soon after five we left
by train, and were back at Knowsley by seven. . . . In the
evening we actually danced! *October* 13.— . . . We took
leave of the party, excepting Lord Cowper, Valletort, and
Mr. Lumley, who went with us, and drove to Huyton, whence
a slowish train landed us at Tring about 6.30. The Manchesters and Jim had joined the train at Colwick, and our
three *beaux*, who had travelled in a separate compartment,
got into and upon our omnibus at Tring, and away we sped
with four horses up the steep hill to Ashridge. Dearest
Lady Marian received us at the door with a train of guests;
Mr. and Lady Margaret Leveson-Gower, "Poodle" Byng,
Mr. Fortescue, Colonel Percy, Colonel Haygarth, Colonel
Percy Herbert, Mr. Percy Cust, Mr. Augustus Stafford, and
Mr. Woolward. We sat downstairs till 8.45 awaiting our
luggage, and then dressed in a hurry. On going down at
9.20 we at once went in to dinner, a party of twenty-seven,
including Lady Craven, Bettine and Evelyn,[1] Lord Granville
and Lord Cowper. . . .

Ashridge, October 14.—Breakfast over, Lady Marian carried
us all off into the library, which was being fitted up as a
theatre, to hear Mr. Stafford read his extravaganza of *Hearts*

---

[1] Lady Elizabeth and Lady Evelyn Craven.

and Tarts. The piece being unanimously agreed to, the gentlemen went out shooting, and I spent the morning in copying out my part as "Queen of Hearts" and devising music for the songs, or rather choruses. Lady Augusta Proby and Lady Sophia Macnamara arrived about noon to take part in our theatricals, and later in the morning Sir Thomas Sebright, accompanied by Miss Treherne [1] (1st singing Maid of Honour to the Queen of Hearts), a Cornish beauty with a lovely voice. Mr. Monckton Milnes also joined the Ashridge party as a guest. We lunched at two, and in the afternoon Louise Manchester and I took a charming drive in the sociable through the Park and round by Berkhamstead Common. . . . Had tea in the drawing-room, and then rehearsed with Lord Granville, Mr. Stafford, and Bettine till dressing-time. George, the Clarendons, and Constance Villiers arrived, also Sir Thomas Sebright and Miss Treherne to dinner, and we were a party of thirty-two. . . . In the evening we had a rehearsal, more regular than the former one, each reading his or her part, and practised the choruses with *l'accompagnateur.* On returning to the drawing-room Miss Treherne sang, and made *furore* with Bosio's Echo song in *L'Étoile du Nord;* we went to our rooms about half-past twelve, and I sat up till two o'clock learning my part.

October 15.—Breakfasted at ten, and then rehearsed with the little boys (*Baker* pages) and the gentlemen, until they went out shooting; afterwards I practised the *minuet* with Augusta Proby,[2] Sophia Macnamara,[3] and the four Maids of Honour. . . . At 3.30 Lady Craven and I drove in walking attire to the coverts where the gentlemen were shooting; crossing a dewy meadow we joined them at a halt, and then accompanied them and saw all the sport—such fun! About five we set out to walk home, carrying off two of the actors, the Duke of Manchester and Lord Granville, with whom I rehearsed the whole way. On reaching the house I hurried to my room to dress in part, and then went down for a short rehearsal with the gentlemen (choruses included) before finishing my toilette. At dinner Lord Granville and the Duke of Manchester sat on either side of me, and I had a charming time of it, as our conversation chiefly ran on poetry. The gentlemen left the table with us, as the dining-room

[1] Now Mrs. Weldon.
[2] Lady Augusta Proby, afterwards Countess of Carysfort.
[3] Lady Sophia Macnamara, now Lady-in-Waiting to the Princess Louise, Marchioness of Lorne.

had to be prepared for the dance, and the actors adjourned at once to the theatre, where we were presently joined by the absent "Maids of Honour," and had a satisfactory rehearsal till about ten, when we joined the rest of the society, and found the neighbours arriving for the ball, which began shortly after, and was kept up with much spirit till past three o'clock, though I left with Mama at 2.30. Geraldine sat with me after I was undressed, and I went over my part again before retiring to rest.

October 16. . . . Lady Marian and I got up in the middle of breakfast to persuade George, who was writing in his room, to come back for the play, but all in vain. He departed with Lord Clarendon, who, however, was to return after the Council. Lord Granville had gone up at ten for the day. I rehearsed with the Duke of Manchester *sotto voce*, as I was rather hoarse; the little boys went through their parts amongst themselves and with me; then the Maids of Honour minuet had to be practised, after which I went to Lady Marian's room, the others being all employed in the green room preparing costumes, and presently had my dress tried on, and crown cut out. In the afternoon we returned to the green room, where Lord Valletort and Mr. Lumley were assisting the ladies in cutting out hearts, and I rehearsed my part with Jim for an audience. Soon after five the actors, with the exception of Lord Granville ("The Knave"), began to assemble, and at half-past the final rehearsal took place in presence of a few spectators, and went so badly that we all thought it would be a failure. . . . Dressed and dined at eight, a party of thirty-six; the Duke of Manchester ("King of Hearts") and Lord Valletort were on either side of me.

Directly after dinner the actors hurried to their rooms to dress, and then assembled in the green room, Lord Granville joining us about ten o'clock. I was very nervous, but had hardly time to think of it, when to my horror I found the piece had begun without, as we had hoped, a last short rehearsal. In fear and trembling I went on the stage, but the audience were indulgent, the actors all did their very best, and the extravaganza of *Hearts and Tarts* came off triumphantly. The *impromptu* chorus at the end, my suggestion as a tribute to Lady Marian, told well, and brought the *tears* to our hostess's "beautiful eyes." At its conclusion I changed my dress, keeping on, however, the crown and veil, and on going down again found the small room opening into the hall prepared for dancing. After one valse we went into the dining-room to a sit-down supper, at which I found

myself between Lord Clarendon and Lord Granville; we
kept up the dance till past two, when I departed to bed, the
others having one more valse.

(BILL OF THE PLAY.)

HEARTS AND TARTS; OR, THE KNAVE TURNED HONEST.

An Extravaganza written for the occasion, and humbly dedicated to
H.R.H. the Duchess of Cambridge, by AUGUSTUS STAFFORD.

The King of Hearts	.	THE DUKE OF MANCHESTER.
The Queen .	.	H.R.H. THE PRINCESS MARY OF CAMBRIDGE.
The Knave .	.	THE EARL GRANVILLE.
The Ten	.	THE EARL COWPER.
The Nine	.	THE VISCOUNT VALLETORT.
The Eight .	.	MISS TREHERNE.
The Seven .	.	THE LADY ELIZABETH CRAVEN.
The Six	.	MR. AUGUSTUS LUMLEY.
The Five	.	THE LADY AUGUSTA PROBY.
The Four	.	THE LADY SOPHIA MACNAMARA.
The Deuce .	.	THE HONBLE. A. CUST.
The Ace	.	THE EARL BROWNLOW.
Pages of the Bakehouse		THE HONBLE. N. GROSVENOR, MASTERS SEBRIGHT, WELLESLEY MAUDE, MARTIN, AND FITZPATRICK.

Stage Manager :	Prompter :
THE EARL OF CLARENDON.	THE HONBLE. FREDERICK BYNG.

October 17.—I was dressed by ten, and went down to
secure the photographs of the guests who were leaving
early. . . . Those who remained sat together in the drawing-
rooms; Mr. Stafford then read us actors, four in number,
the Prologue, and afterwards Monckton Milnes' Lines on
India to the society in general. Lady Harry Vane made
herself very agreeable, Lord Valletort drew in Mama's catalogue, Lord Cowper forgot his shyness, and Lady Marian
brought her drawings for inspection, so that the morning
wore away most pleasantly and but too quickly. . . . At
3.10 we bade adieu to dearest Lady Marian and started for
the Berkhamstead station, where the train conveyed us as
far as Willesden, whence we drove to Kew, where Knese
welcomed us, and Frazer arrived about 5.30, looking quite
blooming and radiant with joy to find herself "at home"
again ! Dear old soul !

Letter to a Friend.

Cambridge Cottage, October 20, 1857.

. . . During my six visits to the Manchester Exhibition I managed to get a very good idea of the whole collection of pictures. England, I am proud to say, held her own, thanks to the Sir Joshuas, Gainsboroughs, etc., water-colours, and a very good gallery of modern paintings. The Spanish and Dutch schools were perhaps the most splendidly represented, although the Italian and old German, but more especially the former, contributed many priceless gems. The rooms I coveted most were the Murillo vestibule and the one hung with Sir Joshuas and Gainsboroughs. . . .

Journal.—Windsor Castle, October 28.— . . . We reached Windsor Castle at six o'clock. Albert came at once to see us, followed somewhat later by the Queen, who stayed till dressing-time. . . . In the evening Albert and I played at *rabouge.* . . . *October 29.*—I was dressed in good time, and we breakfasted at nine ; sat talking till ten, and then went out walking with Her Majesty, Albert, Victoria, and Alice. It was so mild that on Mama and Albert going in, we four sat in the summer-house basking in the sun. On our return home about a quarter to twelve, I went to the green drawing-room to hear Victoria sing and see her sketch-books; after she had left me I looked over her music and tried some of her songs until startled by hearing the clock strike two. Later we were taken to the Rubens room to see Albert's portrait by Mr. Philips, and I sang to him and the children in the oak room. . . . We drove in the Park till five, and on our return I joined Albert in the oak room to hear him sing ; presently the Queen came in, and sang also. . . . *October* 30.—I was up about 7.30 and breakfasted with the others ; as it rained, we drove down to Frogmore with the Queen and Victoria. . . . At two some of the children fetched me to luncheon, and later on I was chaperoned by Geraldine to the Deanery. We walked back to the Castle, and after a snug cose I obtained leave from Her Majesty and trotted up to see darling Beatrice in her bath. I brought Leo down and took him to the Queen and sang in her room till half-past seven. We dined punctually at eight, and I sat next the Prince of Wales, who now dines with the party twice a week and wore the Windsor uniform for the first time. . . . *October 31.*—Soon after ten we took leave of the Queen, and at 11.15 left the Castle for Kew. . . .

Cambridge Cottage, November 13.— . . . I drove over with
Mama to Orleans House to see the d'Aumales, who feel
the sad blow [1] keenly; their touching description of the
circumstances of the terrible calamity cost me many tears.
November 19.—Whilst dressing I heard of the death of Mr.
Stafford, which quite upset me. To think how lately he
presided over the "Ashridge revels" and now he is gone!
And we shall never more see him or listen to his sparkling
wit. This is a solemn warning to us all. . . . In the afternoon we drove to Claremont and paid our sad visit to
the bereaved Queen Marie Amélie, the Duc de Nemours,
who is quite bowed down with affliction, and the Princesse de Joinville. [2] Their grief is quite heartrending to
witness. . . .

November 27.—My birthday and the dawn of a new year!
May God bless and keep me, drawing my heart more and
more to Himself throughout this and many succeeding years
of as much happiness as He, in His mercy, sees fit to bestow
upon me. Was *visited* whilst dressing by sundry well-
wishers, finally by dear Mama. Soon after 10.30 I was
summoned to the drawing-room where my charming birthday presents were arranged. . . . We went over to the
school with Sir Benjamin Hall and Knese, and found the
children gathered round the tea-tables, spread with plum-
cake and buns, at my expense. Little Luff read an
address to me, after which the *feast* began in good earnest!
We hastened home to see the Duchess of Inverness, and then
unpacked the gown from Paris and looked at the rest of my
pretty presents. . . . We dined with George, who had come
up from Lord Huntingfield's in honour of the day. . . .
Lady Marian Alford, M. de Jaucourt, Count Chotek, Quin,
Purves, and Colonel Tyrwhitt were the guests, and we had a
round game and were all very lively.

December 3.—At eleven o'clock I left Kew, for St. James's,
where Major Purves received me. . . . Mr. Hancock brought
the tiara of stars, and I began to dress. Just as I was
attired in all the splendour of black tulle, diamonds, pearls,
and feathers, Mama arrived to see me off with Emily
Somerset in the Queen's carriage. We had to wait some
little time at Buckingham Palace for Victoria, but soon
after 1.30 she and I, with Emily and Lord Charles Fitzroy,
started for the grand entrance of the Houses of Parliament,

---

[1] The Duchesse de Nemours died suddenly November 10, 1857.

[2] Sister of the Emperor Pedro of Brazil, and wife of the Prince de
Joinville.

followed by Lady Caroline Barrington and Biddulph [1] in the second carriage. We were taken into the Queen's robing-room, where Lords Lansdowne, Harrowby, and Granville came up and spoke to us, and thence, on Her Majesty's approach, to the House of Lords. The gallery crowded with spectators made *me very nervous*, but my alarm reached its pitch when the Peers and all present rose on our entrance, and we had to bow our way to the *Woolsack—* the *shyest* seat I ever occupied! Crimson with fright, and with our backs to the House, we awaited the arrival of the Procession; with it my alarm gave way to interest, and the Queen having seated herself on the throne, I ventured to look round and catch a glimpse of the *rush* of the House of Commons to the Bar.

Then came the Speech, alluding chiefly to the Act of Indemnity to be passed for relaxing the Bank Charter as a means of remedying the present money crisis, and to the Mutiny in India, which the Queen read very distinctly, and *so well;* after this we followed the Royal procession out of the House and into the robing-room, where Her Majesty, having unrobed, she took her departure, and as soon as possible we did the same, reaching the Palace in time to see the procession return from the centre window. The Queen then saw me for some time, and afterwards Albert took me to Victoria and Alice, with whom I had some coffee. About four I returned home. . . . Attended by Emily and the Major, we went down to the House soon after five to hear the Debate. Lord Portman, in a long-winded speech, moved the Address, which Lord Carew seconded; then came a very fine speech from Lord Derby, ably responded to by Lord Granville, and a few emphatic words from Lord Ellenborough. . . . At ten we left, having found the latter part rather wearisome; we waited at the Duchess of Beaufort's for the brougham, and drove home in the pouring rain. Supped at 11.30, and then to bed.

[1] General, afterwards Sir Thomas, Biddulph, Keeper of Her Majesty's Privy Purse.

CHAPTER XI.

A TOUR IN SWITZERLAND.

1858-1859.

Marriage of the Princess Royal—Prince of Wales's Confirmation—Studying Italian—The Queen of Portugal—Death of the Duchesse d'Orleans—New Opera House at Covent Garden—Prince of Wales at White Lodge—Death of Lady Wilton—Death of Baron Knesebeck—Large family gathering at Rumpenheim—Ulm—Zürich and neighbourhood—Lucerne — Tell's chapel — Thun — Interlaken — Grindelwald — Lauterbrunnen—Berne—Geneva—Marriage of Lady Louisa Hamilton.

THE next State ceremonial in which Princess Mary took part was the marriage of the Princess Royal. A great friendship existed between the cousins and Princess Mary entered heartily into the preparations for the wedding. Both Queen and people did their utmost to welcome and show hospitality to the bridegroom, Prince Frederick William of Prussia,[1] and the festivities which marked the occasion began some days before the nuptials were celebrated. "We are living in a whirl of excitement," writes Princess Mary to a friend, "and I have scarce time to collect my thoughts. You will be amused to hear that I do not dislike the influx of foreign royalty at all, but have made great friends with several of the Prussian Princes."

Following close upon the marriage of his sister came the Prince of Wales's Confirmation, and after a short visit to Ireland, His Royal Highness took up his residence at the White Lodge with Mr. Gibbs and Mr. Tarver,[2] "so as to be away

---

[1] Eldest son of William I., King of Prussia and first German Emperor: he succeeded his father in 1888.

[2] The Rev. Charles Tarver (afterwards one of the Canons of Chester),

from the world and devote himself exclusively to study and prepare for a military examination." [1] At the same time Lord Valletort, Major Teesdale,[2] and Major Lindsay,[3] were appointed companions to the Prince, and, to use his father's own words, occupied "in monthly rotation a kind of equerry's place about him." During this period the Prince of Wales saw much of his relations at Cambridge Cottage; he often rowed up from Richmond or Mortlake, and mooring his boat alongside the landing-stage at Brentford Ferry, would get out and take a stroll in the gardens with his aunt and cousin. The first dinner-party the Heir-Apparent attended was at the Cottage on Kew Green.

Of late the Duchess of Cambridge had begun to weary somewhat of London society, and spent as much time as possible at her country home, where she loved to sit in the garden admiring what she called "*la belle nature.*" Writing from St. James's Palace to Mr. Harrison she says:

I need not tell you that I felt much happier at Kew than I do here in this hot and noisy town, and I do hope and believe that Mary agrees with me in this; but in our station of life we unfortunately cannot always do what we like, and I am sure, therefore, that you will understand and feel for us.

Although the Duchess continued to go out a good deal, she gave up attending drawing-rooms, finding the fatigue of standing too great; but this partial retirement was not allowed to interfere with her daughter's pleasure, and Princess Mary, often chaperoned by the Hereditary Grand Duchess of Mecklenburg-Strelitz, had a very gay season. An amusing incident occurred at a ball given by Lady Inglis to celebrate

classical tutor to the Prince of Wales. After Mr. Gibbs's retirement in 1858 Mr. Tarver was appointed Director of Studies and Chaplain to His Royal Highness, and remained with the Prince until the autumn of 1859.

[1] Extract from a letter written by the Prince Consort to Baron Stockmar. ("Life of the Prince Consort," vol. iv. p. 206.)

[2] Afterwards Sir Christopher Teesdale and Equerry to the Prince of Wales.

[3] The present Lord Wantage.

the coming out of her youngest sister.[1] The Princess had arranged to dance a quadrille with her host,[2] but when the time came the hero of Lucknow was nowhere to be found. After an awkward pause Lady Inglis, much discomforted, went up to Princess Mary and explained that her husband was so alarmed at the idea of dancing with his royal guest that he had left the ballroom, begging her to make his excuses.

Princess Mary [writes a lady who made the Princess's acquaintance in 1858] was very beautiful; she had fair hair, *blond cendré*, a creamy complexion, and dark blue eyes, with long eyelashes and well-marked eyebrows. She was always kind, sweet, and gracious, and gifted in an eminent degree with what the French call *la joie de vivre*. When present at a public or social gathering, her bright manner and beaming smiles soon won all hearts; this manner was perfectly natural, and really expressed the enjoyment she felt.

Whenever any Court function was going on Princess Mary never forgot her village friends, often sending for them to St. James's Palace in order that they might see her in full dress. One who was thus favoured retains the following recollections:—

When I was ushered into Her Royal Highness's presence her *toilette* for the Drawing-room was just completed. "What do you think of me?" she said. The dress was of white satin, trimmed with Honiton lace and sprays of scarlet poppies—quite a new departure for the Princess, who wore blue so much. I was looking at the general effect, mostly at the bodice, and front of the dress which was beautifully draped and looped with clusters of poppies. "Look at my *head*," said Her Royal Highness; "what do you think of my *head*?" Then for the first time I noticed a large scarlet poppy and trail of leaves and buds at the side of her head below the plumes and falling amongst the folds of the gold-spangled white tulle veil. The charming effect was enhanced by the rich flush of colour in her cheeks, for she was somewhat anxious regarding the new shade that she was wearing.

[1] The Honble. Mary Thesiger, youngest daughter of the first Lord Chelmsford; afterwards Lady-in-Waiting to the Duchess of Teck.
[2] Major-General Sir John Inglis, Colonel of the 32nd Foot.

Her whole appearance was very beautiful, and on my saying so the Princess gave me one of her lovely smiles, and, nodding approval of my opinion, in which others present joined, she went out of the room " to show myself to Mama."

Another day Her Royal Highness allowed me to see many costly things she was going to wear at the Drawing-room, and when nearly dressed said to me, " Now you shall pin my order[1] on," knowing the pleasure this would give. When all had been accomplished to her satisfaction, the Princess bade me fasten on her bracelet, adding, " But mind, don't pinch my arm." I promised that I would be careful, but as I clasped the jewelled band on the exquisite white wrist I caught a little piece in the snap. Her Royal Highness called out, and I quickly undid the bracelet, but she was not the least vexed or impatient, and allowed me to have another trial. The second time I was more fortunate. On the Princess's return she came to the room where I was sitting, and as she entered I saw something fall to the ground. I ran to pick it up, and found it to be a diamond and turquoise ornament which had been stitched on to the skirt of her dress, but had evidently caught in something and been torn away. The Princess exclaimed, as I gave it to her, " Ah! my dear, what a good thing it dropped here; that cost a great deal of money." I had often noticed that Her Royal Highness was rather care- less with her jewels, frequently leaving them about on tables and in unlocked drawers. I think the reason was that she trusted every one.

About this time an incident happened which shows that Princess Mary was not exempt from the annoyances that people of high station have frequently to endure. For some months a man, who subsequently turned out to be of weak intellect, had been following the Princess wherever she went, and persecuting her with his attentions. Not satisfied with this unmannerly behaviour, he frequently despatched letters and flowers to the Princess. One day the Queen, with her usual kindness, sent her cousin a wreath, especially chosen to match the dress she was to appear in at the Palace the same night. Noticing that the Princess was not wearing

[1] An Order given by George IV. to the members of his immediate Family, consisting of a fine miniature head of the King, surrounded with large single stone diamonds. It was attached to a blue watered silk bow (the ribbon of the Hanoverian Guelph Order), and worn on the shoulder.

the wreath, Her Majesty asked the reason. Princess Mary replied that she had never received the flowers, and much concerned, made every inquiry upon her return home, when it was discovered that the gift had duly arrived, but Baron Knesebeck, supposing the Queen's flowers to have come from the impertinent stranger, with scant ceremony had directed that the box and its contents should be thrown away.

Journal.—St. James's Palace, January 16.— . . . Soon after four o'clock the Prussian Princes, Frederick Charles,[1] F. Albrecht, and Adalbert, with Ernest Coburg[2] and Prince Hohenzollern, came to see us. . . . Dressed early, and dined at the Palace; we were sixty-nine at dinner, and I sat between Prince Hohenzollern and Prince Albrecht (junior). In the evening we had "the round table," and in addition to the band a pianoforte player. *January* 18.— . . . A little before twelve I went with Geraldine to the Palace, but by some mistake missed seeing Victoria, and took a turn in the Park. About four we drove to the Palace to call on the Princess of Prussia, who was out, and the Duchess of Coburg, who received us. When we reached home we found that Prince Albrecht had called. . . . We dined at the Palace, a party of seventy-one, and in the evening there was a dance, ending with supper.

January 19.— . . . Accompanied by Geraldine I went to the Palace to pay Victoria a visit, when she gave me her portrait as a bracelet. Mama fetched me, and in the afternoon we received the Prince of Prussia and the King of the Belgians. At 8.30 we were at the Opera to meet the Queen. *Macbeth* and *Twice Killed* were given; the former a poor performance—Mr. Phelps ranted, and Miss Faucit was indistinct—the latter, capital fun with the Keeleys. "God save the Queen" and a buffet of refreshments divided the performances. *January* 20.— . . . I dressed after dinner and drove at 9.30 to the State Ball. *January* 23.—. . . . We went to the Opera to welcome the

[1] Commonly called the "Red Prince." He was a nephew of William I. of Prussia, and father of the Duchess of Connaught.

[2] Duke of Saxe-Coburg and Gotha, and elder brother of the Prince Consort. He married, in 1842, the Princess Alexandrina, eldest daughter of Leopold, Grand Duke of Baden, and was succeeded in 1893 by his nephew, the Duke of Edinburgh.

bridegroom, who had arrived shortly before two o'clock; after the performance the young couple had to acknowledge the cheers of the audience. *January* 24.— . . . I arranged my album for the royal autographs, and then walked with Mama to the Palace to give Victoria our presents. We saw the Queen, and were shown the wedding-presents, which are beautiful, then called upon Aunt Kent, and later I tried on my Court dress, which, alas! did not fit. . . . We sat down eighty-three to dinner at the Palace, the guests being Lord Clarendon, Lord Palmerston, and Prince Reuss of the Prussian Legation.

January 25.—. . . . Dearest Vicky's wedding-day! May she ever look back to it with heartfelt pleasure, and may it prove the dawn of a happy future! I was up about 8.30, had breakfast in my room, tried on my train, which Madame Descou and two girls had been altering since 7.30, had my hair done, and was ready by a quarter-past eleven. Mrs. Barry, Mrs. Laumann, Maria,[1] and Mrs. Gold came to see us dressed. Geraldine and Arabella West (*my Lady-in-waiting*) practised carrying our trains, and about half-past we drove with the escort to St. James's Palace, and awaited Her Majesty in the Closet.[2] The foreign Princes having passed through, the children and Aunt Kent came in, followed shortly by the Queen, and then the procession was at once formed, which I had the unenviable privilege of *opening*. The rooms and corridors we had to pass through were lined with spectators, and the Chapel looked *beautiful* with its decorations and full-dress occupants. The Archbishop[3] performed the service very inaudibly, but the bridegroom's replies were heard all through the Chapel in firm and feeling accents, and dear Victoria's, though softer, were very distinct. At the close there was a good deal of embracing between the young couple and their mutual parents, before the processions returned to the Throne-room, where the marriage register was signed by all present. We then followed the Queen to the Palace, where we had a grand breakfast or luncheon *en famille*, with the addition of the Orleans (3) and Aumales (3); my neighbours were Prince Frederick Charles of Prussia and Edward Weimar. Soon afterwards we bade

[1] Housemaid at Gloucester House.
[2] "I went into the Closet where Mama, looking so handsome in violet velvet trimmed with ermine and white silk and velvet, and the Cambridges were." (Queen's Diary, "Life of Prince Consort," vol. iv. p. 161.)
[3] The Archbishop of Canterbury, who was assisted by the Bishops of London, Oxford, and Chester, the Dean of Windsor, and Dr. West,

adieu, and were home by a quarter to four, when I changed
my dress with lightning speed, and walked back (skirting as
much as possible the crowd) to the Palace to see Vicky off,
with George as my chaperon.   We were in very good time, and
after bidding her a tearful good-bye with the rest, I followed
the Queen to a room overlooking the Park, whence we heard
the loud cheers that greeted the young couple on all sides as
they drove off in the direction of the Paddington station.[1]
Home by five; George sat with us a little in the boudoir, and
we had tea. . . . At 9.30 we went to the State Concert in
the grand Ballroom at the Palace.   The music I thought
rather too heavy: we said farewell to the foreign guests, and
reached home at a quarter to two.

January 27.— . . . I read aloud to Mama the *Daily News*,
which contains a first-rate account of the wedding. . . . We
had a dinner-party of sixteen in honour of Prince Albrecht
of Prussia, and a reception in the evening, which went off
very well.   *January 29.*— . . . We drove round and round
Hyde Park, in the vain hope of meeting the royal party on
their return from Windsor, and were at the Opera in Aunt
Kent's box at 7.15: a little later the Queen and the young
couple arrived, and were received with "God save the
Queen" and cheers.   *The Rivals*, by the Haymarket company,
followed by a second National Anthem and *The Spitalfields
Weaver*, by the Adelphi company, were the plays chosen.
January 30.—I occupied myself until it was time to dress
for the drawing-room: there were no *presentations*, only
congratulations, and all was over a little before four.
Victoria wore her wedding-dress and train.[2] . . . We dined
at the Palace, and I was next to the Prince of Wales and
Count Bernstorff.   In the evening the *eight bridesmaids*[3]
and their respective parents—but no "*young men*"—came,
and we danced till midnight.   *January 31.*— . . . In the
afternoon Victoria and Fritz W. of Prussia, attended by
the Perponchers,[4] came to see us.   Dined with George;
the party included besides Lord Wilton and Lord Eglinton,

[1] *En route* for Windsor Castle.
[2] The Princess Royal's wedding-dress was of white *moiré antique*, ornamented with three flounces of Honiton lace beautifully designed; bordering
each flounce were wreaths of orange and myrtle blossoms—the latter the
bridal flower of Germany.
[3] Lady Susan Pelham Clinton, Lady Emma Stanley, Lady Susan Murray,
Lady Victoria Noel, Lady Cecilia Gordon Lennox, Lady Katherine Hamilton,
Lady Constance Villiers, and Lady Cecilia Molyneux.
[4] The Count and Countess Perponcher, *Kammerherr* and *Oberhofmeisterin*
to the Crown Prince and Princess.

who sat on either side of me, Princess Edward, the Duchess
of Beaufort, Lord Winchester, Lord Stratford de Redcliffe,
and Lord Stanley of Alderley. Very pleasant ! *February* 1.—
I went with Geraldine on foot to the Palace to see Victoria.
She was in her dressing-room; Fritz came in and presently
Albert for a few minutes. She burst into tears as she parted
from me, and with a *very heavy heart* I went to Alice's room
for a little while. . . .

February 2.—*A very gloomy, tearful* day ! At 11.30 we
drove to the Palace to see poor dear Vicky off. It was our
intention to wait downstairs; but we were sent for, and
found dear Victoria surrounded by a number of crying
relations in the Queen's Closet. It was a sad and trying
scene ! We all accompanied her to the carriage, and, after
bidding her adieu, Mama and I hurried to one of the front
rooms to see her drive up the Mall *en cortége*[1] in an open
carriage, in spite of a heavy snowstorm. We were home
by twelve, and after a good cry and talk with Mama, I sat
down to the piano, but was interrupted by the arrival of
Miss Coutts, who came to report Vicky's touching progress
through the City.[2] . . . I felt too sleepy to do anything all
the evening but watch Mama play at patiences. On going
into my room I remarked a strong smell of smoke; but as
Frazer assured me it was caused by taking off the fire in her
room, I betook myself to bed. At 2.30 the noise of footsteps
overhead awoke me, and after a few minutes Frazer came to
me from the Baron's sitting-room and told me the smoke
came from a smouldering beam under his grate, and that the
firemen had been sent for. She had remained awake, and,
finding the smell of smoke increase, had risen and discovered
it to proceed from the room above; thither she hurried, and,
as she opened the door, Knese had appeared at the opposite
one, a violent fit of coughing brought on by the smoke
having awakened him. I got up at once, and, wrapping
myself up, went round to the breakfast-room. All the
establishment save Mama, who slept through it all, were
up, and Mr. Cantrall[3] was on the spot in no time. The
firemen sawed away the beam, which in parts was terribly
charred, and after wandering about the rooms for three

[1] The Prince Consort and the Prince of Wales accompanied the bride and
bridegroom as far as Gravesend, where the Royal yacht was waiting to take
them to Antwerp.

[2] The route taken was through the Strand, Fleet Street, Cheapside, and
over London Bridge.

[3] Chief Clerk at the Board of Works.

hours and having some tea I went to bed again, truly thankful for our providential escape.

February 4.— . . . Soon after five we drove to the House of Lords to hear the opening debate of this year's session. Lord Derby[1] made an admirable speech, in which he touched upon the horrible attempt upon the French Emperor's life and the Refugee question. Lord Granville, Lord Grey, and Lord Brougham, also spoke. . . . *February 8.*— . . . We went to the House of Commons to hear the Vote of Thanks to the Indian army,[2] and Lord Palmerston moved the Anti-conspiracy Bill.[3] D'Israeli spoke in answer to Palmerston on the Vote of Thanks. At 7.30 we were conducted by Lord Charles Russell to his rooms, where Lady Charles and family gave us tea. We thereby lost Lord John Russell's and Sidney Herbert's speeches. After Palmerston had brought in his Bill, numberless radicals—Fox,[4] the Unitarian

---

[1] Parliament reassembled on February 4, after the adjournment, when Lord Derby, as leader of the Opposition in the House of Lords, called attention to the fact that no Ministerial Statement had been made. In the course of his speech he specially referred to the recent attempt by Orsini to kill the Emperor and Empress of the French by means of bombs, as their Majesties were entering the Opera House in Paris. Orsini had been resident for some time in England, and went direct from this country to commit the crime. This unnatural abuse of our hospitality to foreign refugees raised the greatest indignation here. At the same time a strong feeling prevailed amongst certain classes in France that the law of England afforded an improper degree of shelter, and gave countenance to men of the Orsini type. This feeling unfortunately spread, with the result that at the date when Parliament reassembled, the relations between this country and France were somewhat strained. Lord Derby thought the opportunity should be taken to make some declaration of policy. His Lordship was answered by Lord Granville.

[2] Lord Palmerston moved a Vote of Thanks to Lord Canning, Governor-General of India, and to the civil and military officers and servants in India. Mr. Disraeli replied, lamenting the introduction of Lord Canning's name, and moved the previous question. Finally, Lord Palmerston declared that he did not consider the House bound by the Vote to approve Lord Canning's general conduct, whereupon Mr. Disraeli withdrew his motion, and the Vote was agreed to.

[3] Lord Palmerston had already brought in his Conspiracy Bill, which proposed to make conspiracy to murder a felony, punishable with penal servitude, and to apply it to all persons with respect to conspiracies to murder wherever intended, and on February 8 the second reading was arranged to be taken. Sound as the measure was in principle, it was subject to much hostile criticism on the ground that if the House were to pass it we should be yielding to the dictation of France. Ultimately the Government was defeated.

[4] Mr. W. J. Fox.

preacher, Kinglake, and Gilpin rose and ranted, and at
11.30 we came away, fairly tired out. *February* 10.— . . .
We dined at the Palace to celebrate the anniversary of the
Queen's wedding-day, a party of thirty-six. In the evening
"Dr. Marsh and his little men" (a band of forty children)
performed; the solos were very good, and the whole per-
formance wonderful. *February* 13.— . . . The Queen and
Alice arrived about 4.30; the former very kindly with a
pocket full of letters from Berlin. . . . We dined at Lord
Eglinton's; a most agreeable party. *February* 20.— . . .
Count Kielmansegge came to announce that Lord Palmerston
had resigned.[1] . . .

March 13.— . . . About midday we drove to the Kensington Museum; wandered through the departments devoted
chiefly to machinery, furniture, china, glass, and frescoes,
and inspected the Sheepshanks collection of pictures. . . .
Took my first singing lesson with Marras, and saw Don
Juan of Spain.[2] . . . Dined at the Salisburys', and sat
between our host and Lord Derby; a very enjoyable evening.
March 21.— . . . Mama dropped me at the Palace. I went
out walking with Alice, and met the four younger children;
soon after the Queen joined us, and Albert also some time
later. We did not go in before six, when I had tea with
Alice and the Prince of Wales. On reaching home I found
dearest little Madame de Persigny with Mama, in tears,
the French Emperor having accepted Persigny's proposal to
resign his post. *We all wept.* . . . George dined with us,
and after dinner read aloud a description of the Masquerade
at Hanover. *March 28, Sunday.*—Directly after breakfast
we left for Quebec Chapel, but the service not commencing
before half-past eleven, we drove round Hyde Park to fill
up the time. . . . Dr. Goulburn[3] gave us a most excellent
sermon on Sunday trading in London.

Windsor Castle, April 1.—Breakfasted at nine, and soon
afterwards Alice came to us for a little while; then I wrote
till it was time to dress for the Confirmation. We assembled
shortly before twelve in the Queen's Closet; and thence

---

[1] After the adverse vote on the Conspiracy Bill, Lord Palmerston resigned,
and Lord Derby undertook the task of forming a Conservative Government.
Although Lord Palmerston's resignation took place on February 20, it was
not announced in Parliament until two days later.

[2] Father of the present Don Carlos, Duke of Madrid.

[3] The Rev. Edward Meyrick Goulburn, D.D. He became Minister of
Quebec Chapel and Prebendary of St. Paul's in 1850, and was afterwards
Dean of Norwich.

proceeded to the Chapel, where the Archbishop confirmed the Prince of Wales, who seemed much impressed. May he have strength given him from above to keep the vow he has taken upon himself, and may this be a turning-point for good in his life! The ceremony concluded, we repaired to the green drawing-room, where the guests were conversed with; it was a treat to see Conservative Ministers and Court in attendance. We then withdrew to the late King's room to give our presents to Wales, and afterwards lunched as usual *en famille.* Soon after two we took leave of Her Majesty, and occupied ourselves in our own apartments till 4.30, when we started on our return journey.

Cambridge Cottage, April 8.—Took my first Italian lesson with Signora Calimberti, Libbet Yorke's *protégée,* a nice lady-like person. We studied away for two hours, time flying only too swiftly. . . . We drank tea at the Cadogans', where I ascended to the second floor to pay poor *grippé* Lord Cadogan a visit. . . . In the evening Mama read aloud whilst I worked; the subject was one of absorbing interest —Joseph and the army and his bride Isabella of Parma.[1]

April 17.— . . . On returning from our walk we found the Duchesse d'Aumale and the Princesse Salerno awaiting us; on their departure the Duchess of Beaufort, Emily, and Edith were announced. After tea, as Edith and I were sitting in my room, who should arrive but Her Majesty with Albert and little Arthur, and I accompanied them through the Gardens.

May 4.—I wrote Italian before breakfast, and again afterwards till twelve. Later on I had a visit from dear Ellinor Dalrymple, whom I had not seen for upwards of four years. . . . We went to the Haymarket, where we heard Titiens, Alboni, and Giuglini in the *Trovatore.* The first named, a German, has a fine voice, and acts well, but does not touch one; *l'anima* is wanting. . . . *May* 7.— . . . We dined at the Palace in the supper-room, a party of eighty-seven, to meet the young Queen of Portugal,[2] a lovely little rosebud, with a wonderful degree of manner, and something to say to all who were presented to her, on her way to her unknown spouse and her new home.

St. James's Palace, May 8.— . . . Katty accompanied us to Mr. Rarey's, the American horse-tamer; Burghersh, Adza,[3]

---

[1] "Kaiser Joseph der Zweiter und sein Hof," by Mühlbach.

[2] Princess Stéphanie of Hohenzollern. She married Pedro V., King of Portugal, and died from diphtheria a year later.

[3] Lady Burghersh, now the Dowager Countess of Westmorland.

and the Duchess of Beaufort awaited us at the Round House, where Rarey exhibited on Cruizer, the famous wild horse belonging to Lord Dorchester, and subdued in *seven* minutes a mare belonging to the Duke of Manchester; the former is now as docile as a lamb! It was *most* interesting, as Rarey showed and explained his whole system and method to us; it is based on kind treatment and carried out by forcing the horse to lie down against his will. . . .

Cambridge Cottage, May 11.— . . . Lord Ellenborough resigned in consequence of the despatch to Lord Canning.[1]

May 18.—While dressing I heard the sad news of the death of the poor Duchesse d'Orleans,[2] who went off quite suddenly, the Doctors only being alarmed on the previous evening, when she had begun gradually to sink. . . . Geraldine read us the debate on Canning's Proclamation and Lord Ellenborough's censuring despatch. . . . We drank tea at the Duchess of Beaufort's, where we heard that news had arrived from India which greatly vindicated Lord Ellenborough, and indirectly showed up Vernon Smith's treachery in retaining Canning's letter.[3]

May 19.— . . . After lunch we started for Hampton Court, and met the Duc d'Aumale; the Avenue of Chestnut trees was in its full glory, and this year is finer than it has been for several seasons. . . . We proceeded to Bushey, where we got out and went through part of the house, which is filled with pictures and boxes belonging to the French family. In the wilderness of a garden, who should we see but Heath, the late gardener at the King of Hanover's, quite

---

[1] Lord Ellenborough, who had succeeded Mr. Vernon Smith as President of the Board of Control, wrote a celebrated despatch to Lord Canning, severely censuring the Governor-General of India for his Proclamation to the inhabitants of Oude. So great was the opposition shown to Lord Ellenborough's action that to relieve the Government from further embarrassment he resigned his office.

[2] The Duchesse d'Orleans died at Cranbourne House, Richmond, of influenza. She was the daughter of the Grand Duke of Mecklenburg-Schwerin, and married the Duc d'Orleans in 1837.

[3] Soon after Lord Ellenborough had resigned it transpired that Mr. Vernon Smith, since his retirement from office, had received a private letter from Lord Canning, in which the Governor-General of India had stated that the Proclamation he was about to issue would probably require some future explanation, which pressure of business prevented him from giving at the moment. This letter Mr. Vernon Smith did not communicate to his successor. Had he done so, Lord Ellenborough's despatch, which had provoked so much hostility against himself and the Government, would probably not have been written.

beside himself with joy at meeting us again. Thence we drove to Orleans House, where we found the Queen, Albert, and Alice paying a visit of condolence to the Aumales, the poor Comte de Paris,[1] the Duc de Chartres,[2] and the Duc de Nemours. It was quite affecting to see the poor sons bowed down by grief and hardly able to utter a word. We had tea, and took our departure soon after Her Majesty. . . . *May* 23. —We went to the Opera and heard Mario and Grisi in the *Huguenots* at *Covent Garden*.[3] We were lost in admiration of the new house, which is in perfect taste, the soft red of the curtains relieved by the white and gold decorations. The Wiltons and M. de Bentinck were with us in the Queen's box, which is, alas! on the opposite side of the stage to what it used to be.

May 30, *Sunday.*—As we finished breakfast Wales arrived, with Lord Valletort, Mr. Gibbs and Mr. Tarver, and went with us to church ; afterwards we walked in the Gardens and Park, taking Gouramma with us, and paid Mrs. Murphy[4] a visit. Home to luncheon, a party of eight. Wales stayed till four o'clock, having indulged in several games of curling. Then Karolyi and Chotek came, and we had tea out in the garden. . . . *May* 31.— . . . In the afternoon we sat under the trees, and soon after five o'clock walked down to the river to meet Wales, who had rowed up from Richmond with Lord Valletort ; they came ashore and walked with us to the azaleas and rhododendrons where we picked and made a beautiful bouquet, which was put in the prow of their boat. As they shoved off I threw a handful of flowers into her and christened her the *Mary Adelaide.* . . . *June* 1.—Sat under the chestnut tree all the morning. Geraldine read aloud. . . . At five we drove over to the White Lodge to pay Wales a visit. . . .

St. James's Palace, June 22.—George breakfasted with us in his regimentals, and Leo and Beatrice also assisted at our morning meal. . . . I then had to write for Mama, and while thus occupied the Bishop of London arrived. Soon afterwards we, accompanied by Tiny and Katy[5] Hamilton and

---

[1] The Comte de Paris was the eldest son of the Duc d'Orleans ; he married, in 1864, the daughter of the late Duc de Montpensier, and died in 1894.

[2] Younger brother of the Comte de Paris ; he married, in 1863, a daughter of the Prince de Joinville.

[3] The opening night of the present Opera House in Covent Garden.

[4] See p. 21.

[5] Lady Katherine Hamilton, fourth daughter of the first Duke of Abercorn. She married Lord Valletort, afterwards Earl of Mount-Edgcombe, in 1858.

Count Palffy, started for the Tower, where Prince Edward and Lord de Ros received us. We lunched in the mess-room, and then explored all the points of interest: Colonel Windham's apartment, the jewels, chapel, prisons, etc., ending with the ramparts, whence we saw soldiers undergoing punishment. . . . On our return home we had a visit from Peppy and May de Ros, who came to announce Grey's marriage with Bettine Craven. . . . In the evening we attended the ball at Willis's Rooms in aid of the Cambridge Asylum; it was not as full as we could wish, but a great many of *la crème* were there which made it very pleasant.

Letter to the Honble. Mrs. Dalrymple.

Cambridge Cottage, December, 1858.

. . . After Fritz and Adolphus had departed in the second week of August, we had Augusta to ourselves for a little while, and in the first days of September, accompanied her as far as Dover, where we spent a week very pleasantly, after the sad parting with my sister was over. George stayed with us on his way to Germany, and reviewed the troops at Dover, Shorncliffe, and Hythe, we accompanying him, which we much enjoyed. From Dover we went to Tunbridge Wells, one of the prettiest spots I know, and visited most of the *lions*, in the way of country seats, in the vicinity. The weather was delightful, and we found the Abercorns staying there; they did all in their power to make our *séjour* a pleasant one. Ever since the 18th of September, with the exception of a few visits, we have been at Kew, and have generally had some one staying at the Cottage. The year has closed very sadly for us, and one friend after another has been taken away. Scarcely had we recovered from the shock of poor dear Clementina's [1] death, when a far heavier blow came upon us in the loss of our much-loved friend, dearest, kindest Lady Wilton. Words cannot say what we have lost in *her* whom poor dear Mama mourns as a sister. . . . She was, as you know, Mama's oldest friend in England. . . .

During the summer of the following year (1859) a great sorrow befell the inmates of Cambridge Cottage. To the inexpressible grief of his royal mistress, Baron Knesebeck, the trusted friend of so many years, died rather unexpectedly on

[1] Lady Clementina Villiers.

the 24th of June; and in a letter penned some few weeks later, Princess Mary gives expression to the deep affection that she and her mother entertained for their devoted servant and constant companion.

Letters to a Friend.

... We have had a sad, sad trial in the death of our faithful friend dear Knesebeck. He was taken ill the day after Augusta arrived, at a little dinner *en famille* at George's. After an illness of six days he died from exhaustion, following upon an attack of pleurisy and bronchitis. He was, as you know, *everything* to us, and· his loss is irreparable, to poor Mama especially, as, besides his devotion to the family, he was almost her last link with the past. It has been soothing to us in our deep grief to know that others entered into our feelings, and in a measure shared our regret. You who are acquainted with our daily life can picture to yourself how sad the future appears to my mother, and indeed to me, without the *one* who made it his hourly task to ease our life, as far as lay in his power, of every burden and care. But God's will be done ! ... It is a comfort to us (all four) to have been with him at the last. We love to think of him in a better and happier world, reunited with the much-beloved master, whom he so long and faithfully served, and at whose feet his earthly remains repose. ... His death has caused a terrible blank, and each day brings more vividly before us the extent of our loss. Mama cannot at all get over it as yet, but I hope change of scene may be of benefit to her. ... Early in August we propose going abroad for a couple of months. ...

... We left home on the 4th of August, and in less than two days found ourselves in the midst of the most numerous family circle ever known at Rumpenheim—from 20 to 30, without the different suites. A terrible fire in the farm immediately adjoining the *Château*, which, however, mercifully escaped all damage, and the death of poor Count Decken [1] the very day fortnight after we arrived, formed a sad beginning to our *séjour*. We have had, however, the comfort of

[1] See p. 9.

THE PALACE AT RUMPENHEIM.

From a Sketch at Gloucester House.

knowing that we were the greatest possible blessing to dear
Aunt Louisa, who bore her sad affliction with truly Christian
resignation, and whose simple unaffected grief is very touching
to see, and we have been more *united* and affectionate than I
ever remember in any former gathering to have been the
case. I struck up the tenderest of friendships for Anna,[1]
who is really quite, quite charming, and we spent as much of
our leisure as possible together *en tête-à-tête*, or with Fraulein
Steuber, who is a very superior and thoroughly pleasing
person. I also saw a great deal of Louise's children, and to
the *4 eldest*[2] I have completely lost my heart. Augusta,
Fritz, and Adolphus are included in the circle, which was
also joined by my brother for a fortnight. We have now
spent six weeks here, and start to-morrow for Switzerland. . . .

Journal.—Ulm, September 17.—We left Rumpenheim in
the rain amidst general regret, at 9.25, a party of five: Mama,
Augusta, Geraldine, Colonel Purves, and I. Sir Alexander
Malet and Consul Koch met us at the Frankfort station.
Hermann Weimar[3] and the Duc de Chartres accompanied us
alternately, the former as far as Stuttgart, the latter only to
Heidelberg. At Bruchsal we changed carriages, and stayed
for some time in the royal waiting-room. At Ludwigsburg—
in which town my aunt, the late Queen of Wurtemberg, lived
as a widow, and died in the *Château*—the Queen of Holland,
attended by our old friend Hügel,[4] met us, and went with
us as far as Stuttgart, which is very prettily situated and
surrounded by hills. The weather had cleared up, and as we
had to wait for a quarter of an hour, the Queen took us into
the town to see the Schloss-Platz. We then bade her adieu.
The country now became more and more picturesque as we
proceeded; at Esslingen there are three curiously carved
towers, and before you reach Geisslingen, the road winds,
up the hills, affording a lovely view of the surrounding
valleys. We reached Ulm at six, an old picturesque-looking
and strongly-fortified town, and took up our quarters at the
Rothe Rath, a clean old-fashioned inn, with the best rooms

[1] Daughter of Prince and Princess Charles of Prussia.
[2] Prince Frederick, now Heir-Apparent to the Danish throne; Princess
Alexandra, now Princess of Wales; Prince William, elected, in 1863, King of
Greece, under the title of George I.; Princess Marie Dagmar, now Dowager
Empress of Russia.
[3] Prince Hermann of Saxe-Weimar.
[4] Baron Karl Hügel, an Austrian Diplomatist.

up two pair of stairs. We dined at seven; a capital dinner, *mine host* waiting upon us.   Later in the evening an old lady walked in and besieged us with carved ivory things, of which we purchased largely, and whilst we were undressing, we were regaled with a *Ständchen* in the street not far from us.

Ulm, September 18.—Up at 6.30, and hurried to the Dom directly after breakfast; it is now a Protestant church, having originally been built by the congregation, and converted by them, shortly after the Reformation, into a Lutheran church; its length is very great, and the Gothic arches and pillars and stained-glass windows are fine; the carved seats in the Chancel are curious, and on one side is an old and very quaint chapel, belonging to the Bessarer family.   We stayed to hear the organ until morning service was about to begin, and then, alas! drove to the station and went by train to Friederichshafen, where we embarked on the Lake of Constance; it had rained all the way, but fortunately cleared as we went on board. . . . The scenery of the Lake is lovely, and the view of Friederichshafen very pretty, but the Alps were hidden, and the weather was cloudy.   We landed at Romanshorn, whence we proceeded at once by train to Zürich.   The first thing that struck us on entering Switzerland, was the *verdure* of the country, which kept rising gradually until we made a most picturesque descent into Zürich.   The pointed brown church spires come out particularly well in the landscape, and form a great feature in the country.   This being a *jour de fête*, the peasants were to be seen everywhere in their smart dresses. At Winterthurm they congregated in great numbers at the station.   On reaching Zürich we drove to the Hôtel Baur on the Lake to make choice of our rooms, and then, as it was scarcely five o'clock, walked into the town, in spite of the rain.   It is beautifully situated, and rises up on the slope of a hill from the Lake; it is very clean, too, the houses being chiefly white, and the suburbs are formed of villas dotted about and interspersed with vineyards.   We saw the exterior of the church that Zwingli was wont to preach in, and on which is a figure of Charlemagne seated with a mace across his knees. . . . Had a visit from Count Colloredo, who is busy settling the Italian question [1] here. . . .

Zürich, September 19.— . . . Started by the 10.15 steamer for the other extremity of the Lake.   The weather, which

[1] After the Franco-Austrian campaign of 1859 the peace negotiations were conducted at Zürich, and Count Colloredo was the Austrian Plenipotentiary.

looked threatening at first, cleared as we proceeded, and we had a *charming* excursion. The scenery of the Lake of Zürich is very fine; numberless small towns and villages with picturesque spires enliven its cultivated and wood-clad shores. At Wädenschwyl, one of the places we touched at, we saw dozens of bales of cotton hanging out of a manufactory; at Aufnau, the only island on the lake, Ulrich von Hutten, the friend of Luther, took refuge when persecuted, and died there. We reached Rapperschwyl, our destination, at noon, and walked up through the town, chiefly remarkable for paintings on the houses, to the ruins of Grafenburg, a castle on a hill, overhanging the town, that once belonged to a family of that name; some portion of it still seems inhabited by poor people. We had our luncheon on the terrace of the Castle, from both sides of which there is a glorious view of the lake. After returning through the town we went on the bridge of planks, without any balustrade, that stretches from here to the opposite side, a distance of three-quarters of a mile. . . . A steamboat passed through it as we were going along. At two we re-embarked, and had not gone far before two of the *snow*-mountains were slightly visible! The afternoon was delightful, and on landing at Zürich about four, we walked into the town, and leaving Mama to the Colonel's care, went up to the Hohe Promenade, whence we had a lovely view of Zürich and the lake; descended the other side of the hill to a very pretty cemetery with a burying chapel, and finished up with a visit to an apothecary's shop, kept by Lavater, the great-nephew of the celebrated clergyman and phrenologist of that name, to see a good portrait in oils of Lavater. As we crossed the bridge on our return, a *ridge* of snow-mountains presented itself to our delighted gaze! We sat for a while with Mama in the garden of our hotel, on the borders of the Lake, watching the mountains. Dined at 6.30, and afterwards had a visit from M. de Bourqueney, the French Plenipotentiary.

September 20.— . . . The morning was heavenly, and the whole chain of snow-hills in sight. I took leave of my pretty corner room, with its balcony overlooking the Limmath, with regret, and started at nine o'clock in the first carriage with Geraldo,[1] Brand, and Macquean[2]—Mama, Gussy, and the Colonel following in the second—for Lucerne *viâ* the Albis. Our route lay at the back of the hills skirting the Lake, through

[1] Lady Geraldine Somerset.
[2] Dresser to the Hereditary Grand Duchess of Mecklenburg-Strelitz.

pretty villages and fields perfumed with a smell of hay and shining with dew; as the road wound up the sides of the hills the view of the snowy range became more and more beautiful, and the music of the bells of a village church added to the charm of all around.   After going down into a valley, we crossed the river Sihl at Adliswyl, and then ascended the Ober-Albis in zigzag terraces.   We got out at the village near its summit, where we saw pear trees blossoming a second time, and after climbing up a steep ascent, walked along the brow of the hill, the path winding between fir trees and flowery meadows, until we reached the very tiptop, *die Hochwacht* or *Signal*, whence we had one of the most glorious views I ever beheld!   The whole extent of the Lake of Zürich lay before us on one side, whilst on the other were the lakes of Zug and Türl; and beyond, between the hills, we had a peep of the Vierwaldstätter-See enclosed between the Rigi and Pilatus.   The spire of Kappel was visible beneath us, where Zwingli fell, and, to crown all, the chain of snow-mountains from the Säntis to the Jungfrau, including the Dödi, Glärnisch, etc.   Mama and Colonel Purves joining us at the Hochwacht, we returned to the carriages, and drove down by the Türl Lake and through several pretty villages to Kappel.   Just before reaching Kappel, we got out by the roadside to read the inscription engraved on metal plates on a massive block of stone, raised as a monument to Zwingli, in place of the tree that marked the spot where he fell in the midst of his flock in 1531 in the fight with the Roman Catholic cantons.   In front of the monument is a trellis covered with Virginian creeper.

Thence we proceeded to Zug, on the lake of the same name, where our horses had another rest of an hour, and we walked down to a kind of landing-place by the lake, where we had a beautiful view of the Rigi.   After lunching at the *Hirsch* on excellent potatoes and Gruyère cheese, butter, and honey, we left Zug—*sweet place!*—and rounded the lake passing through Chaam, the pretty church and steeple of which we saw from the Hochwacht.   We then continued our route inland, and enjoyed the picturesque pastoral scenery, which was quite a rest after the excitement of the morning. This is the first day that we have seen the regular Swiss houses all along the route.   At about six o'clock we arrived at the Schweizer Hof, Lucerne, a large hotel fronting the Lake of Lucerne or Vierwaldstätter-See, but the sky was overcast, and the first impression I had of Lucerne from our balcony was rather grand than pleasing.   There is far less cultivation on the shores of the lake than on those of Zürich, and the hills, which are much higher and more imposing, rise at once from the water, pine-clad and sombre, with but seldom a meadow at the base. My room is a narrow slip at the back of the house, with no view save on the old fortifications. We dined at seven, and afterwards wrote and dried our flowers.

Lucerne, September 21.—A lovely morning! We left by the early steamboat with a good many of our countrymen and the Leiningens, and touched first at Weggis at the foot of the Rigi; next at Beckenried, a lovely village on what I may almost call a second lake, as it narrows to a strait ere you reach this place; somewhat later at Gersau, for four centuries an independent state, the tiniest in Europe; and then at Brunnen, behind which rise the peaks of the Mythen; here the Leiningens left us. From our steamer we saw the three figures painted *al fresco* on the warehouse to represent Walther Fürst, Werner Stauffacher, and Arnold Melchthal. Close by, on the opposite shore is a small meadow called the Rütli, the spot where these three men took the famous oath to which Switzerland owes its freedom. The Lake now becomes very narrow, and in a bend of it on the rocks we came upon *Tell's Chapel.* Soon after the snow-hills of Uri-Rothstock, and rising behind Flüelen, the Bristenstock met our view. We landed at Flüelen, and drove thence through a lovely valley to Altdorf, where the spots on which Tell stood to shoot the arrow and that over which Gessler's hat was suspended, and on which the boy stood with the apple, are marked by fountains, the former surmounted by the figures of Tell and his son, the latter by that of Gessler. Close behind the last-named fountain is an old tower covered with frescoes chiefly relating to these historical events, and on many of the houses Tell is depicted. Just before we reached the barracks, the road turned off to the left, and we proceeded up the Schächenthal, a charming valley, along which tumbles and tosses the river Schächen in its rocky bed, to Bürglen, once the abode of Tell. The latter part of the ascent is steep; after crossing by a covered bridge the Schächen, which comes down as a waterfall, we got out at the top to see the little chapel, erected in 1522 on the site where Tell's house stood; it is painted all over with the events of his life. At the back stands an old tower overgrown with ivy. From the churchyard we had a lovely view.

We walked down the hill, and then returned by carriage *via* Altorf to Flüelen, whence we were rowed up the *green* lake, quite a contrast to the *blue* waters of Zürich. We landed to explore Tell's Chapel, which is soon done, as it is open to the lake, with a flight of steps from the rocks leading up to it; the walls inside are covered with pictures of Tell's life on a larger scale than those in the Chapel at Bürglen, but half defaced. Tell's Chapel was erected in 1388, on the very spot where he sprang ashore out of Gessler's boat during the storm in the presence of 114 persons, all of whom had known Tell, and could identify the spot. Our three boatmen, good-natured, though anything but savoury, and barely intelligible, rowed us home to Brunnen, where we landed, and having an hour to spare we three ladies walked through the town and up a little way into the country, but being rather scared by some frisky cattle in a field, Mama and I left the others to pursue their walk, and returned to the landing-place, where the Colonel awaited us; talked to the peasants, and were presently joined by the Leiningens. At 4.45 the steamboat picked us up, and landed us again after a delightful passage; the evening lights and shades on the hills were charming. After dinner we wrote our journals, and I finally carried mine to Geraldo's room, and scribbled till late.

September 22.—A pouringly wet morning. At twelve the weather cleared, and we walked up to the Löwen-Denkmal, the monument to the Swiss guards who fell in defence of Louis XVI., in August, 1792. It is a lion, hewn out of the rock, at the point of death; one paw still covers the Bourbon shield, the *fleur-de-lis*, the other hangs down powerless; at its head is the Swiss banner. The agony depicted in the countenance of the animal, and its attitude are *quite beautiful.* Thorwaldsen designed it, and Ahorn, a sculptor from Constance, executed it. Below the rock is a pond fenced in with shrubs, and fronting it a shop, where I bought a photograph of the lion. . . . We passed our hotel and walked on to the Capellbrücke, which crosses close to where the Reuss flows out of the lake; it is a covered bridge with very curious old pictures in the cross-beams or gables (154 in number), representing historical events and occurrences in the lives of Lucerne's patron saints; at an angle of the bridge rises out of the water the old Wasserthurm, which is supposed once upon a time to have been a lighthouse, and thus to have given its name to the town. We returned to the Hotel to luncheon, and at two o'clock started, during a slight shower, in a very nice carriage, covered at the top and open at the sides, for Küssnacht.

The route lay first by the lake, and after winding up a steep hill continued for a while inland, when we again emerged considerably above the lake; the ruined towers of Neu-Habsburg, once the *château de chasse* of the Emperor Rudolph, and the spot where the legend, commemorated by Schiller in his ballad "Der Graf von Habsburg," is said to have taken place, lay beneath us. We drove through a succession of orchards, the peasants gathering the fruit as we passed, and then down a very steep hill to the town of Küssnacht, beyond which is the "hohle gasse," at the entrance to which Tell shot Gessler. It no longer answers to that description, as the wood which enclosed it has by degrees been cleared away. It is now only a closeish avenue overhanging the road up a little hill, at the top of which, by the roadside, is a small open Chapel, built on the spot where Gessler fell, and painted inside with frescoes commemorative of the event. We climbed a grassy hill, and had a lovely view of the town of Küssnacht and the lake; then walked on while they watered the horses, until we came upon the lake of Zug, nestling amongst the hills, with the pretty little town of Arth in the distance. We entered the carriage again, and returned the same way, having thoroughly enjoyed our drive, the afternoon having turned out so fine.

September 23.—Up before six; a cloudy morning, but no rain, and at eight o'clock started (Gussy, Geraldo, and I), with Poslier as our chaperon, in the steamer for Alpnach. After touching at Stansstadt we steered through a narrow strait into the pretty bay or lake of Alpnach, a branch of the lake of Lucerne, and landed at Alpnach-Gestad, where we took a carriage. Our road lay through meadows bounded on either side by a range of wooded hills; we passed the village of Alpnach and its large Church, built with the proceeds of the timber cut down on Mount Pilate; next the town of Sarnen. . . . On the outskirts lies the lake of Sarnen, along which we drove; then through the villages of Saxeln and Giswyl, and ascended the steep hill called the Kaiserstuhl. About halfway up, we got out to see the waterfall formed by letting off the waters from the Lake of Lungern by means of a tunnel cut in the rock; the fall itself is very fine, and we scrambled over a rough piece of ground to see the mouth of the tunnel. On reaching the top of the hill our road wound along the Lake of Lungern, or rather above it, and the pathway being wooded, we had charming peeps of the lake through the trees.

The village itself is a very large one, and very straggling,

the houses standing mostly apart, and surrounded by several
fields.   The high-road being above it affords a very good
view, and we were favoured with sunshine; we stopped at
the inn about noon, and, after ordering luncheon, walked on
to a field at the foot of the ascent to the Brünig, and
clambered about amongst some delightful rocks, or rather
stones covered with moss.   It was *enchanting*; they brought
us our luncheon of potatoes, cheese, and pears, by dint of
much persuasion, under the trees in our pet field, and we sat
enjoying the pastoral scenery until two o'clock or so, when
we started on our return.   We stopped at Saxeln to see its
large church, with a portico resting on black marble pillars,
and similar marble decorations inside; in a small chapel at
the back is a stone effigy in relief of St. Nicholas von der
Flüe, a far-famed hermit of these parts, who was canonised
after his death in 1487.   A peasant woman informed us that
the sticks we saw lying under the effigy had miraculous
powers of healing—for a believer!   We waited some little
time for the steamer, which called for us shortly before five;
the sunset was glorious, and for the first time we beheld
the so-called *Alpen-glühen*, when the snow is tinged with a
pink glow and the hills with purple!   We landed at six, and
Geraldo and I walked with the Colonel through the principal
street of the town (very stinkey-pinky) to the Mühlenbrücke
over the Reuss, a covered bridge, with the dance of death
painted on its crossbeams; and home *viâ* the other side, where
the Swiss soldiers were cleaning their guns, and over the
Capellbrücke.

September 24.— . . . Directly after breakfast we hurried
with the Colonel to the Stiftskirche, to see in particular the
cloisters round the churchyard with monuments and pictures
in them, and every now and then a lovely peep of the Lake
and hills through the open arches.   It was a *heavenly* morning, and the snow range quite blue and dazzling.   At ten
o'clock we left by train, and for some time had a beautiful
view of the Rigi and Pilatus, and the chain of snow-hills
behind, passed by Sempach, and soon after saw the Jungfrau,
Eiger and Mönch, and the Altels in all their glory!   I was
much struck with Aarburg, the only hill fortress in Switzerland; the fortifications and old walls stand out in relief,
looking very picturesque.   At Olten we had half an hour
to wait, which we passed in a kind of summer-house, or
large arbor; here we changed carriages, and returning by
Aarburg, took the Berne line.   As we approached Berne we
had a splendid view of the whole range of the Alps, with the

Jungfrau in its glory, and we crossed the famous bridge over the Aar, with the valley on either side of us. After endless *pourparlers* respecting the feasibility of a rush to the *Plateforme* and back in the 30 minutes *d'attente*, we determined on the advice of a charming guard to risk it. Jumped into a carriage and drove full gallop through the principal street of Berne, by numberless fountains, to the *Plateforme* close by the Cathedral. The view on three sides of it is very fine, commanding the town below, and facing the Alps; we *ran* round it, and returned to the station just in time to get in the train, which the officials had delayed for a few minutes on our account.

Three-quarters of an hour's journey brought us to Thun, where we had the pleasure of seeing the Baron de S——'s party take possession of all the carriages, and had to wait for some time until one of them could return. Drove through the picturesque town of Thun, and under its old Castle with four turrets, to the Hôtel Bellevue, which is situated in a kind of pleasure-ground on the other side of the town; the rooms are small and low, in the cottage style, leading one into the other; the salon is a nice room, and opens upon a balcony, which continues along the bedrooms, and from which one has a lovely view of the Lake, with the snow-mountains Jungfrau, Eiger and Mönch in the background. The balcony upon which Geraldo's and my rooms open is quite shut in by trees, and over the kitchen, but decorated with a mass of Virginian creepers. It was four o'clock when we arrived, and about five we three young ladies[1] walked up through the grounds, passing the little English Chapel on our way to the temple, on the Jacobshügel, and to a seat at the very tip-top, whence we beheld a gorgeous sunset, the Alps glowing in the distance, and the lake of Thun at our feet. It was beyond all description beautiful. Before returning we went up to the *châlet* on the summit. . . .

Thun, September 25, *Sunday.*—We walked up to the English Chapel, and had a good sermon; I felt quite happy at being once again in our own church. On our return I wrote on the balcony, lunched, and worked away at my journal till past three. Then I joined Mama and Augusta in the garden, and after sitting for a while by the wall and watching the peasants pass in their picturesque dresses, we walked up the high-road to La Chartreuse, a place belonging to M. and Mdme. de Parpart; Gussy inquired for them, but they had

---

[1] Princess Mary, the Hereditary Grand Duchess of Mecklenburg-Strelitz, and Lady Geraldine Somerset.

left that morning for Berne. We strolled round the garden and into the house, which seems very pretty, and then along the riverside whilst Gussy ran out to get us a boat, in which we were rowed past the Schadau, M. Rougemont's place, and some way up the Lake. The sunset was beautiful. As we were returning we recognised Geraldo and the Colonel in a boat. . . .

September 26.—We—Geraldo, the Colonel, and I—started by steamer at 7.30. The lake of Thun is not as grand in its scenery as that of Lucerne, but far more so than the lake of Zürich, though much smaller; the Aar, on which the town is built, flows through it; the highest hills near are the Niesen, and on the summit of one of these hills the Prince of Wales shot a chamois. We passed Oberhofen, Count Pourtalès's place, and Spiez, close to which is a Castle belonging to M. de Erlach, and the so-called Beatenhöhle, a kind of waterfall issuing from a cavern in the rock. We landed within the hour at Neuhaus, and drove thence *viâ* Unterseen, a picturesque, but very wretched-looking place with a square, rather in the Italian style, and over two bridges affording a splendid view of the Jungfrau to Interlaken. This place consists of a long row of fine hotels and *pensions* with very good shops between, facing a large meadow with trees, the Jungfrau in the distance. We got out at the *débarcadaire* and were waylaid by three girls with carved wares under a covered bridge as we were about to explore Interlaken. At 9.30 we embarked on the Lake of Brienz, through which the Aar also flows, and which bears very much the character of a highland Lake with bare-peaked hills covered at their base with fir forests. We landed soon after ten at the Giessbach, and climbed up a slippery ascent to the top of the first cascade, then by *détours* I went up to the restaurant, whence one has the finest view of the upper part of the Cascade with its background of dark fir trees; the Giessbach is a succession of falls, seven in number, and though we were told it was very poor compared with other years, we thought it very fine. After changing my boots at the pretty hotel, I ascended to the first bridge, crossed the fall and recrossed it by the second bridge, which passes *under* the cascade. . . . We returned to the inn perfectly enchanted with our expedition, and lunched in a nice little room with a view of the Lake—*un beau* (?) singing Mario's songs with immense *prétension* and quite out of tune the while in an adjoining room. At two o'clock we returned by the steamer to Interlaken, passing very near the mouth of the river Lutschine. Lady Newburgh and her

niece met us at the *débarcadaire*, and walked with us along
the shops until our coachman hurried us away.   Mama and
Gussy greeted us on our arrival about five o'clock at Thun.

September 27.—We again left by the 7.30 steamer.   Brand
and Hardy .were of the party.   On board we made the
acquaintance of a charming boy, the little *Erbprinz* of Wied,[1]
and Mama cultivated his tutor, Herr Gelzer, a *bien-pensant*
professor of Basle.   At Neuhaus we secured three carriages,
and drove through Interlaken and up the valley through
which the Lütschine flows over a rocky bed to the village
of Zweilütschinen.   Here the Weisse and Schwarze Lütschine flow one into the other.   We passed on our way the
ruins of the Burg Unspunnen, sung by Byron, and the rocky
hill of Rothenfluh, where a Herr von Rothenfluh killed his
brother.   Thence we turned to the left and followed the
course of the Schwarze Lütschine, and wound up a steep
road through a charming valley with most picturesque brown
châlets shut in by hills.   About twelve o'clock we reached
the village of Grindelwald, which is scattered all over the
hill, and walked down by a pretty and easy path to the
untere Gletscher; the glacier is a rough mass of ice and
snow, earth and stones, stretching far, to the very foot of the
mountain, flowers and grass growing almost on its edges.
We went into a grotto they had hollowed out in the *untere
Gletscher*, which proceeds from the Fischerhorn, and actually
stood in the ice, which had a kind of greenish hue.   We then
climbed up the hill, in the broiling heat of a meridian sun,
as far as the inn, *der Adler*, where we lunched. . . . Left
again at 1.30, landing at Thun the same time as yesterday.

September 28.—I walked with Geraldo and the Colonel
through the town up to the Church which stands on a hill,
and from a turreted arbor in the corner of the churchyard
there is a lovely view of the Lake and the Jungfrau.   The
inside of the church is not remarkable, but at one end is
an arched kind of porch painted over with frescoes, which
was part of the old church built by Bertha, Queen of
Burgundy, in the 10th century.   Close by is a stone tablet
in memory of some young men and girls drowned in the
Lake during the 18th century.   On an adjoining hill, somewhat higher, stands the old Castle of the Counts of Kyburg,
the Lords of Thun; the wife of the *concierge* took us up
several dark, steep staircases to a huge kind of attic, more
like a barn than anything else, around which wooden cells
had been constructed, most of which, the woman informed

---

[1] Now the reigning Prince of Wied.

us, were tenanted. This gave me the *creeps!* Climbed up
a ladder to a similar attic above, with four turrets at the
corners, under each of which were cells. We got up into
the turret overlooking the town, and gazed down into the
streets below where the fair was going on. Then we descended
to an immense hall with an ancient fireplace, once the state-
room of the Kyburgs, and came out by the cellar. We went
down a long flight of steps into the very heart of the town,
and walked about the fair: the crowd jostled us considerably, but to see the peasants in their different dresses was
great fun.

After lunch M. and Mdme. de Parpart fetched us for a drive.
We drove on the other side of the Lake through the Simmen-
Thal, turned off by the Castle of Wimmis, and back by the
Kander-Thal; a charming drive, by a rolling river, rocky
hills, and pretty meadows. About 4.30 we reached the
Chartreuse *viâ* Thun, and M. de Parpart took us up to his
Library and *cabinet d'antiquités*, at the top of the house: he
showed us a very curious collection of majolica, gems and
rare specimens of Sèvres and Dresden. After seeing the
artistic *salon d'automne* upstairs, we walked up the hill
and into the wood, through which charming vistas, like
vignettes, of Thun and the Schadau have been cut; then
visited the kitchen and flower garden in one, with very good
hot-houses, and at 7.30 sat down ten to dinner, my neighbour being a nice old gentleman, Count de Müllinen. The
dining-room and drawing-room are delightful. Home by ten,
much pleased with our hosts and our day.

September 29.— . . . Took the steamer to Neuhaus, where
Geraldo, the Colonel, and I separated from Mama and
drove to Zweilütschinen, whence we turned to the right
and went along the Weisse Lütschine to Lauterbrunnen.
The valley of Lauterbrunnen, which takes its name from the
numberless tiny waterfalls that come down from the hills, is
certainly the most picturesque we have yet seen. The rocky
mountains almost shut in the road, which winds along the
river, having on the other side fir woods and fields stretching
up to the hills. We got out at the village, and, taking a guide,
walked to the foot of the Staubbach waterfall, which comes
down perpendicularly a height of 925 feet. Towards the
bottom the water resembles dust, powdering the grass and
leaves around; hence the name. The body of water was not
great, so that the waterfall reminded one of a transparent veil.
We then passed through the village and ascended the very
steep hill on the opposite side, pausing frequently to rest,

the heat being intense, and to admire the view down into
the valley. The others outstripped me, and I followed
leisurely with the guide; the view from the last resting-
place up the ascent is too lovely! commanding the whole
extent of the valley, closed in by the snowy peaks of the
Breithorn and part of the Jungfrau.

Not far from the village of Wengern I was overtaken by
two porters with a chair, who finally, by dint of great persuasion, carried me up to the village, which is charmingly
situated on the brow of the hill, the wooden houses being
dotted about. Leaving the chair at the inn, I climbed up a
meadow with my faithful guide, and seated myself on the
roots of a tree to await the return of the others, who had
ascended higher; but they chose another path, so that I
went back to the inn for a glass of excellent milk, and then
ran down the first part, and afterwards suffered myself to
be carried, until we had rejoined the rest. About half-
past one we started on our return. Before long the sky
clouded over, and there was every indication of a coming
storm; however, we reached the Jungfrauenblick, an inn
close by Interlaken, before the rain had come on at all
heavily, and lunched in a sort of closed verandah; mine
host looked in upon us with a half-vacant, half-ironical grin,
and a pretty girl waited on us. The view, of course, was
obliterated by the rain, which came down in torrents, and we
hurried into our carriage and drove post-haste to Neuhaus,
where we found Mama and Gussy sheltering themselves
under a shed for wood after a successful expedition to the
Giessbach. We had to go down into the cabin, which was
crammed full, stuffy, and smoky; fortunately there was a
tiny side cabin, which they opened for us. The weather
cleared directly after our return to the Bellevue. . . .

September 30.—We were up at six o'clock, and left the
Bellevue soon after eight. M. de Parpart met us at the station,
and the three Müllinens accompanied us as far as Berne, which
was reached about ten. Mama and Count Müllinen started off
in a carriage, but the rest of us walked. First to the Kleine
Schanze, a promenade at the entrance of the town, whence
we had a good view of the Palais Fédéral and the new hotel,
Berner Hof; then to the old tower at the head of the principal street, with a huge wooden figure in a recess on one
side, whence it derives its name of Goliath-thurm; it is used
as a prison, but is now to be pulled down. The *trottoirs* on
either side of the streets of Berne run under arches in front
of the houses several steps above the carriage road. We

walked to the Kindlifresser-brunnen (Saturn devouring his children), the most curious of the many fountains in the streets of Berne, on most of which a *bear*, the arms of Berne, is represented; then along the shops under the arches, into a print-shop and pastry-cook's and to the *Plateforme*. We looked at the bronze statue of Barthold, Fifth Duke of Zähringen, founder of Berne; thence to the Cathedral, which bears a strong resemblance to the one at Ulm, and was built by the same architect, but the interior is completely spoilt by a screen, which shuts out the choir with its handsomely-carved seats and fine old stained windows; the organ is second only to the one at Freiberg. The front porch is beautifully carved in stone, with a representation of the last judgment, and in the square in front of the Cathedral is an equestrian statue of Rudolph of Erlach, in bronze. We then walked to the further end of the town (past the Müllinens' house) to the Bärengraben by the bridge over the Aar, where we fed four bears, kept by the town as a tribute to the arms of Berne, and returned to the Zeitglockenthurm in the centre of the town, to see the curious old clock strike twelve. Shortly before the hour, a troupe of tiny bears pass and a cock crows; a clown, shaking his leg, strikes the quarters, and a bearded old man with a sceptre and hour-glass, which he turns, opens his mouth at every stroke. It is ingenious and curious, but very inferior to the clock at Strasburg.

At the Zeitglockenthurm we took leave of the Müllinens and drove to the station, where Gussy and Geraldo mounted into the *coupé* of the diligence, the servants and baggage being stowed inside and outside, Mama, the Colonel, and I preceding them in an open carriage, and thus pursued our journey to Freiburg. The country is pretty but tame. We changed horses at Singine, and just before entering Freiburg had a magnificent view of the town and suspension bridge from the top of a hill, where the whole panorama burst on our view. Below is the valley with the river Saane flowing through it, the town nestling against the opposite hill, and hanging as it were in mid-air, the wonderful bridge (157 feet high) connecting the two hills. Getting out, we crossed it on foot; it swayed with the carriages, and the planks seemed to creak and shake beneath our feet. At the other end stands the hotel, Zähringer Hof, which we reached by three o'clock. The rooms having been apportioned, we walked up to the old lime tree supported by stone pillars, supposed to have sprung from a twig borne home by a young Freiburger after the battle of Murten; he hurried back to apprise his townsmen of the victory, and died of exhaustion and loss of blood on the spot where this lime tree was afterwards planted.

We walked up the hill along the rue de Lausanne to an open square with a convent and Hospital, whence we had a view of the town and valley, and on our way back went into the Cathedral (Roman Catholic); the porch is finely carved with grotesque figures. . . . After dinner we returned to the Cathedral to hear the celebrated organ; it was quite dark save here and there the faint flickering of a lamp in the distance. At seven o'clock the music burst upon us, grand and effective, then died away, and it was as if angel voices were singing to us and the winds were bearing their songs back to heaven. Then followed some parts of "Robert le Diable," the Russian Anthem, and a fugue of Bach, divine! lastly *a storm*, perfectly marvellous, with thunder and rain and the alarm of the people, their prayer for deliverance, and thanksgiving after the danger had passed! At eight o'clock all was over, and I still remained rapt as if in a delicious dream from which one feared to be awakened, for within and around all was peace. . . . Trudged home by the light of a lantern, had our dessert, and to bed early.

October 1.—Up at six, and started at 8.30; Geraldo, Colonel Purves, and I in the *coupé* of the diligence, Mama and Gussy in the open carriage in advance. The country we passed through was very uninteresting; we met numbers of peasants coming to market, and played at the game of "the road!" Ascending a hill we had a glorious view of the mountains behind us, and somewhat later of Mont Blanc in the far west; reached Payerne by eleven o'clock, and were detained there an hour or more, as we found no horses had been ordered; Payerne with its one long dreary street is quite a French town, with endless memories of La Reine Berthe. Thence on to Yverdun; *en route* we had a view of the Lake of Neuchâtel and the chain of the Jura rising behind it before we descended to the Lake itself through the old town of Estavayé, which is situated on its banks. We reached Yverdun soon after three, and had to wait some time for the train, as the steamer had not arrived from Neuchâtel. . . . After being whirled through a very pretty country as far as Lausanne, where we had our first view of the Lake of Geneva, we returned some little way on the same line, and then followed the Lake, stopping at Morges, where we had a magnificent view of Mont Blanc, Rolle, and Coppet, where M. de Necker and his daughter Madame de Stael lived. The scenery is beautiful; to our right vineyards and towns, rising

above them the chain of the Jura; on our left the lake with
its deep blue waters, and the opposite shore bounded by the
Savoy hills, Mont Blanc occasionally visible in the distance.
We reached Geneva soon after six, and drove through a new
town with large houses, some of them still unfinished, and a
very wide street, crossing the Rhône by the pont des Bergues
to our hotel, L'Écu de Genève, situated close to the bridge.
The selection of rooms was then made; a very snug one
between Mama's and the salon fell to my share, with a
window opening upon the balcony, our suite having the view
on the Rhône and up the Lake.

Geneva, October 2, Sunday. — Slept *so* comfortably.
Mama and Gussy went to the Cathedral (French service).
We others walked across the bridge and halfway up the
rue du Mont Blanc to the English Church founded by the
Bishop of Winchester (Sumner). The service, which began at
eleven, was well attended, and was performed by a Mr. ——,
who preached well, though his nervous fidgety manner disturbed one greatly. The singing very good. . . . The weather
was delicious, warm, and fine, and the sky of a deep Italian
blue. Drove through the town and by a part of the old
fortifications, now being demolished, up a hill and by numberless *campagnes* or villas and vineyards to the villa Diodati,
or Byron, which once belonged to our great poet. It now
looks very deserted, the balcony overgrown with jessamine
and creepers, and the garden a wilderness, with beautiful rose
trees quite untrimmed, and rank grass growing over the
borders; the view upon the Lake and Geneva is beautiful
and very *inspiring*. Thence we pursued our drive along the
hill and through a village where a fair was going on down to
the side of the Lake; the sunset was divine. On returning
to our hotel we found we had plenty of time to spare, so
drove over the bridge and through the old streets on the
opposite side, till it was time to go to the English church for
evening service; the heat was intense.

October 3. — After breakfast we went out shopping. . . .
Returned to the hotel for lunch, and then drove out, across
the bridge and up the town by Prégny, once the residence of
Calvin, Rothschild's new *campagne*, to the villa Haldiman,
built by an Englishman, belonging now to a Genevan family.
The house is quite in the English style, and the chintzes
looked so pretty and homelike through the windows; the
outside is covered with Virginian creeper. . . . Altogether
a very livable spot. Thence, *viâ* numberless *campagnes*,
amongst others that belonging to M. de Saussura (who was

the first to ascend Mont Blanc); down the hill, by the village of Chambésy, passed the Empress Marie Louise's *campagne*, now belonging to M. Maculotte, and Sir Robert Peel's villa, to the Villa Bartoloni, charmingly situated on the borders of the Lake; the house is quite in the Italian style, with pillars and statues. Garden too lovely, beautifully laid out, and such a terrace! A railing runs along a part of the grounds overhanging the lake, and we leant over it for a while gazing down into the clear deep blue waters. From there we drove to the *campagne* of a M. Riccofinguerlin to see *la vendange*, this being the opening day. We walked into the vineyard, and the people brought us bunch upon bunch of the most delicious grapes, and were so civil, showing us the process. The juice of the grapes when pressed tasted rather like bad honey. Finally we drove to the *Jonction du Rhône et de l'Arve*, which we saw from the height above, whence also we had a fine view of Geneva *without* the Lake, and of Mont Blanc with the *setting sun* upon it, tracing a very remarkable likeness in its snowy outline, not as is said to old Napoleon, but to Lord Brougham in his Chancellor's wig! We drove home by Les Délicats, once the residence of Voltaire. . . .

October 4.—About 11.30 we steamed off through a country of vineyards, crossed the French frontier at Collonges, went up a narrow valley through which the Rhône flows, and passing under the Fort de l'Écluse, were carried through a seven minutes' long tunnel to Bellegarde. Here we had to go in with the crowd to the *salle des douanes* whilst their luggage was being examined. The French *douaniers* very uncivil! At length we were let out, and in the burning sun walked down by the Valserine Viaduct through a wretched little town to a bridge over the Perte du Rhône. Owing to the rocks having been blasted, the river, instead of disappearing a hundred feet, now only loses itself for a few yards here and there. On the other side of the bridge we found ourselves on the Sardinian territory, guarded by two *douaniers*, and we climbed up the rocks to see the fall of the Rhône, which rushes down, foaming and tumbling, to vanish amongst the rocks and emerge again very quietly beyond the bridge. Sat for a while on a huge stone, then wandered about a little, and finally returned slowly to the station, where we were locked into a room and let out to get into the train. The only available carriage had one passenger in it, a civil old Frenchman, whom Gussy cultivated! We were then moved on to another line and detained for three-quarters of an hour by the arrival of a special train with King Leopold, whom we watched *congédier* the French *préfets* in regal style! We did not reach Geneva till 4.30. On our way back we went to the little island of Jean Jacques Rousseau, which is joined to the middle of the pont des Barques by a suspension bridge. Home shortly before six o'clock, at which hour we dined.

The Journal which the Princess had kept with such regularity during her tour in Switzerland here breaks off abruptly, but from other sources it is known that the royal party remained on the Lake of Geneva for another fortnight, and were joined at the Hôtel Byron, Villeneuve, by the Hereditary Grand Duke of Mecklenburg-Strelitz. "Fritz," writes Princess Mary, "enjoyed sharing in our excursions of all things! poor dear fellow, he has travelled so much in Switzerland that he knows its glorious scenery by heart, and our rapture about it quite delighted him, as it seemed to recall to his mind his own sensations on first beholding its beauties. He is wonderfully cheerful in spite of his misfortune, and was so *happy* with us that it added much to our pleasure. We spent his birthday with him at Vevey, and on October the 20th returned to Rumpenheim, where a small circle was still assembled, for one week ere we bent our steps homewards."

Letter to the Honble. Mrs. Dalrymple.

Cambridge Cottage, November 11, 1859.

. . . Ages have indeed gone by since I last wrote to you, and endless thanks are due to you for overlooking my silence, and sending me so dear an account of my little *namesake* (I suppose I dare not say *godchild*). But though silent I assure you I am not forgetful of *old tried friends*, and you cannot think the pleasure your kind letter afforded me. I am so rejoiced to hear that little Mary Adelaide is such a rosy pet, and so forward for her age, but I feel bound, as *godmother*, to put in a word against your spoiling her, though I feel sure if I were with you I should forget my *Episcopalian* duties and *responsibility*, and make as much fuss with the little darling as you or Mr. Dalrymple. We had the pleasure of seeing a good deal of your dear mother this spring, who is, I hope, as well and *allante* as ever; I think I never saw her in better looks. . . . In the course of the year we have had to mourn -the loss of some of our nearest and dearest friends, amongst others Lady Suffield, who was, as you may remember, Mama's Lady-in-Waiting, although from ill health she resigned her duties during the last four years. But I will not sadden you with an account of our sorrows, but rather turn to a brighter subject.

We had the very great pleasure of a visit from my sister this summer; you know the Queen gave her a small apartment in St. James's Palace, adjoining ours, and she came over in June and spent several weeks with us, Fritz and Adolphus joining her in July. My poor brother-in-law is quite blind, but he bears his affliction with touching resignation, and is wonderfully cheerful. Adolphus is a great big schoolboy, far too old and tall to be petted! but a very fine boy, with good abilities, and fond of his lessons. . . . We started on the 17th of September for dear delightful Switzerland, which I had never before visited, and explored its glorious scenery in almost uninterrupted sunshine, with Augusta for our cicerone, and a most capital one she made. . . . Poor Mama, though much improved in health and spirits for the change of air and scene, has felt the return to our old Kew life and accustomed pursuits, without our dear Baron, very much. Nowhere do we miss him more painfully than in our tiny circle at the Cottage, where everything so constantly reminds us of him—the vacant place, the empty arm-chair. . . . To-day we are going to Windsor, which I rejoice at, as I am longing to meet dear Princess Royal. . . . I went up to town last week to see Louisa (Tiny) Hamilton and her 147 presents and pretty trousseau. She is quite, quite charming, and Lord Dalkeith, who seems devoted to her, and no wonder! could not have made a better choice. Poor Lady Harewood's death has, of course, put off the wedding until the 22nd, but the Duchess of Buccleuch is most kind about it, and Tiny is *charmed* with both the Duke and Duchess. . . . Adieu, dearest Ellinor. Ever your loving friend,

MARY ADELAIDE.

CHAPTER XII.

A NATIONAL SORROW.

1860–1861.

Ode to Lady Marian Alford—Changes at Gloucester House—Gardening at Kew—Learning to drive—Autumn at Brighton—A merry Christmas—Princess Mary sits to the Queen for her portrait—Mr. Magee at Quebec Chapel—Death of the Duchess of Kent—The Queen's grief—First game of croquet—Her Majesty at White Lodge—State opening of the Horticultural Gardens at South Kensington—Adelina Patti—The Prince of Wales's first Drawing-room—Second visit to Baden—A trip to Cassel—Charles Dickens at Brighton—Swimming lessons at Brill's Baths—Death of the King of Portugal—Princess Mary's twenty-eighth birthday—Illness and death of the Prince Consort.

AFTER spending Christmas at Kew amidst the usual scenes of domestic festivity, distributing the prizes to the school children, and dispensing the customary gifts amongst the poor of the parish, the Duchess of Cambridge and Princess Mary began the new year with a round of country-house visits. During the first few days of January they were the guests of Lord and Lady Ebury at Moor Park, going on to Hazlewood, Lord Rokeby's place. Here the Princess had, to use her own words, "plenty of fun and gaiety." Then came a visit to Windsor Castle—the third [1] since the Duchess's return from abroad—and a very enjoyable week at Ashridge, where Princess Mary again appeared on the amateur stage, and at the close of the performance recited most effectively the following lines, written by herself:—

[1] The second visit to Windsor was during the festivities arranged for the birthday of the Crown Princess of Prussia (the Princess Royal), when the Queen gave a dance at the Castle.

ODE TO LADY MARIAN ALFORD.

While Ashridge halls still beam with light
And revels gay awake the night
Our hearts' best homage we would pay
To Her who now inspires our lay.
With courteous grace and gentle hand
Dispensing gifts throughout this land,
The poor man's friend, the rich man's joy
In Her we find without alloy
Whate'er can charm and raise the mind,   '
For she is *noble* as she's kind.

MARY ADELAIDE.

A short stay was made at the Grove with Lord and Lady Clarendon—"our host as charming as ever," remarks the Princess—and on the 23rd of January the Duchess of Cambridge and her daughter returned to London to meet the Prince of Orange, before visiting the Duke and Duchess of Beaufort at Badminton for a few days. "Mama had not been there since the poor Duke's death," Princess Mary records. "They had a splendid lawn meet in our honour, the first that has taken place in this Duke's time, at which 1,800 farmers and tenantry had luncheon in the servants' hall; the evening before we left there was a very pretty ball. And this ended our visits for the winter." Commenting on the Prince of Orange's stay in England, the Princess says:—

It has given rise to all manner of reports which cannot boast a word of truth. In the first place both parties are far too young for a matrimonial engagement to be thought of, and, secondly, I do not think the Prince has any intention of marrying, at any rate at present. We all like what we have seen of him, as he is particularly straightforward and unaffected; he is, besides, very nice looking, and bids fair to be very handsome. He is just now travelling about Wales and England, having made a short stay at Badminton, but returns to London for a few days before going back to Holland.

Letter to a Friend.

St. James's Palace, February 21, 1860.

. . . We have been very anxious of late by very indifferent

accounts from Strelitz of the dear old Grand Duke's[1] health. Symptoms threatening a general break up of the system have shown themselves, and greatly alarmed the family; however, he has since rallied again, and the doctors give every hope of his recovery for *a time*, for at *80* years of age what else can one hope for, much more expect? It will be a terrible blow to the family (my sister included) whenever it pleases God to take the dear old man, for they are all devoted to him. . . . George has at length made up his mind, and is going to Gloucester House shortly, his horses having been moved to the stables this week. . . .

Some first-rate amateur theatricals at the Turkish Embassy, got up chiefly by the members of the Corps diplomatique, a ball given by the Duc and Duchesse d'Aumale at Orleans House, and a succession of pleasant little dinners, preceded the gathering of the Royal Family at Windsor on the 4th of April, the eve of Prince Alfred's Confirmation, when Princess Mary was again the guest of the Queen.

Letter to Miss Ella Taylor.[2]

Cambridge Cottage, April 27, 1860.

. . . A thousand thanks for your dear kind letter, breathing at every line such heartfelt regret—*solches Heimweh.* . . . We dined the other night at Gloucester House, a party of eight at a round table in the small front drawing-room upstairs. The staircase was brilliantly illuminated, as if for a *rout*, which horrified poor dear George at the outset, and to make matters worse, Kielmansegge had the folly to congratulate him on his change of abode, and enlarge on the charms of his house, which you know George still considers in the light of an *hotel* or *pied à terre.* This very nearly upset the Commander in Chief, who looked more inclined to cry than to smile. After dinner we sat in a large back drawing-room, which George has made his sitting-room, and which opens into a slip of a conservatory, leading at one end into a cosy little room, that we mean to get George to let us use when we are a small party. His sitting-room is a very handsome, and, with a little judicious arrangement, may be made a very livable room.

---

[1] The Grand Duke of Mecklenburg-Strelitz.
[2] When Lady Geraldine Somerset was away, her place at Cambridge Cottage was often taken by Miss Ella Taylor.

It is fitted up with a good deal of his own furniture (Buhl cabinets, etc.) from St. James's. Colonel Purves has since told me that George showed him his own room the other day, and appealed to him, whether he did not think it looked nice, and the pictures were well hung? So that I begin to hope he is getting somewhat more reconciled to the change from his snug little apartment to the spacious though comfortable rooms of this really fine house.

The Apponyis and Count Brandenburg[1] came down to see us on Sunday afternoon and had tea, *wobei vielerlei geschwätz wurde*. She is giving a ball on the 14th of May, to my great joy. On Monday afternoon we had a tea-visit from the Cadogans and Baron Bentinck. Next day we went up to St. James's for my music lesson, and I tried on my black glacé train and tulle skirt trimmed with large bows of silk ribbon embroidered with jet for to-morrow's drawing-room, which fitted to perfection, and with which I purpose wearing a black tulle veil and white plume, diamond tiara, and for a relief the turquoise *stomacher*. Yesterday we went over to Orleans House early in the afternoon. As it was the birthday of the old Queen and of the Duchesse d'Aumale the whole Claremont party lunched at Twickenham. On Sunday Dean Trench is to preach our charity sermon for the school. We have not had time to read much of an evening since you left, but have gone on with "David Copperfield," which we find very interesting. . . . The weather during the whole month has been so terribly unfavourable that Mama in despair has at last decided to move the establishment to town and make St. James's our headquarters. . . .

Letters to the Honble. Mrs. Dalrymple.

Cambridge Cottage, September 29, 1860.

. . . Fritz and Adolphus arrived about the second week in July, and we all went down to Kew, where we spent a very happy time together, until, alas! a telegram from Strelitz brought us the sad news of the poor dear old Grand Duke's serious illness. Augusta and Fritz left as soon as possible, and had the comfort and satisfaction of being with the dear old man during the last ten days of his life, and of assisting at the sad scene on the 6th of September. The dear Grand Duke, who you know was our Uncle, having married Mama's sister, had ever been most kind to Augusta,

---

[1] First Secretary at the Prussian Embassy.

whom he loved with a fatherly affection, mingled with much
of the chivalry of by-gone days, and she has felt his death
very, very deeply. A new sphere of action now lies before
her, and the duties she is entering upon will doubtless lend
additional interest to her everyday life. Poor Fritz feels
his sad privation more acutely than ever, now that the well-
being of so many are entrusted to his care and rule, and in
his speech at the ceremony of taking the oath of allegiance
he made a very touching allusion to his blindness. God
help him in the new duties imposed upon him, to which
he devotes himself with all possible zeal and the heartfelt
desire to walk in his father's footsteps, who was universally
beloved and revered.

Ever since Augusta's departure we have been staying
quietly here, leading a very pleasant busy life. I have of
late taken to gardening, and Sir William Hooker has in
a measure made over the arrangement and colouring of the
flower-beds to me, so that I have plenty to do—and the
Scotch flower-gardener, a nice, intelligent man, and I, work
away together in grand style. I *invent* and he draws out
the plans and carries them out. I cannot tell you the amusement that it is to me! Many and many a morning do I
spend in this pleasant occupation, for I like to get my work
done by the time the public is admitted, and I have just
now a good many improvements on hand for next year. I
have felt greatly encouraged in my efforts by seeing them
highly praised in the *Cottage Gardener*, without of course
the writer's knowing whose ideas they were. Besides this
charming *passe-temps*, I have another novel amusement in
the shape of a pair of very pretty black ponies, which I am
learning to drive. Geraldine Somerset has been staying
with us ever since the beginning of August, and, thanks to
the Queen's kindness, Colonel Purves and his family now
occupy the house adjoining ours, which you may remember
formerly belonged to the King of Hanover, who lent it to
Papa for the equerries; so that we have never been quite
alone, which I however rather regret, as I delight in a *tête-à-
tête* with Mama.

23, Brunswick Terrace, Brighton, October 29, 1860.

. . . You will very naturally ask what takes us to Brighton?
Well, for the last year or more Mama has suffered from stiffness
in her limbs and pain in bending the joints; believing it to
be in part weakness and in part rheumatism, our doctor
insisted on her leaving Kew at the fall of the leaf and

advised her to take warm sea-baths. She therefore decided
on moving to Brighton, which we did on the 24th, and
upon undergoing a course of baths that I hope will prove
beneficial.   We have secured a comfortable house with a
sunny aspect and a view of the sea, and purpose (D.V.)
remaining here until the end of November, when we return
to Kew.   We are leading a very healthy life, and spend
most of the early part of the day (I mean from eleven or so)
out-of-doors, returning home at sundown, when it gets very
cold.   Since our arrival the weather has been exceptionally
fine; for four days we were favoured with perfect summer,
so that we sat out on the beach reading and knitting.   Our
drives in the surrounding country are very pleasant, and my
ponies are a daily amusement to me.   Unfortunately there
is a dearth of acquaintances, and with the exception of the
Rokebys we know scarcely any one.   The Brighton season
is just now at its height, and it is great fun to walk along
the streets and promenades and watch the crowds of smartly
dressed pedestrians, the long lines of carriages, and the large
riding parties, consisting of a riding-master followed by *half
a dozen* ladies, or even more!

Journal.—Brighton, October 30.—A lovely summer's day!
Geraldo and I walked up the Marine Parade, in the hope of
meeting Mrs. Stonestreet,[1] which we did, and brought her back
with us to the spot where Mama had established herself in all
the glory of a straw arm-chair and footstool. . . . We went out
in the pony-phaeton, Colonel Purves driving me through the
town, when I took the reins; we chose the Lewes road, and,
turning in at Lord Chichester's Park gates, passed the house
and ascended a steep hill to the Downs—a very pretty bit of
country, and the green *so* refreshing after the glare of the sea.
The road, steep and stony, wound up along the Downs, and
then descended abruptly into the town.   We were home by
five, and before tea I went to the stables and fed my ponies.
October 31.—Soon after breakfast we started in the sociable,
and made for Thunder's Barrow on the Downs beyond Hove to
see the Harriers meet.   They had thrown off before we arrived,
but we saw a very pretty run from the top of the Downs,
returning home in time for lunch.   *November* 2.— . . . The
wind was piercingly cold, and the clouds of dust made
walking unpleasant, so Lord William Paulet and I set off
in the phaeton, and went as far as the town of Lewes;
the road is pretty, but rather hilly, and passes close by the

[1] See footnote, p. 80.

gaol where the Russian prisoners of war were confined. The town itself is built on the slope of a hill. On our way back we watered the ponies at a tiny roadside cottage, turned in at the Barracks, and saw the 5th Dragoons at foot drill. *November* 6.— . . . We drove up Montpellier Road, and then to the left along a country road, which brought us to Portslade, a picturesque village with a Manor House, old, grey church with ivy-clad tower, and a charming cottage *orné* called "Raglan Villa." Leaving the carriage at the top of the hill, we walked back through the village, which we explored. Home by the Shoreham Road and Hove. . . .

November 8.— . . . We made an expedition to the Devil's Dyke, and, getting out at the Inn, walked first to the Devil's Punchbowl, down the steep side of which a Captain Beecher once performed the reckless feat of riding, and then to the Dyke, a narrow slip between two gorges. The cold was very piercing, and we walked back part of the way, the road being so terribly rough and rutty.

November 9.—Geraldine, Colonel Purves, and I left by an early train for Portsmouth. On our way we passed Arundel Castle, Dale Park, Goodwood, and the city of Chichester with its beautiful Cathedral. Lord William Paulet[1] and his A.D.C. received us at the station, whence we drove to the dockyard through the town of Portsea. Admiral Grey was away, but his secretary was in attendance. First we went on board the *Duke of Wellington*, a three-decker (121 guns), and after seeing over the ship visited the *Himalaya*, a huge transport. Captain Seacombe showed us everything, and accompanied us round the dockyard. We passed the *Trafalgar* and the slips on which several ships are building, and saw the gunboats in the distance. Then we were taken into the smithy to see the Nasmyth hammer at work, and afterwards over the planing-house and block machinery. Lord William's *barge* was waiting to convey us to the Victoria Pier, where we landed, and walked through the streets of Portsmouth to Government House. Lord William has everything very nice and in apple-pie order; he gave us a capital luncheon, and directly afterwards we drove to the station *en route* for Brighton.

Sunday, November 11.—We attended Divine service at the church of St. John the Baptist, and Mr. Reid preached a good sermon. We then had a walk, and I called in to see Lady Exeter,[2] to consult with her about an evening service for us;

[1] At this time Governor of Portsmouth.
[2] Wife of the second Marquis of Exeter and daughter of Mr. Poyntz.

we decided to go to St. Margaret's,[1] a very unadorned church, rather in the French Protestant style, with pulpit and reading-desk in one, and that a kind of box over the communion-table. The reading was very indifferent, but the singing nicely done, and Mr. Clay, the preacher, gave us a fine and forcible sermon upon the building of the Ark, in which he warned us against the Maurice views.

November 12.—A very fine day! After breakfast the band of the 5th Dragoons played in front of our windows for an hour or more, when the Colonel, Sir Thomas Macmahon, paid his respects to Mama to the strains of his very good band! . . . *November* 14.— . . . We drove along the upper road to old Shoreham; the road is pretty as it passes Bucknam, a gentleman's place, and comes out close by the church we had come to see. With the aid of a lovely little girl we inspected the interior; it is one of the oldest Norman churches still standing, and built in the shape of a Latin cross, but the upper part is destroyed; the inside here and there has been restored, and in good taste. . . . In the evening I read "David Copperfield" till past eleven, when it came on to blow heavily, and the roaring of the sea was very grand and awful at night. *November* 15.—I walked down to the beach to watch the foaming waves coming in; a splendid sight! . . . In the afternoon we drove in the sociable along the coast beyond Rottingdean, and on our way back I took the Colonel round the pretty village; it was so windy that I narrowly escaped losing my hat. We had tea with the Rokebys, and Mama flirted with his Lordship whilst I showed my Kew gardening plans to Lady Rokeby for approval. . . . The Prince of Wales landed this morning at Plymouth, after 27 days' passage. Thank God![2] *November* 16.—We paid a visit to the 5th Dragoon Guards' barracks. Sir Thomas Macmahon and the officers received us, and we at once went up into a low gallery at one end of the riding-school to see a *ride*, then visited the school, and heard the children read and answer questions remarkably well. After looking round the stables, we had lunch in the mess-room, and left, very much pleased with our visit. *November* 17.—I went with Mama to the new Ladies' Swimming Bath at Brill's, which we were, so to say, to inaugurate. Mr. and Mrs. Brill received us, and we saw

[1] St. Margaret's Church, Cannon Place. For many years the principal Evangelical church in Brighton.

[2] His Royal Highness had returned from his tour in Canada and the United States.

their two little girls swim in the magnificent bath just completed. . . . We then drove to the Chain Pier,[1] and walked to the end; Brighton looked very pretty as it lay before us *dans toute son étendue* in the bright sunshine. *November* 23.— . . . About one o'clock we left for the race-course *via* Kemp Town; the panoramic view is very fine, extending to the sea and taking in the town and the Downs. Passing the Stand, we drove down a steepish hill into the Lewes Road, and thence to the Cemetery, which is prettily situated on the slope of a hill, somewhat like *Père la Chaise*, only laid out with far greater taste. *November* 26.— . . . I drove with Mama to Mr. Attree's place called Queen's Park,[2] and after passing through the pleasure grounds, which are charmingly planted with shrubs in large sweeps, we approached the house or rather Villa, for it is built in that style. As Mr. Attree is 83 and an invalid, we got out of the carriage. Our visit greatly delighted the old man, who is a loyal *attaché* of the House of Hanover; he was present at three coronations, and well known to George IV. and William IV. We saw his niece, a lively agreeable person, rather like Lady Dufferin. On our way home we stopped at a Tunbridge-ware shop to purchase of a poor old *protégée* of my aunt's, now greatly reduced in circumstances. In the evening I sang, Geraldo accompanying me on the organino. George, who had arrived about tea time, left at 10.30 for his hotel, when I went to bed, taking leave of the old year with regret, though looking forward with hopeful trust to what my new year may have in store for me, and praying for a blessing on the future.

November 27.—A very fine sunny day, quite *un jour à commande !* My 27th birthday ! God grant it may prove the harbinger of a happy year. Brand awoke me with Frazer's letter and presents. I prayed fervently for every *spiritual* as well as *temporal* blessing. Dear Mama and George gave me my presents, which are more numerous and lovely than ever. I went out walking with him up and down the Esplanade and along the beach, and had a charming *tête-à-tête.* We were then joined by Mama and Geraldo, and dropped George at the Bedford Hotel on our way home. In the afternoon the review of the 5th Dragoon Guards took place on the Downs. George was much pleased with the Regiment, and

---

[1] The Chain Pier faced the New Steine. In the time of George IV. and William IV. it was a fashionable *rendez-vous*, and during the earlier part of Queen Victoria's reign a favourite promenade for Brighton visitors. It was destroyed by a gale in 1896.

[2] Now a public park.

everything went off well; it was one of the prettiest sights imaginable, and the view over the Downs was lovely—the soft tints quite *southern*. *November* 29.—We left Brighton by the 1.20 train, and reached the Victoria station, Pimlico, about a quarter to four. As the station was not yet completed, we found it very wet overhead and underfoot, on our way to the carriage. When we arrived at Gloucester House we had an excellent tea, but alas! without our host.

Cambridge Cottage, December 4.—I drove my ponies *viâ* Sheen round Richmond Park and home through Richmond, which feat I accomplished triumphantly; then saw Sellé, our organist, about some new chaunts, and played on my new and beautiful piano for an hour and a half, Frazer keeping me company most of the time. . . . Marian Alford, dear soul! arrived for dinner, and we had a delightful evening; we said good-bye for six months, as she is on the eve of starting for Rome. *December* 5.— . . . On returning from a shopping expedition, to my grief and consternation, I found poor Frazer very ill and in great pain. Sent immediately for Mr. Hills . . . to her room later, and found her somewhat easier for his remedies. *December* 6.—As soon as I was up I paid Frazer a visit. Thank God! she was free from pain, though very weak. . . . *December* 9.—Just as I was dressing Mama sent me a letter from George, with the horrible news from China about the English prisoners.[1] Poor Willy de Normann and a Captain Anderson died from the effects of ill-treatment! It made my blood run cold. Alas! for the poor dear Mother. God help her! . . . Shortly before four o'clock we had a visit from Count Brandenburg, who was followed in quick succession by Counts Blücher, Wimpffen,[2]

[1] At this date the Allies (France and Great Britain) were engaged in hostilities with China, and the combined forces were marching on Pekin. On the way Lord Elgin received peace overtures from the Chinese, and a point was fixed about five miles from Tung-chow for the final camp of the Allied army. On September 17, Mr. Parkes, afterwards Sir Harry Parkes, accompanied by Mr. de Normann, attached to Mr. Bruce's Legation, Lieutenant Anderson, commanding the escort, and others, left the camp for Tung-chow to complete arrangements for a meeting between the Chinese Commissioners and the Allied Ambassadors, but notwithstanding that the party carried a flag of truce, they were made prisoners, and fifteen of them brutally murdered. "We are certain of the deaths of Lieutenant Anderson and de Normann," writes Sir Harry Parkes in his Diary (October 14), "two noble fellows, especially the latter, who had become well known to me. He is the only son of the Baroness de Normann. Anderson had greatly signalised himself in the Indian campaigns."

[2] Secretary at the Austrian Embassy, afterwards Austrian Ambassador at Paris.

and Kalnocki.[1] I then wrote till eight o'clock. . . . *December*
13.—Sir William Hooker came directly after breakfast to
see George about some terrible innovation in the pleasure-
gardens; and in the afternoon, after preparing for Windsor, I
did some gardening with Craig[2] and Aldridge, returning home
about 4.30, just in time to change my dress and get into the
carriage which was waiting to take us to the Richmond Station.
On our arrival at the Castle, Helena came at once to see
us. . . . I then had my hair plaited, and on returning to the
sitting-room found Albert, Helena, and Louise with Mama;
the Queen and Alice came about seven, followed by Prince
Louis of Hesse Darmstadt, Alice's *fiancé!* Dressed in haste
for dinner at eight; we sat down a party of thirty, Prince
Consort and the Duke of Athol being my neighbours.

Windsor Castle, December 14.— . . . I took Beatrice up to the
nursery, and helped to put on her walking things, saw Leo,
and shortly before eleven drove out with the Queen and
Alice by Old Windsor and round to the Shore farm, where
we got out and walked to the Castle. After lunch I paid my
respects to Aunt Kent for a few minutes, and found the
Queen had just left her. Alfred escorted me back, and I
played duets with him in Alice's room, where we had tea. . . .
In the evening the Haymarket Company acted *The Babes in
the Wood* in St. George's Hall. The piece is amusing and
clever, though wanting, perhaps, in action. *December 15.*—
I was up at 7.30 and Beatrice fetched me to breakfast, after
which we took leave of the Queen and drove to the Flemish
Farm, where we found Albert, Alfred, Prince Louis, and
Du Plat, and saw the threshing-machine at work. We
admired the Hereford cattle, and were then taken to see the
steam plough, but had not time to make a complete inspection as we were obliged to hurry back to get off by the
train. . . . Kew was reached soon after twelve, and in the
afternoon I went over to the church to practice, the choir and
all the school children together. I sang with them till four.

Cambridge Cottage, December 16.— . . . About 2.30 the
Prince of Wales arrived with Alfred, and very soon after-
wards we went down to luncheon and found the gentlemen,
Captain Keppel,[3] Major Cowell,[4] and Colonel Purves, in the

[1] Councillor at the Austrian Embassy, afterwards Minister of Foreign Affairs at Vienna.
[2] Foreman of the Floral Department at Kew Gardens.
[3] Now Admiral Sir Harry Keppel.
[4] Major, afterwards Sir John, Cowell, Governor to Prince Alfred, and subsequently to Prince Leopold. He became Master of the Queen's Household in 1866.

library. It being Alfred's first visit to Kew, we showed
him our rooms, and after he had amused himself by playing
at curling, I took my two cousins into the Gardens and
through some of the houses, but we had to scamper back as
they were obliged to leave. Wales has much improved in
looks since his American journey. *December* 24.—I went
over to Ella Taylor's room to welcome her. . . . Joined
Hardy in the drawing-room, and helped to hang on the *smart*
bonbons; next collected the different presents, arranged our
photographs in their screens, and whilst the servants were at
tea, spread out the things for them under our Christmas-tree,
and afterwards distributed them. Finally Mama and I
settled the present-tables. . . . We dined about 7.30, our
guests being George, the Duchess of Inverness, Falbe,[1]
Edward Weimar, Mr. Swinton, Purey Cust,[2] the Purveses, and
Quin, who did not arrive till 8.15 owing to his horse having
come down in Hyde Park. We had a very merry dinner, and
about 9.30 the tree was lighted and the bell rung. It was
a blaze of light and looked beautiful. My presents were
delightful, every wish I had expressed having been fulfilled,
and everybody seemed pleased with their souvenirs. Quin
was of course the life of the party, and nearly killed us with
laughing. Our little Duchess was decidedly jolly; in short,
our guests and their hostesses enjoyed themselves to their
hearts' content. About 11.30 the former departed, we sitting
up till twelve to examine our things and talk over the
events of the evening.

Christmas Day.—Sir William Dunbar's brother-in-law read
prayers very impressively, and the children sang the "Song
of the Angels," the hymns, and other parts of the service
particularly well. . . . In the afternoon they again sang very
nicely without the organ. . . . *December* 26.— . . . We had
another little dinner-party, and at eleven o'clock went
in a body to the servants' hall to see our people dance.
We all took part in the fun, and I danced Sir Roger de
Coverley with Ebeling. It was a merry scene, and the
gentlemen and ladies waltzed away till after midnight. To
bed very tired. *December* 27.—A bitterly cold day, and a
heavy fall of snow added still more to the wintriness of the
landscape. I got up late, and on going down to breakfast
found Mr. Taylor[3] there and Colonel Purves. We all went

[1] Baron de Falbe. He was attached to the Danish Legation, and subsequently represented his Sovereign at the Court of St. James's.
[2] Captain Purey Cust, afterwards Equerry to the Duchess of Cambridge.
[3] Now Colonel du Plat Taylor.

out for a walk, and amused ourselves by *snowballing* each
other, and, with the help of a gardener, we made a snow man!
It was great fun. *December* 29.— . . . I cried bitterly
over poor broken-hearted Madame de Normann's touchingly
resigned and *high-souled* letter about poor Willy. . . .
Joined Ella in the little room, and made a selection of toys
for presents to the servants' children. . . . At five o'clock
the *nine* children arrived, and we went down to see them at
their tea. The tree was then lighted, and we played with the
little things in the hall till 7.30. Little Jemmy Thompson
was quite *le roi de la fête!* All seemed very happy, and
went away laden with presents.

December 31.— . . . At 6.30 we drove to church for
evening service, it being the last day of the old year. On
our return home we dined almost immediately, and then
dressed for the *soirée* at Colonel Purves's, getting there at
nine o'clock, and were ushered into the drawing-room to tea,
where we found all the Dunbars, Hookey, and Mrs. Eden (Mrs.
Purves's sister) and her husband and Colonel Strange. Presently we went down to the dining-room, part of which had
been turned into a stage, and there witnessed a very amusing
performance by Colonel Purves and Colonel Strange of *An
Unwarrantable Intrusion.* When that was over we returned
to the drawing-room, and had a round game—a new kind of
vingt-et-un, which was very exciting. At 11.30 we left,
much pleased with our evening's diversion, and on reaching
home I went to Mama for a little while to see the old year
out and the new year in.

Windsor Castle, January 23, 1861.— . . . We reached the
Castle about six o'clock, and found Geraldo at the door to
receive us. It was not long before Helena and Louise came,
followed by Alice, Albert, the Queen, and Beatrice. I
dressed in haste, Helena and Louise in the room, and we had
a very pleasant dinner of thirty. I sat between General
Bonin [1] and Lord John Russell, the other guests being the
Westminsters, Tankervilles, D'Israelis, [2] Lord Campbell, [3] the
Speaker, [4] Bernstorff, and two Prussian officers. The Queen
stood talking till a quarter to eleven! *January* 24.— . . .
A little before eleven o'clock we left the Castle in two
carriages, the Queen, Mama, Alice, and I in the first, for New
Lodge, the Van de Weyer's place. Our arrival took them quite
by surprise; His Excellency was reading the papers, Madame

---

[1] Prussian Minister of War.
[2] Mr. and Mrs. Benjamin Disraeli.   [3] Then Lord Chancellor.
[4] Mr. J. Evelyn Denison, afterwards Viscount Ossington.

H.R.H. The Princess Mary of Cambridge.

busy with her bills, and the servants goodness knows where, as we knocked for an age before we could obtain admittance. The host and hostess showed us all over the house, which is charming, and fitted up in perfect taste. Home by one. . . . In the evening *Richelieu* was acted; Phelps, Madame Vezin, and Miss Heath were particularly good. *January 25.—* Vicky's wedding-day! . . . I went to the Queen's room to sit to Her Majesty, and after luncheon, as it rained, I again sat for the completion of the portrait, and then played at battledore and shuttlecock with the Queen in the corridor. About five o'clock Alice sent for me to have tea with her, and we sang together till past seven, when Walter the gardener brought his drawings for us to see. On going over to Mama's apartments I found the Queen and Beatrice with her; Her Majesty stayed to see my new wreath put on. . . . *January 26.—*A beautiful spring day, warm and sunny. I was up in good time, and we lingered in the breakfast-room till ten o'clock, when we took leave of the Queen. . . . After packing my things we drove down to the station, attended by Captain Cust, who told us *en route* of the household marriage—Miss Bulteel to Colonel Ponsonby.[1]

St. James's Palace, February 5.—The opening of Parliament. . . . We walked with Captain Cust into the Green Park, and saw Her Majesty's procession pass up the Mall, then spent some time in the Park before going into Aunt Kent's garden, whence we had a good view of the procession on its return from the House of Lords. . . . After a visit from the Duke of Manchester, who assisted at our luncheon-dinner at a quarter to five, and hurrying over dressing, we drove to the House of Lords attended by Nony[2] and Captain Cust, to hear Lord Derby. As we took our places Lord —— was mumbling the last words of his speech. Lord Derby's oration I thought very fine, but Lord Granville's attempt at a reply was weak and unsuccessful. The House broke up before our carriage had come, so we waited in the Prince's chamber and talked to peers till past eight. *February 8.—* . . . We all went to the British Institution to see the works of British artists. Alas! the good pictures were very few and far between! J. Gilbert[3] and Patten[4]

---

[1] Equerry to the Prince Consort. Afterwards Sir Henry Ponsonby, and for many years Private Secretary to the Queen. He married the Honble. Mary Bulteel, Maid-of-Honour to Her Majesty, and died in 1897.

[2] Lady Honoria Cadogan.

[3] Afterwards Sir John Gilbert, R.A.

[4] Mr. George Patten, A.R.A., portrait painter in ordinary to the Prince Consort.

were the best. Lord Powis and Mr. Augustus Lumley received us, and Albert joined us there with Dudley de Ros. About five the new French Ambassador and his Lady came, and after their departure I saw Brunnow *en audience* as Ambassador. He was particularly agreeable, and stayed some time. . . . *February* 11.—Little Beatrice arrived quite early, and I gave the darling child her luncheon at my breakfast. She left with Thirston shortly before twelve. Then I joined Mama, who was sitting to Mr. Swinton, and George came in for a little while. The portrait was unanimously approved of, and pronounced almost finished. In the afternoon I paid Louisa Dalkeith a visit in Belgrave Square, and found Katy Valletort with her. Tiny looked as flourishing and pretty as possible on her sofa, and showed me with no small pride her son![1] On my return I made out a list of people for a "tail" for our dinner on the 16th. Wrote to Alice, and after an early dinner we went to the Haymarket to see *The Rivals*, a standard piece, which was well acted, and amused us very much, Buckstone especially was great fun.

February 16.— . . . The Civil Service Volunteers with Lord Bury[2] at their head marched through our yard[3] *pour nos beaux yeux*. After this I put the finishing touches to the room, went to see Hargrave about the dessert, and had a professional visit from Quin, then dressed for our dinner at home. George, the Apponyis, Van de Weyers, Lady Ely,[4] Count Pahlen, Lord Malmesbury,[5] Sir Hamilton Seymour, and Captain Cust were the guests at a round table. In the evening we had a few people, merely a "tail," amounting in all to twenty-five. It went off very well, and the rooms looked charming. All left soon after eleven to go on to Lady Palmerston's. *February* 17.—We went with George to hear Mr. Magee[6] at Quebec Chapel, and had great difficulty in making our way along the densely crowded aisle to the pew. His sermon on the elder brother in the parable of the prodigal

[1] The late Earl of Dalkeith, accidentally killed while deer-stalking in September, 1886.

[2] Afterwards Earl of Albemarle. As Lord Bury he took the greatest interest in the Volunteer movement, and was honorary colonel of the 2nd battalion Manchester Regiment, and the 5th battalion King's Royal Rifles.

[3] Ambassadors' Court.

[4] Lady-of-the-Bedchamber to the Queen.

[5] The third Earl of Malmesbury; was Foreign Secretary in Lord Derby's Administration, 1858–59, and Lord Keeper of the Privy Seal in Lord Derby's last Government, 1866–68.

[6] The Rev. William Connor Magee, afterwards Bishop of Peterborough. In 1891 he was made Archbishop of York, and died a few months later.

son was splendid! The flow of language and ideas so
wonderful that he carried one along with him. I quite
hung on his words. . . . Soon after four I drove to the Palace
to call upon Aunt Kent. The Queen came over to see us, and
then Alice carried me off to her room to tea, where I saw
Helena, Beatrice, and Tilla.[1] Alice kept me with her till
seven. *February* 18.—Hélène Hay, Mama, and I went down
to the dining-room to hear Blumner play on his own instrument. He played with great feeling, and has a soft clear
touch, but it is more that of a woman than of a man. We
listened to him for over an hour, and I much enjoyed it. We
dined at the Palace, and I sat next to Lord Salisbury. The
guests included the Brunnows, Sydneys, Lady Salisbury,
Lord Churchill,[2] Lord Edward Howard,[3] and Sir Frederick
Grey. Poor Albert was suffering agonies from face and
toothache.

February 19.— . . . I drove with Mama down to Kew,
and gardened with Sir William Hooker, Aldridge, and Craig
till quite late in the afternoon ; Sir William showed me the
plants of Peruvian bark which are to be sent on to the East
Indies for cultivation. Directly we got home I had some
tea, and dressed early to enable Frazer and Brand to go to the
Adelphi. *February* 20.— . . . I wrote till luncheon-time,
taking occasional peeps at the smart coats for the levée. . . .
Alice arrived about five, and we went over to the music-room
to play and sing. I sang pretty well, in spite of my cold,
Alice accompanying me. *February* 21.—Hallé came at
eleven, and soon afterwards Alice, to hear me play with him.
She herself played several duets with Hallé. After dining
with George we went on to Drury Lane, where Miss Coutts
had lent us her box, to see Kean in *Louis XI.* Both Mr.
and Mrs. Kean acted admirably. Later in the evening Miss
Coutts joined us. *February* 24.—The 87th anniversary of
dear Papa's birthday. We went to St. Philip's Church, where
Mr. Pigou gave us a clever sermon on demoniacal possession
in the olden times. Soon after luncheon Albert came in,
and on his departure we drove over to the Palace to see the
Queen, but I was at once carried off by Helena to play at
" Volant " with Albert, who, however, had to leave very soon to

[1] Miss Hildyard.

[2] Lord Churchill married, in 1849, Lady Jane Conyngham, daughter of
the Marquis of Conyngham, and Lady-of-the-Bedchamber to the Queen.

[3] Second son of the thirteenth Duke of Norfolk. He was Vice-Chamber-
lain to the Queen 1846–52, Deputy Earl-Marshal 1866–68, and was created
Baron Howard of Glossop in 1869.

see Count Bernstorff; I sat with Alice and Helena for some time before returning home, when I wrote a *volume* to the Princess Royal before dressing for dinner.

March 1.— . . . A very busy unsettled afternoon! We had to arrange the drawing-room and boudoir without poor Hardy's aid, and worked away till past five, when I got Mama some tea. Hardy's injury is pronounced to be indentation of a rib; he is in great pain, but I am glad to say not feverish. After inspecting the dessert I dressed for our dinner-party, which included the Shelburnes, Rokebys, Sydneys, Lord St. Germans,[1] Mr. Henry Greville, and George. *March 5.*— . . . We called on Lord Lyndhurst,[2] and spent some time with the dear old man. . . . Dressed in great agitation, as my *nouvelle coiffure* took a long time! But we reached the Duchess of Inverness's by eight, where we had a very merry and pleasant dinner. In the evening we had a round game ("Fright") for a book, which Mr. Peel won after playing the game out with me. *March 8.*—Major Dormer [3] came to present me (thanks to Lord Clyde) [4] with a splendid Chinese dressing-gown from Pekin! of the colour only worn by the Imperial family. After his visit we drove down to Kew, where I worked away in the gardens, and was getting on capitally till Hookey came and spoilt all my arrangements. When we reached home we had a most agreeable visit from Lord Stratford de Redclyffe, and after a

---

[1] The third Earl of St. Germans. As Lord Eliot he was sent as Envoy to Spain in 1835, and concluded the famous "Eliot Convention," and six years later filled the post of Secretary of State for Ireland in Sir Robert Peel's last Administration. He succeeded his father in 1845, and the same year was appointed Postmaster-General. In Lord Aberdeen's Government, 1852–55, he was Lord-Lieutenant of Ireland, and under Lord Palmerston held the office of Lord Steward of the Household.

[2] Lord Lyndhurst was then in his 90th year. He was Lord Chancellor in Mr. Canning's Government of 1827, and remained in office till 1830, during the successive Administrations of Viscount Goderich and the Duke of Wellington. When Sir Robert Peel came into power in 1834 Lord Lyndhurst again became Lord Chancellor, and returned for the fifth time to the wool-sack in 1841. He died in 1863.

[3] Afterwards General Sir James Dormer.

[4] As Sir Colin Campbell he commanded the Highland Brigade which formed the left wing of the Duke of Cambridge's Division in the Crimean War, and the repulse of the Russian attack on Balaclava was mainly due to his intrepidity. As Commander-in-Chief of the Indian Army he showed great energy and resource, and by his skilful tactics finally crushed the Mutiny and preserved British rule in India. For these services he was raised to the peerage as Baron Clyde.

very merry dinner, at which Sir Richard Airey[1] and the Captain assisted, we adjourned to the Strand Theatre, where Marie Wilton[2] acted charmingly in *Court Favour*, but the extravaganza *Cinderella* is very *peu de chose*. . . . Sat up some little time talking to Fracky[3] and Brand, who had been to the St. James's Theatre.

March 15.— . . . We had quite a levée all the afternoon. Lily Wellesley came just as I had settled myself to write. Augusta Cadogan fell into the visit, but took herself off very shortly. Peppy and little May de Ros followed next in succession, and I had just a peep of Lady Rokeby. I then went to Mama's room, where I saw Miss Mitford and Lady Derby, and as a *finale* had a visit from Emma Talbot. Albert called somewhat later with a satisfactory report of Aunt Kent. . . . Dined with Lady Jersey, meeting Lord William Osborne, Lord Bath, Count Kielmansegge, and Sir Richard Airey. The dinner was a very merry one, and Lord William Osborne quite the life of the party. We had just settled ourselves with Lady Jersey in the drawing-room, when Lord Redesdale, who we knew was to dine at the Palace, walked in, to our surprise, and informed us that at seven o'clock the dinner had been *postponed*. Mama and I at once guessed that bad accounts had reached the Queen from Frogmore, and our hearts misgave us. Later in the evening our fears were confirmed by George Cavendish,[4] who had learned through his sister[5] that poor dear Aunt Kent had been taken alarmingly ill in the afternoon, and that the Queen had gone down to Frogmore at seven o'clock. Several people dropped in, so that we numbered seventeen in all, but I was so upset that I found it almost impossible to converse, and listened to what was going on around me as if in a dream. On our return home at twelve o'clock we found a letter from Phipps, and a telegraph from Grey, confirming what we had heard at Lady Jersey's. I did not get to bed much before two o'clock, and prayed earnestly for my poor dear Aunt. *March* 16.—A cold rainy day, and oh, so cheerless! Up rather late, and whilst dressing received two telegrams sent over by Phipps, the first preparing us for the worst, the second bringing the sad news that at 9.30 all was over, and dear Aunt released

---

[1] Quartermaster-General on Lord Raglan's Staff in the Crimea, and later on attached to the Head-quarter Staff at the Horse Guards.

[2] Now Lady Bancroft.

[3] Louisa Fraser.   [4] The present Lord Waterpark.

[5] The Honble. Adelaide Cavendish, Maid-of-Honour to the Queen, now the Honble. Mrs. Clowes.

from her sufferings. The shock seemed to chill one, but after
the first moment I could only think of the poor Queen.
Shortly after breakfast Mama received a telegram from
Albert. . . . I wrote to Alice.

March 17, *Sunday.—* . . . At 11.30 I went to Mama, who
had just heard from Albert, and began making arrangements
for our journey down to Windsor. Later on I read prayers
with Mama, and at 1.15, after we had a little luncheon in the
boudoir, Captain Cust arrived; he accompanied us to the
Paddington Station, where George met us, and chaperoned
us down to Windsor *à nous trois.* We were in a terrible
state of nervous anxiety at the thought of the interview.
The Prince of Wales received us on arriving at the Castle,
and we were shown into our usual sitting-room, where Albert
at once joined us, and gave us very feelingly all the sad
details before the entrance of the poor dear Queen, who came
in with Alice. She was very much overcome just at first,
and sobbed audibly as she threw herself into Mama's and my
arms, but recovered her composure in a measure afterwards,
and was able to speak of her dear mother and her last hours.
Altogether it was *very touching.* The Queen left us after
nearly an hour, and Helena and Louise stayed with us till it
was time to drive back to the station.

Windsor Castle, March 24, *Sunday.—* . . . We reached
Windsor by train soon after three o'clock, and drove down to
Frogmore at once, leaving the Colonel to proceed to the
Castle. Poor dear Augusta Bruce[1] and Lady Fanny Howard
received us, and we visited all Her rooms in their company,
learning the while from their lips further particulars of her
last hours. Everything has been left untouched in those
pretty rooms, which her presence would still seem to *hallow*
though no longer animate, and the sight of them quite overcame us. After resting in Lady Fanny's room we hurried
out to meet the Queen. A little later, Albert, Victoria, and
the rest of the children came, and we all proceeded to the
Large Drawing-room, which was decorated with flowers. At
one end stood the coffin, covered with a silken pall, and
ornamented very tastefully with wreaths and bouquets of
white flowers, violets, and palm branches, and at the other,
chairs were placed for us and dear Aunt's household. The
Dean of Windsor officiated, and the service consisted of

[1] Lady Augusta Bruce, daughter of the seventh Earl of Elgin, Lady-in-
Waiting to the Duchess of Kent, and afterwards Lady-of-the-Bedchamber to
the Queen. She married, in 1863, the Very Rev. Arthur Stanley, Dean of
Westminster.

portions of the Burial and Evening services, and of the Litany, the 90th Psalm, and the 14th Chapter of St. John. At its close we withdrew to the room next Her large sitting-room, where, after a time, the poor dear Queen came to us to wish us good-bye. Her manner touched us to tears. God bless and comfort her, as He alone can! Then—alas! without being able to breathe a prayer by the coffin, as we had longed to do—we were carried off to the Castle by Victoria and Alice. We sat together, and had tea in the Lancaster Tower, and at seven took leave of them and returned home.

The death of the revered mother of the Sovereign was much felt by the inmates of Cambridge Cottage. "The sad, sad event," writes Princess Mary, a few days later, " has crushed all our gaiety, and sent us back to Kew with saddened hearts, for not only do we feel *her* loss most keenly, but our sympathy with the poor dear Queen is very *deep* and *real*. Poor thing! it is her first experience of the trials of life, and she is stunned and overwhelmed by it. I cannot express how touching it is to see her all gentleness and affection in her deep sorrow, ever mindful of others, and seeking comfort in religion. . . . Of course our deep mourning will keep us at Kew until the middle of June." Very shortly after the funeral, Her Majesty, with the Prince Consort and the royal children, retired to the White Lodge, where they remained some little time, and the sorrowing Queen derived genuine consolation from the never-failing love and sympathy of her aunt and cousin.

Princess Mary had now become an experienced whip, and her pony-phaeton was a familiar sight about Richmond Park and the neighbourhood. She delighted to take her friends for drives, and on these expeditions was often accompanied by Princess Alice. The two months' sojourn at Kew afforded every opportunity for horticultural pursuits, and even after settling in town for the season, the Princess and her mother often drove down to Kew for a day's gardening, leaving St. James's soon after breakfast, and returning just in time to dress for dinner, or to attend an evening party. From Saturday till Monday it was quite the exception for them to be in London, and Cambridge Cottage became a favourite *rendez-vous*, on Sunday afternoon, for their London friends. Referring to her week-end visits, Princess Mary writes: "You cannot think how refreshing these glimpses of the country are to us after the hot rooms and late hours, and I feel sure, if steadily persevered in, will do Mama a world of good. . . . The wistaria and lilies-of-the-valley are shedding a delicious perfume over my pretty room."

Journal.—Cambridge Cottage, March 26.—Up early, and started for town to breakfast with dear George in honour of the day; we gave him the Queen's and our birthday gift—two book-stands, with which he seemed charmed. We then drove back to Kew, and after doing some gardening, I returned home to arrange the china baskets, joined the others at tea, and set out on a fresh expedition for leaves. Met Hookey, who cut in grand style for us *à deux reprises*, and finally put the finishing stroke to the baskets for the dinner-table. . . .
April 1, Easter Monday.— . . . I read the Lessons and Epistle and Gospel for the day with Mama, after which I wasted some time in waiting for the Volunteers, whom we were more than once April-fooled into believing were coming over the bridge, and in making an April fool of Brand, and finally settled down to write, as the weather put an end to our planned expedition to Wimbledon to see the Volunteer sham fight. After luncheon I made Oppermann very happy by giving him a presentation to Christ's Hospital for his youngest boy. Then mounted into the phaeton, when, before I could take the reins, the naughty ponies bolted off for about twenty yards, dragging the second postillion, Kirby and Thompson, along. They succeeded, however, most providentially in stopping them by Willis's gate, and a merciful escape we all had, for, thank God, no one was hurt. I drove the ponies round by Mortlake, Barnes Common, Richmond Park and Town, but they pulled tremendously after their escapade. . . .
April 13.—I went over all our own flower-beds with Craig, planning and revising, and gardened in front of the windows, . . . then drove the Colonel, the sociable preceding us, through Richmond and the Park, to Mr. Byam Martin's to see the camellia tree, which a fortnight ago was at its best with 2000 blossoms on it. . . . In the evening I read aloud the Duc d'Aumale's pamphlet entitled "Une Lettre sur l'Histoire de France," and addressed to Plonplon.

It is admirably written, and its accusations quite unanswerable for the Buonapartes. *April* 17.— . . . George rode down to breakfast, and we were much upset by his announcing to us that Coombe was to be given up for villas. . . . We showed Captain Cust the palm-house, and then took him over the Old Palace, and hunted out the quaint pictures. . . . Later on we drove to the Cambridge Asylum, where we visited well-nigh all the old ladies. . . . *April* 25.—Up at seven o'clock to write to Alice, dressed, and then read *Hamlet* with Geraldo. After breakfast we went over to the King of Hanover's garden, where Hookey had arranged a croquet[1] ground for us; the Captain established the croquet hoops, and he and I played against Geraldo and the Colonel. . . . We returned to the croquet ground in the afternoon, and played for nearly three hours! first a "four," and finally a "two," under the Captain's guidance; Mama sitting near to watch the game, or wandering up and down listening to the nightingales the while. . . . After dinner I read "Hypatia" aloud till 11.30. We none of us like the book, or can feel any interest in its leading characters, and agree in thinking it very coarse in thought and language, very unworthy of a clergyman, and tedious to a degree in its philosophic dissertations.

April 29.— . . . I drove the ponies to Hanworth *viâ* Richmond and Twickenham, and on the way we stopped at Mr. Perkins's (of the firm Barclay and Co.), and got out at the invitation of his gardener and steward, who took us to see the remains of what is supposed to have been Queen Elizabeth's kitchen and a part of the old house given by Charles II. to Nell Gwynne, now converted into the farm. After visiting the vinery, figgery, with figs nearly ripe, and the kitchen garden, we went into a charming wood, where we gathered primroses and periwinkles. *May* 1.— . . . We paid a visit to the White Lodge, and had a glimpse of Arthur and Leo, who were just starting on their return to town, and found Alice and the two younger girls settling themselves in the breakfast corridor or gallery. Beatrice, Albert, and the dear Queen looked in upon us, and we stayed till six or so, and then returned home. *May* 2.—I finished the play of *Hamlet* with Geraldo before going down to breakfast, and directly afterwards we hurried to the pleasure-grounds to see the flagstaff set up by sailors and shipwrights before the delighted eyes of the frantically excited Hookey, the astonished eyes of Kewites of all classes, and the disapproving eyes of our

---

[1] The game was just becoming popular in England.

party, who consider it highly tea-gardeny! The ceremony over, we proceeded to the Royal Academy, where George and a party received us, and Sir Charles Eastlake took us round. The sculpture-gallery has been much enlarged, and the Exhibition is, I think, a very good and pleasing one; there are, perhaps, fewer pictures of note, but the average is much better than usual. . . .

May 4.— . . . I was sent for into the Gardens to meet " the Princesses," and sallied out in quest of them. After hunting about for some time, I came upon the Queen and the three elder girls by the old Victoria House, and walked with them up to Williamson's Gate, where the carriage was waiting. On my way back solo, I had to take shelter under the old archway during a pelting shower. . . . In the afternoon I drove in my brougham to the White Lodge and carried off Alice to Cambridge Cottage. I showed her the stables, fed the ponies, and after giving her some tea drove her home. On my return I found Mr. Harrison arrived. *May 5, Sunday.*—About ten o'clock Mr. Harrison came to my room, where we were joined by Mama, and he read and talked to us until church time. He preached a most beautiful and soul-stirring sermon on St. John, 5th Chapter, and 12th verse, and then, assisted by Sir William Dunbar, administered the Holy Sacrament, which I received for the first time at his hands.

May 7.— . . . At three o'clock Mama and I started for town, to hear Fechter read in French at Miss Coutts's. He had selected the play *Ruy Blas*, in 4 acts, and *most admirably* did he read it, rendering each character to perfection, and bringing out the grand and touching *scenes* and *bits* with an emphasis and feeling which went to one's heart. His voice was rather weak at first, but he warmed with his subject, and seemed to gather strength as he proceeded. He read for about two hours, when we had to descend from the *ideal* and return to the material, which we very effectually did by refreshing ourselves with tea and strawberries. *May 8.—* . . . At one o'clock the Queen, Albert, and Alice paid us a visit, and I showed them my room. In the afternoon we arranged the conservatory and sat in Mama's room till five o'clock, when I drove to the White Lodge and stayed with Alice till seven, playing duets with and singing to her. Beatrice and Fraulein Bauer [1] formed our audience. . . . In the evening I read " Hypatia " to breathless hearers, and we were so painfully interested in the appalling and horrible *dénoûment* of

---

[1] The Princesses' German governess,

this strange tale, that it was nearly twelve o'clock ere I closed the book.

May 10.— . . . I drove my ponies up to the White Lodge and carried off Alice, gave her a charming drive, out at the Robin Hood Gate, through the Coombe rabbit warren, down the lane to Malden, stopping by a field for Kirby to gather us some cowslips, round to the right by the Cambridge Common, turning up the high-road from Kingston to Wimbledon Common, and back to the White Lodge by the Robin Hood Gate. I got out and saw Albert, who took me into the living-rooms, and finally into the Queen's sitting-room, where Her Majesty kept me talking for some time; the two little boys arrived from town just as I took my leave. Home the shortest way. . . . I went with Lady Dunbar to the church to practise the boys for Sunday. . . . Looked into the rooms that are being prepared for Katty. *May* 12, *Sunday*.—The Bishop of Oxford[1] preached the anniversary sermon for our school, and gave us a very eloquent and practical one. The collection amounted to £47 16s. 7d.! We were home soon after one o'clock, the Bishop following. We received him in the Drawing-Room, and Sir William and Lady Dunbar having arrived, sat down to luncheon a party of eight, including the Colonel. The Bishop left about three o'clock, and we betook ourselves to the piano in the library, Katty and I alternately singing and accompanying, whilst Mama remained in the drawing-room listening. . . .

May 13.—We three young ladies (Geraldo, Katty, and I) went into the Gardens; Helena and Louise being in the Palm House with Hookey I followed them there to give a message for Alice, who was with her parents at the Old Palace. . . . On our return, *laden* with flowers, I drove Katty in the pony-phaeton as far as Hammersmith Suspension Bridge. There we parted, she going on in her sociable, and I, in solitary glory *per prima volta*, with Kirby on the *seat behind*. . . . Mama and I paid a visit to the Queen, who had Beatrice with her, and in the evening we drove up to the St. James's Theatre to see Mr. and Mrs. Wigan in *A Scrap of Paper*, a very pretty and interesting piece, and most admirably acted. *May* 25.—We all went out into the garden after breakfast, when George and Mama weeded! *à qui mieux mieux*. . . . At three o'clock we started for Orleans House, just to see Lina[2] *en passant* at her request, going on to

---

[1] The Right Rev. Samuel Wilberforce, D.D., Chancellor of the Order of the Garter, and Lord High Almoner to the Queen.

[2] The Duchesse d'Aumale.

Claremont, where we saw the dear old Queen, the Duc de
Nemours, Joinvilles, and Chartres. The Queen has aged
very much, and her voice has grown feeble. After an early
dinner we went to the "Princess's" to see Fechter in *Hamlet*.
His *acting* is *perfect*, and his conception of the part very grand!
but now and then his French accent rather distressed me.

St. James's Palace, June 3.—We drove to the new Horticultural Gardens, where Mr. Dilke [1] and Mr. Westmacott
received us, and we were presently met by Albert, who
shewed us all over them. The glass-house is in perfect
taste, and the plan of the grounds and colonnades seem
admirable, though the whole is in a very unfinished
state. George and Jim joined us there. . . . *June 5.*— . . .
At four o'clock I saw dear Marian Alford, who was to
accompany Mama to the Horticultural Gardens, and at a
quarter past I drove there in state with George, Geraldine,
and the Captain, and we awaited the Consort and children.[2]
On their arrival Albert [3] gave me his arm, and we marched in
procession, preceded by *du bas et du haut* formed of gardeners,
masons, and noble commissioners of the Exhibition of 1851,
and Bishops (the men *chapeau bas*), along the wet and muddy
gravel walks, up the centre of the grounds to the glass-house,
at the entrance to which an endlessly long address was read
and responded to and, to my mind, an ill-timed prayer offered
up. Albert then planted a Wellingtonia, and we marched
into the colonnades under which the flower show was arranged
to great advantage, I thought. We passed through the glass-
house, where the roses were, to the refreshment stall, when
we halted and had to "partake of ice." Thence along the
garden to the lower colonnade to inspect the competition
for the decoration of the dinner-table (Lady Rokeby won
the 2nd prize), and finally back to the starting-point, where
before leaving we inscribed our names. . . . Dressed for a
grand dinner at Apsley House. Count Apponyi and the
Duke of Wellington were my neighbours.

June 10.— . . . We drove to the Regent's Park, up to
Hampstead Heath, and back by the Finchley Road, where

---

[1] Mr. Charles Wentworth Dilke, a distinguished member of the Society
of Arts, the Royal Horticultural and other learned societies. He took a
prominent part in the Exhibitions of 1851 and 1862, and was created a
baronet for his services.

[2] The Prince of Wales, Prince Arthur, Princess Alice, Princess Helena,
and Princess Louise.

[3] The occasion was memorable as the last public ceremonial in London at
which the Prince Consort was present.

we came upon the open country! Buildings are, however, springing up everywhere, and doing away with the fresh green fields. . . . We heard Patti[1] in the *Sonnambula*. She has a sweet, clear, and very high voice, which will improve, I fancy, as she grows older, for it wants power in the lower and middle notes. She sings with much feeling and expression, acts charmingly, and is very pretty. Tiberini, the new tenor, has a good voice, but is unpleasing in appearance and manner. . . . *June* 12.—The flower show of the Regent's Park Botanic was excellent, and the geraniums and fruit very fine. Emily Peel and her sister Julia accompanied us round, and we afterwards sat in the shade and watched the smart people arrive to the strains of three bands. . . . *June* 19.— . . . Mrs. Lindley brought my jet tiara, which was approved of, and shortly before one o'clock I began to dress for the drawing-room. Mrs. James[2] came in for a minute, and Mama assisted at my toilet. *J'étais magnifique* in crape and jet. Geraldo and the Colonel accompanied me. The drawing-room lasted from two o'clock till four, and was very sombre, as every one was in black save the presentations. I stood between the Prince of Wales (it was his first drawing-room) and Alice. Home dead tired soon after four.

June 20.—I took my first singing lesson with Signor Pinsuti. . . . Attended the *fête* at the Wellington Barracks; the heat was intense. There were hundreds of people, chiefly ladies, collected in the barrack yard, and we sat under some trees and listened to the performance of the three bands of the Guards united, led by old Godfrey. Dressed and dined at the Combermeres' *à* 22 at eight o'clock. The heat quite overpowering. In the evening there was a dance, and I walked quadrilles. *June* 22.— . . . Wrote my journal with Mama's help, amid sundry interruptions (the Colonel coming in perpetually with the invitation list for the Breakfast at Kew) until luncheon-time. . . . The King of the Belgians called, and on his departure we dressed for the tea at the riding-school in the Regent's Park Barracks, given by the Blues, to which we went about five. The band played very well indeed, but it was very hot, and people were at first too shy to come up and speak to us. Home by Hyde Park to see George's Regiment of Volunteers. We dined with Lady Waldegrave and Mr. Harcourt,[3] *à* 20, and I sat

---

[1] Mdlle. Patti made her *début* in England on May 14, 1861, at the Royal Italian Opera.

[2] Princess Mary's dressmaker.

[3] Mr. Harcourt of Nuneham-Courtenay married, secondly, the Dowager Countess of Waldegrave.

between the Ducs de Chartres and d'Aumale. After dinner
we remained in a kind of library downstairs until 10.30,
when we were ushered upstairs into the drawing-rooms, one
of which was fitted up as a stage, to witness the performance
of a piece called *The Dowager*, by Lady Waldegrave, Mary
Boyle, Mrs. W. Harcourt, Mr. Mitford, Villiers Lyster,
and Mr. F. Stonor.[1] Lady Waldegrave and Mr. Mitford
acted to perfection. Mary Boyle *well*, but it was too young
a part for her. *La soirée était une pillule dorée*, for the play
was charming.

July 4.— . . . Left St. James's with Mama for Kew in
the rain, and on our arrival at 1.30 we found Lady Rokeby
hard at work in the rooms, arranging the furniture with
Hardy and the others. Smith and Craig awaited their orders
in the garden, and from the windows of the conservatory
she directed how the plants in pots were to be arranged.
We all helped, both in the rooms and garden, and about five
o'clock sat down to tea in the little room. We then spent
an hour in the dining-room, settling with the Colonel how
the tables were to be placed.[2] . . . We did not get back to
Town before a quarter before eight!

July 10.— . . . About 10.30 p.m. I drove with Mama in the
brougham, preceded by the Captain and Count Wimpffen, to
Cremorne, to see the famous Léotard fly from swinging pole
to pole in the easiest and most graceful manner. We were
in a box and saw *à merveille*, and stayed for the fireworks
and "Fire King," who, enveloped in a fireproof costume,
walked through flames, and departed mighty pleased with our
expedition. We drove round by Piccadilly, Waterloo Place,
the Haymarket, and Pall Mall, to look at the illuminations
in honour of the Queen's State Birthday. *July* 12.— . . . I
was sent for to see the Duc and Duchesse de Montpensier and
their eldest girl Isabella.[3] We dined at Gloucester House,
and went on to Etta Morant's for a concert, which would have
been perfection had there not been rather too much instrumental music. It was not over till 1.45! And we at length
listened to Mario and Graziani as in a dream.

[1] The Honble. Francis Stonor, father of the fourth Lord Camoys; he
married Eliza daughter of Sir Robert Peel, Bart., afterwards Bedchamber
Woman to the Princess of Wales.

[2] These arrangements were being made for a Breakfast which the Duchess
of Cambridge gave at Kew, but the Journal contains no record of the party.

[3] Afterwards the Comtesse de Paris.

Letter to a Friend.

Pavilion, Baden, July 26, 1861.

. . . The English courier leaves for "Home, sweet home!" this evening, and he shall not depart without a few lines to you, my dear old pet. I hope George obeyed the commands I addressed to him from Calais, and sent my letter on for your perusal, for in it I described the misery of our passage. My forebodings were, alas! but too fully realised, and though I did not actually suffer, thanks to the chloroform, I felt thoroughly uncomfortable and wretched. Poor dear Mama was more dead than alive when we reached Calais. . . . The Dessin Hotel is no longer the one you remember, opening into an old-fashioned garden, but is situated in the middle of the town in a narrow street, the fragrant odours from which were not very refreshing to sea-sick travellers. Captain Smithett dined with us as usual, and complimented me on being so good a sailor, but in truth I consider myself quite a phenomenon in the sailing line.

We started at twelve next day for Paris. Our railway journey was marked by but one incident—the loss of poor Geraldine's straw hat, which blew off and went spinning over the fields to her and our despairing consternation, though we could not help laughing. Wonderful to relate, the hat has since been recovered in a very wearable state, having been picked up and sent after us to Baden. Lord Cowley met us at the station, and took us to the Embassy in the sociable, so that we might see a little of the Boulevards. We dined, and took the eight o'clock train to Baden, an Imperial carriage being placed at our disposal for the whole journey, and reached our destination at 10.30 the next morning. Gussy, Dolphus, and the Duchess of Hamilton received us and accompanied us to this charming abode, in which we are most comfortably installed, and which certainly has contributed greatly to the charm of the place. Picture to yourself a large cottage, or small villa, very prettily and comfortably furnished in the English style, chintzed and carpeted, surrounded by a nice garden, which shuts out all the surrounding houses, and situated on a hill, commanding a very pretty view of Baden itself and the opposite range of wooded hills,—and you have our residence. The garden takes the place of the promenade, which we only resort to just to hear the music, the society not being nearly so agreeable as on our former visit.

The royalties here include the King, Queen, and Prince

and Princess Charles of Prussia (Anna's parents), the Grand
Duke of Baden and the Grand Duchess, with whom I have
struck up a great friendship. We have seen much of Marie
Hamilton, and taken advantage of the glorious weather to
make many expeditions. . . .

Journal.—Baden, July 29.— . . . We set out in three
carriages, without the Captain,[1] for the Alt Schloss, and
on reaching the ruins took a most charming walk along a
shady path under the rocks and looking down into the woods.
Leaving the others to sit or wander about, Geraldo, Lühe,
Dops,[2] M. de Engel, and I clambered up the steep ascent and
took the road leading to the Felsen-Brücke, pausing to enjoy
the view from the different points of rock that jutted out.
We returned by the ruins, and having refreshed ourselves
with some cake, entered the carriages again and drove home
by Ebersteinburg and the Teufelskanzel. . . . We were caught
in a violent shower and had to make our way to Marie
Hamilton's in a regular downpour. Their Prussian Majesties
and Baden Grand-ducal pair had tea at Marie's with us.
We were a party of ten, and it was the dullest and slowest
affair possible! We scarcely uttered, and were absorbed in
photograph albums till ten o'clock, when, thank Heaven, it
was over. We found the Captain at the door and took him
up to the Pavilion in our carriage *pour nous désennuyer.*

August 5.— . . . I wrote a little before breakfast, into
which the dear King of Saxony tumbled. He paid us a
flying visit, and soon afterwards Countess Blücher, Countess
Thérèse Hardenberg, and the Grand Duke of Oldenburg
came. . . . At two o'clock or so we were off to Neuweier *viâ*
Geroldsau. The road winds up through pine woods, and as
we descended the hill on the other side, a glorious view of the
plain bounded by the Vosges burst upon us. We got out
at the inn "Zum Goldenen Baum," and after choosing a
place to dine at, sat in the shade of an orchard, for the heat
was well-nigh overpowering, until our repast was ready. . . .
Dinner over, we younger ones climbed up an adjoining hill,
and witnessed a glorious sunset behind the Vosges. . . .
The evening was divine and we remained sitting out in the
garden till eleven o'clock in rapt admiration of the canopy of
stars above us. *August 6.*— . . . Quite late in the afternoon we had a charming drive up to the Iburg; the cool
shade of the woods was delightful. We youngsters scrambled

[1] Captain Purey Cust.
[2] The Hereditary Grand Duke of Mecklenburg-Strelitz.

up to the ruin, leaving Mama and Gussy in the carriage, and after enjoying the view over Neuweier and Steinbach to Strasburg from the lower part of the ruin, we ascended the tower by means of ladders, and had a very extensive view of the Black Forest. We walked till we overtook Mama's carriage, then drove back to Baden. I went with Gussy to the Hotel to be tidied, and then to the Queen of Prussia's to tea, where we found the Badens and Oldenburgs. . . .

August 7.— . . . We made an early start in two carriages for Forbach : the first part of the way lay along the Eberstein-schloss route, then down to Gernsbach, under Eberstein, and up a charming rocky and wooded valley through which the Murg runs tossing over its stony bed. The scenery from the high-road, which is not completed, and runs halfway up the side of the valley, is beautiful, and the drive was most enjoyable. Passing through several pretty villages we crossed the river by a covered bridge, drove through Forbach and selected a charming spot in a field under some fruit trees just beyond the town for our gipsy encampment. The Captain was our cook, and in a short time a fire had been kindled and our stew-pan put on it. We watched his culinary proceedings with hungry anxiety (for it was past four when we reached Forbach) and about six we had a first-rate repast of trout, potatoes in their skins, the Captain's stew, ice and cakes. . . . The drive home was delightful.

Letters to a Friend.

Rumpenheim, September, 1861. ˙

I liked our stay at Baden very much, although it was not quite so pleasant as the former one, which you so well remember. We left on the 10th of August for Rumpenheim, and found a large party already assembled here. My three Uncles and two Aunts unchanged, the Landgravine aged, Mimi of Dessau and her girls, Louise of Denmark and her three girls [1]—the eldest strikingly handsome, the second sweetly pretty—and youngest boy,[2] a fine little fellow, Lilli of Mecklenburg, who I think much altered, and my brother-in-law. A few days later our circle was further increased by the arrival of Christian [3] and his two eldest sons, my brother

[1] Princess Alexandra, Princess Marie Dagmar (see footnote, p. 321), and Princess Thyra, now Duchess of Cumberland.

[2] Prince Waldemar, who married in 1885 Princess Marie d'Orleans, eldest daughter of the Duc de Chartres.

[3] Prince Christian, afterwards King of Denmark.

Gussy, and my cousin Fritz of Hesse. We were a very merry party in spite of the intense heat, and as united as possible considering our very different views on certain political and other points. As Adelheid of Nassau was staying at Köningstein, a charming villa the Duke had given her up in the Tannus hills, Mama advised me to accept her invitation to spend a couple of days with her, which accordingly I did. I enjoyed my visit very much, and especially the expeditions to the ruined castles which form a leading feature of that very pretty scenery. Adelheid was very dear and nice, and I think enjoyed having me all to herself. . . . On the 28th we brought our gay doings to a climax by a very merry dance amongst ourselves. With this impromptu hop, however, all our fun ended, for on the very next day poor dear Uncle William was taken ill. The attack, two days later, assumed so serious a character that for some time we fluctuated between hope and fear. . . . He is now, I am glad to say, much better, although still very weak. During the most anxious time of his illness I had one great happiness in the society of dear Anna, who was at once telegraphed for from Berlin. We spent ten days together, and most thankful was I for even this brief reunion with one I so fondly love.

On the 13th George departed for Brühl, to see something of the Prussian manœuvres, and a few days later we bade adieu to Louise and Christian and their charming children. My Uncle being really better, I indulged in a little dissipation, and went to the Austrian General's at Frankfort to hear the famous Austrian band from Mayence (70 strong), which was sent for in our honour. I was also present at the sham fight between the Nassau troops and the troops quartered at Frankfort, and took lunch with the Duke of Nassau in his camp. Adelheid was on horseback during the whole affair, and rode extremely well. The Elector[1] is just now our neighbour at Philipsruhe, whence he has been over twice to see us, and Mama intends to take advantage of his absence to run over to Cassel for a few days, in order to show us the beauties of the place. . . . I have had a very happy letter from Katty since her marriage;[2] her father gave her away. Only conceive, Mr. Hutchinson is going to be married! I am speechless with astonishment! . . .

[1] Of Hesse.
[2] Lady Katherine Grey-Egerton had married (July 22, 1861) the Honble. Henry John Coke, brother to the present Earl of Leicester.

Cambridge Cottage, October 15, 1861.

... I must go back to where my last letter left off—
our trip to Cassel. We started a party of five, including
Gussy, for Marburg, where we spent some hours seeing
the fine old church, which was erected to the memory
of our ancestress, "Die Heilige Elizabeth," and has lately
been restored; thence proceeding the same evening to Cassel.
Judge of our dismay on learning, immediately on our arrival,
that the Elector was expected the following day! Next
morning we drove up to Wilhelmshöhe, the Elector's summer
residence, a beautiful place, backed by hills and splendid
woods, with here and there an autumn tint upon them. The
display of cascades and fountains (six in succession) was
quite the finest thing I have seen of the kind, and the
happiest blending of art and nature imaginable. The Wilhelmshöhe park and woods and the Auggarten, a kind of
park close to the town, reminded me more of England than
anything I have yet seen on the Continent. The beautiful
marble bath in the Auggarten is full of Italian statues, and
the orangery contains some magnificent orange trees in full
blossom. As we were on our way to the sixth waterfall, the
Elector drove up; he was very civil, and the following day
again sought us out on our drive. I was much interested in
seeing the Belvedere Palace, in which Mama and Papa were
married, and which contains a very choice collection of pictures. We were all so charmed with Cassel that we were
very sorry to leave it again so soon. Captain Cust pronounced it to be "a thoroughly gentlemanlike place," and in
the truth of this remark I quite agree.

Soon after our return to Rumpenheim we made an expedition to Philipsruhe, where Wilhelm Hanau received us. We
went all over the château, which contains a long suite of
fair-sized rooms, handsomely furnished, and some good
modern pictures. After a rapid survey of the garden and
peep at the river, we drove on to the Schloss at Hanau, with
its endless succession of low rooms, poorly-furnished, and in
bad repair. In one fine saal are some good pictures of Wilhelmshöhe. Young Hanau invited us into his own apartments, which are cheerful and comfortable. Thence we
proceeded to Wilhelmsbad, where we got out at the Burg,
which we also inspected. The first Elector fitted it up in
rococo style. Up a winding staircase is a circular room
hung with the portraits of the Landgraves, beginning with
Philip der Edelmüthig down to the Elector, and above is a
platform commanding a pretty view of the woods. The day

following our trip to Philipsruhe I made the acquaintance of Prince Wilhelm of Schaumburg-Lippe, formerly in the Austrian service, *un sposeur* and a *bon parti!* We bade adieu to the rest of the Rumpenheim circle on the 7th, always a trying affair, but on this occasion more particularly so, as the parting from dear Uncle William cost our hearts a severe pang.

A delay at Mayence on account of the trains enabled us to see its beautiful cathedral, which is now in process of repair, and will, when the decoration of the roof, or rather ceiling, is completed, be a great object of attraction for all lovers of the beautiful. . . . We had, I am thankful to say, a very fair passage, although the swell in Dover harbour upset poor Mama. This, however, I could scarcely regret, as it settled the question of our remaining at Dover for the night, which on Mama's account I was anxious to do, thinking it too much to go on to Kew that evening after her emotion at Rumpenheim and the great fatigue of the journey. We slept at the "Lord Warden," the Birminghams having given up the dear old Ship, and came up to town next day, reaching dear Kew in the afternoon of the 10th.

Journal.—23, *Brunswick Terrace, Brighton, October* 24.—... We came down here by road in the brougham, posting the whole way under six hours. The country we passed through was charming, gentlemen's country-seats positively lining the road! The ponies, of course, accompanied us hither. . . . *November* 2.— . . . Wrote till one o'clock, when we had a visit from dear old Miss Adams, who had come over from Worthing to see us. . . . We drove out (I in the phaeton), taking the Lewes Road, and walked part of the way back. I had the luck to find a pony's and a horse's shoe! *November* 5.—Such a morning I never before beheld or experienced! The sea rolling mountains high, and the gale so tremendous there was no standing against it. . . . At twelve o'clock we prepared for our expedition to Coolhurst. It began to rain as we got into the landau to drive to the station, and we steamed off in a perfect deluge, the rain coming into the carriage. Nothing could look more hopeless, but we were thankful to get away from the roar of the sea, and as we approached our destination the weather suddenly cleared up and the sun burst forth. Mr. C. Dickins and Captain Cust received us at the Horsham station, whence an omnibus conveyed the whole party to Coolhurst, where Lady Elizabeth, Mr. and Mrs. Dickins, Marian, Addy,[1] and Mr.

---

[1] The present Earl Brownlow.

Lane[1] awaited us. The house is charming, and the grounds seem beautiful. The library or sitting-room, opening into a conservatory, is quite the perfection of a room. After luncheon we saw dearest Madame de Normann, who is more lovable and admirable than ever in her touching resignation to the Divine will. We sat with her and dear Marian for a while, and then I joined the others in a game at rolling billiards. Soon after five o'clock we took our leave, "Uncle Charles"[2] and the Captain accompanying us to Horsham.

November 8.— . . . We went to the Town Hall at eight o'clock to attend Charles Dickens's reading of "Nicholas Nickleby" at Dotheboys Hall, and the Trial in "Pickwick." He *renders*, rather than reads his subject, and is admirable in his change of voice and manner, especially in the comic parts, which he gives with a great deal of drollery and humour. The first part was deeply interesting—the second immensely amusing. *November* 9.— . . . Home by two o'clock to dress and have our luncheon, before driving to the Pavilion to hear Charles Dickens read "David Copperfield" in six chapters, four containing the pith of the history of *Em'ly* and Steerforth, Mr. Peggotty and Ham, one devoted to David's bachelor dinner at the Micawbers', and the sixth to his courtship and marriage with Dora. In the two last named Dickens's comic drollery was irresistible, whilst his rendering of the pathetic parts was finer and more touching than in "Nicholas Nickleby." It was over, I thought, too soon. Lord Robert Clinton[3] was there in his chair, and thoroughly enjoyed it.

November 12.— . . . During dinner we learned the death of the poor young King of Portugal. He fell a victim to typhus fever a few days after one of his younger brothers had died of it. His has been a sad fate, poor fellow![4] *November* 13.— . . . In the afternoon I was busy writing, when the Grand Duke and Grand Duchess Constantine of Russia, with their little

[1] The Vicar of Ashridge.
[2] Mr. Charles Scrase Dickins.
[3] Sixth son of the fourth Duke of Newcastle. He was a great invalid.
[4] Don Pedro V. (see footnote, p. 316). He died at the early age of 25. In her Diary for the day Her Majesty writes: "Such a fearful loss . .'. the only thought which has comfort in it, is that he—dear, pure, excellent Pedro —is united to his darling angel Stephanie. . . . But it is an irreparable loss for the country, which adored him; for his and our family, of which he was the brightest ornament; for Europe—in short, for every one. . . . My Albert was very fond of him, loved him like a son (as I did too), while he had unbounded confidence in Albert, and was worthy of him" ("Life of the Prince Consort," vol. v. p. 410).

girl, Olga,[1] were announced. The telegram they had sent to apprise us of their coming did not arrive till an hour later; it was therefore a great surprise, but a *very pleasant* one. She is charming, so unaffected and affectionate. He *très sur son beau dire*, and immensely improved in manner. We fed them with tea, sandwiches and buns, wine, and bread and cheese, which they did ample justice to, and they took their departure just before five o'clock in our carriage, *en route* for the station. . . .

November 14.— . . . Before breakfast we drove down to the swimming-bath to see the *swimmer* and Mr. Brill's little girls and boy exhibit. Geraldo and I resolved to try the art!

November 15.—A fine, cold day. Up at seven, dressed, and drove at nine to the swimming-bath, for Geraldo and me to take our first lesson. After getting over our nervousness we both managed very well, thanks to the swimmer, Miss Ragless, and quite enjoyed it. After breakfast I started solo in the phaeton for the old Steine, where I picked up Yaddy Spencer,[2] and drove her to Lewes. There we got out, and walked down into the town. After poking about we discovered the picturesque ruins of the old Castle of Saxon origin, and Geraldo and I climbed up the steps, for it is situated on the top of a steep hill commanding the town. Ascending the tower, now converted into a museum, we had a fine view, then hastening down again we joined the others at Southover Church, a very pretty edifice, with a western chapel in good taste adjoining it, containing the marble tombstone of Gundrada, the daughter of William the Conqueror, together with her bones, and those of her husband, Earl Warenne, in two *leaden coffers*. I drove back, passing through Lewes by perilous back streets too steep to be pleasant, and finally accomplished the feat of driving down the Cliff at the fashionable hour, for we were not home till four.

November 16.— . . . I occupied myself till twelve o'clock, when we had a walk up and down the West Cliff, and then started on a long drive in the sociable. Taking the Patcham road we turned into the old London one, leaving it after we had descended the steep hill over Clayton tunnel, the scene of the recent railway accident, to seek for a lane into Danny Park, but this being under repair, we crossed some fields and returned to the high-road, turning off into Danny Park on the

---

[1] Now the Queen of Greece.

[2] Daughter of Sir Horace Beauchamp Seymour and second wife of the fourth Earl Spencer.

other side. It is a fine old country squire's seat, dating from
the Tudors, the house bearing the stamp of the Elizabethan
era on it. Mr. Campion, junior, admitted us, and in the
absence of his parents shewed us the fine hall and sitting-
rooms, all hung with old portraits. Thence we proceeded
through the large village of Hurstpierpoint, which is very
pretty, and is in part made up of the Brighton tradesmen's
villas, back into the Horsham and Patcham road, and did not
reach home till just upon five o'clock. . . . *November* 18.—
. . . We drove towards Hove Church, turning into two *culs
de sac* before reaching it, and got out to see a pretty stone
monument in the churchyard, erected to the memory of a
sister of Lady Stradbroke, and carved by her "intended," a
Mr. Beauclerc. Thence by the lanes at the back of the town
to the old *Brighthelmstone* Church, to see the monument to
Phœbe Hessel, who enlisted in the last century, and served
during the '45. She died here in 1821, aged 108. . . .
November 20.—A blowy day and keen air. The sky of the
deepest blue! Up before eight, and then to the swimming-
bath—my fifth lesson—to exhibit before Mama, who was
agreeably surprised at our proficiency in the art. I swam
alone two-thirds of the length, and performed sundry feats.
When we were dressed we stayed some time looking at a
school of young ladies swimming. . . . After dropping the
Dickinses at Lady Georgina Bathurst's, and taking leave of
Count Wimpffen, and quite a flirtation with Lord Robert, I
went in to lunch. . . . *November* 25.—Up at 6.30 by candle-
light, and shortly before eight drove to Brill's to take our last
swimming lesson! It was eminently successful. . . . Packed
my box, and at 10.50 left our Brighton domicile for the
station. . . . On our arrival at Kew, dear old Fracky welcomed me after an absence of four months.

Cambridge Cottage, November 26.— . . . Felt sad at parting
with my 27th year, which has, thank God, been a pleasant
one, though content to leave my future to Him Who doeth
all things well. *November* 27.— . . . My 28th birthday.
May it usher in a happy, joyful, *care-less* year! and may
I grow in grace therein. I awoke early, Fracky brought me
numberless pretty offerings, and I was up before eight o'clock.
The morning was sunshiny. George kindly surprised us
about ten o'clock, when I was admitted to the drawing-
room. . . . George gave a very handsome, merry dinner in
my honour. . . . *December* 4.— . . . Hancock's little girl
played to us most charmingly, and certainly wonderfully well
for not quite twelve! whilst we looked at his things. . . .

December 6.—Heard of poor dear Lady Canning's death of cholera out in India. . . . Inspected a number of beautiful prints Graves had sent for choice, and shortly before one o'clock we started in the cane landau for St. James's, where dear Katty Coke paid me a visit—our first meeting since her marriage! . . . In the evening Mama finished Mrs. St. George's Journal,[1] kept during her visit to Germany in 1799 and 1800, to us. . . . *December* 7.— . . . George and Sir Richard Airey dined with us, and brought us the startling news that war with America is expected, and that two battalions of Guards are under orders to embark at once for Canada. 30,000 stand of arms were shipped to-day. Alas! that we are again to be engaged in war,[2] but may God give us the victory. . . . I finished young Bulwer's poem of "Lucile" aloud. We are all charmed with it. His metaphors are so beautiful, and some of the passages very striking.

December 11.— . . . At two o'clock Helena, Louise, and Marie Leiningen, accompanied by Miss Byng, arrived. They said but little about poor Albert's illness, trying to make light of it, and assured us he had had three good nights. . . .

December 12.— . . . Just as we were starting for town Mr. Whitehurst came about the railway to Kew, and detained us till nearly twelve o'clock; when he had left we drove up to Gloucester House and saw George, who alarmed us about Albert. Mama and I then did some shopping together. . . .

December 13.— . . . I had a better account of Albert from Lady Augusta Bruce this morning. . . . *December* 14.—A bright sunshiny day, but oh! how sad an one! Up at eight o'clock, and whilst dressing was sent for to Mama, who had received a letter from George saying that Albert was in *imminent*

[1] See p. 4.
[2] The firing upon the British steamer *Trent* by an American warship, and the subsequent arrest of four passengers, had produced such a feeling of indignation throughout this country that for a time it seemed open hostilities must follow. Thanks in no small measure to the amendment, proposed by the Prince Consort, in Lord Palmerston's despatch, so terrible a calamity was averted. The American Government informed the Foreign Secretary that the captain of the warship had acted without instructions, and that the four persons taken from the *Trent* should "be cheerfully liberated." This welcome intelligence reached London on January 9, 1862, and was communicated at once to the Queen, who in her reply said, "Lord Palmerston cannot but look on this peaceful issue of the American quarrel as greatly owing to her beloved Prince, who wrote the observations upon the Draft to Lord Lyons, in which Lord Palmerston so entirely concurred. It was the last thing he ever wrote" ("Life of the Prince Consort," vol. v. p. 426).

danger, and the doctors *dreaded* the night for him. George was to go to Windsor by the seven o'clock train. *Terrible* tidings these! Hastened down to join the others at breakfast, who, like myself, could not at all realise them. After taking a touching farewell of poor old Willis, who was to depart for his lodge at the Kingston Gate, I went up with Mama to her room, and presently tried to settle down to my accounts in my own sanctum. . . . In the middle of luncheon we had a second letter from George to say that poor Albert was a shade better, the breathing being less oppressed, but the danger was still imminent. An hour or so later the Colonel brought me a very *un*satisfactory telegram from Phipps. . . .

December 15, *Sunday.*—A greyish day, and a *wretched one!* At 8.30 I received the terrible tidings communicated by a telegram from Phipps to Mama, that poor dear Albert had breathed his last shortly before eleven o'clock on the preceding night. The poor unhappy Queen! How will she ever bear it? and those poor children, to whom he was *everything!* God help them! I hastened to Mama, who, like myself, was quite stunned by the shock, and could not find relief in tears, then dressed and went down to breakfast. Little did we dream last night, with all our fears, of the terrible scene that was just then passing at Windsor! and that *he*, who had been the ruling head, the very life of that family and household, and the idol of our poor beloved Queen, had gone to his long rest. At two o'clock I left with Geraldo and the Colonel for the Richmond station *en route* for Windsor, where we arrived just before three o'clock. We walked up the *hundred steps* to the Castle, which, with all its blinds drawn down, looked dreary and dismal indeed. I went in at the Lancaster Tower entrance, and in the corridor met Marie Leiningen and Victor Hohenlohe: a little way further down we came upon poor Alice, Helena, Louise, and Arthur, who all broke down at sight of me, though they strove to regain composure, and to remain as calm as possible for their widowed mother's sake. Alice hurried me to the poor Queen's door, in the hope she would see me, but came out again with the message, "She had not the heart to see me—that day." We therefore returned to the corridor, where I found Wales with Leiningen and the Duc de Nemours. After Alice had exchanged a few words with the Duc, he took his leave, and we all went out for a while, and met little Beatrice and Thirston, who joined us. We walked on the terrace, and as far as the kennel, then separated from Wales and his cousins, and retraced our steps to the Castle. I accompanïèd the girls to their room, where we had tea.

Wales presently joined us, and took me later to see poor dear Albert. He lay on a small bed in the *blue* room (of late years Mama's bedroom), a wreath of white flowers at the head and single ones laid on his breast, and scattered on the white coverlid. With a bursting heart I gazed on those handsome features, more beautiful far than in life, on which death had set so soft a seal, that it seemed almost as if he were sleeping, and looked my *tearful last* on them! The eyelids were scarcely closed, and there was a smile on the lips, which, I like to think, told (as I fondly hoped and prayed it might) of *happiness beyond the grave.* I would have given much to have been able to kneel down by the bedside, but there were men in the room, Mr. Corbould, Dr. Brown, and the page, and I could not therefore give way to my feelings. Wales was very nice, as we went out together; we then sat in the corridor, the doctors, Sir James Clark, Sir Henry Holland, and Dr. Jenner[1] passing to and fro and stopping to talk to us; Alice went away with Marie Leiningen, and I remained with Wales and wrote two telegrams for him. At six o'clock George, who had just arrived from town, joined us. Alice and Marie gave me many interesting details of His illness, and about seven little Arthur put me into the carriage with Geraldo and the Colonel to drive to the station, and I reached home soon after eight.

December 21. — . . . I saw from Mama's window the brake go by, drawn by our six horses in the state harness (preparatory to Monday's sad ceremony). . . . *December* 22, *Sunday.* — A cold grey day. . . . After the congregation had gone in I slipped into Church. Sir William preached on our recent loss, and at the conclusion of the service Sellé played the Dead March in Saul. We stayed till all had dispersed and then went home and for a short walk, in which I lost sight of Mama whilst feeding the birds. . . . At 2.30 we drove up to Gloucester House and found George very unwell indeed, his nerves terribly upset. He had called in Dr. Fergusson, who with the other doctors, forbade his

---

[1] Sir James Clark, Bart., and Dr. Jenner were in attendance on the Prince Consort during the early stages of his illness, but as His Royal Highness's case became more critical it was thought advisable to call in further assistance, and the services of Dr. Thomas Watson and Sir Henry Holland, Bart., father of the present Lord Knutsford, were requisitioned. Both Dr. Jenner and Dr. Watson were subsequently created baronets.

attending the funeral, in spite of which George declared he *would* go. The worry and excitement had well-nigh driven him into a fever. Edward Weimar came in and sat with us for some time, and at five o'clock or so we started on our return, considerably anxious at heart. . . . I telegraphed to Alice.

December 23.— . . . A grey, *cheerless* day! The very air felt heavy with the general gloom. Up at eight. . . . The tolling of the bell and the minute-guns in St. James's Park informed us that the last sad ceremony in St. George's Chapel, Windsor, was about to take place. After a short interval, I began to write to poor dear Vicky, and when luncheon was over went on with my letter: towards four o'clock the Colonel returned from the funeral, and gave us all the melancholy particulars of the sad and striking scene.

Christmas Day! but oh! how different to former years. I breakfasted in my sitting-room, where the Colonel came to wish me *happier returns* of the day. Sir William gave us a *very appropriate* sermon: after lunch we drove up to Gloucester House, and were glad to find George rather better and decidedly more cheerful about himself. *December* 31.— I went to Evening Service with Ellinor Dunbar, and sat in their pew. Sir William finished his sermon with a very touching prayer. . . . I assisted at dear Mama's undressing, then spent the last ten minutes of the Old Year and the first few of 1862 in *reading* and *prayer* for all dear to me and for myself.

CHAPTER XIII.

WEDDING BELLS.

1862–1866.

Letter upon the death of the Prince Consort—Visit to the British Museum
—Princess Alice at New Lodge—Pictures at Christie's Rooms—
Touching interview with the Queen—The Rev. Charles Kingsley at
the Chapel Royal—Dr. Magee at St. Paul's—Opening of the International Exhibition, 1862—Princess Mary's impressions of the Exhibition—Visit to Lincoln's Inn and the Temple—Marriage of Princess
Alice—Princess Mary's maiden speech—The Prince of Wales attains
his majority — Letter to Louisa Frazer — Princess Alexandra of
Denmark at Windsor—A merry Christmas and New ,Year—Lawn
meet at Badminton—The Prince of Wales takes his seat in the House
of Lords—Marriage of the Prince of Wales—Guards' ball—The
Comte de Paris married—Betrothal of Princess Mary to Prince Teck
—His characteristics—Trousseau confined to British manufactures—
Princess Mary's wedding-day—Honeymoon at Ashridge—Sudden
departure for Vienna—The Duchess of Cambridge and the war—
First six months of married life.

THE great and unexpected affliction that in the closing days
of 1861 had fallen upon the Royal Family and plunged a
nation into mourning cast an abiding sadness over the new
year. Sorrow was universal, and the loss one that extended
to every class of the community. To Princess Mary the
death of the Prince Consort was a great grief, but her first
thought was for the bereaved Queen and the Royal children,
and truly characteristic of her warm heart and tender,
sympathetic nature is the following letter, written a few
weeks after the funeral had taken place :—

Letter to a Friend.

Cambridge Cottage, January, 1862.

. . . I trust you will accept, together with my grateful
and heartfelt thanks for the sympathy so kindly conveyed

in your letter to me, the expression of my unfeigned regret
at not being able to write to you before this. . . . But every
post brought me letters of condolence, and my poor bereaved
cousins are so continually writing to me, and assure me that
my letters are *a comfort* to them, that I have never had a
moment's leisure. . . . It has, as you may imagine, been a
time of great sorrow to *us*, although of course every feeling
of personal grief is absorbed by the thought of the overwhelming affliction of our widowed Queen and the deep
sympathy awakened for her in every breast, and most
especially so in the hearts of the members of her own
family. Hers is indeed the bitterness of woe, and beyond
all words do I pity her, for after a life of almost unequalled
happiness she is draining the cup of sorrow to its very
dregs.

It sends a pang to my heart when I think that she is left
thus early on her lonely eminence to meet the duties of
her exalted station and face the trials of life *alone,* and yet
not alone, if, as I pray she will, she turns to her God in her
hour of need. Oh! may she find Him a very ready help in
trouble. He alone can bind up the broken heart and speak
peace to the mourner. We must all unite in prayer for her
and her poor sorrowing children, who for their mother's sake
have struggled to bear up under this terrible visitation.
You know how devotedly they loved their dear Father, and
can therefore, in a measure, estimate the extent of their
bereavement and the load of sorrow that is weighing down
their young hearts.

I saw the poor Queen on the Monday following the terrible
event, and I cannot describe to you the misery of that
meeting. I felt myself in the presence of a sorrow too sacred
for words, and which the deepest, tenderest sympathy could
in no wise alleviate. Her voice in its touching plaintiveness
wrung my very heart, and her words and manner quite overcame me. I saw that her *life* had passed away with *his,* and
that henceforth she would drag on a weary existence alone.
Since then the accounts from Osborne have been, and are, as
satisfactory as we could hope, and only three days ago we
saw the King of the Belgians, who confirms this. He says
our poor Queen occupies herself with business, and is, on the
whole, tolerably calm and composed. Helena wrote me
word yesterday that she sleeps well now, which is a great
blessing, as also that she takes exercise; but I hear that she
is grown *thin* and *pale.* Poor thing! she says that her life
from henceforth will be one of labour, that she will toil on,

for her happiness in this life is all gone. I have had a heart-rending letter of eight pages from her, and she most kindly and thoughtfully sent Mama and me a tiny photograph of poor dear Albert's head enclosed in a locket. I mention all these particulars, knowing how much they will interest you.

I think if anything on *earth* can tend to soothe our Queen's grief, it will be the *great* feeling shown throughout the country. All classes seem to unite, not only in loyal sympathy for their bereaved Sovereign, but in heartfelt sorrow for *him*, to whose great and eminently useful qualities one and all now bear a ready testimony, and in whom I may in truth say the nation has suffered an irreparable loss. You have particularly mentioned the poor dear Princess Royal in your letter, and I must, therefore, tell you that I have had a most touching letter from her, telling me how inexpressibly wretched she is. She is coming over in a few weeks. Poor darling! What a terrible return to the home of her childhood! Alfred, too, is very shortly expected. . . .

Journal.—Cambridge Cottage, January 1, 1862.—A new year! Oh! may it be fraught with joys and happiness for *me* and *mine*, and as free from care as possible, and may God's blessing rest upon us throughout its course, and that of many and many succeeding years. . . . *January* 10.— . . . Mama and I drove up to see George, and sat with him : he is better, and as *cross* as possible! Dear Marian Alford arrived, and we had tea. . . . On our way back we went to Daniell's for a *dab*, and thence home. . . . *January* 12, *Sunday.*— . . . Mr. Birch assisted Sir William Dunbar in the service this morning, and preached a very strange sermon, the first part being *anti-doctrinal*, as it represented the serpent's form for Satan to be a mere *metaphor*. . . . About five o'clock I had a visit from Sir William, who roused me to a new view of the coming of the Saviour and my own *personal* interest in being "uplifted." . . . After he left I sat in Mama's room, and we shed many tears over the poor Queen's *heartrending* letters.

January 17.— . . . We went on to Gloucester House, expecting to meet King Leopold there, but found instead a note from George, saying that the King was unwell, where-upon Mama wrote to the latter proposing to call upon him. . . . We then drove to Buckingham Palace, and paid the King a long visit, afterwards calling on Lady Jersey, and found D'Israeli with her. She was *très causante* and gracious,

and gave us some tea. *January* 23.— . . . Mama received
a letter from Mimi [1] to inform us of Tilla's *betrothal* to Lippe! [2]
He proposed again, and was accepted. Mimi is *highly
pleased*, and I am delighted, and wish them every happiness.
After our excitement at the news had somewhat subsided,
we settled down to some reading. . . . We dined *à trois*. It
was a very strange dinner, as all the *fried* things *misglückten*,
poor Oppermann having *completely* lost his head! *January*
28.— . . . Lina conveyed us in her landau to Claremont,
where we found the poor dear old Queen painfully weak.
The Duc de Nemours and Princesse Joinville received us,
and presently Ciquite Joinville took me up to see her room,
which is full of birds, alive and stuffed, and curiosities. She
also showed me her mother's tiny salon. Then Lina fetched
us down to tea, when I found Marguerite and Blanche [3] had
joined the party. The room looked quite cosy lighted up. . . .
In the evening I read a pamphlet, by a secret agent of
Cavour's, entitled "Revelations," and containing horrible
stories about Italy. *January* 31.—Drove with Charlie
Purves [4] over to Orleans House to leave a message, and on
my way home, having seen a wretched-looking labourer
shaking all over, as if in a fit, close to Lord Russell's, [5] I
turned up a grass road, all mud and ruts, towards Lucas's
cottage, and sent him to look after the poor man. After
luncheon Ella and I went to the school (Mama following
somewhat later), and there assisted at the tea I annually
regale the children with. Seventy boys and girls were
feasted, and, tea over, they sang several pieces very nicely,
led by Mrs. Moore, the new schoolmistress, finally cheering
us most vociferously.

St. James's Palace, February 10.—Our *poor* Queen's
Wedding Day! . . . *February* 15.—The Captain came in
full of the affair of my photograph as "Summer," now most
improperly published. . . . Mama and I went out in the
brougham, and ferreted out Katty Coke's house in Warwick
Square, where I was deposited. Scarcely had I been *warmly*
welcomed by Katty, when she summoned her husband and
presented him to me, and there we sat *à trois* in her pretty
drawing-room for an hour or more, I cultivating assiduously
Mr. Coke! . . . To dinner with the Duchess of Inverness.
We were a party of eight, and dined in the tent-room. The

---

[1] Princess Marie of Anhalt-Dessau, mother of Princess Bathildis.
[2] Princess Bathildis of Anhalt-Dessau (see p. 79).
[3] Daughters of the Duc de Nemours.　　[4] Son of Colonel Purves.
[5] Pembroke Lodge, Richmond Park.

conversation was general and animated, and superseded any round game.

February 22.— . . . We set out, almost directly after luncheon, for the British Museum, where we were met by the Duchess of Beaufort, and received by Milman, the Dean of St. Paul's, Mr. Jones, one of the librarians, and other gentlemen. Panizzi *made himself scarce, or was invisible* during our visit. Our guides conducted us first into the new reading-room—a grand circular hall with book-shelves all round it, containing from 60,000 to 70,000 volumes, with seats and accommodation for 320 readers and a splendid dome, altogether the finest thing of the kind now existing. Thence we were conducted into the old library, and shown some interesting autographs, George III.'s reading-desk, and his own library,[1] containing specimens of very early English and foreign printing. We also saw Magna Charta (an original copy), several most curious and beautiful missals, and some original sketches by the Old Masters, together with books illustrated by them. Two delightful hours were spent in this manner, when we were obliged to tear ourselves away.

February 24.— . . . Mama and I started for Kew, where, after inspecting the bolts and bars of the rooms, in case of thieves, who, during the last week, have been busy at Kew, and seeing poor Hepburn, who is still laid up with his leg, we visited dear Papa's mausoleum and placed two wreaths on the coffin. . . . *February* 25.—I drove with George to the Paddington Station in time for the 11.15 train for Windsor, whence a landau and four conveyed us to New Lodge, where the Van de Weyers and Lady Caroline Barrington received us. Almost immediately I went up to Alice's little sitting-room, and remained talking with her until luncheon-time. I thought her *looking* better than I expected, but she is far from strong, evidently worn out bodily and mentally. She was tolerably cheerful, and entered, in a quiet way, into the conversation at the luncheon-table, at which we sat down a party of thirteen, including the two sons and their tutors. We adjourned to the drawing-room for a little while, when Alice accompanied me upstairs to put on my things, and we took our leave, returning in the same manner as we had come down.

February 28.—Shortly before one o'clock we left for the

---

[1] George III.'s library, which included many very rare books and had cost His Majesty £135,000, was presented to the British Museum by George IV.

Great Exhibition,[1] where George and Count Brandenburg met us; we were received by Lord Granville, the Duke of Buckingham, Mr. Fairbairn, and Sir Charles Dilke, who conducted us over the building, now greatly advanced and in process of being painted. The transept and the domes at either end are grand and striking, but I miss the centre dome sadly, and fear the unrelieved length of the building will appear very flat and spoil the general effect. *March* 7.— Before I had finished my breakfast Mama had gone to dress for our pedestrian expedition to Christie's Rooms, to see a collection of pictures, chiefly pre-Raphaelites, to be sold there by auction. We found a good many people assembled, but managed to get a view of the pictures; it was a curious and interesting collection, in which Ley's picture of a preacher in a Dutch town, "Elaine," and Millais's "Black Brunswicker" figured conspicuously. Of the water-colour drawings we saw but few, as the majority had already been removed. *March* 8.—I had an interview with the lawyer about my will, and as soon as he had departed I carried off the Colonel to my room to talk over my "little job" for Miss Coutts (the shirt contract for Spitalfields). Mama then drove with me down to Kew, and leaving her with Lady Dunbar I hastened to Hookey's and carried him off. . . . I hurried on to the Broad Walk, where I met Craig and settled with him the colouring of the beds in front of the Palm House. I then held a council with my three A.D.C.'s on the subject of the raised bed, spoke to the German gardener, and finally returned home to tea, the Dunbars assisting at our repast to talk over school matters.

March 10.—The midday train conveyed us in the company of Lord Sydney to Windsor, where Alfred received us most affectionately, and took us to the Princess Royal's rooms; we found her particularly well and better in spirits than we had expected. Alice and Helena joined us, and we went to luncheon in the usual room, where poor Albert's *vacant place* quite upset me. As Louise was not well, we were only a party of six. Beatrice came in at dessert. After luncheon we were shown into the little audience-room recently done up, and a few minutes later the poor Queen came in, rigid as stone, and the picture of desolate misery. We sat down and talked, chiefly of *Him,* for some little time, then Mama took leave of the Queen, who directly afterwards broke down, and

---

[1] The second Great English International Exhibition was held in London in a large building erected on the ground adjoining the gardens of the Royal Horticultural Society at South Kensington.

throwing herself into my arms sobbed convulsively. She kept me with her until Alice came to ask her to go out. ... At four or so we left the Castle. *March 12.—* ... Mama dropped me at Buckingham Palace, where I found Alice in her own rooms, in all the bustle and confusion of looking over her things, previous to sorting them for packing. She took me to her bedroom where she lay down, and we had a snug talk. We had a high tea *à cinque*, including Lady Caroline Barrington and Tilla. Afterwards Alice and I promenaded the passages for a while, and then, with Alfred, visited poor Albert's and the Queen's private suite of rooms. ... A smart dinner at George's finished the day. Prince and Princess Edward, the Duchess of Manchester, the Derbys, Bessboroughs, Lord Malmesbury, Quin, and Mr. Wenman Coke [1] were among the guests.

March 17.— ... Soon after three o'clock we had a visit from Sir Richard Airey, *so agreeable*, and on his departure Quin arrived with the thinning *régime!* We drove over to Stafford House to tea (though to me it was forbidden fruit). Annie Sutherland received us in the downstairs suite of rooms, and we found Lady Bessborough with her. After a while Princess Camporeale, *née* Acton, came in, and her lively and engaging manners made a very favourable impression on us both: we had a *causette à quatre*, and were not home till quite late. *March 19.—* ... We drove down to the South Kensington Horticultural Gardens. The Flower Show was most *tastefully* arranged in the Council Room, and consisted chiefly of *hyacinths*, tulips, cut roses, and one or two standards in pots, lilies of the valley, primulas, narcissus, and new leaved plants. Sight and smell were equally delighted. The Duke of Buckingham joined us, and we walked through the Gardens up to the conservatory, which has been charmingly decorated inside with basket flower-stands! After spending some time in the conservatory we retraced our steps, and were home at 1.30. ... *March 25.—* ... I walked over with Colonel Purves to Stafford House to be *weighed*, which feat the Duke accomplished, and in the afternoon we paid a visit to Countess Apponyi, to hear her sing, which she did *most charmingly* with Mr. Woodhouse. Brandenburg, Falbe, and M. de Sabouroff were the only other listeners besides her family. M. de Sabouroff played beautifully on the piano between the songs. *Es war ein wahrer Genusz!*

*March 26.—*Dearest George's birthday! May he be long spared to us, and may God's blessing rest on him, and

---

[1] Fourth son of the late Earl of Leicester.

every earthly blessing be his besides, above all *health.* . . .
We gave a dinner of twelve in honour of the day—George,
the Edward Weimars, Derbys, Lord Malmesbury, Airey, Jim,
Quin, and the Colonel.   Afterwards we had a little party,
which I can*not* say *some* of our *beaux* did their best to
enliven.   *March* 27.— . . . Countess Apponyi arrived soon
after twelve to assist at my singing lesson with Pinsuti.   I
was very nervous, and my voice not as clear as usual, in
spite of which the Countess thought me much improved;
she sang some duets with me and stayed till after one
o'clock. . . . We dined at eight, and spent a very wretched
evening, for scarcely had I read a few pages of "Good for
Nothing," when Freieisen rushed in, *in tears,* to tell us of
the death of dear old Alsfeldt, who breathed her last at
Vilsen on Sunday, March 20th.   She was only alarmingly
ill for twenty-four hours, and was buried on *this* very morning.   It was a terrible shock to poor Mama and me, coming
so totally unexpectedly too, *doch Ihr ist wohl, denn sie sehnte
sich nach einem besseren Leben,* and she has found rest and
peace.   I had a good cry, and about eleven we retired *very,
very* sad at heart.
    March 28.—I went to Mama's room, and arranged with
her and the Colonel how we were to sit at dinner . . . drove
to the Nursery Ground, and after going over the whole place
and only selecting two little azalea trees for the dinner-table,
which I presented to Mama, we returned home to dress, our
guests being the Flahaults,[1] Wellingtons, Lady Ely, Lady
Palmerston (*he* has the gout), Lord Clyde, Lord Chelsea
Henry Greville, and Falbe.   In the evening we had a small
party, which seemed more successful than the last one, as
the *hommes* talked away and did the agreeable.   *March* 29.—
Edward Weimar met us (Colonel and Mrs. Purves and I)
at the Paddington station, whence we proceeded together to
Windsor. . . . In the corridor we met Alice, Helena, and
Louise, and after taking off my things in their room, Vicky
joined us, and we went in to luncheon, Louise lunching with
the Queen. . . . I found Tilla and old Bachelor with Alice,
who took me downstairs to see all that had, as yet, been
unpacked of her trousseau, chiefly beautiful lace, *lingerie,*
and pieces of grey and lilac silk and moiré.   I bade her and
Vicky good-bye, and set out for a walk with Helena and
Louise down to Frogmore, to visit dear Aunt Kent's mausoleum and the site of poor Albert's.   The former is in a

---

[1] Comte and Comtesse de Flahault.   He had succeeded M. de Persigny
as French Ambassador at the Court of St. James's.

quiet spot, and the banks of violets and primroses that slope down on either side are very sweet and pretty. On our way back we met the Queen in a carriage with Vicky, Alice, and Beatrice (Alfred riding behind). Her Majesty stopped to speak to me, and I thought her looking better and more cheerful. On my return to the Castle the two girls and Tilla made me have some tea, and I hurried off to catch the train, which landed us at Waterloo, after affording me a peep of the dear Kew Pagoda. We dined at Stafford House, the Duke and Lord Derby being my neighbours; and a very amusing dinner it was, for Lord Derby and Lord Granville kept *chaffing* each other across the table In the evening there was a small and pleasant party. We were in the downstairs suite of rooms, which is a very pretty one.

April 2.—Attended divine service at Portman Chapel with Lady Sydney, where we had a beautiful sermon from Mr. Reeve; the application at the end was particularly impressive, and cannot fail to have gone to every one's heart; I know it came home to mine. The sermon must have been a long one—for the service was not over till past one—though we did not find it so. . . . About 4.30 I had a visit from Ellinor Dalrymple and her first-born George, a nice tall boy of six, full of life and spirits. Ellinor and I had a cosy chat together. *April* 4.—Mama being unwell, Lady Sydney accompanied me to the Chapel Royal to hear the celebrated Charles Kingsley, in whose honour the Chapel was crowded He gave us a wonderful sermon, more like a lecture than anything else, and more *startling* than *edifying*. His delivery is slow and measured, to conceal an impediment in his speech, and his voice is not at all powerful. The subject he selected was *death.* . . . The greater part of the afternoon I spent talking and reading to Mama, who was established on her sofa. At seven I left her and went down to my solitary dinner, at which, to my alarm, the footman waited in scarlet! *April* 5.— . . . I put the finishing touch to the luncheon and music rooms for the evening's use, and was fetched by Freieisen to look at her sitting-room, in which it was decided Mama should sleep. . . . We had a dinner-party; Lady Marian, the two Cadogans, George, Lord William Osborne, Lord Clanwilliam,[1] Cecil Forester, Mr. Bentinck, William Peel, and Captain Cust. I had to receive the guests, and Mama came in when all were assembled It was very pleasant and would have been perfect could Mama

---

[1] Sometime our Ambassador at Berlin.

but have been quite up to it.   She left at 10.30, and
we had a good deal of fun, Mr. Bentinck and Lord William
chaffing Cecil Forester till half-past eleven, when they departed. . . . *April* 6, *Sunday.*— . . . Marian Alford, Augusta
Cadogan and the Captain went with me to St. Paul's Cathedral for the special service at seven o'clock.   We sat in the
Dean's seats at the end of the choir; the centre under the
dome was crowded, and the service and singing were as
thrillingly beautiful and impressive as on former occasions.
Dr. Magee preached on "Thy will be done in earth, as it is
in heaven," and gave us a fine sermon, though perhaps a
little too much spun out.   *April* 8.—Mama had another bad
night, and had coughed incessantly. . . . Started with
Frazer on a shopping expedition for Helena's confirmation
gift. . . . I dined with George to meet the Aumales, the
party consisting of the Sydneys, Shelburnes, Lord William
Osborne, Count Bradenburg, Count Pahlen, and Colonel
Tyrwhitt.   It was very successful, but I missed Mama, and
felt shy at having to do the honours.

Letter to a Friend.

Cambridge Cottage, April, 1862.

. . . Mama was for ten days or so very seriously unwell,
and I even at one time felt rather uneasy about her.   She
had a bad sore throat, owing, I believe, in a great measure to
an offensive odour that at times pervaded her bedroom, and
which has since been discovered to have been caused by *dead
rats!* poisoned by Her Majesty's *rat-catcher!* . . . On April 12,
I am glad to say, we were able to move her down to Kew;
the pure air of the country did wonders for the dear invalid,
and the unfavourable symptoms gradually disappeared.   For
some time, however, after our *délogement*, she had to keep
very quiet, and I read to her a good deal, "East Lynne"
forming our *lecture* just then.   In my few leisure moments I
had to answer endless notes of inquiry, and besides this there
were the daily services during Passion Week and Easter.
. . . A few days ago we had the happiness of welcoming
my dear sister, who is looking wonderfully well, and is
delighted to find herself once more in dear old England.
I think her arrival has proved a tonic in Mama's case,
for she has ever since been able to undergo all manner
of fatigue, bodily and mental, without feeling at all the
worse. . . .

Public attention was now focussed on the Great International Exhibition, which was nearing completion, when the Prince Consort, who had been the moving spirit of the undertaking, was suddenly called away to his long rest. In the altered circumstances an informal opening of the building would certainly have been permissible, but even in these, her days of early widowhood, the Queen was most anxious that her personal sorrow should not interfere with the State function in contemplation at the time of her severe bereavement. Accordingly, Her Majesty notified her desire that the proceedings should bear as much as possible the character of a national ceremonial, and the Exhibition was inaugurated by an imposing pageant. No royal ladies, however, accompanied the procession, in which the Duke of Cambridge, the Crown Prince of Prussia, and Prince Oscar of Sweden took part, but the Duchess of Cambridge and Princess Mary were present at South Kensington, and as their carriage drove up to the entrance they were received by a royal salute. On this memorable occasion the Duke of Cambridge was the central figure, and after receiving from Lord Granville the humble Address to the Throne, by the Queen's command, His Royal Highness declared the Exhibition open.

Journal.—St. James's Palace, May 1.—I was up at 8.30, dressed, and was down a little before eleven, and found Mama being *coiffée* by Régnier. The Colonel and the Captain assisted at my breakfast, and I then went up to finish my smart toilet. I was ready by twelve—in black, with new lace shawl and mauve crape bonnet! We (Mama, Gussy, and I) drove, *viâ* the Parks and Albert Road, to the Cromwell Road entrance of the Exhibition. We passed up the *lined* Transept to the Eastern Dome, and there waited. The *music* was grand! After the prayer we had more music, and then left with the Princes, reaching home at a quarter to three. George and Prince Oscar of Sweden came in for a second. . . . In the evening we went to a grand banquet at Stafford House, and sat down a party of forty-three.

Letter to Miss Ella Taylor.

Cambridge Cottage, May 13, 1862.

. . . After making her *début* on the 30th at Apsley House, Mama was able to accompany us to the opening ceremony of the Great Exhibition, which I thought very fine and grand, although, of course, a sad contrast to the one of '51; and also to be present at the *fête* given at Stafford House the same evening. Next day we returned to Kew, and on the following morning again drove up to the Exhibition, where we spent some hours in the picture-galleries, which to my mind are as yet the only well done and arranged portion of the work. The rest at present gives one the idea of a huge bazaar, the Pantheon on a colossal scale; the blocking up of the nave with all kinds of *trophies* (as they are called, though applied to toys, piled up one above the other, and raw products), telescopes, lighthouses and such-like is the greatest mistake of all, and one the commissioners are setting to work to remedy. Had *I* the management of the thing, I should have the nave cleared, and allow only sculpture and works of art, and perhaps guns, to be placed in it, interspersed with trees, flowers, and fountains. This would have the effect of turning it into a promenade, and thus making it at once useful and ornamental.

As a *whole* I think we can be justly proud of the British collection of pictures, although I miss many of the gems exhibited at Manchester in '57, and many of the modern artists are not represented by their best works. Of the foreign collections the *Belgian* ranks decidedly highest, for with but few exceptions *every* picture is a remarkable one. Holland and Norway are *very well* represented, and Spain and France boast several gems. From the 4th to the 8th of May we rested and ruralised, enjoying the beauty and sweetness of Kew, which was literally *one mass* of blossom, the lilacs, laburnums, azaleas, and chestnut trees being in full bloom. . . . We went up to St. James's on the 8th for my first Ball, and on the day following again visited the Exhibition, devoting our time and energies to English china (lovely!), jewellery (splendid!), the English furniture department, with which we are delighted, and to the French court, which, I think, when completed, will be very fine, the tapestry is *quite beautiful*.

Mama has had a letter from Helena with a somewhat better account of the poor Queen, who felt the return to Balmoral without *Him* most terribly, and quite broke down at first. Poor thing! Her *habitual* load of sorrow has, if possible, been increased of late by her anxiety on the King of the Belgians'· account. He has been very seriously ill, but the telegraph has brought much better news the last few days, and I really believe that his recovery is steady and progressive. . . .

Journal.—St. James's Palace, June 10.—We started with the Captain in the barouche on a sight-seeing expedition. First to Lincoln's Inn, where we saw the fine dining-hall, with a fresco by Watts, representing the earliest law-givers down to the era of Magna Charta; the withdrawing-room hung with the portraits of all the great lawyers, the very handsome library, in which we inscribed our names in a book bearing the signatures of Charles II. and James II., and lastly the chapel, with old carving and stained-glass windows. After thanking the Treasurer for taking us round, and a glance at Pitt's house, we drove on to the Middle Temple, where we visited the dining-hall, bearing date 1570, the carving of which is beautiful, and the wood supposed to have been the hulks of some of the Spanish Armada. Our conductor, Mr. Hopney White, then took us to the new library, which to my mind, would be more adapted for a chapel, and after showing us the garden whence the York and Lancaster factions are said to have taken the white and red roses, escorted us to the Temple church built by Henry L, Stephen and John, and beautiful in its noble simplicity. It contains the tombs of the Templars, their statues recumbent, the crusaders only, it is said, with their legs crossed. The pillars are of Purbeck marble, and beautiful in design. This is one of the few round churches in England.

Sad indeed as the Prince Consort's death was to all his children, in the case of Princess Alice circumstances lent additional pathos to the melancholy event, for it was while engaged in directing the preparations for her wedding that the much-beloved father was stricken down. Everything had been arranged by him, even to the design of the bridal dress, but instead of the joyful wedding which all were looking forward to, the Princess was married quietly at Osborne on the 1st of July, 1862, some six months later than the date originally fixed. The Duchess of Cambridge and Princess Mary were among the near relatives assembled for the marriage, and at the conclusion of the ceremony had a touching interview with the Queen, who attended the service in the most private manner. Unfortunately Princess Mary kept no record of her stay at Osborne.

Letter to Miss Ella Taylor.

Cambridge Cottage, August 29, 1862.

... I have been leading a very pleasant though remarkably unsettled country life, with now and then a *dash* of London in it. Mama and I moved down to this place on the 23rd of July, as Mama wished to spend her birthday amongst the flowers, but we dined with George in the evening of the 25th, and I slept in town that night to give myself a long morning at the Exhibition with Lady Marian Alford, returning here late on the Saturday night, after a dinner and party at Mary Craven's, at which I joined Mama, and took my leave of London society for the time being. Next day Augusta, Fritz, and Adolphus came down to us, and all that week we took advantage of the lovely weather to extend our drives, and show the Mecklenburg suite the *lions* of this place and its neighbourhood, and the prettiest bits of scenery hereabouts, with all which they were as much delighted as *I even* could possibly desire! The pony phaeton was consequently in great request, and its owner thoroughly gratified by the admiration the ponies excited.

We went to Ashridge for the first week in August, and after spending a quiet Sunday with the family and two or three *élus*, such as Mary Boyle, the Bishop of Oxford, Lord Shelburne, and Lord Stratford de Redclyffe, we plunged on the Monday into all the dissipation attendant upon a large party, comprising from thirty to forty guests. Amongst these were the Clarendons, Seftons, Dufferins (*mère et fils!*), Probyns, the Duke of Newcastle, Lord Granville (on crutches, as he was suffering from gout), Quin, Falbe, Lord Lyons of American fame,[1] Count Wimpffen, and Lord Cowper. Croquet formed the chief morning's occupation, broken by singing, and cutting out flowers to be pasted on a screen, as a *souvenir* of the party, each member having to select and cut out one (*at least*) of the flower prints. Of an evening there was dancing or round games, and on one occasion we had some

[1] Our Ambassador at Washington at the time of the negotiations between Great Britain and the United States concerning the "Trent" affair, 1861.

very successful theatricals. The day before we left the Hertfordshire Volunteer rifle shooting came off in Ashridge Park, and during a portion of the day we were present at it. A grand early dinner of 150, in the conservatory and a long tent, followed, after which I had, in *fear* and *trembling*, to make a short speech, and distribute the prizes to the Volunteers. I am assured that I acquitted myself well, and the hearty cheers which greeted me and mine fully repaid me for the nervousness I had suffered on the occasion of making my *maiden speech!* The day's proceedings terminated with a dance, which we kept up till midnight. . . .

I have been gardening at a great rate lately, chiefly studying improvements to be carried out next year (D.V.), and you will be glad to hear that the flower-beds are considered *very good* this summer, and that Lady Rokeby (my instructress in the art) bestowed great praise upon her pupil after going over the gardens (*public and private*) very systematically with me. We have had *no end* of visitors of late, and indeed may expect some nearly every day, for not only do they come down from London, but several of our friends are staying in the neighbourhood: Lady Jersey is at Osterley, her own place, where we are going over to luncheon to-morrow; Lady Westmorland has taken a charming villa at Wimbledon, which opens into a very pretty garden; and Falbe has a cottage at Richmond. The Aumales are away, Lina having left the end of July for Spa, where the Duke joined her a few days ago, having been telegraphed for in consequence of the alarming illness of the poor old Princesse de Salerno, *her* mother, who has been at death's door. The last accounts from Spa were somewhat better, though I fear the poor dear old lady is still in a very precarious state. The two Austrian Archdukes, younger brothers of the Emperor, the Brabants and the Crown Prince of Saxony, with his brother Prince George, came down to pay us a visit, and possibly before long we shall see the Grand Duke and Grand Duchess Michael here. . . . I am to be godmother to the Princess Royal's little boy,[1] a very fine child, I am told. . . .

Journal.—Cambridge Cottage, September 2.—We had the happiness of breaking to Lady Dunbar, and later to Sir William, that the Lord Chancellor (Lord Westbury) had given him the Vicarage of Dronfield. They left at about twelve in oh! such joy and thankfulness of heart, and we

[1] Prince Henry of Prussia; he married in 1888 Princess Irene of Hesse Darmstadt.

H.R.H. THE DUKE OF CAMBRIDGE.

H.R.H. THE DUCHESS OF CAMBRIDGE.   H.R.H. THE GRAND DUCHESS OF MECKLENBURG-STRELITZ.

H.R.H. THE GRAND DUKE OF MECKLENBURG-STRELITZ.   H.R.H. THE HEREDITARY GRAND DUKE OF MECKLENBURG-STRELITZ.

H.R.H. PRINCESS MARY OF CAMBRIDGE,

[1864.]

hurried off into the Gardens to meet Mr. Blashfield and Hookey by the raised bed. The *tazza* had been fixed, and was approved of, and we decided on the height of the coping; I then walked on a little by Mama's basket carriage, and finally went into the propagating part of the garden before returning home. . . . *October* 1.—After breakfast I joined Craig in the broad walk, settled the flower-beds with him, and consulted with Hooker about the Maltese crosses. . . . *October* 2.—Gardened with Craig, and afterwards with Smith, in front of the Old Museum by the cactus house, where I am trying for a long diamonded bed. . . . *October 3.*— . . . Gave my attention to the locket and necklace bed, and to a chain of beds to be introduced at the back of the palm house. . . . Hunted out old Hookey from his den, and dragged him round the shrubberies, but all to no purpose. Home in a rage with the old piece of obstinacy! to find Lady Dunbar waiting to accompany me to the school, where I assisted at the children's examination and awarded the prizes.

Recalling his early years at Kew, the Keeper[1] of the Museum says—

Princess Mary and the Duchess of Cambridge took daily morning walks in the Royal Gardens, which at that time were not open to the public till one o'clock. From the attention paid by the Princess to the Duchess it was apparent, even to an outsider, how devoted she was to her mother. They usually walked arm-in-arm, and were often unattended; and when the Duchess drove about in a little pony-carriage, only large enough to carry herself, the Princess was generally seen walking by the side. Sometimes, perchance in consequence of a passing shower, their Royal Highnesses sought shelter in the Museum, and on these occasions I used to take them chairs from my room. Princess Mary in the pleasantest manner possible asked me to tell them something about the objects in the cases near at hand, and never omitted to thank me for having done so. The Princess was known to every one employed in the Gardens, and as showing the personal interest she took in the men, it may be mentioned that when the assistant Curator, Donald Macleod by name, fell ill, and was ordered away for change, the Princess at once missed him, and expressed her great regret when I told her the cause of his

---

[1] Mr. J. R. Jackson; he first came to Kew in 1858.

absence. Soon after Macleod's return he was passing along the Kew road, near the present Cumberland Gate, and the Princess was driving with her mother in an opposite direction. On seeing him the carriage was at once stopped and a kindly expressed inquiry made after his health.

Ever since the informal meeting at Heidelberg in September, 1861, when the Prince of Wales was travelling with his tutor, and Prince Christian of Denmark and his daughter were on their way to join the family gathering at Rumpenheim, it was apparent, to use the Prince Consort's words, that " the young people had taken a warm liking to each other." As soon as the Princess arrived at the Hessian Palace, her cousins were most anxious to hear all about the meeting, and much excitement followed when Princess Alexandra, producing a photograph from her pocket, laughingly exclaimed, " I have got him here ! " The formal betrothal took place just a year later, during the Queen's visit to the Continent, and soon afterwards, as recorded by Princess Mary, Prince Christian brought his daughter over here to stay with the Queen at Osborne, but the public announcement of the engagement was not made until the day preceding the Prince of Wales's twenty-first birthday. The Royal nuptials were peculiarly gratifying to the Duchess of Cambridge, for the bride elect was her great-niece. Princess Mary had passed many weeks with her cousin at Rumpenheim, and when quite a child Princess Alexandra visited this country to make the acquaintance of her Cambridge relations. In the circumstances she naturally looked to them for any assistance she might require in the preparation of her trousseau, the greater part of which was made in England. The assistance was joyfully rendered, and, as may be imagined, Princess Mary's good taste was of signal service in a matter of this kind.

Journal.—Brighton, November 9.—The Prince of Wales— God bless him !—attains his majority (21) to-day. It blew a gale all night and poured with rain all the morning. After luncheon we watched anxiously for the expected and longed-for arrival of dear Christian, who was on his way

back to Copenhagen, having established Alix[1] at Osborne.
At half-past three we had the happiness of welcoming him,
and for upwards of three hours sat talking over the *Verlo-
bung*[2] of Alix and Bertie. We had much to hear and dis-
cuss, and while fully sharing his happiness at the marriage
we could enter into his feelings at leaving Alix thus for the
first time. We dined at eight o'clock, a party of five, and
toasted our dear Prince in champagne.

November 10.—Down by 8.30 for Christian's breakfast,
who left soon after nine. . . . At six Geraldo and I
drove up to Mr. Lee's school, where Mr. and Mrs. Lee
and the Somerset boys[3] received us and took us into the
drawing-room, from the windows of which we saw the fireworks, consisting of Roman candles, rockets, serpents or the
D—— among the tailors, a Chinese edifice, a Maltese star,
and ending with a transparency—a large C surmounted by
a crown!—and the bonfire in honour of Wales's birthday.
Before leaving I passed through the two dining-rooms, where
supper was laid out for the boys.

Cambridge Cottage, November 21.— . . . We reached
Windsor Castle about twelve and were shown into our old
Lancaster tower rooms, where we were presently joined
by darling Alix,—too overjoyed at the meeting to speak!—
dear Alice and Louis; after a while Alix took me to her
room. . . . I then returned to the others, and we went with
Alice to see her rooms in the Devil's tower, where Louis was
being *sketched;* here the poor dear Queen joined us and remained
with us for some time. We lunched without Her Majesty,
and Beatrice came in afterwards. . . . Went into Alix's room
again and played to her *en souvenir de Rumpenheim,* afterwards
accompanying her into all the state-rooms, Mama, Alice,
Louis, and Helena being also of the party. On our return
Mama and I were summoned to the Queen's Closet, and had
a nice little talk with her, ending with tea. We were hurried
off shortly before five, Alix, Alice, and the others rushing
after us to bid us good-bye.

November 24.— . . . Welcomed dear Christian, whom
George had driven down *en surprise.* Soon afterwards Alix,
Alice, Louisa, and Helena arrived, attended by Miss Wortley,
Fräulein von Schenck,[4] Westerweller,[5] and Dudley de Ros.

---

[1] Princess Alexandra of Denmark, now Princess of Wales.
[2] Betrothal.
[3] Lords Henry, Arthur, and Edward, sons of the eighth Duke of Beaufort.
[4] Lady-in-waiting to Princess Alice.
[5] Baron Westerweller, aide-de-camp to Prince Louis of Hesse.

As soon as Alix had taken off her things in my room, I left her with her father in my sitting-room to an undisturbed *tête-à-tête nach dem ersten Wiedersehn.* . . . After luncheon we adjourned to the drawing-room and conservatory, the suite occupying the library. George and Christian left soon after three, but the others remained till past four o'clock, when they left for Richmond, where a special train awaited them. Mama and I sat for a while talking over the pleasant visit. . . . Drove up to dine at Gloucester House in Christian's honour —a very agreeable party of twelve. *November* 25.— . . . I saw Mrs. James with patterns of Honiton and *modèles* of gowns for Alix's trousseau. Shortly afterwards Christian arrived, accompanied by Captain Falbe; they lunched with us, and after a tender farewell Christian left *en route* for Windsor; he starts with Alix on their return to-morrow. . . . I worked at the Rumpenheim carpet, my first commencement.

Letter to Louisa Frazer.

Cambridge Cottage, November 26, 1862.

MY DEAREST FRACKY,— . . . You will have gleaned the chief particulars of our *séjour* at Brighton from Brand's [1] and Freieisen's letters. . . . We were fortunate in having the Barringtons (Mary Sartoris, my particular friend, included) and Gomms to associate with. They arrived the last week in October, and were available at all hours for walking and driving. Sir William Gomm is a beautiful reader of poetry, and many a pleasant evening did we spend at home listening to his readings of Shakespeare, Tennyson, and of his own admirable translations of Schiller. Lord Robert Clinton, too, was again established at Brighton, and able this year to be wheeled into our dining-room after dinner, and carried up into the drawing-room, so that we had his agreeable company now and then of an evening. . . . Geraldo and I took a much greater delight in our swimming lessons than heretofore, having quite made ourselves *mistresses* of the art. I hope you admire my delicate attention in writing to you on the paper on which the scene of our lessons (Brill's Baths) is depicted; you can thus form some idea of the size of the bath round which I am proud to say I now swim with ease. My last lesson was a most successful one, as I took a

---

[1] Princess Mary's second Dresser.

header from the *top step*, and swam the *whole length* of the bath!

Our Brighton dissipations consisted of going to two concerts at the Pavilion to protect and hear a Spanish guitar player; in giving a little party at which to introduce him to all our friends there; and in attending a performance got up by the 9th Lancers for the benefit of Lancashire. We were received by Colonel Drysdale and Colonel Steele, and conducted to the box which was very nicely fitted up for us. The theatre is a pretty one, though small. The first piece, *The Pride of the Market*, was carried through by Celeste's acting, whilst the last, an extravaganza, *The Happy Man*, was capital fun, thanks to the chief actor in it, a Captain Mahon. . . . I must reserve the rest of my account for another day, being anxious that these pages should reach you on my twenty-ninth birthday, and prove to you that, though, alas! absent from me, I am ever mindful of you, and near you in spirit. Dearest Fracky, let us pray that the act of self-denial we are both practising for your good may be rewarded, and that you may return to me about the middle of next month stronger and more like your old self, thanks to the course of treatment I hope you will steadily persevere in. . . . Brand desires me to say with her love that she has this morning sent off a box containing your warm cloak, and that she will write to-morrow. God Almighty bless you, my own old Fracky, and spare us for many years to be a blessing to each other. Ever your loving,

MARY ADELAIDE.

Journal.—Cambridge Cottage, November 27.—My twenty-ninth birthday! May God give me what *He* deems best in the year I am now entering upon, and may His blessing ever attend me and those I love! Oh that I may grow daily in every Christian grace and in favour with God and man! . . . After receiving my lovely presents, I remained in the drawing-room until a packet from the Queen hurried me up to my room to write. Mr. Nepean and Mr. Hutchinson arrived, and we sat down six to a capital luncheon, at which Lord Llanover's saddle of Welsh mutton was done ample justice to. It was carried out a bone! . . .

December 6.—Mama and I looked out old wraps and shawls with Brand for the families of the very poor clergy, and at one o'clock we left for Gloucester House, whence we drove, George and Colonel Tyrwhitt following us, to Islington, to see the great cattle show. The *fat beasts*—oxen, sheep, and pigs—were shown in a magnificent hall built in the Exhibition style. We were received by Lord Feversham and other members of the committee, who accompanied us round. *December* 9.—Wales, attended by Captain Grey, arrived shortly before two, and we received him upstairs; it was our first meeting since his engagement to Alix. . . . Sat with Bertie in the drawing-room till four, when he took his departure, and I adjourned to Mama's room and read our deeply interesting book "It's never too late to mend," Mama working the while at the carpet in her frame.

December 10. — . . . From Windsor station we drove straight to Frogmore, where the Queen and Helena met us. We went into dear Aunt Kent's two sitting-rooms downstairs, where *everything* had been left as in her time, even to the *flowers;* then walked to her Mausoleum, which Mama now visited for the first time; the temple at the top of the hill in which her statue is to be placed is not yet finished. Thence we passed over the little bridge to poor Albert's destined Mausoleum, which is sufficiently advanced to admit of the coffin being removed to it. The walls are temporarily of brickwork, but will ultimately be stone. Returning to Frogmore, we saw the Queen drive off in her pony phaeton with Helena, and followed in our carriage up to the Castle. . . . I had a nice chat with Alice, and Wales and Louis having returned from shooting, we lunched a little before two o'clock, saw Mrs. Thornycroft's bust of Alix, and after taking leave of the Queen and Beatrice in the Audience-room, hurried off to catch the train. *December* 12.—I drove Mama *viâ* Richmond to Edson's cottage in the rabbit-warren; we stopped and spoke to the nurse, and gave her a bottle of brandy for the poor fellow, who still lingers in great suffering and is almost unconscious. . . . I went out with Mama and the Captain to look for a pine tree for our garden; after a while Mama got into her basket-carriage, and we walked briskly alongside.

December 24.— . . . I joined Mama in the Christmas-room, and helped to arrange the tables, furniture, decorations, and the white china on the dinner-table. . . . Visited the guest chambers, carried the presents into the Christmas-room, saw Lady Dunbar and gave her a bonnet, Mama adding a cloak, arranged the presents for the upper servants on a table in front of the tree, and after some delay and rushing about, got them together and distributed my gifts to each. *One and all* seemed delighted! After settling how Mama's things were to be arranged, I looked into Freieisen's room, where her presents from Mama were displayed. I then gave my Christmas-boxes of money to some of the other servants, went up to welcome Ella Taylor, and visited Quin by the way, and, after presenting Bus with an overcoat, hastened to my room to dress. George, Sir Richard Airey, Swinton, the Purveses, Cust and Quin, Ella and our two selves made up the party. Dinner over, the tree was lighted, and a charming one it was. Our presents met with much approval and success, and I was quite delighted with mine. At eleven o'clock our London guests left, but the home party of six talked on pleasantly and merrily enough till past twelve.

Christmas Day.—May all its sacred blessings be ours. . . . We dined at Gloucester House, where dinner was served upstairs, and I sat all the evening in George's own sitting-room, trying to cheer and amuse poor wheezy Quin, who was terribly suffering and *short breathed. December 26.*—I drove Charlie Purves to Coombe, and going into the Rabbit Warren by Dr. Marsden's gate, we came upon the five *chasseurs*—George, Colonel Purves, Liddell, Mildmay, and Tyrwhitt. I there learnt that poor Edson had died that morning. The gentlemen making for the wood, I turned back and stopped close to his cottage in order to speak to his broken-hearted brother—poor fellow! . . . *December* 30. —I started in the phaeton with the Colonel, and drove through Richmond and up to Sawyer's house in the Park, where the Colonel got out, as Sawyer [1] was in bed with the gout, to ask him for particulars about the Edson family. . . . *December* 30.— . . . About ten o'clock we adjourned to the servants' hall to see the dancing. There were plenty of *danseurs*, and George's three maids (good-looking girls) were quite the *belles* of the ball! All seemed *thoroughly* to enjoy themselves, and it was a merry pretty scene. It was past midnight when we went upstairs. *December* 31.— . . . After bidding Mama good night in 1862, I went to my room, and the dawn of the New Year 1863 found me on my knees in prayer for myself and all dear to me. *Old Year! good night—good night.*

New Year's Day, 1863.—A happy new year to all those I love . . . and many happy returns of the same. I pray that much happiness may be in store for us in this year, much good effected by us, and care and sorrow warded off by a Fatherly and Almighty hand. . . . We

[1] Head keeper of Richmond Park.

had a charming visit from Mr. Tarver, on whose departure Ella joined us, and finished "Lady Audley's Secret," which I think a *provoking* book. It *feverishly* interests one, and one *hurries* on to know the secret and end (both of which are disappointing), without caring to look back at any page or passage, even for the writing's sake. . . . *January* 2.—I went into the Christmas-room and rearranged the table for the evening. . . . Old and young seemed delighted with their presents and the tree. After a while we younger ones adjourned to the library, and pushing aside the sofas, played at "Post," "The hissing game," and "Railway," and then danced to our own playing and *singing*, and finally to *Pitt's violin*. To crown all, I had by general desire to sing at the end, and managed, in spite of the dancing, to have a *little* voice. We broke up at twelve, having spent a very happy evening.

January 3.—After breakfast we remained for some time talking, and were full of Alice's merciful escape (she was thrown out of a phaeton on the 31st). . . . At 7.10 we started for Marble Hill, to dine with the Peels, and instead of finding, as we *expected*, only the family, we sat down to dinner a party of thirteen. I was between the General and Lord Russell, and among the guests were Count Wachmeister, Prince Gortschakoff,[1] M. de Cadore, and Alice Morier;[2] I had to talk to the foreigners all the evening. *January* 10.— . . . Poor Mama not feeling well enough to venture out, I went with Ella to Gloucester House, where we dined, a party of ten, upstairs, and sat in the large drawing-room. *I number one!* Rather fun! A very pleasant evening.

January 12.—Tidied my things, put away letters in my new box, and collected my music with Brand for Badminton. . . . We drove *viâ* Shepherd's Bush, Notting Hill, and Bayswater, to the Paddington station, where George, Jim, the Colonel and the Captain received us. We found Quin stowed away in our saloon carriage, and he, George, and the Colonel travelled down with us. Our train was a fast one, only stopping three times, and at Chippenham the Duke of Beaufort's landau and four awaited us. It had come on to rain heavily in the afternoon, and poured in torrents as we reached Badminton and got out at the side door. The Duke

---

[1] Russian plenipotentiary at the Vienna Conference in 1855.

[2] Daughter of General Peel. She married in 1861 Sir Robert Morier, who was successively ambassador to Portugal, Madrid, and St. Petersburg.

and Nina,[1] with the Dowager Duchess and the girls, received us, and after a while Nina took us to our rooms —mine a Chinese one. We dined, a liberal eight, in the hall, the party consisting of Worcester, Penna,[2] Lord Beaumont, Lord Coventry, the Binghams, the Jim Macdonalds, Lords Westmorland and Proby (whose wives had not arrived in time to be ready for dinner) and Courtenay, Colonel Baillie (Blues), Captain Edwardes (Coldstream Guards), Mr. De Vœux, Mr. Naper, Mr. Baldwin, and Captain Little. Adza appeared after dinner in the now *chintzed* grand drawing-room, where we danced later in the evening, the sofas being pushed away; but the circle thus made was an awfully formal one, and made the dancing rather a stiff affair.

Badminton, January 13.— . . . Nina took Cuckoo[3] and me into the kennel where we saw two packs, kitchen garden, stables, and dairy, and on returning to the house showed me the steward's room, housekeeper's room, servants' hall, and kitchen. I then rested until tea-time, when I went to the library, where the two girls appeared in *dressing-gowns*. We sat down twenty-eight to dinner *senza* poor Quin, who was a prisoner in his room. In the evening I paid him a visit, or rather a *visitation*, and was driven away by our host and Jim, and caught in the passage coming out! Soon after I had joined the rest, the drawing-room was cleared for dancing; but thanks to Mama's suggestion, the circle was a much less formal one, and we danced away merrily till past midnight. *January* 14.—Down at 10.30 to the great breakfast in the hall in honour of the lawn meet! The day was a lovely one, bright and sunshiny and fresh, but not too cold. From the hall windows we watched the riders and carriages arrive before equipping ourselves for the drive. . . . I went in the second carriage (a britschka) with Mrs. Macdonald. We drove off amidst loyal cheers, and had a good view of the "field," numbering about 1200 on horse-back, as they moved from the house up the park—to my mind the prettiest sight of all! Geraldo sat her horse beautifully; ditto Adza, Emmy, and Nina. They drew the first covert blank, and we went on with the field until they left us far behind, the ground being *very deep*. . . . In the afternoon I set out for a walk with the "Jims," across the fields to the farm, the basket-carriage following us. We had, in some places, to all but wade through the mud, and after complying with the chivalrous and most loyal

[1] The Duchess of Beaufort.   [2] Lord Henry Somerset.
[3] Countess of Lucan.

request of a farmer's son that I would place a tiny ivy-leaf
in his pocket-book, I trudged on ahead with Jim, his little
wife betaking herself to the carriage. I walked all the way
back, reaching home about five. After tea we adjourned to
the landing-place on the oaken staircase, where Nina's singing
class or choir were assembled, and heard them sing a number
of glees very nicely, Nina joining in. We were thirty-two
at dinner, the guests being two Codringtons and two Walshes.

January 15.— . . . We went into the red room adjoining
the library, the drawing-room being in preparation for the
ball, and listened to Lady Proby's charming singing, I
working away at my carpet. After a while Adza sang, and
lastly I—"The Bridge." Directly after luncheon the two
girls, Mrs. Jim, and I, attended by Mr. Baldwin, Mr. Naper,
and Captain Little, started out on foot to join the shooters,
who were peppering away in the preserves not far from the
kitchen garden. We got into the thick of it, seeing very
pretty sport; I followed George, and saw him bring down two
birds. We walked home with the shooters. . . . Dinner was
at seven, Mr. Symons, the Oxford surgeon, being the only
addition to the house party, and afterwards I went up to my
room to change my dress for the ball. Geraldo and I looked
into Quin's room to display our *costumes de bal* to his admiring eyes. After we had all assembled in the Library the
Duke conducted me to the drawing-room, where the guests
were beginning to arrive, and the ball opened with a valse to
warm the room for Mama. I danced away all night, only
skipping the valses, just while the room was too crowded,
and enjoyed myself to my heart's content! The guests numbered, I should think, upwards of 200. The Duke took me
to supper in the hall about midnight, and Mama left at
half-past one, but I remained till the end, and after winding
up with some pleasant valses, *une bande joyeuse* burst into
the hall at four o'clock clamouring for some more supper!
At half-past I went upstairs with poor dear ——, who was
put out and low, and whom I spent three-quarters of an hour
nearly in striving to comfort; so that I was not in bed till
six o'clock!

January 16.—I came down about one o'clock, and found
the girls and Jim in the library; they asked me to join
them at indoor croquet. Our *very absurd* game was interrupted by luncheon. . . . Mr. Baldwin brought me his
charming photograph album, and we sat together looking
over it until tea-time, and again afterwards. It was quite the
old country-house life, with the gentlemen coming in and

out all day, and very cheery! Later on I went upstairs and
paid Geraldo a visit in her own room, little Edward[1] joining
us *en negligé*. . . . After dinner I looked in upon Quin before
joining the ladies in the drawing-room.   It was a remarkably
pleasant evening; Lady Proby sang sweetly, the Bath band
played very nicely at intervals between, and we all talked
cosily.   Before separating I collected the autographs of some
of the guests.

St. James's Palace, February 5.— . . . Mama and I drove
with Geraldo and the Captain to the House of Lords.   When
prayers were over, the Prince of Wales took his seat *in form ;*[2]
the two Archbishops were sworn in, and then, after a little
delay, the address was moved by Lord Ward! and seconded
by Lord Granard; Lord Derby (able) and Lord Russell[3] (lame)
spoke, and we did not get home till half-past eight.   All the
evening I sorted, arranged, and weeded letters of '62.
February 6.— . . . Shortly before three o'clock the Prince of
Wales, whom we were expecting, arrived and sat with us for
some time, and then escorted me on foot to Marlborough
House, which he took us over.   We dined early, and went to
the Lyceum to see *The Duke's Motto*—too charming!   Saw
the French family in Wales's boudoir.   *February 7.*—Mrs.
James came, after I had finished dressing, with Alix's lace,
and I had Régnier for the arrangement of my diadem and
feathers, Mama giving me her taste; we chose our gowns
for the wedding and others to be done up. . . . Fanny
Marlborough and Lady Vane came to see me, then the
Foresters, followed by Hookey, *mollified* and repentant, the
Alstons,[4] and General Knollys.[5]   Dressed in a hurry, dined,
and went to the Adelphi, the Aumales joining us in the
Wales's box.   The two pieces, entitled *A Grey Mare* and
A Ticket of Leave, and the pantomime were not worth

[1] Lord Edward Somerset.
[2] The Prince of Wales entered the House of Lords accompanied by the
Duke of Cambridge and other peers wearing their robes of state.   The Prince
wore his ducal robes over the uniform of a General.   It was the opening day
of the session, and the Queen's Speech invited Parliament to ratify the
Treaty made with the King of Denmark respecting His Royal Highness's
marriage with Princess Alexandra, and to make provision for such an
establishment as legislators might think suitable "to the rank and dignity
of the Heir Apparent to the Crown of these realms."
[3] Lord John Russell was raised to the peerage as Earl Russell in 1861.
[4] The eldest daughter of Mrs. Bridges Taylor had just married Mr.,
now Sir Francis, Alston.
[5] General Sir William Knollys.   His son, now Sir Francis Knollys, is
Private Secretary to the Prince of Wales.

going to see, the first and last from their utter stupidity, the second from the very low style of acting. *Je souffrais* all the time for our guests. *February* 17.— . . . Drove into Hyde Park and walked in Rotten Row escorted by Sir Hamilton Seymour; thence to Gloucester House, where we met Jim on the stairs as we were coming away, full of Wales's visit to Savernake. Home at five to change our dress and rush off again to the tea at the Duchess of Marlborough's, and found a party of *eight* ladies, Count Vitzthum coming in just at the end. . . . Captain Cust dined with us, and read Kinglake's most interesting and well-written but mischievous book[1] to us all the evening.

February 22, *Sunday.*—We went to St. Philip's; Mr. Pigou read prayers and preached a very impressive sermon on the words "Is it not a little one?" After the service Mama and I drove to the South Kensington Horticultural; a man let us in, though the garden is not generally open till two, and we paced it in melancholy solitude, funereal urns, vases, and dark evergreens meeting the eye *everywhere!* The conservatory, however, was bright and gay with choice and sweet flowers, and we sat and walked in it till we returned home at 2.45 to luncheon, after which I read the "Gospel in Ezekiel" to Mama, and was beginning the evening Lessons when Sir Richard Airey was announced. . . . *February* 23.— Directly after breakfast I went to Mama's boudoir to choose my wedding-present for Alix—a diamond bracelet! . . . I sat with poor nervous Frazer for a while, when dear old Lady Napier was announced. I first saw her in my room and then took her over to the boudoir. Drove in my brougham to Nina Munster's to meet her friend Mr. Molyneux, the clergyman; a very earnest man, a little in Mr. Harrison's line, and had tea with Katty Coke in Warwick Square, where I saw my godson. During dinner a rather disquieting telegram came about Alfred, who is ill at Malta with fever, from the Duke of Newcastle. In the evening I read the *Times* article on Kinglake's book.

February 25.—Saw Mrs. James about the orange blossom for Alix, and watched the gentlemen arrive to attend the Prince's Levée.[2] Mama joined me at my bedroom window, but we were soon called away to see Captain Falbe just returned from Copenhagen. . . . Sir William and Lady Davison were announced, into whose visitation the Colonel and Mrs. Purves tumbled, the former dead tired after the Levée,

---

[1] "The Invasion of the Crimea," by A. W. Kinglake.
[2] This was the first *Levée* held by the Prince of Wales.

which had lasted from two o'clock till 5.15! *February* 27.—
At twelve I went to the Chapel Royal, Edith Somerset
accompanying me to the door, which was crowded in Mr.
Kingsley's honour: His sermon, taken from the third chapter
of Genesis, refuting Colenso's [1] views respecting the Pentateuch, was very clever and very impressive. In the afternoon
Miss Coutts came and I took her to my room, where she sat
talking over charities with me for some time. Dined *à deux*
at eight and in the evening I showed Mama a letter from
Wales and my *seven* valentines, and read aloud little scraps
of news about Alix. *March* 3.— . . . I was called away
from my singing lesson with Pinsuti to see the wedding lace
and veil for Alix, which is of Honiton manufacture and
quite beautiful! [2]

Princess Alexandra of Denmark left Copenhagen on the
26th of February, amidst scenes of the greatest enthusiasm,
and her reception by the people of England will long live in
the annals of this country. On the 10th of March the marriage
took place in the Chapel Royal, Windsor Castle. The procession was an imposing one, and to the Duke of Cambridge
was assigned the place of honour in the carriage occupied by
the bride and her father, the Duchess of Cambridge and
Princess Mary taking their customary place, immediately
before the younger children of the Queen. Bishop Wilberforce, referring to the scene in the Chapel, notes, "The
wedding was certainly the most moving sight I ever saw.
The Queen above all looking down added such a wonderful
chord of feeling to all the lighter notes of joyfulness and
show. Every one behaved quite at their best. The Princess
of Wales, calm, feeling, self-possessed, the Prince with more
depth of manner than ever before. Princess Mary's entrance
was grand." [3]

After the wedding of the Heir Apparent the usual routine
at Court, which had been interrupted by the death of the

---

[1] The Rt. Rev. J. W. Colenso, D.D., Bishop of Natal, had just published the second part of "The Pentateuch and Book of Joshua critically
examined," a work which occasioned much hostile comment in clerical
circles.

[2] The Journal breaks off here.

[3] "Life of Bishop Wilberforce," vol. iii. p. 88.

Prince Consort, was resumed. But the very deep affliction of the Queen made it impossible for her to appear at State functions, and for a time Her Majesty's place was filled by the Prince and Princess of Wales, who thus, at the onset of their married life, were called upon to perform the public duties of the Sovereign, duties that, during the past year, had in some measure necessarily devolved upon the Duke of Cambridge and his family.

Society did its utmost to give the beautiful young bride a right royal welcome, and the season was a joyous one. An event which attracted a good deal of attention was the Guards' ball in honour of the Prince and Princess of Wales, held in the picture-galleries of the International Exhibition. The decorations were of the most lavish character, and the Queen graciously lent the accessories used on similar occasions at Buckingham Palace. Following Her Majesty's example, many members of the aristocracy placed at the disposal of the Duke of Cambridge, as head of the Committee, their collections of gold and silver plate, the contributions being valued at £2,000,000. The guests, limited in number to 1400, began to arrive at nine o'clock, and soon after ten the ball was opened by a royal quadrille, in which eight couples took part, the Duke of Cambridge dancing with the Princess of Wales, and the Prince of Wales with Princess Mary, whose appearance called forth general admiration. The supper-room presented a magnificent sight, and the Prince and Princess of Wales showed their appreciation of the regal entertainment which their soldier hosts had provided, by remaining till the approach of daylight. A lady who was present at the ball says—

Princess Mary shone as a great beauty. She was dressed in white, trimmed with red and blue, the Guards' colours, and wore a wreath of poppies, cornflowers, and daisies. She danced a quadrille, having the Prince of Wales as partner and the Duchesse d'Aumale and Prince Edward of Saxe-Weimar for *vis-à-vis*. The Princess of Wales danced with a guardsman (I think it was General Sir Francis Seymour), and opposite to them were the Duchess of Manchester and the Duke of Cambridge. Among the side-couples were some of the greatest beauties in London, including the three lovely Miss Moncrieffes [1] and Lady Mary Craven. When the royalties had departed, a Scotch reel was danced with great animation, but it seemed to me this was scarcely suitable for the occasion, and a fair young man, with a broad orange-coloured ribbon across his breast, appeared to share my opinion. It was the Prince of Orange.

In July the Duchess of Cambridge and her daughter left England for Rumpenheim, where they met Princess Louis of Hesse, who was staying at Kranichstein. Writing to the Queen on August 1, Princess Alice makes allusion to the meeting: "Yesterday we were all day at Rumpenheim: so kindly received! The Landgrave, his two brothers Frederick and George, the Dowager Grand Duchess of Mecklenburg-Strelitz, her daughter Duchess Caroline, Aunt Cambridge, Mary, Augusta and Adolphus; Fritz and Anna of Hesse, and good Princess Louise, kindness itself. Aunt Cambridge was very amiable, and spoke most tenderly of you." [2]

Letter to Lady Elizabeth Adeane.

80, Adelaide Crescent, Brighton, November 15, 1863.

MY DEAREST LIBBET,— . . . I need scarcely tell you that I am overjoyed to find myself in dear Old England! Though I must say the three months we spent abroad, eleven weeks of them at Rumpenheim, surrounded by nearly the whole of Mama's family, and ten charming days in Paris, were pleasant enough in their way. We had a very interesting and amusing time of it during the three weeks of the Congress at Frankfort, and either made or renewed acquaintance with nearly all the leading members of the "Almanach de Gotha." We returned home on the 21st of last month, and after about a fortnight of Kew, during which we had a brief visit from my Danish cousins, came down here on the 7th and took possession of the only house then to be had large enough to contain our-selves and servants; alas! *not* facing the sea. . . . But we have made the drawing-rooms thoroughly liveable and com-fortable, and the bedrooms were so from the first, so that

---

[1] Afterwards Countess of Dudley, Lady Mordaunt, and Lady Forbes of Newe.

[2] "Princess Alice's Letters to the Queen," p. 65.

there is nothing to complain of about the house save its situation. We are here for a month. . . .

The poor dear Duchess of Hamilton and her little Mary are here, having taken Mr. Lawrence Peel's house in Kemptown for six months; and we see as much of them as the twenty minutes' distance between our respective abodes will admit of. The Duchess is, I think, somewhat more cheerful than when we saw her at Baden on our way home. Lady Spencer (Dowager) is also here with her children, and Lady Gainsborough, to recruit her strength. . . . Lord Bathurst and dear Lady Georgina, who, alas! is a great invalid, and our friend Lord Robert Clinton, are staying in our more immediate vicinity, and we shortly expect some more friends, so that you see that we are not badly off in the way of society. . . . I hear the Queen told Dean Stanley that he was going to deprive her of her best treasure.[1] We were at Windsor two days before coming here, and thought her looking very well, and more cheerful in spirits. . . . On Friday afternoon I hope to hear Fanny Kemble (Mrs. Butler) read, "As You Like It," never having heard her. Ever your most affectionate friend,

MARY ADELAIDE.

Except that Sandringham was added to the list of country houses visited by the Duchess of Cambridge and Princess Mary, there is little to record during the years 1864 and 1865. The Journal, which broke off abruptly in March, 1863, is not resumed till some time later, nor do the Princess's letters throw much light upon this period of her life. She attended the christening of Prince Albert Victor at Buckingham Palace on the anniversary of his parents' wedding-day, and on the 24th of May assisted at the first State celebration of the Queen's birthday that had taken place since the death of the Prince Consort. To the great joy of the nation Her Majesty had made her reappearance in public some weeks before at the Royal Horticultural Gardens, which twelve months earlier the Prince of Wales had formally inaugurated as a Memorial to his late father.

Shortly afterwards the Comte de Paris was married to Princess Isabella d'Orleans, eldest daughter of the Duc and Duchesse de Montpensier and niece to the reigning Queen

---

[1] See footnote, p. 358.

H.R.H. Princess Mary of Cambridge in 1864.
From a portrait at White Lodge.

of Spain. The wedding was celebrated at the Roman Catholic church at Kingston and made the occasion of a great gathering of the house of Orleans. At the *déjeuner* given by Queen Marie Amélie at Claremont, the French royal party was augmented by the presence of the Prince and Princess of Wales, the Duchess of Cambridge, the Duke of Cambridge, the Grand Duke and Grand Duchess of Mecklenburg-Strelitz, and Princess Mary, who looked very handsome in a dress of pale salmon-coloured silk. The Duc and Duchesse de Chartres gave a ball the same evening at Morgan House, Ham Common, which Princess Mary also attended.

Letter to Mrs. Barry.

Cambridge Cottage, March 15, 1865.

DEAR DRAPERCHEN,—I am charmed to find you are once more in England. Your last letter reached me when I was peculiarly busy in the writing line, and I foolishly put off answering it until far too late for my reply to have reached you at Aix. I can assure you, dear Draperchen, that you have been amply avenged, for I have never worn the deliciously warm grey rabbit's wool mittens you so kindly sent me, without experiencing a severe prick of conscience at the recollection of never having thanked you for so amiably thinking of me. It will be a real pleasure to me to see you again, and to prove to my *exaltée* little friend that my silence was not caused by any " error or errors," as she terms it, of hers, but resulted from procrastination in the first place, and in the last from the fact of not knowing where to address a letter. Will it be agreeable for you to come to me on Friday or Saturday next ? . . . Hoping to be forgiven for the pain I have most unwillingly caused you, I remain ever, dear Draperchen, your affectionate

MARY ADELAIDE.

Letter to Mrs. Bridges Taylor.

Cambridge Cottage, April 27, 1865.

MY DEAR EMILY,—Mama bids me say she hopes you will *dedommager* us for yesterday's disappointment by spending Saturday afternoon with us, and coming down with your dear little girls soon after three. I shall be delighted to hide the Easter eggs again for their especial benefit, after which I hope you will all do justice to a *country tea!* Your kind sympathy in poor dear Minny's [1] sorrow and the blight which has fallen upon her young life, was most welcome to our hearts. All we know at present is that she was with him to the last, and that Louise purposes returning at once with Minny to Denmark *viâ* Rumpenheim, I suppose for a few days' rest. Ever, dear Emily, affectionately yours,

MARY ADELAIDE.

Princess Alice writes to the Queen on the 19th of June, 1865, from Seeheim : "Dear Mary Cambridge has been here, and we enjoyed her visit so much. We took her back to Frankfort to-day, where we gave her and Aunt Cambridge a luncheon at Uncle Louis' Palais." And in a letter dated Kranichstein, a month later, the Princess again writes, "Mary has been so kind as to give us a boat, which we expect shortly. It is to be christened 'Mary Adelaide,' after her." [2] The Duchess of Cambridge stood godmother to Prince George of Wales, who was christened at Windsor Castle on July 7, but being abroad at the time, she was represented on the occasion by Princess Helena. The Duke of Cambridge was also one of Prince George's sponsors.

The year 1866 was destined to be a very eventful one for Princess Mary. Early in March she met her future husband, Prince Teck, at a dinner given by the Duchess of Cambridge at St. James's Palace to the Duc and Duchesse d'Aumale. The attraction from the beginning was mutual, and it may indeed be said to have been a case of love at first sight. "The wooing was but a short affair," writes Princess Mary. "Francis only arrived in England on the 6th of March, and we met for the first time on the 7th at St. James's. One month's acquaintance settled the question, and on the 6th of April he proposed in *Kew Gardens* and was accepted." The following week the Duchess of

---

[1] Princess Dagmar of Denmark. Her betrothed, the Cesarewitch Nicholas, died at Nice, April 24, 1865. She subsequently married the late Emperor Alexander III.

[2] "Princess Alice's Letters to the Queen," pp. 94, 95.

Cambridge, Princess Mary, and Prince Teck went on a visit to the Prince and Princess of Wales at Sandringham, where the engagement was announced.

Letter to Earl Granville.

St. James's Palace, April 16, 1866.

MY DEAR LORD GRANVILLE,—I shall be in town on Wednesday next, and as I am desirous of seeing you and flatter myself you will be glad to avail yourself of an *early* opportunity to congratulate me on my bright and happy prospects, I would propose to give you a *rendez-vous* at Gloucester House at five o'clock, if agreeable to you. I do not name an earlier hour, as I presume you have a Cabinet Council, but should three o'clock or so suit your convenience, do not scruple to say so. Hoping for a line in reply, I remain ever, my dear Lord Granville, very sincerely yours,

MARY ADELAIDE.

The bridegroom elect was the only son of Duke Alexander of Würtemberg, who in 1835 married Claudine, Comtesse de Rhédey, but not being of royal birth she could not take the rank of her husband nor could her children succeed to the throne of Würtemberg.[1] The Emperor of Austria conferred on her the title of Comtesse de Hohenstein, but she did not long survive her marriage, being killed four years later in a most tragic manner while attending a review of the Austrian troops. Her horse ran away with her, and the unfortunate lady was trampled to death by a squadron of cavalry. Count Hohenstein, afterwards Prince Teck, was four years younger [2] than Princess Mary. He was brought up at Vienna, and entered the Austrian army, serving as a lieutenant in the Imperial Gendarmerie Guard, and at the battle of Solferino[3]

[1] Otherwise the Duke of Teck would be heir apparent to the throne of Würtemberg.

[2] He was born at Vienna, August 27, 1837.

[3] The continued difference of opinion between Austria and Sardinia as to the policy of the former power in Italy led to a growing coolness with France, and ultimately war broke out. The allies (France and Sardinia) were victorious, and the last battle was fought near the village of Solferino, on

was attached to the General's staff, acting as aide-de-camp. Both the Emperor and Empress had a warm regard for Count Hohenstein, and he accompanied Her Imperial Majesty when she went to Madeira [1] after her serious illness in 1860. He was also very popular with his brother officers and much liked in Viennese society, where his good looks gained for him the sobriquet of *der schöner Uhlan*. In September, 1863, Count Hohenstein was created Prince Teck [2] with the rank of Serene Highness.

The Prince and Princess of Wales made his acquaintance when they were staying with the King and Queen of Hanover in the autumn of 1864, and taking a personal liking to the handsome young officer, invited him to stay with them at Sandringham in the following December. Owing, however, to some misunderstanding, he arrived in London a week sooner than was expected, and Prince Edward of Saxe-Weimar [3] was his host until he could be received at Sandringham. Prince Teck passed several weeks in England during 1865, and made many friends in London society. He was at the Garden Party given at Marlborough House, and at the close of the season went to Goodwood races with the Dowager Lady Ailesbury's party, going on to Cowes at the invitation of the Prince of Wales. Later in the year he again visited Sandringham.

Much public interest was naturally taken in Princess Mary's *fiancé*, and his photograph was in great request. Anticipating this demand, an enterprising firm of photographers ascertained that the Prince had given a sitting to a local man at Chichester, and immediately opened negotiations with the possessor of the copyright. The Prince, however, had laid strict injunctions upon the artist on no account to publish the portrait, as it showed him with a beard. In his

June 24, 1859. Terms of peace were then arranged, and a conference was afterwards held at Zürich, when a treaty was signed (see p. 322).

[1] Her Majesty made the voyage in the Royal yacht *Victoria and Albert*, which the Queen had placed at her disposal.

[2] Teck is one of the titles of the Kings of Würtemberg.

[3] Prince Hermann of Saxe-Weimar, a brother of Prince Edward's, married a sister of the King of Würtemberg.

dilemma the man applied to Prince Edward of Saxe-Weimar, who, thinking the photograph an excellent likeness, advised publication, and before many days were over Prince Teck, to his dismay, saw himself represented, with a beard, in every shop window in London.

Her future husband possessed the attributes that most appealed to Princess Mary. He was high principled, domesticated, a thorough soldier, and, above all, a strong Protestant.[1] They had, besides, many tastes in common; he was endowed with much natural talent for music and also for drawing, and had these gifts been cultivated, he could scarcely have failed to attain success, either as a musician or as an artist. "I long to tell you how happy I am," Princess Mary writes to a friend of her early girlhood, "and with what confiding hope I can (D.V.) look forward to a future of bright promise, as *he* is not only all *I* could wish, but all Mama's heart could possibly desire for her child. I know I shall have your prayers and best wishes on the 12th of June, on the afternoon of which *all important* day we purpose going to Ashridge, which Lord Brownlow and Lady Marian Alford have lent us for a fortnight. Pray send Colonel Purves your address, that he may forward you some of the wedding-cake." The Duchess of Cambridge was almost as pleased as her daughter with the engagement, and in a letter written shortly before the marriage, says, "I am happy to say I feel sure of dear Mary's future happiness. Prince Teck seems to be a most excellent young man, good principled, most religious, perfect manners —in short, I call Mary a most fortunate creature to have found such a husband."

The charge of the trousseau was duly confided to Mrs. James, but with the express directions that it should only be composed of English, Irish, and Scotch manufactures, and an additional embargo was laid upon the milliner that the family tradesmen should, as far as possible, supply the materials. By the Princess's desire the greater portion of the *lingerie*

---

[1] The royal family of Würtemberg is Protestant, but as the crown cannot pass in the female line, on the death of the present King, the throne goes to a Roman Catholic branch.

was entrusted to girls of the various charitable and industrial schools with which she was connected, and although it was pointed out to her that this arrangement must necessarily cause delay in the completion of the work, she declined to deprive the children of a task which she knew would give them so much pleasure.

A week before the wedding the Duchess of Cambridge celebrated the approaching nuptials with a banquet, followed by a ball, at Cambridge Cottage. No pains were spared to make the entertainment worthy of the occasion, and so august a gathering had not been seen at Kew since the days of George III. For the adequate accommodation of the guests two tents were erected in the garden, and one hundred and forty persons sat down to dinner, including the Prince and Princess of Wales and other members of the Royal Family. A still greater number of people were invited to the ball in the evening, when the garden was beautifully illuminated, the most conspicuous device showing the initials of Princess Mary and Prince Teck encircled by a true-lover's knot.

It was Princess Mary's wish to be married in the village she loved so well, and, as she herself expressed it, amongst her own people. Accordingly the ceremony was fixed to take place at the parish church, endeared to her by many memories, and where she had worshipped from the days of her childhood. The Surrey hamlet was *en fête* for the occasion, and the inhabitants vied with one another in doing all they could to show their devotion to the much-beloved bride, and their appreciation of the benefits conferred upon them by her family. A triumphal arch of flowers and evergreens spanned Kew Bridge Road, while other floral decorations were specially arranged by the ladies of Kew; and if further proof were wanting to show the affection and esteem in which the Princess was held, it was seen in the eagerness of the parishioners to place the church at the disposal of the Duchess of Cambridge, in order that adequate accommodation might be provided for her Royal and other distinguished guests.

A space was cleared in the centre of the building, the

floor carpeted, and on either side of a wide aisle, thus temporarily formed, chairs, sent from Buckingham Palace, were placed, but with this exception, and the introduction of a few flowers, little attempt was made at decoration. The pews that remained intact were set apart for privileged persons, including members of the household, and tradesmen patronised by the family. In fact, no one was forgotten, and seats were found for all who had enjoyed the friendship of the bride, either in social or domestic life. Princess Mary, always mindful of what would give the most pleasure, decided to walk to church, so that the village folk might see her as she passed along in wedding attire. The awning, erected over the improvised pathway in case of rain, was left open at the sides, and space reserved along the route for the parishioners, while a favoured few were enabled to witness the procession from a raised platform. .

The pageantry customary at State functions was absent, but the gathering was none the less representative, nor the enthusiasm less genuine. The Queen and the Royal family, the Ambassadors, Cabinet Ministers, and many other personages of distinction were present, but only in a private capacity. There was no Lord Chamberlain to arrange the ceremonial, everything being done by Colonel Purves, and in the most unostentatious manner. Morning dress was worn, the prevailing colour of the ladies' gowns being pale blue, out of compliment to the bride, whose favourite colour it was. In some instances the men donned their stars and ribbons, but not a few, including the Prince of Wales, wore no orders of any kind. Princess Mary wished her wedding to be a country wedding in the true sense of the word, and this wish was carefully responded to by her mother's guests. The same sentiment pervaded everything in connection with the ceremony. Little or no restriction was placed upon the people, who were permitted, within reasonable limits, to go where they liked, and do as they pleased.

From an early hour it was evident that something very unusual was on foot in the village, and soon after daybreak Kew Green was alive with people, who, in spite of drops of

rain and threatening clouds, had come from London and
many miles round to greet Princess Mary on her wedding
morn. But while the throng was great, there was no over-
crowding, no rough play, no attempt to take advantage of the
mere nominal guard which the authorities had sent down
"to preserve order." The scene was essentially a rural one,
more like what might have been expected in the olden time
before the days of telegraphs and railways. The guests, both
invited and uninvited, entered fully into the spirit of the
occasion, and universal kindliness and tender feeling towards
Princess Mary animated all classes.

The Queen, who was accompanied by Prince Arthur,
Princess Helena, and Princess Louise, occupied a chair on
the right of the altar. Facing Her Majesty were the Duchess
of Cambridge, the Prince and Princess of Wales, the Duke
of Edinburgh, the Crown Prince of Denmark, and the Grand
Duke and Grand Duchess of Mecklenburg-Strelitz, with the
Dowager Grand Duchess and the Duchess Caroline. As
soon as the Royal guests had taken their seats, Prince Teck
arrived, accompanied by Count Apponyi, and attended by
Count Wimpffen and Baron Varnbüler. He wore the
customary blue coat, with black velvet collar, and, apart from
his position as bridegroom, his handsome face and gallant
bearing made him the cynosure of every eye.

By twelve o'clock all signs of rain had disappeared, and
the sun shone forth brightly as the bride's procession entered
the ivy-clad porch ; and Princess Mary, who appeared deeply
moved, advanced to the altar leaning on her brother's arm,
the choir meanwhile singing " How welcome was the call."
She bore herself royally, and her stately grace left an impression upon the illustrious assembly which time has not
effaced. The wedding dress was entirely of white satin
trimmed with exquisite Honiton lace, looped up with orange
flowers and myrtle. The bodice was cut square at the throat,
and the rich satin *manteau de cour* fell from her shoulders.
Her head was crowned with a wreath of orange blossoms,
intermixed with myrtle gathered in Kew Gardens, and a
spray of diamonds fastened a veil of Honiton lace of the

finest description, designed in a sequence of cornucopiæ, filled with roses, thistles, and shamrocks, emblematic of England, Scotland, and Ireland. The Princess was attended by four bridesmaids, Lady Georgina Hamilton, Lady Cornelia Churchill, Lady Cecilia Molyneux, and Lady Agneta Yorke, wearing dresses of white tarlatan over blue silk and small bonnets with long veils. Lady Arabella Bannerman and Colonel Clifton [1] closed the procession.

The Duke of Cambridge gave his sister away, and the ceremony was impressively performed by the Archbishop of Canterbury,[2] a personal friend of Princess Mary's, assisted by the Bishop of Winchester, the Vicar of Kew and his curate. At the conclusion of the service the whole congregation knelt in silent prayer for the royal couple, and on rising from his knees Prince Teck, in good old-fashioned style, kissed his bride, who was immediately afterwards clasped in her mother's arms, and affectionately embraced by the Queen. The organ burst forth with the strains of Beethoven's symphony, "The Ode to Joy," which, by Her Majesty's express desire, was substituted for Mendelssohn's "Wedding March," and amidst a murmur of admiration the handsome pair passed slowly down the aisle, followed immediately by the Queen and the Duke of Cambridge. The bride looked radiantly happy, and smilingly acknowledged the salutations of her more intimate friends. As she emerged from the porch on the arm of her husband, the girls from the village school, attired in blue frocks, white tippets, and straw hats to match, strewed the pathway to Cambridge Cottage with flowers.

After the register had been signed and attested in the drawing-room, the wedding breakfast began, the royal table being laid in the library, and the rest of the party sitting down in the gaily decorated tent which had been used for

[1] At the time of the Princess's marriage, Colonel Clifton was attached to the Duke of Cambridge's Household, but obtained leave to attend Princess Mary and act as her Equerry. When the Princess gave up Kensington Palace, Colonel Clifton retired from Her Royal Highness's service and resumed his duties as Equerry to the Duke of Cambridge.

[2] The Most Rev. Charles Thomas Longley, D.D.

the ball. In due course the Duke of Cambridge proposed the health of the bride and bridegroom, who, when the Queen had retired, joined the party in the tent, where Lord Derby, in an appropriate speech, wished them a long and happy married life. At three o'clock Her Majesty left, but not before signifying her intention of conferring upon Prince Teck the Grand Cross of the Order of the Bath.

An hour later the Royal couple drove off amidst the cheers of the spectators and a shower of old shoes, thrown by relatives and friends assembled at the door of the Cottage to wish them God-speed. As the carriage passed through Kew, Princess Mary saw one of her village acquaintances holding up a small bunch of flowers, as if to ask permission to throw it. The Princess returned an encouraging smile, and the nosegay was at once thrown and as quickly caught. Looking back, the bride nodded her thanks, and the spectators redoubled their cheers, pleased alike at the gracious act and the smartness of the catch. Enthusiastic crowds lined the road, and cheered and cheered again as the happy pair proceeded on their way to Ashridge. It was the spontaneous wish of everybody, high and low, rich and poor, to do honour to one so universally beloved, and the drive from Kew to London was one continual triumphal progress.

Letter from the Grand Duchess of Mecklenburg-Strelitz to the Honble. Mrs. Dalrymple.

Strelitz, July 20, 1866.

MY DEAREST ELLINOR,—You will think me the most heartless of creatures never yet to have answered your dear letter, written for Mary's Marriage Day, but if you consider what I have had to undergo since then, and what has taken place since that *happy day*, I hope you will excuse me. I gave Mary the kiss you sent her, told her of your promised gift, which enchanted her, and fully intended to have written to you all about the ceremony and the handsome bride and bridegroom, when I was quite suddenly called away, together with the Grand Duke, to return to this poor country where war and horrors of all kind are being committed. The seat of war is not close to us, but we feel the effects of it, and have to bear the degradation of being drawn into it. . . .

But to return to Mary! Poor Mary, her happiness was but of short duration! All looked so bright on June 12th, when she drove off to Ashridge, and after a fortnight of anxiety and indecision as to what Francis was to do, they left for Germany, first going to Stuttgart, where he left Mary with his family, whilst he went on to offer his services to the Emperor at Vienna. Only to-day have I heard from Mary that she is there with him, but she does not say where he is to be sent to. Vienna may fall any day into the enemy's hands, and what is to become of Mary then I know not! I fancy she will join the Imperial family at Buda. Poor Mama is much shaken by all she has had to undergo and suffer for *our* sakes! Both her poor daughters in divided camps, though our hearts are naturally all in the one camp of right and justice. . . . Poor Hanover! What is to become of our old dynasty? My son of sixteen is with me to-day, but he is to return to his studies at Dresden soon. He is tall and nice-looking, a young man with a child's heart and an affection for his Mama. I forgot to say Mary sent you a thousand loves and so many thanks for your present. . . . Believe me ever yours very affectionately,

AUGUSTA CAROLINE.

Letter from the Duchess of Cambridge to the same.

Cambridge Cottage, September 6, 1866.

MY DEAREST ELLINOR,—I had so much to write, and such a painful time when your dear letter reached me, that I had no heart to answer you, dearest, best! Alas! all the dearest countries that my heart loved best have been *stolen* (I can't give it another name). . . . Hanover, which is the cradle of our English family, Hesse is mine, and Nassau was my dearest own mother's; so you may judge of my feelings at this moment. . . . I can't think it can be God's *will*—but *He* permits it, and I try to submit myself, and to hope for better days to come.

You will know that Mary is still at Vienna, therefore you had better keep the picture of *your* little Mary till *mine* has returned. Though I know and hear from all sides that she *is* and *looks* very happy, I can't give you any particulars about her, as her letters are scarce and short! And now God bless you, dearest Ellinor, and believe me ever yours sincerely,

AUGUSTA.

Letter from Princess Mary to the same.

Cambridge Cottage, December 31, 1866.

. . . How can I find words sufficiently to thank you and Mr. Dalrymple for the wedding-gift you have so kindly and thoughtfully selected for me, than which nothing can possibly have given me greater pleasure? The portrait is a charming likeness of your darling child, and what with her bright sweet face and flowers, she is a perfect emblem of Spring, and will shed sunshine o'er my boudoir as she looks down on me from its walls! This present has touched me more than I can express, as it is such a very pretty attention on your part, and one that *affection* alone can have prompted. Therefore please to accept yourself, my own friend, and to convey to your *caro sposo* all the gratitude my heart can offer for this precious tribute of love and devotion, and assure my dearly loved god-child of the pleasure it affords me to possess her portrait, and be thus enabled to picture to myself her sweet little face. . . .

The bright hopes of wedded bliss I indulged in before our marriage I am most thankful to say bid fair to be fully realised, as we are *thoroughly happy*, and as *united* and *devoted* a couple as our friends can possibly desire. But let me give you a brief sketch of the past, ere I enter into particulars touching the present. . . . On the second day after our engagement, matters on the continent began to look very black, and the war, which till then there had been strong hopes of warding off, became imminent. As Francis had only quitted the Austrian service in March, he of course felt it to be his duty to offer his services to the Emperor in the event of the war breaking out, so that during the nine weeks which intervened between the 5th of April and 12th of June, we were in constant dread of his having to hurry off to Vienna. However, fortunately for us, things did not come to a crisis until after the eventful day. But our fortnight among the roses of dear beautiful Ashridge was sadly disturbed by the sudden and hurried departure of Fritz and Augusta, and the anxious news that reached us from abroad; and we were but too soon awakened from our bright dream of life to its terrible reality, by having to get ready and start at *two days'* notice to enable Francis to join the army.

After dropping me at Ludwigsburg, once the summer residence of my Aunt, the late Princess Royal and Queen of Würtemberg, where he left me under the care of his Aunt, the Queen Mother of Würtemberg, Francis went on to

Vienna on the 1st of July, and reached it just as the disastrous news of the defeat of Königgrätz had arrived. After a week of cruel uncertainty for him and terrible anxiety for me, during which he vainly sought for an audience, and never even succeeded in seeing any of the military authorities, so great was the general confusion, he gave it up in despair and came back to me, and a week later we proceeded together to Vienna, where I spent a most interesting time. For five weeks we were at the Hôtel Munsch, Francis in hourly expectation of an appointment which he only succeeded in obtaining just before the peace was signed, after which, on the 20th of August, we moved to my father-in-law's Villa at Liesing, an hour's drive from Vienna, and there spent two months very pleasantly with his family.

They had all been absent in Styria, where my married sister-in-law Amélie has a place close to Gratz, during our *séjour* at Vienna, having left at the time of the panic, but they returned to Liesing to receive us, bringing Amélie with them. Francis's elder unmarried sister Claudine had accompanied them to Ludwigsburg, and passed three days with us there, so that they were not all strangers to me when we established ourselves at Liesing, and I very soon learnt to care for them all and feel thoroughly at home with them. In short, I may consider myself very fortunate to have married into so nice and pleasant a family, my father-in-law, Duke Alexander, making a great pet of me, and Claudine and Amélie being *utterly* devoted to their new sister! We paid a ten days' visit to Amélie about the middle of October in her home amidst the Styrian hills, and I was delighted with the splendid scenery of the pass over the Semmering Alps and the picturesque beauty of Styria, the mountainous air of which did me a world of good.

On the 12th of November we started on our homeward journey, stopping *en route* at Stuttgart, Rumpenheim,— where we spent four days with several members of dear Mama's family, who, owing to the sad and terrible issue of the war, are now either *exiles* or *homeless!* and have settled at Rumpenheim for at any rate the winter,—Brussels, and Paris, in order that I might sit to Winterhalter for a head, which is now opposite me and considered very like. We landed at Dover on the 28th after a wretched passage, and for the last six weeks have been Mama's guests at Cambridge Cottage. You can picture to yourself my delight at finding myself once more in my dear old home, and spending my birthday and Christmas in the old familiar way, and in a spot endeared to me by past and *recent* memories! To crown all, dearest Mama was in the best of health and spirits, and overjoyed at having us with her, so that our visit has been in every respect a most pleasant one.

January 8, 1867.

After having been snowed and frozen up for five days, not an omnibus even able to attempt the passage to London, we came up here (11, Prince's Gate, a corner house belonging to my friend Lady Marian Alford, which we have taken for the next five months) yesterday, and are beginning life on our own account, having just completed our small establishment. It is, of course, a great interest and amusement to us both, and you would laugh could you hear me consulting with the steward and *lady*-cook, and giving my orders *en bonne maîtresse de maison!* I am thankful to say that the Queen has given us the greater portion of the apartment she and Aunt Kent occupied at Kensington Palace in days of yore, which the Board of Works promise to get ready for us by the month of May, and which, if they please to spend a little money upon it, may be made a very charming abode, as the rooms are handsome and comfortable. . . . I am finishing this letter after dinner in Francis's sitting-room, whilst he is amusing himself at the piano. I mention this to give you an idea of our *tête-à-tête* evenings, which are very cosy—in the *Darby* and *Joan* fashion. But I really must not run on any longer in this way, lest I should weary you, so I will take my leave with every good and heartfelt wish for your happiness and those dear to you in 1867, and many, many bright years to come. I enclose a photograph done of us at Vienna, and one of *l'objet aimé*, that you may be able to picture him to yourself, and remain ever, my own dear Ellinor, your loving friend,

MARY ADELAIDE.

END OF VOL. I.

LONDON : PRINTED BY WILLIAM CLOWES AND SONS, LIMITED, STAMFORD STREET AND CHARING CROSS.

Lightning Source UK Ltd.
Milton Keynes UK
UKOW031809230312

189493UK00006B/23/P